The American Spirit

Selected and Edited with
Introduction and Commentary by

David M. Kennedy

Stanford University

Thomas A. Bailey

The American Spirit

United States History
as Seen by Contemporaries

Tenth Edition

Volume II: Since 1865

Houghton Mifflin Company
Boston   New York

Editor-in-Chief: Jean L. Woy
Sponsoring Editor: Mary Dougherty
Assistant Editor: Michael Kerns
Senior Project Editor: Rosemary R. Jaffe
Associate Production/Design Coordinator: Christine Gervais
Senior Manufacturing Coordinator: Marie Barnes
Senior Marketing Manager: Sandra McGuire

Cover Image: *The Migration of the Negro,* Panel No. 3, by Jacob Lawrence, 1940–1941. The Philips Collection, Washington, D.C.

Printed in the United States of America.

Library of Congress Control Number: 2001131514

International Standard Book Number: 0-618-12218-4

6   7   8   9-DOC-05   04   03

About the Authors

David M. Kennedy is the Donald J. McLachlan Professor of History at Stanford University, where he has taught for more than three decades. Born and raised in Seattle, he received his undergraduate education at Stanford and did his graduate training at Yale in American Studies, combining the fields of history, economics, and literature. His first book, *Birth Control in America: The Career of Margaret Sanger* (1970) was honored with both the Bancroft Prize and the John Gilmary Shea Prize. His study of World War I, *Over Here: The First World War and American Society* (1980) was a Pulitzer Prize finalist. In 1999 he published *Freedom from Fear: The American People in Depression and War, 1929–1945,* which won the Pulitzer Prize for History, as well as the Francis Parkman Prize, the English-Speaking Union's Ambassador's Prize, and the Commonwealth Club of California's Gold Medal for Literature. At Stanford he teaches courses in American political, diplomatic, intellectual, and social history, and in American literature. He has received several teaching awards, including the Dean's Award for Distinguished Teaching. He has been a visiting professor at the University of Florence, Italy, and in 1995–1996 served as the Harmsworth Professor of American History at Oxford University. He has also served on the Advisory Board for the PBS television series, *The American Experience,* and as a consultant to several documentary films, including *The Great War, Cadillac Desert,* and *Woodrow Wilson.* From 1990 to 1995 he chaired the Test Development Committee for the Advanced Placement United States History examination. He is an elected Fellow of the American Academy of Arts and Sciences and of the American Philosophical Society. Married and the father of two sons and a daughter, in his leisure time he enjoys hiking, bicycling, river-rafting, and fly-fishing.

Thomas A. Bailey (1903–1983) taught history for nearly forty years at Stanford University, his alma mater. Long regarded as one of the nation's leading historians of American diplomacy, he was honored by his colleagues in 1968 with election to the presidencies of both the Organization of American Historians and the Society for Historians of American Foreign Relations. He was the author, editor, or co-editor of some twenty books, but the work in which he took most pride was *The American Pageant* through which, he liked to say, he had taught American history to several million students.

Contents

23 *Political Paralysis in the Gilded Age, 1869–1896* **37**

24 *Industry Comes of Age, 1865–1900* **65**

25   *America Moves to the City, 1865–1900*   *99*

26 The Great West and the Agricultural Revolution, 1865–1896   **131**

27 The Path of Empire, 1890–1899   **174**

28
America on the World Stage, 1899–1909   *186*

29
Progressivism and the Republican Roosevelt, 1901–1912   *200*

30   *Wilsonian Progressivism at Home and Abroad, 1912–1916*   *231*

31   *The War to End War, 1917–1918*   *248*

32   *American Life in the "Roaring Twenties", 1919–1929*   *274*

35 *Franklin D. Roosevelt and the Shadow of War, 1933–1941*   *344*

38   *The Eisenhower Era, 1952–1960*   *437*

39 The Stormy Sixties, 1960–1968 **467**

40 The Stalemated Seventies, 1968–1980 **514**

41 *The Resurgence of Conservatism, 1980–2000*   557

42 The American People Face a New Century 603

Maps

Preface

The documents collected in *The American Spirit* are meant to recapture the spirit of the American past as expressed by the men and women who lived it. Movers and shakers who tried to sculpt the contours of history share these pages with the humble folk whose lives were grooved by a course of events they sometimes only dimly understood, and not infrequently resented. In all cases I have tried to present clear and pungent documents that combine intrinsic human interest with instructive historical perspectives. Students in American history courses will discover in these selections the satisfaction of working with primary documents—the raw human record from which meaningful historical accounts are assembled.

Taken together, the readings in the pages that follow convey a vivid sense of the wonder and the woe, the passion and the perplexity, with which Americans have confronted their lives and their times. *The American Spirit* seeks especially to stimulate reflection on the richness, variety, and complexity of American history, and an appreciation of both the problems and the prejudices of people in the past. Accordingly, it devotes much attention to the clash of opinion and judgment, including the unpopular or unsuccessful side of controversial issues. It gives special emphasis to problems of social justice, including the plight of religious, ethnic, and racial minorities; the evolving status of women; the problems of the poor; the responsibilities of world power; and the ongoing debate about the meaning of democracy itself.

I have revised the tenth edition of *The American Spirit* to make it fully compatible with its companion text, the twelfth edition of *The American Pageant*. Every chapter in the *Pageant* has a corresponding chapter of the same title in the *Spirit*. Instructors and students may use the two books together if they choose, but the chronological organization of the *Spirit* and its extensive explanatory materials make it usable with virtually any American history text. It may also be read on its own. Prologues for each chapter, headnotes for each document, explanatory inserts, and questions at the end of each headnote and at the end of every chapter will guide students in learning to appraise the documents thoughtfully and critically.

In many chapters, readers will find visual materials—cartoons, paintings, or posters, for example—that are treated as documents in their own right, fully equivalent in their evidentiary value and their historical interest to the more traditional verbal texts. These visual documents are here presented with the same kind of explanatory and other editorial apparatus that frames the conventional texts. It is my hope that students will thereby be encouraged to interrogate the past in new ways—not only by analyzing the written record, but by developing a critical attitude toward other kinds of historical evidence as well.

Like the twelfth edition of *The American Pageant*, this edition of the *Spirit* has been substantially revised to emphasize the interaction of social, economic, and cultural developments with political history. It contains many new documents on Native Americans, the slave trade, indentured servants in the colonial era, disputes over governance and authority in the Revolutionary era, the environmental consequences of settlement and industrialization, the westward movement, and women's history. In response to suggestions from users, I have also undertaken to shorten some documents so that their essential significance might be more accessible and apparent to readers.

The result of these revisions, I hope, is a fresher and more provocative *Spirit* whose documents will enable students to savor the taste and to feel the texture of the American past, while engaging themselves in its frequently emotional and sometimes explosive controversies.

D. M. K.

The American Spirit

22

The Ordeal
of Reconstruction,
1865–1877

The years of war tried our devotion to the Union;
the time of peace may test the sincerity of our faith
in democracy.

Herman Melville, c. 1866

Prologue: President Johnson, a rough-hewn Tennessean, favored reconstruction of the seceded states on a "soft" basis. But he soon ran afoul of the congressional Republicans. Though divided into hard-line ("radical") and more accommodating ("moderate") factions, Republicans agreed that the seceding states should not be readmitted until they had adopted the Fourteenth Amendment. This amendment (ratified in 1868) would guarantee civil rights to the blacks while reducing congressional representation in states where the ex-slave was denied a vote. But such terms were spurned by ten of the eleven high-spirited Southern states. The Republicans in Congress thereupon passed the drastic military reconstruction acts of 1867, under which black suffrage was forced upon the white South. The Congress also came within a hairsbreadth, in 1868, of removing the obstructive President Johnson by impeachment. Meanwhile the partly black Southern legislatures, despite grievous excesses, passed stacks of long-overdue social and economic legislation. The whites struck back through secret terrorist organizations, and ultimately secured control of their state governments by fraud, fright, and force.

A. The Status of the South

1. Carl Schurz Reports Southern Defiance (1865)

President Johnson sent Carl Schurz—the lanky, bewhiskered, and bespectacled German-American reformer—into the devastated South to report objectively on conditions there. But Schurz was predisposed to see continued defiance. He was on intimate terms with the radical Republican leaders, who favored a severe reconstruction of the South, and in addition he was financially obligated to the radical Charles

---

[1]Joseph H. Mahaffrey, ed. "Carl Schurz's Letters from the South," *Georgia Historical Quarterly* 35 (September 1951): 244–247. Courtesy of the Georgia Historical Society.

Sumner. President Johnson, evidently hoping for evidence that would support his lenient policies, brushed aside Schurz's elaborate report with ill-concealed annoyance. Schurz partially financed his trip by selling a series of letters under an assumed name to the Boston Advertiser, *which presumably welcomed his pro-radical bias. In the following letter, which he wrote from Savannah to the newspaper, what class of people does he deem responsible for the trouble? What motivated them? Why were their outbursts not more serious?*

But there is another class of people here [in Savannah], mostly younger men, who are still in the swearing mood. You can overhear their conversations as you pass them on the streets or even sit near them on the stoop of a hotel. They are "not conquered but only overpowered." They are only smothered for a time. They want to fight the war over again, and they are sure in five years they are going to have a war bigger than any we have seen yet. They are meaning to get rid of this d——d military despotism. They will show us what stuff Southern men are made of. They will send their own men to Congress and show us that we cannot violate the Constitution with impunity.

They have a rope ready for this and that Union man when the Yankee bayonets are gone. They will show the Northern interlopers that have settled down here to live on their substance the way home. They will deal largely in tar and feathers. They have been in the country and visited this and that place where a fine business is done in the way of killing Negroes. They will let the Negro know what freedom is, only let the Yankee soldiers be withdrawn.

Such is their talk. You can hear it every day, if you have your ears open. You see their sullen, frowning faces at every street corner. Now, there may be much of the old Southern braggadocio in this, and I do not believe that such men will again resort to open insurrection. But they will practice private vengeance whenever they can do it with impunity, and I have heard sober-minded Union people express their apprehension of it. This spirit is certainly no evidence of true loyalty.

It was this spirit which was active in an occurrence which disgraced this city on the Fourth of July. Perhaps you have heard of it. The colored firemen of this city desired to parade their engine on the anniversary of our independence. If nobody else would, they felt like celebrating that day. A number will deny that it was a legitimate desire. At first the engineer of the fire department, who is a citizen of this town, refused his permission. Finally, by an interposition of an officer of the "Freedmen's Bureau,"* he was prevailed upon to give his consent, and the parade took place. In the principal street of the city the procession was attacked with clubs and stones by a mob opposed to the element above described, and by a crowd of boys all swearing at the d——d niggers. The colored firemen were knocked down, some of them severely injured, their engine was taken away from them, and the peaceable procession dispersed. Down with the d——d niggers. A northern gentleman who loudly expressed his indignation at the proceedings was in danger of being mobbed, and had to seek safety in a house. . . .

To return to the "unconquered" in Savannah—the occurrence of the Fourth of July shows what they are capable of doing even while the Yankee bayonets are still

---

*A federal agency designed to help the ex-slaves adjust to freedom.

here. If from this we infer what they will be capable of doing when the Yankee bayonets are withdrawn, the prospect is not altogether pleasant, and Union people, white and black, in this city and neighborhood may well entertain serious apprehensions. . . .

Unfortunately, this spirit receives much encouragement from the fair sex. We have heard so much of the bitter resentment of the Southern ladies that the tale becomes stale by frequent repetition, but when inquiring into the feelings of the people, this element must not be omitted. There are certainly a good many sensible women in the South who have arrived at a just appreciation of the circumstances with which they are surrounded. But there is a large number of Southern women who are as vindictive and defiant as ever, and whose temper does not permit them to lay their tongues under any restraint. You can see them in every hotel, and they will treat you to the most ridiculous exhibitions, whenever an occasion offers.

A day or two ago a Union officer, yielding to an impulse of politeness, handed a dish of pickles to a Southern Lady at the dinner-table of a hotel in this city. A look of unspeakable scorn and indignation met him. "So you think," said the lady, "a Southern woman will take a dish of pickles from a hand that is dripping with the blood of her countrymen?"

It is remarkable upon what trifling material this female wrath is feeding and growing fat. In a certain district in South Carolina, the ladies were some time ago, and perhaps are now, dreadfully exercised about the veil question. You may ask me what the veil question is. Formerly, under the old order of things, Negro women were not permitted to wear veils. Now, under the new order of things, a great many are wearing veils. This is an outrage which cannot be submitted to; the white ladies of the neighborhood agree in being indignant beyond measure. Some of them declare that whenever they meet a colored woman wearing a veil they will tear the veil from her face. Others, mindful of the consequences which such an act of violence might draw after it, under this same new order of things, declare their resolve never to wear veils themselves as long as colored women wear veils. This is the veil question, and this is the way it stands at present.

Such things may seem trifling and ridiculous. But it is a well-known fact that a silly woman is sometimes able to exercise a powerful influence over a man not half as silly, and the class of "unconquered" above described is undoubtedly in a great measure composed of individuals that are apt to be influenced by silly women. It has frequently been said that had it not been for the spirit of the Southern women, the rebellion would have broken down long ago, and there is, no doubt, a grain of truth in it.

2. General Ulysses S. Grant Is Optimistic (1865)

President Johnson, hoping to capitalize on Grant's enormous prestige, also sent the general on a fact-finding trip to the South. Grant spent less than a week hurriedly visiting leading cities in four states. Schurz had ranged far more widely over a longer period, from July to September 1865. But just as Schurz was predisposed to see

---

[2]*Senate Executive Documents,* 39th Cong., 1st sess., I, no. 2, pp. 106–107.

defiance, Grant was predisposed to see compliance. Bear in mind also that Schurz was an idealist, strongly pro-black, and a leading Republican politician closely in touch with the radicals. Grant was none of these. Which of their reports is more credible?

I am satisfied that the mass of thinking men of the South accept the present situation of affairs in good faith. The questions which have heretofore divided the sentiment of the people of the two sections—slavery and state rights, or the right of a state to secede from the Union—they regard as having been settled forever by the highest tribunal—arms—that man can resort to. I was pleased to learn from the leading men whom I met that they not only accepted the decision arrived at as final, but, now that the smoke of battle has cleared away and time has been given for reflection, that this decision has been a fortunate one for the whole country, they receiving like benefits from it with those who opposed them in the field and in council.

Four years of war, during which law was executed only at the point of the bayonet throughout the states in rebellion, have left the people possibly in a condition not to yield that ready obedience to civil authority the American people have generally been in the habit of yielding. This would render the presence of small garrisons throughout those states necessary until such time as labor returns to its proper channel, and civil authority is fully established. I did not meet anyone, either those holding places under the government or citizens of the Southern states, who think it practicable to withdraw the military from the South at present. The white and the black mutually require the protection of the general government.

There is such universal acquiescence in the authority of the general government throughout the portions of country visited by me that the mere presence of a military force, without regard to numbers, is sufficient to maintain order. . . .

My observations lead me to the conclusion that the citizens of the Southern states are anxious to return to self-government, within the Union, as soon as possible; that whilst reconstructing they want and require protection from the government; that they are in earnest in wishing to do what they think is required by the government, not humiliating to them as citizens, and that if such a course were pointed out they would pursue it in good faith.

3. The Former Slaves Confront Freedom (1901)

The reactions of the freed slaves to their new liberty ran the gamut of human emotions from jubilation to anxiety. Attitudes toward former masters—and toward whites generally—ranged from resentment and fear to pity. Booker T. Washington was a young boy no more than eight years of age when the day of freedom came. What was his response? From what he describes as the first reactions of his family members and other freed slaves, what might one conclude were the worst deprivations suffered in slavery?

---

[3]Booker T. Washington, *Up from Slavery* (New York: A. L. Burt, 1901), pp. 224–227.

Finally the war closed, and the day of freedom came. It was a momentous and eventful day to all upon our plantation. We had been expecting it. Freedom was in the air, and had been for months. Deserting soldiers returning to their homes were to be seen every day. Others who had been discharged, or whose regiments had been paroled, were constantly passing near our place. The "grape-vine telegraph" was kept busy night and day. The news and mutterings of great events were swiftly carried from one plantation to another. In the fear of "Yankee" invasions, the silverware and other valuables were taken from the "big house," buried in the woods, and guarded by trusted slaves. Woe be to any one who would have attempted to disturb the buried treasure. The slaves would give the Yankee soldiers food, drink, clothing—anything but that which had been specifically intrusted to their care and honour. As the great day drew nearer, there was more singing in the slave quarters than usual. It was bolder, had more ring, and lasted later into the night. Most of the verses of the plantation songs had some reference to freedom. True, they had sung those same verses before, but they had been careful to explain that the "freedom" in these songs referred to the next world, and had no connection with life in this world. Now they gradually threw off the mask, and were not afraid to let it be known that the "freedom" in their songs meant freedom of the body in this world. The night before the eventful day, word was sent to the slave quarters to the effect that something unusual was going to take place at the "big house" the next morning. There was little, if any, sleep that night. All was excitement and expectancy. Early the next morning word was sent to all the slaves, old and young, to gather at the house. In company with my mother, brother, and sister, and a large number of other slaves, I went to the master's house. All of our master's family were either standing or seated on the veranda of the house, where they could see what was to take place and hear what was said. There was a feeling of deep interest, or perhaps sadness, on their faces, but not bitterness. As I now recall the impression they made upon me, they did not at the moment seem to be sad because of the loss of property, but rather because of parting with those whom they had reared and who were in many ways very close to them. The most distinct thing that I now recall in connection with the scene was that some man who seemed to be a stranger (a United States officer, I presume) made a little speech and then read a rather long paper— the Emancipation Proclamation, I think. After the reading we were told that we were all free, and could go when and where we pleased. My mother, who was standing by my side, leaned over and kissed her children, while tears of joy ran down her cheeks. She explained to us what it all meant, that this was the day for which she had been so long praying, but fearing that she would never live to see.

For some minutes there was great rejoicing, and thanksgiving, and wild scenes of ecstasy. But there was no feeling of bitterness. In fact, there was pity among the slaves for our former owners. The wild rejoicing on the part of the emancipated coloured people lasted but for a brief period, for I noticed that by the time they returned to their cabins there was a change in their feelings. The great responsibility of being free, or having charge of themselves, of having to think and plan for themselves and their children, seemed to take possession of them. It was very much like suddenly turning a youth of ten or twelve years out into the world to provide for himself. In a few hours the great questions with which the Anglo-Saxon race had been grappling for centuries had been thrown upon these people to be solved. These were the questions of a home, a living, the rearing of children, education, citizenship, and the establishment and support of churches. Was it any wonder that within a few hours the wild rejoicing ceased and a feeling of deep gloom seemed to pervade the slave quarters? To some it seemed that, now that they were in actual possession of it, freedom was a more serious thing than they had expected to find it. Some of the slaves were seventy or eighty years old; their best days were gone. They had no strength with which to earn a living in a strange place and among strange people, even if they had been sure where to find a new place of abode. To this class the problem seemed especially hard. Besides, deep down in their hearts there was a strange and peculiar attachment to "old Marster" and "old Missus," and to their children, which they found it hard to think of breaking off. With these they had spent in some cases nearly a half-century, and it was no light thing to think of parting. Gradually, one by one, stealthily at first, the older slaves began to wander from the slave quarters back to the "big house" to have whispered conversation with their former owners as to the future. . . .

After the coming of freedom there were two points upon which practically all the people on our place were agreed, and I find that this was generally true throughout the South: that they must change their names, and that they must leave the old plantation for at least a few days or weeks in order that they might really feel sure that they were free.

In some way a feeling got among the coloured people that it was far from proper for them to bear the surname of their former owners, and a great many of them took other surnames. This was one of the first signs of freedom. When they were slaves, a coloured person was simply called "John" or "Susan." There was seldom occasion for more than the use of the one name. If "John" or "Susan" belonged to a white man by the name of "Hatcher," sometimes he was called "John Hatcher," or as often "Hatcher's John." But there was a feeling that "John Hatcher" or "Hatcher's John" was not the proper title by which to denote a freeman; and so in many cases "John Hatcher" was changed to "John S. Lincoln" or "John S. Sherman," the initial "S" standing for no name, it being simply a part of what the coloured man proudly called his "entitles."

As I have stated, most of the coloured people left the old plantation for a short while at least, so as to be sure, it seemed, that they could leave and try their freedom on to see how it felt. After they had remained away for a time, many of the older slaves, especially, returned to their old homes and made some kind of contact with their former owners by which they remained on the estate.

My mother's husband, who was the stepfather of my brother John and myself, did not belong to the same owners as did my mother. In fact, he seldom came to our plantation. I remember seeing him there perhaps once a year, that being about Christmas time. In some way, during the war, by running away and following the Federal soldiers, it seems, he found his way into the new state of West Virginia. As soon as freedom was declared, he sent for my mother to come to the Kanawha Valley, in West Virginia. At that time a journey from Virginia over the mountains to West Virginia was rather a tedious and in some cases a painful undertaking. What little clothing and few household goods we had were placed in a cart, but the children walked the greater portion of the distance, which was several hundred miles.

4. Emancipation Violence in Texas (c. 1865)

In the following recollection by a former slave woman in Texas, what is revealed about the response of some slaveowners to emancipation? What implications did such responses have for the future of the freed slaves? for federal policy during Reconstruction?

I heard about freedom in September and they were picking cotton and a white man rode up to master's house on a big, white horse and the houseboy told master a man wanted to see him and he hollered, "Light, stranger." It was a government man and he had the big book and a bunch of papers and said why hadn't master turned the niggers loose. Master said he was trying to get the crop out and he told master to have the slaves in. Uncle Steven blew the cow horn that they used to call to eat and all the niggers came running, because that horn meant, "Come to the big house, quick." The man read the paper telling us we were free, but master made us work several months after that. He said we would get 20 acres of land and a mule but we didn't get it.

Lots of niggers were killed after freedom, because the slaves in Harrison County were turned loose right at freedom and those in Rusk County weren't. But they heard about it and ran away to freedom in Harrison County and their owners had them bushwhacked, then shot down. You could see lots of niggers hanging from trees in Sabine bottom right after freedom, because they caught them swimming across Sabine River and shot them. There sure are going to be lots of souls crying against them in judgment!

B. The Debate on Reconstruction Policy

1. Southern Blacks Ask for Help (1865)

As the smoke of war cleared, blacks throughout the South gathered in "Conventions of Freedmen" to determine the best strategies for protecting their fragile freedom. Several of these conventions formally petitioned the Congress for help. In the following petition from a convention meeting in Alexandria, Virginia, in August 1865, what forms of support are deemed most essential? What is the freedmen's greatest fear?

We, the undersigned members of a Convention of colored citizens of the State of Virginia, would respectfully represent that, although we have been held as slaves, and denied all recognition as a constituent of your nationality for almost the entire period of the duration of your Government, and that by *your permission* we have been denied either home or country, and deprived of the dearest rights of human nature; yet when you and our immediate oppressors met in deadly conflict upon the

[4]George P. Rawick, ed., *The American Slave: A Composite Autobiography* (Westport, Conn.: Greenwood Publishing Company, 1972), vol. 5, Texas Narratives, part 3, p. 78.

[1]"Proceedings of the Convention of the Colored People of Virginia, Held in the City of Alexandria, August 2, 3, 4, 5, 1865" (Alexandria, Va., 1865), in W. L. Fleming, ed., *Documentary History of Reconstruction* (Cleveland, Ohio, 1906), vol. 1, pp. 195–196.

field of battle—the one to destroy and the other to save your Government and nationality, *we,* with scarce an exception, in our inmost souls espoused your cause, and watched, and prayed, and waited, and labored for your success. . . .

When the contest waxed long, and the result hung doubtfully, you appealed to us for help, and how well we answered is written in the rosters of the two hundred thousand colored troops now enrolled in your service; and as to our undying devotion to your cause, let the uniform acclamation of escaped prisoners, "whenever we saw a black face we felt sure of a friend," answer.

Well, the war is over, the rebellion is "put down," and we are *declared* free! Four fifths of our enemies are paroled or amnestied, and the other fifth are being pardoned, and the President has, in his efforts at the reconstruction of the civil government of the States, late in rebellion, left us entirely at the mercy of these subjugated but unconverted rebels, in *everything* save the privilege of bringing us, our wives and little ones, to the auction block. . . . We *know* these men—know them *well*— and we assure you that, with the majority of them, loyalty is only "lip deep," and that their professions of loyalty are used as a cover to the cherished design of getting restored to their former relations with the Federal Government, and then, by all sorts of "unfriendly legislation," to render the freedom you have given us more intolerable than the slavery they intended for us.

We warn you in time that our only safety is in keeping them under Governors of the *military persuasion* until you have so amended the Federal Constitution that it will prohibit the States from making any distinction between citizens on account of race or color. In one word, the only salvation for us besides the power of the Government, is in the *possession of the ballot.* Give us this, and we will protect ourselves. . . . But, 'tis said we are ignorant. Admit it. Yet who denies we *know* a traitor from a loyal man, a gentleman from a rowdy, a friend from an enemy? . . . All we ask is an *equal chance* with the white *traitors* varnished and japanned with the oath of amnesty. Can you deny us this and still keep faith with us? . . .

We are "sheep in the midst of wolves," and nothing but the military arm of the Government prevents us and all the *truly* loyal white men from being driven from the land of our birth. Do not then, we beseech you, give to one of these "wayward sisters" the rights they abandoned and forfeited when they rebelled until you have secured *our* rights by the aforementioned amendment to the Constitution. . . .

2. The White South Asks for Unconditional Reintegration into the Union (1866)

The Joint Committee on Reconstruction, composed of nine congressional representatives and six senators, held extensive hearings in the spring of 1866 about the condition of the South and various proposals for reintegrating the Southern states into the Union. One leading proposal was the legislation that eventually became the Fourteenth Amendment to the Constitution. It was designed to reduce the representation in Congress of any state that denied the freedmen the right to vote. Congressional Republicans wanted to make any state's restoration to the Union conditional on its rat-

---

[2]*Report of the Joint Committee on Reconstruction* (Washington, D.C., 1866), Part III, pp. 163ff.

ification of the amendment. In the following testimony, former Confederate Vice President Alexander Stephens comments on the congressional plan. What are his main objections to it? What alternatives does he propose? Does his statement confirm or cast doubt on the concerns of blacks presented in the preceding selection?

I think the people of the State would be unwilling to do more than they have done for restoration. Restricted or limited suffrage would not be so objectionable as general or universal. But it is a matter that belongs to the State to regulate. The question of suffrage, whether universal or restricted, is one of State policy exclusively, as they believe. Individually I should not be opposed to a proper system of restricted or limited suffrage to this class of our population. . . . The only view in their opinion that could possibly justify the war that was carried on by the federal government against them was the idea of the indissolubleness of the Union; that those who held the administration for the time were bound to enforce the execution of the laws and the maintenance of the integrity of the country under the Constitution. . . . They expected as soon as the confederate cause was abandoned that immediately the States would be brought back into their practical relations with the government as previously constituted. That is what they looked to. They expected that the States would immediately have their representatives in the Senate and in the House; and they expected in good faith, as loyal men, as the term is frequently used—loyal to law, order, and the Constitution—to support the government under the Constitution. . . . Towards the Constitution of the United States the great mass of our people were always as much devoted in their feelings as any people ever were towards any laws or people . . . they resorted to secession with a view of more securely maintaining these principles. And when they found they were not successful in their object in perfect good faith, as far as I can judge from meeting with them and conversing with them, looking to the future development of their country . . . their earnest desire and expectation was to allow the past struggle . . . to pass by and to co-operate with . . . those of all sections who earnestly desire the preservation of constitutional liberty and the perpetuaion of the government in its purity. They have been . . . disappointed in this, and are . . . patiently waiting, however, and believing that when the passions of the hour have passed away this delay in representation will cease. . . .

My own opinion is, that these terms ought not to be offered as conditions precedent. . . . It would be best for the peace, harmony, and prosperity of the whole country that there should be an immediate restoration, an immediate bringing back of the States into their original practical relations; and let all these questions then be discussed in common council. Then the representatives from the south could be heard, and you and all could judge much better of the tone and temper of the people than you could from the opinions given by any individuals. . . . My judgment, therefore, is very decided, that it would have been better as soon as the lamentable conflict was over, when the people of the south abandoned their cause and agreed to accept the issue, desiring as they do to resume their places for the future in the Union, and to look to the arena of reason and justice for the protection of their rights in the Union—it would have been better to have allowed that result to take place, to follow under the policy adopted by the administration, than to delay or hinder it by propositions to amend the Constitution in respect to suffrage. . . . I think the people of all the southern States would in the halls of Congress discuss these questions calmly and deliberately, and if they did not show that the views they entertained were just and proper, such as to control the judgment of the people of the other sections and States, they would quietly . . . yield to whatever should be constitutionally determined in common council. But I think they feel very sensitively the offer to them of propositions to accept while they are denied all voice . . . in the discussion of these propositions. I think they feel very sensitively that they are denied the right to be heard.

3. The Radical Republicans Take a Hard Line (1866)

After weeks of testimony, the Joint Committee on Reconstruction made its report. With only three Democrats among its fifteen members, and dominated by the imperious Thaddeus Stevens, the committee reflected radical Republican views on Reconstruction policy. What were its principal conclusions? In the light of the evidence provided in the previous two selections, were the committee's views justified?

A claim for the immediate admission of senators and representatives from the so-called Confederate States has been urged, which seems to your committee not to be founded either in reason or in law, and which cannot be passed without comment. Stated in a few words, it amounts to this: That inasmuch as the lately insurgent States had no legal right to separate themselves from the Union, they still retain their position as States, and consequently the people thereof have a right to immediate representation in Congress without the interposition of any conditions whatever. . . . It has even been contended that until such admission all legislation affecting their interests is, if not unconstitutional, at least unjustifiable and oppressive.

It is believed by your Committee that these propositions are not only wholly untenable, but, if admitted, would tend to the destruction of the government. . . . It cannot, we think, be denied that the war thus waged was a civil war of the greatest magnitude. The people waging it were necessarily subject to all the rules which, by the law of nations, control a contest of that character, and to all the legitimate consequences following it. One of these consequences was that, within the limits prescribed by humanity, the conquered rebels were at the mercy of the conquerors. . . .

It is moreover contended . . . that from the peculiar nature and character of our government . . . from the moment rebellion lays down its arms and actual hostilities cease all political rights of rebellious communities are at once restored; that because the people of a state of the Union were once an organized community within the Union, they necessarily so remain, and their right to be represented in Congress at any and all times, and to participate in the government of the country under all circumstances, admits of neither question nor dispute. If this is indeed true, then is the government of the United States powerless for its own protection, and flagrant rebellion, carried to the extreme of civil war, is a pastime which any state may play at, not only certain that it can lose nothing in any event, but may even be the gainer by defeat?

It is the opinion of your committee—

---

[3]*Report of the Joint Committee on Reconstruction* (Washington, D.C., 1866), pp. 4ff.

I. That the States lately in rebellion were, at the close of the war, disorganized communities, without civil government, and without constitutions or other forms, by virtue of which political relation could legally exist between them and the federal government.

II. That Congress cannot be expected to recognize as valid the election of representatives from disorganized communities, which, from the very nature of the case, were unable to present their claim to representation under those established and recognized rules, the observance of which has been hitherto required.

III. That Congress would not be justified in admitting such communities to a participation in the government of the country without first providing such constitutional or other guarantees as will tend to secure the civil rights of all citizens of the republic; a just equality of representation; protection against claims founded in rebellion and crime; a temporary restoration of the right of suffrage to those who have not actively participated in the efforts to destroy the Union and overthrow the government, and the exclusion from position of public trust of, at least, a portion of those whose crimes have proved them to be enemies of the Union, and unworthy of public confidence. . . .

The necessity of providing adequate safeguards for the future, before restoring the insurrectionary States to a participation in the direction of public affairs, is apparent from the bitter hostility to the government and people of the United States yet existing throughout the conquered territory. . . .

The conclusion of your committee therefore is, that the so-called Confederate States are not, at present, entitled to representation in the Congress of the United States. . . .

4. President Andrew Johnson Tries to Restrain Congress (1867)

Alarmed by the outbreak of race riots in several Southern cities, and frustrated by the South's rejection of the Fourteenth Amendment, Congress passed the First Reconstruction Act on March 2, 1867. The act divided the South into military districts subject to martial law. It also stipulated that the seceding states could be restored to the Union only when they had called constitutional conventions, on the basis of universal manhood suffrage, which must guarantee black voting rights and ratify the Fourteenth Amendment. President Johnson promptly vetoed the bill, which just as promptly was passed over his veto. In his veto message, which follows, what reasons does he offer for his action? Are his arguments sound? Why might they have especially provoked the Republicans in Congress?

Washington, March 2, 1867

To the House of Representatives:

I have examined the bill "to provide for the more efficient government of the rebel States" with the care and anxiety which its transcendent importance is calcu-

---

[4]J. D. Richardson, ed., *Messages and Papers of the Presidents* (New York: Bureau of National Literature, 1911), vol. 5, pp. 3690–3696.

lated to awaken. I am unable to give it my assent, for reasons so grave that I hope a statement of them may have some influence on the minds of the patriotic and enlightened men with whom the decision must ultimately rest.

The bill places all the people of the ten States therein named under the absolute domination of military rulers; and the preamble undertakes to give the reason upon which the measure is based and the ground upon which it is justified. It declares that there exists in those States no legal governments and no adequate protection for life or property, and asserts the necessity of enforcing peace and good order within their limits. Is this true as matter of fact? . . .

Have we the power to establish and carry into execution a measure like this? I answer, Certainly not, if we derive our authority from the Constitution and if we are bound by the limitations which it imposes.

This proposition is perfectly clear, that no branch of the Federal Government—executive, legislative, or judicial—can have any just powers except those which it derives through and exercises under the organic law of the Union. Outside of the Constitution we have no legal authority more than private citizens, and within it we have only so much as that instrument gives us. This broad principle limits all our functions and applies to all subjects. It protects not only the citizens of States which are within the Union, but it shields every human being who comes or is brought under our jurisdiction. We have no right to do in one place more than in another that which the Constitution says we shall not do at all. If, therefore, the Southern States were in truth out of the Union, we could not treat their people in a way which the fundamental law forbids.

Some persons assume that the success of our arms in crushing the opposition which was made in some of the States to the execution of the Federal laws reduced those States and all their people—the innocent as well as the guilty—to the condition of vassalage and gave us a power over them which the Constitution does not bestow or define or limit. No fallacy can be more transparent than this. Our victories subjected the insurgents to legal obedience, not to the yoke of an arbitrary despotism. . . .

Invasion, insurrection, rebellion, and domestic violence were anticipated when the Government was framed, and the means of repelling and suppressing them were wisely provided for in the Constitution; but it was not thought necessary to declare that the States in which they might occur should be expelled from the Union. Rebellions, which were invariably suppressed, occurred prior to that out of which these questions grow; but the States continued to exist and the Union remained unbroken. In Massachusetts, in Pennsylvania, in Rhode Island, and in New York, at different periods in our history, violent and armed opposition to the United States was carried on; but the relations of those States with the Federal Government were not supposed to be interrupted or changed thereby after the rebellious portions of their population were defeated and put down. It is true that in these earlier cases there was no formal expression of a determination to withdraw from the Union, but it is also true that in the Southern States the ordinances of secession were treated by all the friends of the Union as mere nullities and are now acknowledged to be so by the States themselves. If we admit that they had any force or validity or that they did in fact take the States in which they were passed out of the Union, we sweep from under our feet all the grounds upon which we stand in justifying the use of Federal force to maintain the integrity of the Government. . . .

The United States are bound to guarantee to each State a republican form of government. Can it be pretended that this obligation is not probably broken if we carry out a measure like this, which wipes away every vestige of republican government in ten States and puts the life, property, liberty, and honor of all the people in each of them under the domination of a single person clothed with unlimited authority?

The purpose and object of the bill—the general intent which pervades it from beginning to end—is to change the entire structure and character of the State governments and to compel them by force to the adoption of organic laws and regulations which they are unwilling to accept if left to themselves. The negroes have not asked for the privilege of voting; the vast majority of them have no idea what it means. This bill not only thrusts it into their hands, but compels them, as well as the whites, to use it in a particular way. If they do not form a constitution with prescribed articles in it and afterwards elect a legislature which will act upon certain measures in a prescribed way, neither blacks nor whites can be relieved from the slavery which the bill imposes upon them. Without pausing here to consider the policy or impolicy of Africanizing the southern part of our territory, I would simply ask the attention of Congress to that manifest, well-known, and universally acknowledged rule of constitutional law which declares that the Federal Government has no jurisdiction, authority, or power to regulate such subjects for any State. To force the right of suffrage out of the hands of the white people and into the hands of the negroes is an arbitrary violation of this principle. . . .

The bill also denies the legality of the governments of ten of the States which participated in the ratification of the amendment to the Federal Constitution abolishing slavery forever within the jurisdiction of the United States [the Thirteenth Amendment] and practically excludes them from the Union. If this assumption of the bill be correct, their concurrence can not be considered as having been legally given, and the important fact is made to appear that the consent of three-fourths of the States—the requisite number—has not been constitutionally obtained to the ratification of that amendment, thus leaving the question of slavery where it stood before the amendment was officially declared to have become a part of the Constitution.

That the measure proposed by this bill does violate the Constitution in the particulars mentioned and in many other ways which I forbear to enumerate is too clear to admit of the least doubt. . . .

It is part of our public history which can never be forgotten that both Houses of Congress, in July, 1861, declared in the form of a solemn resolution that the war was and should be carried on for no purpose of subjugation, but solely to enforce the Constitution and laws, and that when this was yielded by the parties in rebellion the contest should cease, with the constitutional rights of the States and of individuals unimpaired. This resolution was adopted and sent forth to the world unanimously by the Senate and with only two dissenting voices in the House. It was accepted by the friends of the Union in the South as well as in the North as expressing honestly and truly the object of the war. On the faith of it many thousands of persons in both sections gave their lives and their fortunes to the cause. To repudiate it now by refusing to the States and to the individuals within them the rights which the Constitution and laws of the Union would secure to them is a breach of our plighted honor for which I can imagine no excuse and to which I can not voluntarily become a party. . . .

5. *The Controversy over the Fifteenth Amendment (1866, 1870)*

The Fifteenth Amendment guaranteed all adult males, regardless of race, the right to vote, and the campaign to have it ratified produced bitter arguments between the radical Republicans and their opponents. The first illustration below, entitled The Constitutional Amendment, *was first published during a heated election campaign in Pennsylvania in 1866. Supporters of the Democratic candidate for governor circulated this image in an attempt to defeat the Republican gubernatorial nominee. What are its most pointed arguments? The second image,* The Fifteenth Amendment and Its Results, *appeared in Baltimore in 1870 to celebrate the enactment of the Fifteenth Amendment. What does it find most praiseworthy about the new law? How are blacks depicted in the two prints? Were there any principled arguments against the Fifteenth Amendment?*

CELEBRATION AT BALTIMORE ON MAY 19ᵗ 1870.

THE FIFTEENTH AMENDMENT AND ITS RESULTS.

Respectfully dedicated to the colored Citizens of the U.S.of America A.D.1870. by Schneider & Fuchs 184 N.Eutaw St. Baltimore Mᵈ

C. Impeaching the President

1. Johnson's Cleveland Speech (1866)

A tactless and stubborn President Johnson clashed openly with the Republicans in Congress, including the embittered Thaddeus Stevens, when he vetoed a series of reconstruction bills. Two of the measures designed to help the former slaves—the Civil Rights Bill and the New Freedmen's Bureau Bill—were speedily repassed over his veto. Undaunted, Johnson embarked on a speech-making tour to urge the election of

---

[1]Edward McPherson, *The Political History of the United States of America during the Period of Reconstruction,* 3rd ed. (Washington, D.C.: Philip and Salomons, 1871), pp. 134–136.

congressmen favorable to his policies. But the public was in an ugly mood. Former President Jefferson Davis, though still in prison, was untried and unhanged, as were other former Confederates. A recent antiblack riot in New Orleans had resulted in some two hundred casualties. Johnson had earlier distinguished himself as a rough-and-ready stump speaker in Tennessee, but, as Secretary Seward remarked, the president of the United States should not be a stump speaker. Johnson's undignified harangue in Cleveland contained passages (here italicized) that formed the basis of some of the impeachment charges later brought by the House. What criticisms can be legitimately leveled against this speech? Which one is the most serious?

Notwithstanding the subsidized gang of hirelings and traducers [in Congress?], I have discharged all my duties and fulfilled all my pledges, and I say here tonight that if my predecessor had lived, the vials of wrath would have been poured out upon him. [Cries of "Never!" "Three cheers for the Congress of the United States!"]

. . . Where is the man or woman who can place his finger upon one single act of mine deviating from any pledge of mine or in violation of the Constitution of the country? [Cheers.] . . . Who can come and place his finger on one pledge I ever violated, or one principle I ever proved false to? [A voice, "How about New Orleans?" Another voice, "Hang Jeff Davis."] Hang Jeff Davis, he says. [Cries of "No," and "Down with him!"] . . . Hang Jeff Davis. Why don't you hang him? [Cries of "Give us the opportunity."] Have not you got the court? Have not you got the Attorney General? . . .

I will tell you what I did do. I called upon your Congress that is trying to break up the government. [Emphasis added.] [Cries, "You be d———d!" and cheers mingled with hisses. Great confusion. "Don't get mad, Andy!"] Well, I will tell you who is mad. "Whom the gods wish to destroy, they first make mad." Did your Congress order any of them to be tried? ["Three cheers for Congress."] . . .

You pretend now to have great respect and sympathy for the poor brave fellow who has left an arm on the battlefield. [Cries, "Is this dignified?"] I understand you. . . . I care not for dignity. . . . [A voice, "Traitor!"] I wish I could see that man. I would bet you now that if the light fell on your face, cowardice and treachery would be seen in it. Show yourself. Come out here where I can see you. [Shouts of laughter.] If you ever shoot a man you will do it in the dark, and pull the trigger when no one is by to see you. [Cheers.]

I understand traitors. I have been fighting them at the south end of the line, and we are now fighting them in the other direction. [Laughter and cheers.] I come here neither to criminate or recriminate, but when attacked, my plan is to defend myself. [Cheers.] . . . As Chief Magistrate, I felt so after taking the oath to support the Constitution, and when I saw encroachments upon your Constitution and rights, as an honest man I dared to sound the tocsin of alarm. ["Three cheers for Andrew Johnson."] . . .

I love my country. Every public act of my life testifies that is so. Where is the man that can put his finger upon any one act of mine that goes to prove the contrary? And what is my offending? [A voice, "Because you are not a Radical," and cry of "Veto."] Somebody says veto. Veto of what? What is called the Freedmen's Bureau bill? . . . I might refer to the Civil Rights Bill, the results of which are very similar. I tell you, my countrymen, that though the powers of hell and Thad Stevens and his gang were by, they could not turn me from my purpose. . . .

In conclusion, beside that, Congress had taken such pains to poison their constituents against him. But what had Congress done? Had they done anything to restore the Union of these states? No; on the contrary, they had done everything to prevent it; and because he stood now where he did when the rebellion commenced, he had been denounced as a traitor. Who had run greater risks or made greater sacrifices than himself? But Congress, factious and domineering, had [under]taken to poison the minds of the American people.* [Emphasis added.]

2. Senator Lyman Trumbull Defends Johnson (1868)

Johnson's unrestrained oratory backfired, and at the polls in November the Republicans won control of a two-thirds majority in both houses of Congress. They proceeded to pass the Tenure of Office Act, which was designed to entrap Johnson. Doubting its constitutionality (by indirection it was later judged unconstitutional) and seeking to bring a test case, he deliberately challenged it by removing Secretary William Stanton. The House thereupon impeached Johnson for "high crimes and misdemeanors." Most of its indictment related to Johnson's alleged violation of the Tenure of Office Act; other charges related to his "scandalous harangues." Particularly objectionable was a speech at the White House in which the president had declared that acts of Congress were not binding upon him because the South did not enjoy proper representation in it. One of the ablest of those who spoke for Johnson was Senator Lyman Trumbull of Illinois, a brilliant constitutional lawyer and a former associate of Lincoln. As one who followed principle rather than partisanship, he changed parties three times during his career. In the following speech, what is his main reason for thinking that Johnson's removal would be unfortunate?

In coming to the conclusion that the President is not guilty of any of the high crimes and misdemeanors with which he stands charged, I have endeavored to be governed by the case made, without reference to other acts of his not contained in the record, and without giving the least heed to the clamor of intemperate zealots who demand the conviction of Andrew Johnson as a test of party faith, or seek to identify with and make responsible for his acts those who from convictions of duty feel compelled, on the case made, to vote for his acquittal.

His speeches and the general course of his administration have been as distasteful to me as to anyone, and I should consider it the great calamity of the age if the disloyal element, so often encouraged by his measures, should gain political ascendancy. If the question was, Is Andrew Johnson a fit person for President? I should answer, no; but it is not a party question, nor upon Andrew Johnson's deeds and acts, except so far as they are made to appear in the record, that I am to decide.

---

*The reporter now lapses into the third person.

[2]*Congressional Globe,* 40th Cong., 2d sess. (May 7, 1868), Supplement, p. 420.

Painful as it is to disagree with so many political associates and friends whose conscientious convictions have led them to a different result, I must, nevertheless, in the discharge of the high responsibility under which I act, be governed by what my reason and judgment tell me is the truth, and the justice and law of this case. . . .

Once set the example of impeaching a President for what, when the excitement of the hour shall have subsided, will be regarded as insufficient causes, as several of those now alleged against the President were decided to be by the House of Representatives only a few months since, and no future President will be safe who happens to differ with a majority of the House and two-thirds of the Senate on any measure deemed by them important, particularly if of a political character. Blinded by partisan zeal, with such an example before them, they will not scruple to remove out of the way any obstacle to the accomplishment of their purposes, and what then becomes of the checks and balances of the Constitution, so carefully devised and so vital to its perpetuity? They are all gone.

In view of the consequences likely to flow from this day's proceedings, should they result in conviction on what my judgment tells me are insufficient charges and profits, I tremble for the future of my country. I cannot be an instrument or produce such a result; and at the hazard of the ties even of friendship and affection, till calmer times shall do justice to my motives, no alternative is left me but the inflexible discharge of duty.

[President Johnson escaped removal by the margin of a single vote, and only because seven conscientious Republican senators, including Trumbull, risked political suicide by refusing to go along with the majority.]

D. "Black Reconstruction"

1. Thaddeus Stevens Demands Black Suffrage (1867)

The most influential radical Republican in the House, crippled and vindictive Thaddeus Stevens of Pennsylvania, loathed slavery, slaveholders, and slave breeders. He felt a deep compassion for blacks and, in fact, arranged to be buried in a black cemetery. But in his demands for black suffrage he was motivated, like many other Republicans, by a mixture of idealism and opportunism. Of the arguments for black voting that he set forth in the following speech in the House, which ones were the most selfish? the most idealistic?

There are several good reasons for the passage of this bill [for reconstructing the South].

---

[1]*Congressional Globe,* 39th Cong., 2d sess. (January 3, 1867), p. 252.

In the first place, it is just. I am now confining my argument to Negro suffrage in the rebel states. Have not loyal blacks quite as good a right to choose rulers and make laws as rebel whites?

In the second place, it is a necessity in order to protect the loyal white men in the seceded states. The white Union men are in a great minority in each of those states. With them the blacks would act in a body; and it is believed that in each of said states, except one, the two united would form a majority, control the states, and protect themselves. Now they are the victims of daily murder. They must suffer constant persecution, or be exiled. . . .

Another good reason is, it would insure the ascendancy of the Union [Republican] Party. "Do you avow the party purpose?" exclaims some horror-stricken demagogue. I do. For I believe, on my conscience, that on the continued ascendancy of that party depends the safety of this great nation.

If impartial suffrage is excluded in the rebel states, then every one of them is sure to send a solid rebel representative delegation to Congress, and cast a solid rebel electoral vote. They, with their kindred Copperheads of the North, would always elect the President and control Congress. While Slavery sat upon her defiant throne, and insulted and intimidated the trembling North, the South frequently divided on questions of policy between Whigs and Democrats, and gave victory alternately to the sections. Now, you must divide them between loyalists, without regard to color, and disloyalists, or you will be the perpetual vassals of the free-trade, irritated, revengeful South.

For these, among other reasons, I am for Negro suffrage in every rebel state. If it be just, it should not be denied; if it be necessary, it should be adopted; if it be a punishment to traitors, they deserve it.

2. Black and White Legislatures (c. 1876)

Black suffrage was finally forced on the Southern whites by their new state constitutions and by the Fifteenth Amendment to the federal Constitution (1870). Tension grew worse as designing Northern "carpetbaggers" and Unionist Southern whites ("scalawags") moved in to exploit the inexperienced former slaves. J. W. Leigh, an English clergyman turned Georgia rice planter, recorded the following observations in a personal letter. What conditions were most galling to the former Confederates?

The fact is, the poor Negro has since the war been placed in an entirely false position, and is therefore not to be blamed for many of the absurdities he has committed, seeing that he has been urged on by Northern "carpetbaggers" and Southern "scalawags," who have used him as a tool to further their own nefarious ends.

The great mistake committed by the North was giving the Negroes the franchise so soon after their emancipation, when they were not the least prepared for it. In

---

[2]Frances B. Leigh, *Ten Years on a Georgia Plantation since the War* (London: R. Bentley and Sons, 1883), pp. 268–292 (Appendix).

1865 slavery was abolished, and no one even among the Southerners, I venture to say, would wish it back. In 1868 they [Negroes] were declared citizens of the United States, and in 1870 they had the right of voting given them, and at the same time persons concerned in the rebellion were excluded from public trusts by what was called the "iron-clad" oath. And as if this was not enough, last year [1875] the Civil Rights Bill was passed, by which Negroes were to be placed on a perfect equality with whites, who were to be compelled to travel in the same cars with them, and to send their children to the same schools.

The consequence of all this is that where there is a majority of Negroes, as is the case in the states of Louisiana, Mississippi, and South Carolina, these states are placed completely under Negro rule, and scenes occur in the state legislatures which baffle description.

I recollect at the beginning of 1870 being at Montgomery, the capital of Alabama, and paying a visit to the State House there, when a discussion was going on with respect to a large grant which was to be made for the building of the Alabama and Chattanooga Railway, the real object of which was to put money into the pockets of certain carpetbaggers, who, in order to gain their object, had bribed all the Negroes to vote for the passing of the bill.

The scene was an exciting one. Several Negro members were present, with their legs stuck up on the desks in front of them, and spitting all about them in free and independent fashion. One gentleman having spoken for some time against the bill, and having reiterated his condemnation of it as a fraudulent speculation, a stout Negro member from Mobile sprung up and said, "Mister Speaker, when yesterday I spoke, I was not allowed to go on because you said I spoke twice on the same subject. Now what is sauce for the goose is sauce for the gander. Dis Member is saying over and over again de same thing; why don't you tell him to sit down? for what is sauce for," etc. To which the Speaker said, "Sit down yourself, sir." Another member (a carpetbagger) jumped up and shook his fist in the speaking member's face, and told him he was a liar, and if he would come outside he would give him satisfaction.

This is nothing, however, to what has been going on in South Carolina this last session. Poor South Carolina, formerly the proudest state in America, boasting of her ancient families, remarkable for her wealth, culture, and refinement, now prostrate in the dust, ruled over by her former slaves, an old aristocratic society replaced by the most ignorant democracy that mankind ever saw invested with the functions of government. Of the 124 representatives, there are but 23 representatives of her old civilization, and these few can only look on at the squabbling crowd amongst whom they sit as silent enforced auditors. Of the 101 remaining, 94 are colored, and 7 their white allies. The few honest amongst them see plundering and corruption going on on all sides, and can do nothing. . . .

The Negroes have it all their own way, and rob and plunder as they please. The Governor of South Carolina lives in luxury, and treats his soldiers to champagne, while the miserable planters have to pay taxes amounting to half their income, and if they fail to pay, their property is confiscated.

Louisiana and Mississippi are not much better off. The former has a Negro barber for its Lieutenant-governor, and the latter has just selected a Negro steamboat porter as its United States Senator, filling the place once occupied by Jefferson Davis.

3. W. E. B. Du Bois Justifies Black Legislators (1910)

W. E. B. Du Bois, a Massachusetts-born black of French Huguenot extraction, received his Ph.D. from Harvard University in 1895. Distinguished as a teacher, lecturer, historian, economist, sociologist, novelist, poet, and propagandist, he became a militant advocate of equal rights. A founder of the National Association for the Advancement of Colored People (NAACP), he served for twenty-four years as editor of its chief organ. Du Bois, who was born the day before the House impeached Johnson, here writes as a scholar. In what important respects does he argue that Reconstruction legislatures have been unfairly represented? In what ways were these bodies responsible for significant achievements?

Undoubtedly there were many ridiculous things connected with Reconstruction governments: the placing of ignorant field-hands who could neither read nor write in the legislature, the gold spittoons of South Carolina, the enormous public printing bill of Mississippi—all these were extravagant and funny; and yet somehow, to one who sees, beneath all that is bizarre, the real human tragedy of the upward striving of downtrodden men, the groping for light among people born in darkness, there is less tendency to laugh and jibe than among shallower minds and easier consciences. All that is funny is not bad.

Then, too, a careful examination of the alleged stealing in the South reveals much. First, there is repeated exaggeration. For instance, it is said that the taxation in Mississippi was fourteen times as great in 1874 as in 1869. This sounds staggering until we learn that the state taxation in 1869 was only ten cents on one hundred dollars, and that the expenses of government in 1874 were only twice as great as in 1860, and that too with a depreciated currency. . . .

The character of the real thieving shows that white men must have been the chief beneficiaries. . . . The frauds through the manipulation of state and railway bonds and of banknotes must have inured chiefly to the benefit of experienced white men, and this must have been largely the case in the furnishing and printing frauds. . . .

That the Negroes, led by astute thieves, became tools and received a small share of the spoils is true. But . . . much of the legislation which resulted in fraud was represented to the Negroes as good legislation, and thus their votes were secured by deliberate misrepresentation. . . .

Granted, then, that the Negroes were to some extent venal but to a much larger extent ignorant and deceived, the question is: Did they show any signs of a disposition to learn better things? The theory of democratic governments is not that the will of the people is always right, but rather that normal human beings of average intelligence will, if given a chance, learn the right and best course by bitter experience. This is precisely what Negro voters showed indubitable signs of doing. First, they strove for schools to abolish ignorance, and, second, a large and growing number of them revolted against the carnival of extravagance and stealing that marred the beginning of Reconstruction, and joined with the best elements to institute reform. . . .

---

[3]*American Historical Review* 15 (1910): 791–799, passim.

We may recognize three things which Negro rule gave to the South:

1. Democratic government.
2. Free public schools.
3. New social legislation. . . .

In South Carolina there was before the war a property qualification for office-holders, and, in part, for voters. The [Reconstruction] constitution of 1868, on the other hand, was a modern democratic document . . . preceded by a broad Declaration of Rights which did away with property qualifications and based representation directly on population instead of property. It especially took up new subjects of social legislation, declaring navigable rivers free public highways, instituting homestead exemptions, establishing boards of county commissioners, providing for a new penal code of laws, establishing universal manhood suffrage "without distinction of race or color," devoting six sections to charitable and penal institutions and six to corporations, providing separate property for married women, etc. Above all, eleven sections of the Tenth Article were devoted to the establishment of a complete public-school system.

So satisfactory was the constitution thus adopted by Negro suffrage and by a convention composed of a majority of blacks that the state lived twenty-seven years under it without essential change. And when the constitution was revised in 1895, the revision was practically nothing more than an amplification of the constitution of 1868. No essential advance step of the former document was changed except the suffrage article. . . .

There is no doubt but that the thirst of the black man for knowledge—a thirst which has been too persistent and durable to be mere curiosity or whim—gave birth to the public free-school system of the South. It was the question upon which black voters and legislators insisted more than anything else, and while it is possible to find some vestiges of free schools in some of the Southern states before the war, yet a universal, well-established system dates from the day that the black man got political power. . . .

Finally, in legislation covering property, the wider functions of the state, the punishment of crime, and the like, it is sufficient to say that the laws on these points established by Reconstruction legislatures were not only different from and even revolutionary to the laws in the older South, but they were so wise and so well suited to the needs of the new South that in spite of a retrogressive movement following the overthrow of Negro governments, the mass of this legislation, with elaboration and development, still stands on the statute books of the South.

4. Benjamin Tillman's Antiblack Tirade (1907)

Reared in a slaveowning family, Senator Benjamin R. Tillman of South Carolina had participated in antiblack outrages during Reconstruction days. His face contorted, his one good eye glowing like a live coal, and his voice rising to a whine, "Till-

---

[4]*Congressional Record,* 59th Cong., 2d sess. (January 21, 1907), p. 1440.

man the Terrible" shocked the Senate and the nation with wild speeches in which he boasted that "we took the government away [from blacks]," we "stuffed the ballot boxes," we used "tissue ballots," "we shot them," "we are not ashamed of it," and "we will do it again." Whom does he blame most for the alleged conditions to which he refers?

It was in 1876, thirty years ago, and the people of South Carolina had been living under Negro rule for eight years. There was a condition bordering upon anarchy. Misrule, robbery, and murder were holding high carnival. The people's substance was being stolen, and there was no incentive to labor. Our legislature was composed of a majority of Negroes, most of whom could neither read nor write. They were the easy dupes and tools of as dirty a band of vampires and robbers as ever preyed upon a prostrate people. . . . Life ceased to be worth having on the terms under which we were living, and in desperation we determined to take the government away from the Negroes.

We reorganized the Democratic party [of South Carolina] with one plank, and only one plank, namely, that "this is a white man's country, and white men must govern it." Under that banner we went to battle.

We had 8000 Negro militia organized by carpetbaggers. . . . They used to drum up and down the roads with their fifes and their gleaming bayonets, equipped with new Springfield rifles and dressed in the regulation uniform. It was lawful, I suppose, but these Negro soldiers—or this Negro militia, for they were never soldiers—growing more and more bold, let drop talk among themselves where the white children might hear their purpose, and it came to our ears. This is what they said: "The President [Grant] is our friend. The North is with us. We intend to kill all the white men, take the land, marry the white women, and then these white children will wait on us." . . .

We knew—who knew better—that the North then was a unit in its opposition to Southern ideas, and that it was their purpose to perpetuate Negro governments in those states where it could be done by reason of their being a Negro majority. Having made up our minds, we set about it as practical men. . . .

Clashes came. The Negro militia grew unbearable and more and more insolent. I am not speaking of what I have read; I am speaking of what I know, of what I saw. There were two militia companies in my township and a regiment in my county. We had clashes with these Negro militiamen. The Hamburg riot was one clash, in which seven Negroes and one white man were killed. A month later we had the Ellenton riot, in which no one ever knew how many Negroes were killed, but there were forty or fifty or a hundred. It was a fight between barbarism and civilization, between the African and the Caucasian, for mastery.

It was then that "we shot them"; it was then that "we killed them"; it was then that "we stuffed ballot boxes." After the [federal] troops came and told us, "You must stop this rioting," we had decided to take the government away from men so debased as were the Negroes. . . .

[President] Grant sent troops to maintain the carpetbag government in power and to protect the Negroes in the right to vote. He merely obeyed the law. . . . Then it was that "we stuffed ballot boxes," because desperate diseases require desperate remedies, and having resolved to take the state away, we hesitated at nothing. . . .

I want to say now that we have not shot any Negroes in South Carolina on account of politics since 1876. We have not found it necessary. Eighteen hundred and seventy-six happened to be the hundredth anniversary of the Declaration of Independence, and the action of the white men of South Carolina in taking the state away from the Negroes we regard as a second declaration of independence by the Caucasian from African barbarism.

E. The Ku Klux Klan's Reign of Terror

1. Alfred Richardson Testifies about Reconstruction-Era Georgia (1871)

In 1871, a special congressional committee took testimony, in hearings conducted in both Washington and the South, about the mounting violence that was being visited upon the newly freed blacks, especially by the Ku Klux Klan. The extensive record of the committee's investigation provides grisly evidence of the dangerous situation in which black men and women found themselves in the post–Civil War South. The testimony excerpted below was given by Alfred Richardson. He was born a slave in Georgia in about 1837 and supported his wife and three children after emancipation by working as a carpenter. He was also politically active in the Republican party, an affiliation that brought down upon him the savage wrath of his white neighbors, virtually all of them Democrats. What does his testimony suggest about the political situation in the Reconstruction-era South? about the situation of black women? By what means did whites assert political and economic control over blacks? In the light of this testimony, how should the success or failure of Reconstruction policy be judged?

Washington, D.C., July 7, 1871

Alfred Richardson (colored) sworn and examined.

Question. Since you became a freeman have you voted?
Answer. Yes, sir.
Question. With what party have you voted?
Answer. The republican party.
Question. State to the committee whether you have been attacked in any way by anybody; if so, when and how. Tell us the whole story about it.
Answer. Yes, sir; I was attacked twice. The first time was just before last Christmas; I cannot recollect exactly what day.
Question. Tell us all the particulars.
Answer. There was a set of men came down to about a quarter of a mile of where I live. They were all disguised. They had taken out an old man by the name of

---

[1]Alfred Richardson, in *Testimony Taken by the Joint Select Committee to Inquire into the Condition of Affairs in the Late Insurrectionary States; Georgia, Volume I*, pp. 1–2, 12–13. *Report* No. 41, Part 6, 42d Cong., 2d sess. Senate (Washington, D.C.: Government Printing Office, 1872).

Charles Watson. They commenced beating him. His wife and children all ran out, and screamed and hallooed for help to stop the men from beating him to death. We, who were in town, came out to see what was the matter.

Question. You heard the outcry?

Answer. Yes, sir, and came out to see what was the matter. We went up the street a piece, out on the edge of the town, and heard a great parcel of men talking beside the fence. It was the Ku-Klux, who had this old man down in the corner of the fence, knocking him and telling him he had to tell where Alfred Richardson was, and had to go with them to his house and show how he was fixed up. The old man seemed to be sort of dilatory in telling them, and they rapped him over the head again and told him he had to go.

Question. They wanted him to tell where you were?

Answer. Yes, sir; they wanted him to tell where I was, and how I was fixed up; they said he had to go and get me out. In the mean time, while they were telling him this, a crowd of boys came on behind me, and we all ran up, after we heard what they were up to. They all broke and ran, and carried this old man with them. We followed them to the forks of the road, about three hundred yards from where we met them. They all stopped and got over into the field, taking the old man with them. I ran up, and looked first up one road and then the other, to see which way they had gone. I could not see anybody for a long time; a cloud had got over the moon. After a while I saw one fellow slipping alongside the fence. He had a pistol in his hand, as if to shoot me. When I saw him doing that, I took my pistol, and shot at him. When I shot at him there were three or four men who shot me from through the fence. I did not see them. They shot about twenty shots into my leg and hip. I went off home, and went to the doctor's office. The doctor examined me, and fixed my wounds up. In three or four days I got so that I could travel very well. Things went on till after Christmas. On the 18th of January a man by the name of John O. Thrasher came to me———

Question. Was he a white man?

Answer. Yes, sir; a very wealthy man. He came to me. My brother was keeping a family grocery; and I was in with him. I did not stay in the store; I worked at my trade.

Question. Were you a partner in the concern?

Answer. Yes, sir. This man told me, "There are some men about here that have something against you; and they intend to kill you or break you up. They say you are making too much money; that they do not allow any nigger to rise that way; that you can control all the colored votes; and they intend to break you up, and then they can rule the balance of the niggers when they get you off." He said, "They said they wanted me to join their party, but I told them I did not want to do it; I never knew you to do anything wrong, and these are a parcel of low-down men, and I don't want to join any such business; but I tell you, you had better keep your eyes open, for they are after you." He talked to me about it that evening for three or four hours. I told him I didn't know why they had anything against me. I talked to the ordinary, and the clerk of the court, and several other citizens. They said they didn't see why anybody wanted to interrupt me; that I had always kept the peace between the colored and the white people; that when there was a fuss I was the only man that could break it up and make the colored people behave themselves; that they hated to let me go away. I talked with all the citizens, and they told me they did not see why anybody had anything against me. I said, "I am told that some men are coming to kill me or run me off, and I think I had better go away. I don't know whether I can stay safely." They told me, "No, don't move away; they are just talking that way to scare you, I reckon." The same night this man was telling me that, I went to bed about 9 o'clock. Between 12 and 1 o'clock these men came; there were about twenty or twenty-five of them, I reckon. About eight or ten of them got abreast and ran against my door. I sort of expected them, and had my door barred very tight; I had long staples at the side, and scantling across the door. They ran against the door and tried to burst it in. They could not do it. One fellow had a new patent ax with him; and he commenced cutting down the door. One lit a candle and put it down in the piazza; the other man cut the door till he cut it down. I stood and looked at him until he cut it spang through. Then I thought I had better go up-stairs. I did so. I thought I would stand at the head of the stair-steps and shoot them as they came up. But they broke in the lower door and came up-stairs firing in every direction. I could not stand in the stairway to shoot at them. I had some small arms back in the garret. There was a door up there about large enough for one man to creep in. I thought I had better go in there, and maybe they would not find me—probably they would miss me, and I could make my escape. They all came up-stairs. My wife opened the window to call out for help, and a fellow shot at her some twelve or fifteen times through that window while she was hallooing. A whole crowd came up, and when they saw that window open, they said, "He has jumped out of the window," and they hallooed to the fellows on the ground to shoot on top of the house. Thinking I had gone out of the window, they all went down-stairs except one man. He went and looked in the cuddy-hole where I was, and saw me there. He hallooed to the rest of the fellows that he had found me; but they had got down-stairs, and some of them were on the piazza. Then he commenced firing, and shot me three times. He lodged two balls in my side, and one in the right arm. That weakened me pretty smartly. After he had shot his loads all out, he said to the rest of them, "Come back up here; I have got him; and I have shot him, but he is not quite dead; let us go up and finish him." I crept from the door of the little room where I was to the stairway; they came up-stairs with their pistols in their hands, and a man behind with a light. I shot one of them as he got on the top step. They gathered him up by the legs; and then they all ran and left me. I never saw any more of them that night; and I have not seen them since. . . .

Question. Do these bands of men ever whip women?

Answer. Yes, sir.

Question. Why do they whip women? They do not vote.

Answer. Many times, you know, a white lady has a colored lady for cook or waiting in the house, or something of that sort. They have some quarrel, and sometimes probably the colored women gives the lady a little jaw. In a night or two a crowd will come in and take her out and whip her.

Question. For talking saucily to her mistress?

Answer. Yes, sir.

Question. Does that state of things control colored labor down there? Do these bands make the negroes work for whomever they please?

Answer. Do you mean the Ku-Klux?

Question. Yes, sir.

Answer. Well, they go sometimes so far as this: When a man is hired, if he and his employer have any dispute about the price, and there are hard words between them about the amount of money to be paid, they whip the colored man for disputing the white man's word, or having any words with him.

Question. They whip the colored man for having any dispute with his employer about what shall be paid him?

Answer. Yes, sir.

Question. Is that common?

Answer. Yes, sir; that has been done several times. Sometimes colored people are working for a part of the crop. They work on till the crop is nearly completed and ready for gathering. Then a fuss arises between them and the employer, and they are whipped off—whipped off by these men in disguise. If they do not whip a man, they come and knock his door down and run him out, and he gets scared and moves away, leaving his share of the crop. He will sometimes go to the employer, and the man will say, "Your crop in the field is worth such and such a price, and that is all I will give you." The man will have to take what he can get and move off. Some of the colored people swear that they do not intend to farm any more, excepting they can have peace to gather what they plant. Now, they work a part of the year and then get run off and make nothing. So they conclude it is best to go to some city and work by the day for what they can get. Every town in our State where there is any protection is overrun with colored people. Many of the farm hands are there; and there is a great mass of loafers who stand round town because they have got no work to do. Yet people's fields around in the country are running away with grass. Some men go to town and try to get hands. The colored men will ask, "In what part of the country do you live?" The man will mention such and such a place. They will say, "We can't go down there; the Ku-Klux is down there. If it wasn't for the Ku-Klux we would go down and work for you."

Question. Are there many white republicans in your county?

Answer. No, sir; I do not suppose there are over four or five. In the city of Athens the man who attends the post office, I think, is a republican; then he has got two or three sons who are clerks in the post office; then there is the tax collector. They are republicans; they vote the republican ticket. . . .

2. Maria Carter Describes an Encounter with the Klan (1871)

Maria Carter, a twenty-eight-year-old slave from South Carolina, lived in Georgia at the time she gave the following testimony to the Joint Select Committee at its hearing

---

[2]Maria Carter, in *Testimony Taken by the Joint Select Committee to Inquire into the Condition of Affairs in the Late Insurrectionary States; Georgia, Volume I.* pp. 411–412. *Report* No. 41, Part 6, 42d Cong., 2d sess. Senate (Washington, D.C.: Government Printing Office, 1872).

in Atlanta. She describes a Klan raid on her house and that of a neighbor, John Walthall. What was Walthall's alleged offense? How might one account for the ferocity of the assault on Carter's family and Walthall?

Atlanta, Georgia, October 21, 1871

Maria Carter (colored) sworn and examined.

Question. How old are you, where were you born, and where do you now live?
Answer. I will be twenty-eight years old on the 4th day of next March; I was born in South Carolina; and I live in Haralson County now.
Question. Are you married or single?
Answer. I am married.
Question. What is your husband's name?
Answer. Jasper Carter.
Question. Where were you on the night that John Walthall was shot?
Answer. In my house, next to his house; not more than one hundred yards from his house.
Question. Did any persons come to your house that night?
Answer. Yes, sir, lots of them; I expect about forty or fifty of them.
Question. What did they do at your house?
Answer. They just came there and called; we did not get up when they first called. We heard them talking as they got over the fence. They came hollering and knocking at the door, and they scared my husband so bad he could not speak when they first came. I answered them. They hollered, "Open the door," I said, "Yes, sir." They were at the other door, and they said, "Kindle a light." My husband went to kindle a light, and they busted both doors open and ran in—two in one door and two in the other. I heard the others coming on behind them, jumping over the fence in the yard. One put his gun down to him and said, "Is this John Walthall?" They had been hunting him a long time. They had gone to my brother-in-law's hunting him, and had whipped one of my sisters-in-law powerfully and two more men on account of him. They said they were going to kill him when they got hold of him. They asked my husband if he was John Walthall. He was so scared he could not say anything. I said, "No." I never got up at all. They asked where he was, and we told them he was up to the next house. They jerked my husband up and said that he had to go up there. I heard them up there hollering "Open the door," and I heard them break the door down. While they were talking about our house, just before they broke open our door, I heard a chair fall over in John Walthall's house. He raised a plank then and tried to get under the house. A parcel of them ran ahead and broke the door down and jerked his wife out of the bed. I did not see them, for I was afraid to go out of doors. They knocked his wife about powerfully. I heard them cursing her. She commenced hollering, and I heard some of them say, "God damn her, shoot her." They struck her over the head with a pistol. The house looked next morning as if somebody had been killing hogs there. Some of them said, "Fetch a light here, quick;" and some of them said to her, "Hold a light." They said she held it, and they put their guns down on him and shot him. I

heard him holler, and some of them said, "Pull him out, pull him out." When they pulled him out the hole was too small, and I heard them jerk a plank part off the house and I heard it fly back. At that time four men came in my house and drew a gun on me; I was sitting in my bed and the baby was yelling. They asked, "Where is John Walthall?" I said, "Up yonder." They said, "Who lives here?" I said, "Jasper Carter." They said, "Where is John Walthall?" I said, "Them folks have got him." They said, "What folks?" I said, "Them folks up there." They came in and out all the time. I heard John holler when they commenced whipping him, They said, "Don't holler, or we'll kill you in a minute." I undertook to try and count, but they scared me so bad that I stopped counting; but I think they hit him about three hundred licks after they shot him. I heard them clear down to our house ask him if he felt like sleeping with some more white women; and they said, "You steal, too, God damn you." John said, "No, sir." They said, "Hush your mouth, God damn your eyes, you do steal." I heard them talking, but that was all I heard plain. They beat him powerfully. She said they made her put her arms around his neck and then they whipped them both together. I saw where they struck her head with a pistol and bumped her head against the house, and the blood is there yet. They asked me where my husband's gun was; I said he had no gun, and they said I was a damned liar. One of them had a sort of gown on, and he put his gun in my face and I pushed it up. The other said, "Don't you shoot her." He then went and looked in a trunk among the things. I allowed they were hunting for a pistol. My husband had had one, but he sold it. Another said, "Let's go away from here." They brought in old Uncle Charlie and sat him down there. They had a light at the time, and I got to see some of them good. I knew two of them, but the others I could not tell. There was a very large light in the house, and they went to the fire and I saw them. They came there at about 12 o'clock and staid there until 1. They went on back to old Uncle Charley's then, to whip his girls and his wife. They did not whip her any to hurt her at all. They jabbed me on the head with a gun, and I heard the trigger pop. It scared me and I throwed my hand up. He put it back again, and I pushed it away again.

Question. How old was your baby?

Answer. Not quite three weeks old.

Question. You were still in bed?

Answer. Yes, sir; I never got up at all.

Question. Did they interrupt your husband in any way?

Answer. Yes, sir; they whipped him mightily; I do not know how much. They took him away up the road, over a quarter, I expect. I saw the blood running down when he came back. Old Uncle Charley was in there. They did not carry him back home. They said, "Old man, you don't steal." He said, "No." They sat him down and said to him, "You just stay here." Just as my husband got back to one door and stepped in, three men came in the other door. They left a man at John's house while they were ripping around. As they came back by the house they said, "By God, good-bye, hallelujah!" I was scared nearly to death, and my husband tried to keep it hid from me. I asked him if he had been whipped much. He said, "No." I saw his clothes were bloody, and the next morning they stuck to him, and his shoulder was almost like jelly.

3. Henry Lowther Falls Victim to the Klan (1871)

Forty-one-year-old Henry Lowther was jailed on a charge of conspiring to kill a black man by the name of Rack Bell, who allegedly collaborated with the Ku Klux Klan. What does his gruesome account reveal about the Ku Klux Klan's tactics? What role do you think the physician played?

Atlanta, Georgia, October 20, 1871

Henry Lowther (colored) sworn and examined.

I was put in jail Saturday evening; my son was put in there with me. They said they had a warrant for him, but they did not have any. . . . I said, "Tell Captain Cummins to come here." A gentleman came with him by the name of Beaman. Captain Cummins sat down and talked with me about an hour, but there was nothing he said that I thought had any substance in it, only when he went to leave he said, "Harry, are you willing to give up your stones to save your life?" I sat there for a moment, and then I told him, "Yes." Said he, "If they come for you will you make fight?" I said "No." He said, "No fuss whatever?" I said, "No." That was about an hour by sun. I lay right down then and went to sleep, and did not wake up until 2 o'clock in the morning. Then I saw one Ku-Klux in jail with a light. I raised up, and he caught my arm and told me to come out. I came out and looked around, and the whole town was covered with them.

Question. Covered with what?

Answer. Ku-Klux. There were supposed to be one hundred and eighty of them. When they first took me out they tied me and carried me off from the jail-house about a hundred yards; they then divided into four parties, and about twenty of them carried me off into a swamp about two miles. Well, within a hundred yards of the swamp they all stopped and called numbers, began with number one, and went up as high as number ten. When they got to number ten they went for a rope, and I was satisfied they were going to hang me. I begged for my life. They told me if they did not kill me I would shoot into the Ku-Klux again. I told them I had not done it. They asked me who it was; I told them who I heard it was, but I did not know. One of them who was standing by told the other who was talking to me to hush up and ask no questions, because he knew more about it than I did. They went on then into the swamp, and came to a halt again, and stood there and talked awhile. There were eight men walking with me—one hold of each arm, three in front of me with guns, and three right behind me. After some conversation, just before they were ordered to march, or something was said, every man cocked his gun and looked right at me. I thought they were going to shoot me, and leave me right there. The moon was shining bright, and I could see them. I was satisfied they were going to kill me, and I did not care much then. They asked me whether I preferred to be altered [castrated] or to be killed. I said I preferred to be altered. After laying me down

---

[3]Henry Lowther, in *Testimony Taken by the Joint Select Committee to Inquire into the Condition of Affairs in the Late Insurrectionary States; Georgia, Volume I.* pp. 356–358. *Report* No. 41, Part 6, 42d Cong., 2d sess. Senate (Washington, D.C.: Government Printing Office, 1872).

and getting through they said: "Now, as soon as you can get to a doctor go to one; you know the doctors in this country, and as soon as you are able to leave do it, or we will kill you next time." I asked how long it would take to get well, and they said five or six weeks. I was naked and bleeding very much. It was two miles and a quarter to a doctor's. The first man's house I got to was the jailer's. I called him up and asked him to go to the jail-house and get my clothes. He said he could not go; I said, "You must; I am naked and nearly froze to death." That was about 3 o'clock in the night. He had a light in the house, and there was a party of men standing in the door. I told him I wanted him to come out and give me some attention. He said he could not come. I could hardly walk then. I went on about ten steps further and I met the jailer's son-in-law. I asked him to go and get my clothes; and he said, "No," and told me to go up and lie down. I went right on and got up to a store; there were a great many men sitting along on the store piazza; I knew some of them, but I did not look at them much. They asked me what I wanted; I said I wanted a doctor. They told me to go on and lie down. I had then to stop and hold on to the side of the house to keep from falling. I staid there a few minutes, and then went on to a doctor's house, about a quarter of a mile, and called him aloud twice. He did not answer me. The next thing I knew I was lying on the sidewalk in the street—seemed to have just waked up out of a sleep. I thought to myself, "Did I lie down here and go to sleep?" I wanted some water; I had to go about a quarter of a mile to get some water; I was getting short of breath, but the water helped me considerably. I went to a house about fifty yards further. I called to a colored woman to wake my wife up; she was in town. I happened to find my son there, and he went back for a doctor. When he got there the doctor answered the first time he called him. The reason he did not answer me was that he was off on this raid. I asked the doctor where he was when I was at his house, and he said he was asleep. I said, "I was at your house." The men kept coming in and saying to me that I did not get to the doctor's house, and I said that I did. After two or three times I took the hint, and said nothing more about that. But I told my son the next morning to go there and see if there was not a large puddle of blood at the gate. They would not let him go. But some colored women came to see me and told me that the blood was all over town; at the doctor's gate, and everywhere else. It was running a stream all the time I was trying to find the doctor, and I thought I would bleed to death. My son tended me until I got so I could travel. Doctor Cummins came there to my house on Tuesday evening, between sunset and dark, and said, "I am told you say the reason I did not come to you was that I was out on the raid with the Ku-Klux." I said, "I did not say so." He said, "That is what I heard;" and he seemed to be mad about it. He said, "I am a practicing physician, and am liable to be called at night, and must go; I was in my horse-lot then." He talked a long while, and then he said he was in his stable. He kept talking, and after awhile he said he was in his drug-store. So I never knew where he was. He said the reason he was hiding about so was he was afraid of the Ku-Klux. In a day or two he came to the house and said, "The white people have got up a story here, and say I am the man who castrated you; now, this talk must stop." I said, "Doctor, I can't help it; I don't know who did it; I didn't start the story." He said it had to be stopped; and then he began to tell me where he was; that the Ku-Klux came in, and he went right off to hide. In a few days his brother, Captain Cummins, came in and said, "Harry, I am told you make a threat of what you are going to do when you get well." I said, "What can I do?" He shook his head. I said, "Do the people believe it?" He said, "Yes, some of the most responsible people in town do believe it." I said, "I am very sorry." I then said, "Do you think the Ku-Klux will bother me any more?" He said, "If this talk dies out, I do not think they will pester you any more." I had been in the house about seventeen days; I was not able to walk, but I was uneasy; they came to me so many times that I began to be uneasy, and I left there. Just before I left they sent old man Bush and Mr. Hatfield to me to know if I would stay here and turn state's evidence against them. I said, "I am in a close place; the Ku-Klux have ordered me to leave; but I reckon I will try and stay." When I got so I could travel—I believe I lay there twenty-one days—I think it was the 22d of September, I left there. Now, I want you to understand that there was a man by the name of Lavender, who got up a company of men after they came to my house on a Monday night. I had run away. They told my wife to tell me that they would give me five days to leave in. . . .

F. The Legacy of Reconstruction

1. Editor E. L. Godkin Grieves (1871)

Irish-born E. L. Godkin, a fearless liberal, founded the distinguished and long-lived New York Nation *in 1865. So biting were his criticisms that the magazine was dubbed "the weekly day of judgment." His views on the blunders of Reconstruction were aired with incisiveness. He argued that there were two ways of dealing with the postwar South: (1) reorganize the section "from top to bottom" or (2) treat the whole community as made up of "unfortunate Americans, equally entitled to care and protection, demoralized by an accursed institution for which the whole Union was responsible, and which the whole Union had connived at, and, down to 1860, had profited by." But the North, wrote Godkin, followed neither course. Which aspects of Reconstruction does he regard as the most regrettable?*

The condition of the Negro after emancipation . . . attracted the carpetbagger as naturally as a dead ox attracts the buzzard. The lower class of demagogue scents an unenlightened constituency at an almost incredible distance, and travels towards it over mountain, valley, and river with the certainty of the mariner's compass.

But then we hastened his coming by our legislation. We deliberately, and for an indefinite period, excluded all the leading Southern men from active participation in the management of their local affairs, by a discrimination not unlike that which would be worked in this city [New York], but very much worse, if every man who

---

[1]*The Nation* (New York) 13 (December 7, 1871): 364.

had not at some time belonged to the Tammany Society were declared incapable of holding office.

It was before the war the time-honored custom of the Southern states, and a very good custom too, to put their ablest men, and men of the highest social standing and character, in office. The consequence was that it was these men who figured most prominently in the steps which led to the rebellion, and in the rebellion itself. When the war was over, we singled these men out, and not unnaturally, for punishment by the 14th Amendment and other legislation.

But we forgot that, as the President points out, they were no worse, so far as disloyalty went, than the rest of the community. They broke their oaths of allegiance to the United States, but the other white men of the South would have done the same thing if they had got the chance of doing it by being elevated to office, either under the United States or under the Confederacy. We forgot, too, that when putting a mutinous crew in irons, the most justly indignant captain leaves at liberty enough able-bodied seamen to work the ship. . . .

The results . . . have been positively infernal. In the idea that we were befriending the Negroes, we gave them possession of the government, and deprived them of the aid of all the local capacity and experience in the management of it, thus offering the states as a prey to Northern adventurers, and thus inflicting on the freedmen the very worst calamity which could befall a race newly emerged from barbarism— that is, familiarity, in the very first movements of enfranchisement, with the process of a corrupt administration, carried on by gangs of depraved vagabonds, in which the public money was stolen, the public faith made an article of traffic, the legislature openly corrupted, and all that the community contained of talent, probity, and social respectability put under a legal ban as something worthless and disreputable.

We do not hesitate to say that a better mode of debauching the freedmen, and making them permanently unfit for civil government, could hardly have been hit on had the North had such an object deliberately in view. Instead of establishing equal rights for all, we set up the government of a class, and this class the least competent, the most ignorant and inexperienced, and a class, too, whose history and antecedents made its rule peculiarly obnoxious to the rest of the community.

Out of this state of things Ku-Kluxing has grown . . . naturally. . . . We cannot gainsay anything anybody says of the atrocity of riding about the country at night with one's face blackened, murdering and whipping people. But we confess we condemn Ku-Kluxing very much as we condemn the cholera. . . . There is no more use in getting in a rage with Ku-Kluxery, and sending cavalry and artillery after it, than of legislating against pestilence, as long as nothing is done to remove the causes.

2. Frederick Douglass Complains (1882)

The incredible former slave Frederick Douglass (see p. 351) raised two famous black regiments in Massachusetts during the Civil War. Among the first recruits were his

---

[2]*Life and Times of Frederick Douglass* (Hartford Park Publishing Company, 1881), pp. 458–459.

own sons. Continuing his campaign for civil rights and suffrage for the freedmen, he wrote the following bitter commentary in his autobiography. One of his keenest regrets was that the federal government, despite the urgings of Thaddeus Stevens and others, failed to provide land for the freed slaves. In the light of his observations, how would free land have alleviated the conditions he describes? Why did the former slaveowners make life extremely difficult for the former slaves?

Though slavery was abolished, the wrongs of my people were not ended. Though they were not slaves, they were not yet quite free. No man can be truly free whose liberty is dependent upon the thought, feeling, and action of others, and who has himself no means in his own hands for guarding, protecting, defending, and maintaining that liberty. Yet the Negro after his emancipation was precisely in this state of destitution.

The law on the side of freedom is of great advantage only where there is power to make that law respected. I know no class of my fellow men, however just, enlightened, and humane, which can be wisely and safely trusted absolutely with the liberties of any other class. Protestants are excellent people, but it would not be wise for Catholics to depend entirely upon them to look after their rights and interests. Catholics are a pretty good sort of people (though there is a soul-shuddering history behind them); yet no enlightened Protestants would commit their liberty to their care and keeping.

And yet the government had left the freedmen in a worse condition than either of these. It felt that it had done enough for him. It had made him free, and henceforth he must make his own way in the world, or, as the slang phrase has it, "root, pig, or die." Yet he had none of the conditions for self-preservation or self-protection.

He was free from the individual master, but the slave of society. He had neither money, property, nor friends. He was free from the old plantation, but he had nothing but the dusty road under his feet. He was free from the old quarter that once gave him shelter, but a slave to the rains of summer and the frosts of winter. He was, in a word, literally turned loose, naked, hungry, and destitute, to the open sky.

The first feeling toward him by the old master classes was full of bitterness and wrath. They resented his emancipation as an act of hostility toward them, and, since they could not punish the emancipator, they felt like punishing the object which that act had emancipated. Hence they drove him off the old plantation, and told him he was no longer wanted there. They not only hated him because he had been freed as a punishment to them, but because they felt that they had been robbed of his labor.

An element of greater bitterness still came into their hearts: the freedman had been the friend of the government, and many of his class had borne arms against them during the war. The thought of paying cash for labor that they could formerly extort by the lash did not in any wise improve their disposition to the emancipated slave, or improve his own condition.

Now, since poverty has, and can have, no chance against wealth, the landless against the landowner, the ignorant against the intelligent, the freedman was powerless. He had nothing left him but a slavery-distorted and diseased body, and lame and twisted limbs, with which to fight the battle of life.

3. Booker T. Washington Reflects (1901)

Booker T. Washington was reared in a one-room, dirt-floored shanty, and never slept on a bed until after emancipation. Obtaining an education under grave hardships, he ultimately became the head of the famed industrial institute at Tuskegee, Alabama. The acknowledged leader of his race after Frederick Douglass died in 1895, he won additional fame as an orator and as an apostle of "gradualism" in achieving equality with the whites. He believed that blacks should acquire manual skills and otherwise prove themselves worthy of a place beside whites. Black intellectuals like W. E. B. Du Bois (see p. 509) criticized this conservative "Uncle Tomism" as condemning the race to permanent inferiority. In the following selection from Washington's justly famous autobiography, what does the author regard as the chief mistakes made by both whites and blacks in Reconstruction?

Though I was but little more than a youth during the period of Reconstruction, I had the feeling that mistakes were being made, and that things could not remain in the condition that they were in then very long. I felt that the Reconstruction policy, so far as it related to my race, was in a large measure on a false foundation, was artificial and forced. In many cases it seemed to me that the ignorance of my race was being used as a tool with which to help white men into office, and that there was an element in the North which wanted to punish the Southern white men by forcing the Negro into positions over the heads of the Southern whites. I felt that the Negro would be the one to suffer for this in the end. Besides, the general political agitation drew the attention of our people away from the more fundamental matters of perfecting themselves in the industries at their doors and in securing property.

The temptations to enter political life were so alluring that I came very near yielding to them at one time, but I was kept from doing so by the feeling that I would be helping in a more substantial way by assisting in the laying of the foundation of the race through a generous education of the hand, head, and heart. I saw colored men who were members of the state legislatures, and county officers, who, in some cases, could not read or write, and whose morals were as weak as their education.

Not long ago, when passing through the streets of a certain city in the South, I heard some brick-masons calling out, from the top of a two-story brick building on which they were working, for the "Governor" to "hurry up and bring up some more bricks." Several times I heard the command, "Hurry up, Governor!" "Hurry up, Governor!" My curiosity was aroused to such an extent that I made inquiry as to who the "Governor" was, and soon found that he was a colored man who at one time had held the position of Lieutenant-Governor of his state.

But not all the colored people who were in office during Reconstruction were unworthy of their positions, by any means. Some of them, like the late Senator B. K. Bruce, Governor Pinchback, and many others, were strong, upright, useful men. Neither were all the class designated as carpetbaggers dishonorable men. Some of them, like ex-Governor Bullock of Georgia, were men of high character and usefulness.

---

[3]Booker T. Washington, *Up from Slavery* (New York: A. L. Burt, 1901), pp. 83–86.

Of course the colored people, so largely without education, and wholly without experience in government, made tremendous mistakes, just as any people similarly situated would have done. Many of the Southern whites have a feeling that, if the Negro is permitted to exercise his political rights now to any degree, the mistakes of the Reconstruction period will repeat themselves. I do not think this would be true, because the Negro is a much stronger and wiser man than he was thirty-five years ago, and he is fast learning the lesson that he cannot afford to act in a manner that will alienate his Southern white neighbors from him. . . .

During the whole of the Reconstruction period our people throughout the South looked to the federal government for everything, very much as a child looks to its mother. This was not unnatural. The central government gave them freedom, and the whole nation had been enriched for more than two centuries by the labor of the Negro. Even as a youth, and later in manhood, I had the feeling that it was cruelly wrong in the central government, at the beginning of our freedom, to fail to make some provision for the general education of our people in addition to what the states might do, so that the people would be the better prepared for the duties of citizenship.

It is easy to find fault, to remark what might have been done, and perhaps, after all, and under all the circumstances, those in charge of the conduct of affairs did the only thing that could be done at the time. Still, as I look back now over the entire period of our freedom, I cannot help feeling that it would have been wiser if some plan could have been put in operation which would have made the possession of a certain amount of education or property, or both, a test for the exercise of the franchise, and a way provided by which this test should be made to apply honestly and squarely to both the white and black races.

Thought Provokers

1. Was the white South ever really defeated in spirit? Would the results have been more satisfactory from its point of view if it had accepted the rule of the conqueror with better grace?
2. What were the major differences between presidential and congressional Reconstruction plans? What accounts for those different approaches? Who had the better constitutional arguments? Who advocated the soundest policies?
3. It has been said that Johnson was his own worst enemy and that the white Southerners were damaged by his determination to befriend them with a "soft" policy. Comment critically.
4. Present the cases for and against *immediate* and *gradual* black suffrage. Form conclusions. Why have the excesses of the black–white legislatures been overplayed and their achievements downgraded?
5. Why did organizations like the Ku Klux Klan flourish in the Reconstruction South? In what ways did the KKK resemble a modern "terrorist" group?
6. Identify the most serious long-run mistake made during Reconstruction. What have been the effects of that mistake?

23

Political Paralysis in the Gilded Age, 1869–1896

The lessons of paternalism ought to be unlearned and the better lesson taught that while the people should patriotically and cheerfully support their government, its functions do not include the support of the people.

Grover Cleveland, Inaugural Address, 1893

Prologue: War hero Ulysses S. Grant came to the White House in 1869, when corruption abounded at many levels of government. A great general, the politically infantile Grant proved to be a great disappointment as president. Disaffected Republicans, unable to stomach Grant for a second term, organized the Liberal Republican party in 1872 and, together with the Democrats, chose the outspoken—and outrageous—Horace Greeley as their presidential standard-bearer. Greeley went down to inglorious defeat. Politics at the national level turned into a petty and highly partisan stalemate, as the delicately balanced major parties hesitated to upset the shaky electoral standoff by emphasizing controversial issues. Rutherford B. Hayes narrowly triumphed over Democrat Samuel Tilden in 1877. As part of the arrangements that eventually secured his election, Hayes effectively ended Reconstruction in the South. With the withdrawal of federal troops from the South following Hayes's election, a regime of strict segregation relegated African-Americans to second-class status. Meanwhile, mounting economic distress nurtured a rising protest movement in the agricultural regions of the South and the Midwest. In the gutter-low presidential contest of 1884, Grover Cleveland emerged triumphant. Cleveland, the first Democratic president since 1861, displayed a fierce commitment to fiscal orthodoxy and to lowering sky-high Republican-passed tariffs.

A. The South After Reconstruction _____

1. Rutherford B. Hayes Believes Himself Defrauded (1876)

In 1876 the Republicans nominated, as Grant's successor, Governor Rutherford B. Hayes of Ohio. Hayes was a political puritan so serious-minded that at the age of twelve he had written in his diary that it was necessary to read law books rather than frivolous newspapers. The Democrats nominated a multimillionaire bachelor, Governor Samuel J. Tilden of New York, a prominent corporation lawyer and a noted but overrated reformer. The first electoral returns, though not the later ones, indicated a Democratic landslide, and Hayes privately conceded defeat in his diary. Why does he feel that he would have won in a fair election?

Sunday, November 12.—The news this morning is not conclusive. The headlines of the morning papers are as follows: the *News,* "Nip and Tuck"; "Tuck has it"; "The Mammoth National Doubt"; and the *Herald* heads its news column, "Which?" But to my mind the figures indicate that Florida has been carried by the Democrats. No doubt both fraud and violence intervened to produce the result. But the same is true in many Southern states.

We shall, the fair-minded men of the country will, history will hold that the Republicans were by fraud, violence, and intimidation, by a nullification of the 15th Amendment, deprived of the victory which they fairly won. But we must, I now think, prepare ourselves to accept the inevitable. I do it with composure and cheerfulness. To me the result is no personal calamity.

I would like the opportunity to improve the civil service. It seems to me I could do more than any Democrat to put Southern Affairs on a sound basis. I do not apprehend any great or permanent injury to the financial affairs of the country by the victory of the Democrats. The hard-money wing of the party is at the helm. . . .

We are in a minority in the electoral colleges; we lose the administration. But in the former free states—the states that were always loyal—we are still in a majority. We carry eighteen of the twenty-two and have two hundred thousand majority of the popular vote. In the old slave states, if the recent Amendments were cheerfully obeyed, if there had been neither violence nor intimidation nor other improper interference with the rights of the colored people, we should have carried enough Southern states to have held the country and to have secured a decided popular majority in the nation.

Our adversaries are in power, but they are supported by a minority only of the lawful voters of the country. A fair election in the South would undoubtedly have given us a large majority of the electoral votes, and a decided preponderance of the popular vote.

---

[1]C. R. Williams, ed., *Diary and Letters of Rutherford Birchard Hayes* (1924), vol. 3, pp. 377–378.

2. Zachariah Chandler Assails the Solid South (1879)

With the electoral vote of three southern states in hot dispute, the Hayes-Tilden dead-lock of 1876 was broken in 1877 by the specially constituted Electoral Commission of fifteen men. Its questionable decision for Hayes was grudgingly accepted by the Democrats. But they did not yield until they had received assurances that federal bayonets would no longer prop up Republican regimes in Louisiana and South Carolina, the last of the states under military reconstruction. Hayes honored this pledge and withdrew the troops, despite Republican outcries. The two states then went over to the Democratic solid South. Senator Zachariah Chandler of Michigan, who had been an outspoken antislaveryite, deplored these developments in a fiery speech in Chicago. (He died the next day.) The Democrats at that time controlled both houses of Congress. Why does he regard the southern states as grossly overrepresented?

They [the Confederates] have forfeited all their property—we gave it back to them. We found them naked, and we clothed them. They were without the rights of citizenship, and we restored to them those rights. We took them to our bosoms as brethren, believing that they had repented of their sins. We killed for them the fatted calf and invited them to the feast, and they gravely informed us that they had always owned that animal, and were not grateful for the invitation.

By the laws of war, and by the laws of nations, they were bound to pay every dollar of the expense incurred in putting down that rebellion. But we forgave them that debt, and today you are being taxed heavily to pay the interest on the debt that they ought to have paid. Such magnanimity as was exhibited by this nation to these rebels has never been witnessed on the earth since God made it, and, in my humble judgment, it will never be witnessed again.

Mistakes we undoubtedly made, errors we committed, but, in my judgment, the greatest mistake we made, and the gravest error we committed, was in not hanging enough of these rebels to make treason forever odious.

Today, in Congress, the men have changed but not the measures. Twenty years ago they said: "Do this, or fail to do that, and we will shoot your government to death." If I am to die, I would rather be shot to death with musketry than starved to death. These rebels (for they are just as rebellious now as they were twenty years ago; there is not a particle of difference—I know them better than any other living mortal man; I have summered and wintered with them)—these rebels today have thirty-six members on the floor of the House of Representatives. Without one single constituent, and in violation of law, those thirty-six members represent 4,000,000 people, lately slaves, who are absolutely disfranchised as if they lived in another sphere, through shotguns, and whips, and tissue-ballots. For the law [the Fourteenth Amendment] expressly says that wherever a race or class is disfranchised, they shall not be represented upon the floor of the House. And these thirty-six members thus elected constitute three times the whole of their majority upon the floor.*

---

[2]C. M. Depew, ed., *The Library of Oratory* (New York: The Globe Publishing Company, 1902), vol. 8, pp. 448–451 (October 31, 1879).
*The House numbered 149 Democrats and 130 Republicans; the Senate, 42 Democrats and 33 Republicans.

This is not only a violation of the law, but it is an outrage upon all the loyal men of the United States. It ought not to be. It must not be. And it shall not be. Twelve members of the Senate—more than their whole majority—occupy their seats upon the floor by fraud and violence; and I am saying no more to you than I said to those rebel generals. With majorities thus obtained by fraud and violence in both Houses, they dared to dictate terms to the loyal men of these United States. . . .

What they want is not free elections, but free fraud at elections. They have got a Solid South by fraud and violence. Give them permission to perpetrate the same fraud and violence in New York City and Cincinnati, and New York and Ohio, with the Solid South, will give them the Presidency, and that once obtained by fraud and violence, they would hold it for a generation. Today 8,000,000 of people in the Southern states control the legislation of the country through caucus dictation, as they controlled their slaves when slavery existed.

[Chandler was partially correct. The Democratic party that finally won the White House under Grover Cleveland, Woodrow Wilson, and Franklin Roosevelt was basically the solid South plus the Democratic machines of the large northeastern and midwestern cities.]

3. Reconstruction and Redemption (1882)

During military reconstruction (c. 1867–1877), U.S. troops closed the heavy hand of federal government power over much of the defeated South. Reconstruction officially ended when the last troops were withdrawn in 1877, and "Redeemer" governments returned to power in all the southern states. The white South rejoiced at the restoration of "home rule." This pro-southern cartoon draws a stark constrast between the Reconstruction and Redemption eras. What does it depict as the principal differences between the two regimes? What image of the federal government does it convey? Were there any southerners who would have disagreed with the message of this cartoon?

---

[3]*Puck.*

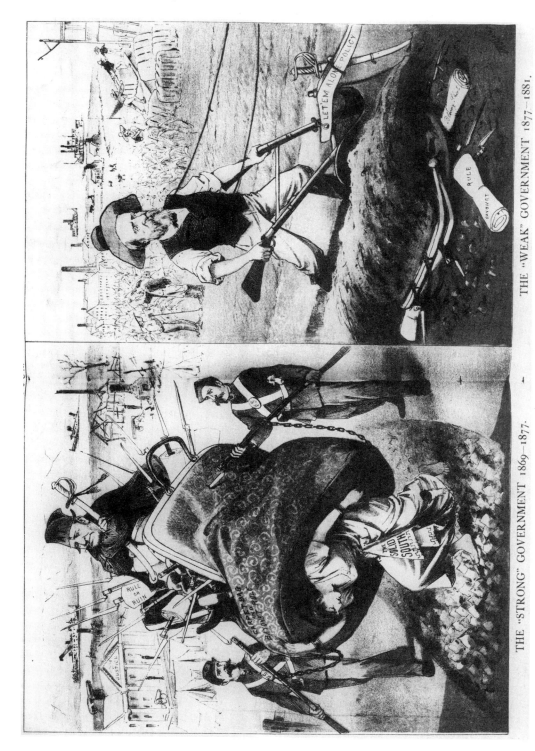

B. Race Divides the South

1. A Southern Senator Defends Jim Crow (1900)

Following Rutherford B. Hayes's election, the last federal troops were withdrawn from the South, and Reconstruction effectively ended. The white South proceeded rapidly to roll back the political, economic, and social gains that the freedmen had achieved with federal help in the Reconstruction era. In the following speech, a notorious racist, South Carolina senator "Pitchfork Ben" Tillman, unabashedly defends the disfranchisement of African-Americans and mocks the philanthropic educational work of northern whites in the South. On what premises about Africans and African-Americans does his defense rest? What is his attitude toward the institution of slavery itself?

The slaves of the South were a superior set of men and women to freedmen of today, and . . . the poison in their minds—the race hatred of the whites—is the result of the teachings of Northern fanatics. Ravishing a woman, white or black, was never known to occur in the South till after the Reconstruction era. So much for that phase of the subject. . . .

As white men we are not sorry . . . for anything we have done. . . . We took the government away from [the carpetbag Negro government] in 1876. We did take it. If no other Senator has come here previous to this time who would acknowledge it, more is the pity. We have had no fraud in our elections in South Carolina since 1884. There has been no organized Republican party in the State.

We did not disfranchise the Negroes until 1895. Then we had a constitutional convention convened which took the matter up calmly, deliberately, and avowedly with the purpose of disfranchising as many of them as we could under the Fourteenth and Fifteenth Amendments. We adopted the educational qualification as the only means left to us, and the Negro is as contented and as prosperous and as well protected in South Carolina to-day as in any State of the Union south of the Potomac. He is not meddling with politics, for he found that the more he meddled with them the worse off he got. As to his "rights"—I will not discuss them now. We of the South have never recognized the right of the Negro to govern white men, and we never will. We have never believed him to be equal to the white man, and we will not submit to his gratifying his lust on our wives and daughters without lynching him. I would to God the last one of them was in Africa, and that none of them had ever been brought to our shores. . . .

Some people have been ready to believe and to contend that the Negro is a white man with a black skin. All history disproves that. Go to Africa. What do you find there? From one hundred and fifty million to two hundred million savages.

I happened in my boyhood, when I was about 12 years old, to see some real Africans fresh from their native jungles. The last cargo of slaves imported into this

---

[1]*The Congressional Record,* March 29, 1900, February 24, 1903.

country were brought here in 1858 on the yacht Wanderer, landed on an island below Savannah, and sneaked by the United States marshal up the Savannah River and landed a little distance below Augusta, and my family bought some thirty of them.

Therefore I had a chance to see just what kind of people these were, and to compare the African as he is to-day in Africa with the African who, after two centuries of slavery, was brought side by side to be judged. The difference was as "Hyperion to a satyr." Those poor wretches, half starved as they had been on their voyage across the Atlantic, shut down and battened under the hatches and fed a little rice, several hundred of them, were the most miserable lot of human beings—the nearest to the missing link with the monkey—I have ever put my eyes on. . . .

Then if God in His providence ordained slavery and had these people transported over here for the purpose of civilizing enough of them to form a nucleus and to become missionaries back to their native heath, that is a question. . . . But the thing I want to call your attention to is that slavery was not an unmitigated evil for the Negro, because whatever of progress the colored race has shown itself capable of achieving has come from slavery; and whether among those four million there were not more good men and women than could be found among the nine million now is to my mind a question. I would not like to assert it; but I am strongly of that belief from the facts I know in regard to the demoralization that has come to those people down there by having liberty thrust upon them in the way it was, and then having the ballot and the burdens of government, and being subjected to the strain of being tempted and misled and duped and used as tools by designing white men who went there among them. . . .

All of the millions that are being sent there by Northern philanthropy has been but to create an antagonism between the poorer classes of our citizens and these people upon whose level they are in the labor market. There has been no contribution to elevate the white people in the South, to aid and assist the Anglo-Saxon Americans, the men who are descended from the people who fought with Marion and Sumter.* They are followed to struggle in poverty and in ignorance, and to do everything they can to get along, and they see Northern people pouring in thousands and thousands to help build up an African domination.

2. A Spokesman for the "New South" Describes Race Relations in the 1880s (1889)

Henry W. Grady, editor of the Atlanta Constitution, *championed the cause of the "New South"—a South that would emulate its northern neighbors by industrializing and modernizing its economy. Grady and other New South advocates knew that they needed the goodwill, the markets, and the capital of the North if they were to succeed. Overshadowing northern attitudes toward the region was the question of*

---

*Francis Marion and Thomas Sumter were American military heroes in the South during the War for American independence.

[2]Edwin DuBois Shurter, ed., *The Complete Orations of Henry W. Grady* (New York: 1910), pp. 192–220.

race relations in the decades after slavery's end. In the following speech delivered in Boston in 1889, how does Grady describe the condition of the recently emancipated African-Americans? Why did the North generally prove willing to believe him, and to acquiesce in the discriminatory arrangements that were directed against blacks?

I thank God as heartily as you do that human slavery is gone forever from the American soil.

But the freedman remains. With him a problem without precedent or parallel. Note its appalling conditions. Two utterly dissimilar races on the same soil; with equal political and civil rights, almost equal in numbers but terribly unequal in intelligence and responsibility; each pledged against fusion, one for a century in servitude to the other and freed at last by a desolating war; the experiment sought by neither, but approached by both with doubt—these are the conditions. Under these, adverse at every point, we are required to carry these two races in peace and honor to the end. Never, sir, has such a task been given to mortal stewardship. Never before in this republic has the white race divided on the rights of an alien race. The red man was cut down as a weed because he hindered the way of the American citizen. The yellow man was shut out of this republic because he is an alien and inferior. The red man was owner of the land, the yellow man highly civilized and assimilable—but they hindered both sections and are gone!

But the black man, affecting but one section, is clothed with every privilege of government and pinned to the soil, and my people commanded to make good at any hazard and at any cost, his full and equal heirship of American privilege and prosperity. . . . It matters not that wherever the whites and blacks have touched, in any era or any clime, there has been irreconcilable violence. It matters not that no two races, however similar, have lived anywhere, at any time, on the same soil with equal rights in peace. In spite of these things we are commanded to make good this change of American policy which has not perhaps changed American prejudice; to make certain here what has elsewhere been impossible between whites and blacks; and to reverse, under the very worst conditions, the universal verdict of racial history. And driven, sir, to this superhuman task with an impatience that brooks no delay, a rigor that accepts no excuse, and a suspicion that discourages frankness and sincerity. . . .

We give to the world this year a crop of 7,500,000 bales of cotton, worth $45 million, and its cash equivalent in grain, grasses, and fruit. This enormous crop could not have come from the hands of sullen and discontented labor. It comes from peaceful fields, in which laughter and gossip rise above the hum of industry and contentment runs with the singing plow.

It is claimed that this ignorant labor is defrauded of its just hire. I present the tax books of Georgia, which show that the Negro, twenty-five years ago a slave, has in Georgia alone $10 million of assessed property, worth twice that much. Does not that record honor him and vindicate his neighbors? What people, penniless, illiterate, has done so well? For every Afro-American agitator, stirring the strife in which alone he prospers, I can show you a thousand Negroes, happy in their cabin homes, tilling their own land by day, and at night taking from the lips of their children the helpful message their state sends them from the schoolhouse door.

And the schoolhouse itself bears testimony. In Georgia we added last year $250,000 to the school fund, making a total of more than $1 million—and this in the face of prejudice not yet conquered—of the fact that the whites are assessed for $368 million, the blacks for $10 million, and yet 49 percent of their beneficiaries are black children—and in the doubt of many wise men if education helps, or can help, our problem. Charleston, with her taxable values cut half in two since 1860, pays more in proportion for public schools than Boston. . . . The South since 1865 has spent $122 million in education, and this year is pledged to $37 million for state and city schools, although the blacks, paying one-thirtieth of the taxes, get nearly one-half of the fund.

Go into our fields and see whites and blacks working side by side, on our buildings in the same squad, in our shops at the same forge. Often the blacks crowd the whites from work, or lower wages by greater need or simpler habits, and yet are permitted because we want to bar them from no avenue in which their feet are fitted to tread. They could not there be elected orators of the white universities, as they have been here, but they do enter there a hundred useful trades that are closed against them here. We hold it better and wiser to tend the weeds in the garden than to water the exotic in the window.

In the South, there are Negro lawyers, teachers, editors, dentists, doctors, preachers, multiplying with the increasing ability of their race to support them. In villages and towns they have their military companies equipped from the armories of the state, their churches and societies built and supported largely by their neighbors. What is the testimony of the courts? In penal legislation we have steadily reduced felonies to misdemeanors, and have led the world in mitigating punishment for crime that we might save, as far as possible, this dependent race from its own weakness. In our penitentiary record 60 percent of the prosecutors are Negroes, and in every court the Negro criminal strikes the colored juror, that white men may judge his case. In the North, one Negro in every 466 is in jail; in the South only one in 1,865. In the North the percentage of Negro prisoners is six times as great as native whites; in the South, only four times as great. If prejudice wrongs him in Southern courts, the record shows it to be deeper in Northern courts. . . .

Now, Mr. President, can it be seriously maintained that we are terrorizing the people from whose willing hands come every year $1 billion of farm crops? Or have robbed a people, who twenty-five years from unrewarded slavery have amassed in one state $20 million of property?

Or that we intend to oppress the people we are arming every day? Or deceive them when we are educating them to the utmost limit of our ability? Or outlaw them when we work side by side with them? Or reenslave them under legal forms when for their benefit we have imprudently narrowed the limit of felonies and mitigated the severity of law? My fellow countryman, as you yourself may sometimes have to appeal to the bar of human judgment for justice and for right, give to my people tonight the fair and unanswerable conclusion of these incontestible facts. . . .

When will the black cast a free ballot? When ignorance anywhere is not dominated by the will of the intelligent; when the laborer anywhere casts a vote unhindered by his boss; when the vote of the poor anywhere is not influenced by the power of the rich; when the strong and the steadfast do not everywhere control the suffrage of the weak and shiftless—then and not till then will the ballot of the Negro be free. . . .

Here is this vast ignorant and purchasable vote—clannish, credulous, impulsive, and passionate—tempting every art of the demagogue, but insensible to the appeal of the statesman. Wrongly started, in that it was led into alienation from its neighbor and taught to rely on the protection of an outside force, it cannot be merged and lost in the two great parties through logical currents, for it lacks political conviction and even that information on which conviction must be based. It must remain a faction, strong enough in every community to control on the slightest division of the whites. Under that division it becomes the prey of the cunning and unscrupulous of both parties. Its credulity is imposed on, its patience inflamed, its cupidity tempted, its impulses misdirected, and even its superstition made to play its part in a campaign in which every interest of society is jeopardized and every approach to the ballot box debauched.

It is against such campaigns as this—the folly and the bitterness and the danger of which every Southern community has drunk deeply—that the white people of the South are banded together. Just as you in Massachusetts would be banded if 300,000 black men—not one in a hundred able to read his ballot—banded in a race instinct, holding against you the memory of a century of slavery, taught by your late conquerors to distrust and oppose you, had already travestied legislation from your statehouse, and in every species of folly or villainy had wasted your substance and exhausted your credit. . . .

3. An African-American Minister Answers Henry Grady (1890)

The Reverend Joshua A. Brockett, pastor of St. Paul's African Methodist Episcopal Church in Cambridge, Massachusetts, was deeply offended by Grady's description of life in the South and made this reply in January 1890. To which of Grady's arguments is his response most vigorous? Why do those particular issues bother him? What are his most telling rebuttals?

Henry W. Grady, of Atlanta, Ga., delivered an address before the Boston Merchants' Association at their annual banquet, on Thursday evening, December 13, 1889. . . . In that address, beneath the glamor of eloquence, the old rebel spirit, and the old South is seen throughout. In every expression of every line in which the Negro is mentioned the old spirit of Negro hatred is manifest. . . .

The gentleman asks the question when will the black cast a free ballot? His reply is, when ignorance anywhere is not dominated by the will of the intelligent; when the laborer casts his vote unhindered by his boss; when the strong and steadfast do not everywhere control the suffrage of the weak and shiftless. Then and not till then will the Negro be free. He also says that the Negro vote can never again control in the South. He asks of the North, "Can we solve this question?" and answers, "God knows."

---

³*Philadelphia Christian Recorder,* January 16, 1890.

Consistency, thou art a jewel! It is declared that the Negro is peaceful and industrious on the one hand, weak and shiftless on the other. If he is peaceful surely the South has small need to fear an uprising. Politics, then, is the only source whence danger can come to the whites. If the black vote is never to control again, why should Mr. Grady state that the condition of the people is fraught with danger from the presence of a shiftless people? Whence the need of that wail for sympathy, if, as Mr. Grady says, the colored man must down, and the white partisan might as well understand it? If the colored man is never to rise, why waste so much eloquence upon a useless subject? The problem is already solved.

Mr. Grady asserts that nearly one-half of the school fund is used to educate the Negro. If the South is leagued together to maintain itself against this beleaguering black host, why educate it?

Has Mr. Grady to learn that education and power are inseparable? I will give Mr. Grady fair warning if they continue to give one-half or thereabouts to the school fund to educate a black man, then he will rise against the greatest odds that the South can oppose; not God alone, but even I know when the black man will be free.

Mr. Grady says that the Negro has not a basis upon which to rest his political conviction, and that of 300,000 voters, not 1 in 100 can read his ballot. That is a splendid compliment to the educational system which costs the South so dear. Either the South is amazingly stupid to pay so dearly for such meager results, or the Negro is incapable of learning, or the money is not paid.

Mr. Grady states that the Negro, by every species of villainy and folly, has wasted his substance and exhausted his credit. By the side of that statement I will place another of Mr. Grady's statements, namely, that from the Negroes' willing hands comes $1 billion of farm crops. If the latter statement is true, then the character of the Negro in the former statement has been falsified. Does Mr. Grady desire to make a strong case against this villainous race at the expense of the truth? And if the former statement is true, that the Negro is villainously wasteful, the $1 billion crops are but a creation of fancy, and the Northern sons with their modest patrimony would do well to remain standing in their doors, or turn their gaze in any direction but southward.

Again, with childlike innocence, Mr. Grady asks, can it be seriously maintained that we are terrorizing the people from whose willing hands comes every year $1 billion in crops? Or that we have robbed a people who, twenty-five years from unrewarded slavery, have amassed in one state $20 million worth of property?

In Georgia, Mr. Grady's own state, the Negro's real wealth accumulated since the war, is $20 million. Its population of Negroes is 725,132. Twenty millions of dollars divided among that number will give to each person $27.58. Upon the same basis of calculation the total wealth of the Negro in the 15 Southern states, including the District of Columbia, is $146,189,834. The colored population of these states is 5,305,149. It seems an enormous sum. In those 15 states the Negro has, by the exceedingly friendly aid of their best friends, amassed a fortune of $1 a year.

Should they not, because of this rapid accumulation of wealth, balance their little account, clutch to the mule, jog down the furrow, and let the world wag on?

Look now for a moment at those billion-dollar yearly crops accumulating for 27 years, giving us the almost inconceivable sum of $27 billion, which, divided between a number of whites equal to that of blacks, each one would from this $27 billion, receive $5,089.39. Thus the blacks receive for their willing toil through 27 years $27.58, while the whites receive $5,089.39. These are both sides of the Grady picture of Negro wealth which was intended to deceive the North. Gaze upon it. . . .

4. Booker T. Washington Portrays the Plight of Black Tenant Farmers (1889)

In the late nineteenth century, most southern blacks remained unskilled agricultural workers—especially in the cottonfields—just as they had been under slavery. Many became tenant farmers, renting plots of land from big landholders and paying their rent by the delivery of some share of their crops. Financing for the tenant farmers was often provided by local merchants, who were also often their landlords. Frequently criticized as shiftless and lacking in ambition, tenant farmers (white as well as black) were among the poorest and sorriest southerners in the post–Civil War years. Here noted black leader Booker T. Washington describes their plight, and especially the role of the merchant in perpetuating it. What are the most objectionable features of the system Washington depicts?

. . . When the [Civil] war ended the colored people had nothing much on which to live. . . . They had to get the local merchant or someone else to supply the food for the family to eat while the first crop was being made. For every dollar's worth of provisions so advanced the local merchant charged from 12 to 30 per cent interest. In order to be sure that he secured his principal and interest a mortgage or lien was taken on the crop, in most cases not then planted. Of course the farmers could pay no such interest and the end of the first year found them in debt—the 2nd year they tried again, but there was the old debt and the new interest to pay, and in this way the "mortgage system" has gotten a hold on everything that it seems impossible to shake off. Its evils have grown instead of decreasing, until it is safe to say that ⅞ of the colored farmers mortgage their crops every year. Not only their crops before, in many cases, they are actually planted, but their wives sign a release from the homestead law and in most every case mules, cows, wagons, plows and often all household furniture is covered by the lien.

At a glance one is not likely to get the full force of the figures representing the amount of interest charged. Example, if a man makes a mortgage with a merchant for $200 on which to "run" during the year the farmer is likely to get about $50 of this amount in February or March, $50 in May, $50 in June or July and the remainder in Aug. or Sept. By the middle of September the farmer begins returning the money in cotton and by the last of Oct. whatever he can pay the farmer has paid, but the merchant charges as much for the money gotten in July or Aug. as for that gotten in Feb. The farmer is charged interest on all for the one year of 12 months. And as the "advance" is made in most cases in provisions rather than cash, the farmer, in addition to paying the interest mentioned, is charged more for the same goods than one buying for cash. If a farmer has 6 in a family, say wife and 4 chil-

⁴Booker T. Washington to George W. Cable, October 8, 1889, as reprinted in *Journal of Negro History* 17 (April 1948). Reprinted by permission of The Associated Publishers, Inc.

dren, the merchant has it in his power to feed only those who work and sometimes he says to the farmer if he sends his children to school no rations can be drawn for them while they are attending school.

After a merchant has "run" a farmer for 5 or 6 years and he does not "pay out" or decides to try mortgaging with another merchant the first merchant in such cases usually "cleans up" the farmer, that is takes everything, mules, cows, plows, chicken's fodder—everything except wife and children. . . .

The result of all this is seen in the "general run down" condition of ⅘ of the farms in Alabama—houses unpainted—fences tumbling down, animals poorly cared for, and the land growing poorer every year. Many of the colored farmers have almost given up hope and do just enough work to secure their "advances." One of the strongest things that can be said in favor of the colored people is, that in almost every community there are one or two who have shaken off this yoke of slavery and have bought farms of their own and are making money—and there are a *few* who rent land and "mortgage" and still do something. . . .

5. A Southern Black Woman Reflects on the Jim Crow System (1902)

Political disfranchisement and economic impoverishment were not the only penalties endured by southern blacks after Reconstruction ended. Blacks felt the stigma of discrimination and restriction in all aspects of social life. How did "Jim Crow" affect the life of this southern black woman? How—or why—did she put up with the conditions she describes?

. . . I am a colored woman, wife and mother. I have lived all my life in the South, and have often thought what a peculiar fact it is that the more ignorant the Southern whites are of us the more vehement they are in their denunciation of us. They boast that they have little intercourse with us, never see us in our homes, churches or places of amusement, but still they know us thoroughly.

They also admit that they know us in no capacity except as servants, yet they say we are at our best in that single capacity. What philosophers they are! The Southerners say we Negroes are a happy, laughing set of people, with no thought of tomorrow. How mistaken they are! The educated, thinking Negro is just the opposite. There is a feeling of unrest, insecurity, almost panic among the best class of Negroes in the South. In our homes, in our churches, wherever two or three are gathered together, there is a discussion of what is best to do. Must we remain in the South or go elsewhere? Where can we go to feel that security which other people feel? Is it best to go in great numbers or only in several families? These and many other things are discussed over and over. . . .

I know of houses occupied by poor Negroes in which a respectable farmer would not keep his cattle. It is impossible for them to rent elsewhere. All Southern real estate agents have "white property" and "colored property." In one of the largest Southern cities there is a colored minister, a graduate of Harvard, whose wife

---

[5]"The Negro Problem: How It Appears to a Southern Colored Woman," *Independent* 54 (September 18, 1902).

is an educated, Christian woman, who lived for weeks in a tumble-down rookery because he could neither rent nor buy in a respectable locality.

Many colored women who wash, iron, scrub, cook or sew all the week to help pay the rent for these miserable hovels and help fill the many small mouths, would deny themselves some of the necessaries of life if they could take their little children and teething babies on the cars to the parks of a Sunday afternoon and sit under trees, enjoy the cool breezes and breathe God's pure air for only two or three hours; but this is denied them. Some of the parks have signs, "No Negroes allowed on these grounds except as servants." Pitiful, pitiful customs and laws that make war on women and babes! There is no wonder that we die; the wonder is that we persist in living.

Fourteen years ago I had just married. My husband had saved sufficient money to buy a small home. On account of our limited means we went to the suburbs, on unpaved streets, to look for a home, only asking for a high, healthy locality. Some real estate agents were "sorry, but had nothing to suit," some had "just the thing," but we discovered on investigation that they had "just the thing" for an unhealthy pigsty. Others had no "colored property." One agent said that he had what we wanted, but we should have to go to see the lot after dark, or walk by and give the place a casual look; for, he said, "all the white people in the neighborhood would be down on me." Finally, we bought this lot. When the house was being built we went to see it. Consternation reigned. We had ruined his neighborhood of poor people; poor as we, poorer in manners at least. The people who lived next door received the sympathy of their friends. When we walked on the street (there were no sidewalks) we were embarrassed by the stare of many unfriendly eyes.

Two years passed before a single woman spoke to me, and only then because I helped one of them when a little sudden trouble came to her. Such was the reception, I a happy young woman, just married, received from people among whom I wanted to make a home. Fourteen years have now passed, four children have been born to us, and one has died in this same home, among these same neighbors. Although the neighbors speak to us, and occasionally one will send a child to borrow the morning's paper or ask the loan of a pattern, not one woman has ever been inside of my house, not even at the times when a woman would doubly appreciate the slightest attention of a neighbor. . . .

A colored woman, however respectable, is lower than the white prostitute. The Southern white woman will declare that no Negro women are virtuous, yet she placed her innocent children in their care. . . .

White agents and other chance visitors who come into our homes ask questions that we must not dare ask their wives. They express surprise that our children have clean faces and that their hair is combed. . . .

We were delighted to know that some of our Spanish-American heroes were coming where we could get a glimpse of them. Had not black men helped in a small way to give them their honors? In the cities of the South, where these heroes went, the white school children were assembled, flags waved, flowers strewn, speeches made, and "My Country, 'tis of Thee, Sweet Land of Liberty," was sung. Our children who need to be taught so much, were not assembled, their hands waved no flags, they threw no flowers, heard no thrilling speech, sang no song of their country. And this is the South's idea of justice. Is it surprising that feeling grows more bitter, when the white mother teaches her boy to hate my boy, not because he is mean, but because his skin is dark? I have seen very small white children hang their black dolls. It is not the child's fault, he is simply an apt pupil. . . .

C. The Populist Crusade in the South

1. Tom Watson Supports a Black-White Political Alliance (1892)

Populism in the South seemed to offer the prospect of a political alliance of poor farmers, black as well as white, that would be strong enough to overthrow the conservative "Bourbon" regimes holding power in the southern states. Some forward-looking Populist leaders, among them Georgia's Tom Watson, tried to overcome the racial differences that, they argued, irrationally overshadowed the common economic interests of black and white agrarians and that kept the Bourbons in control. On one occasion in 1892, Watson summoned dozens of armed white farmers to his home to protect a black colleague who had taken refuge from a lynch mob. Only a few years later, when the Populist dream of an interracial political alliance had died, Watson reversed his views and emerged as one of the South's premier racists. In the selection below, whom does Watson blame for the racial tensions of the postbellum South? What are the limits of his program for interracial cooperation?

The Negro Question in the South has been for nearly thirty years a source of danger, discord, and bloodshed. It is an ever-present irritant and menace.

Several millions of slaves were told that they were the prime cause of the civil war; that their emancipation was the result of the triumph of the North over the South; that the ballot was placed in their hands as a weapon of defence against their former masters; that the war-won political equality of the black man with the white, must be asserted promptly and aggressively, under the leadership of adventurers who had swooped down upon the conquered section in the wake of the Union armies.

No one, who wishes to be fair, can fail to see that, in such a condition of things, strife between the freedman and his former owner was inevitable. In the clashing of interests and of feelings, bitterness was born. The black man was kept in a continual fever of suspicion that we meant to put him back into slavery. . . .

Quick to take advantage of this deplorable situation, the politicians have based the fortunes of the old parties upon it. Northern leaders have felt that at the cry of "Southern outrage" they could not only "fire the Northern heart," but also win a unanimous vote from the colored people. Southern politicians have felt that at the cry of "Negro domination" they could drive into solid phalanx every white man in all the Southern states.

Both the old parties have done this thing until they have constructed as perfect a "slot machine" as the world ever saw. Drop the old, worn nickel of the "party slogan" into the slot, and the machine does the rest. You might beseech a Southern white

---

[1] Thomas Watson, "The Negro Question in the South," *The Arena* 6 (October 1892): 540–550.

tenant to listen to you upon questions of finance, taxation, and transportation; you might demonstrate with mathematical precision that herein lay his way out of poverty into comfort; you might have him "almost persuaded" to the truth, but if the merchant who furnished his farm supplies (at tremendous usury) or the town politician (who never spoke to him excepting at election times) came along and cried, "Negro rule!" the entire fabric of reason and common sense which you had patiently constructed would fall, and the poor tenant would joyously hug the chains of an actual wretchedness rather than do any experimenting on a question of mere sentiment.

Thus the Northern Democrats have ruled the South with a rod of iron for twenty years. We have had to acquiesce when the time-honored principles we loved were sent to the rear and new doctrines and policies we despised were engrafted on our platform. All this we have had to do to obtain the assistance of Northern Democrats to prevent what was called "Negro supremacy." In other words, the Negro has been as valuable a portion of the stock in trade of a Democrat as he was of a Republican. Let the South ask relief from Wall Street; let it plead for equal and just laws on finance; let it beg for mercy against crushing taxation, and Northern Democracy, with all the coldness, cruelty, and subtlety of Mephistopheles, would hint "Negro rule!" and the white farmer and laborer of the South had to choke down his grievance and march under Tammany's orders.

Reverse the statement, and we have the method by which the black man was managed by the Republicans.

Reminded constantly that the North had emancipated him; that the North had given him the ballot; that the North had upheld him in his citizenship; that the South was his enemy, and meant to deprive him of his suffrage and put him "back into slavery," it is no wonder he has played as nicely into the hands of the Republicans as his former owner has played into the hands of the Northern Democrats.

Now consider: here were two distinct races dwelling together, with political equality established between them by law. They lived in the same section; won their livelihood by the same pursuits; cultivated adjoining fields on the same terms; enjoyed together the bounties of a generous climate; suffered together the rigors of cruelly unjust laws; spoke the same language; bought and sold in the same markets; classified themselves into churches under the same denominational teachings; neither race antagonizing the other in any branch of industry; each absolutely dependent on the other in all the avenues of labor and employment; and yet, instead of being allies, as every dictate of reason and prudence and self-interest and justice said they should be, they were kept apart, in dangerous hostility, that the sordid aims of partisan politics might be served!

Not completely has this scheme succeeded that the Southern black man almost instinctively supports any measure the Southern white man condemns, while the latter almost universally antagonizes any proposition suggested by a Northern Republican. We have, then, a solid South as opposed to a solid North; and in the South itself, a solid black vote against the solid white.

That such a condition is most ominous to both sections and both races, is apparent to all.

If we were dealing with a few tribes of red men or a few sporadic Chinese, the question would be easily disposed of. The Anglo-Saxon would probably do just as he pleased, whether right or wrong, and the weaker man would go under.

But the Negroes number 8,000,000. They are interwoven with our business, political, and labor systems. They assimilate with our customs, our religion, our civilization. They meet us at every turn,—in the fields, the shops, the mines. They are a part of our system, and they are here to stay. . . .

The People's Party will settle the race question. First, by enacting the Australian ballot system [The "secret" ballot, which protects the confidentiality of the voter's choice—so-called because it originated in Australia.]. Second, by offering to white and black a rallying point which is free from the odium of former discords and strifes. Third, by presenting a platform immensely beneficial to both races and injurious to neither. Fourth, by making it to the *interest* of both races to act together for the success of the platform. Fifth, by making it to the *interest* of the colored man to have the same patriotic zeal for the welfare of the South that the whites possess. . . .

The white tenant lives adjoining the colored tenant. Their houses are almost equally destitute of comforts. Their living is confined to bare necessities. They are equally burdened with heavy taxes. They pay the same high rent for gullied and impoverished land.

They pay the same enormous prices for farm supplies. Christmas finds them both without any satisfactory return for a year's toil. Dull and heavy and unhappy, they both start the plows again when "New Year's" passes.

Now the People's Party says to these two men, "You are kept apart that you may be separately fleeced of your earnings. You are made to hate each other because upon that hatred is rested the keystone of the arch of financial despotism which enslaves you both. You are deceived and blinded that you may not see how this race antagonism perpetuates a monetary system which beggars both."

This is so obviously true it is no wonder both these unhappy laborers stop to listen. No wonder they begin to realize that no change of law can benefit the white tenant which does not benefit the black one likewise; that no system which now does injustice to one of them can fail to injure both. Their every material interest is identical. The moment this becomes a conviction, mere selfishness, the mere desire to better their conditions, escape onerous taxes, avoid usurious charges, lighten their rents, or change their precarious tenements into smiling, happy homes, will drive these two men together, just as their mutually inflamed prejudices now drive them apart. . . .

The question of social equality does not enter into the calculation at all. That is a thing each citizen decides for himself. No statute ever yet drew the latch of the humblest home—or ever will. Each citizen regulates his own visiting list—and always will.

The conclusion, then, seems to me to be this: the crushing burdens which now oppress both races in the South will cause each to make an effort to cast them off. They will see a similarity of cause and a similarity of remedy. They will recognize that each should help the other in the work of repealing bad laws and enacting good ones. They will become political allies, and neither can injure the other without weakening both. It will be to the interest of both that each should have justice. And on these broad lines of mutual interest, mutual forbearance, and mutual support the present will be made the stepping-stone to future peace and prosperity.

2. A Black-Alliance Man Urges
Interracial Cooperation (1891)

The Reverend J. L. Moore, author of the selection below, was the superintendent of the Colored Farmers' Alliance in Putnam County, Florida. In the selection reprinted here, a reply to a newspaper editorial, he urges congressional passage of a civil-rights bill, sometimes called the force bill, to ensure black political participation in the South. In what ways does his position resemble that of Tom Watson, described in the previous selection?

I notice you,* as others, call it the force bill, and you remarked, "How the force bill could benefit the Negro even in the slightest degree passes comprehension. . . ." But our object was to have protection of the ballot boxes, because none sees the need of reform more than we do. How is that reform to be brought about while the present parties have control of the ballot boxes (unless it comes through the now existing parties, which is not likely if their past history argues anything)? . . .

In all the discussions of the whites in all the various meetings they attend and the different resolutions, remarks, and speeches they make against the Negro, I never hear you, Mr. Editor, nor any of the other leading journals, once criticize their action or say they are antagonizing the races, neither do you ever call a halt. But let the Negro speak once, and what do you hear? Antagonizing races, Negro uprising, Negro domination, etc. Anything to keep the reading public hostile toward the Negro, not allowing him the privilege to speak his opinion, and if that opinion be wrong show him by argument, and not at once make it a race issue . . . as members of the Colored Farmers' Alliance we avowed that we were going to vote with and for the man or party that will secure for the farmer or laboring man his just rights and privileges, and in order that he may enjoy them without experiencing a burden.

We want protection at the ballot box, so that the laboring man may have an equal showing, and the various labor organizations to secure their just rights, we will join hands with them irrespective of party, "and those fellows will have to walk." We are aware of the fact that the laboring colored man's interests and the laboring white man's interests are one and the same. Especially is this true at the South. Anything that can be brought about to benefit the workingman, will also benefit the Negro more than any other legislation that can be enacted. . . . So I for one have fully decided to vote with and work for that party, or those who favor the workingman, let them belong to the Democratic, or Republican, or the People's Party. I know I speak the sentiment of that convention, representing as we do one-fifth of the laborers of this country, seven-eighths of our race in this country being engaged in agricultural pursuits.

Can you wonder why we have turned our attention from the few pitiful offices a few of our members could secure, and turned our attention toward benefiting the mass of our race, and why we are willing to legislate that this must be benefited? And we ask Congress to protect the ballot box, so they may be justly dealt with in their effort to gain that power. We know and you know that neither of the now ex-

---

[2]J. L. Moore, "The Florida Colored Farmers' Alliance, 1891," *National Economist,* March 7, 1891.

*The editors of the Jacksonville, Florida, newspaper to whom Moore was replying.

isting parties is going to legislate in the interest of the farmers or laboring men except so far as it does not conflict with their interest to do so. . . .

Now, Mr. Editor, I wish to say, if the laboring men of the United States will lay down party issues and combine to enact laws for the benefit of the laboring man, I, as county superintendent of Putnam County Colored Farmers' Alliance, and member of the National Colored Farmers, know that I voice the sentiment of that body, representing as we did 750,000 votes, when I say we are willing and ready to lay down the past, take hold with them irrespective of party, race, or creed, until the cry shall be heard from the Heights of Abraham of the North, to the Everglades of Florida, and from the rock-bound coast of the East, to the Golden Eldorado of the West, that we can heartily endorse the motto, "Equal rights to all and special privileges to none."

3. The Wilmington Massacre (1898)

In 1894 white Populists and black Republicans in North Carolina formed a successful anti-Bourbon coalition and gained control of the state government. Four years later, conservative Bourbon Democrats overturned the Populist-Republican "fusion" government in a campaign marked by flagrant fraud and intimidation. The climax came in Wilmington, North Carolina, on November 11, 1898, when a mob murdered several African-Americans and deposed by force the elected city administration. The following eyewitness account describes the uprising in detail. In what ways does this account shed light on the death of the Populist dream of interracial political action? How does the speaker draw on the contemporary developments in the Spanish-American War to drive home his point?

Nine Negroes massacred outright; a score wounded and hunted like partridges on the mountain; one man, brave enough to fight against such odds would be hailed as a hero anywhere else, was given the privilege of running the gauntlet up a broad street, where he sank ankle deep in the sand, while crowds of men lined the sidewalks and riddled him with a pint of bullets as he ran bleeding past their doors; another Negro shot twenty times in the back as he scrambled empty handed over a fence; thousands of women and children fleeing in terror from their humble homes in the darkness of the night, out under a gray and angry sky, from which falls a cold and bone-chilling rain, out to the dark and tangled ooze of the swamp amid the crawling things of night, fearing to light a fire, startled at every footstep, cowering, shivering, shuddering, trembling, praying in gloom and terror: half-clad and barefooted mothers, with their babies wrapped only in a shawl, whimpering with cold and hunger at their icy breasts, crouched in terror from the vengeance of those who, in the name of civilization, and with the benediction of the ministers of the Prince of Peace, inaugurated the reformation of the city of Wilmington the day after the election by driving out one set of white office holders and filling their places with another set of white office holders—the one being Republican and the other Democrat. . . . All this happened, not in Turkey, nor in Russia, nor in Spain, not in

[3]Charles S. Morris, speech to the Interdenominational Association of Colored Clergymen, Boston, January 1899. From the papers of Charles H. Williams, Wisconsin State Historical Society, Madison, Wisconsin.

the gardens of Nero, nor in the dungeons of Torquemada, but within three hundred miles of the White House, in the best State in the South, within a year of the twentieth century, while the nation was on its knees thanking God for having enabled it to break the Spanish yoke from the neck of Cuba. This is our civilization. This is Cuba's kindergarten of ethics and good government. This is Protestant religion in the United States, that is planning a wholesale missionary crusade against Catholic Cuba. This is the golden rule as interpreted by the white pulpit of Wilmington.

Over this drunken and blood-thirsty mob they stretch their hands and invoke the blessings of a just God. We have waited two hundred and fifty years for liberty, and this is what it is when it comes. O Liberty, what crimes are committed in thy name! A rent and bloody mantle of citizenship that has covered as with a garment of fire, wrapped in which as in a shroud, forty thousand of my people have fallen around Southern ballot boxes. . . . A score of intelligent colored men, able to pass even a South Carolina election officer, shot down at Phoenix, South Carolina, for no reason whatever, except as the Charleston *News and Courier* said, because the baser elements of the community loved to kill and destroy. The pitiful privilege of dying like cattle in the red gutters of Wilmington, or crouching waist deep in the icy waters of neighboring swamps, where terrified women give birth to a dozen infants, most of whom died of exposure and cold. This is Negro citizenship! This is what the nation fought for from Bull Run to Appomattox!

What caused all this bitterness, strife, arson, murder, revolution and anarchy at Wilmington? We hear the answer on all sides—"Negro domination." I deny the charge. It is utterly false, and no one knows it better than the men who use it to justify crimes that threaten the very foundation of republican government; crimes that make the South red with blood, white with bones and gray with ashes; crimes no other civilized government would tolerate for a single day. The colored people comprise one-third of the population of the State of North Carolina; in the Legislature there are one hundred and twenty representatives, seven of whom are colored. There are fifty senators, two of whom are colored—nine in all out of one hundred and seventy. Can nine Negroes dominate one hundred and sixty white men? That would be a fair sample of the tail wagging the dog. Not a colored man holds a state office in North Carolina; the whole race has less than five per cent of all the offices in the state. In the city of Wilmington the Mayor was white, six out of ten members of the board of aldermen, and sixteen out of twenty-six members of the police force were white; the city attorney was white, the city clerk was white, the city treasurer was white, the superintendent of streets was white, the superintendent of garbage was white, the superintendent of health was white, and all the nurses in the white wards were white; the superintendent of the public schools was white, the chief and assistant chief of the fire department, and three out of five fire companies were white; the school committee has always been composed of two white men and one colored; the board of audit and finance is composed of five members, four of whom were white, and the one Negro was reported to be worth more than any of his white associates. The tax rate under this miscalled Negro regime was less than under its predecessors; this is Negro domination in Wilmington. This is a fair sample of that Southern scarecrow—conjured by these masters of the black art everywhere. . . .

The Good Samaritan did not leave his own eldest son robbed and bleeding at his own threshold, while he went way off down the road between Jerusalem and

Jericho to hunt for a man that had fallen among thieves. Nor can America afford to go eight thousand miles from home to set up a republican government in the Philippines while the blood of citizens whose ancestors came here before the Mayflower, is crying out to God against her from the gutters of Wilmington.

D. The Spread of Segregation

1. The Supreme Court Declares That Separate Is Equal (1896)

In the closing years of the nineteenth century, most southern states passed Jim Crow laws mandating segregated public facilities for whites and blacks. Louisiana passed a statute in 1890 that provided for "equal but separate accommodations for the white and colored races" on railroads in the state, and prohibited persons from occupying a railcar or waiting room other than those reserved for their race. Black Louisianans brought suit against this law, as a way of challenging the spreading practice of segregation. Interestingly, the plaintiffs had some support from the railroads, which objected to the added costs entailed by providing separate cars. By a seven-to-one majority, however, the U.S. Supreme Court upheld the Louisiana statute in the case of Plessy v. Ferguson, *thus helping to cement the system of segregation into place until it was dismantled by the civil rights movement in the post–World War II period. (The lone dissenter was Justice John Harlan, a former slave owner.) In the following excerpt from the majority's opinion, what are the principal rationales offered for the Court's conclusions? In what ways did the opinion ultimately prove vulnerable? (It was reversed in the case of* Brown v. Topeka Board of Education *in 1954, which held that separate educational facilities are inherently unequal.)*

By the Fourteenth Amendment, all persons born or naturalized in the United States, and subject to the jurisdiction thereof, are made citizens of the United States and of the State wherein they reside; and the States are forbidden from making or enforcing any law which shall abridge the privileges or immunities of citizens of the United States, or shall deprive any person of life, liberty or property without due process of law, or deny to any person within their jurisdiction the equal protection of the laws.

The proper construction of this amendment was first called to the attention of this court in the *Slaughter-house cases* [1873], which involved, however, not a question of race, but one of exclusive privileges. The case did not call for any expression of opinion as to the exact rights it was intended to secure to the colored race, but it was said generally that its main purpose was to establish the citizenship of the negro; to give definitions of citizenship of the United States and of the States, and to protect from the hostile legislation of the States the privileges and immunities of citizens of the United States, as distinguished from those of citizens of the States

---

[1]*United States Reports* (1896), vol. 163, p. 537.

The object of the amendment was undoubtedly to enforce the absolute equality of the two races before the law, but in the nature of things it could not have been intended to abolish distinctions based upon color, or to enforce social, as distinguished from political equality, or a commingling of the two races upon terms unsatisfactory to either. Laws permitting, and even requiring, their separation in places where they are liable to be brought into contact do not necessarily imply the inferiority of either race to the other, and have been generally, if not universally, recognized as within the competency of the state legislatures in the exercise of their police power. The most common instance of this is connected with the establishment of separate schools for white and colored children, which has been held to be a valid exercise of the legislative power even by courts of States where the political rights of the colored race have been longest and most earnestly enforced. . . .

So far, then, as a conflict with the Fourteenth Amendment is occurred, the case reduces itself to the question whether the statute of Louisiana is a reasonable regulation, and with respect to this there must necessarily be a large discretion on the part of the legislature. In determining the question of reasonableness it is at liberty to act with reference to the established usages, customs and traditions of the people, and with a view to the promotion of their comfort, and the preservation of the public peace and good order. Gauged by this standard, we cannot say that a law which authorizes or even requires the separation of the two races in public conveyances is unreasonable, or more obnoxious to the Fourteenth Amendment than the acts of Congress requiring separate schools for colored children in the District of Columbia, the constitutionality of which does not seem to have been questioned, or the corresponding acts of state legislatures.

We consider the underlying fallacy of the plaintiff's argument to consist in the assumption that the enforced separation of the two races stamps the colored race with a badge of inferiority. If this be so, it is not by reason of anything found in the act, but solely because the colored race chooses to put that construction upon it. The argument necessarily assumes that if, as has been more than once the case, and is not unlikely to be so again, the colored race should become the dominant power in the state legislature, and should enact a law in precisely similar terms, it would thereby relegate the white race to an inferior position. We imagine that the white race, at least, would not acquiesce in this assumption. The argument also assumes that social prejudices may be overcome by legislation, and that equal rights cannot be secured to the negro except by an enforced commingling of the two races. We cannot accept this proposition. If the two races are to meet upon terms of social equality, it must be the result of natural affinities, a mutual appreciation of each other's merits and a voluntary consent of individuals. As was said by the Court of Appeals of New York in *People* v. *Gallagher,* "this end can neither be accomplished nor promoted by laws which conflict with the general sentiment of the community upon whom they are designed to operate. When the government, therefore, has secured to each of its citizens equal rights before the law and equal opportunities for improvement and progress, it has accomplished the end for which it was organized and performed all of the functions respecting social advantages with which it is endowed." Legislation is powerless to eradicate racial instincts or to abolish distinctions based upon physical differences, and the attempt to do so can only result in accentuating the difficulties of the present situation. If the civil and political rights of both races be equal one cannot be inferior to the other civilly or politically. If one race be inferior to the other socially, the Constitution of the United States cannot put them upon the same plane. . . .

2. A Justice of the Peace Denies Justice (1939)

The Jim Crow system that emerged in the South at the end of the nineteenth century denied black southerners the right to vote. For more than half a century, various tactics were employed to ensure that blacks could not exercise political power at the ballot box. In the selection that follows, a justice of the peace in North Carolina describes how he foiled black attempts to register to vote. What were his principal methods? How does he justify his actions?

. . . In 1900 I was a Red Shirt;* that was what they called us, though we didn't actually wear red shirts as they did in some sections. But the legislature had fixed it so we could disfranchise the nigger, and we aimed to tote our part in gettin' it done. Judge Farmer organized the county; they was about thirty-five of us around here that called ourselves Red Shirts. Up to 1900 the niggers had rushed in to register whether or no, and with control of the vote they had put in nigger officeholders all over the county. They wa'n't but one white family in the county that could get a office under the nigger rule of the time, and that was Dr. Hughes's. Dr. Hughes was so good to all the pore folks, goin' when they sent for him and not chargin' 'em a cent, that they'd give him anything he asked for. When the registration book was opened in 1900, the Red Shirts was ordered to get their rifles and shotguns and protect the registration from the niggers. When the word come to me, I remember I was in the field plowin'. I got my gun and hurried out to where the rest of the Red Shirts was assembled with shotguns.

Word come that the federal authorities was comin' to protect the nigger vote; if they had, it would o' meant war. We wa'n't totin' shotguns just for show. Well, the upshot was not a nigger come nigh the registration book that day, from sunrise to sunset. Nigger rule was over!

Two years after, when I first took hold o' registerin' voters, a right smart o' niggers come to register at first, claimin' they could meet the requirements. Some wrote the Constitution, I reckon, as good as a lot o' white men, but I'd find somethin' unsatisfactory, maybe an *i* not dotted or a *t* not crossed, enough for me to disqualify 'em. The law said "satisfactory to the registrar." A few could get by the grandfather clause,† for they was some free niggers before the Civil War, but they couldn't get by an undotted *i* or a uncrossed *t*. They wa'n't no Republicans in the South before the Civil War; the free niggers always voted like their old masters told 'em to—and

---

[2]From *Such As Us: Southern Voices of the Thirties* edited by Tom E. Terrill and Jerrold Hirsch. Copyright © 1978 by the University of North Carolina Press. Used by permission of the publisher.

*A vigilante group that intimidated blacks.

†If a man's father or grandfather could have voted on 1 January 1867, he did not have to meet other voting requirements.

'twa'n't Republican! That's what the war was fought over, politics; they didn't care so much about freein' the slaves as they did the Republican party. . . .

Politics is the rottenest thing in the world. I ought to know, for I've been in it thirty years and over. Not meanin' to brag, I can say I've been honest and my hands is clean. I wouldn't twist a principle for no man. That's how come I got the influence I have in the county. The candidates come to me for advice and want me to get out and work for 'em, because they know I know practically everybody in the county— they ain't a man over forty I don't know—and can't nobody bring nothin' against my integrity. Not meanin' to brag now, my life counts much as my word; folks'll listen to a honest man. My methods ain't like some; I don't get out in the final heat of the campaign and hurrah and shout. By that time my work's all done. It's durin' the off season like this, when nobody's thinkin' politics much, that I do my workin', in a quiet homely way. I get votes pledged to my candidate—a man that won't stand by his pledge ain't worth his salt—and when the campaign gets hot I stay out'n the fight, knowin' the precincts is already lined up for my man. . . .

E. Cleveland and the Tariff

1. Cleveland Pleads for Tariff Reduction (1885)

The financial embarrassments of Cleveland's first administration, oddly enough, stemmed from too much money in the Treasury. The great bulk of federal revenue then came from tariff duties, which the consumer repaid as a hidden tax in the increased price of the import. The only feasible way to reduce the unnecessarily large inflow to the Treasury was to reduce the tariff, and such a reduction was bound to arouse the high-protectionists, mostly Republicans but some Democrats as well. Cleveland, never one to shrink from disagreeable duty, courageously recommended such a remedy in his first annual message to Congress. Is he really hostile to protection? Why does he single out a certain class of items for reduction?

The fact that our revenues are in excess of the actual needs of an economical administration of the government justifies a reduction in the amount exacted from the people for its support. Our government is but the means established by the will of a free people, by which certain principles are applied which they have adopted for their benefit and protection. And it is never better administered, and its true spirit is never better observed, than when the people's taxation for its support is scrupulously limited to the actual necessity of expenditure, and distributed according to a just and equitable plan.

The proposition with which we have to deal is the reduction of the revenue received by the government, and indirectly paid by the people, from customs duties. The question of free trade is not involved, nor is there now any occasion for the general discussion of the wisdom or expediency of a protective system.

---

[1]J. D. Richardson, ed., *Messages and Papers of the Presidents* (New York: Bureau of National Literature, 1897), vol. 8, p. 341.

Justice and fairness dictate that, in any modification of our present laws relating to revenue, the industries and interests which have been encouraged by such laws, and in which our citizens have large investments, should not be ruthlessly injured or destroyed.

We should also deal with the subject in such manner as to protect the interests of American labor, which is the capital of our workingmen. Its stability and proper remuneration furnish the most justifiable pretext for a protective policy.

Within these limitations a certain reduction should be made in our customs revenue. The amount of such reduction having been determined, the inquiry follows: Where can it best be remitted and what articles can best be released from duty in the interest of our citizens?

I think the reductions should be made in the revenue derived from a tax upon the imported necessaries of life. We thus directly lessen the cost of living in every family of the land, and release to the people in every humble home a larger measure of the rewards of frugal industry.

2. Philadelphians Criticize Cleveland (1887)

To Cleveland's repeated pleas for tariff reduction, the protectionists, both Republicans and Democrats, turned a deaf ear. The president finally decided to arouse the country by taking the unprecedented step of devoting his entire annual message to one subject: the tariff and its implications. Old-line Democratic politicians, fearful that such boat-rocking tactics would lose the next presidential election, in vain urged him to reconsider. But as one of his critics remarked, he would rather be wrong than be president. In his sensational tariff message of 1887, he declared that the surplus confronted the nation with a "condition" and "not a theory." He called for a "slight reduction" of the tariff and branded as "irrelevant" and "mischievous" Republican charges of "free trade." In what particular is the following reaction of the Philadelphia Press (Republican) most unfair?

A thousand thanks to President Cleveland for the bold, manly, and unequivocal avowal of his extreme free-trade purposes! And a thousand rebukes and defeats for the false, dangerous, and destructive policy which he thus frankly and unreservedly proclaims!

The message deserves all the glory of courage, all the praise of high public issue, all the condemnation of utter, ruinous heresy.

It is a surprise in its method and a still greater surprise in its matter. It comes like the sudden, echoing boom of a great gun signaling a crucial fight on unexpected ground. In its immediate flash of light and in its broad bearings it looms up as one of the most momentous political events since the war.

It plants the President and his party squarely on free trade; it clarifies the next presidential battle as by a lightning stroke; it makes free trade *vs.* protection the overshadowing issue; it dwarfs and dismisses all other questions; it clears away all cowardly evasions and juggling subterfuges; it ends all pitiful personal bespattering; and it summons the American people to decide the supreme question whether the

---

[2]Quoted in *Public Opinion* 4, no. 193 (December 10, 1887).

grand protective system which has built up our splendid industries shall be over-thrown or not!

For the distinct and emphatic manner in which the President has faced and forced this paramount issue he deserves all credit; for the wrongs, the perils, and the inevitable disasters of his policy he must be crushed unless the people would have their own vital interests crushed.

3. The New York Times *Acclaims Courage* (1887)

The New York Times, *an independent newspaper with Democratic leanings, regarded Cleveland's tariff message as statesmanlike but politically unwise. Explain why, in the light of this editorial.*

Mr. Cleveland has done an act of statesmanship in the best sense. Recognizing a great duty, he has performed it with courage, with firmness, and at the right time. And he has performed it so that every honest man must see that it is an honest act—disinterested, faithful to the requirements of conscience, without hope or purpose of personal or party advantage except such as comes from the public recognition of public service.

Judged by an ordinary standard of political expediency the President's act is in-expedient. He has forced upon his party an issue as to which the party is divided, and so divided that unless the minority yield, it can defeat the will of the majority. He has done this on the eve of a national context in which a considerable number of men of influence in the party have been urging him to avoid this issue, and threatening him and the party with disaster if he did not avoid it.

On the other hand, there is nothing in this issue, thus presented, by which Mr. Cleveland could hope to draw from the Republican Party any votes to compensate those he is in danger of losing, and which he has been warned over and again by leaders of his own party that he would lose.

Nor this alone, for if the protectionist faction in the Democratic Party carry out their own desires, or do what they have continually declared that they would do, Mr. Cleveland has done the one thing by which he could imperil the prospect of his own renomination. From the point of view of the politician, he has shown a courage that is temerity in the pursuit of an end of no value to himself.

[The Cleveland-Harrison presidential canvas of 1888 hinged on the tariff, not the private morals of the candidates, and the Republican Harrison won. The tariff message of 1887 is commonly blamed for the Democratic defeat. But Cleveland actually polled in excess of 100,000 more popular votes than his opponent, and he showed increased strength in states like New Jersey and Rhode Island, where manufacturing was strong. Other factors were no doubt important in tipping the scales, notably the blundering interference of the British minister in Washington, Sackville-West, who declared in effect that a vote for Cleveland was a vote for England.]

---

[3]*New York Times,* December 7, 1887.

4. A Cartoonist Criticizes the Tariff (1884)

"It is a condition which confronts us—not a theory," Grover Cleveland proclaimed in discussing the tariff issue in 1887. In theory, high protective tariffs should have insulated American workers from low-wage foreign competition and bolstered their incomes. In practice, however, the condition of labor was extremely precarious, even behind America's high-tariff protective shield. The drawing below, The Slave Market of To-day, *calls attention to labor's condition in 1884. How are trade unions portrayed in this scene? Why did the protective tariff not protect workers? Was this "wage slavery" comparable to slavery in the South prior to the Civil War?*

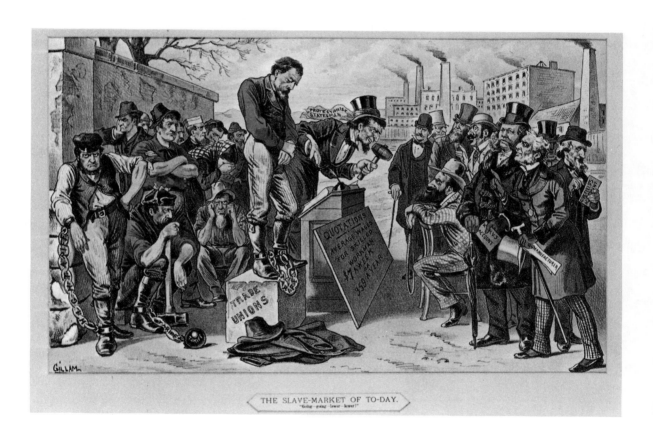

THE SLAVE-MARKET OF TO-DAY.
"Going—going—lower—lower!"

---

[4]Courtesy of The Chicago Historical Society.

Thought Provokers

1. How might one explain the fact that Grant was a success as a general but an embarrassment as a president?
2. What might have been the consequences for whites and blacks in the South if the election of 1876 had gone to Tilden?
3. In the light of the conditions in the South in the late nineteenth century, could Reconstruction be considered a success or a failure? Why has this period been called the darkest hour in the history of African-Americans?
4. What were the strengths and weaknesses of populism in the South? Did the Populist crusade advance or hinder the struggle of black southerners for social justice?
5. How and why did legally sanctioned segregation emerge in the South? Why did the segregationist regime endure for so long?
6. With reference to the tariff-surplus problem, what did Cleveland mean when he said that "unnecessary taxation is unjust taxation"? In what ways might the "surplus" have been legitimately spent?

24

Industry Comes of Age, 1865–1900

That is the most perfect government in which an injury to one is the concern of all.

Motto of the Knights of Labor

Prologue: A few of the railroad companies after 1865 had more employees than a number of the state governments—and more power to inflict harm. When cutthroat competition failed to eliminate abuses, Congress finally passed the precedent-shattering Interstate Commerce Act of 1887. But this pioneer measure fell far short of providing adequate safeguards. Competing industries had meanwhile been merging as monopolistic trusts, notably Rockefeller's Standard Oil Company. Congress belatedly tried to restrain these monsters with the rather toothless Sherman Anti-Trust Act of 1890. The emerging "Titans of Industry"—notably Andrew Carnegie—also developed an articulate social and economic philosophy to justify the new social order they were helping to create. The new industrial regime transformed the lives of working Americans and stimulated the trade union movement. The Knights of Labor, who in the 1870s and 1880s made the most successful attempt until then to organize the nation's army of toilers, amassed considerable numerical strength. But they overreached themselves in the 1880s, and the wage-conscious American Federation of Labor, with its component skilled unions, forged to the front. Advancing industrialization, meanwhile, inflicted incalculable damage on the environment—and on the humans who inhabited it.

A. The Problem of the Railroads

1. A Defense of Long-Haul Rates (1885)

A serious grievance against the "railroad rascals" was discrimination. Their rates were often lower where a line had competition and higher elsewhere. Charges were sometimes heavier for a short haul than for a long haul over the same track. At one time, the freight rate on cotton goods shipped from Boston to Denver was $1.79 a

---

[1]Report of the Senate Select Committee on Interstate Commerce, 49th Cong., 1st sess., *Senate Reports,* no. 46, vol. 2, part 1, Appendix, pp. 130–131.

hundredweight; if the shipment went fourteen hundred miles farther, to San Fran-cisco, the total charge was only $1.50. Is the following justification of this practice by a southern railroad manager (H. S. Haines) convincing? Why did certain farmers favor this type of discrimination?

If it costs $600,000 per annum to keep up a [rail]road, then the money must come out of the freight and passengers that are obliged to pass over it. Whether the amount of business be small or large, the money to keep up the road must be forth-coming, or it will go to decay.

If 100,000 bales of cotton were the only freight that passed over a road which carried no passengers, that cotton would have to pay a freight of $6 per bale if it cost $600,000 per annum to maintain the road, and no legislation could make it oth-erwise. But if the quantity of cotton to be transported could be increased to 200,000 bales, then the cost of transportation could be fixed at $3 per bale, to the great joy and relief of the shippers of the first 100,000 bales; and yet the $600,000 required to operate the road would be forthcoming.

Now, suppose that the community which raised this second 100,000 bales had a water route to market and said to the railroad company, "It only costs a dollar per bale to ship our cotton by water, but we prefer to ship it by rail at the same price." Who would be benefited if the company took the cotton at a dollar per bale? Who but the local shippers themselves, for without this addition to the business of the road they would have to pay $600,000 per year, or $6 per bale, to keep up the road, while with the $100,000 obtained from the other 100,000 bales of competitive or through cotton they would have to pay but $500,000 or $5 per bale on their own cot-ton. Should they turn around upon the managers of the railroad and say that it was unjust to the local shippers to charge only a dollar per bale on the through cotton?

No, it is not only just, but to the benefit of the local shippers, that the railroad which they are obliged to use should get all the business it can from those who are not obliged to use it, and at any rate the latter choose to pay, provided—and it is a very important provision—that such competitive business adds something to the net revenue of the road; or, in other words, if it be carried at anything above the actual cost of transportation.

2. Railroad President Sidney Dillon Supports Stock Watering (1891)

Critics of the railroads especially condemned "stock watering"—the practice of issu-ing stocks and bonds grossly in excess of the value of the property. The more the stock was watered, the higher the freight and passenger rates would have to be to ensure a normal return on the investment. Sidney Dillon, a later president of the Union Pa-cific Railroad, stoutly defended stock watering. Beginning his career at the age of seven as a water boy—appropriately enough—on a New York railway, he ultimately amassed a fortune by building railroads, including the Union Pacific. Present at the "wedding of the rails" in Utah in 1869, he retained one of the final silver spikes until

---

[2]Sidney Dillon, "The West and the Railroads," *North American Review* 152 (April 1891): 445–448, passim.

his death. Here he attacks regulatory legislation in an article for a popular maga-zine. What is his social philosophy? Why does he place his faith in competition and the courts?

Statutory enactments interfere with the business of the railway, even to the mi-nutest details, and always to its detriment. This sort of legislation proceeds on the theory that the railroad is a public enemy; that it has its origin in the selfish desire of a company of men to make money out of the public; that it will destroy the public unless it is kept within bounds; and that it is impossible to enact too many laws tending to restrain the monster. The advocates of these statutes may not state their theory in these exact words. But these words certainly embody their theory, if they have any theory at all beyond such prejudices as are born of the marriage between ignorance and demagogism.

Many of the grievances that are urged against railways are too puerile to be se-riously noticed, but the reader will pardon a few words as to "overcapitaliza-tion." . . .

Now, it is impossible to estimate in advance the productive power of this useful and untiring servant. Sometimes a railway is capitalized too largely, and then it pays smaller dividends; sometimes not largely enough, and then the dividends are much in excess of the usual interest of money. In the former case stockholders are willing to reduce the face of their shares, or wait until increase of population increases rev-enue; in the latter they accept an enlarged issue. But, as a matter of reason and prin-ciple, the question of capitalization concerns the stockholders, and the stockholders only. A citizen, simply as a citizen, commits an impertinence when he questions the right of any corporation to capitalize its properties at any sum whatever. . . .

Then as to prices, these will always be taken care of by the great law of competition, which obtains wherever any human service is to be performed for a pecuniary consideration. That any railway, anywhere in a republic, should be a monopoly is not a supposable case. If between two points, A and B, a railway is constructed, and its charges for fares and freight are burdensome to the public and unduly profitable to itself, it will not be a long time before another railway will be laid between these points, and then competition may be safely trusted to reduce prices. We may state it as an axiom that no common carrier can ever maintain bur-densome and oppressive rates of service permanently or for a long period. . . .

Given a company of men pursuing a lawful and useful occupation,—why inter-fere with them? Why empower a body of other men, fortuitously assembled, not possessing superior knowledge, and accessible often to unworthy influences, to dic-tate to these citizens how they shall manage their private affairs? Wherever such management conflicts with public policy or private rights, there are district attorneys and competent lawyers and upright courts to take care that the commonwealth or the citizen shall receive no detriment. . . .

3. General James B. Weaver Deplores
Stock Watering (1892)

General James B. Weaver, a walrus-mustached veteran of the Civil War, had early experienced extortion when he had to borrow $100 at 33⅓ percent interest to finish law school. Fiery orator and relentless foe of the railroads and other "predatory" corporations, he won the presidential nomination of the People's party (Populists) in 1892. (See p. 160.) His book A Call to Action, *published during the campaign, condemned stock waterers. To what extent does the following excerpt from it cast doubts on the testimony of President Dillon, whose article, presented in the previous selection, he sharply attacks? What is Weaver's view of the citizens' "impertinence"?*

In their delirium of greed the managers of our transportation systems disregard both private right and the public welfare. Today they will combine and bankrupt their weak rivals, and by the expenditure of a trifling sum possess themselves of properties which cost the outlay of millions. Tomorrow they will capitalize their booty for five times the cost, issue their bonds, and proceed to levy tariffs upon the people to pay dividends upon the fraud.

Take for example the Kansas Midland. It cost $10,200 per mile. It is capitalized at $53,024 per mile. How are the plain plodding people to defend themselves against such flagrant injustice?

Mr. Sidney Dillon, president of the Union Pacific, . . . is many times a millionaire, and the road over which he presides was built wholly by public funds and by appropriations of the public domain. The road never cost Mr. Dillon nor his associates a single penny. It is now capitalized at $106,000 per mile! This company owes the government $50,000,000 with accruing interest which is destined to accumulate for many years. The public lien exceeds the entire cost of the road, and yet this government, which Mr. Dillon defies, meekly holds a second mortgage to secure its claim. . . .

It is pretty clear that it would not be safe for the public to take the advice of either Mr. Dillon or Mr. Gould [a railroad promoter] as to the best method of dealing with the transportation problem.

[Responding to a mounting public outcry, in 1887 Congress passed the Interstate Commerce Act, the first regulatory legislation of its kind in U.S. history. Among various reforms, it forbade unreasonable or unjust rates, discriminatory rates or practices, the payment of rebates, the pooling of profits among competing lines, and a higher charge for a short haul than for a long haul. In practice, however, the law proved to be riddled with loopholes, and subsequent legislation was required to provide adequate safeguards.]

---

[3]J. B. Weaver, *A Call to Action* (Des Moines: Iowa Printing Company, 1892), pp. 412–413.

B. The Trust and Monopoly

1. John D. Rockefeller Justifies Rebates (1909)

John D. Rockefeller, who amassed a fortune of nearly $1 billion dollars, lived to give away more than half of his "oil-gotten gains" in philanthropy. A prominent lay Baptist, he yearly donated one-tenth of his income to charities and, in 1859, helped a Cincinnati black man to buy his slave wife. As a founding father of the mighty Standard Oil Company, he here puts the best possible face on railroad rebates, which were finally banned by the Interstate Commerce Act. He tactfully neglects to add that at one time his company also extorted secret payments ("drawbacks") from the railways on shipments by his competitors. What were the advantages to the railroads of the rebate system? To what extent did they, rather than Standard Oil, profit from these under-the-counter deals?

Of all the subjects that seem to have attracted the attention of the public to the affairs of the Standard Oil Company, the matter of rebates from railroads has perhaps been uppermost. The Standard Oil Company of Ohio, of which I was president, did receive rebates from the railroads prior to 1880, but received no advantages for which it did not give full compensation.

The reason for rebates was that such was the railroads' method of business. A public rate was made and collected by the railroad companies, but, so far as my knowledge extends, was seldom retained in full; a portion of it was repaid to the shippers as a rebate.

By this method the real rate of freight which any shipper paid was not known by his competitors nor by other railroad companies, the amount being a matter of bargain with the carrying company. Each shipper made the best bargain that he could, but whether he was doing better than his competitor was only a matter of conjecture. Much depended upon whether the shipper had the advantage of competition of carriers.

The Standard Oil Company of Ohio, being situated at Cleveland, had the advantage of different carrying lines, as well as of water transportation in the summer. Taking advantage of those facilities, it made the best bargains possible for its freights. Other companies sought to do the same.

The Standard gave advantages to the railroads for the purpose of reducing the cost of transportation of freight. It offered freights in large quantity, carloads and trainloads. It furnished loading facilities and discharging facilities at great cost. It provided regular traffic, so that a railroad could conduct its transportation to the best advantage and use its equipment to the full extent of its hauling capacity without waiting for the refiner's convenience. It exempted railroads from liability for fire and carried its own insurance. It provided at its own expense terminal facilities which permitted economies in handling. For these services it obtained contracts for special allowances on freights. But notwithstanding these special allowances, this traffic

---

[1]J. D. Rockefeller, *Random Reminiscences of Men and Events* (1909), pp. 107–109, 111–112. Copyright 1909, Doubleday & Company, Inc.

from the Standard Oil Company was far more profitable to the railroad companies than the smaller and irregular traffic, which might have paid a higher rate.

To understand the situation which affected the giving and taking of rebates, it must be remembered that the railroads were all eager to enlarge their freight traffic. They were competing with the facilities and rates offered by the boats on lake and canal and by the pipe lines. All these means of transporting oil cut into the business of the railroads, and they were desperately anxious to successfully meet this competition. . . .

The profits of the Standard Oil Company did not come from advantages given by railroads. The railroads, rather, were the ones who profited by the traffic of the Standard Oil Company, and whatever advantage it received in its constant efforts to reduce rates of freight was only one of the many elements of lessening cost to the consumer which enabled us to increase our volume of business the world over because we could reduce the selling price.

How general was the complicated bargaining for rates can hardly be imagined; everyone got the best rate that he could. After the passage of the Interstate Commerce Act, it was learned that many small companies which shipped limited quantities had received lower rates than we had been able to secure, notwithstanding the fact that we had made large investments to provide for terminal facilities, regular shipments, and other economies.

I well remember a bright man from Boston who had much to say about rebates and drawbacks. He was an old and experienced merchant, and looked after his affairs with a cautious and watchful eye. He feared that some of his competitors were doing better than he in bargaining for rates, and he delivered himself of this conviction:

"I am opposed on principle to the whole system of rebates and drawbacks—unless I am in it."

2. An Oil Man Goes Bankrupt (1899)

Rockefeller's great passion was not so much a love of power or money as a dislike of waste and inefficiency. Having begun as a $3.50-a-week employee, he ultimately moved into the chaotically competitive oil business with a vision that enabled him to see far ahead, and then "around the corner." Overlooking no detail, he insisted that every drop of solder used on his oil cans be counted. By acquiring or controlling warehouses, pipelines, tankers, railroads, oil fields, and refineries, he helped forge the United States's first great trust in 1882. He produced a superior product at a lower price but, in line with existing ethics, resorted to such "refined robbery" as ruthless price cutting, dictation to dealers, deception, espionage, and rebates. George Rice, one of his ill-starred competitors, here complains to the U.S. Industrial Commission. What are his principal grievances?

---

[2]*Report of the U.S. Industrial Commission,* vol. 1 (Washington, D.C.: Government Printing Office, 1899), pp. 687, 704.

I am a citizen of the United States, born in the state of Vermont. Producer of petroleum for more than thirty years, and a refiner of same for twenty years. But my refinery has been shut down during the past three years, owing to the powerful and all-prevailing machinations of the Standard Oil Trust, in criminal collusion and conspiracy with the railroads to destroy my business of twenty years of patient industry, toil, and money in building up, wholly by and through unlawful freight discriminations.

I have been driven from pillar to post, from one railway line to another, for twenty years, in the absolutely vain endeavor to get equal and just freight rates with the Standard Oil Trust, so as to be able to run my refinery at anything approaching a profit, but which I have been utterly unable to do. I have had to consequently shut down, with my business absolutely ruined and my refinery idle.

This has been a very sad, bitter, and ruinous experience for me to endure, but I have endeavored to the best of my circumstances and ability to combat it the utmost I could for many a long waiting year, expecting relief through the honest and proper execution of our laws, which have [has] as, however, never come. But I am still living in hopes, though I may die in despair. . . .

Outside of rebates or freight discriminations, I had no show with the Standard Oil Trust, because of their unlawfully acquired monopoly, by which they could temporarily cut only my customers' prices, and below cost, leaving the balance of the town, nine-tenths, uncut. This they can easily do without any appreciable harm to their general trade, and thus effectually wipe out all competition, as fully set forth. Standard Oil prices generally were so high that I could sell my goods 2 to 3 cents a gallon below their prices and make a nice profit, but these savage attacks and [price] cuts upon my customers' goods . . . plainly showed . . . their power for evil, and the uselessness to contend against such odds. . . .

3. Weaver Attacks the Trusts (1892)

Rockefeller's Standard Oil of Ohio was not authorized to operate outside the state, so in 1882 the Standard Oil Trust, the first of its kind, was born. "A corporation of corporations," it secretly merged forty-one different concerns. In 1892 the courts held this trust to be illegally in restraint of trade, but Rockefeller and his associates were able to achieve their semimonopolistic ends by less formal agreements. General Weaver, the fiery Populist candidate for president in 1892 (see p. 160), here assails the trusts, whose unwritten motto was said to be, "Let us prey." Note his enumeration of the evils of the trusts. What does he make of the monopolists' claim that the elimination of wasteful competition is advantageous to the consumer?

The trust is organized commerce with the Golden Rule excluded and the trustees exempted from the restraints of conscience.

They argue that competition means war and is therefore destructive. The trust is eminently docile and hence seeks to destroy competition in order that we may have peace. But the peace which they give us is like that which exists after the leopard

---

[3]J. B. Weaver, *A Call to Action* (Des Moines: Iowa Printing Company, 1892), pp. 392–393.

has devoured the kid. This professed desire for peace is a false pretense. They dread the war of competition because the people share in the spoils. When rid of that, they always turn their guns upon the masses and deprecate without limit or mercy.

The main weapons of the trust are threats, intimidation, bribery, fraud, wreck, and pillage. Take one well-authenticated instance in the history of the Oat Meal Trust as an example. In 1887 this trust decided that part of their mills should stand idle. They were accordingly closed. This resulted in the discharge of a large number of laborers who had to suffer in consequence. The mills which were continued in operation would produce seven million barrels of meal during the year. Shortly after shutting down, the trust advanced the price of meal one dollar per barrel, and the public was forced to stand the assessment. The mills were more profitable when idle than when in operation.

The Sugar Trust has it within its power to levy a tribute of $30,000,000 upon the people of the United States by simply advancing the price of sugar one cent per pound for one year. If popular tumult breaks out and legislation in restraint of these depredations is threatened, they can advance prices, extort campaign expenses and corruption funds from the people, and force the disgruntled multitude to furnish the sinews of war for their own destruction. They not only have the power to do these things, but it is their known mode of warfare, and they actually practice it from year to year.

The most distressing feature of this war of the trusts is the fact that they control the articles which the plain people consume in their daily life. It cuts off their accumulations and deprives them of the staff upon which they fain would lean in their old age.

C. The New Philosophy of Materialism

1. Andrew Carnegie's Gospel of Wealth (1889)

Andrew Carnegie, the ambitious Scottish steel magnate, spent the first part of his life in the United States making a half-billion or so dollars and the rest of it giving his fortune away. Not a gambler or speculator at heart, he gambled everything on the future prosperity of the United States. His social conscience led him to preach "the gospel of wealth," notably in the following magazine article. Why does he believe that the millionaire is a trustee for the poor and that direct charity is an evil?

This, then, is held to be the duty of the man of wealth: first, to set an example of modest, unostentatious living, shunning display or extravagance; to provide moderately for the legitimate wants of those dependent upon him; and after doing so to consider all surplus revenues which come to him simply as trust funds, which he is called upon to administer, and strictly bound as a matter of duty to administer in the manner which, in his judgment, is best calculated to produce the most beneficial results for the community—the man of wealth thus becoming the mere agent and

---

[1]Andrew Carnegie, "Wealth," *North American Review* 148 (June 1889): 661–664.

trustee for his poorer brethren, bringing to their service his superior wisdom, experience, and ability to administer, doing for them better than they would or could do for themselves. . . .

Those who would administer wisely must, indeed, be wise, for one of the serious obstacles to the improvement of our race is indiscriminate charity. It were better for mankind that the millions of the rich were thrown into the sea than so spent as to encourage the slothful, the drunken, the unworthy. Of every thousand dollars spent in so-called charity today, it is probable that $950 is unwisely spent; so spent, indeed, as to produce the very evils which it proposes to mitigate or cure.

A well-known writer of philosophic books admitted the other day that he had given a quarter of a dollar to a man who approached him as he was coming to visit the house of his friend. He knew nothing of the habits of this beggar; knew not the use that would be made of this money, although he had every reason to suspect that it would be spent improperly. This man professed to be a disciple of [conservative English social theorist] Herbert Spencer; yet the quarter-dollar given that night will probably work more injury than all the money which its thoughtless donor will ever be able to give in true charity will do good. He only gratified his own feelings, saved himself from annoyance—and this was probably one of the most selfish and very worst actions of his life, for in all respects he is most worthy.

In bestowing charity, the main consideration should be to help those who will help themselves; to provide part of the means by which those who desire to improve may do so; to give those who desire to rise the aids by which they may rise; to assist, but rarely or never to do all. Neither the individual nor the race is improved by almsgiving. Those worthy of assistance, except in rare cases, seldom require assistance. The really valuable men of the race never do, except in cases of accident or sudden change. Everyone has, of course, cases of individuals brought to his own knowledge where temporary assistance can do genuine good, and these he will not overlook.

But the amount which can be wisely given by the individual for individuals is necessarily limited by his lack of knowledge of the circumstances connected with each. He is the only true reformer who is as careful and as anxious not to aid the unworthy as he is to aid the worthy, and, perhaps, even more so, for in almsgiving more injury is probably done by rewarding vice than by relieving virtue.

The rich man is thus almost restricted to following the examples of Peter Cooper, Enoch Pratt of Baltimore, Mr. Pratt of Brooklyn, Senator Stanford,* and others, who know that the best means of benefiting the community is to place within its reach the ladders upon which the aspiring can rise—parks, and means of recreation, by which men are helped in body and mind; works of art, certain to give pleasure and improve the public taste; and public institutions of various kinds, which will improve the general condition of the people;—in this manner returning their surplus wealth to the mass of their fellows in the forms best calculated to do them lasting good. . . .

---

*Cooper founded an institute in New York City for educating the working classes; Enoch Pratt established a free library in Baltimore; Charles Pratt created an institute in Brooklyn for training skilled workers; and Leland Stanford endowed Stanford University.

The man who dies leaving behind him millions of available wealth, which was his to administer during life, will pass away "unwept, unhonored, and unsung," no matter to what uses he leaves the dross which he cannot take with him. Of such as these the public verdict will then be: "The man who dies thus rich dies disgraced."

Such, in my opinion, is the true Gospel concerning Wealth, obedience to which is destined some day to solve the problem of the Rich and the Poor, and to bring "Peace on earth, among men good will."

2. The Nation *Challenges Carnegie (1901)*

Carnegie avoided the "disgrace" of dying rich. He gave away $350 million of the fortune he had accumulated. Some $60 million went to public municipal libraries, many named after himself. Finley Peter Dunne ("Mr. Dooley") poked fun at this immodest arrangement, especially the feature that required the community to provide the site, the books, the upkeep: "Ivry time he [Carnegie] dhrops a dollar, it makes a noise like a waither [waiter] fallin' downstairs with a tray iv dishes." The New York Nation *reviewed rather critically Carnegie's essay on the gospel of wealth when it was published in book form. Does Carnegie or the* Nation *have the better of the argument as to the baleful effects of inherited riches? How have these issues changed since Carnegie's day?*

Mr. Carnegie's philosophy is perfectly simple, and it is stated clearly and forcibly. He holds, first, that the present competitive system, which necessarily creates millionaires, or allows men to get rich, is essential to progress, and should not be altered. Secondly, rich men should not leave their fortunes to their children, because their children will be demoralized by having money to spend which they have not earned. Thirdly, rich men should not indulge in luxury. Fourthly, they should dispose of their fortunes while living, or the government should confiscate them at their death. Fifthly, the only practical way of disposing of them is to found libraries and other public institutions, requiring the public to contribute to their support.

Evidently, this system assumes that millionaires are sinners above other men. The number of persons who have wealth sufficient to maintain their children in idleness is very large, and such persons are able to indulge in many luxuries. We cannot concede that the children of millionaires will go straight to perdition if they inherit their parents' wealth, while those who get but a hundred thousand shall be immune. Everyone familiar with the life of the common people knows that an inheritance of a very few thousand dollars may demoralize a young man, and this principle has been illustrated on a prodigious scale in our pension largesses.

On the other hand, virtue among the children of millionaires is not quite so rare as Mr. Carnegie intimates. Instances are known where inherited wealth has been wisely administered by men of respectable and even irreproachable habits. Mr. Carnegie's dictim, "I would as soon leave to my son a curse as the almighty dollar,"

---

[2]*Nation* (New York) 62 (January 17, 1901): 55.

is too sweeping. Millions of people who are not millionaires desire to give their children the advantages of wealth, and this desire is one of the greatest incentives to accumulation. Provided they educate their children wisely, it is impossible to maintain that the gift of these advantages is necessarily injurious.

On this point Mr. Carnegie and Mr. Gladstone [a British statesman] had some debate; the latter contending that "the heriditary transmission of wealth and position, in conjunction with the calls of occupation and of responsibility, is a good and not an evil thing." Of course, this is nothing but the old conflict between the ideals of democracy and aristocracy, and we need not restate it. . . .

Probably we shall see the experiment of confiscating large fortunes at the death of their owners tried on an increasing scale, together with progressive taxes on incomes.

3. Russell Conwell Deifies the Dollar (c. 1900)

The Reverend Russell H. Conwell was a remarkable Baptist preacher from Philadelphia who founded Temple University and had a large hand in establishing three hospitals. He delivered his famous lecture, "Acres of Diamonds," more than six thousand times. The proceeds went toward the education of some ten thousand young men. His basic theme was that in seeking riches, people were likely to overlook the opportunities (the "acres of diamonds") in their own backyards. Critics charged that Conwell was merely throwing the cloak of religion about the materialistic ideals of his time, especially since he combined philanthropy with dollar chasing. In the following excerpt from his famous lecture, what is his attitude toward the poor? How might one reconcile this brand of Christianity with the teachings of Christ, who said to the young man, "Go and sell that thou hast, and give to the poor" (Matthew 19:21)?

You have no right to be poor. It is your duty to be rich.

Oh, I know well that there are some things higher, sublimer than money! Ah, yes, there are some things sweeter, holier than gold! Yet I also know that there is not one of those things but is greatly enhanced by the use of money.

"Oh," you will say, "Mr. Conwell, can you, as a Christian teacher, tell the young people to spend their lives making money?"

Yes, I do. Three times I say, I do, I do, I do. You ought to make money. Money is power. Think how much good you could do if you had money now. Money is power, and it ought to be in the hands of good men. It would be in the hands of good men if we comply with the Scripture teachings, where God promises prosperity to the righteous man. That means more than being a goody-good—it means the all-round righteous man. You should be a righteous man. If you were, you would be rich.

I need to guard myself right here. Because one of my theological students came to me once to labor with me, for heresy, inasmuch as I had said that money was power.

---

[3]R. H. Conwell, *Acres of Diamonds* (1901), pp. 145–147, 151. Reprinted from *Modern Eloquence.*

He said: "Mr. Conwell, I feel it my duty to tell you that the Scriptures say that money 'is the root of all evil.'" . . .

So he read: "The *love* of money is the root of all evil." Indeed it is. The *love* of money is the root of all evil. The love of money, rather than the *love* of the good it secures, is a dangerous evil in the community. The desire to get hold of money, and to hold on to it, "hugging the dollar until the eagle squeals," is the root of all evil. But it is a grand ambition for men to have the desire to gain money, that they may use it for the benefit of their fellow men.

Young man! you may never have the opportunity to charge at the head of your nation's troops on some Santiago's heights. Young woman! you may never be called on to go out in the seas like Grace Darling to save suffering humanity.* But every one of you can earn money honestly, and with that money you can fight the battles of peace; and the victories of peace are always grander than those of war. I say then to you that you ought to be rich. . . .

No man has a right to go into business and not make money. It is a crime to go into business and lose money, because it is a curse to the rest of the community. No man has a moral right to transact business unless he makes something out of it. He has also no right to transact business unless the man he deals with has an opportunity also to make something. Unless he lives and lets live, he is not an honest man in business. There are no exceptions to this great rule. . . .

It is cruel to slander the rich because they have been successful. It is a shame to "look down" upon the rich the way we do. They are not scoundrels because they have gotten money. They have blessed the world. They have gone into great enterprises that have enriched the nation and the nation has enriched them. It is all wrong for us to accuse a rich man of dishonesty simply because he secured money. Go through this city and your very best people are among your richest people. Owners of property are always the best citizens. It is all wrong to say they are not good.

D. The Rise of the New South

1. Henry Grady Issues a Challenge (1889)

The industrialized South—the new South—was slow to rise from the ashes of civil conflict. A kind of inferiority complex settled over the area. Henry W. Grady, eloquent editor of the Atlanta Constitution, *did more than anyone else to break the spell. With Irish wit he preached the need for diversified crops, a readjustment of the freed slaves, the encouragement of manufacturing, and the development of local resources. In demand as a speaker, he broadcast his message widely and with demonstrable effect. The South of the 1880s was experiencing a marvelous economic boom, and new industries were spreading like its own honeysuckle. Following is a selection*

---

*Grace Darling was the daughter of a British lighthouse keeper who heroically helped her father rescue passengers from a shipwreck in 1838.

[1]Joel C. Harris, *Life of Henry W. Grady* (New York: Cassell and Company, Ltd., 1890), pp. 204–205. Shortly after delivering this speech, Grady contracted pneumonia and died.

from a speech in Boston in which Grady contrasted the broken-down South of Reconstruction days with the new industrialized South. What major lesson must this passage have impressed upon his northern listeners?

I attended a funeral once in Pickens county in my state [Georgia]. A funeral is not usually a cheerful object to me unless I could select the subject. I think I could, perhaps, without going a hundred miles from here, find the material for one or two cheerful funerals. Still, this funeral was peculiarly sad. It was a poor "one-gallus" fellow, whose breeches struck him under the armpits and hit him at the other end about the knee—he didn't believe in décolleté clothes.

They buried him in the midst of a marble quarry—they cut through solid marble to make his grave—and yet a little tombstone they put above him was from Vermont. They buried him in the heart of a pine forest, and yet the pine coffin was imported from Cincinnati. They buried him within the touch of an iron mine, and yet the nails in his coffin and the iron in the shovel that dug his grave were imported from Pittsburgh. They buried him by the side of the best sheep-grazing country on earth, and yet the wool in the coffin bands and the coffin bands themselves were brought from the North. The South didn't furnish a thing on earth for that funeral but the corpse and the hole in the ground.

There they put him away and the clods rattled down on his coffin, and they buried him in a New York coat and a Boston pair of shoes and a pair of breeches from Chicago and a shirt from Cincinnati, leaving him nothing to carry into the next world with him to remind him of the country in which he lived, and for which he fought for four years, but the chill of blood in his veins and the marrow in his bones.

Now we have improved on that. We have got the biggest marble-cutting establishment on earth within a hundred yards of that grave. We have got a half-dozen woolen mills right around it, and iron mines, and iron furnaces, and iron factories. We are coming to meet you. We are going to take a noble revenge, as my friend Mr. Carnegie said last night, by invading every inch of your territory with iron, as you invaded ours [in the Civil War] twenty-nine years ago.

2. A Yankee Visits the New South (1887)

New England–born Charles Dudley Warner—lecturer, newspaper editor, essayist, and novelist—shone as one of the literary lights of the post–Civil War years. World traveler and humorist, he collaborated with his friend and neighbor Mark Twain in writing a satirical novel that gave a name to an era, The Gilded Age *(1873). He revisited the South, after a two-year absence, on an extensive six-week tour. The result was the charming magazine article from which the following selection is excerpted. What is most remarkable about the industrial flowering of the South, and who or what was primarily responsible for it?*

When we come to the New Industrial South, the change is marvelous. . . . Instead of a South devoted to agriculture and politics, we find a South wide awake to

---

[2]C. D. Warner, "The South Revisited," *Harper's New Monthly Magazine* 74 (March 1887): 638–639.

business, excited and even astonished at the development of its own immense re-sources in metals, marbles, coal, timber, fertilizers, eagerly laying lines of communication, rapidly opening mines, building furnaces, foundries, and all sorts of shops for utilizing the native riches.

It is like the discovery of a new world. When the Northerner finds great foundries in Virginia using only (with slight exceptions) the products of Virginia iron and coal mines; when he finds Alabama and Tennessee making iron so good and so cheap that it finds ready market in Pennsylvania, and foundries multiplying near the great furnaces for supplying Northern markets; when he finds cotton mills running to full capacity on grades of cheap cottons universally in demand throughout the South and Southwest; when he finds small industries, such as paper box factories and wooden bucket and tub factories, sending all they can make into the North and widely over the West; when he sees the loads of most beautiful marbles shipped North; when he learns that some of the largest and most important engines and mill machinery were made in Southern shops; when he finds in Richmond a "pole locomotive," made to run on logs laid end to end, and drag out from Michigan forests and Southern swamps lumber hitherto inaccessible; when he sees worn-out highlands in Georgia and Carolina bear more cotton than ever before by help of a fertilizer the base of which is the cotton seed itself (worth more as a fertilizer than it was before the oil was extracted from it); when he sees a multitude of small shops giving employment to men, women, and children who never had any work of that sort to do before; and when he sees Roanoke iron cast in Richmond into car irons, and returned to a car factory in Roanoke which last year sold three hundred cars to the New York and New England Railroad—he begins to open his eyes.

The South is manufacturing a great variety of things needed in the house, on the farm, and in the shops, for home consumption, and already sends to the North and West several manufactured products. With iron, coal, timber contiguous and easily obtained, the amount sent out is certain to increase as the labor becomes more skillful. The most striking industrial development today is in iron, coal, lumber, and marbles; the more encouraging for the self-sustaining life of the Southern people is the multiplication of small industries in nearly every city I visited.

When I have been asked what impressed me most in this hasty tour, I have always said that the most notable thing was that everybody was at work. In many cities this was literally true: every man, woman, and child was actively employed, and in most there were fewer idlers than in many Northern towns. There are, of course, slow places, antiquated methods, easygoing ways, a-hundred-years-behind-the-time make-shifts, but the spirit in all the centers, and leavening the whole country, is work. Perhaps the greatest revolution of all in Southern sentiment is in regard to the dignity of labor. Labor is honorable, made so by the example of the best in the land. There are, no doubt, fossils or Bourbons, sitting in the midst of the ruins of their estates, martyrs to an ancient pride; but usually the leaders in business and enterprise bear names well known in politics and society. The nonsense that it is beneath the dignity of any man or woman to work for a living is pretty much eliminated from the Southern mind. It still remains true that the purely American type is prevalent in the South, but in all the cities the business signboards show that the enterprising Hebrew is increasingly prominent as merchant and trader, and he is becoming a plantation owner as well.

It cannot be too strongly impressed upon the public mind that the South, to use a comprehensible phrase, "has joined the procession." Its mind is turned to the development of its resources, to business, to enterprise, to education, to economic problems; it is marching with the North in the same purpose of wealth by industry. It is true that the railways, mines, and furnaces could not have been without enormous investments of Northern capital, but I was continually surprised to find so many and important local industries the result solely of home capital, made and saved since the war.

3. Life in a Southern Mill (1910)

From Charles Dickens's England to the modern-day Third World, the onset of industrialization has repeatedly wrenched people out of traditional habits of life and forced harsh accommodation to the cruel discipline of the factory floor. The rapidly industrializing late-nineteenth-century South was no exception, as the following excerpt from a congressional investigation illustrates. What were the hardest conditions of life in the southern textile mills? Were there any distinctively southern aspects to these millworkers' plight?

In many mill villages the mill whistles blow at 4.30 or 5 A.M. to awaken the inhabitants, and in winter employees begin work in the mills before daybreak and they work until after nightfall.

When a mill is operated longer than its nominal working schedule, the machinery is started before the announced time of beginning work in the morning and at noon, and, in some cases, continues to run later than the announced time of stopping work at noon and in the evening. Mill managers, when questioned as to this practice, said that employees are not required to work before or after the announced scheduled time. In reality, however, employees are required to be at their machines whenever the machines are running. Otherwise the work gets in bad condition, and in the case of weavers dockage is made for imperfections, which are liable to occur when the weaver is not attending the looms.

The practice of requiring employees to begin before the announced beginning time and to work after the announced stopping time is called by them "stealing time." . . .

Taking the 28 North Carolina mills which employed women or children at night, all together, the children working by day in all these mills were 25.32 per cent of all the day employees there, and the 437 children working by night in all these mills were 26.29 per cent of all the night workers. . . .

In only 2 establishments investigated did the night force work more than 5 nights a week. In each of these mills, both of which were in North Carolina, an additional half day's work on Saturday was demanded, and this demand caused much dissatisfaction. In 1 of these 2 establishments the night shift worked 11 hours and 15 minutes nightly from Monday to Friday, inclusive, and on Saturday resumed at noon and worked until 6.15 in the evening, making a total of 62 hours and 30 minutes a

---

[3]*Report on Condition of Woman and Child Wage-Earners in the United States,* U.S. Congress, 61st Cong., 2d sess., Senate Document No. 645 (Washington, D.C.: Government Printing Office, 1910), pp. 280–291.

week. In the other mill the night shift worked 11 hours and 30 minutes nightly, from Monday to Friday, inclusive, and on Saturday resumed at 3 P.M. and worked until 10 P.M., making a total of 64 hours and 30 minutes. Other mills which had had such a schedule had discontinued the Saturday work for its night workers, because of the dissatisfaction which such a time-table caused. . . .

In interviewing cotton-mill operatives, women expressed more dissatisfaction with night work than children did. Many of the latter claimed that they much preferred to work at night. Spinners asserted that the "work runs better at night," because the increased moisture in the air keeps the threads from breaking so frequently. In consequence the young spinners received less reproof from the overseers.

Then, with the exception of 2 mills in North Carolina the night shifts worked only 5 nights a week, from Monday to Friday, inclusive. This means that three full days were given for rest, Saturday, Sunday, and Monday. If the children should sleep on Saturday, as they ought to do, but rarely do, they would see that they have very little more spare time than the day workers—only the one night, Saturday, which they surely need for recuperation after their sixty hours' work at night. Mothers complain that the children who work at night are nervous.

In visiting families of cotton-mill operatives who worked at night, night workers were often found sitting drowsily before a scant fire between 9 and 11 o'clock in the morning. They had begun work the night before at 6, had quit at 6 A.M., and at 11 o'clock they had had no sleep. Usually they arose at 4 or 5 in the afternoon and again took their seats before the fire, too weary and sluggish to think of a walk in the open air. Even when they went to bed early in the morning, sleep was not continuous throughout the day, nor could it be sound sleep. In the small houses, with thin wood partitions, every sound in the house can be heard by the night worker, even though he may sleep in a separate room. Moreover, night workers often sleep in the same room occupied by the nonworkers during the day. The nonworkers frequently include children and the room can not be kept quiet.

In cases where both the mother and father worked at night, the mother nearly always did her housework, including her washing and ironing. This means that on one day at least the mother went from 18 to 24 hours without sleeping. One woman, who gave as her reason for working at night that she could take care of her home, garden, cow, and boy during the day, was found at 11 in the morning hanging up her clothes. She had had no sleep during the preceding 24 hours.

Shocking abuses in connection with night work were found in two small mills in North Carolina, where night employees frequently worked in the daytime in addition to their regular night work, and where day employees frequently worked at night after a full day's work. These cases are not cited here as typical, but they are given to show the extremes to which unregulated labor of women and children can go in the absence of legal regulation or of efficient means of enforcement, and to show the callous disregard of every consideration for a child wage-earner that can be shown by his employer and his natural protector alike.

In one of these mills the day shift worked 66 hours per week and the night shift 60 hours. Owing to a scarcity of help, day workers were frequently requested to return to the mill immediately after supper and work until midnight, and frequently some one was sent to the homes of employees early in the evening or at midnight to request day workers to come and work half of the night. Some employees usually declined to do overtime work. Others worked alternate nights as a regular custom.

Ordinarily this overtime work was paid for at the time it was performed and there was no record to show its extent. In the case of one family, however, the names of workers were entered on both the day roll and the night roll and this record showed that 4 children, 2 boys, doffers, one 10 and one 15 years old, and 2 girls, spinners, one 11 and one 13, and also a youth 17 years old, all members of the same family, had been paid for 78 to 84 hours of work per week. They had worked this number of hours, less a little time for supper and breakfast, on days when extra work was done. It was found that during a considerable part of the eight months that this family had been at this mill these children had worked two or three half nights each week, in addition to day work. After working from 6 A.M. to 6 P.M., with 35 minutes for dinner, they had returned to the mill, usually every other night, immediately after supper and worked until midnight, when they went home for four or five hours of sleep before beginning the next day's work; or, they had been aroused at midnight and sent to the mill for the second half of the night, where they remained until 6 o'clock the following afternoon, except when eating breakfast and dinner. In either case, they were on duty for a working day of 17 hours, with no rest period save for meals. Those who worked the second half of the night went home for a hurried breakfast just before 6 A.M. The mill stopped only 35 minutes out of the 24 hours, from 12 M. to 12.35 P.M. On one or two occasions two younger children of the same family, one a girl spinner and spooler-helper 7 years old, and the other a male doffer, reported 10 years old but apparently 8, had worked half of the night in addition to day work.

The father of this family was apparently an active, hard-working man. He expressed the opinion that night work in addition to day work was rather hard on the children, but said that he was trying to get money to buy a home. He also said that as the children were in two sets, part his and part his wife's, he must be careful not to show any favor to either portion of the family. No member of this family could read or write. . . .

E. Labor in Industrial America

1. In Praise of Mechanization (1897)

As capitalists competed for markets and profits, they pushed their workers ever harder. Factory laborers came to dread the "speedup"—the order to produce more goods in less time. The already screeching din of the shop floor then whined to an even higher pitch, as machines were made to run faster—and more dangerously. Some observers claimed that the peculiarly profit-hungry and competitive U.S. business environment rendered the conditions of labor in the United States particularly intolerable. Yet new workers by the millions fled the farms of both America and Europe to seek work tending the rattling industrial machines. In the following

[1]E. Levasseur, "The Concentration of Industry, and Machinery in the United States," *Annals of the American Academy of Political and Social Science* 9, no. 2 (March 1897): 12–14, 18–19, 21–24.

comments by a French economist who visited the United States near the end of the nineteenth century, how does he appraise the overall impact of mechanization? Is he convincing? What differences does he see between work conditions in Europe and those in the United States? What does he identify as the principal complaints of U.S. workers? Does he consider them justified?

"The pay here is good, but the labor is hard," said an Alsatian blacksmith employed in a large factory. I could verify nearly everywhere the truth of this remark, for I have seen such activity both in the small industry, where the tailors in the sweating-shops in New York worked with feverish rapidity, and in the great industry, where the butchers of the Armour packing house prepared 5800 hogs a day, where the cotton weavers tended as many as eight looms, or where the rolling-mill in Chicago turned out 1000 tons of rails in a day. Everywhere the machine goes very rapidly, and it commands; the workman has to follow. . . .

In the Senate inquiry of 1883, upon education and labor, a weaver of Fall River, who had been a member of the Massachusetts Legislature, and who was then secretary of the Weavers' Union, said that he had worked seventeen years in England, and that conditions were much better than in America. The manufacturers there were not so desirous as they are here of working their men like horses or slaves; they do not work with the extraordinary rapidity which is customary at Fall River. In England, one man manages a pair of looms with two assistants; one between the looms and the other behind. In America, the manufacturer, with one or two exceptions, will not hear of that, and whatever the number of spindles they do not wish that a man shall have more than one assistant. The spindle is turned more rapidly; the laborers have more to do and for each loom Fall River produces more. . . .

The manufacturers judge that the movement [to mechanize] has been advantageous to workmen, as sellers of labor, because the level of salaries has been raised, as consumers of products, because they purchase more with the same sum, and as laborers, because their task has become less onerous, the machine doing nearly everything which requires great strength; the workman, instead of bringing his muscles into play, has become an inspector, using his intelligence. He is told that his specialized labor is degrading because monotonous. Is it more monotonous to overlook with the eye for ten hours several automatic looms, and to attach, from time to time, one thread to another with the finger, than to push for fourteen hours against the breast the arm of a hand-loom, pressing at the same time the pedals with the feet?

In proportion as the machines require more room, the ceilings become higher, the workshops larger, the hygienic conditions better. From a sanitary standpoint, there is no comparison between the large factory to-day and the hut of the peasant, or the tenement of the sweating system. The improvement of machinery and the growing power of industrial establishments, have diminished the price of a great number of goods, and this is one of the most laudable forward movements of industry whose object is to satisfy, as well as possible, the needs of man.

The laboring classes do not share this optimism. They reproach the machine with exhausting the physical powers of the laborer; but this can only apply to a very small number of cases, to those where the workman is at the same time the motive power, as in certain sewing-machines. They reproach it with demanding such continued attention that it enervates, and of leaving no respite to the laborer, through the continuity of its movement. This second complaint may be applicable in a much larger number of cases, particularly in the spinning industries and in weaving, where the workman manages more than four looms. They reproach the machine with degrading man by transforming him into a machine, which knows how to make but one movement, and that always the same. They reproach it with diminishing the number of skilled laborers, permitting in many cases the substitution of unskilled workers and lowering the average level of wages. They reproach it with depriving, momentarily at least, every time that an invention modifies the work of the factory, a certain number of workmen of their means of subsistence, thus rendering the condition of all uncertain. They reproach it, finally, with reducing absolutely and permanently the number of persons employed for wages, and thus being indirectly injurious to all wage-earners who make among themselves a more disastrous competition, the more the opportunities for labor are restricted.

In one of the reports of the census of 1880, Mr. [Carroll D.] Wright examined other accusations which have been brought generally against manufacturing: (1) necessitating the employment of an excessive number of women and children, it tends to destroy the family ties; (2) it is injurious to health; (3) it tends toward intemperance, prodigality, and pauperism; (4) it encourages prostitution and criminality. It was not difficult to prove that these accusations rest upon errors or exaggerations.

To these grievances political economy replies by the general results of statistics, which show that the total number of laborers, far from having diminished, has steadily increased from one census to another in the United States; that, on the other hand, the total wages paid to laborers shows an increase of average wages, that the diminution in the price of goods is advantageous to consumers among whom are to be reckoned the wage-earners. These three facts are indisputable.

However, the American laborer is not reassured by such a reply, because he rarely consumes the goods he manufactures, because the average wages of the country is not necessarily the measure of his wages; because when dismissed in consequence of an improvement of machinery, he runs great risk of finding no employment in the same industry, while in another he finds it generally only after long delays; in the meantime, he has a family to support. Although the American is more mobile than the European, the transition is not easy either for one or the other. And on both sides of the Atlantic, there is individual misery and professional crises which touch painfully, very cruelly sometimes, the laboring classes. That fact is not to be disputed.

The chief of the Labor Bureau of New York has made a suggestive comparison: the United States and Great Britain, he says, are the countries which own and use the most machines. Compare the general condition of laborers in those countries with that of any country whatever in the world, where machines are unknown, except in the most primitive forms. Where is the superiority? It is almost a paradox, and yet it is a truth that machines bring about a much larger employment and improvement, not only because they increase production, but because they multiply the chances of employment, and incidentally the consumption of products. In fact, the census of the United States shows that the proportion of laborers to the total number of inhabitants has increased in the same period that the machine has taken most complete possession of manufactures. From 1860 to 1890, while the population of the United States doubled, the number of persons employed in industry increased nearly threefold (increase of 172 per cent), and at the same time the mechanical power, measured by horse-power, increased fourfold. Inventions have created new industries, such as photography, electricity, telegraphy, electrotyping, railroading, manufacture of bicycles, etc., and have thus given to labor much more employment than they have withdrawn from it. Thus, even in old industries, transformed by machinery, the progress of consumption has generally maintained a demand for hands.

There is no social evolution which does not produce friction. That which urges industry toward machinery and large factories appears to me to-day irresistible, because it leads to cheapness, which the consumer seeks first of all, and which is one of the objects of economic civilization. It is Utopia to believe that the world could come back by some modification of the social order, or of mechanical motive powers to the system of the little family workshop. Such a workshop is far from being an ideal, as the sweating system proves.

2. A Tailor Testifies (1883)

In 1883 a Senate investigating committee heard the testimony of several workers about the conditions of labor in the United States' burgeoning industries. The witness who gave the following account had been a tailor for some thirty years. What changes in work conditions had he seen in his lifetime? Were they for good or ill? What did they imply for his family life?

Senator Pugh. Please give us any information that you may have as to the relation existing between the employers and the employees in the tailoring business in this city, as to wages, as to treatment of the one by the other class, as to the feeling that exists between the employers and the employed generally, and all that you know in regard to the subject that we are authorized to inquire into?

A. During the time I have been here the tailoring business is altered in three different ways. Before we had sewing machines we worked piecework with our wives, and very often our children. We had no trouble then with our neighbors, nor with the landlord, because it was a very still business, very quiet; but in 1854 or 1855, and later, the sewing machine was invented and introduced, and it stitched very nicely, nicer than the tailor could do; and the bosses said: "We want you to use the sewing machine; you have to buy one." Many of the tailors had a few dollars in the bank, and they took the money and bought machines. Many others had no money, but must help themselves; so they brought their stitching, the coat or vest, to the other tailors who had sewing machines, and paid them a few cents for the stitching. Later, when the money was given out

---

[2]U.S. Congress, Senate Committee on Education and Labor, *Report of the Committee of the Senate Upon the Relations Between Labor and Capital* (Washington, D.C.: Government Printing Office, 1885), vol. 1, pp. 413–421.

for the work, we found out that we could earn no more than we could without the machine; but the money for the machine was gone now, and we found that the machine was only for the profit of the bosses; that they got their work quicker, and it was done nicer. . . . The machine makes too much noise in the place, and the neighbors want to sleep, and we have to stop sewing earlier; so we have to work faster. We work now in excitement—in a hurry. It is hunting; it is not work at all; it is a hunt.

Q. You turn out two or three times as much work per day now as you did in prior times before the war?

A. Yes, sir; two or three times as much; and we have to do it, because the wages are two-thirds lower than they were five or ten years back. . . .

Senator Blair. What proportion of them are women and what proportion men, according to your best judgment?

A. I guess there are many more women than men.

Q. The pay of the women is the same as the pay of the men for the same quantity of work, I suppose?

A. Yes; in cases where a manufacturer—that is, a middleman—gets work from the shop and brings it into his store and employs hands to make it, women get paid by the piece also. If the manufacturer gets $.25 for a piece, he pays for the machine work on that piece so many cents to the machine-worker, he pays so many cents to the presser, so many cents to the finisher, and so many to the button-sewer—so much to each one—and what remains is to pay his rent and to pay for the machinery.

Q. What is your knowledge as to the amount that workers of that class are able to save from their wages?

A. I don't know any one that does save except those manufacturers.

Q. As a class, then, the workers save nothing?

A. No.

Q. What sort of house-room do they have? What is the character, in general, of the food and clothing which they are able to purchase with what they can make by their labor?

A. They live in tenement houses four or five stories high, and have two or three rooms.

Q. What is the character of their clothing?

A. They buy the clothing that they make—the cheapest of it.

Q. What about the character of food that they are able to provide for themselves?

A. Food? They have no time to eat dinner. They have a sandwich in the middle of the day, and in the evening when they go away from work it is the same, and they drink lager or anything they can get.

Q. They are kept busy all the time and have but little opportunity for rest?

A. Yes.

Q. What is the state of feeling between the employers and their employees in that business? How do you workingmen feel towards the people who employ you and pay you?

A. Well, I must say the workingmen are discouraged. If I speak with them they go back and don't like to speak much about the business and the pay. They fear that if they say how it is they will get sent out of the shop. They hate the bosses and the foremen more than the bosses, and that feeling is deep.

3. The Life of a Sweatshop Girl (1902)

Sadie Frowne was approximately sixteen years old when she dictated the following account of her life to a reporter from The Independent *magazine in 1902. What are the greatest differences between her life in Poland and her life in the United States? What are the best and worst parts of her job in a garment factory? What is her attitude toward her job? Toward her labor union?*

My mother was a tall, handsome, dark complexioned woman with red cheeks, large brown eyes and a great quantity of jet black, wavy hair. She was well educated, being able to talk in Russian, German, Polish and French, and even to read English print, tho[ugh], of course, she did not know what it meant. She kept a little grocer's shop in the little village where we lived at first. That was in Poland, somewhere on the frontier, and mother had charge of a gate between the countries, so that everybody who came through the gate had to show her a pass. She was much looked up to by the people, who used to come and ask her for advice. Her word was like law among them.

She had a wagon in which she used to drive around the country, selling her groceries, and sometimes she worked in the fields with my father.

The grocer's shop was only one story high, and had one window, with very small panes of glass. We had two rooms behind it, and were happy while my father lived, altho[ugh] we had to work very hard. By the time I was six years of age I was able to wash dishes and scrub floors, and by the time I was eight I attended to the shop while my mother was away driving her wagon or working in the fields with my father. She was strong and could work like a man.

When I was a little more than ten years of age my father died. He was a good man and a steady worker, and we never knew what it was to be hungry while he lived. After he died troubles began, for the rent of our shop was about $6 a month and then there were food and clothes to provide. We needed little, it is true, but even soup, black bread and onions we could not always get.

We struggled along till I was nearly thirteen years of age and quite handy at housework and shop keeping, so far as I could learn them there. But we fell behind in the rent and mother kept thinking more and more that we should have to leave Poland and go across the sea to America where we heard it was much easier to make money. Mother wrote to Aunt Fanny, who lived in New York, and told her how hard it was to live in Poland, and Aunt Fanny advised her to come and bring me. I was out at service at this time and mother thought she would leave me—as I had a good place—and come to this country alone, sending for me afterward. But Aunt Fanny would not hear of this. She said we should come at once, and she went around among our relatives in New York and took up a subscription for our passage.

---

[3]"The Story of a Sweatshop Girl," *The Independent* 54, no. 2808 (September 25, 1902): 2279–2282.

We came by steerage on a steamship in a very dark place that smelt dreadfully. There were hundreds of other people packed in with us, men, women and children, and almost all of them were sick. It took us twelve days to cross the sea, and we thought we should die, but at last the voyage was over, and we came up and saw the beautiful bay and the big woman with the spikes on her head and the lamp that is lighted at night in her hand [Statue of Liberty]. . . .

Aunt Fanny and her husband met us at the gate of this country and were very good to us, and soon I had a place to live out (domestic servant), while my mother got work in a factory making white goods.

I was only a little over thirteen years of age and a greenhorn, so I received $9 a month and board and lodging, which I thought was doing well. Mother, who, as I have said, was very clever, made $9 a week on white goods, which means all sorts of underclothing, and is high class work.

But mother had a very gay disposition. She liked to go around and see everything, and friends took her about New York at night and she caught a bad cold and coughed and coughed. . . . [A]t last she died and I was left alone. I had saved money while out at service, but mother's sickness and funeral swept it all away and now I had to begin all over again.

Aunt Fanny had always been anxious for me to get an education, as I did not know how to read or write, and she thought that was wrong. Schools are different in Poland from what they are in this country, and I was always too busy to learn to read and write. So when mother died I thought I would try to learn a trade and then I could go to school at night and learn to speak the English language well.

So I went to work in Allen street (Manhattan) in what they call a sweatshop, making skirts by machine. I was new at the work and the foreman scolded me a great deal.

"Now, then," he would say, "this place is not for you to be looking around in. Attend to your work. That is what you have to do."

I did not know at first that you must not look around and talk, and I made many mistakes with the sewing, so that I was often called a "stupid animal." But I made $4 a week by working six days in the week. For there are two Sabbaths here—our own Sabbath, that comes on a Saturday, and the Christian Sabbath that comes on a Sunday. It is against our law to work on our own Sabbath, so we work on their Sabbath.

In Poland I and my father and mother used to go to the synagogue on the Sabbath, but here the women don't go to the synagogue much, tho[ugh] the men do. They are shut up working hard all the week long and when the Sabbath comes they like to sleep long in bed and afterward they must go out where they can breathe the air. The rabbis are strict here, but not so strict as in the old country.

I lived at this time with a girl named Ella, who worked in the same factory and made $5 a week. We had the room all to ourselves, paying $1.50 a week for it, and doing light housekeeping. It was in Allen street, and the window looked out of the back, which was good, because there was an elevated railroad in front, and in summer time a great deal of dust and dirt came in at the front windows. We were on the fourth story and could see all that was going on in the back rooms of the houses behind us, and early in the morning the sun used to come in our window.

We did our cooking on an oil stove, and lived well, as this list of our expenses for one week will show:

Ella and Sadie for Food (one week)

Tea	$0.06
Cocoa	.10
Bread and rolls	.40
Canned vegetables	.20
Potatoes	.10
Milk	.21
Fruit	.20
Butter	.15
Meat	.60
Fish	.15
Laundry	.25
Total	$2.42
Add rent	1.50
Grand total	$3.92

Of course, we could have lived cheaper, but we are both fond of good things and felt that we could afford them.

We paid 18 cents for a half pound of tea so as to get it good, and it lasted us three weeks, because we had cocoa for breakfast. We paid 5 cents for six rolls and 5 cents a loaf for bread, which was the best quality. Oatmeal cost us 10 cents for three and one-half pounds, and we often had it in the morning, or Indian meal porridge in the place of it, costing about the same. Half a dozen eggs cost about 13 cents on an average, and we could get all the meat we wanted for a good hearty meal for 20 cents—two pounds of chops, or a steak, or a bit of veal, or a neck of lamb—something like that. Fish included butter fish, porgies, codfish and smelts, averaging about 8 cents a pound. . . .

It cost me $2 a week to live, and I had a dollar a week to spend on clothing and pleasure, and saved the other dollar. I went to night school, but it was hard work learning at first as I did not know much English.

Two years ago I came to this place, Brownsville, where so many of my people are, and where I have friends. I got work in a factory making underskirts—all sorts of cheap underskirts, like cotton and calico for the summer and woolen for the winter, but never the silk, satin or velvet underskirts. I earned $4.50 a week and lived on $2 a week, the same as before. . . .

It isn't piecework in our factory, but one is paid by the amount of work done just the same. So it is like piecework. All the hands get different amounts, some as low as $3.50 and some of the men as high as $16 a week. The factory is in the third story of a brick building. It is in a room twenty feet long and fourteen broad. There are fourteen machines in it. I and the daughter of the people with whom I live work two of these machines. The other operators are all men, some young and some old.

At first a few of the young men were rude. When they passed me they would touch my hair and talk about my eyes and my red cheeks, and make jokes. I cried and said that if they did not stop I would leave the place. The boss said that that should not be, that no one must annoy me. Some of the other men stood up for me, too, especially Henry, who said two or three times that he wanted to fight. Now the men all treat me very nicely. It was just that some of them did not know better, not being educated.

Henry is tall and dark, and he has a small mustache. His eyes are brown and large. He is pale and much educated, having been to school. He knows a great many things and has some money saved. I think nearly $400. He is not going to be in a sweatshop all the time, but will soon be in the real estate business, for a lawyer that knows him well has promised to open an office and pay him to manage it.

Henry has seen me home every night for a long time and makes love to me. He wants me to marry him, but I am not seventeen yet, and I think that is too young. He is only nineteen, so we can wait. . . .

I get up at half-past five o'clock every morning and make myself a cup of coffee on the oil stove. I eat a bit of bread and perhaps some fruit and then go to work. Often I get there soon after six o'clock so as to be in good time, tho[ugh] the factory does not open till seven. I have heard that there is a sort of clock that calls you at the very time you want to get up, but I can't believe that because I don't see how the clock would know.

At seven o'clock we all sit down to our machines and the boss brings to each one the pile of work that he or she is to finish during the day, what they call in English their "stint." This pile is put down beside the machine and as soon as a skirt is done it is laid on the other side of the machine. Sometimes the work is not all finished by six o'clock and then the one who is behind must work overtime. Sometimes one is finished ahead of time and gets away at four or five o'clock, but generally we are not done till six o'clock.

The machines go like mad all day, because the faster you work the more money you get. Sometimes in my haste I get my finger caught and the needle goes right through it. It goes so quick, tho[ugh], that it does not hurt much. I bind the finger up with a piece of cotton and go on working. We all have accidents like that. Where the needle goes through the nail it makes a sore finger, or where it splinters a bone it does much harm. Sometimes a finger has to come off. Generally, tho[ugh], one can be cured by a salve.

All the time we are working the boss walks about examining the finished garments and making us do them over again if they are not just right. So we have to be careful as well as swift. But I am getting so good at the work that within a year I will be making $7 a week, and then I can save at least $3.50 a week. I have over $200 saved now.

The machines are all run by foot power, and at the end of the day one feels so weak that there is a great temptation to lie right down and sleep. But you must go out and get air, and have some pleasure. So instead of lying down I go out, generally with Henry. Sometimes we go to Coney Island, where there are good dancing places, and sometimes we go to Ulmer Park to picnics. I am very fond of dancing, and, in fact, all sorts of pleasure. I go to the theater quite often, and like those plays that make you cry a great deal. "The Two Orphans" is good. Last time I saw it I cried all night because of the hard times that the children had in the play. I am going to see it again when it comes here.

For the last two winters I have been going to night school at Public School 84 on Glenmore avenue. I have learned reading, writing and arithmetic. I can read quite well in English now and I look at the newspapers every day. I read English books, too, sometimes. The last one that I read was "A Mad Marriage," by Charlotte Braeme. She's a grand writer and makes things just like real to you. You feel as if you were the poor girl yourself going to get married to a rich duke.

I am going back to night school again this winter. Plenty of my friends go there. Some of the women in my class are more than forty years of age. Like me, they did not have a chance to learn anything in the old country. It is good to have an education; it makes you feel higher. Ignorant people are all low. People say now that I am clever and fine in conversation.

We have just finished a strike in our business. It spread all over and the United Brotherhood of Garment Workers was in it. That takes in the cloakmakers, coatmakers, and all the others. We struck for shorter hours, and after being out four weeks won the fight. We only have to work nine and a half hours a day and we get the same pay as before. So the union does good after all in spite of what some people say against it—that it just takes our money and does nothing.

I pay 25 cents a month to the union, but I do not begrudge that because it is for our benefit. The next strike is going to be for a raise of wages, which we all ought to have. But tho[ugh] I belong to the Union I am not a Socialist or an Anarchist. I don't know exactly what those things mean. There is a little expense for charity, too. If any worker is injured or sick we all give money to help.

Some of the women blame me very much because I spend so much money on clothes. They say that instead of a dollar a week I ought not to spend more than twenty-five cents a week on clothes, and that I should save the rest. But a girl must have clothes if she is to go into high society at Ulmer Park or Coney Island or the theatre. Those who blame me are the old country people who have old-fashioned notions, but the people who have been here a long time know better. A girl who does not dress well is stuck in a corner, even if she is pretty, and Aunt Fanny says that I do just right to put on plenty of style.

I have many friends and we often have jolly parties. Many of the young men like to talk to me, but I don't go out with any except Henry.

Lately he has been urging me more and more to get married—but I think I'll wait.

4. The Knights of Labor Champion Reform (1887)

The blue-eyed, ruddy-complexioned Terence V. Powderly, a nimble-witted son of Irish immigrants, became a machinist and joined the secret order of the all-embracing Knights of Labor. He ultimately rose to be its influential head as Grand Master Workman and saw the organization attain a maximum strength of some 700,000 members—skilled and unskilled, white and black. But lawyers, bankers, gamblers, and liquor dealers were barred. The Knights strove primarily for social and economic reform on a broad front, rather than the piecemeal raising of wages that was the chief concern of the skilled-crafts unions. Powderly favored the substitution of arbitration for strikes, the regulation of trusts and monopolies, and the replacement of the wage system with producers' cooperatives. Shot at from the front by conservatives, who accused him of communism, he was sniped at from the rear by some of his own

---

[4]*Journal of United Labor,* July 16, 1887, in *Public Opinion* 3 (July 23, 1887): 318.

following. In the following selection, Powderly defends the Knights against charges in 1887 that they were "breaking up." What does he identify as the Knights's most important goals? Which of these goals would be approved by the modern-day labor movement? How relevant were they to the problems of workers in late-nineteenth-century America?

It is true, the Knights are breaking up. We are at last forced to acknowledge the truth so long, so stubbornly, resisted. We are breaking up—breaking up as the plowman breaks up the soil for the sowing of new seed. We are breaking up old traditions. We are breaking up hereditary rights, and planting everywhere the seed of universal rights. We are breaking up the idea that money makes the man and not moral worth. We are breaking up the idea that might makes right. We are breaking up the idea that legislation is alone for the rich. We are breaking up the idea that the Congress of the United States must be run by millionaires for the benefit of millionaires. We are breaking up the idea that a few men may hold millions of acres of untilled land while other men starve for the want of one acre. We are breaking up the practice of putting the labor of criminals [convict labor] into competition with honest, industrious labor and starving it to death. We are breaking up the practice of importing [European] ignorance, bred of monarchies and dynamite, in order to depreciate intelligent, skilled labor at home. We are breaking up the practice of employing little children in factories, thus breeding a race of deformed, ignorant, and profligate. We are breaking up the idea that a man who works with his hands has need neither of education nor of civilized refinements. We are breaking up the idea that the accident of sex puts one-half of the human race beyond the pale of constitutional rights. We are breaking up the practice of paying woman one-third the wages paid man simply because she is a woman. We are breaking up the idea that a man may debauch an infant [minor] girl and shield himself from the penalty behind a law he himself has made. We are breaking up ignorance and intemperance, crime and oppression, of whatever character and wherever found.

Yes, the Knights of Labor are breaking up, and they will continue their appointed work of breaking up until universal rights shall prevail; and while they may not bring in the millennium, they will do their part in the evolution of moral forces that are working for the emancipation of the race.

[With Samuel Gompers at the helm, the skilled-crafts American Federation of Labor emerged in 1886. By 1890 it had overshadowed the fast-fading Knights of Labor. Skilled carpenters, striking for their own narrow objectives, could not easily be replaced by strikebreakers; unskilled workers could be. The skilled crafts became weary of sacrificing themselves on the altar of large social objectives. This, in brief, was the epitaph of the Knights of Labor.]

5. Samuel Gompers Condemns the Knights (c. 1886)

Samuel Gompers, a stocky Jewish cigarmaker who had been born in a London tenement, emerged as the potent leader of the skilled-crafts American Federation of Labor. Once asked what organized labor wanted, he is said to have replied, "More"—by which he meant more wages, more power, more liberty, more leisure, more benefits. He and his skilled-crafts workers battled the unskilled laborers of the Knights of Labor to defeat revolutionary schemes for remaking U.S. society. What are the principal weaknesses of the Knights of Labor from the skilled-union point of view? Which one is the most serious in the eyes of Gompers?

In 1886 a definite order went out from D.A. [District Assembly No.] 49 [of the Knights of Labor] to make war on the International Cigarmakers' Unions. It was the culmination of years of friction developing over Knights of Labor encroachments on trade union functions.

The two movements were inherently different. Trade unions endeavored to organize for collective responsibility persons with common trade problems. They sought economic betterment in order to place in the hands of wage-earners the means to wider opportunities.

The Knights of Labor was a social or fraternal organization. It was based upon a principle of cooperation, and its purpose was reform. The Knights of Labor prided itself upon being something higher and grander than a trade union or political party. Unfortunately, its purposes were not always exemplified through the declarations and the acts of its members.

The order admitted to membership any person, excluding only lawyers and saloonkeepers. This policy included employers among those eligible. Larger employers gradually withdrew from the order, but the small employers and small businessmen and politicians remained.

The order was a hodgepodge with no basis for solidarity, with the exception of a comparatively few trade assemblies. The aggressive policy inaugurated in 1886 [against the Cigarmakers' Unions] was not due to any change of heart or program, but solely to the great increase in the membership of the Knights of Labor that made it seem safe to put declarations into effect.

When the order began to encroach upon the economic field, trouble was inevitable, for such invasion was equivalent to setting up a dual organization to perform a task for which they were entirely unfitted. It was particularly unfortunate when it endeavored to conduct strikes. The Knights of Labor was a highly centralized organization, and this often placed decision upon essential trade policies in the hands of officers outside the trade concerned. Strikes are essentially an expression of collective purpose of workers who perform related services and who have the spirit of union growing out of joint employment. . . .

Talk of harmony with the Knights of Labor is bosh. They are just as great enemies of trade unions as any employer can be, only more vindictive. I tell you they

---

[5]From *Seventy Years of Life and Labor* by Samuel Gompers. Copyright 1925 by Samuel Gompers, renewed © 1953 by Gertrude Gleaves Gompers. Used by permission of Dutton, a division of Penguin Putnam, Inc.

will give us no quarter, and I would give them their own medicine. It is no use trying to placate them or even to be friendly. They will not cooperate with a mere trades union, as they call our organization. The time will come, however, when the workingmen of the country will see and distinguish between a natural and an artificial organization.

6. Capital Versus Labor (1871)

The contest between labor and capital in nineteenth-century America was often bitter and always complicated. Workers were generally praised for their industriousness, but they were also frequently blamed for strikes and for the unrest that sometimes violently rocked the nation. Capitalists, on the other hand, were admired for their ingenuity and entrepreneurial energy, but were also criticized for their alleged greed and their supposed insensitivity to the circumstances of their employees. In the cartoon on the next page, the famous illustrator Thomas Nast portrays both sides of this complex relationship between labor and capital. Why does Nast choose to depict the laborer with his family and the capitalist alone at the office? In what ways was organized labor oppressive? Who had more at risk: the laborer or the capitalist? Which side does Nast favor? Why?

---

[6]Thomas Nast, *Harper's Weekly,* courtesy of the Harvard College Library.

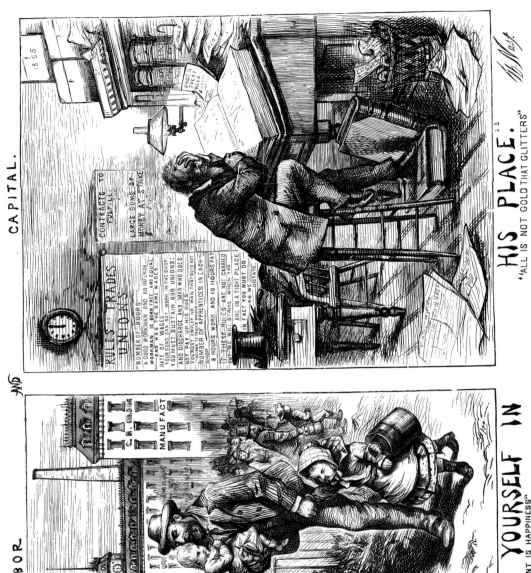

F. The Environmental Impact of Industrialization

1. Upton Sinclair Describes the Chicago Stockyards (1906)

In The Jungle, *one of the most provocative novels ever written about social conditions in the United States, the muckraking writer Upton Sinclair penned a devastating description of Chicago's meat-packing industry at the opening of the twentieth century. In the passage below, the novel's protagonist, Lithuanian immigrant Jurgis Rudkus, first encounters Chicago. The city's landscape and its very atmosphere have been transformed by the huge slaughterhouse complex around the city's sprawling, fetid stockyards. What were the most noxious environmental effects of the meat-packing industry? Why did the city of Chicago tolerate them? How did the particular technologies of the era contribute to this environmental catastrophe?*

A full hour before the party [Rudkus and his traveling companions] reached the city they had begun to note the perplexing changes in the atmosphere. It grew darker all the time, and upon the earth the grass seemed to grow less green. Every minute, as the train sped on, the colours of things became dingier; the fields were grown parched and yellow, the landscape hideous and bare. And along with the thickening smoke they began to notice another circumstance, a strange, pungent odour. They were not sure that it was unpleasant, this odour; some might have called it sickening, but their taste in odours was not developed, and they were only sure that it was curious. Now, sitting in the trolley car, they realized that they were on their way to the home of it—that they had travelled all the way from Lithuania to it. It was now no longer something far off and faint, that you caught in whiffs; you could literally taste it, as well as smell it—you could take hold of it, almost, and examine it at your leisure. They were divided in their opinions about it. It was an elemental odour, raw and crude; it was rich, almost rancid, sensual and strong. There were some who drank it in as if it were an intoxicant; there were others who put their handkerchiefs to their faces. The new emigrants were still tasting it, lost in wonder, when suddenly the car came to a halt, and the door was flung open, and a voice shouted—"Stockyards!"

They were left standing upon the corner, staring; down a side street there were two rows of brick houses, and between them a vista: half a dozen chimeys, tall as the tallest of buildings, touching the very sky, and leaping from them half a dozen columns of smoke, thick, oily, and black as night. It might have come from the centre of the world, this smoke, where the fires of the ages still smoulder. It came as if self-imperilled, driving all before it, a perpetual explosion. It was inexhaustible; one stared, waiting to see it stop, but still the great streams rolled out. They spread in vast clouds overhead, writhing, curling; then, uniting in one giant river, they streamed away down the sky, stretching a black pall as far as the eye could reach.

Then the party became aware of another strange thing. This, too, like the odour, was a thing elemental; it was a sound—a sound made up of ten thousand little sounds. You scarcely noticed it at first—it sunk into your consciousness, a vague

---

[1]From *The Jungle* by Upton Sinclair, copyright 1905, 1906 by Upton Sinclair. Used by permission of Viking Penguin, a division of Penguin Putnam, Inc.

disturbance, a trouble. It was like the murmuring of the bees in the spring, the whispering of the forest; it suggested endless activity, the rumblings of a world in motion. It was only by an effort that one could realize that it was made by animals, that it was the distant lowing of ten thousand cattle, the distant grunting of ten thousand swine. . . .

There were two hundred and fifty miles of track within the yards, their guide went on to tell them. They brought about ten thousand head of cattle every day, and as many hogs, and half as many sheep—which meant some eight or ten million live creatures turned into food every year. One stood and watched, and little by little caught the drift of the tide, as it set in the direction of the packing houses. There were groups of cattle being driven to the chutes, which were roadways about fifteen feet wide, raised high above the pens. In these chutes the stream of animals was continuous; it was quite uncanny to watch them, pressing on to their fate, all unsuspicious—a very river of death. . . .

2. *An Engineer Describes Smoke Pollution (1911)*

Herbert Wilson, chief engineer for the U.S. Geological Survey, undertook a comprehensive survey of air quality in major American cities in the first years of the twentieth century. In the following report, he describes the effects of smoke pollution, mostly from coal-burning furnaces. What are the worst kinds of damage inflicted by coal burning? What would it have been like to live in a city perpetually enshrouded by coal smoke and dust? What problems associated with burning fossil fuels persist today?

The smoke nuisance is one of the greatest dangers of modern times, insidiously attacking the health of the individual, lowering his vitality, increasing the death rate, and causing untold loss and injury to property. The damage which this evil inflicts can hardly be estimated in money; it is equally impossible to estimate the amount of suffering, disease and death and the general effect of lowered vitality caused by this nuisance. . . .

The Smoke Committee of Cleveland, discussing the losses occasioned by smoke, reported:

> There are approximately 400 retail dry goods stores in Cleveland doing business of from $10,000 to $3,000,000 or $4,000,000 a year. The owners of some of these stores estimate, and the same estimate is given in other cities, that on all white goods a clear loss of 10 per cent must be figured. Taking the single items of underwear, shirt waists, linens and white dress goods for the eleven department stores, the proprietors conservatively estimate their combined loss at $25,000. . . .
>
> But a greater cost than all of these must be considered in the loss to the 100,000 homes in Cleveland. The constant need of cleaning walls, ceilings, windows, carpets, rugs and draperies, for redecorating and renewing, can be realized only by the house owner or housekeeper. To this should be added the increased laundry bills for household linen, the dry cleaning for clothing, and the great additional wear resulting from this constant renovation, necessitating frequent renewal. Consider also the permanent injury to books, pictures and similar articles. Though impossible of computation, it will be seen that the total of these items aggregates millions of dollars.

---

[2]Herbert M. Wilson, *The American City* 4 (May, 1911): 210–212.

The City Forester of St. Louis declared that more than 4 per cent of the city trees are killed every year by smoke. In that city it has been found impossible to grow evergreen conifers, except the dwarf juniper and the Austrian pine. Only the hardiest of roses grow in that city. The trees which suffer the greatest injury are the oaks, hickories and conifers, and these are especially ideal park trees and far more valuable for beauty and permanence than the softer wooded varieties. . . .

Turning now to the losses in fuel combustion: our present method of burning coal with smoke is costing the people of this country, unnecessarily, $90,000,000. It is estimated that 8 per cent of the coal used in the production of power, light and heat, or in all about 20,000,000 tons of coal, are going up the chimneys each year in smoke.

The prime source of the pollution of the atmosphere is smoke. The death rate is higher in the city than in the country, and the larger the city the higher the death rate. . . .

It must be understood that smoke, aside from the looks and tangible shapes in which it presents itself, is one of the most poisonous gases polluting the very air we breathe. So apparent is this fact that physicians in our larger cities state their ability to tell at a moment's glance at the lungs in a post-mortem examination whether the man has lived more than thirty days in such a city or not. In the former case their examination proves that the blood, instead of showing red, is black as soot can make it.

Medical men the world over are unanimous in the declaration that the breathing of coal smoke predisposes the lungs to tuberculosis and even more violent lung trouble, such as pneumonia, as well as to many other acute diseases. We know that lung diseases are more prevalent in smoky cities; that the death rate of children due to diseases of the respiratory organs is especially great in coal and iron districts; that tuberculosis is more rapidly fatal in smoky regions.

In addition to all the above, there is the psychological effect of smoke. The city enveloped in a sooty fog is a gloomy city and the children reared therein are in danger of growing up with too much toleration for dirt and too little of that full enthusiasm for the beautiful and clean things of life which sunlight and God's blue sky encourage about as well as anything else in this world.

Thought Provokers

1. Which of the so-called railroad abuses of the post–Civil War period are the easiest to justify? The hardest? In view of the fact that railway rates were becoming progressively lower when the Interstate Commerce Act was passed in 1887, why should the public have complained?
2. Comment critically on the advantages and disadvantages of the monopolistic trust from the standpoint of the consumer. Was the attempted distinction between "good" and "bad" trusts a valid one?

3. To what extent was Carnegie selfish in his gospel of wealth? Is it better to have large private benefactions or to have the government tax wealth and engage in benefactions itself? Why is it difficult to give away large sums of money intelligently?

4. Why was the South, which has many natural resources and is being rapidly industrialized today, so slow to be industrialized after the Civil War?

5. What features of working-class life must have been most troubling to laborers in the late nineteenth century? How is industrial labor different today?

6. Is organized labor today tending toward the Gompers or the Powderly approach? Explain. Why does the United States not have a labor party?

7. Why did nineteenth-century Americans tolerate the environmental ravages of rampant industrialization?

25

America Moves to the City, 1865–1900

Th' worst thing we can do f'r anny man is to do him good.

F. P. Dunne ("Mr. Dooley"), paraphrasing Andrew Carnegie, 1906

Prologue: The robust growth of cities transformed the face of the United States in the decades following the Civil War. The inpouring of the New Immigration from southern and eastern Europe, beginning conspicuously in the 1880s, raised vexing social questions. It aggravated already festering slum conditions, stimulated agitation to halt cheap foreign labor, and revived anti-Catholic outcries. Protestant denominations, already disturbed by the numerical primacy of the Roman Catholic church in the United States, were alarmed by its hundreds of thousands of new communicants. At the same time, Protestantism was profoundly shaken by the impact of Darwinism. One manifestation was a heated debate between the rock-ribbed Fundamentalists and the more adaptable Modernists, who came to see in evolution a more glorious revelation of a wonder-working God. White reformers now largely left the recently freed blacks to their own devices. The temperance crusade intensified, as did the still-frustrated campaign for women's suffrage. Meanwhile, new work patterns in the booming cities provided new opportunities and challenges for women, which in turn sparked fresh debate on women's role, marital relations, and sexual morality.

A. The Lures and Liabilities of City Life

1. Frederick Law Olmsted Applauds the City's Attractions (1871)

In the late nineteenth century, rural Americans flocked to the burgeoning cities, where they were joined by multitudes of immigrants from overseas. Some tradition-

---

[1]Frederick Law Olmsted, "Public Parks and the Enlargement of Towns," *Journal of Social Science* 3 (1871): 1–3, 5–6.

alists decried the alleged evils of city life, but other commentators found in the urban environment a new frontier of excitement and opportunity, especially for women. Frederick Law Olmsted (1822–1903), one of the United States' greatest landscape architects, recognized the irresistible allure of the big cities and strove to humanize the cityscape with parks and open spaces. His works included New York City's Central Park; the grounds of the national Capitol in Washington, D.C.; the municipal park systems of Boston and Louisville; and the campuses of Stanford University and the University of California at Berkeley. In the following passage, what does he identify as the city's principal attractions? What does he find particularly appealing to women?

The last "Overland Monthly" tells us that in California "only an inferior class of people can be induced to live out of towns. There is something in the country which repels men. In the city alone can they nourish the juices of life."

This newly built and but half-equipped cities, where the people are never quite free from dread of earthquakes, and of a country in which the productions of agriculture and horticulture are more varied, and the rewards of rural enterprise larger, than in any other under civilized government! With a hundred million acres of arable and grazing land, with thousands of outcropping gold veins, with the finest forests in the world, fully half the white people live in towns, a quarter of all in one town, and this quarter pays more than half the taxes of all. "Over the mountains the miners," says Mr. Bowles, "talk of going to San Francisco as to Paradise," and the rural members of the legislature declare that "San Francisco sucks the life out of the country."

At the same time all our great interior towns are reputed to be growing rapidly; their newspapers complain that wheat and gold fall much faster than house-rents, and especially that builders fail to meet the demand for such dwellings as are mostly sought by new-comers, who are mainly men of small means and young families, anxious to make a lodgment in the city on any terms which will give them a chance of earning a right to remain. In Chicago alone, it is said, that there are twenty thousand people seeking employment.

To this I can add, from personal observation, that if we stand, any day before noon, at the railway stations of these cities, we may notice women and girls arriving by the score, who, it will be apparent, have just run in to do a little shopping, intending to return by supper time to farms perhaps a few hundred miles away.

It used to be a matter of pride with the better sort of our country people that they could raise on their own land or manufacture within their own households almost everything needed for domestic consumption. But if now you leave the rail, at whatever remote station, the very advertisements on its walls will manifest how greatly this is changed. Push out over the prairie and make your way to the house of any long-settled and prosperous farmer, and the intimacy of his family with the town will constantly appear, in dress, furniture, viands, and in all the conversation. If there is a piano, they will be expecting a man from town to tune it. If the baby has outgrown its shoes, the measure is to be sent to town. If a tooth is troublesome, an appointment is to be arranged by telegraph with the dentist. The railway time-table hangs with the almanac. The housewife complains of her servants. There is no difficulty in getting them from the intelligence offices in town, such as they are; but only the poorest, who cannot find employment in the city, will come to the country, and these as soon as they have got a few dollars ahead, are crazy to get back to town. It is much the same with the men, the farmer will add; he has to run up in the morning and get some one to take "Wolf's" place. You will find, too, that one of his sons is in a lawyer's office, another at a commercial college, and his oldest daughter at an "institute," all in town. I know several girls who travel eighty miles a day to attend school in Chicago. . . .

We all recognize that the tastes and dispositions of women are more and more potent in shaping the course of civilized progress, and we may see that women are even more susceptible to this townward drift than men. Ofttimes the husband and father gives up his country occupations, taking others less attractive to him in town, out of consideration for his wife and daughters. Not long since I conveyed to a very sensible and provident man what I thought to be an offer of great preferment. I was surprised that he hesitated to accept it, until the question was referred to his wife, a bright, tidy American-born woman, who promptly said: "If I were offered a deed of the best farm that I ever saw, on condition of going back to the country to live, I would not take it. I would rather face starvation in town." She had been brought up and lived the greater part of her life in one of the most convenient and agreeable farming countries in the United States.

Is it astonishing? Compare advantages in respect simply to schools, libraries, music, and the fine arts. People of the greatest wealth can hardly command as much of these in the country as the poorest work-girl is offered here in Boston at the mere cost of a walk for a short distance over a good firm, clean pathway, lighted at night and made interesting to her by shop fronts and the variety of people passing.

It is true the poorer work-girls make little use of these special advantages, but this simply because they are not yet educated up to them. When, however, they come from the country to town, are they not moving in the way of this education? In all probability, as is indicated by the report (in the "New York Tribune") of a recent skillful examination of the condition and habits of the poor sewing women of that city, a frantic desire to escape from the dull lives which they have seen before them in the country, a craving for recreation, especially for more companionship in yielding to playful girlish impulses, innocent in themselves, drives more young women to the town than anything else. Dr. Holmes* may exaggerate the clumsiness and dreariness of New England village social parties; but go further back into the country among the outlying farms, and if you have ever had part in the working up of some of the rare occasions in which what stands for festivity is attempted, you will hardly think that the ardent desire of a young woman to escape to the town is wholly unreasonable.

2. Sister Carrie Is Bedazzled by Chicago (1900)

In his novel Sister Carrie, *Theodore Dreiser painted a classic portrait of a young woman from the countryside who seeks her fate in the big city—in this case,*

---

*Oliver Wendell Holmes, New England author and physician, and the father of Supreme Court justice Oliver Wendell Holmes, Jr. The elder Holmes's works include *The Autocrat of the Breakfast Table* (1858).

[2]Theodore Dreiser, *Sister Carrie* (New York: New American Library, 1961; first published 1900), pp. 25–27.

Chicago. Among the features of urban life that the novel's heroine, Carrie Meeber, finds most alluring are the huge department stores. Dreiser considered department stores such a distinctive innovation that he paused in his narrative to describe them at length. What effect do they have on Carrie Meeber? In what ways do they symbolize the new cultural realities of urban life?

At that time the department store was in its earliest form of successful operation, and there were not many. The first three in the United States, established about 1884, were in Chicago. Carrie was familiar with the names of several through the advertisements in the *Daily News,* and now proceeded to seek them. The words of Mr. McManus [a store manager who had interviewed Carrie for a job] had somehow managed to restore her courage, which had fallen low, and she dared to hope that this new line would offer her something. Some time she spent in wandering up and down, thinking to encounter the buildings by chance, so readily is the mind, bent upon prosecuting a hard but needful errand, eased by that self-deception which the semblance of search, without the reality, gives. At last she inquired of a police officer, and was directed to proceed "two blocks up," where she would find The Fair.

The nature of these vast retail combinations, should they ever permanently disappear, will form an interesting chapter in the commercial history of our nation. Such a flowering out of a modest trade principle the world had never witnessed up to that time. They were along the line of the most effective retail organization, with hundreds of stores co-ordinated into one and laid out upon the most imposing and economic basis. They were handsome, bustling, successful affairs, with a host of clerks and a swarm of patrons. Carrie passed along the busy aisles, much affected by the remarkable displays of trinkets, dress goods, stationery, and jewelry. Each separate counter was a showplace of dazzling interest and attraction. She could not help feeling the claim of each trinket and valuable upon her personally, and yet she did not stop. There was nothing there which she could not have used—nothing which she did not long to own. The dainty slippers and stockings, the delicately frilled skirts and petticoats, the laces, ribbons, haircombs, purses, all touched her with individual desire, and she felt keenly the fact that not any of these things were in the range of her purchase. She was a work seeker, an outcast without employment, one whom the average employee could tell at a glance was poor and in need of a situation.

It must not be thought that anyone could have mistaken her for a nervous, sensitive, high-strung nature, cast unduly upon a cold, calculating, and unpoetic world. Such certainly she was not. But women are peculiarly sensitive to their adornment.

Not only did Carrie feel the drag of desire for all which was new and pleasing in apparel for women, but she noticed too, with a touch at the heart, the fine ladies who elbowed and ignored her, brushing past in utter disregard of her presence, themselves eagerly enlisted in the materials which the store contained. Carrie was not familiar with the appearance of her more fortunate sisters of the city. Neither had she before known the nature and appearance of the shopgirls with whom she now compared poorly. They were pretty in the main, some even handsome, with an air of independence and indifference which added, in the case of the more favored, a certain piquancy. Their clothes were neat, in many instances fine, and wherever she encountered the eye of one it was only to recognize in it a keen analysis of her own position—her individual shortcomings of dress and that shadow of manner which she thought must hang about her and make clear to all who and what she was. A flame of envy lighted in her heart. She realized in a dim way how much the city held—wealth, fashion, ease—every adornment for women, and she longed for dress and beauty with a whole heart. . . .

3. Cleaning Up New York (1897)

The cities grew so fast that municipal governments were hard pressed to provide adequate sanitation facilities and other essential urban services. New York City commissioner George F. Waring, Jr., here describes the situation in late-nineteenth-century New York before a concerted effort was made to clean up the city. What features of urban life were the worst contributors to unsanitary conditions? Which city dwellers suffered the most from those conditions?

Before 1895 the streets were almost universally in a filthy state. In wet weather they were covered with slime, and in dry weather their air was filled with dust. Artificial sprinkling in summer converted the dust into mud, and the drying winds changed the mud to powder. Rubbish of all kinds, garbage, and ashes lay neglected in the streets, and in the hot weather the city stank with the emanations of putrefying organic matter. It was not always possible to see the pavement, because of the dirt that covered it. One expert, a former contractor of street-cleaning, told me that West Broadway could not be cleaned, because it was so coated with grease from wagon-axles; it was really coated with slimy mud. The sewer inlets were clogged with refuse. Dirty paper was prevalent everywhere, and black rottenness was seen and smelled on every hand.

The practice of standing unharnessed trucks and wagons in the public streets was well-nigh universal in all except the main thoroughfares and the better residence districts. The Board of Health made an enumeration of vehicles so standing on Sunday, counting twenty-five thousand on a portion of one side of the city; they reached the conclusion that there were in all more than sixty thousand. These trucks not only restricted traffic and made complete street-cleaning practically impossible, but they were harbors of vice and crime. Thieves and highwaymen made them their dens, toughs caroused in them, both sexes resorted to them, and they were used for the vilest purposes, until they became, both figuratively and literally, a stench in the nostrils of the people. In the crowded districts they were a veritable nocturnal hell. Against all this the poor people were powerless to get relief. The highest city officials, after feeble attempts at removal, declared that New York was so peculiarly constructed (having no alleys through which the rear of the lots could be reached) that its commerce could not be carried on unless this privilege were given to its truckmen; in short, the removal of the trucks was "an impossibility. . . ."

The condition of the streets, of the force, and of the stock was the fault of no man and of no set of men. It was the fault of the system. The department was

---

[3]George E. Waring, Jr., *Street-Cleaning* (New York: Doubleday and McClure, 1897), pp. 13–21.

throttled by partizan control—so throttled it could neither do good work, command its own respect and that of the public, nor maintain its material in good order. It was run as an adjunct of a political organization. In that capacity it was a marked success. It paid fat tribute; it fed thousands of voters, and it gave power and influence to hundreds of political leaders. It had this appointed function, and it performed it well. . . .

New York is now thoroughly clean in every part, the empty vehicles are gone. . . . "Clean streets" means much more than the casual observer is apt to think. It has justly been said that "cleanliness is catching," and clean streets are leading to clean hallways, and staircases and cleaner living-rooms. A recent writer says:

> It is not merely justification of a theory to say that the improvement noticed in the past two and a half years in the streets of New York has led to an improvement in the interior of its tenement-houses. A sense of personal pride has been awakened in the women and children, the results of which have been noticeable to every one engaged in philanthropic work among the tenement dwellers. When, early in the present administration, a woman in the Five Points district was heard to say to another, "Well, I don't care; my street is cleaner than yours is, anyhow," it was felt that the battle was won.

Few realize the many minor ways in which the work of the department has benefited the people at large. For example, there is far less injury from dust to clothing, to furniture, and to goods in shops; mud is not tracked from the streets on to the sidewalks, and thence into the houses; boots require far less cleaning; the wearing of overshoes has been largely abandoned; wet feet and bedraggled skirts are mainly things of the past; and children now make free use as a playground of streets which were formerly impossible to them. "Scratches," a skin disease of horses due to mud and slush, used to entail very serious cost on truckmen and liverymen. It is now almost unknown. Horses used to "pick up a nail" with alarming frequency, and this caused great loss of service, and, like scratches, made the bill of the veterinary surgeon a serious matter. There are practically no nails now to be found in the streets.

The great, the almost inestimable, beneficial effect of the work of the department is shown in the large reduction of the death-rate and in the less keenly realized but still more important reduction in the sick-rate. As compared with the average death-rate of 26.78 of 1882–94, that of 1895 was 23.10, that of 1896 was 21.52, and that of the first half of 1897 was 19.63. If this latter figure is maintained throughout the year, there will have been fifteen thousand fewer deaths than there would have been had the average rate of the thirteen previous years prevailed. The report of the Board of Health for 1896, basing its calculations on diarrheal diseases in July, August, and September, in the filthiest wards, in the most crowded wards, and in the remainder of the city, shows a very marked reduction in all, and the largest reduction in the first two classes.

4. Jacob Riis Goes Slumming (1890)

Police reporter Jacob A. Riis, a Danish-born immigrant who had known rat-infested tenements in Denmark, aimed his talented pen at the scandalous slums of New York.

---

[4]J. A. Riis, *How the Other Half Lives* (New York: Charles Scribner's Sons, 1890), pp. 43–44.

He was shocked by the absence of privacy, sanitation, and playgrounds, and by the presence of dirt, stench, and vermin. One tenement area in New York was known as the "Lung Block" because of the prevalence of tuberculosis. Despite the opposition of heartless landlords, who worked hand-in-glove with corrupt politicians, Riis helped to eliminate some of these foul firetraps, especially the dark "rear tenements." What does he regard as the chief obstacles to good health and good morals in these slums?

Suppose we look into one? No.—Cherry Street. Be a little careful, please! The hall is dark and you might stumble over the children pitching pennies back there. Not that it would hurt them; kicks and cuffs are their daily diet. They have little else.

Here where the hall turns and dives into utter darkness is a step, and another, another. A flight of stairs. You can feel your way, if you cannot see it. Close? Yes! What would you have? All the fresh air that ever enters these stairs comes from the hall-door that is forever slamming, and from the windows of dark bedrooms that in turn receive from the stairs their sole supply of elements God meant to be free, but man deals out with such niggardly hand.

That was a woman filling her pail by the hydrant you just bumped against. The sinks are in the hallway, that all the tenants may have access—and all to be poisoned alike by their summer stenches.

Hear the pump squeak! It is the lullaby of tenement-house babes. In summer, when a thousand thirsty throats pant for a cooling drink in this block, it is worked in vain. But the saloon, whose open door you passed in the hall, is always there. The smell of it has followed you up.

Here is a door. Listen! That short hacking cough, that tiny, helpless wail—what do they mean? They mean that the soiled bow of white you saw on the door downstairs will have another story to tell—oh! a sadly familiar story—before the day is at an end. The child is dying with measles. With half a chance it might have lived; but it had none. The dark bedroom killed it.

"It was took all of a suddint," says the mother, smoothing the throbbing little body with trembling hands. There is no unkindness in the rough voice of the man in the jumper, who sits by the window grimly smoking a clay pipe, with the little life ebbing out in his sight, bitter as his words sound: "Hush, Mary! if we cannot keep the baby, need we complain—such as we?"

Such as we! What if the words ring in your ears as we grope our way up the stairs and down from floor to floor, listening to the sounds behind the closed doors—some of quarreling, some of coarse songs, more of profanity. They are true. When the summer heats come with their suffering, they have meaning more terrible than words can tell.

Come over here. Step carefully over this baby—it is a baby, spite of its rags and dirt—under these iron bridges called fire-escapes, but loaded down, despite the incessant watchfulness of the firemen, with broken household goods, with washtubs and barrels, over which no man could climb from a fire.

This gap between dingy brick walls is the yard. The strip of smoke-colored sky up there is the heaven of these people. Do you wonder the name does not attract them to churches?

That baby's parents live in the rear tenement here. She is at least as clean as the steps we are now climbing. There are plenty of houses with half a hundred such in. The tenement is much like the one in front we just left, only fouler, closer, darker—we will not say more cheerless. The word is a mockery. A hundred thousand people lived in rear tenements in New York last year.

B. The New Immigration

1. Mary Antin Praises America (1894)

The bomb-assassination of Czar Alexander II in 1881 touched off an outburst of anti-Semitism in Russia that resulted in countless riots, burnings, pillagings, rapes, and murders. Tens of thousands of Jewish refugees fled to America then and later. Mary Antin, a thirteen-year-old Polish Jew, joined her father in Boston in 1894. She later distinguished herself as an author and a welfare worker. In her autobiographical account, excerpted here, what did these Jewish immigrants find most gratifying in America?

In our flat we did not think of such a thing as storing the coal in the bathtub. There was no bathtub. So in the evening of the first day my father conducted us to the public baths. As we moved along in a little procession, I was delighted with the illumination of the streets. So many lamps, and they burned until morning, my father said, and so people did not need to carry lanterns.

In America, then, everything was free, as we had heard in Russia; the streets were as bright as a synagogue on a holy day. Music was free; we had been serenaded, to our gaping delight, by a brass band of many pieces, soon after our installation on Union Place.

Education was free. That subject my father had written about repeatedly, as comprising his chief hope for us children, the essence of American opportunity, the treasure that no thief could touch, nor even misfortune or poverty. It was the one thing that he was able to promise us when he sent for us; surer, safer, than bread or shelter.

On our second day I was thrilled with the realization of what this freedom of education meant. A little girl from across the alley came and offered to conduct us to school. My father was out, but we five between us had a few words of English by this time. We knew the word *school*. We understood. This child, who had never seen us till yesterday, who could not pronounce our names, who was not much better dressed than we, was able to offer us the freedom of the schools of Boston! No application made, no questions asked, no examinations, rulings, exclusions; no machinations, no fees. The doors stood open for every one of us. The smallest child could show us the way.

---

[1]From *The Promised Land* by Mary Antin. Copyright 1912 by Houghton Mifflin Company.

The incident impressed me more than anything I had heard in advance of the freedom of education in America. It was a concrete proof—almost the thing itself. One had to experience it to understand it.

[Distressingly common was the experience of Anzia Yezierska, whose impoverished family came from Russia to New York City in 1901. Buoyed up by the hope of finding green fields and open places, she found herself in a smelly, crowded slum. God's blue sky was not visible; the landscape was the brick wall of the next building; and there was no place for the pasty-faced children to play. One of her despairing companions said, "In Russia, you could hope to run away from your troubles in America. But from America where can you go?"]

2. The American Protective Association Hates Catholics (1893)

The flood of cheap southern European labor in the 1880s, predominantly Roman Catholic, rearoused nativist bigots. The most powerful group, the secretive American Protective Association (APA), claimed a million members by 1896. Among its various activities, it circulated forged documents revealing alleged papal orders to "exterminate" non-Catholics. In Toledo, Ohio, the local branch gathered Winchester rifles for defense. The APA was especially alarmed by the Irish-Catholic political machines, which in cities like New York and Chicago had secured a semimonopoly of public offices, including the fire department and the police department. In the following secret oath of the APA, are the economic or the political prohibitions more damaging?

I do most solemnly promise and swear that I will always, to the utmost of my ability, labor, plead, and wage a continuous warfare against ignorance and fanaticism; that I will use my utmost power to strike the shackles and chains of blind obedience to the Roman Catholic Church from the hampered and bound consciences of a priest-ridden and church-oppressed people; that I will never allow anyone, a member of the Roman Catholic Church, to become a member of this order, I knowing him to be such; and I will use my influence to promote the interest of all Protestants everywhere in the world that I may be; that I will not employ a Roman Catholic in any capacity, if I can procure the services of a Protestant.

I furthermore promise and swear that I will not aid in building or maintaining, by my resources, any Roman Catholic church or institution of their sect or creed whatsoever, but will do all in my power to retard and break down the power of the Pope, in this country or any other; that I will not enter into any controversy with a Roman Catholic upon the subject of this order, nor will I enter into any agreement with a Roman Catholic to strike or create a disturbance whereby the Catholic employees may undermine and substitute their Protestant co-workers; that in all grievances I will seek only Protestants, and counsel with them to the exclusion of all

---

[2]From *Documents of American Catholic History*, edited by J. Tracy Ellis. Copyright © 1951. Reprinted by permission of Prentice-Hall, Inc., Upper Saddle River, NJ.

Roman Catholics, and will not make known to them anything of any nature matured at such conferences.

I furthermore promise and swear that I will not countenance the nomination, in any caucus or convention, of a Roman Catholic for any office in the gift of the American people, and that I will not vote for, or counsel others to vote for, any Roman Catholic, but will vote only for a Protestant, so far as may lie in my power (should there be two Roman Catholics in opposite tickets, I will erase the name on the ticket I vote); that I will at times endeavor to place the political positions of this government in the hands of Protestants, to the entire exclusion of the Roman Catholic Church, of the members thereof, and the mandate of the Pope.

To all of which I do most solemnly promise and swear, so help me God. Amen.

3. Henry Cabot Lodge Urges a Literacy Test (1896)

The continued influx of hordes of impoverished and illiterate southern Europeans during the depression of the 1890s intensified outcries for their exclusion. Organized labor objected to their low wages; religious bigots, to their Catholicism; city planners, to their slum residence; believers in racial purity, to their "degenerate" stock. Senator Henry Cabot Lodge, a Massachusetts blue blood and later the arch-foe of Woodrow Wilson, here argues for a bill that would establish a literacy test. Which group was he trying to exclude? Would the best interests of the nation have been served by his proposal?

It is found, in the first place, that the illiteracy test will bear most heavily upon the Italians, Russians, Poles, Hungarians, Greeks, and Asiatics, and very lightly, or not at all, upon English-speaking emigrants or Germans, Scandinavians, and French.

In other words, the races most affected by the illiteracy test are those whose emigration to this country has begun within the last twenty years and swelled rapidly to enormous proportions, races with which the English-speaking people have never hitherto assimilated, and who are most alien to the great body of the people of the United States.

On the other hand, emigrants from the United Kingdom and of those races which are most closely related to the English-speaking people, and who with the English-speaking people themselves founded the American colonies and built up the United States, are affected but little by the proposed test. These races would not be prevented by this law from coming to this country in practically undiminished numbers.

These kindred races also are those who alone go to the Western and Southern states, where immigrants are desired, and take up our unoccupied lands. The races which would suffer most seriously by exclusion under the proposed bill furnish the immigrants who do not go to the West or South, where immigration is needed, but who remain on the Atlantic seaboard, where immigration is not needed and where their presence is most injurious and undesirable.

---

[3]*Congressional Record,* 54th Cong., 1st sess. (March 16, 1896), p. 2817.

The statistics prepared by the committee show further that the immigrants excluded by the illiteracy test are those who remain for the most part in congested masses in our great cities. They furnish, as other tables show, a large proportion of the population of the slums. The committee's report proves that illiteracy runs parallel with the slum population, with criminals, paupers, and juvenile delinquents of foreign birth, or parentage, whose percentage is out of all proportion to their share of the total population when compared with the percentage of the same classes among the native-born.

It also appears from investigations which have been made that the immigrants who would be shut out by the illiteracy test are those who bring least money to the country, and come most quickly upon private or public charity for support.

4. President Cleveland Vetoes a Literacy Test (1897)

In 1897 Congress finally passed a bill excluding all prospective immigrants who could not read or write twenty-five words of the Constitution of the United States in some language. One of the several goals of the exclusionists was to bar anarchists and other radical labor agitators. Cleveland, ever ruggedly independent, vetoed the bill. What is his most effective argument against it?

It is not claimed, I believe, that the time has come for the further restriction of immigration on the ground that an excess of population overcrowds our land.

It is said, however, that the quality of recent immigration is undesirable. The time is quite within recent memory when the same thing was said of immigrants who, with their descendants, are now numbered among our best citizens.

It is said that too many immigrants settle in our cities, thus dangerously increasing their idle and vicious population. This is certainly a disadvantage. It cannot be shown, however, that it affects all our cities, nor that it is permanent; nor does it appear that this condition, where it exists, demands as its remedy the reversal of our present immigration policy.

The claim is also made that the influx of foreign laborers deprives of the opportunity to work those who are better entitled than they to the privilege of earning their livelihood by daily toil. An unfortunate condition is certainly presented when any who are willing to labor are unemployed, but so far as this condition now exists among our people, it must be conceded to be a result of phenomenal business depression and the stagnation of all enterprises in which labor is a factor. With the advent of settled and wholesome financial and economic governmental policies, and consequent encouragement to the activity of capital, the misfortunes of unemployed labor should, to a great extent at least, be remedied. If it continues, its natural consequences must be to check the further immigration to our cities of foreign laborers and to deplete the ranks of those already there. In the meantime those most willing and best entitled ought to be able to secure the advantages of such work as there is to do. . . .

[4]J. D. Richardson, ed., *Messages and Papers of the Presidents* (New York: Bureau of National Literature, 1897), vol. 9, pp. 758–759.

The best reason that could be given for this radical restriction of immigration is the necessity of protecting our population against degeneration and saving our national peace and quiet from imported turbulence and disorder.

I cannot believe that we would be protected against these evils by limiting immigration to those who can read and write in any language twenty-five words of our Constitution. In my opinion, it is infinitely more safe to admit a hundred thousand immigrants who, though unable to read and write, seek among us only a home and opportunity to work than to admit one of those unruly agitators and enemies of governmental control who can not only read and write, but delight in arousing by inflammatory speech the illiterate and peacefully inclined to discontent and tumult.

Violence and disorder do not originate with illiterate laborers. They are, rather, the victims of the educated agitator. The ability to read and write, as required in this bill, in and of itself affords, in my opinion, a misleading test of contented industry and supplies unsatisfactory evidence of desirable citizenship or a proper apprehension of the benefits of our institutions.

If any particular element of our illiterate immigration is to be feared for other causes than illiteracy, these causes should be dealt with directly, instead of making illiteracy the pretext for exclusion, to the detriment of other illiterate immigrants against whom the real cause of complaint cannot be alleged.

[President Taft, following Cleveland's example in 1897, successfully vetoed a literacy test in 1913, as did President Wilson in 1915. Finally, in 1917, such a restriction was passed over Wilson's veto. Wilson had declared that the prohibition was "not a test of character, of quality, or of personal fitness." In fact, a literacy test denied further opportunity to those who had already been denied opportunity.]

5. Four Views of the Statue of Liberty (1881, 1885, 1886)

The Statue of Liberty was a gift from the French people to the American people, intended to symbolize the friendship between the two republics. Even before the dedication ceremonies in 1886, the statue had become a symbol of America itself. What particular aspects of America did the statue symbolize? At the dedication ceremonies, President Grover Cleveland and other speakers explained that the statue represented the beneficent effect of American ideals, and they emphasized the theme of international friendship and peace. Later, Lady Liberty came to signify a warm welcome to foreign immigrants. The prints below provide four images of the statue and four images of America. What interpretations of the meaning of America are being expressed in these images? What different groups or perspectives are represented in these prints? Are there any similarities among the four images?

---

[5]p. 111, Thomas Nast, *Harper's Weekly* April 2, 1881; p. 112, Daniel McCarthy, *Judge,* May 23, 1885; p. 113, Victor Gillam, *Judge,* September 4, 1886; p. 114 C. Jay Taylor, *Puck,* October 27, 1886. All four illustrations appear courtesy of The Harvard College Library.

The Warning Light, 1881

Bartenders' Statue of License Lightening New York, 1885

Erecting the New York Political Statue, 1886

Our Statue of Liberty—She Can Stand It, 1886

C. The Church on the Defensive

1. The Shock of Darwinism (1896)

The theory of evolution, popularized by Charles Darwin's On the Origin of Species *(1859), directly challenged the biblical story of creation. (In 1654 a distinguished English scholar had declared the date of creation to be "the 26th of October, 4004 B.C. at 9 o'clock in the morning.") Orthodox religionists flooded the New York publishers of Darwin's volume with letters demanding its suppression. Andrew D. White, a prominent U.S. educator, scholar, and diplomat, here describes in a famous book some of the reactions in the United States. How might one explain the violence of these comments?*

Darwin's *Origin of Species* had come into the theological world like a plough into an anthill. Everywhere those thus rudely awakened from their old comfort and repose had swarmed forth angry and confused. Reviews, sermons, books light and heavy, came flying at the new thinker from all sides. . . .

Echoes came from America. One review, the organ of the most widespread of American religious sects, declared that Darwin was "attempting to befog and to pettifog the whole question"; another denounced Darwin's views as "infidelity"; another, representing the American branch of the Anglican Church, poured contempt over Darwin as "sophistical and illogical," and then plunged into an exceedingly dangerous line of argument in the following words: "If this hypothesis be true, then is the Bible an unbearable fiction; . . . then have Christians for nearly two thousand years been duped by a monstrous lie. . . . Darwin requires us to disbelieve the authoritative word of the Creator."

A leading journal representing the same church took pains to show the evolution theory to be as contrary to the explicit declarations of the New Testament as to those of the Old, and said: "If we have all, men and monkeys, oysters and eagles, developed from an original germ, then is St. Paul's grand deliverance—'All flesh is not the same flesh; there is one kind of flesh of men, another of beasts, another of fishes, and another of birds'—untrue." . . .

But a far more determined opponent was the Rev. Dr. Hodge, of Princeton. His anger toward the evolution doctrine was bitter: he denounced it as thoroughly "atheistic"; he insisted that Christians "have a right to protest against the arraying of probabilities against the clear evidence of the Scriptures"; he even censured so orthodox a writer as the Duke of Argyll, and declared that the Darwinian theory of natural selection is "utterly inconsistent with the Scriptures," and that "an absent God, who does nothing, is to us no God"; that "to ignore the design as manifested in God's creation is to dethrone God"; that "a denial of design in Nature is virtually a denial of God"; and that "no teleologist can be a Darwinian."

Even more uncompromising was another of the leading authorities at the same university—the Rev. Dr. Duffield. He declared war not only against Darwin but even against men like Asa Gray, Le Conte, and others, who attempted to reconcile the new theory with the Bible. He insisted that "evolutionism and the Scriptural account

[1]A. D. White, *A History of the Warfare of Science with Theology in Christendom* (New York: D. Appleton and Company, 1896), vol. 1, pp. 70, 71–72, 79–80.

of the origin of men are irreconcilable"—that the Darwinian theory is "in direct conflict with the teaching of the apostle, 'All Scripture is given by inspiration of God.'" He pointed out, in his opposition to Darwin's *Descent of Man* and Lyell's *Antiquity of Man,* that in the Bible "the genealogical links which connect the Israelites in Egypt with Adam and Eve and Eden are explicitly given."

These utterances of Prof. Duffield culminated in a declaration which deserves to be cited as showing that a Presbyterian minister can "deal damnation round the land" *ex cathedra* [literally, "from the throne," the figurative position of the Pope when he speaks officially] in a fashion quite equal to that of popes and bishops. It is as follows: "If the development theory of the origin of man," wrote Dr. Duffield in the *Princeton Review,* "shall in a little while take its place—as doubtless it will—with other exploded scientific speculations, then they who accept it with its proper logical consequences will in the life to come have their portion with those who in this life 'know not God and obey not the gospel of His Son.'"

2. Henry Ward Beecher Accepts Evolution (1886)

The Reverend Henry Ward Beecher, a famed Congregational minister, was the most popular and influential preacher of his day. Like his sister, Harriet Beecher Stowe, he crusaded against slavery and, in a mock auction in his Brooklyn church, raised money to redeem a black girl from slavery. Although besmirched by a notorious adultery trial, which ended in a hung jury, he continued to preach religion and discuss public issues with eloquence and boldness. His disbelief in a literal hell, combined with his belief in evolution, generated friction with orthodox members of the clergy and led to his withdrawal from the Association of Congregational Ministers. He customarily preached to twenty-five hundred people; after he died, forty thousand viewed his body. Why does he accept Darwin's views, and why does he believe that evolution will help true religion?

As thus set forth, it may be said that Evolution is accepted as the method of creation by the whole scientific world, and that the period of controversy is passed and closed. A few venerable men yet live with many doubts; but it may be said that 99 percent—as has been declared by an eminent physicist—99 percent of scientific men and working scientists of the world are using this theory without any doubt of its validity. . . .

This science of Evolution is taught in all advanced academies, in all colleges and universities, in all medical and surgical schools, and our children are receiving it as they are the elements of astronomy or botany or chemistry. That in another generation Evolution will be regarded as uncontradictable as the Copernican system of astronomy, or the Newtonian doctrine of gravitation, can scarcely be doubted. Each of these passed through the same contradiction by theologians. They were charged by the Church, as is Evolution now, with fostering materialism, infidelity, and atheism.

We know what befell Galileo for telling the truth of God's primitive revelation. We know, or do not know, at least, how Newton stood charged with infidelity and with atheism when he announced the doctrine of gravitation.

---

[2]H. W. Beecher, *Evolution and Religion* (Chicago: The Pilgrim Press, 1885), pp. 50–54.

Who doubts the heliocentric theory [of Copernicus] today? Who doubts whether it is the sun which is moving round the earth or the earth round the sun? Who doubts that the law of attraction, as developed by Newton, is God's material law universally? The time is coming when the doctrine of Evolution, or the method of God in the creation of the world, will be just as universally accepted as either of these great physical doctrines. The whole Church fought them; yet they stand, conquerors. . . .

Evolution is substantially held by men of profound Christian faith: by the now venerable and universally honored scientific teacher, Professor Dana of Yale College, a devout Christian and communicant of a Congregational Church; by Professor Le Conte of the University of California, an elder in the Presbyterian Church; by President McCosh of Princeton College, a Presbyterian of the Presbyterians, and a Scotch Presbyterian at that; by Professor Asa Gray of Harvard University, a communicant of the Christian Church; by increasing numbers of Christian preachers in America; by Catholics like Mivart, in England. . . .

To the fearful and the timid let me say that while Evolution is certain to oblige theology to reconstruct its system, it will take nothing away from the grounds of true religion. It will strip off Saul's unmanageable armor from David, to give him greater power over the giant. Simple religion is the unfolding of the best nature of man towards God, and man has been hindered and embittered by the outrageous complexity of unbearable systems of theology that have existed. If you can change theology, you will emancipate religion; yet men are continually confounding the two terms, religion and theology. . . .

Evolution, applied to religion, will influence it only as the hidden temples are restored, by removing the sands which have drifted in from the arid deserts of scholastic and medieval theologies. It will change theology, but only to bring out the simple temple of God in clearer and more beautiful lines and proportions. . . .

In every view, then, it is the duty of the friends and simple and unadulterated Christianity to hail the rising light and to uncover every element of religious teaching to its wholesome beams. Old men may be charitably permitted to die in peace, but young men and men in their prime are by God's providence laid under the most solemn obligations to thus discern the signs of the times, and to make themselves acquainted with the knowledge which science is laying before them. And above all, those zealots of the pulpit who make faces at a science which they do not understand, and who reason from prejudice to ignorance; who not only will not lead their people, but hold up to scorn those who strive to take off the burden of ignorance from their shoulders— these men are found to open their eyes and see God's sun shining in the heavens.

D. The Anti-Saloon Crusade

1. Frances Willard Prays in a Saloon (1874)

An independent girl, Frances E. Willard defied her novel-hating father by openly reading Scott's Ivanhoe *on her eighteenth birthday. At first an educator of females,*

---

[1]Frances E. Willard, *Glimpses of Fifty Years* (Women's Temperance Publishing Association, 1892), pp. 340–341.

she gained fame as an advocate of temperance and women's suffrage. She was one of the founders of the Woman's Christian Temperance Union (WCTU), which grew out of the praying-in-saloons crusade of 1873–1874. Willard stressed not so much the social and economic evils of drinking as the need for protecting the home and the Christian way of life. The saloon, often in league with gambling and prostitution, was riding high from 1870 to 1900. Some towns had one for every two hundred inhabitants; and the swinging doors, the heavy brass rails, and the nude Venus over the huge gilded mirror were familiar sights. Willard here describes her experiences in Pittsburgh. How effective is this approach, and how would it be received today?

We paused in front of the saloon that I have mentioned. The ladies ranged themselves along the curbstone, for they had been forbidden in any wise to incommode the passers-by, being dealt with much more strictly than a drunken man or a heap of dry-goods boxes would be.

At a signal from our gray-haired leader, a sweet-voiced woman began to sing, "Jesus the water of life will give," all our voices soon blending in that sweet song. I think it was the most novel spectacle that I recall. There stood women of undoubted religious devotion and the highest character, most of them crowned with the glory of gray hairs. Along the stony pavement of that stoniest of cities rumbled the heavy wagons, many of them carriers of beer; between us and the saloon in front of which we were drawn up in line, passed the motley throng, almost every man lifting his hat and even the little newsboys doing the same. It was American manhood's tribute to Christianity and to womanhood, and it was significant and full of pathos.

The leader had already asked the saloonkeeper if we might enter, and he had declined, else the prayer meeting would have occurred inside his door. A sorrowful old lady, whose only son had gone to ruin through that very death-trap, knelt on the cold, moist pavement and offered a broken-hearted prayer, while all our heads were bowed.

At a signal we moved on and the next saloonkeeper permitted us to enter. I had no more idea of the inward appearance of a saloon than if there had been no such place on earth. I knew nothing of its high, heavily corniced bar, its barrels with the ends all pointed toward the looker-on, each barrel being furnished with a faucet, its shelves glittering with decanters and cut glass, its floors thickly strewn with sawdust, and here and there a round table with chairs—nor of its abundant fumes, sickening to healthful nostrils.

The tall, stately lady who led us placed her Bible on the bar and read a psalm, whether hortatory or imprecatory I do not remember, but the spirit of these crusaders was so gentle, I think it must have been the former.

Then we sang "Rock of Ages" as I thought I had never heard it sung before, with a tender confidence to the height of which one does not rise in the easy-going, regulation prayer meeting, and then one of the older women whispered to me softly the leader wished to know if I would pray. It was strange, perhaps, but I felt not the least reluctance, and kneeling on the sawdust floor, with a group of earnest hearts around me, and behind them, filling every corner and extending out into the street, a crowd of unwashed, unkempt, hard-looking drinking men, I was conscious that perhaps never in my life, save beside my sister Mary's dying bed, had I prayed as truly as I did then. This was my Crusade baptism. The next day I went on to the West and within a week had been made president of the Chicago W.C.T.U.

2. Samuel Gompers Defends the Saloon (c. 1886)

The Knights of Labor, joining the foes of the saloon, refused to admit liquor sellers to their membership. Their leader, Terence V. Powderly, even accused certain employers of encouraging drink so that the employees would become more content with their underpaid lot. (This argument assumes that docility is preferable to efficiency.) But Samuel Gompers of the American Federation of Labor had a good word to say for the attractively lighted "poor man's club," even though it drained away the family's grocery money. Did the advantages offset the disadvantages?

The saloon was the only club the workingmen had then. For a few cents we could buy a glass of beer and hours of congenial society. Talk in these meeting places had a peculiar freedom from formality that engendered good-fellowship and exchange of genuine intimacies.

The saloon rendered a variety of industrial services. Frequently, wages were paid there—in checks which the saloonkeeper cashed. Of course, it was embarrassing to accept that service without spending money with him.

All too frequently the saloonkeeper also served as an employment agent. But on the other hand the saloonkeeper was often a friend in time of strikes and the free lunch [salty foods to stimulate thirst] he served was a boon to many a hungry striker.

Nearly every saloon had a room or a hall back of it or over it that could be rented for a nominal sum. Of course, the saloon was counting on increased receipts due to gatherings held in the hall. These rooms were practically the only meeting places available to unions, which were poor and small in numbers.

[The continued callousness of "booze barons" resulted in the launching of the Anti-Saloon League in 1893. It supplemented the efforts of the Prohibition party, organized in 1869, and the Woman's Christian Temperance Union, organized in 1874. With mounting zeal the reformers harped on the following arguments: (1) Alcohol was a debauching force in U.S. politics. (2) The rapid mechanization of industry required sobriety for safety and efficiency. (3) The liquor sellers were saddling the taxpayers with the occupants of prisons and poorhouses. But prohibition in the localities and the states was slow in coming. By 1905 only four states had entered the "dry" column: Kansas, Maine, Nebraska, and North Dakota. Success was slowest in the large urban areas, where huge colonies of immigrants had brought with them Old World drinking habits.]

---

[2]From *Seventy Years of Life and Labor* by Samuel Gompers. Copyright 1925 by Samuel Gompers, renewed © 1953 by Gertrude Gleaves Gompers. Used by permission of Dutton, a division of Penguin Putnam, Inc.

E. The Changing Role of Women

1. Victoria Woodhull Advocates Free Love (1871)

Victoria Woodhull, a brilliant, beautiful, and erratic woman, arrived in New York in 1868 with her sister, Tennessee Celeste Claflin. They quickly emerged as outspoken champions of women's suffrage and of a new egalitarian standard of sexual morality. Woodhull gained wide support from leaders of the suffrage movement when she persuaded the House Judiciary Committee in 1871 to hold hearings on a suffrage amendment. But many of her fellow feminists began to wonder about Woodhull's usefulness to their cause when she accused Horace Greeley, who favored women's suffrage but opposed "free love," of ruining his wife's health and causing the deaths of five of his seven children. She also denounced Catharine Beecher (see Vol. I, p. 331) as among those "who now clog the wheels of progress, and stand forth as the enemies of their sex . . . doing their utmost to cement the chains of their degradation, giving to man the same power over them as he possesses over his horses and dogs." Finally, in 1872, Woodhull accused Henry Ward Beecher, probably the most famous American preacher of his day and another friend of women's suffrage, of carrying on an adulterous relationship—an accusation that resulted in a sensational trial that ended in a "jury disagreement." In the article excerpted here, what are Woodhull's views of marriage? How do they differ from those of Catharine Beecher and other traditional women of the day? What might have been the relationship between these views and Woodhull's advocacy of women's suffrage?

Many are the tales of horror and brutal violence that have been related of negro slavery, where the lash of the driver was depicted until their hearers almost felt its stings in their own flesh, and almost the red streams flowing down their own backs, and these appealed to the souls of men and women until they were ready to do whatever was needed to destroy a monster that could cause such suffering to a single human being. But I am fully convinced that all the suffering of all the negro slaves combined, is as nothing in comparison to that which women, as a whole, suffer. There were several millions of negro slaves. There are twenty millions of women slaves. The negroes were dependent upon their masters for all the comforts of life they enjoyed; but it was to the interest of their masters to give them all of these that health demanded. Women are as much dependent upon men for their sustenance as were the negroes upon their masters, lacking the interest that they had in the negroes as personal property.

It is an unpleasant thing to say that women, in many senses, are as much slaves as were the negroes, but if it be true, ought it not to be said? I say, a thousand times, yes! And when the slavery to which they are subjected is compared to that which the negro endured, the demand for its consideration increases again, still a thousand times more.

Perhaps it may be denied that women are slaves, sexually, sold and delivered to man. But I tell you, as a class, that they are, and the conclusion cannot be escaped.

---

[1]Victoria C. Woodhull, *The Scarecrows of Sexual Slavery* (1874), pp. 19–22.

Let me convince all doubters of this. Stand before me, all ye married women, and tell me how many of you would remain mistresses of your husbands' homes if you should refuse to cohabit sexually with them? Answer ye this, and then tell me that ye are free, if ye can! I tell ye that you are the sexual slaves of your husbands, bound by as terrible bonds to serve them sexually as ever a negro was bound to serve his owner, physically; and if you don't quite believe it, go home and endeavor to assert your freedom, and see to what it will lead! You may not be made to feel the inevitable lash that followed rebellion on the part of the negro, but even this is not certain; yet lashes of some sort will surely be dealt. Refuse to yield to the sexual demands of your legal master, and ten to one he will turn you into the street, or in lieu of this, perhaps, give you personal violence, even to compelling you to submit by force. Tell me that wives are not slaves! As well might you have done the same of the negroes, who, as the women do not, did not realize their condition!

I offer it as a well-grounded conclusion that I have come to, after years of inquiry and observation, that nine of every ten wives, at some time during their marriage, are compelled, according to the injunction of St. Paul, to submit themselves to their husbands, when every sentiment of their souls revolts to the act; and I feel an answering response coming up to me from many sick souls among you, that shrink in horror from the contemplation of the terrible scenes to which they have been compelled.

Remember, I do not say this is universally true; I do not say that all wives, at all times, are thus situated. Neither were all negro slaves at all times subjected to the lash or to other brutal treatment. The large majority of negroes were well treated and comparatively happy; but they were slaves, nevertheless. The cases of extreme cruelty were really rarer than is generally believed, but they were enough to condemn the system and to cause its terrible washing out by the blood of hundreds of thousands of the brightest souls of the country. So, also, are the cases of extreme cruelty on the part of the husbands not exceedingly common, but they are sufficiently so to condemn the whole system, and to demand, if need be, that it, too, be washed out by the blood, if necessary, of millions of human beings.

For my part I would rather be the labor slave of a master, with his whip cracking continually about my ears, my whole life, than the forced sexual slave of any man a single hour; and I know that every woman who has freedom born in her soul will shout in deepest and earnest response to this—Amen! I know what it is to be both these. I have traveled the city pavements of New York in mid-winter, seeking employment, with nothing on my feet except an old pair of india-rubber shoes, and a common calico dress only to cover my body, while the man who called me wife and who made me his sexual slave, spent his money upon other women. I am not speaking whereof I know not. My case may be thought an extreme one, but I know of thousands even worse. Then tell me I shall not have the right to denounce this damned system! Tell me I shall be sent to Sing Sing [a prison in New York] if I dare expose these things! Open your Sing Sings a thousand times, but none of their terrors shall stop a single word. I will tell the world, so long as I have a tongue and the strength to move it, of all the infernal misery hidden behind this horrible thing called marriage, though the Young Men's Christian Association sentence me to prison a year for every word. I have seen horrors beside which stone walls and iron bars are heaven, and I will not hold my peace so long as a system, that can produce such damnation and by which, as its author, heaven is blasphemed, exists.

Would to Heaven I could thunder these facts forth until women should be moved by a comprehension of the low degradation to which they have fallen, to open rebellion; until they should rise *en masse* and declare themselves free, resisting all sexual subjection, and utterly refusing to yield their bodies up to man, until they shall grant them perfect freedom. It was not the slaves themselves who obtained their own freedom. It was their noble white brothers of the North, who, seeing their condition, and realizing that though they were black, still that they were brothers, sacrificed themselves for the time to emancipate them. So it will not be the most suffering slaves of this horrible slavery who will accomplish its abolition; but it must be those who know and appreciate the terrible condition, who must, for the time, sacrifice ourselves, that their sisters may come to themselves and to own themselves.

Go preach this doctrine, then, ye who have the strength and the moral courage: No more sexual intercourse for men who do not fully consent that all women shall be free, and who do not besides this, also join the standard of the rebellion. It matters not if you be wife or not, raise your voice for your suffering sex, let the consequences to yourself be what they may. They say I have come to break up the family; I say amen to that with all my heart. I hope I may break up every family in the world that exists by virtue of sexual slavery, and I feel that the smiles of angels, the smiles of those who have gone on before, who suffered here what I have suffered and what thousands are suffering, will give me strength to brave all opposition, and to stand even upon the scaffold, if need be, that my sisters all over the world may be emancipated, may rise from slavery to the full dignity of womanhood.

2. The Life of a Working Girl (1905)

Dorothy Richardson, a fairly well-educated, obviously middle-class young woman, was compelled by necessity to seek employment in a New York sweatshop around the turn of the century. She recorded her experiences in a remarkable book, The Long Day, *excerpted here. What is her attitude toward the immigrant working-class girls who became her companions and workmates? Why did these young women work? How were their working conditions different from those of today? Elsewhere in her book, Richardson quoted one of her fellow workers who spoke of "long ago, when they used to treat the girls so bad. Things is ever so much better now." How might the conditions here described have been worse in an earlier day?*

Bessie met Eunice and me at the lower right-hand corner of Broadway and Grand Street, and together we applied for work in the R——— Underwear Company, which had advertised that morning for twenty operators.

---

[2]From Dorothy Richardson, *The Long Day: The Story of the New York Working Girl as Told by Herself* (Century Company, 1905), as it appears in William L. O'Neill, *Women at Work* (Quadrangle, 1972), pp. 203–214.

"Ever run a power Singer?" queried the foreman.

"No, but we can learn. We're all quick," answered Bessie, who had volunteered to act as spokesman.

"Yes, I guess you can learn all right, but you won't make very much at first. All come together? . . . So! Well, then, I guess you'll want to work in the same room," and with that he ushered us into a very inferno of sound, a great, yawning chaos of terrific noise. The girls, who sat in long rows up and down the length of the great room, did not raise their eyes to the newcomers, as is the rule in less strenuous workrooms. Every pair of eyes seemed to be held in fascination upon the flying and endless strip of white that raced through a pair of hands to feed itself into the insatiable maw of the electric sewing-machine. Every face, tense and stony, bespoke a superb effort to concentrate mind and body, and soul itself, literally upon the point of a needle. Every form was crouched in the effort to guide the seam through the presser-foot. And piled between the opposing phalanxes of set faces were billows upon billows of foamy white muslin and lace—the finished garments wrought by the so-many dozen per hour, for the so-many cents per day,—and wrought, too, in this terrific, nerve-racking noise.

The foreman led us into the middle of the room, which was lighted by gas-jets that hung directly over the girls' heads, although the ends of the shop had bright sunshine from the windows. He seemed a good-natured, respectable sort of man, of about forty, and was a Jew. Bessie and me he placed at machines side by side, and Eunice a little farther down the line. Then my first lesson began. He showed me how to thread bobbin and needle, how to operate ruffler and tucker, and also how to turn off and on the electric current which operated the machinery. My first attempt to do the latter was productive of a shock to the nerves that could not have been greater if, instead of pressing the harmless little lever under the machine with my knee, I had accidently exploded a bomb. The foreman laughed good-naturedly at my fright.

"You'll get used to it by and by," he shouted above the noise; "but like as not for a while you won't sleep very good nights—kind of nervous; but you'll get over that in a week or so," and he ducked his head under the machine to adjust the belt. . . .

I leaned over the machine and practised at running a straight seam. Ah, the skill of these women and girls, and of the strange creature opposite, who can make a living at this torturing labor! How many different, how infinitely harder it is, as compared with running an ordinary sewing-machine. The goods that my nervous fingers tried to guide ran every wrong way. I had no control whatever over the fearful velocity with which the needle danced along the seam. In utter discouragement, I stopped trying for a moment, and watched the girl at my right. She was a swarthy, thick-lipped Jewess, of the type most common in such places, but I looked at her with awe and admiration. In Rachel Goldberg's case the making of muslin, lace-trimmed corset-covers was an art rather than a craft. She was a remarkable operator even among scores of experts at the R———. Under her stubby, ill-kept hands ruffles and tucks and insertion bands and lace frills were wrought with a beauty and softness of finish, and a speed and precision of workmanship, that made her the wonder and envy of the shop. . . .

Result of my first hour's work: I had spoiled a dozen garments. Try as I would, I invariably lost all control of my materials, and the needle plunged right and left—everywhere, in fact, except along the straight and narrow way laid out for it. . . .

As I spoiled each garment I thrust it into the bottom of a green pasteboard box under the table, which held my allotment of work, and from the top of the box grabbed up a fresh piece. I glanced over my shoulder and saw that Bessie was doing the same thing, although what we were going to do with them, or how account for such wholesale devastation of goods, we were too perturbed to consider. At last, however, after repeated trials, and by guiding the seam with laborious care, I succeeded in completing one garment without disaster; and I had just started another, when—crash!—flying shuttles and spinning bobbins and swirling wheels came to a standstill. My sewing-machine was silent, as were all the others in the great workroom. Something had happened to the dynamo.

There was a howl of disappointment. . . .

Rachel Goldberg had finished four dozen of extrafine garments, which meant seventy-five cents, and it was not yet eleven o'clock. She would make at least one dollar and sixty cents before the day was over, provided we did not have any serious breakdowns. She watched the clock impatiently—every minute she was idle meant a certain fraction of a penny lost,—and crouched sullenly over her machine for the signal. . . .

In half an hour we had resumed work, and at half-past twelve we stopped for another half-hour and ate luncheon—Bessie, Eunice, and I in a corner by ourselves.

We held a conference, and compared notes of the morning's progress, which had been even more discouraging to poor Eunice than to us; for to her it had brought the added misfortune of a row of stitches in her right forefinger. We counted up our profits for the morning, and the aggregate earnings of the three of us did not amount to ten cents. Of course we would learn to do better, but it would take a long, long time, Bessie was firmly convinced, before we could even make enough to buy our lunches. It was decided that one of us should resign the job that night, and the other two keep at it until the delegate found something better for us all and had tested the new job to her satisfaction. Bessie was of course appointed, and the next morning Eunice and I went alone, with plausible excuses for the absent Bessie, for we had a certain delicacy about telling the real facts to so kind a foreman as "Abe."

The second day we had no better luck, and the pain between the shoulderblades was unceasing. All night long I had tossed on my narrow cot, with aching back and nerves wrought up to such a tension that the moment I began to doze off I was wakened by a spasmodic jerk of the right arm as it reached forward to grasp a visionary strip of lace. That evening, as we filed out at six o'clock, Bessie was waiting for us, her gentle face full of radiance and good news. Even the miserable Eunice was affected by her hopefulness.

"Oh, girls, I've got something that's really good—three dollars a week while you're learning, and an awful nice shop; and just think, girls!—the hours—I never had anything like it before, and I've knocked around at eighteen different jobs—half-past eight to five, and—" she paused for breath to announce the glorious fact—"Girls, just think of it!—*Saturday afternoons off,* all the year round."

3. An Italian Immigrant Woman Faces Life Alone in the Big City (c. 1896)

Rosa Cavalleri came from her native Lombardy, in Italy, to Chicago in 1884. Although she never knew her exact birth date, she was probably about eighteen years old when she arrived in the United States. In later years she recounted her life story to Marie Hall Ets, who was a social worker at the Chicago Commons, a settlement house founded in 1894 by Dr. Graham Taylor, an associate of the pioneering urban reformer Jane Addams. What might have been Rosa Cavalleri's response to Victoria Woodhull's call for free love? What were the most important concerns in Cavalleri's life? Who helped her? What evidence does this account provide of the existence of an immigrant "community"? What was the role of the municipal government in Rosa Cavalleri's life?

The year my Leo was born I was home alone and struggled along with my children. My husband went away because he was sick—he went by a doctor in St. Louis to get cured. The doctor said he must stay away from his home one year and gave him a job to do all the janitor work around his house for five dollars a month and his board. So me, I used to go all around to find the clothes to wash and the scrubbing. The city hall was helping me again in that time—they gave me a little coal and sometimes the basket of food. Bob, the sign painter downstairs, he helped me the most. He was such a good young man. He used to bring a big chunk of coal and chop it up right in my kitchen and fix the stove.

I was to the end of my nine months, but the baby never came. So I went by one woman, Mis' Thomas, and I got part of the clothes washed. Then I said, "Oh Mis' Thomas, I've got to go. I've got the terrible pains!"

She said, "You can go when you finish. You've got to finish first."

"No, I go. Otherwise I'll have to stay in your bed." When I said that she got scared I would have the baby there, so she let me go.

I went by the midwife, Mis' Marino, and told her to come; then I went home. When I saw it was my time, I told Domenico something and sent him with all the children to the wife of Tomaso. I told those people before, when they see the children come they must keep them all night—it's my time. It was really, really my time, and I had such a scare that I would be alone a second time. So when I heard a lady come in the building—she lived downstairs—I called to her. She said, "I have no time." And she didn't come up.

I was on my bed all alone by myself and then I prayed Sant' Antoni with all my heart. I don't know why I prayed Sant' Antoni—the Madonna put it in my mind. And then, just when the baby was born, I saw Sant' Antoni right there! He appeared in the room by me! I don't think it was really Sant' Antoni there, but in my imagination I saw him—all light like the sun. I saw Sant' Antoni there by my bed, and right then the door opened and the midwife came in to take care of the baby! It was February seventh and six below zero. There I had him born all alone, but Mis' Marino came

---

[3]From Marie Hall Ets, *Rosa: The Life of an Italian Immigrant* (1970), pp. 228–231. University of Minnesota Press, Minneapolis. Copyright © 1970 by the University of Minnesota. Reprinted by permission of the publisher.

when I prayed Sant' Antoni. She washed the baby and put him by me, but then she ran away. She didn't light the fire or nothing.

Oh, that night it was *so* cold! And me in my little wooden house in the alley with the walls all frosting—thick white frosting. I was crying and praying, "How am I going to live?" I said. "Oh, Sant' Antoni, I'll never live till tomorrow morning! I'll never live till the morning!"

And just as I prayed my door opened and a lady came in. She had a black shawl twice around her neck and head and that shawl came down to her nose. All I could see was half the nose and the mouth. She came in and lighted both the stoves. Then she came and looked at me, but I couldn't see her face. I said, "God bless you!"

She just nodded her head up and down and all the time said not one word, only "Sh, sh."

Then she went down in the basement herself, nobody telling her nothing, and she got the coal and fixed the fire. Pretty soon she found that little package of camomile tea I had there on the dresser and she made a little tea with the hot water. And that woman stayed by me almost till daylight. But all the time she put her finger to her mouth to tell me to keep still when I tried to thank her. And I never knew where that lady came from! I don't know yet! Maybe she was the spirit of that kind girl, Annina, in Canaletto? I don't know. I really don't know! I was *so* sick and I didn't hear her voice or see her face. All the time she put her finger on her mouth and said, "Sh, sh." And when the daylight came she was gone.

About seven o'clock morning my children came home. And Mis' Marino, that midwife, she came at eight o'clock and said, "It's so cold I thought I'd find you dead!"

Then here came the city hall, or somebody, with a wagon. They wanted to take me and my new baby to the hospital. But how could I leave all my children? I started to cry—I didn't want to go. And my children cried too—they didn't want me to leave them. So then they didn't make me. They pulled my bed away from the frosting on the wall and put it in the front room by the stove. And my baby, I had him wrapped up in a pad I made from the underskirt like we do in *Italia*. But that baby froze when he was born; he couldn't cry like other babies—he was crying weak, weak.

My Visella was bringing up the wood and the coal and trying to make that room warm. But she was only a little girl, she didn't know, and she filled that stove so full that all the pipes on the ceiling caught fire. I had to jump up from the bed and throw the pails of water so the house wouldn't burn down. Then God sent me help again. He sent that Miss Mildred from the settlement house. She didn't know about me and my Leo born; she was looking for some other lady and she came to my door and saw me. She said, "Oh, I have the wrong place."

"I said, "No, lady, you find the right place."

So she came in and found out all. Then she ran away and brought back all those little things the babies in America have. She felt sorry to see my baby banded up like I had him. She didn't know then, Miss Mildred, that the women in *Italia* always band their babies that way. And she brought me something to eat too—for me and for my children. That night another young lady from the Commons, Miss May, she came and slept in my house to take care of the fire. She was afraid for the children—maybe they would burn themselves and the house. Oh, that Miss Mildred and Miss May, they were angels to come and help me like that! Four nights Miss May stayed there and kept the fire going. They were high-up educated girls—they were used to sleeping in the warm house with the plumbing—and there they came and slept in my wooden house in the alley, and for a toilet they had to go down to that shed under the sidewalk. They were really, really friends! That time I had my Leo nobody knew I was going to have the baby—I looked kind of fat, that's all. These women in the settlement house were so surprised. They said, "Why you didn't tell us before, Mis' Cavalleri, so we can help you?"

You know that Mis' Thomas—I was washing her clothes when the baby started to come—she wanted a boy and she got a baby girl right after my baby was born. When I went there the next week to do the washing I had to carry my baby with me. When she saw him she said, "Well better I have a girl than I have a boy that looks like your baby! He looks for sure like a monkey!"

In the first beginning he did look like a monkey, but in a few weeks he got pretty. He got so pretty all the people from the settlement house came to see him. After two or three months there was no baby in Chicago prettier than that baby.

When the year was over for him, my husband came home from St. Louis. He didn't send me the money when he was there—just two times the five dollars—so he brought twenty-five dollars when he came back. Oh, he was so happy when he saw that baby with exactly, exactly his face and everything—the same dark gold hair and everything—and so beautiful. But he saw that baby was so thin and pale and couldn't cry like the other babies. "Better I go by a good doctor and see," he said. "I've got twenty-five dollars—I'm going to get a good doctor." So he did.

But the doctor said, "That baby can't live. He was touched in the lungs with the cold. Both lungs got froze when he was born."

And sure enough he was all the time sick and when it was nine months he died. My first Leo and my second Leo I lose them both. Oh, I was brokenhearted to lose such a beautiful baby! . . .

4. Jane Addams Demands the Vote for Women (1910)

Jane Addams (1860–1935) was a multitalented reformer who battled for women's rights, urban reform, and international peace (she was awarded the Nobel Peace Prize in 1931). In 1889 she helped to found Chicago's Hull-House, one of the earliest settlement houses that worked to improve living conditions in the slums. A keen observer of the conditions that shaped people's lives in the new environment of the cities, she soon found in the movement toward urbanization a powerful set of arguments on behalf of granting the vote to women. In the following selection, what points are most effective in her demand for the suffrage? Does she view the suffrage as an extension of women's traditional role or as a means for transforming that role?

This paper is an attempt to show that many women today are failing to discharge their duties to their own households properly simply because they do not perceive that as society grows more complicated it is necessary that woman shall

---

[4]Jane Addams, "Why Women Should Vote," *Ladies' Home Journal* 27 (January 1910): 21–22.

extend her sense of responsibility to many things outside of her own home if she would continue to preserve the home in its entirety. One could illustrate in many ways. A woman's simplest duty, one would say, is to keep her house clean and wholesome and to feed her children properly. Yet if she lives in a tenement house, as so many of my neighbors do, she cannot fulfill these simple obligations by her own efforts because she is utterly dependent upon the city administration for the conditions which render decent living possible. Her basement will not be dry, her stairways will not be fireproof, her house will not be provided with sufficient windows to give light and air, nor will it be equipped with sanitary plumbing, unless the Public Works Department sends inspectors who constantly insist that these elementary decencies be provided. Women who live in the country sweep their own dooryards and may either feed the refuse of the table to a flock of chickens or allow it innocently to decay in the open air and sunshine. In a crowded city quarter, however, if the street is not cleaned by the city authorities no amount of private sweeping will keep the tenement free from grime; if the garbage is not properly collected and destroyed a tenement-house mother may see her children sicken and die of diseases from which she alone is powerless to shield them, although her tenderness and devotion are unbounded. She cannot even secure untainted meat for her household, she cannot provide fresh fruit, unless the meat has been inspected by city officials and [unless] the decayed fruit, which is so often placed upon sale in the tenement districts, has been destroyed in the interests of public health. In short, if woman would keep on with her old business of caring for her house and rearing her children she will have to have some conscience in regard to public affairs lying quite outside of her immediate household. The individual conscience and devotion are no longer effective. . . .

. . . [There] are certain primary duties which belong to even the most conservative women. . . . The first of these . . . is woman's responsibility for the members of her own household that they may be properly fed and clothed and surrounded by hygienic conditions. The second is a responsibility for the education of children: (a) that they may be provided with good schools; (b) that they may be kept free from vicious influences on the street; (c) that when working they may be protected by adequate child-labor legislation.

(a) The duty of a woman toward the schools which her children attend is so obvious that it is not necessary to dwell upon it. But even this simple obligation cannot be effectively carried out without some form of social organization as the mothers' school clubs and mothers' congresses testify, and to which the most conservative women belong because they feel the need for wider reading and discussion concerning the many problems of childhood. It is, therefore, perhaps natural that the public should have been more willing to accord a vote to women in school matters than in any other, and yet women have never been members of a Board of Education in sufficient numbers to influence largely actual school curriculi. If they had been kindergartens, domestic science courses and school playgrounds would be far more numerous than they are. More than once woman has been convinced of the need of the ballot by the futility of her efforts in persuading a business man that young children need nurture in something besides the three r's. Perhaps, too, only women realize the influence which the school might exert upon the home if a proper adaptation to actual needs were considered. An Italian girl who has had lessons in cooking at the public school will help her mother to connect the entire family with American food and household habits. . . .

(b) But women are also beginning to realize that children need attention outside of school hours; that much of the petty vice in cities is merely the love of pleasure gone wrong, the overrestrained boy or girl seeking improper recreation and excitement. It is obvious that a little study of the needs of children, a sympathetic understanding of the conditions under which they go astray, might save hundreds of them. Women traditionally have had an opportunity to observe the plays of children and the needs of youth, and yet in Chicago, at least they had done singularly little in this vexed problem of juvenile delinquency until they helped to inaugurate the Juvenile Court movement a dozen years ago. . . .

. . . (c) As the education of her children has been more and more transferred to the school, so that even children four years old go to the kindergarten, the woman has been left in a household of constantly-narrowing interests, not only because the children are away, but also because one industry after another is slipping from the household into the factory. Ever since steam power has been applied to the process of weaving and spinning woman's traditional work has been carried on largely outside of the home. The clothing and household linen are not only spun and woven, but also usually sewed, by machinery; the preparation of many foods has also passed into the factory and necessarily a certain number of women have been obliged to follow their work there, although it is doubtful, in spite of the large number of factory girls, whether women now are doing as large a portion of the world's work as they used to do. Because many thousands of those working in factories and shops are girls between the ages of fourteen and twenty-two there is a necessity that older women should be interested in the conditions of industry. The very fact that these girls are not going to remain in industry permanently makes it more important that some one should see to it that they shall not be incapacitated for their future family life because they work for exhausting hours and under unsanitary conditions.

If woman's sense of obligation had enlarged as the industrial conditions changed she might naturally and almost imperceptibly have inaugurated the movements for social amelioration in the line of factory legislation and shop sanitation. That she has not done so is doubtless due to the fact that her conscience is slow to recognize any obligation outside of her own family circle, and because she was so absorbed in her own household that she failed to see what the conditions outside actually were. It would be interesting to know how far the consciousness that she had no vote and could not change matters operated in this direction. After all, we see only those things to which our attention has been drawn, we feel responsibility for those things which are brought to us as matters of responsibility. If conscientious women were convinced that it was a civic duty to be informed in regard to these grave industrial affairs, and then to express the conclusions which they had reached by depositing a piece of paper in a ballot-box, one cannot imagine that they would shirk simply because the action ran counter to old traditions. . . .

In a complex community like the modern city all points of view need to be represented; the resultants of diverse experiences need to be pooled if the community would make for sane and balanced progress. If it would meet fairly each problem as it arises, whether it be connected with a freight tunnel having to do largely with business men, or with the increasing death rate among children under five years of age, a problem in which women are vitally concerned, or with the question of more adequate street-car transfers, in which both men and women might be said to be equally interested, it must not ignore the judgments of its entire adult population.

To turn the administration of our civic affairs wholly over to men may mean that the American city will continue to push forward in its commercial and industrial development, and continue to lag behind in those things which make a city healthful and beautiful. After all, woman's traditional function has been to make her dwelling-place both clean and fair. Is that dreariness in city life, that lack of domesticity which the humblest farm dwelling presents, due to a withdrawal of one of the naturally coöperating forces? If women have in any sense been responsible for the gentler side of life which softens and blurs some of its harsher conditions, may they not have a duty to perform in our American cities?

In closing, may I recapitulate that if woman would fulfill her traditional responsibility to her own children; if she would educate and protect from danger factory children who must find their recreation on the street; if she would bring the cultural forces to bear upon our materialistic civilization; and if she would do it all with the dignity and directness fitting one who carries on her immemorial duties, then she must bring herself to the use of the ballot—that latest implement for self-government. May we not fairly say that American women need this implement in order to preserve the home?

Thought Provokers

---

1. What was most novel about city life? How are cities different today?
2. If the New Immigrants were disillusioned by America, why didn't more of them return to the Old Country? Why did they congregate in slums?
3. Was a literacy test fairer than restricting immigrants by quota? Why was the immigrant less welcome in the 1890s than in the 1790s?
4. It has been said that Darwin jolted orthodox Christianity more severely than Copernicus did three hundred years earlier with his discoveries regarding the solar system. Explain. Why was it so difficult to reconcile evolution with a literal reading of the Bible?
5. Critics have charged that one reason that the saloon prospered was that the churches and the community failed to provide wholesome alternatives. Discuss.
6. What was new about the "new woman" at the end of the nineteenth century? Why did women in growing numbers work for wages? Did female workers deserve special protection? How did the movement to the city help the campaign for women's suffrage?

26

The Great West and the Agricultural Revolution, 1865–1896

Many, if not most, of our Indian wars have had
their origin in broken promises and acts of injustice
upon our part.

President Hayes, 1877

Prologue: The fence-erecting white men inevitably clashed with the wide-roaming Indians of the plains. As land greed undermined ethical standards, many settlers acted as though the Indians had no more rights than the buffalo, which were also ruthlessly slaughtered. The seemingly endless frontier wars ended finally when the Native Americans, cooped up in reservations, were forced to adopt in part the economic life of their conquerors. The honest farmer and the fraudulent speculator were now free to open the Far West under the Homestead Act of 1862—the United States' first big giveaway program. Much of the settlement occurred in areas with only scanty rainfall, and when crops failed, or when overproduction came, the farmer was trapped. Agitation for relief vented itself most spectacularly in 1892, when the Populist party waged a colorful campaign for the presidency under General James B. Weaver. Although he carried six western states, he ran well behind the second-place Republicans as the Democrats again swept Grover Cleveland to victory.

A. The Plight of the Indian

1. The U.S. Army Negotiates a Treaty with the Sioux (1868)

In the pre–Civil War years, the U.S. government had signed treaties with the Native Americans of the Great Plains, guaranteeing them huge northern and southern "reservation" areas on either side of a relatively narrow corridor of white settlement that generally followed the course of the Platte River across the central Plains. But the uncontrollable advance of the whites onto the Plains after the Civil War, especially

---

[1]From Vine V. Deloria, Jr., and Ramond DeMallie, eds., *Proceedings of the Great Peace Commission, 1867–1868,* pp. 106–109. Copyright © 1975. Reprinted by permission of Vine V. Deloria, Jr.

along the "Bozeman Trail" to newly discovered gold fields in present-day Montana, sparked repeated clashes with the native peoples. The government built a series of forts along the Bozeman Trail, but following a series of successful Native American attacks, agreed in 1868 to abandon them, and reaffirmed its intentions to establish peaceful relations with the Indians. (Just six years later, George Armstrong Custer was to violate these agreements when he led an armed party into Sioux territory in the Black Hills of South Dakota, a provocation that led to the fateful clash on the Little Big Horn River in 1876 that cost Custer his life.) In the negotiations of April 28, 1868, recorded here, what do the U.S. Army representatives cite as their principal difficulty in maintaining peace between the whites and the Native Americans? What arguments do they use to persuade the Native Americans to sign the new treaty? What appears to be their attitude toward the Native Americans? How do the Native Americans regard the whites?

General Sanborn. We . . . offer you peace to save your nations from destruction. We speak the truth. But the truth is often unwelcome and grates harshly upon the ear. You will not believe me when I tell you that you can not protect yourselves from the white people. You will not believe me when I tell you that this military officer now here, a commissioner to meet you, had to use his authority to keep a great body of whites out of your country last year. You will not believe me when I tell you that the white soldiers whom you were killing and trying to kill last year were driving back the whites from your country and trying to save the country for you and to prevent your destruction. But all this is true, and you must have the protection of the President of the United States and his white soldiers or disappear from the earth.

We want you to see this yourselves, and not be compelled to believe it because we say so. That you may see how the case stands we request you to send some of your chiefs and braves to Washington now. Any of your friends among the whites that you desire may go along with you. You will then see and know what we know, and can determine what course it is best for your nations to take. You do not see the white soldiers when they are fighting the whites and keeping them out of your country, but only when they resist your attacks made upon them when marching along the road. The questions between you and the whites must soon be finally and forever settled.

If you continue to fight the whites you can not expect the President nor your friends among them to protect you in your country from those who are waiting to go there in large numbers. If you continue at war your country will soon be all overrun by white people. Military posts will be located on all the rivers. Your game and yourselves will be destroyed. This is the last effort of the President to make peace with you and save for you a country and home.

We therefore propose that you now make a treaty by which you can and will abide. By this treaty we will agree to protect you from the inroads of our people and keep them out of a portion of your present country described in the treaty. We shall agree to furnish you supplies in clothing and other useful articles while you continue to roam and hunt. We shall agree to furnish cattle, horses, cows, and implements to work the ground to each of your people as may at any time settle down and build a home and wish to live like the whites. Under this treaty you can roam and hunt while you remain at peace and game lasts; and when the game is gone you will have a home and means of supporting yourselves and your children. But you must understand that if peace is not now made all efforts on our part to make it are at an end.

We ask you now to consider this matter with the understanding of men and not with the malice of children; and when you reply speak your whole thoughts and feelings. If there are any here who do not design to remain at peace, we do not want them to sign any treaty. If there are any here who design to disturb the railroads or any of the ranches or white people south of the Platte River, we do not want them to sign any treaty, for such acts repeated will force the President to send soldiers into your country and to make war. But all who now conclude to make peace and abide by it, who intend to meet the whites in a friendly manner, and receive aid and protection from the President, we now request to sign the treaty tomorrow morning at 10 o'clock. This is all that we have been told to say to you.

General Harney. I am afraid you do not understand why we want to make peace. Perhaps you think we are afraid. You can not be such fools as that, I hope. We do not want to go to war with you because you are a small nation, a handful compared with us, and we want you to live. If we go to war we shall send out to meet you a large army. Suppose you kill the whole army, we have another to send in its place. A great many of you will be killed and you have nobody to take their places. We are kind to you here. You have true hearts and we want you to live. We have not been making war with you. You are at war with us. We have not commenced yet. I hope you will not drive us to war.

Iron Shell (Brulé). I am getting to be an old man. The talk you have just made is what I have always gone by since I was a young man. When I was about 30 years old I joined the sensible men and have been with them ever since. When I was a young man I looked for nothing good, but everything that was bad. I was out hunting buffalo, and I heard that there were some good men here waiting to see me and I came in. I heard that General Harney had left the warpath and was ready for peace, so I came in.

My father and grandfather used to be with the whites, and I have been with them, too. We used to treat them well, I do not recollect that there was any war while we were with the whites. We used to take pity on one another and did nothing bad to each other while we were together. I know that the whites are like the grass on the prairie. Anybody that takes anything from the whites must pay for it. You have come into my country without my consent and spread your soldiers all over it. I have looked around for the cause of the trouble and I can not see that my young men were the cause of it. All the bad things that have been done, you have made the road for it. That is my truth. I love the whites. You whites went all over my country, killing my young men, and disturbing everything in my country. My heart is not made out of rock, but of flesh, but I have a strong heart. All the bad deeds that have been done I have had no hand in, neither have any of our young men. I want to hear you give us good advice. I came here for that purpose. We helped you to stop this war between us and the whites. You have put us in misery; also these old traders whom the war has stopped. We want you to set us all right and put us back the same as in old times.

We want you to take away the forts from the country. That will leave big room for the Indians to live in. If you succeed about the forests all the game will come back and we will have plenty to eat. If you want the Indian to live do that and we will have a chance to live. One above us has created all of us, the whites the same as the Indians, and he will take pity on us. Our God has put us on earth to live in the way we do, to live on game. Our great father we depend on at Washington. We do not deliberate for ourselves, and we want him to take pity on us. Do you think that our God is for us the same as for the whites? I have prayed to God and asked him to make me succeed, and He has allowed it to me. I succeeded often. Your commissioners want to make peace and take pity on the Indians. Take away all these things if you intend to make peace, and we will live happy and be at peace. All we have is the land and the sky above. This war has set an example to our young men to make war on the whites. If it had not been for that we should have been at peace all the time.

You generally pick on bad white men to give them office which is the cause of our being put in trouble. From this our young men have learned all these bad things and we are in misery and have a hard time. Me and some others of the sensible men have been put in trouble by you. I have listened to your advice, General Sanborn, and I told the others to listen to you. You sent messengers to us last winter and we have come in to you. A few of us are inclined to do well out of way that are for war, and we have pushed for you to make peace with you. The Single Horn [a chief, probably Lone Horn or One Horn] went to the Missouri. I brought a chief of the Sans Arcs to you, and I want you to send word by him to the Sans Arcs when he goes away.

You are passing over the foolish acts of our young men, and we are pleased at that. Try to get all the Indians in and give them good advice and it will be all right. Push, push as hard as you can, and in that way you will take great pity on me. I want to live. It goes slow, and there are a great many Indians who are pushing for peace. Go slow yourselves and you will succeed. Get through with the Brulés at once. I want to go home. You will have plenty of Indians in and will have enough to do. You will hear pretty much the same from the different tribes of Indians as you have heard from me. Three moons is too long in which to move the forts. I would like them to be moved before. Winter will come before that time.

General Sanborn. The forts will be removed as soon as possible.

Iron Shell. Those forts are all that is in the way—wagons coming backward and forward. You have taken Spotted Tail away from me and have him to go around with you. That is good. I expect you will listen to him when he talks with you. You are right in bringing him here. There are a very few who are out yet. Often when you are persecuting me and the Indians with papers we do not get well thought of. I have one recommendation which I take good care of. I always talk to the whites in a good way and they generally listen to me. Today you tell us you will take pity on us. I have listened to it all. I will recollect all you have to say.

Our country is filling up with whites. Our great father has no sense; he lets our country be filled up. That is the way I think sometimes. Our great father is shutting up on us and making us a very small country. That is bad. For all that I have a strong heart. I have patience and pass over it, although you come over here and get all our gold, minerals, and skins. I pass over it all and do not get mad. I have always given the whites more than they have given me.

Yesterday you tell us we would have a council and last night I did not sleep; I was so glad. Now, I would like you to pick some good sensible young men, from one to four, and send them out, men who can be depended upon. I name Blue Horse, myself, and I want him to pick the others. We have been speaking very well together, and I am glad we get along so smoothly. The last thing I have to ask you about are the forts. This is sufficient and all right. We have got through talking. Give us our share of the goods and send them over to our village. We want to get back immediately as our children are crying for food. What you are doing with the Brulés will be a good example to the others. It will encourage them. We do not want to stay here and loaf upon you.

General Harney. We know very well that you have been treated very badly for years past. You have been cheated by everybody, and everybody has told lies to you, but now we want to commence anew. You have killed our people and have taken enough of our property and you ought to be satisfied. It is not the fault of your great father in Washington. He sends people out here that he thinks are honest, but they are people who cheat you and treat you badly. We will take care that you shall not be treated so any more. We will begin to move the forts as soon as possible. They will be removed as soon as the treaty is made with all the Indians. . . .

Iron Shell. I will always sign any treaty you ask me to do, but you have always made away with them, broke them. The whites always break them, and that is the way that war has come up.

(The treaty was here signed by the chiefs and head soldiers of the Brulés.)

2. Harper's Weekly Decries the Battle of Little Big Horn (1876)

As the white men closed in, the western Indians were forced to make numerous treaties with Washington that confined them to reservations and guaranteed needed supplies. But rascally government contractors cheated them with moldy flour, rotten beef, and moth-eaten blankets. In 1875 the discovery of gold on the Sioux reservation in the Dakotas brought stampeding thousands of miners, who brutally ignored treaty guarantees. The Indians fled the reservation (many had never agreed to live there in the first place), and the U.S. Army was sent to bring them back. The dashing General George Custer with only 264 men rashly attacked a hostile force that turned out to number several thousand. In 1876 Custer and his entire command were wiped out near the Little Big Horn River (Montana), in what the white men call a "massacre" and the Indians a "battle," and legend has long described as "Custer's last stand." What does this account in the reformist Harper's Weekly *see as the*

[2]*Harper's Weekly* 20 (August 5, 1876): 630–631.

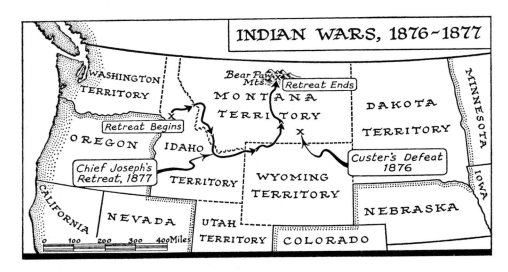

principal mistake in dealing with Native Americans? Who was basically responsible for the situation that had developed?

The fate of the brave and gallant Custer had deeply touched the public heart, which sees only a fearless soldier leading a charge against an ambushed [lurking] foe, and falling at the head of his men and in the thick of the fray. A monument is proposed, and subscriptions have been made. But a truer monument, more enduring than brass or marble, would be an Indian policy intelligent, moral, and efficient. Custer would not have fallen in vain if such a policy should be the result of his death.

It is a permanent accusation of our humanity and ability that over the Canadian line the relations between Indians and whites are so tranquil, while upon our side they are summed up in perpetual treachery, waste, and war. When he was a young lieutenant on the frontier, General Grant saw this, and watching attentively, he came to the conclusion that the reason of the difference was that the English respected the rights of the Indians and kept faith with them, while we make solemn treaties with them as if they were civilized and powerful nations, and then practically regard them as vermin to be exterminated.

The folly of making treaties with the Indian tribes may be as great as treating with a herd of buffaloes. But the infamy of violating treaties when we have made them is undeniable, and we are guilty both of the folly and the infamy.

We make treaties—that is, we pledge our faith—and then leave swindlers and knaves of all kinds to execute them. We maintain and breed pauper colonies. The savages, who know us, and who will neither be pauperized nor trust our word, we pursue, and slay if we can, at an incredible expense. The flower of our young officers is lost in inglorious forays, and one of the intelligent students of the whole subject rises in Congress and says, "The fact is that these Indians, with whom we have made a solemn treaty that their territory should not be invaded, and that they should receive supplies upon their reservations, have seen from one thousand to fifteen hundred [gold] miners during the present season entering and occupying their territory, while the Indians, owing to the failure of this and the last Congress to make adequate appropriations for their subsistence, instead of being fattened, as the gentleman says, by the support of this government, have simply been starved." . . .

It is plain that so long as we undertake to support the Indians as paupers, and then fail to supply the food; to respect their rights to reservations, and then permit the reservations to be overrun; to give them the best weapons and ammunition, and then furnish the pretense of their using them against us; to treat with them as men, and then hunt them like skunks—so long we shall have the most costly and bloody Indian wars, and the most tragical ambuscades, slaughters, and assassinations.

The Indian is undoubtedly a savage, and a savage greatly spoiled by the kind of contact with civilization which he gets at the West. There is no romance, there is generally no interest whatever, in him or his fate. But there should be some interest in our own good faith and humanity, in the lives of our soldiers and frontier settlers, and in the taxation to support our Indian policy. All this should certainly be enough to arouse a public demand for a thorough consideration of the subject, and the adoption of a system which should neither be puerile nor disgraceful, and which would tend to spare us the constant repetition of such sorrowful events as the slaughter of Custer and his brave men.

3. She Walks with Her Shawl Remembers the Battle of the Little Big Horn (1876)

The Indian encampment that Custer attacked on June 25, 1876, composed one of the largest gatherings of Indians ever to assemble on the Great Plains—including Hunkpapas, Oglalas, Minneconjous, Brulés, Blackfeet, Two Kettles, Sans Arcs, and Northern Cheyennes, among others. She Walks with Her Shawl was a young Hunkpapa woman who witnessed the Battle of Little Big Horn and gave the following account to an interviewer fifty-five years later, in 1931. In what ways might the Indians' account of the battle have differed from the whites' account? How reliable is testimony that has been filtered through more than a half-century of memory?

I was born seventy-seven winters ago, near Grand River, [in present] South Dakota. My father, Slohan, was the bravest man among our people. Fifty-five years ago we packed our tents and went with other Indians to Peji-sla-wakpa (Greasy Grass). We were then living on the Standing Rock Indian reservation [Great Sioux Reservation, Standing Rock Agency]. I belonged to Sitting Bull's band. They were great fighters. We called ourselves Hunkpapa. This means confederated bands. When I was still a young girl (about seventeen) I accompanied a Sioux war party which made war against the Crow Indians in Montana. My father went to war 70 times. He was wounded nearly a dozen times.

But I am going to tell you of the greatest battle. This was a fight against Pehin-hanska (General Custer). I was several miles from the Hunkpapa camp when I saw a cloud of dust rise beyond a ridge of bluffs in the east. The morning was hot and

[3]From Jerome A. Greene, ed., *Lakota and Cheyenne: Indian Views of the Great Sioux Wars, 1876–1877,* 1994, pp. 42–46. Reprinted by permission of the University of Oklahoma Press.

sultry. Several of us Indian girls were digging wild turnips. I was then 23 years old. We girls looked towards the camp and saw a warrior ride swiftly, shouting that the soldiers were only a few miles away and that the women and children including old men should run for the hills in an opposite direction.

I dropped the pointed ash stick which I had used in digging turnips and ran towards my tipi. I saw my father running towards the horses. When I got to my tent, mother told me that news was brought to her that my brother had been killed by the soldiers. My brother had gone early that morning in search for a horse that strayed from our herd. In a few moments we saw soldiers on horseback on a bluff just across the Greasy Grass (Little Big Horn) river. I knew that there would be a battle because I saw warriors getting their horses and tomahawks.

I heard Hawkman shout, Ho-ka-he! Ho-ka-he! (Charge.) The soldiers began firing into our camp. Then they ceased firing. I saw my father preparing to go to battle. I sang a death song for my brother who had been killed.

My heart was bad. Revenge! Revenge! For my brother's death. I thought of the death of my young brother, One Hawk. Brown Eagle, my brother's companion on that morning had escaped and gave the alarm to the camp that the soldiers were coming. I ran to a nearby thicket and got my black horse. I painted my face with crimson and unbraided my black hair. I was mourning. I was a woman, but I was not afraid.

By this time the soldiers (Reno's men) were forming a battle line in the bottom about a half mile away. In another moment I heard a terrific volley of carbines. The bullets shattered the tipi poles. Women and children were running away from the gunfire. In the tumult I heard old men and women singing death songs for their warriors who were now ready to attack the soldiers. The chanting of death songs made me brave, although I was a woman. I saw a warrior adjusting his quiver and grasping his tomahawk. He started running towards his horse when he suddenly recoiled and dropped dead. He was killed near his tipi.

Warriors were given orders by Hawkman to mount their horses and follow the fringe of a forest and wait until commands were given to charge. The soldiers kept on firing. Some women were also killed. Horses and dogs too! The camp was in great commotion.

Father led my black horse up to me and I mounted. We galloped towards the soldiers. Other warriors joined in with us. When we were nearing the fringe of the woods an order was given by Hawkman to charge. Ho-ka-he! Ho-ka-he! Charge! Charge! The warriors were now near the soliders. The troopers were all on foot. They shot straight, because I saw our leader killed as he rode with his warriors.

The charge was so stubborn that the soldiers ran to their horses and, mounting them, rode swiftly towards the river. The Greasy Grass river was very deep. Their horses had to swim to get across. Some of the warriors rode into the water and tomahawked the soldiers. In the charge the Indians rode among the troopers and with tomahawks unhorsed several of them. The soldiers were very excited. Some of them shot into the air. The Indians chased the soldiers across the river and up over a bluff.

Then the warriors returned to the bottom where the first battle took place. We heard a commotion far down the valley. The warriors rode in a column of fives.

They sang a victory song. Someone said that another body of soldiers were attacking the lower end of the village. I heard afterwards that the soliders were under the command of Long Hair (Custer). With my father and other youthful warriors I rode in that direction.

We crossed the Greasy Grass below a beaver dam (the water is not so deep there) and came upon many horses. One soldier was holding the reins of eight or ten horses. An Indian waved his blanket and scared all the horses. They got away from the men (troopers). On the ridge just north of us I saw blue-clad men running up a ravine, firing as they ran.

The dust created from the stampeding horses and powder smoke made everything dark and black. Flashes from carbines could be seen. The valley was dense with powder smoke. I never heard such whooping and shouting. "There was never a better day to die," shouted Red Horse. In the battle I heard cries from troopers, but could not understand what they were saying. I do not speak English.

Long Hair's troopers were trapped in an enclosure. There were Indians everywhere. The Cheyennes attacked the soldiers from the north and Crow King from the South. The Sioux Indians encircled the troopers. Not one got away! The Sioux used tomahawks. It was not a massacre, but [a] hotly contested battle between two armed forces. Very few soldiers were mutilated, as oft has been said by the whites. Not a single soldier was burned at the stake. Sioux Indians do not torture their victims.

After the battle the Indians took all the equipment and horses belonging to the soldiers. The brave men who came to punish us that morning were defeated; but in the end, the Indians lost. We saw the body of Long Hair. Of course, we did not know who the soldiers were until an interpreter told us that the men came from Fort Lincoln, then [in] Dakota Territory. On the saddle blankets were the cross saber insignia and the letter seven.

The victorious warriors returned to the camp, as did the women and children who could see the battle from where they took refuge. Over sixty Indians were killed and they were also brought back to the camp for scaffold-burial.* The Indians did not stage a victory dance that night. They were mourning for their own dead. . . .

4. Chief Joseph's Lament (1879)

Chief Joseph, a noble-featured and humane Nez Percé (Pierced Nose) Indian, resisted being removed from his ancestral lands in Oregon and penned up on a reservation in Idaho. After an amazing flight of about a thousand miles, he was finally captured in 1877 near the Canadian border. The miserable remnants of his band were deported to Indian Territory (now Oklahoma), where many died of malaria and other afflictions. Chief Joseph appealed personally to the president, and subsequently the Nez Percés were returned to the Pacific Northwest. In the following narrative, what formula does he offer for ending white-Indian wars?

---

*Native Americans often buried their dead not in the ground, but by laying them out on aerial scaffoldings.

[4]*North American Review* 128 (April 1879): 431–432.

At last I was granted permission to come to Washington and bring my friend Yellow Bull and our interpreter with me. I am glad I came. I have shaken hands with a good many friends, but there are some things I want to know which no one seems able to explain. I cannot understand how the government sends a man out to fight us, as it did General Miles, and then breaks his word. Such a government has something wrong about it. . . .

I have heard talk and talk, but nothing is done. Good words do not last long unless they amount to something. Words do not pay for my dead people. They do not pay for my country, now overrun by white men. They do not protect my father's grave. They do not pay for my horses and cattle.

Good words do not give me back my children. Good words will not make good the promise of your war chief, General Miles. Good words will not give my people good health and stop them from dying. Good words will not get my people a home where they can live in peace and take care of themselves.

I am tired of talk that comes to nothing. It makes my heart sick when I remember all the good words and all the broken promises. There has been too much talking by men who had no right to talk. Too many misinterpretations have been made; too many misunderstandings have come up between the white men and the Indians.

If the white man wants to live in peace with the Indian, he can live in peace. There need be no trouble. Treat all men alike. Give them the same laws. Give them all an even chance to live and grow.

All men are made by the same Great Spirit Chief. They are all brothers. The earth is the mother of all people, and all people should have equal rights upon it. You might as well expect all rivers to run backward as that any man who was born a free man should be contented penned up and denied liberty to go where he pleases. If you tie a horse to a stake, do you expect he will grow fat? If you pen an Indian up on a small spot of earth and compel him to stay there, he will not be contented nor will he grow and prosper.

I have asked some of the Great White Chiefs where they get their authority to say to the Indian that he shall stay in one place, while he sees white men going where they please. They cannot tell me.

I only ask of the government to be treated as all other men are treated. If I cannot go to my own home, let me have a home in a country where my people will not die so fast. I would like to go to Bitter Root Valley [western Montana]. There my people would be healthy; where they are now, they are dying. Three have died since I left my camp to come to Washington. When I think of our condition, my heart is heavy. I see men of my own race treated as outlaws and driven from country to country, or shot down like animals.

I know that my race must change. We cannot hold our own with the white men as we are. We only ask an even chance to live as other men live. We ask to be recognized as men. We ask that the same law shall work alike on all men. If an Indian breaks the law, punish him by the law. If a white man breaks the law, punish him also.

Let me be a free man—free to travel, free to stop, free to work, free to trade where I choose, free to choose my own teachers, free to follow the religion of my fathers, free to think and talk and act for myself—and I will obey every law or submit to the penalty.

Whenever the white man treats the Indian as they treat each other, then we shall have no more wars. We shall all be alike—brothers of one father and mother, with one sky above us and one country around us and one government for all. Then the Great Spirit Chief who rules above will smile upon this land and send rain to wash out the bloody spots made by brothers' hands upon the face of the earth. For this time the Indian race are waiting and praying. I hope no more groans of wounded men and women will ever go to the ear of the Great Spirit Chief above, and that all people may be one people.

5. Theodore Roosevelt Downgrades the Indians (1885)

Sickly and bespectacled young Theodore Roosevelt, the future president, invested more than $50,000 of his patrimony in ranch lands in Dakota Territory. He lost most of his investment but gained robust health and valuable experience. With little sympathy for Native Americans, he felt that the government had "erred quite as often on the side of too much leniency as on the side of too much severity." The following account, based in part on firsthand observations, appears in one of his earliest books. What light do his observations cast on the allegation that whites robbed Native Americans of their lands? What is his proposed solution to the problem?

There are now no Indians left in my immediate neighborhood, though a small party of harmless Grosventres occasionally passes through. Yet it is but six years since the Sioux surprised and killed five men in a log station just south of me, where the Fort Keogh trail crosses the river; and, two years ago, when I went down on the prairies toward the Black Hills, there was still danger from Indians. That summer the buffalo hunters had killed a couple of Crows, and while we were on the prairie a long-range skirmish occurred near us between some Cheyennes and a number of cowboys. In fact, we ourselves were one day scared by what we thought to be a party of Sioux; but on riding toward them they proved to be half-breed Crees, who were more afraid of us than we were of them.

During the past century a good deal of sentimental nonsense has been talked about our taking the Indians' land. Now, I do not mean to say for a moment that gross wrong has not been done the Indians, both by government and individuals, again and again. The government makes promises impossible to perform, and then fails to do even what it might toward their fulfilment; and where brutal and reckless frontiersmen are brought into contact with a set of treacherous, revengeful, and fiendishly cruel savages a long series of outrages by both sides is sure to follow.

But as regards taking the land, at least from the Western Indians, the simple truth is that the latter never had any real ownership in it at all. Where the game was plenty, there they hunted; they followed it when it moved away to new hunting-

---

[5]Theodore Roosevelt, *Hunting Trips of a Ranchman* (New York: G. P. Putnam's Sons, 1885), pp. 17–19.

grounds, unless they were prevented by stronger rivals; and to most of the land on which we found them they had no stronger claim than that of having a few years previously butchered the original occupants.

When my cattle came to the Little Missouri the region was only inhabited by a score or so of white hunters; their title to it was quite as good as that of most Indian tribes to the lands they claim; yet nobody dreamed of saying that these hunters owned the country. Each could eventually have kept his own claim of 160 acres, and no more.

The Indians should be treated in just the same way that we treat the white settlers. Give each his little claim; if, as would generally happen, he declined this, why then let him share the fate of the thousands of white hunters and trappers who have lived on the game that the settlement of the country has exterminated, and let him, like these whites, who will not work, perish from the face of the earth which he cumbers.*

The doctrine seems merciless, and so it is; but it is just and rational for all that. It does not do to be merciful to a few, at the cost of justice to the many. The cattlemen at least keep herds and build houses on the land; yet I would not for a moment debar settlers from the right of entry to the cattle country, though their coming in means in the end the destruction of us and our industry.

6. Carl Schurz Proposes to "Civilize" the Indians (1881)

Carl Schurz, a notable "forty-eighter," or liberal refugee from the failed German revolution of 1848, had a prominent military career on the Union side in the Civil War and in 1877 became secretary of the interior. A lifelong reformer, he fought against slavery and political corruption and considered himself a friend to the Indians. What is his preferred solution to the "Indian problem"? Is he condescending to Native Americans or simply realistic? In what ways do his comments reveal attitudes about gender roles in nineteenth-century America?

. . . I am profoundly convinced that a stubborn maintenance of the system of large Indian reservations must eventually result in the destruction of the red men, however faithfully the Government may endeavor to protect their rights. It is only a question of time. . . . What we can and should do is, in general terms, to fit the Indians, as much as possible, for the habits and occupations of civilized life, by work and education; to individualize them in the possession and appreciation of property, by allotting to them lands in severalty, giving them a fee simple title individually to the parcels of land they cultivate, inalienable for a certain period, and to obtain their consent to a disposition of that part of their lands which they cannot use, for a fair

---

*In the Dawes Act of 1887, Congress made provision for granting the Indians individual allotments, as Roosevelt here suggests.

[6]Carl Schurz, "Present Aspects of the Indian Problem," *North American Review* 133 (July 1881), pp. 6–10, 12–14, 16–18, 20–24.

compensation, in such a manner that they no longer stand in the way of the development of the country as an obstacle, but from part of it and are benefited by it.

The circumstances surrounding them place before the Indians this stern alternative: extermination or civilization. The thought of exterminating a race, once the only occupant of the soil upon which so many millions of our own people have grown prosperous and happy, must be revolting to every American who is not devoid of all sentiments of justice and humanity. To civilize them, which was once only a benevolent fancy, has now become an absolute necessity, if we mean to save them.

Can Indians be civilized? This question is answered in the negative only by those who do not want to civilize them. My experience in the management of Indian affairs, which enabled me to witness the progress made even among the wildest tribes, confirms me in the belief that it is not only possible but easy to introduce civilized habits and occupations among Indians, if only the proper means are employed. We are frequently told that Indians will not work. True, it is difficult to make them work as long as they can live upon hunting. But they will work when their living depends upon it, or when sufficient inducements are offered to them. Of this there is an abundance of proof. To be sure, as to Indian civilization, we must not expect too rapid progress or the attainment of too lofty a standard. We can certainly not transform them at once into great statesmen, or philosophers, or manufacturers, or merchants; but we can make them small farmers and herders. Some of them show even remarkable aptitude for mercantile pursuits on a small scale. I see no reason why the degree of civilization attained by the Indians in the States of New York, Indiana, Michigan, and some tribes in the Indian Territory, should not be attained in the course of time by all. I have no doubt that they can be sufficiently civilized to support themselves, to maintain relations of good neighborship with the people surrounding them, and altogether to cease being a disturbing element in society. The accomplishment of this end, however, will require much considerate care and wise guidance. That care and guidance is necessarily the task of the Government which, as to the Indians at least, must exercise paternal functions until they are sufficiently advanced to take care of themselves. . . .

. . . The failure of Sitting Bull's attempt to maintain himself and a large number of followers on our northern frontier in the old wild ways of Indian life will undoubtedly strengthen the tendency among the wild Indians of the North-west to recognize the situation and to act accordingly. The general state of feeling among the red men is therefore now exceedingly favorable to the civilizing process. . . .

The Indian, in order to be civilized, must not only learn how to read and write, but how to live. . . . Such considerations led the Government, under the last administration, largely to increase the number of Indian pupils at the Normal School at Hampton, Va., and to establish an institution for the education of Indian children at Carlisle, in Pennsylvania, where the young Indians would no longer be under the influence of the Indian camp or village, but in immediate contact with the towns, farms, and factories of civilized people, living and working in the atmosphere of civilization. In these institutions, the Indian children, among whom a large number of tribes are represented, receive the ordinary English education, while there are various shops and a farm for the instruction of the boys, and the girls are kept busy in the kitchen, dining-room, sewing-room, and with other domestic work. In the summer, as many as possible of the boys are placed in the care of intelligent and philanthropic farmers and their families, mostly in Pennsylvania and New England, where they find instructive employment in the field and barn-yard. The pupils are, under proper regulations, permitted to see as much as possible of the country and its inhabitants in the vicinity of the schools. . . .

Especial attention is given in the Indian schools to the education of Indian girls, and at Hampton a new building is being erected for that purpose. This is of peculiar importance. The Indian woman has so far been only a beast of burden. The girl, when arrived at maturity, was disposed of like an article of trade. The Indian wife was treated by her husband alternately with animal fondness, and with the cruel brutality of the slave-driver. Nothing will be more apt to raise the Indians in the scale of civilization than to stimulate their attachment to permanent homes, and it is woman that must make the atmosphere and form the attraction of the home. She must be recognized, with affection and respect, as the center of domestic life. If we want the Indians to respect their women, we must lift up the Indian women to respect themselves. This is the purpose and work of education. If we educate the girls of to-day, we educate the mothers of to-morrow, and in educating those mothers we prepare the ground for the education of generations to come. Every effort made in that direction is, therefore, entitled to especial sympathy and encouragement. . . .

As the third thing necessary for the absorption of the Indians in the great body of American citizenship, I mentioned their individualization in the possession of property by their settlement in severalty upon small farm tracts with a fee simple title. When the Indians are so settled, and have become individual property-owners, holding their farms by the same title under the law by which white men hold theirs, they will feel more readily inclined to part with such of their lands as they cannot themselves cultivate, and from which they can derive profit only if they sell them, either in lots or in bulk, for a fair equivalent in money or in annuities. This done, the Indians will occupy no more ground than so many white people; the large reservations will gradually be opened to general settlement and enterprise, and the Indians, with their possessions, will cease to stand in the way of the "development of the country." The difficulty which has provoked so many encroachments and conflicts will then no longer exist. When the Indians are individual owners of real property, and as individuals enjoy the protection of the laws, their tribal cohesion will necessarily relax, and gradually disappear. They will have advanced an immense step in the direction of the "white man's way." . . .

7. A Native American Tries to Walk the White Man's Road (1890s)

From 1883 to 1890, Sun Elk, a Taos Indian, attended the Carlisle Indian School in Pennsylvania, where he learned typesetting. In the following passage, he describes his return to his pueblo in New Mexico. Did his Carlisle education prove beneficial

---

[7]From Edwin R. Embree, *Indians of the Americas.* Copyright © 1939 by Houghton Mifflin Company. Used by permission.

for him? In what ways does his experience suggest the limitations of the reformers' efforts to "civilize" Native Americans?

When I was about thirteen years old I went down to St. Michael's Catholic School. Other boys were joining the societies and spending their time in the kivas [sacred ceremonial chambers] being purified and learning the secrets. But I wanted to learn the white man's secrets. I thought he had better magic than the Indian. . . . So I drifted a little away from the pueblo life. My father was sad but he was not angry. He wanted me to be a good Indian like all the other boys, but he was willing for me to go to school. He thought I would soon stop. There was plenty of time to go into the kiva.

Then at the first snow one winter . . . a white man—what you call an Indian Agent—came and took all of us who were in that school far off on a train to a new kind of village called Carlisle Indian School, and I stayed there seven years. . . .

Seven years I was there. I set little letters together in the printing shop and we printed papers. For the rest we had lessons. There were games, but I was too slight for foot and hand plays, and there were no horses to ride. I learned to talk English and to read. There was much arithmetic. It was lessons: how to add and take away, and much strange business like you have crossword puzzles only with numbers. The teachers were very solemn and made a great fuss if we did not get the puzzles right.

There was something called Greatest Common Denominator. I remember the name but I never knew it—what it meant. When the teachers asked me I would guess, but I always guessed wrong. We studied little things—fractions. I remember that word too. It is like one half of an apple. And there were immoral fractions. . . .

They told us that Indian ways were bad. They said we must get civilized. I remember that word too. It means "be like the white man." I am willing to be like the white man, but I did not believe Indian ways were wrong. But they kept teaching us for seven years. And the books told how bad the Indians had been to the white men—burning their towns and killing their women and children. But I had seen white men do that to Indians. We all wore white man's clothes and ate white man's food and went to white man's churches and spoke white man's talk. And so after a while we also began to say Indians were bad. We laughed at our own people and their blankets and cooking pots and sacred societies and dances. I tried to learn the lessons—and after seven years I came home. . . .

It was a warm summer evening when I got off the train at Taos station. The first Indian I met, I asked him to run out to the pueblo and tell my family I was home. The Indian couldn't speak English, and I had forgotten all my Pueblo language. But after a while he learned what I meant and started running to tell my father "Tulto is back. . . ."

I went home with my family. And next morning the governor of the pueblo and the two war chiefs and many of the priest chiefs came into my father's house. They did not talk to me; they did not even look at me. When they were all assembled they talked to my father.

The chiefs said to my father, "Your son who calls himself Rafael has lived with the white men. He has been far away from the pueblo. He has not lived in the kiva nor learned the things that Indian boys should learn. He has no hair. He has no blankets. He cannot even speak our language and he has a strange smell. He is not one of us."

The chiefs got up and walked out. My father was very sad. I wanted him to be angry, but he was only sad. So I would not be sad and was very angry instead.

And I walked out of my father's house and out of the pueblo. I did not speak. My mother was in the other room cooking. She stayed in the other room but she made much noise rattling her pots. Some children were on the plaza and they stared at me, keeping very still as I walked away.

I walked until I came to the white man's town, Fernandez de Taos. I found work setting type in a printing shop there. Later I went to Durango and other towns in Wyoming and Colorado, printing and making a good living. But this indoor work was bad for me. It made me slight of health. So then I went outside to the fields. I worked in some blacksmith shops and on farms.

All this time I was a white man. I wore white man's clothes and kept my hair cut. I was not very happy. I made money and I kept a little of it and after many years I came back to Taos.

My father gave me some land from the pueblo fields. He could do this because now the land did not belong to all the people, as it did in the old days; the white man had cut it up and given it in little pieces to each family, so my father gave me a part of his, and I took my money and bought some more land and some cattle. I built a house just outside the pueblo. I would not live in the pueblo so I built outside a house bigger than the pueblo houses all for myself.

My father brought me a girl to marry. Her name was Roberta. Her Indian name was P'ah-tah-zhuli (little deer bean). She was about fifteen years old and she had no father. But she was a good girl and she came to live with me in my new house outside the pueblo.

When we were married I became an Indian again. I let my hair grow, I put on blankets, and I cut the seat out of my pants.

B. The Crusade for Free Homesteads

1. "Vote Yourself a Farm" (1846)

Free homesteads from the public domain found a powerful champion in George H. Evans, an immigrant from England who became a pioneer editor of U.S. labor journals. A confirmed atheist, he was preoccupied with "natural rights" to the soil. He hoped particularly to increase the wages of eastern laborers by luring surplus workers onto free lands in the West. On what grounds does he base the following appeal?

Are you an American citizen? Then you are a joint-owner of the public lands. Why not take enough of your property to provide yourself a home? Why not vote yourself a farm?*

---

[1]J. R. Commons et al., eds., *A Documentary History of American Industrial Society,* vol. 7 (Cleveland: Arthur H. Clarke Company, 1910), pp. 305–307.

*"Vote Yourself a Farm" was a Republican slogan in the Lincoln campaign of 1860.

Remember Poor Richard's saying: "Now I have a sheep and a cow, every one bids me 'good morrow.'" If a man have a house and a home of his own, though it be a thousand miles off, he is well received in other people's houses; while the homeless wretch is turned away. The bare right to a farm, though you should never go near it, would save you from many an insult. Therefore, Vote yourself a farm.

Are you a party follower? Then you have long enough employed your vote to benefit scheming office-seekers; use it for once to benefit yourself—Vote yourself a farm.

Are you tired of slavery—of drudging for others—of poverty and its attendant miseries? Then, Vote yourself a farm.

Are you endowed with reason? Then you must know that your right to life hereby includes the right to a place to live in—the right to a home. Assert this right, so long denied mankind by feudal robbers and their attorneys. Vote yourself a farm.

Are you a believer in the Scriptures? Then assert that the land is the Lord's, because He made it. Resist then the blasphemers who exact money for His work, even as you would resist them should they claim to be worshiped for His holiness. Emancipate the poor from the necessity of encouraging such blasphemy—Vote the freedom of the public lands.

Are you a man? Then assert the sacred rights of man—especially your right to stand upon God's earth, and to till it for your own profit. Vote yourself a farm.

Would you free your country, and the sons of toil everywhere, from the heartless, irresponsible mastery of the aristocracy of avarice? Would you disarm this aristocracy of its chief weapon, the fearful power of banishment from God's earth? . . . Therefore forget not to Vote yourself a farm.

2. A Texan Scorns Futile Charity (1852)

Agitation for free land continued to mount, and a homestead bill was introduced in Congress designed to donate 160 acres of land to every landless head of a family needing it. Easterners objected that this was a giveaway scheme to benefit a few new western states at the expense of the old states. It would drain off factory workers and hence push up wages and jeopardize prosperity. Critics further argued that the public domain, which was then being sold to replenish the Treasury, was the property of all the taxpayers and should not be given away to a favored few. Congressman Volney E. Howard of Texas aired additional objections in Congress. What light do his remarks cast on the safety-valve theory—that is, that impoverished eastern families could reduce economic distress and relieve class conflict by moving west and taking up cheap land?*

But, sir, I deny the constitutional power of Congress to grant away the public property in donations to the poor. This government is not a national almshouse. We

---

[2]*Congressional Globe,* 32d Cong., 1st sess., Appendix, pp. 583–584.

*The safety-valve theory, popularly attributed to the historian Frederick J. Turner, antedated him by many years. As early as 1843 a British journal referred to "the safety-valve of western emigration" in America (*Quarterly Review* 71:522). Only a few eastern mechanics moved to the West, but many incoming immigrants were attracted there who otherwise would have further congested the seaboard cities.

have no right to collect money by taxation and then divide the proceeds among the people generally, or those who are destitute of land, food, or raiment. . . .

There is no sound distinction between giving money by direct appropriations from the Treasury, and land, in the purchase of which [e.g., the Louisiana Purchase] that money has been invested. It is no more the property of the nation in one case than in the other, nor less an appropriation. What right have we to tax the property and industry of all classes of society to purchase homesteads, and enrich those who may not be the possessors of the soil? . . .

It is a great mistake to suppose that you will materially better the condition of the man in the old states, or the Atlantic cities, by giving him 160 acres of land in the Far West. The difficulty with him is not that of procuring the land, but to emigrate himself and family to the country where it is, and to obtain the means of cultivating it. Without this the grant is useless to the poor man.

The gift, to make it efficient, should be followed up by a further donation to enable the beneficiary to stock and cultivate it. It would be a far greater boon to all our citizens, of native and foreign origin, to furnish them, for a few dollars, a rapid means of reaching the land states in the West; and this, in my opinion, may be accomplished by exercising the legitimate powers of the government, and without drawing upon the Treasury, or diminishing the value of the public domain as a source of revenue.

3. President James Buchanan Kills a Homestead Bill (1860)

Free-soilers continued to argue that settlers not only had a "natural right" to western land but that they should receive it as recompense for their own expense and sweat in taming the wilderness. In the 1850s homestead bills thrice passed the House, where the North was dominant, but all met defeat in the Senate, where the South was entrenched. Senator Benjamin F. Wade of Ohio cried inelegantly in 1859 that it was "a question of land to the landless," whereas the southern-sponsored bill to buy Cuba was "a question of niggers to the niggerless." Finally, in 1860, a compromise measure staggered through both houses of Congress. It granted 160 acres of land to bona-fide settlers who would pay the nominal sum of twenty-five cents an acre at the end of five years. President Buchanan, a Pennsylvanian under southern influence, vetoed the measure. Comment critically on his views regarding unfairness to non-farmers and to the older states. Was he correct in arguing that such a law would undermine the nation's moral fiber?

. . . 4. This bill will prove unequal and unjust in its operation, because from its nature it is confined to one class of our people. It is a boon exclusively conferred upon the cultivators of the soil. Whilst it is cheerfully admitted that these are the most numerous and useful class of our fellow citizens, and eminently deserve all the advantages which our laws have already extended to them, yet there should be no new legislation which would operate to the injury or embarrassment of the large

---

[3]J. D. Richardson, ed., *Messages and Papers of the Presidents* (New York: Bureau of National Literature, 1897), vol. 5, pp. 611–614, passim.

body of respectable artisans and laborers. The mechanic who emigrates to the West and pursues his calling must labor long before he can purchase a quarter section of land, whilst the tiller of the soil obtains a farm at once by the bounty of the government. The numerous body of mechanics in our large cities cannot, even by emigrating to the West, take advantage of the provisions of this bill without entering upon a new occupation for which their habits of life have rendered them unfit.

5. This bill is unjust to the old states of the Union in many respects; and amongst these states, so far as the public lands are concerned, we may enumerate every state east of the Mississippi, with the exception of Wisconsin and a portion of Minnesota.

It is a common belief within their limits that the older states of the confederacy [Union] do not derive their proportionate benefit from the public lands. This is not just opinion. It is doubtful whether they could be rendered more beneficial to these states under any other system than that which at present exists. Their proceeds go into the common Treasury to accomplish the objects of the government, and in this manner all of the states are benefited in just proportion. But to give this common inheritance away would deprive the old states of their just proportion of this revenue without holding out any, the least, corresponding advantage. Whilst it is our common glory that the new states have become so prosperous and populous, there is no good reason why the old states should offer premiums to their own citizens to emigrate from them to the West. That land of promise presents in itself sufficient allurements to our young and enterprising citizens without any adventitious aid.

The offer of free farms would probably have a powerful effect in encouraging emigration, especially from states like Illinois, Tennessee, and Kentucky, to the west of the Mississippi, and could not fail to reduce the price of property within their limits. An individual in states thus situated would not pay its fair value for land when, by crossing the Mississippi, he could go upon the public lands and obtain a farm almost without money and without price.

6. This bill will open one vast field for speculation. . . . Large numbers of actual settlers will be carried out by capitalists upon agreements to give them half of the land for the improvement of the other half. This cannot be avoided. Secret agreements of this kind will be numerous.* In the entry of graduated lands the experience of the Land Office justifies this objection. . . .

10. The honest poor man, by frugality and industry, can in any part of our country acquire a competence for himself and his family, and in doing this he feels that he eats the bread of independence. He desires no charity, either from the government or from his neighbors. This bill, which proposes to give him land at an almost nominal price out of the property of the government, will go far to demoralize the people and repress this noble spirit of independence. It may introduce among us those pernicious social theories which have proved so disastrous in other countries.

---

*Buchanan was right. Under the Homestead Act as finally passed, about ten acres were secured by speculators for every acre secured by a bona-fide settler.

C. Life on the Frontier

1. Westward the Course of Empire Takes Its Way (1868)

Images of the western American frontier flooded popular magazines and newspapers in the East (and in Europe) in the mid-nineteenth century. The 1868 print below, by Francis F. Palmer, entitled Across the Continent: "Westward the Course of Empire Takes Its Way," *presents a typical figurative rendering of the frontier, an allegorical scene in which "civilization" meets the wilderness. How does the artist portray the contrast between the East and the West? Which visual elements signify "civilization," and which signify "wilderness"? What role do the Indians play in this image? What awaits settlers in the West? What are they bringing with them?*

ACROSS   THE   CONTINENT.
"WESTWARD THE COURSE OF EMPIRE TAKES ITS WAY."

---

[1]Francis F. Palmer, *Across the Continent: "Westward the Course of Empire Takes Its Way."* Museum of the City of New York, 56.300.107, The Harry T. Peters Collection.

2. A Pioneer Woman Describes the Overland Trail (1862)

Thousands of men, women, and children trekked into the trans-Mississippi West in the nineteenth century. In this description of the overland crossing to California in 1862, what appear to be the greatest hardships the pioneers faced? What is the writer's attitude toward Indians? What might have motivated the Indians to act as they did? Was white settlement compatible with Indian life? Was there a missed opportunity for a different kind of relationship between white settlers and Native Americans?

Monday, July 28 . . . Came past a camp of thirty six wagons who have been camped for some time here in the mountains. They have had their cattle stampeded four or five times. There was a woman died in this train yesterday. She left six children, one of them only two days old. Poor little thing, it had better have died with its mother. They made a good picket fence around the grave. . . .

Sunday, August 3 . . . We passed by the train I have just spoken of. They had just buried the babe of the woman who died days ago, and were just digging a grave for another woman that was run over by the cattle and wagons when they stampeded yesterday. She lived twenty-four hours, she gave birth to a child a short time before she died. The child was buried with her. She leaves a little two year old girl and a husband. They say he is nearly crazy with sorrow. . . .

Tuesday, August 5 . . . Did not start very early. Waited for a train to pass. It seems today as if I *must* go to home to fathers to see them all. I can't wait another minute. If I could only *hear* from them it would do some good, but I suppose I shall have to wait whether I am patient or not. . . .

Sunday, August 10   Traveled five or six miles when we came to Snake River. We stayed till two o'clock then traveled till about four or five, when *we* from the back end of the train saw those on ahead all get out their guns. In a short time the word came back that a train six miles on had been attacked by the Indians, and some killed and that was cause enough for the arming. In a short time were met by two men. They wanted us to go a short distance from the road and bring two dead men to their camp, five miles ahead.

Albert unloaded his little wagon and sent Gus back with them and about forty armed men from both trains, to get them. We learned that a train of eleven wagons had been plundered of all that was in them and the teams taken and the men killed. One was Mr. Bullwinkle who left us the 25th of last month, at the crossing of Green River. He went on with this Adams train. Was intending to wait for us but we had not overtaken him yet. He was shot eight times. His dog was shot four times before he would let them get to the wagon. They took all that he had in his wagon, except his trunks and books and papers. They broke open his trunks and took all that they

---

[2]From *The Diary of Jane Gould Torillott, (Journey from Mitchel Co., Iowa to California by Land)*, as in Lillian Schlissel, ed., *Women's Diaries of the Westward Journey*, 1982, pp. 222–225.

contained. (He had six.) It is supposed that they took six thousand dollars from him, tore the cover from his wagon, it was oilcloth. He had four choice horses. They ran away when he was shot, the harnesses were found on the trail where it was cut from them when they went. It was a nice silver one. The Captain had a daughter shot and wounded severely. This happened yesterday. This morning a part of their train and a part of the Kennedy train went in pursuit of the stock. They were surrounded by Indians on ponies, two killed, several wounded and two supposed to be killed. They were never found. One of those killed was Capt. Adams' son, the other was a young man in the Kennedy train. Those that we carried to camp were those killed this morning. Mr. Bullwinkle and two others were buried before we got to the camp. There were one hundred and fifty wagons there and thirty four of ours. Capt. Kennedy was severely wounded. Capt. Hunter of Iowa City train was killed likewise by an Indian. We camped near Snake River. We could not get George to ride after the news, he *would* walk and carry his loaded pistol to help.

Monday, August 11 . . . The two men we brought up were buried early this morning with the other three, so they laid five men side by side in this vast wilderness, killed by guns and arrows of the red demons. The chief appeared yesterday in a suit of Mr. Bullwinkle's on the battlefield. . . .

Tuesday, August 12   Capt. Adams' daughter died this morning from the effects of her wound. Was buried in a box made of a wagon box. Poor father and mother lost one son and one daughter, all of his teams, clothing and four thousand dollars. Is left dependent on the bounty of strangers. . . . In the evening we took in Mrs. Ellen Ives, one of the ladies of the plundered train. Her husband goes in the wagon just ahead of us. She was married the morning she started for California. Not a very pleasant wedding tour. . . .

Thursday, August 13 . . . After going up the canyon about four miles, we came to a wagon that had been stopped. There was a new harness, or parts of one, some collars and close by we saw the bodies of three dead men, top of the ground. They had been dead two or three weeks. Some one had been along and thrown a little earth over them, but they were mostly uncovered again. One had his head and face out, another his legs, a third, his hands and arms. Oh! it is a horrid thing. I wish all of the Indians in Christendom were exterminated. . . .

Friday, August 15   We were aroused this morning at one o'clock by the firing of guns and yelling of Indians, answered by our men. The Capt. calling, "come on you red devils." It did not take us long to dress, for once. I hurried for the children and had them dress and get into our wagon, put up a mattress and some beds and quilts on the exposed side of the wagon to protect us. The firing was from the willows and from the mouth of the corrall. There were two other trains with us. There are one hundred and eleven wagons of all and two hundred or more men. The firing did not continue long nor do any harm. Our men shot a good many balls into the willows but I presume they were not effectual. We sat and watched and waited till morning. Yoked the cattle and turned them out with a heavy guard and several scouts to clear the bushes. Cooked our breakfast and started. There were ball holes through two or three wagon covers. . . . We nooned in a little valley but kept our eyes open to all that might be hidden in the bushes and behind the rocks. . . .

3. Opening Montana (1867)

Elizabeth Chester Fisk, born in 1846 in Connecticut, was among the first white women to settle in Montana, and in her letters to her New England family, she chronicled its early growth with a sharp but sympathetic eye. What did she find to be the most appealing aspects of life in the rugged frontier town of Helena? What did she miss most about her native Connecticut? What were the raw new community's greatest problems?

Helena, Montana, July [21], 1867

My dear Mother:

Our steamer reached Fort Benton on the afternoon of Sunday last. We came into port amid the firing of cannon and shouts of the people assembled on shore. We had been long and anxiously expected and many fears entertained concerning our safety. Our passengers were more delighted than words can express to know that their long "Misery" was at an end. . . .

Fort Benton was a pleasanter town than I expected to see and wore an air of life and animation. The ox and mule teams awaited their loads of freight were drawn up on the river banks, while further back, on the broad plain on which the town is built, were hundreds of cattle and mules feeding on the rich grass. . . . Our route lay over the most beautiful prairie, a level natural highway. At evening we came to Sun River where we were delayed four hours waiting for the coach from Helena. . . . While our coach stopped to change horses, I stretched myself out on the seat and took a little nap, awoke thoroughly chilled and entering the little cabin warmed myself by the fire and drank a cup of hot tea. Soon we came to the crossing of the Dearborn, and forded the stream and rushed on our way as before. The rain was falling fast and at every steep hill our gentleman passengers (I was the only lady) were obliged to unload and walk up the mountain side. They were wet to the skin and a more dismal looking party could not have been found. . . .

I am much pleased with this country, and can already think of it as home. We passed through Prickly Pear Canyon on our way from Benton. Here is some of the most beautiful scenery in the world. The loftiest mountains, their peaks covered with snow, towered above our heads, while in the valley were the most lovely wild flowers in bloom—roses . . . blue bells, and many other of whose names I cannot tell. The mountains rise all about our home, their sides sometimes covered with pine and cedar and again only with the green grass. The snow still lingers on

[3]© Rex C. Myers, ed., *Lizzie: The Letters of Elizabeth Chester Fisk, 1864–1893.* 1989, Missoula, Montana: Mountain Press Publishing Company. Reprinted by permission.

the tallest peaks and the wind is cold and wintery which sweeps down from their sides. . . .

Helena, Sept. 2nd/67

My dear Fannie:

[F]or two weeks I have been enjoying your most troublesome complaint, diarrhea. . . . [M]edicine seemed to have no effect unless I entriely abstained from food. . . . But I am well again now, which is to be chiefly attributed to the exercise I have taken, both out and in doors, not less than to food better adapted to an invalid. . . .

I made bread on Saturday and would like to send you a piece; it is very nice. Fabricated some pie, too, after my most approved style and sent some to the office hoping to get [an editorial] puff, but it doth not appear. Can you credit my words when I tell you that, in this country where milk well watered is one dollar per gallon, and eggs one dollar and a half per dozen, I made cream pies. And today, I have been guilty of the further extravagance of cooking for supper a spring chicken for which I paid only $1.25 in [gold] dust. Such is the fact, and not a bone is left to tell the tail, but we had visitors at tea, Stuart and Jackey, and we don't have chickens every day.

Today has been election, the day so long [and] anxiously awaited and on which events so much depends. We can as yet have no idea of the result, but can only hope that our territory will have no such delegate in Congress as James M. Cavanaugh.

The day has been one of much interest yet in this city it passed off very quietly. Had it not been for an event which occurred late in the day we might have been proud of the manner in which our citizens conducted themselves. The negroes of course voted and this raised some disaffection among the rebels. Late in the afternoon an Irishman shot a negro without the slightest provocation and for no reason at all, unless it were the color of his skin. The colored man cannot live it is thought, and the son of Erin will without doubt be hung, with little delay and not much of a trial. The Vigilantes keep things in order here, and I truly believe there is less of crime in this city than in any town east, of the same number of inhabitants. This I consider high praise, remembering the elements of which society is in a great measure composed. . . .

What would you think of a town with no grass, no trees, no flowers, only dust and stone in the streets and yards. Such is our town. . . . Nothing grows here without irrigation. This however might easily be accomplished since ditches run through all the principal streets. I intended making a garden another year. Send along the seeds please, both flower and vegetable, as soon as you gather them and they will be in season. . . .

Your sister
Lizzie

Helena, May 24th, 1868

My dear Mother:

. . . I sent you a long letter by Tuesday's mail, but as news has just come to us that the eastward-bound coach was robbed yesterday, near Pleasant Valley [Idaho], I deem it possible that this letter of mine may have been one of those torn up by the desperadoes, and cast to the winds. We seem to be living over again and the early days in the history of our territory when murders, robberies, depredations and lawlessness were on every side and the Vigilantes were engaged in their terrible, awe-inspiring works. These Vigilantes must again organize in every part of our domain and bring miscreants to swift punishment. Mild measures will never do for reckless savages or still more daring white men. . . .

I have not much faith in mankind. The world is selfish, supremely selfish, and no part of it more so than. . . . Montana. People coming here, leave behind all the grace and goodness they ever possessed, and live only for money getting, They are true to no principle of right or justice, make friends only to advance their own interests. . . . The temptation is often great to make my home, when I shall gain it, my world, to seek no companionship outside its little circle.

Could I only decide the question—Shall I, too, selfishly address myself to money getting and ignore the claims of society upon me, or shall my influence be used to bring about a better state of things and beget a little public spirit. I should then with all my heart and soul address myself to the one or the other.

Love untold for all.
L.C. Fisk

4. Sodbusters in Kansas (1877)

Migrants to the treeless prairies had to invent new ways of living—including new kinds of houses—at least until they could import more traditional building materials from the East. The following diary entries were written by a Kansas homesteader in Snyder's Kill Creek, Kansas. What is most novel and what is most traditional about the physical and social setting described in the diary?

Wednesday, March 28, 1877   Noah staked two of the corners of my claim this morning, before he went out to herd the cattle and Jim and I followed him, looking for a place to make our dugout. We found a spot about ¾ mile from Snyders house where a patch of wild sunflowers had killed the grass. Here we began to dig, and by noon had made some progress. We laid off the ground 10 × 14 feet, and we'll have to dig it about 6 feet deep. Just before dinner I wished myself back home, and would have started for Osborne, but Jim persuaded me to stay. After dinner we went back to the hole and in about two hours had dug about half of it to the depth of two feet. And then we were stopped by a shower coming up, which bid fair to

[4]*Sod-House Days,* edited by John Ise. Copyright © 1937 by Columbia University Press. Reprinted by permission of the publisher.

keep on till night, but did not, though the clouds hung very low. We went back to the house, and Snyder fixed the handle to our ax. My dugout is at the head of the prettiest draw on my claim, and if the clouds clear off we will have it finished by the middle of next week. This afternoon Bevvy Neuschwanger rode up to see Mrs. Snyder and while they were talking we made off and put in a little more work on the claim. Talk about hard work will you? Just try digging in the ground out here two feet from the surface—oh, I should have written 6 inches from the surface. The ground is packed just as hard as could be, and it is no fun to pick and shovel it. It is damp as far as we have gone down (some 27 inches) and sticky as putty. Sometimes we can throw out lumps as big as your head. About 3 o'clock we had a little shower and then we quit work and went back to the house. We wanted a little instruction about putting the handle into the axe, and Snyder offered to do it for us, for which we were glad enough and by the time it was dark, the axe was fixed. Now our possessions consist of an axe, shovel and tincup, besides our clothing.

The prairie chickens are about as pretty a bird as you will come across. They are about as big as a half-grown barnyard fowl, and are not much shyer. The folks say they become more numerous as the land is broken up. The law forbids a man shooting them on any claim but his own, but if a poor fellow shoots a couple on somebody else's claim for food, no one thinks of having him up for it. The folks here all talk German more than English, but they can all get along, even if they cannot use the latter tongue very fluently. I talk English altogether and they may talk what they please. . . .

Wednesday, April 4, 1877   About 8 o'clock I got to shoveling the dirt away from the cellar door and got through about 10, when I went digging a place in the hill to put a hen house. Here the cattle and fowls are all put into half-dugouts—that is, part dugout and part log, sod, or stone, with straw roofs. That was mean digging, with the busted pick and in gravelly ground. The gravel is as firmly packed as though it had been rammed down. Finished that about 4 o'clock and then started digging for a well where old man Gsell said there was water. He found it out by the use of a forked branch of a peach tree. That was the first time I ever saw forks used for finding water, but I have heard it said that the black shale will draw the switch as well as water. And when you strike shale before you get to water it is no use to go any deeper, but if you strike the water first, go ahead and make your reservoir in the shale and you will always have a supply. These two days' work were the hardest I have done in 6 months. I got $1 a day and board, so there is $1.50 earned. L. & J. were at work at the house—dugout—while I was away. I got back to Snyder's about 7 o'clock. Had bean soup for supper. It was hot today, and I worked without coat or vest.

Thursday, April 5, 1877   This was another hot day, and we had heavy work too, laying up sod. Snyder broke a lot for us this a. m. and we began laying up the wall. It is 20 inches thick. These "Kansas brick" are from 2 to 4 inches thick, 12 wide and 20 long and the joints between them we fill with ground. Just before sunset we got the ridgepole into position on the crotches, so that the room will be about 7 feet high. We expect to get the roof in and have the place in condition to live in by the end of the week. The sod is heavy and when you take 3 or 4 bricks on a litter or hand barrow, and carry it 50 to 150 feet, I tell you it is no easy work. We quit just before sunset. Had supper about 7:30. I could hardly walk today—the result of that bareback ride. It was awfully hot right after dinner, and Levin fetched water from Snyder's in a jug. That water tasted good.

5. John Wesley Powell Reports on the "Arid Region" (1879)

In 1869, the one-armed explorer John Wesley Powell (1834–1902) led the first party to float down the mighty Colorado River through the Grand Canyon. He later led many scientific expeditions throughout the American West, and he served from 1881 to 1894 as the head of the United States Geological Survey. In 1879 he filed the following report on the topography and climate of the Great Basin, including Utah. (The Great Basin lies between the Sierra Nevada and Rocky Mountain ranges.) What did he identify as the distinguishing geological and meteorological characteristics of the region? What features of this region did Powell find most different from the eastern part of North America? What were the eventual social and environmental effects of his recommended method for making the region suitable for large-scale settlement?

In order to set forth the characteristics of these lands and the conditions under which they can be most profitably utilized, it is deemed best to discuss first a somewhat limited region in detail as a fair type of the whole. . . . It is proposed to take up for this discussion only the area embraced in Utah Territory. . . .

Having determined from the operations of irrigation that one cubic foot per second of water will irrigate from 80 to 100 acres of land when the greatest economy is used, and having determined the volume of water or number of cubic feet per second flowing in the several streams of Utah by the most thorough methods available under the circumstances, it appears that within the territory, excluding a small portion in the southeastern corner where the survey has not yet been completed, the amount of land which it is possible to redeem by this method is about 2,262 square miles, or 1,447,920 acres. Of course this amount does not lie in a continuous body, but is scattered in small tracts along the water courses. . . . That is, 2.8 per cent of the lands under consideration can be cultivated by utilizing all the available streams during the irrigating season. . . .

This statement of the facts relating to the irrigable lands of Utah will serve to give a clearer conception of the extent and condition of the irrigable lands throughout the Arid Region. Such as can be redeemed are scattered along the water courses, and are in general the lowest lands of the several districts to which they belong. . . .

The Arid Region is somewhat more than four-tenths of the total area of the United States, and as the agricultural interests of so great an area are dependent upon irrigation it will be interesting to consider certain questions relating to the economy and practicability of distributing the waters over the lands to be redeemed.

[5]J. W. Powell, *Report on the Lands of the Arid Region of the United States* (Washington, D.C.: Government Printing Office, 1879), pp. 6, 7–10, 23–24.

There are two considerations that make irrigation attractive to the agriculturist. Crops thus cultivated are not subject to the vicissitudes of rainfall; the farmer fears no droughts; his labors are seldom interrupted and his crops rarely injured by storms. This immunity from drought and storm renders agricultural operations much more certain than in regions of greater humidity. Again, the water comes down from the mountains and plateaus freighted with fertilizing materials derived from the decaying vegetation and soils of the upper regions, which are spread by the flowing water over the cultivated lands. It is probable that the benefits derived from this source alone will be full compensation for the cost of the process.

D. The Farmers' Protest Movement

1. An Iowan Assesses Discontent (1893)

Farm distress increased during the 1890s, to a large extent in the South but more spectacularly on the western plains. The four "d's"—drought, debt, deflation, and depression—played their dismal role, but the basic trouble was overproduction of grain. Farmers simply could not control prices that were determined by the world supply, and they vented their spleen on scapegoats nearer at hand, notably the railroads. Freight rates had fallen substantially since the Civil War, but no rates seemed fair to farmers whose grain prices were so low that they could not make a profit. And inequities persisted, despite the Interstate Commerce Act of 1887. A prominent Iowa journalist here analyzes some of the grievances that caused these hardy children of the soil to beat their Farmers' Alliances into a political plowshare. In the following essay, what are the farmers' most pressing complaints?

Nothing has done more to injure the [western] region than these freight rates. The railroads have retarded its growth as much as they first hastened it. The rates are often four times as large as Eastern rates. . . . The extortionate character of the freight rates has been recognized by all parties, and all have pledged themselves to lower them, but no state west of the Missouri has been able to do so.

In the early days, people were so anxious to secure railways that they would grant any sort of concession which the companies asked. There were counties in Iowa and other Western states struggling under heavy loads of bond-taxes, levied twenty-five years ago, to aid railways of which not one foot has been built. Perhaps a little grading would be done, and then the project would be abandoned, the bonds transferred, and the county called upon by the "innocent purchaser" to pay the debt incurred by blind credulity. I have known men to sacrifice fortunes, brains, and lives in fighting vainly this iniquitous bond-swindle.

Railways have often acquired mines and other properties by placing such high freight rates upon their products that the owner was compelled to sell at the railroad company's own terms. These freight rates have been especially burdensome to the farmers, who are far from their selling and buying markets, thus robbing them in both directions.

---

[1]F. B. Tracy, "Why the Farmers Revolted," *Forum* 16 (October 1893): 242–243.

Another fact which has incited the farmer against corporations is the bold and unblushing participation of the railways in politics. At every political convention their emissaries are present with blandishments and passes and other practical arguments to secure the nomination of their friends. The sessions of these legislatures are disgusting scenes of bribery and debauchery. There is not an attorney of prominence in Western towns who does not carry a pass or has not had the opportunity to do so. The passes, of course, compass the end sought. By these means, the railroads have secured an iron grip upon legislatures and officers, while no redress has been given to the farmer.

The land question, also, is a source of righteous complaint. Much of the land of the West, instead of being held for actual settlers, has been bought up by speculators and Eastern syndicates in large tracts. They have done nothing to improve the land and have simply waited for the inevitable settler who bought cheaply a small "patch" and proceeded to cultivate it. When he had prospered so that he needed more land, he found that his own labor had increased tremendously the value of the adjacent land. . . .

Closely connected with the land abuse are the money grievances. As his pecuniary condition grew more serious, the farmer could not make payments on his land. Or he found that, with the ruling prices, he could not sell his produce at a profit. In either case he needed money, to make the payment or maintain himself until prices should rise. When he went to the moneylenders, these men, often dishonest usurers, told him that money was very scarce, that the rate of interest was rapidly rising, etc., so that in the end the farmer paid as much interest a month as the moneylender was paying a year for the same money. In this transaction, the farmer obtained his first glimpse of the idea of "the contraction of the currency at the hands of Eastern money sharks."

Disaster always follows the exaction of such exorbitant rates of interest, and want or eviction quickly came. Consequently, when demagogues went among the farmers to utter their calamitous cries, the scales seemed to drop from the farmers' eyes, and he saw gold bugs, Shylocks, conspiracies, and criminal legislation *ad infinitum*. Like a lightning flash, the idea of political action ran through the Alliances. A few farmers' victories in county campaigns the previous year became a promise of broader conquest, and with one bound the Farmers' Alliance went into politics all over the West.

2. Mrs. Mary Lease Raises More Hell (c. 1890)

As the plains seethed with protest, the Populist party emerged from the Farmers' Alliance. Kansas spawned the most picturesque and vocal group of orators. A flaming speaker in great demand was the Irish-born Mrs. Mary E. Lease, a tall, magnetic lawyer known as "Patrick Henry in petticoats." Noting that corn was so cheap that it was being burned as fuel, she demanded the raising of less corn and "more hell." Noting also the disparity between the wealthy families and the people allegedly living out of garbage cans, she insisted on drastic measures. In the following selection,

[2]Elizabeth N. Barr, "The Populist Uprising," in W. E. Connelley, ed., *History of Kansas, State and People*, vol. 2 (1928), p. 1167.

which are substantial grievances and which are demagogic outpourings? Which of her complaints seem to be the most serious?

This is a nation of inconsistencies. The Puritans fleeing from oppression became oppressors. We fought England for our liberty and put chains on four million of blacks. We wiped out slavery and by our tariff laws and national banks began a system of white wage slavery worse than the first.

Wall Street owns the country. It is no longer a government of the people, by the people, and for the people, but a government of Wall Street, by Wall Street, and for Wall Street.

The great common people of this country are slaves, and monopoly is the master. The West and South are bound and prostrate before the manufacturing East.

Money rules, and our Vice-President is a London banker. Our laws are the output of a system which clothes rascals in robes and honesty in rags.

The parties lie to us and the political speakers mislead us. We were told two years ago to go to work and raise a big crop, that was all we needed. We went to work and plowed and planted; the rains fell, the sun shone, nature smiled, and we raised the big crop that they told us to; and what came of it? Eight-cent corn, ten-cent oats, two-cent beef, and no price at all for butter and eggs—that's what came of it.

Then the politicians said we suffered from overproduction. Overproduction, when 10,000 little children, so statistics tell us, starve to death every year in the United States, and over 10,000 shopgirls in New York are forced to sell their virtue for the bread their niggardly wages deny them.

Tariff is not the paramount question. The main question is the money question. . . . Kansas suffers from two great robbers, the Santa Fe Railroad and the loan companies. The common people are robbed to enrich their masters. . . .

We want money, land, and transportation. We want the abolition of the national banks, and we want the power to make loans direct from the government. We want the accursed foreclosure system wiped out. Land equal to a tract thirty miles wide and ninety miles long has been foreclosed and bought in by loan companies of Kansas in a year.

We will stand by our homes and stay by our fireside by force if necessary, and we will not pay our debts to the loan-shark companies until the government pays its debts to us. The people are at bay; let the bloodhounds of money who have dogged us thus far beware.

3. William Allen White Attacks the Populists (1896)

The embittered farmers and laborites, organized into the People's (Populist) party, met in a frenzied convention in Omaha, Nebraska, in July 1892. They nominated General James B. Weaver for president and adopted a scorching platform. In addition to other grievances, they pilloried corruption among politicians and judges, the subsidized and "muzzled" press, the impoverishment of labor, the shooting of strikers, and the hypocrisy of the two major parties. More specifically, the platform

---

[3]*Emporia Gazette,* August 15, 1896.

demanded distribution of monopolized land to actual settlers; government owner-
ship of the telegraphs, telephones, and railroads ("The railroad corporations will ei-
ther own the people or the people must own the railroads"); reduction of bloated
fortunes by a graduated income tax; and inflation of the currency by issuing more
paper money and coining all silver produced.

Four years later, the Populists nominated William Jennings Bryan and tem-
porarily fused with the Democratic party, which also nominated Bryan, in a bid for
national power. In Emporia, Kansas, newspaperman William Allen White had long
been critical of the Populists and now wrote a famous editorial denouncing them:
"What's the Matter with Kansas?" White's piece was reprinted and widely distributed
by Republicans backing William McKinley for president against Bryan. The editorial
vaulted White to national prominence, and he later became a friend and adviser to
presidents from Theodore Roosevelt to Franklin D. Roosevelt. As White saw matters in
1896, Kansas desperately needed new investment capital from the Northeast, and the
Populist agitation was scaring it away. How valid is his argument? Were the Pop-
ulists not simply the victims of agricultural distress, but in some way also contribu-
tors to it?

Today the Kansas Department of Agriculture sent out a statement which indicates that Kansas has gained less than two thousand people in the past year. There
are about two hundred and twenty-five thousand families in this state, and there
were ten thousand babies born in Kansas, and yet so many people have left the
state that the natural increase is cut down to less than two thousand net.

This has been going on for eight years.

If there had been a high brick wall around the state eight years ago, and not a
soul had been admitted or permitted to leave, Kansas would be a half million souls
better off than she is today. And yet the nation has increased in population. In five
years ten million people have been added to the national population, yet instead of
gaining a share of this—say, half a million—Kansas has apparently been a plague
spot and, in the very garden of the world, has lost population by ten thousands
every year.

Not only has she lost population, but she has lost money. Every moneyed man
in the state who could get out without loss has gone. Every month in every community sees someone who has a little money pack up and leave the state. This has
been going on for eight years. Money has been drained out all the time. In towns
where ten years ago there were three or four or half a dozen money-lending concerns, stimulating industry by furnishing capital, there is now none, or one or two
that are looking after the interests and principal already outstanding.

No one brings any money into Kansas any more. What community knows over
one or two men who have moved in with more than $5,000 in the past three years?
And what community cannot count half a score of men in that time who have left,
taking all the money they could scrape together?

Yet the nation has grown rich; other states have increased in population and
wealth—other neighboring states. Missouri has gained over two million, while
Kansas has been losing half a million. Nebraska has gained in wealth and population while Kansas has gone downhill. Colorado has gained every way, while Kansas
has lost every way since 1888.

What's the matter with Kansas?

There is no substantial city in the state. Every big town save one has lost in population. Yet Kansas City, Omaha, Lincoln, St. Louis, Denver, Colorado Springs, Sedalia, the cities of the Dakotas, St. Paul and Minneapolis and Des Moines—all cities and towns in the West—have steadily grown.

Take up the government blue book and you will see that Kansas is virtually off the map. Two or three little scrubby consular places in yellow-fever-stricken communities that do not aggregate ten thousand dollars a year is all the recognition that Kansas has. Nebraska draws about one hundred thousand dollars; little old North Dakota draws about fifty thousand dollars; Oklahoma doubles Kansas; Missouri leaves her a thousand miles behind; Colorado is almost seven times greater than Kansas—the whole west is ahead of Kansas.

Take it by any standard you please, Kansas is not in it.

Go east and you hear them laugh at Kansas; go west and they sneer at her; go south and they "cuss" her; go north and they have forgotten her. Go into any crowd of intelligent people gathered anywhere on the globe, and you will find the Kansas man on the defensive. The newspaper columns and magazines once devoted to praise of her, to boastful facts and startling figures concerning her resources, are now filled with cartoons, jibes and Pefferian* speeches. Kansas just naturally isn't in it. She has traded places with Arkansas and Timbuctoo.

What's the matter with Kansas?

We all know; yet here we are at it again. We have an old mossback Jacksonian who snorts and howls because there is a bathtub in the State House; we are running that old jay for Governor. We have another shabby, wild-eyed, rattle-brained fanatic who has said openly in a dozen speeches that "the rights of the user are paramount to the rights of the owner"; we are running him for Chief Justice, so that capital will come tumbling over itself to get into the state. We have raked the old ash heap of failure in the state and found an old human hoop skirt who has failed as a businessman, who has failed as an editor, who has failed as a preacher, and we are going to run him for Congressman-at-Large. He will help the looks of the Kansas delegation at Washington. Then we have discovered a kid without a law practice and have decided to run him for Attorney General. Then, for fear some hint that the state had become respectable might percolate through the civilized portions of the nation, we have decided to send three or four harpies out lecturing, telling the people that Kansas is raising hell and letting the corn go to weed.

Oh, this is a state to be proud of! We are a people who can hold up our heads! What we need is not more money, but less capital, fewer white shirts and brains, fewer men with business judgment, and more of those fellows who boast that they are "just ordinary clodhoppers, but they know more in a minute about finance than John Sherman"; we need more men who are "posted," who can bellow about the crime of '73,† who hate prosperity, and who think, because a man believes in national honor, he is a tool of Wall Street. We have had a few of them—some hundred fifty thousand—but we need more.

---

*William A. Peffer was a notoriously long-winded Populist senator from Kansas.

†"The crime of '73" refers to the demonetization of silver in 1873, a development loudly lamented by the pro-inflation Populists.

We need several thousand gibbering idiots to scream about the "Great Red Dragon" of Lombard Street. We don't need population, we don't need wealth, we don't need well-dressed men on the streets, we don't need cities on the fertile prairies; you bet we don't! What we are after is the money power. Because we have become poorer and ornerier and meaner than a spavined, distempered mule, we, the people of Kansas, propose to kick; we don't care to build up, we wish to tear down.

"There are two ideas of government," said our noble [William Jennings] Bryan at Chicago. "There are those who believe that if you legislate to make the well-to-do prosperous, this prosperity will leak through on those below. The Democratic idea has been that if you legislate to make the masses prosperous their prosperity will find its way up and through every class and rest upon them."

That's the stuff! Give the prosperous man the dickens! Legislate the thriftless man into ease, whack the stuffing out of the creditors and tell the debtors who borrowed the money five years ago when money "per capita" was greater than it is now, that the contraction of currency gives him a right to repudiate.

Whoop it up for the ragged trousers; put the lazy, greasy fizzle, who can't pay his debts, on the altar, and bow down and worship him. Let the state ideal be high. What we need is not the respect of our fellow men, but the chance to get something for nothing.

Oh, yes, Kansas is a great state. Here are people fleeing from it by the score every day, capital going out of the state by the hundreds of dollars; and every industry but farming paralyzed, and that crippled, because its products have to go across the ocean before they can find a laboring man at work who can afford to buy them. Let's don't stop this year. Let's drive all the decent, self-respecting men out of the state. Let's keep the old clodhoppers who know it all. Let's encourage the man who is "posted." He can talk, and what we need is not mill hands to eat our meat, nor factory hands to eat our wheat, nor cities to oppress the farmer by consuming his butter and eggs and chickens and produce. What Kansas needs is men who can talk, who have large leisure to argue the currency question while their wives wait at home for that nickel's worth of bluing.

What's the matter with Kansas?

Nothing under the shining sun. She is losing her wealth, population and standing. She has got her statesmen, and the money power is afraid of her. Kansas is all right. She has started in to raise hell, as Mrs. Lease advised, and she seems to have an overproduction. But that doesn't matter. Kansas never did believe in diversified crops. Kansas is all right. There is absolutely nothing wrong with Kansas. "Every prospect pleases and only man is vile."

E. The Pullman Strike

1. A Populist Condemns George Pullman (1894)

George M. Pullman, who invented the popular upper-and-lower-berth Pullman Palace Car, made a fortune in manufacturing and controlling his brainchild. A generous philanthropist with his millions, he built for his employees the model town of Pullman (now in Chicago). But when the depression came and the company slashed wages about 25 percent, the workers struck. They were joined by Eugene V. Debs's powerful American Railway Union. According to Debs, the management had said, "There is nothing to arbitrate." Senator William A. Peffer, a Populist from Kansas who combed his long whiskers with his fingers while delivering even longer speeches, here presents his views. What are the two main grievances of the Pullman workers? How legitimate are they?

Without going into all the details, I will state by way of preface that the Pullman Company established what most people in this world believed to be an ideal community, in which all the citizens should have equal rights, in which none should have special privileges. The object was to build a community where the best modern scientific principles of hygiene, drainage, sewerage, grading, lighting, watering, and every other convenience should abound.

But while the company was doing that, while the world was looking on applauding, the company, like every other corporation of which I have ever known anything, held all of the power, all of the reins within its own grasp. That is to say, while there was sewerage, while there was light, while there was water, while there were parks, and all those desirable things, at the end of every month or of every week, as the case might be, when pay day came around, the charges that were set up against the residents of the town of Pullman for their lots and for their conveniences were deducted from their pay (just as the clothing of a soldier or extra rations or a lost gun were deducted from his pay) and the balance found to be due was paid to these people. Among these charges were rents and stated dues for the purchase of property.

After a while hard times began to pinch the company as it did everybody else, and it began to reduce the pay of the men. The men submitted patiently. Another reduction came and the men again submitted, only asking, however, that their rent charges should be reduced, that their taxes should be reduced, to correspond to the amount of reduction in their wages.

Then it was found that these poor people were absolutely defenseless, absolutely powerless in the hands of a corporation that had no soul. They asked to have a reduction of their rent charges and of other charges; they asked for a little time to turn around.

All these things were denied them. Finally, the Pullman citizens came to the conclusion that they might as well starve in defense of their rights as to starve while the proprietors of the town, the organizers and controllers of the corporation, were

---

[1]*Congressional Record*, 53d Cong., 2d sess. (July 10, 1894), p. 7231.

feasting on the fat things that these men had made for them. Now the trouble is on hand, and the leader of this great corporation [George M. Pullman] is off at the seashore, or on a lake, or on an island, or somewhere, refusing to entertain even a newspaper man, except to say, "I have nothing to say; the company at Chicago will look after the company's interest there"—heartless, soulless, conscienceless, Mr. President, this tyrant of tyrants.

2. Pullman Defends His Company (1894)

The bloody disorders attending the Pullman strike led to an investigation by the U.S. Strike Commission. George M. Pullman took the stand and testified that his company had undertaken to manufacture cars at a loss so as to keep his men employed. But he conceded that it was better to operate at a slight loss than to incur the larger losses resulting from idle factories. He also testified that the salaries of management (including his own) had not been cut; that the Pullman Company still had about $25 million in undivided profits; and that the dividends paid to stockholders had ranged from 12 percent to the current 8 percent. U.S. Commissioner Worthington extracted the following information from Pullman. How sound is Pullman's position on arbitration? How does his general business philosophy square with that prevalent in the United States today?

Commissioner Worthington. Now, let me ask you right there, Mr. Pullman, what do you see that is objectionable, in a business point of view, under the existing state of affairs, . . . in submitting to disinterested persons the question as to whether under all the circumstances wages might not be increased somewhat of your employees?

Mr. Pullman. I think I have made that as plain in this [written] statement as I can make it if I should repeat it a thousand times.

Commissioner Worthington. Is that the only reason you can give?

Mr. Pullman. What do you mean by that, "The only reason"?

Commissioner Worthington. The reason you give here (in the statement), "It must be clear to every businessman and to every thinking workman that no prudent employer could submit to arbitration the question whether he should commit such a piece of business folly." Is that the only answer to it?

Mr. Pullman. Well now, I have a little memorandum here which is practically the same thing on the question of arbitration. Of course there are matters which are proper subjects of arbitration—matters of opinion.

Commissioner Worthington. What are those matters that are proper subjects for arbitration?

Mr. Pullman. A matter of opinion would be a proper subject of arbitration, as, for instance, a question of title, or a disagreement on a matter of opinion. . . . But as to whether a fact that I know to be true is true or not, I could not agree to submit to arbitration. Take the case in hand: the question as to whether the shops at Pullman shall be continuously operated at a loss or not is one which it was impossible for the company, as a matter of principle, to submit to the opinion of any third party; and as to whether they were running at a loss on contract work

---

[2]*Senate Executive Documents,* 53d Cong., 3d sess., vol. 2, no. 7, pp. 555–556.

in general, as explained to the committee of the men in my interview with them—that was a simple fact that I knew to be true, and which could not be made otherwise by the opinion of any third party.

Commissioner Worthington. You use the expression, "Impossible to be submitted." Why is it impossible?

Mr. Pullman. Because it would violate a principle.

Commissioner Worthington. What principle?

Mr. Pullman. The principle that a man should have the right to manage his own property.

Commissioner Worthington. The decision of arbitrators would not be compulsory, would it?

Mr. Pullman. I still think, having managed the property of the Pullman Company for twenty-seven years, that I am perhaps as well calculated to manage it for the interests of its stockholders and for the interests of the public—for the general interest—as some man who is not interested, who comes in to arbitrate certain points.

3. Starvation at Pullman (1894)

The Pullman strike was finally broken by federal bayonets, and the company allegedly imported more docile workers to replace those who had struck. A group signing themselves "The Starving Citizens of Pullman" appealed to Governor John Altgeld of Illinois for relief. After examining conditions personally, the governor wrote the following letter to George M. Pullman. Does the evidence here given support the charge of discrimination?

Sir: I examined the conditions at Pullman yesterday, visited even the kitchens and bedrooms of many of the people. Two representatives of your company were with me and we found the distress as great as it was represented. The men are hungry and the women and children are actually suffering. They have been living on charity for a number of months and it is exhausted. Men who had worked for your company for more than ten years had to apply to the relief society in two weeks after the work stopped.

I learn from your manager that last spring there were 3,260 people on the payroll; yesterday there were 2,220 at work, but over 600 of these are new men, so that only about 1,600 of the old employees have been taken back, thus leaving over 1,600 of the old employees who have not been taken back. A few hundred have left, the remainder have nearly all applied for work, but were told that they were not needed. These are utterly destitute. The relief committee on last Saturday gave out two pounds of oatmeal and two pounds of cornmeal to each family. But even the relief committee has exhausted its resources.

Something must be done and at once. The case differs from instances of destitution found elsewhere, for generally there is somebody in the neighborhood able to give relief; this is not the case at Pullman. Even those who have gone to work are so exhausted that they cannot help their neighbors if they would. I repeat now that

---

[3]John P. Altgeld, *Live Questions* (1899), pp. 422–423. The letter was written on August 21, 1894.

it seems to me your company cannot afford to have me appeal to the charity and humanity of the state to save the lives of your old employees. Four-fifths of those people are women and children. No matter what caused this distress, it must be met.

[Mr. Pullman turned a deaf ear to appeals for relief, and humane citizens were forced to help the destitute. "Mr. Dooley" (F. P. Dunne) referred to the time "whin God quarried his heart." Reconcile Pullman's attitude in this instance with his large private philanthropies, including a bequest of $1.2 million for a free manual training school in Pullman.]

F. The Free-Silver Mirage

1. Coin's Financial School (1894)

By the 1880s and 1890s indebted Americans, especially farmers, were caught in a deflationary pinch. A cry arose for inflating the currency by abandoning the single gold standard and restoring the bimetallic gold-silver standard, dropped by Congress in 1873 ("the Crime of '73"). The silverites specifically demanded the free and unlimited coinage of silver in the ratio of sixteen ounces of silver to one ounce of gold, despite Britain's adherence to the gold standard. William Hope Harvey, a frustrated silver-mine operator from Colorado, came to Chicago and in 1894 published his best-selling tract, Coin's Financial School. *His fictional account tells how Coin, the boy wizard of Chicago, conducted a six-day financial school attended by many leading figures, whom he converted to the gospel of free silver. The 174-page booklet, cleverly but deceptively illustrated, sold upwards of a million copies and was a major propaganda weapon in the free-silver crusade. Why was Harvey bitter against England? Why did the proposed international agreement on bimetallism have little prospect of realization?*

His [Coin's] appearance upon the platform was the signal for an ovation. He had grown immensely popular in those last five days.

He laid his silk hat on the table, and at once stepped to the middle of the platform. He raised his eyes to the audience, slowly turned his head to the right and left, and looked into the sea of faces that confronted him.

"In the midst of plenty, we are in want," he began. "Helpless children and the best womanhood and manhood of America appeal to us for release from a bondage that is destructive of life and liberty. All the nations of the Western Hemisphere turn to their great sister republic for assistance in the emancipation of the people of at least one-half the world.

"The Orient, with its teeming millions of people, and France, the cradle of science and liberty in Europe, look to the United States to lead in the struggle to roll back the accumulated disasters of the last twenty-one years [since "the Crime of '73"]. What shall our answer be? [Applause.]

"If it is claimed we must adopt for our money the metal England selects [gold], and can have no independent choice in the matter, let us make the test and find out

---

[1]W. H. Harvey, *Coin's Financial School* (New York: American News Company 1894), pp. 130–133, passim.

if it is true. It is not American to give up without trying. If it is true, let us attach England to the United States and blot her name out from among the nations of the earth. [Applause.]

"A war with England would be the most popular ever waged on the face of the earth. [Applause]. If it is true that she can dictate the money of the world, and thereby create world-wide misery, it would be the most just war ever waged by man. [Applause.]

"But fortunately this is not necessary. Those who would have you think that we must wait for England, either have not studied this subject, or have the same interest in continuing the present conditions as England. It is a vain hope to expect her voluntarily to consent. England is the creditor nation of the globe, and collects hundreds of millions of dollars in interest annually in gold from the rest of the world. We are paying her two hundred millions yearly in interest. She demands it in gold; the contracts call for it in gold. Do you expect her to voluntarily release any part of it? It has a purchasing power twice what a bimetallic currency would have. She knows it. . . .

"Whenever property interest and humanity have come in conflict, England has ever been the enemy of human liberty. All reforms with those so unfortunate as to be in her power have been won with the sword. She yields only to force. [Applause.]

"The moneylenders in the United States, who own substantially all of our money, have a selfish interest in maintaining the gold standard. They, too, will not yield. They believe that if the gold standard can survive for a few years longer, the people will get used to it—get used to their poverty—and quietly submit.

"To that end they organize international bimetallic committees and say, 'Wait on England, she will be forced to give us bimetallism.' Vain hope! Deception on this subject has been practiced long enough upon a patient and outraged people."

2. William Jennings Bryan's Cross of Gold (1896)

At the Democratic party's presidential nominating convention in Chicago in 1896, William Jennings Bryan of Nebraska made an eloquent and impassioned speech denouncing the gold standard and advocating inflation. Although a well-known ex-congressman and free-silver orator, Bryan was not then regarded as one of the front-runners for the presidential nomination. Tall, lean, smooth-shaven, hawk-nosed, and wide-mouthed, "the Boy Orator of the Platte" hushed the vast assemblage of some fifteen thousand with his masterful presence. The "cross of gold" analogy to the crucifixion of Christ was one he had already used a number of times, but never before so effectively. Projecting his organlike voice to the outer reaches of the vast hall, he had the frenzied crowd cheering his every sentence as he neared the end. The climax swept the delegates off their feet and won Bryan the presidential nomination the next day. How do you account for the success of his memorable speech? To what different kinds of prejudice does Bryan appeal?

I would be presumptuous, indeed, to present myself against the distinguished gentlemen to whom you have listened if this were a mere measuring of abilities. But

---

[2]C. M. Depew, ed., *The Library of Oratory* (New York: The Globe Publishing Company, 1902), vol. 14 pp. 415, 418, 420–425, passim.

this is not a contest between persons. The humblest citizen in all the land, when clad in the armor of a righteous cause, is stronger than all the hosts of error. I come to speak to you in defense of a cause as holy as the cause of liberty—the cause of humanity. . . .

We [silverites] do not come as aggressors. Our war is not a war of conquest. We are fighting in the defense of our homes, our families, and posterity. We have petitioned, and our petitions have been scorned. We have entreated, and our entreaties have been disregarded. We have begged, and they have mocked when our calamity came. We beg no longer; we entreat no more; we petition no more. We defy them! . . .

The gentleman from New York [Senator David Hill] . . . says he wants this country to try to secure an international agreement. Why does he not tell us what he is going to do if he fails to secure an international agreement? . . . Our opponents have tried for twenty years to secure an international agreement, and those are waiting for it most patiently who do not want it at all. . . .

We go forth confident that we shall win. Why? Because upon the paramount issue of this campaign there is not a spot of ground upon which the enemy will dare to challenge battle. If they [the Republicans] tell us that the gold standard is a good thing, we shall point to their platform and tell them that their platform pledges the party to get rid of the gold standard and substitute bimetallism. If the gold standard is a good thing, why try to get rid of it? . . .

Mr. Carlisle* said in 1878 that this was a struggle between "the idle holders of idle capital" and "the struggling masses, who produce the wealth and pay the taxes of the country"; and, my friends, the question we are to decide is: upon which side will the Democratic Party fight—upon the side of "the idle holders of idle capital" or upon the side of "the struggling masses"? That is the question which the party must answer first, and then it must be answered by each individual hereafter. The sympathies of the Democratic Party, as shown by the platform, are on the side of the struggling masses who have ever been the foundation of the Democratic Party.

There are two ideas of government. There are those who believe that, if you will only legislate to make the well-to-do prosperous, their prosperity will leak through on those below. The Democratic idea, however, has been that if you legislate to make the masses prosperous, their prosperity will find its way up through every class which rests upon them.

You come to us and tell us that the great cities are in favor of the gold standard. We reply that the great cities rest upon our broad and fertile prairies. Burn down your cities and leave our farms, and your cities will spring up again as if by magic. But destroy our farms, and the grass will grow in the streets of every city in the country.

My friends, we declare that this nation is able to legislate for its own people on every question, without waiting for the aid or consent of any other nation on earth; and upon that issue we expect to carry every state in the Union. I shall not slander the inhabitants of the fair state of Massachusetts nor the inhabitants of the state of New York by saying that, when they are confronted with the proposition, they will declare that this nation is not able to attend to its own business. It is the issue of

---

*John G. Carlisle of Kentucky, formerly a distinguished member of Congress, was Cleveland's secretary of the treasury in 1896.

1776 over again. Our ancestors, when but three millions in number, had the courage to declare their political independence of every other nation. Shall we, their descendants, when we have grown to seventy millions, declare that we are less independent than our forefathers?

No, my friends, that will never be the verdict of our people. Therefore, we care not upon what lines the battle is fought. If they say bimetallism is good but that we cannot have it until other nations help us, we reply that, instead of having a gold standard because England has, we will restore bimetallism, and then let England have bimetallism because the United States has it. If they dare to come out in the open field and defend the gold standard as a good thing, we will fight them to the uttermost.

Having behind us the producing masses of this nation and the world, supported by the commercial interests, the laboring interests, and the toilers everywhere, we will answer their demand for a gold standard by saying to them: You shall not press down upon the brow of labor this crown of thorns; you shall not crucify mankind upon a cross of gold.

[The Cleveland Democrats, with their devotion to the gold standard, were appalled by the nomination of Bryan. "What a burlesque on a Democratic convention," wrote Postmaster General William Wilson in his diary. "May God help the country!" He stressed the youth, ambition, and Populist leanings of the candidate, while noting that Bryan's "utter ignorance of the great diplomatic, financial, and other questions a President has constantly to dispose of, will be lost sight of in the fanaticism of the one idea he represents." (F. P. Summers, The Cabinet Diary of William L. Wilson, 1896–1897 *[Chapel Hill: University of North Carolina Press, 1957], p. 116.) Conservatives, then and later, generally agreed that Bryan was strong on sound but weak on substance.]*

3. The "Anarchists" Lose Out (1896)

Bryan's whirlwind campaign for free silver gained such momentum in its early stages that he might have won if the election had been held two months earlier. But frightened "gold-bug" Republicans opened wide their purses, and the subsequent deluge of propaganda helped bring victory to William McKinley, the Republican candidate. Many of the gold-standard Cleveland Democrats spurned Bryan and contributed actively to McKinley's victory. The gold-bug East stressed the presence in Bryan's camp of such radicals as Eugene V. Debs, who had headed the Pullman strike of 1894, and Governor John Altgeld of Illinois, who had pardoned the three surviving Haymarket Riot anarchists. In what respects is this editorial in the New York Nation *least fair?*

We have escaped from what a large number of people supposed was an immense danger, the danger of having our currency adulterated and our form of government changed, and a band of ignoramuses and anarchists put at the head of what remained of the great American republic. Probably no man in civil life has succeeded in inspiring so much terror, without taking life, as Bryan. Attila and Tamer-

---

[3]*The Nation* (New York) 63 (November 5, 1896), p. 337.

lane frightened more people, but they killed or threatened to kill them; they hardly destroyed more property.

Bryan succeeded in persuading hundreds of thousands that the great fabric of government which was built up by the wisdom of experience of a thousand years, and cemented by hundreds of thousands of lives, was, almost in the first century of its existence, about to be handed over by the vote of its own people to a knot of silly, half-taught adventurers and anarchists. We were to exchange the Constitution and the Supreme Court for the decrees of Altgeld and Debs and Bryan and Teller, whose principal occupation was to be striking off "cheap money for the poor man."

The whole episode has been utterly discreditable to our politics, as conducted by politicians. Could anything better reveal the character of our nominating system than the fact that the nominating convention of one of our two great parties could be taken possession of by a few adventurers, that the platform could be drawn, in the main, by a noted anarchist [Altgeld], and an unknown young man nominated on it simply because the audience was pleased with one of his metaphors, and that it should drive away from it all the party's men of light and leading before going to the country?

4. Bryan's Afterthoughts (1896)

While his memory of the campaign was still fresh, Bryan recorded his impressions. His then-unprecedented six hundred speeches and his eighteen thousand miles of sweaty travel must have left him in something of a daze. What does his account suggest about the ethics of the opposition, the intellectual level of the campaign, and the assumption that the canvass was a crusade rather than a campaign?

The reminiscences of the campaign of 1896 form such a delightful chapter in memory's book that I am constrained to paraphrase a familiar line and say that it is better to have run and lost than never to have run at all. . . .

Unless I am mistaken, the deep awakening among the people during the campaign just closed will result in a more careful study of political questions by both men and women, and in a more rigid scrutiny of the conduct of public officials by those whom they serve. No matter what may be the ultimate outcome of the struggle over the financial question, better government will result from the political interest which has been aroused. . . .

During the campaign I ran across various evidences of coercion, direct and indirect. One of the most common means of influencing voters was the advertising of orders placed with manufacturers, conditioned upon Republican success at the polls. The following is an illustration. Tuesday morning, November 3rd, there appeared at the head of the last column of the first page of the *Morning News,* of Wilmington, Del.:

Contingent Orders
The Harlan and Hollingsworth Company, of this city, have received a contract for a boat costing $300,000. One clause in the contract provides that in the event of Bryan's election the contract shall be canceled. If the boat is built here, $160,000 of its cost would

---

[4]W. J. Bryan, *The First Battle* (Chicago: Conkey, 1896), pp. 612–624, passim.

be paid to Wilmington workmen for wages. The corporation wanting the boat feel that it would not be justified in having it constructed if Bryan should become President. . . .

I may mention a still more forcible means adopted by many employers. The workingmen were paid off Saturday night before election and notified that they might expect work Wednesday morning in case of Mr. McKinley's election, but that they need not return if I was elected. Whether the employers themselves were actually afraid or whether they merely intended to frighten their employees, the plan worked admirably and exerted a most potent influence on election day. . . .

The ratio of 16 to 1 was scrupulously adhered to during the campaign, and illustrated with infinite variety. At one place our carriage was drawn by sixteen white horses and one yellow horse; at any number of places we were greeted by sixteen young ladies dressed in white and one dressed in yellow, or by sixteen young men dressed in white and one dressed in yellow. But the ratio was most frequently represented in flowers, sixteen white chrysanthemums and one yellow one being the favorite combination. . . .

It is impossible to chronicle all the evidences of kindly feeling given during the campaign; in fact the good will manifested and the intense feeling shown impressed me more than any other feature of the campaign. When the result was announced my composure was more endangered by the sorrow exhibited by friends than it was during all the excitement of the struggle. Men broke down and cried as they expressed their regret, and there rises before me now the face of a laboring man of Lincoln, who, after he dried his tears, held out his hand from which three fingers were missing, and said: "I did not shed a tear when those were taken off."

People have often lightly said that they would die for a cause, but it may be asserted in all truthfulness that during the campaign just closed there were thousands of bimetallists who would have given their lives, had their lives been demanded, in order to secure success to the principles which they advocated. Surely, greater love hath no man than this. . . .

I am proud of the character of my support. Those who voted for me did so of their own volition; neither coercion nor purchase secured their suffrages; their confidence and good will robbed defeat of all its pangs.

5. The London Standard Rejoices (1896)

William McKinley, the high priest of high protection, had expected to emphasize the tariff in the campaign, but Bryan took the play away from him with free silver. The business world on both sides of the Atlantic, unwilling to be paid off in fifty-cent silver dollars, rejoiced over the Republican triumph. London reported that millions of dollars' worth of orders from the United States had been placed in England contingent on Bryan's defeat. Why is the London Standard, *in the following selection, not altogether happy?*

The complete rejection of Bryan's tempting program, addressed to indolence, incapacity, and cupidity, shows that these qualities are less widely distributed in the

---

[5]Quoted in *Public Opinion* 21 (November 12, 1896): 623.

United States than Bryan would have us believe. There has been a revolt of the honest and loyal citizens, who are solicitous for the fair name and fame of the Republic, and the Bryanites astonished the world by the comparative paucity of their numbers. The hopelessly ignorant and savagely covetous waifs and strays of American civilization voted for Bryan, but the bulk of the solid sense, business integrity, and social stability sided with McKinley. The nation is to be heartily congratulated. The victory has drawbacks for Englishmen, and, indeed, for every country in Europe engaged in manufacturing industries. It is a triumph of good faith, but also a triumph of [tariff] protection.

Thought Provokers

1. It has been said that there was no Indian problem but a white problem; no black problem but a white problem. Comment critically. Why were Indian-white relations different in Canada? Did George Armstrong Custer bring on his own death?
2. Did the American settlers have a "natural right" to the free lands? Was selling the public land to replenish the Treasury sound in principle? Why was the Homestead Act so long delayed? Did both the East and the South have legitimate objections to it?
3. What were the best and worst things about life on the frontier? How was the frontier experience for men different from that for women?
4. Farmers, to be successful, had to be good businesspeople, and many failed because they were not. It was charged that they illogically put the blame for their failures on other factors. Comment. Other critics accused them of not doing well because they had fallen into habits of indolence. Would greater energy and larger harvests have cured the basic ills?
5. Is a company like Pullman's justified in cutting wages when it has a large surplus of money? Does management have a higher obligation to the investor than to the laborer? Is the businessperson the best interpreter of the public interest? Is a large-scale business a purely private matter?
6. Explain why the free-silver craze developed the momentum that it did. Comment on the common assumption that the silverites were all ignorant, poor, and basically dishonest. Would disaster have befallen the United States if Bryan had been elected and the Treasury had coined many dollars with the purchasing power of fifty cents each?

27

The Path of Empire,
1890–1899

It has been a splendid little war [with Spain]; begun
with the highest motives, carried on with magnificent
intelligence and spirit, favored by that fortune which
loves the brave.

John Hay, 1898

Prologue: As the century neared its sunset, the American people felt a strange
restlessness. The frontier was filling up; factories and farms were pouring out ex-
portable surpluses; the nation had not had a rousing war for a generation. Spain, trying desperately to crush a rebellion in Cuba with brutal measures, proved to be the
whipping boy. The big-business administration of William McKinley did not want
war; but public opinion, inflamed by the racy new yellow journalism, did. Although
Spain made important eleventh-hour diplomatic concessions, an impatient and outraged Congress declared hostilities. The U.S. Navy was ready and smashed two
badly outmatched Spanish fleets—one at Manila, the other off Cuba. The army, however, was most unready. After some sharp and confused fighting in Cuba, the
Spaniards hoisted the white flag. The imperialistic virus had meanwhile attacked the
American people, and McKinley, their ever-obedient servant, demanded and obtained all of the Philippines in the treaty of peace signed at Paris in December 1898.

A. Yellow Journalism in Flower

1. Joseph Pulitzer Demands Intervention (1897)

*The oppressed Cubans revolted in 1895, and the Spanish commander, General Vale-
riano ("Butcher") Weyler, tried to crush them by herding them into pesthole concentration camps. Atrocities on both sides were inevitable, but the United States heard
little of Cuban misdeeds. The American yellow press, with Joseph Pulitzer's* New York
World *and William Randolph Hearst's* New York Journal *competing in sensationalism, headlined lurid horror tales. The basic principle of the so-called new journalism
seemed to be "Anything to Sell a Paper," regardless of the truth. A* World *reporter
wrote from Cuba that slaughtered rebels were fed to dogs and that children of high-
ranking Spanish families clamored for Cuban ears as playthings. The following edi-*

---

[1]*New York World*, February 13, 1897.

torial in Pulitzer's World *demanded action. What point or points probably made the heaviest impact on the American public?*

How long are the Spaniards to drench Cuba with the blood and tears of her people?

How long is the peasantry of Spain to be drafted away to Cuba to die miserably in a hopeless war, that Spanish nobles and Spanish officers may get medals and honors?

How long shall old [Cuban] men and women and children be murdered by the score, the innocent victims of Spanish rage against the patriot armies they cannot conquer?

How long shall the sound of rifles in Castle Morro [in Cuba] at sunrise proclaim that bound and helpless prisoners of war have been murdered in cold blood?

How long shall Cuban women be the victims of Spanish outrages and lie sobbing and bruised in loathsome prisons?

How long shall women passengers on vessels flying the American flag be unlawfully seized and stripped and searched by brutal, jeering Spanish officers, in violation of the laws of nations and of the honor of the United States?*

How long shall American citizens, arbitrarily arrested while on peaceful and legitimate errands, be immured in foul Spanish prisons without trial?†

How long shall the navy of the United States be used as the sea police of barbarous Spain?

How long shall the United States sit idle and indifferent within sound and hearing of rapine and murder?

How long?

2. William Randolph Hearst Stages a Rescue (1897)

William Randolph Hearst, the irresponsible California playboy who had inherited some $20 million from his father, was even more ingenious than his arch-rival Joseph Pulitzer. He is said to have boasted (with undue credit to himself) that it cost him $3 million to bring on the Spanish-American War. He outdid himself in the case of Evangelina Cisneros, a "tenderly nurtured" Cuban girl of eighteen who was imprisoned in Havana on charges of rebellion and reportedly faced a twenty-year incarceration with depraved fellow inmates. The yellow press pictured her as a beautiful young woman whose only crime had been to preserve her virtue against the lustful advances of a "lecherous" Spanish officer. Hearst's New York Journal whipped up a storm of sympathy for the girl and inspired appeals to the Spanish queen and to the pope. All else failing, a Journal reporter rented a house next to the prison, drugged the inmates, sawed through the cell bars, and—using a forged visa—escaped with Señorita Cisneros disguised as a boy. What does this account in the Journal reveal about the character and the techniques of the new yellow journalism?

---

*The most highly publicized case actually involved an examination by a police matron.

†By 1897 there were few, if any, U.S. citizens in Cuban prisons, even naturalized Americans of Cuban birth.

²*New York Journal,* October 10, 1897.

EVANGELINA CISNEROS RESCUED BY THE JOURNAL

**AN AMERICAN NEWSPAPER ACCOMPLISHES AT A SINGLE
STROKE WHAT THE RED TAPE OF DIPLOMACY
FAILED UTTERLY TO BRING ABOUT IN
MANY MONTHS**

By Charles Duval
(Copyright, 1897, by W. R. Hearst)

Havana, Oct. 7, via Key West, Fla., Oct. 9.—Evangelina Cosio y Cisneros is at liberty, and the *Journal* can place to its credit the greatest journalist coup of this age. It is an illustration of the methods of new journalism and it will find an endorsement in the heart of every woman who has read of the horrible sufferings of the poor girl who has been confined for fifteen long months in Recojidas Prison.

The *Journal,* finding that all other methods were unavailing, decided to secure her liberation through force, and this, as the specially selected commissioner of the *Journal,* I have succeeded in doing.

I have broken the bars of Recojidas and have set free the beautiful captive of monster Weyler, restoring her to her friends and relatives, and doing by strength, skill, and strategy what could not be accomplished by petition and urgent request of the Pope.

Weyler could blind the Queen to [the] real character of Evangelina, but he could not build a jail that would hold against *Journal* enterprise when properly set to work.

Tonight all Havana rings with the story. It is the one topic of conversation; everything else pales into insignificance.

B. The Declaration of War

1. President McKinley Submits a War Message (1898)

Despite Spain's belated concessions, McKinley sent his war message to Congress on April 11, 1898. His nerves were giving way under the constant clamor for war; his heart went out to the mistreated Cubans. (He had anonymously contributed $5,000 for their relief.) He realized that Spain's offer of an armistice, at the discretion of its commander, did not guarantee peace. The rebels had to agree on terms, and Spain had shown a talent for breaking promises and protracting negotiations. Further delay would only worsen the terrible conditions. Among the reasons that McKinley here gives Congress for intervention, which are the soundest and which the weakest? Was there danger in intervening for humanitarian reasons?

The grounds for such intervention may be briefly summarized as follows:

First. In the cause of humanity and to put an end to the barbarities, bloodshed, starvation, and horrible miseries now existing there, and which the parties to the

---

[1]James D. Richardson, ed., *Messages and Papers of the Presidents* (New York: Bureau of National Literature, 1899), vol. 10, pp. 147, 150, passim.

conflict are either unable or unwilling to stop or mitigate. It is no answer to say this is all in another country, belonging to another nation, and is therefore none of our business. It is specially our duty, for it is right at our door.

Second. We owe it to our citizens in Cuba to afford them that protection and indemnity for life and property which no government there can or will afford, and to that end to terminate the conditions that deprive them of legal protection.

Third. The right to intervene may be justified by the very serious injury to the commerce, trade, and business of our people and by the wanton destruction of property and devastation of the island.

Fourth, and which is of the utmost importance. The present condition of affairs in Cuba is a constant menace to our peace, and entails upon this government an enormous expense. With such a conflict waged for years in an island so near us and with which our people have such trade and business relations; when the lives and liberty of our citizens are in constant danger and their property destroyed and themselves ruined; where our trading vessels are liable to seizure and are seized at our very door by warships of a foreign nation; the expeditions of filibustering [freebooting] that we are powerless to prevent altogether, and the irritating questions and entanglements thus arising—all these and others that I need not mention, with the resulting strained relations, are a constant menace to our peace and compel us to keep on a semi-war footing with a nation with which we are at peace.

These elements of danger and disorder already pointed out have been strikingly illustrated by a tragic event which has deeply and justly moved the American people. I have already transmitted to Congress the report of the Naval Court of Inquiry on the destruction of the battleship *Maine* in the harbor of Havana during the night of the 15th of February. The destruction of that noble vessel has filled the national heart with inexpressible horror. Two hundred and fifty-eight brave sailors and marines and two officers of our Navy, reposing in the fancied security of a friendly harbor, have been hurled to death, [and] grief and want brought to their homes and sorrow to the nation.

The Naval Court of Inquiry, which, it is needless to say, commands the unqualified confidence of the government, was unanimous in its conclusion that the destruction of the *Maine* was caused by an exterior explosion—that of a submarine mine.* It did not assume to place the responsibility. That remains to be fixed.

In any event, the destruction of the *Maine,* by whatever exterior cause, is a patent and impressive proof of a state of things in Cuba that is intolerable. That condition is thus shown to be such that the Spanish government cannot assure safety and security to a vessel of the American Navy in the harbor of Havana on a mission of peace, and rightfully there. . . .

[McKinley here refers to the offer by the Spanish minister to arbitrate the Maine, *and simply adds, "To this I have made no reply."]*

The long trial has proved that the object for which Spain has waged the war cannot be attained. The fire of insurrection may flame or may smolder with varying seasons, but it has not been, and it is plain that it cannot be, extinguished by present methods. The only hope of relief and repose from a condition which can no longer

---

*Assuming that the outside-explosion theory is correct—and it has been seriously challenged—the *Maine* might have been blown up by Cuban insurgents seeking to involve the United States in the war.

be endured is the enforced pacification of Cuba. In the name of humanity, in the name of civilization, in behalf of endangered American interests which give us the right and the duty to speak and to act, the war in Cuba must stop. . . .

The issue is now with the Congress. It is a solemn responsibility. I have exhausted every effort to relieve the intolerable condition of affairs which is at our doors. Prepared to execute every obligation imposed upon me by the Constitution and the law, I await your action.

Yesterday, and since the preparation of the foregoing message, official information was received by me that the latest decree of the Queen Regent of Spain directs General Blanco, in order to prepare and facilitate peace, to proclaim a suspension of hostilities, the duration and details of which have not yet been communicated to me.

This fact, with every other pertinent consideration, will, I am sure, have your just and careful attention in the solemn deliberations upon which you are about to enter. If this measure attains a successful result, then our aspirations as a Christian, peace-loving people will be realized. If it fails, it will be only another justification for our contemplated action.

[The president had prepared the foregoing war message a week or so before he submitted it; the delay was primarily to permit U.S. citizens to flee Cuba. A few hours before McKinley finally moved, cablegrams from Minister Stewart Woodford in Madrid brought the news that Spain, having already revoked reconcentration [the policy of herding Cuban rebels into concentration camps], had met the rest of the president's demands by authorizing an armistice. So, at the end of a message that urged war, McKinley casually tacked on the two foregoing paragraphs hinting that hostilities might be avoided. Eight days later a bellicose Congress overwhelmingly passed what was in effect a declaration of war. Several years after the event General Woodford told the journalist and reformer, O. G. Villard, "When I sent that last cable to McKinley, I thought I should wake up the next morning to find myself acclaimed all over the United States for having achieved the greatest diplomatic victory in our history." Instead, he learned of the war message. (O. G. Villard, Fighting Years *[New York: Harcourt, Brace and Co., 1939], p. 136.)]*

2. Professor Charles Eliot Norton's Patriotic Protest (1898)

Lovable and immensely popular, Charles Eliot Norton served for many years at Harvard as professor of the history of the fine arts. After war broke out, he shocked public opinion with a speech in Cambridge urging young men not to enlist. The press denounced him as one of the "intellectual copperheads." McKinley had recommended war in the interests of civilization; Norton here urges an opposite course. Who had the sounder arguments? Was it more patriotic to protest than to acquiesce?

And now of a sudden, without cool deliberation, without prudent preparation, the nation is hurried into war, and America, she who more than any other land was

---

[2]*Public Opinion* 24 (June 23, 1898): 775–776.

pledged to peace and good will on earth, unsheathes her sword, compels a weak and unwilling nation to a fight, rejecting without due consideration her [Spain's] earnest and repeated offers to meet every legitimate demand of the United States. It is a bitter disappointment to the lover of his country; it is a turning back from the path of civilization to that of barbarism.

"There never was a good war," said [Benjamin] Franklin. There have indeed been many wars in which a good man must take part. . . . But if a war be undertaken for the most righteous end, before the resources of peace have been tried and proved vain to secure it, that war has no defense. It is a national crime. The plea that the better government of Cuba, and the relief of the *reconcentrados,* could only be secured by war is the plea either of ignorance or of hypocrisy.

But the war is declared; and on all hands we hear the cry that he is no patriot who fails to shout for it, and to urge the youth of the country to enlist, and to rejoice that they are called to the service of their native land. The sober counsels that were appropriate before the war was entered upon must give way to blind enthusiasm, and the voice of condemnation must be silenced by the thunders of the guns and the hurrahs of the crowd.

Stop! A declaration of war does not change the moral law. "The Ten Commandments will not budge" at a joint resolve of Congress. . . . No! the voice of protest, of warning, of appeal is never more needed than when the clamor of fife and drum, echoed by the press and too often by the pulpit, is bidding all men fall in and keep step and obey in silence the tyrannous word of command. Then, more than ever, it is the duty of the good citizen not to be silent, and spite of obliquity, misrepresentation, and abuse, to insist on being heard, and with sober counsel to maintain the everlasting validity of the principles of the moral law.

C. The Sordid Little War

1. Rough Times for Rough Riders (1898)

Fight-thirsty Theodore Roosevelt was so determined to get into action that he resigned his post as assistant secretary of the navy. He hastily raised a volunteer cavalry outfit and, as lieutenant colonel of these Rough Riders, managed to reach Cuba—without the horses. Exposing himself with reckless courage, he got into the thick of the fray and won renown near Santiago. But commanding General William R. Shafter was too fat for active duty, the "embalmed beef" was vomit inducing, and most of the volunteers were poorly trained and equipped. They betrayed their position with old-fashioned, smoke-emitting powder; and one outfit dragged around a captive balloon, thereby revealing its movements. The easy naval victories, combined with the nation's holiday mood and Secretary of State John Hay's reference to the "splendid little war," left a false impression of glamor. What does Roosevelt's letter to his close friend, Senator Henry Cabot Lodge, suggest about this romantic image of the war? about Roosevelt's character?

---

[1]From *The Letters of Theodore Roosevelt* by E. E. Morrison, ed. Copyright © 1951 by the President and Fellows of Harvard College. Reprinted by permission of Harvard University Press.

Outside Santiago, July 3, 1898

Dear Cabot: Tell the President for Heaven's sake to send us every regiment and, above all, every battle possible. We have won so far at a heavy cost; but the Spaniards fight very hard, and charging these intrenchments against modern rifles is terrible. We are within measurable distance of a terrible military disaster; we *must* have help—thousands of men, batteries, and *food* and ammunition. The other volunteers are at a hideous disadvantage owing to their not having smokeless powder. Our General [Shafter] is poor; he is too unwieldy to get to the front. I commanded my regiment, I think I may say, with honor. We lost a quarter of our men. For three days I have been at the extreme front of the firing line; how I have escaped I know not; I have not blanket or coat; I have not taken off my shoes even; I sleep in the drenching rain, and drink putrid water. Best love to Nannie [Lodge's wife].

2. Disillusionment over the Cubans (1898)

The U.S. press, in playing up Spanish atrocities, had idealized the nondescript Cuban insurgents and their shadowy government. The liberating U.S. troops were speedily disillusioned. They had to restrain their ragged allies from pillaging towns, shooting Spanish prisoners, and butchering the wounded. The insurgents flatly refused to help their deliverers with such menial tasks as building roads and carrying American wounded from the battlefield. U.S. anger and contempt naturally bred Cuban resentment. In the Teller amendment, passed by Congress in 1898, the United States had pledged itself to free Cuba; in the Platt amendment, passed by Congress in 1902, Washington reserved the right to intervene to preserve order. What was the relationship between the Platt amendment and the views expressed in the following editorial in a Virginia newspaper?

Day by day the news from Santiago brings out more clearly the real character of the majority of the Cuban insurgents. Men who have to be prevented by force from killing prisoners and plundering surrendered cities are not likely to make admirable citizens of an independent country. Liberty, according to their conception of it, would truly be synonymous with many crimes.

In the meanwhile, let us be thankful that the President [McKinley] stood so strongly against the recognition of the alleged insurgent government—a step which was urged with ceaseless vehemence by many influential members of Congress, and by innumerable orators and periodicals. Wouldn't we have been in a pretty predicament if we had found ourselves obliged at every point to bow to the wishes of the undisciplined, bloodthirsty guerrillas who seem to compose the majority of the insurgent forces?

Of course, we believe that Cuba will rise from her ruin and show herself fully worthy of the attempt that has been made to save her, but a good many years will pass before it will be safe for the United States to withdraw their troops and leave

---

[2]*Norfolk* (Virginia) *Landmark,* in *Public Opinion* 25 (July 28, 1898): 104.

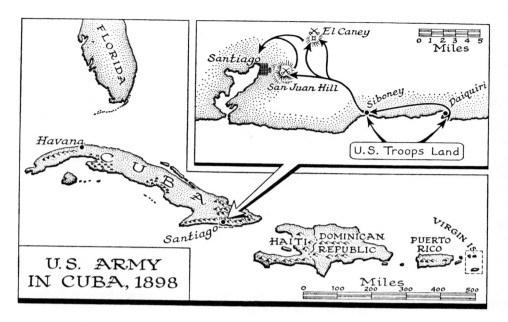

the island to her own devices. Even then, it is a question whether Cuban independence outside of the Union will be a success or a failure.

D. The Siren Song of Imperialism

1. McKinley Prays for Guidance (1898)

What to do with the conquered Philippines? At first President McKinley considered taking only a foothold at Manila, on the main island of Luzon. But this would be rendered militarily untenable if the remaining islands should fall into the hands of an unfriendly power, possibly Germany. The decision then lay between all and nothing. To hand back the islands to Spain was unthinkable. After fighting a war to free Cuba from Spanish misrule, the United States could hardly return the Filipinos, who had risen in revolt, to Spanish misrule. To cut them completely loose, however, might result in a mad scramble among the powers that would touch off a world war into which the United States might be drawn. McKinley had to make the decision while badly upset by the murder of his brother-in-law at the hands of a betrayed woman.

---

[1]This document is a report of an interview with McKinley at the White House, November 21, 1899, written by one of the interviewers and confirmed by others present. Published in *Christian Advocate*, January 22, 1903, it is here reprinted from C. S. Olcott, *The Life of William McKinley* (1916), vol. 2, pp. 110–111.

He later told a group of fellow Methodists how he sought divine guidance, presumably late in October 1898. How sound was McKinley's reasoning? Are there elments of racism in his thinking?

When next I realized that the Philippines had dropped into our laps, I confess I did not know what to do with them. I sought counsel from all sides—Democrats as well as Republicans—but got little help. I thought first we would take only Manila; then Luzon; then other islands, perhaps, also.

I walked the floor of the White House night after night until midnight; and I am not ashamed to tell you, gentlemen, that I went down on my knees and prayed Almighty God for light and guidance more than one night. And one night late it came to me this way—I don't know how it was, but it came:

(1) That we could not give them back to Spain—that would be cowardly and dishonorable;

(2) That we could not turn them over to France or Germany, our commercial rivals in the Orient—that would be bad business and discreditable;

(3) That we could not leave them to themselves—they were unfit for self-government, and they would soon have anarchy and misrule worse than Spain's was; and

(4) That there was nothing left for us to do but to take them all, and to educate the Filipinos, and uplift and civilize and Christianize them and by God's grace do the very best we could by them, as our fellow men, for whom Christ also died.

And then I went to bed and went to sleep, and slept soundly, and the next morning I sent for the chief engineer of the War Department (our map-maker), and I told him to put the Philippines on the map of the United States (pointing to a large map on the wall of his office), and there they are and there they will stay while I am President!

2. Professor William Sumner Spurns Empire (1898)

The "magnificently bald" and "iron-voiced" Professor William G. Sumner of Yale was an immensely popular lecturer and a leading anti-imperialist. Fearlessly outspoken, he offended influential alumni by opposing tariff protection and by turning a cynical eye on the United States' "civilizing mission" in the Philippines. The truth is that the more obvious the natural resources of the islands became, the less capable the inhabitants seemed of self-rule. The moral obligation of the "white man's burden," which the British poet Kipling urged the United States to shoulder, had many of the earmarks of the loot sack. The British welcomed Americans as fellow civilizers, no doubt in part because imperialistic misery loved company. Why did Sumner believe that the conquered peoples would be unlikely to accept U.S. rule, and that such rule was a perversion of American principles?

There is not a civilized nation which does not talk about its civilizing mission just as grandly as we do. The English, who really have more to boast of it in this re-

---

[2]W. G. Sumner, *War and Other Essays* (1919), pp. 303–305.

spect than anybody else, talk least about it, but the Phariseeism with which they correct and instruct other people has made them hated all over the globe. The French believe themselves the guardians of the highest and purest culture, and that the eyes of all mankind are fixed on Paris, whence they expect oracles of thought and taste. The Germans regard themselves as charged with a mission, especially to us Americans, to save us from egoism and materialism. The Russians, in their books and newspapers, talk about the civilizing mission of Russia in language that might be translated from some of the finest paragraphs in our imperialistic newspapers.

The first principle of Mohammedanism is that we Christians are dogs and infidels, fit only to be enslaved or butchered by Moslems. It is a corollary that wherever Mohammedanism extends it carries, in the belief of its votaries, the highest blessings, and that the whole human race would be enormously elevated if Mohammedanism should supplant Christianity everywhere.

To come, last, to Spain, the Spaniards have, for centuries, considered themselves the most zealous and self-sacrificing Christians, especially charged by the Almighty, on this account, to spread true religion and civilization over the globe. They think themselves free and noble, leaders in refinement and the sentiments of personal honor, and they despise us as sordid money-grabbers and heretics. I could bring you passages from peninsular authors of the first rank about the grand rôle of Spain and Portugal in spreading freedom and truth.

Now each nation laughs at all the others when it observes these manifestations of national vanity. You may rely upon it that they are all ridiculous by virtue of these pretensions, including ourselves. The point is that each of them repudiates the standards of the others, and the outlying nations, which are to be civilized, hate all the standards of civilized men.

We assume that what we like and practice, and what we think better, must come as a welcome blessing to Spanish-Americans and Filipinos. This is grossly and obviously untrue. They hate our ways. They are hostile to our ideas. Our religion, language, institutions, and manners offend them. They like their own ways, and if we appear amongst them as rulers, there will be social discord in all the great departments of social interest. The most important thing which we shall inherit from the Spaniards will be the task of suppressing rebellions.

If the United States takes out of the hands of Spain her mission, on the ground that Spain is not executing it well, and if this nation in its turn attempts to be schoolmistress to others, it will shrivel up into the same vanity and self-conceit of which Spain now presents an example. To read our current literature one would think that we were already well on the way to it.

Now, the great reason why all these enterprises which begin by saying to somebody else, "We know what is good for you better than you know yourself and we are going to make you do it," are false and wrong is that they violate liberty; or, to turn the same statement into other words, the reason why liberty, of which we Americans talk so much, is a good thing is that it means leaving people to live out their own lives in their own way, while we do the same.

If we believe in liberty, as an American principle, why do we not stand by it? Why are we going to throw it away to enter upon a Spanish policy of dominion and regulation?

3. Albert Beveridge Trumpets Imperialism (1898)

Albert J. Beveridge delivered this famous speech, "The March of the Flag," at Indianapolis, Indiana, on September 16, 1898, before McKinley had decided to keep the Philippines. Born to an impoverished family, Beveridge had spent his youth at hard manual labor but ultimately secured a college education with prizes won in oratorical contests. The cadences of his spellbinding oratory were such that "Mr. Dooley" (F. P. Dunne) said you could waltz to them. The year after making this address, Beveridge was elected to the U.S. Senate from Indiana at the remarkably youthful age of thirty-six. How convincing is his reply to the anti-imperialists' warnings against the annexation of noncontiguous territory and to their argument that no more land was needed? What were his powers as a prophet?

Distance and oceans are no arguments. The fact that all the territory our fathers bought and seized is contiguous is no argument. In 1819 Florida was further from New York than Porto Rico is from Chicago today; Texas, further from Washington in 1845 than Hawaii is from Boston in 1898; California, more inaccessible in 1847 than the Philippines are now. . . . The ocean does not separate us from lands of our duty and desire—the oceans join us, a river never to be dredged, a canal never to be repaired.

Steam joins us; electricity joins us—the very elements are in league with our destiny. Cuba not contiguous! Porto Rico not contiguous! Hawaii and the Philippines not contiguous! Our navy will make them contiguous. [Admirals] Dewey and Sampson and Schley have made them contiguous, and American speed, American guns, American heart and brain and nerve will keep them contiguous forever.

But the Opposition is right—there is a difference. We did not need the western Mississippi Valley when we acquired it, nor Florida, nor Texas, nor California, nor the royal provinces of the far Northwest. We had no emigrants to people this imperial wilderness, no money to develop it, even no highways to cover it. No trade awaited us in its savage fastnesses. Our productions were not greater than our trade. There was not one reason for the land-lust of our statesmen from Jefferson to Grant, other than the prophet and the Saxon within them.

But today we are raising more than we can consume. Today we are making more than we can use. Today our industrial society is congested; there are more workers than there is work; there is more capital than there is investment. We do not need more money—we need more circulation, more employment. Therefore we must find new markets for our produce, new occupation for our capital, new work for our labor. And so, while we did not need the territory taken during the past century at the time it was acquired, we do need what we have taken in 1898, and we need it now.

Think of the thousands of Americans who will pour into Hawaii and Porto Rico when the republic's laws cover those islands with justice and safety! Think of the tens of thousands of Americans who will invade mine and field and forest in the Philippines when a liberal government, protected and controlled by this republic, if not the government of the republic itself, shall establish order and equity there!

---

[3]C. M. Depew, ed., *The Library of Oratory* (New York: The Globe Publishing Company, 1902), vol. 14, pp. 438–440.

Think of the hundreds of thousands of Americans who will build a soap-and-water, common-school civilization of energy and industry in Cuba, when a government of law replaces the double reign of anarchy and tyranny!—think of the prosperous millions that Empress of Islands will support when, obedient to the law of political gravitation, her people ask for the highest honor liberty can bestow, the sacred Order of the Stars and Stripes, the citizenship of the Great Republic!

What does all this mean for every one of us? It means opportunity for all the glorious young manhood of the republic—the most virile, ambitious, impatient, militant manhood the world has ever seen. It means that the resources and the commerce of these immensely rich dominions will be increased as much as American energy is greater than Spanish sloth; for Americans henceforth will monopolize those resources and that commerce.

[The Treaty of Paris, by which the United States acquired the Philippines, received Senate approval by a close vote on February 6, 1899. The imperialists had little to add to the materialistic-humanitarian arguments presented by McKinley and Beveridge. The anti-imperialists stressed the folly of annexing noncontiguous areas in the tropics thickly populated by alien peoples. They also harped on the folly of departing from the principles of freedom and nonintervention as set forth in the Declaration of Independence, Washington's Farewell Address, the Monroe Doctrine, and the Emancipation Proclamation. Senator George F. Hoar of Massachusetts assailed the imperialists with these words: "If you ask them what they want, you are answered with a shout: 'Three cheers for the flag! Who will dare to haul it down? Hold on to everything you can get. The United States is strong enough to do what it likes. The Declaration of Independence and the counsel of Washington and the Constitution of the United States have grown rusty and musty. They are for little countries and not for great ones. There is no moral law for strong nations. America has outgrown Americanism.'" (Congressional Record, 55th Cong., 3d sess., [1899] p. 495.)]

Thought Provokers

1. Does the press in a democracy have an ethical responsibility to pursue sober policies, even if such tactics hurt circulation? Has the press shown more responsibility in recent years than in 1898?
2. Were patriotic Spaniards justified in resenting American attitudes and accusations in 1897–1898? Should the United States have accepted arbitration of the *Maine* dispute?
3. It has been said that a joint-power intervention in Cuba for humanitarian reasons would have been on sounder ground than the United States' unilateral intervention. Explain. Using McKinley's reasoning, would Spain have been justified in intervening in the American Civil War to prevent continued bloodshed off Cuba's shores? Would a grant of autonomy have solved the Cuban problem?
4. To what extent were the anti-imperialists idealists? Was there anything morally objectionable in their attitude?
5. In the long run, would the United States have been better off if it had kept Cuba and relinquished the Philippines? Did intervention solve the Cuban problem? Has the so-called white man's burden proved to be unselfish or a cover for selfishness?

28

America on the World Stage, 1899–1909

The mission of the United States is one of benevolent assimilation.

President McKinley, 1898

Prologue: The resentful Filipinos, unwilling to be caged by American overlords, revolted in 1899. The insurrection dragged on scandalously for seven years. In 1900 the Democratic presidential candidate, William Jennings Bryan, trumpeting anti-imperialism as the "paramount issue," again ran unsuccessfully against the prosperity president, William McKinley. The victor was fatally shot late in 1901 after serving only six months of his second term. Theodore Roosevelt, moving up from the vice presidency, promptly launched a two-fisted, big-stick foreign policy. By strong-arm methods, he secured a canal zone at Panama and then "made the dirt fly." By devising the Roosevelt corollary to the Monroe Doctrine, he intervened in the bankrupt Dominican Republic to prevent other powers from intervening. By mediating a settlement at the end of the Russo-Japanese War in 1905, he won the Nobel Peace Prize. And by interceding in the quarrel between California and Japan over Japanese immigrants, he worked out the "Gentlemen's Agreement" for amicably halting the inflow.

A. The Bitter Fruits of Imperialism

1. Albert Beveridge Deplores Unpatriotic Talk (1900)

The Filipino troops, under their leader Emilio Aguinaldo, had cooperated loyally with the Americans in capturing Manila. They had received informal promises of freedom, but when these were not honored, they rose in revolt. The fighting between Filipinos and Americans rapidly degenerated into brutal guerrilla warfare. Albert J. Beveridge of Indiana (see p. 184), recently elected to the U.S. Senate, went to the Philippines on a personal tour of inspection and reported his findings in an impressive Senate speech. Should the anti-imperialists have been silenced by his argument?

It has been charged that our conduct of the war has been cruel. Senators, it has been the reverse. I have been in our hospitals and seen the Filipino wounded as

[1]*Congressional Record,* 56th Cong., 1st sess. (January 9, 1900), p. 708.

carefully, tenderly cared for as our own. Within our lines they may plow and sow and reap and go about the affairs of peace with absolute liberty. And yet all this kindness was misunderstood, or rather not understood. Senators must remember that we are not dealing with Americans or Europeans. We are dealing with Orientals. We are dealing with Orientals who are Malays. We are dealing with Malays instructed in Spanish methods. They mistake kindness for weakness, forbearance for fear. . . .

Mr. President, reluctantly and only from a sense of duty am I forced to say that American opposition to the war has been the chief factor in prolonging it. Had Aguinaldo not understood that in America, even in the American Congress, even here in the Senate, he and his cause were supported; had he had not known that it was proclaimed on the stump and in the press of a faction in the United States that every shot his misguided followers fired into the breasts of American soldiers was like the volleys fired by Washington's men against the soldiers of King George, his insurrection would have dissolved before it entirely crystallized.

The utterances of American opponents of the war are read to the ignorant soldiers of Aguinaldo, and repeated in exaggerated form among the common people. Attempts have been made by wretches claiming American citizenship to ship arms and ammunition from Asiatic ports to Filipinos, and these acts of infamy were coupled by the Malays with American assaults on our government at home.

The Filipinos do not understand free speech, and therefore our tolerance of American assaults on the American President and the American government means to them that our President is in the minority or he would not permit what appears to them such treasonable criticism. It is believed and stated in [the islands of] Luzon, Panay, and Cebu that the Filipinos have only to fight, harass, retreat, break up into small parties, if necessary, as they are doing now, but by any means hold out until the next presidential election, and our forces will be withdrawn.

All this has aided the enemy more than climate, arms, and battle. Senators, I have heard these reports myself; I have talked with the people; I have seen our mangled boys in the hospital and field; I have stood on the firing line and beheld our dead soldiers, their faces turned to the pitiless southern sky, and in sorrow rather than anger I say to those whose voices in America have cheered those misguided natives on to shoot our soldiers down, that the blood of those dead and wounded boys of ours is on their hands, and the flood of all the years can never wash that stain away. In sorrow rather than anger I say these words, for I earnestly believe that our brothers knew not what they did.

2. William Jennings Bryan
Vents His Bitterness (1901)

In 1900 the Republican President McKinley, who favored keeping the Philippines, again ran against the Democrat William J. Bryan, who favored giving them independence. Republicans accused Bryan of prolonging the insurrection by holding out false hopes. One popular magazine published a picture of the Filipino leader on its

---

[2]*Commoner,* November 22, 1901.

front cover, with the query, "Who is behind Aguinaldo?" The curious reader lifted a flap and saw the hawklike features of Bryan. McKinley triumphed by a handsome margin, and Republicans misleadingly hailed the results as a national mandate to retain the islands. The next year Bryan expressed his bitterness as follows, several months after the United States had captured Aguinaldo. What is his strongest rebuttal to Republican charges that the Democrats were responsible for prolonging the insurrection? How good a prophet was Bryan?

In the campaign of 1900 the Republican leaders denied that their party contemplated a permanent increase in the standing army. They asserted that a large army was only necessary because of the insurrection in the Philippines, and they boldly declared that the insurrection would cease immediately if the Republican ticket was successful. The Democratic platform and Democratic speakers were blamed for the prolongation of the war. "Just re-elect President McKinley," they said, "and let the Filipinos know they are not to have independence, and they will lay down their arms and our soldiers can come home."

Well, the Republican ticket was elected, and the Filipinos were notified that they were not to have independence. But a month after the election the Republicans rushed through Congress a bill authorizing the President to raise the regular army to 100,000, and now, after a year has elapsed, the insurrection is still in progress and the end is not yet. Some of the worst losses of the year have been suffered by our troops within two months. . . .

After the Republican victory made it impossible for the imperialists to blame the anti-imperialists for the continuation of hostilities, the Republican leaders declared that Aguinaldo, actuated by selfish ambition, was compelling his countrymen to continue the war. But even after his capture and imprisonment—yes, even after his captors had secured from him an address advising his comrades to surrender—the insurrection continued.

How long will it take the imperialists to learn that we can never have peace in the Philippine Islands? That we can suppress open resistance is certain, although the cost may be far beyond any gain that can be derived from a colonial government, but that we can ever make the Filipinos love us or trust us while we rule them through a carpetbag government is absurd.

If the Republicans had read the speeches of Abraham Lincoln as much recently as they did in former years, they would have known that hatred of an alien government is a natural thing and a thing to be expected everywhere. Lincoln said that it was God himself who placed in every human heart the love of liberty. . . .

3. The Nation *Denounces Atrocities* (1902)

Many of the Filipino tribes were simple peoples who knew little of so-called civilized warfare. Some of them would horribly mutilate and torture American captives, sometimes fastening them down to be eaten alive by insects. The infuriated white soldiers retaliated by shooting a few prisoners and by administering the "water cure"— forcing buckets of dirty water into Filipinos, deflating them with rifle butts, and

---

[3]*The Nation* (New York) 74 (May 8, 1902): 357.

repeating the painful process. In certain areas the Americans herded the populace into reconcentration camps, somewhat after the manner of "Butcher" Weyler in Cuba. General Jacob ("Hell Roaring Jake") Smith was "admonished" by the War Department for an order (not carried out) to kill all males over ten years of age on the island of Samar. How sound is the parallel that the New York Nation *here draws between Spanish behavior in Cuba and U.S. behavior in the Philippines?*

Even if the condemnation of barbarous warfare in the Philippines by the imperialist press is somewhat belated, we welcome it, as we welcome everything that compels Americans to give attention to a subject to which too many of them have become increasingly indifferent. Silence, we know, is consistent with shame, and may be one of the signs of its existence; and the fact that only a few of the more unblushing or foolish newspapers have defended Gen. Smith's policy of extermination shows what the general sentiment is.

To allege the provocation which our soldiers had is to set up a defense which President Roosevelt brushed aside in advance. To fall back on the miserable sophistry that "war is hell" is only another way of making out those who engage in that kind of war to be fiends. It is, besides, to offer an excuse for ourselves which we did not tolerate for an instant in the case of Spanish atrocities. That is our present moral humiliation in the eyes of the world.

We made war on Spain four years ago for doing the very things of which we are now guilty ourselves. As the Chicago *News* pointedly observes, we are giving Spain as good reason to interfere with us on the ground of humanity as we had to interfere with her. Doubtless she would interfere if she were strong enough and thought she could acquire some islands in the virtuous act.

4. A San Francisco Weekly Defends the Army (1902)

Moderate defenders of the Republican administration replied that the charges of cruelty were grossly exaggerated, that atrocity stories were being used by Democrats for partisan advantage, and that in any event such tales did not affect the question of the United States' duty in the Philippines. The Outlook *(April 26, 1902) concluded: "The humanity of the army as a whole cannot be discredited by single acts of cruelty, no matter how abhorrent these may be in their character." The extreme imperialists openly avowed a policy of brutality. Shockingly frank was the* San Francisco Argonaut, *a respectable and long-lived weekly magazine. How does it apportion the blame for the existing situation between Republicans and Democrats? What force is there in its case for the army?*

There has been too much hypocrisy about this Philippine business—too much snivel—too much cant. Let us all be frank.

WE DO NOT WANT THE FILIPINOS.

WE WANT THE PHILIPPINES.

All our troubles in this annexation matter have been caused by the presence in the Philippine Islands of the Filipinos. Were it not for them, the Treaty of Paris

---

[4]*San Francisco Argonaut* 50 (May 26, 1902): 342.

would have been an excellent thing; the purchase of the archipelago for twenty millions of dollars would have been cheap. The islands are enormously rich; they abound in dense forests of valuable hardwood timber; they contain mines of the precious metals; their fertile lands will produce immense crops of sugar cane, rice, and tobacco. Touched by the wand of American enterprise, fertilized with American capital, these islands would speedily become richer than Golconda was of old.

But, unfortunately, they are infested by Filipinos. There are many millions of them there, and it is to be feared that their extinction will be slow. Still, every man who believes in developing the islands must admit that it cannot be done successfully while the Filipinos are there. They are indolent. They raise only enough food to live on; they don't care to make money; and they occupy land which might be utilized to much better advantage by Americans. Therefore the more of them killed, the better.

It seems harsh. But they must yield before the superior race, and the American syndicate. How shortsighted, then, to check the army in its warfare upon these savages; particularly when the army is merely carrying out its orders and the duly expressed wishes of the American people, as shown through their elections and their representatives.

Doubtless, many of the excellent gentlemen now in Congress would repudiate these sentiments as brutal. But we are only saying what they are doing. We believe in stripping all hypocritical verbiage from national declarations, and telling the truth simply and boldly. We repeat—the American people, after thought and deliberation, have shown their wishes. THEY DO NOT WANT THE FILIPINOS. THEY WANT THE PHILIPPINES.

It is no one party, no one class, that is responsible for our Philippine policy. It is the people of the United States. The Democratic Party shares equally the responsibility with the Republican Party. The Democratic Party voted for the war with Spain. Had it opposed the fifty-million [arms] appropriation, the war could not have taken place. The Democrats advocated the purchase of the Philippines. For a time the confirmation of the Philippine treaty was in doubt. It was the direct personal lobbying of William J. Bryan with the Democratic Senators which led to the confirmation of the Philippine purchase, and which also led to the present bloody war. Mr. Bryan said at the time that he advocated the confirmation of the treaty in order to put "the Republicans into a hole." He has certainly put his country into a hole. Is he proud of his work?

We are all responsible. You, reader, are responsible. If you are a Republican, your party has made this action part of its national policy. If you are a Democrat, your party, by its vote in the House of Representatives, made the war possible, and by its vote in the Senate turned the scales for the purchase of the Philippines.

But if we, the people of the United States, are responsible for the Philippine campaign, the American army is not. The army is only seventy thousand out of seventy millions. The army did not ask to go there. It was sent. It has fought for four years under tropic suns and torrential rains, in pestilential jungles and miasmatic swamps, patiently bearing the burdens placed upon it by the home country, and with few laurels to be gained as a result of hard and dangerous duty. Nearly every general officer returning from the Philippines has returned to either a wrecked reputation, newspaper odium, or public depreciation. Look at Merritt, Otis, Merriam, MacArthur, Funston. The best treatment that any of them has received is not to be abused. And yet, with these melancholy examples before them, our army toils on uncomplainingly doing its duty.

The army did not bring on the war. We civilians did it. The army is only doing our bidding as faithful servants of their country. And now that they have shown a perfectly human tendency to fight the devil with fire, we must not repudiate their actions, for their actions are our own. They are receiving the fire of the enemy from the front. It is shameful that there should be a fire upon them from the rear.

B. The Panama Revolution

1. John Hay Twists Colombia's Arm (1903)

The Spanish-American War, which netted a far-flung empire, increased public pressure for an isthmian canal. Nicaragua had long been the favored route, but in 1902 Congress approved Colombia's Isthmus of Panama. Secretary of State Hay, by threatening to revert to the Nicaragua route, finally secured a treaty from the reluctant Colombian envoy in Washington. But the Senate of Colombia delayed ratification, for it was dissatisfied with the rather niggardly financial terms offered for this priceless asset—$10 million plus an annual payment of $250,000. Secretary Hay thereupon sent the following telegram to the U.S. minister in Bogotá, the capital of Colombia. Critics have contended that this statement contains an intolerable threat to a sovereign republic. Does it?

Department of State
Washington, June 9, 1903

The Colombian Government apparently does not appreciate the gravity of the situation. The canal negotiations were initiated by Colombia, and were energetically pressed upon this Government for several years. The propositions presented by Colombia, with slight modifications, were finally accepted by us. In virtue of this agreement our Congress reversed its previous judgment [favoring Nicaragua] and decided upon the Panama route. If Colombia should now reject the treaty or unduly delay its ratification, the friendly understanding between the two countries would be so seriously compromised that action might be taken by the Congress next winter which every friend of Colombia would regret. Confidential. Communicate substance of this verbally to the minister of foreign affairs. If he desires it, give him a copy in form of memorandum.

Hay

[When the American envoy in Bogotá conveyed this stern message to the foreign minister, the latter asked whether the threat meant hostile measures against Colombia or the adoption of the Nicaragua route. The American was unable to answer. Actually, Secretary Hay took liberties with the truth when he stated that Colombia had "energetically pressed" canal negotiations for several years. In fact, Washington had done the pressing.]

---

[1] *Foreign Relations of the United States,* 1903 (Washington, D.C.: Government Printing Office, 1904), p. 146.

2. Theodore Roosevelt Hopes for Revolt (1903)

The Colombian Senate unanimously rejected the canal zone treaty on August 12, 1903. Among other motives, it hoped to secure for Colombia an additional $40 million—the sum that Washington was proposing to pay the heirs of the French company that had started the canal in the 1870s. The Panamanians feared that the United States would now turn to Nicaragua, as the law required Roosevelt to do if blocked, and thus deprive the Panamanians of the anticipated prosperity that the canal would bring. They had revolted against Colombia's misrule fifty-three times in the past fifty-seven years (by Roosevelt's count), and they were now riper than ever for rebellion. The following letter that Roosevelt sent to Dr. Albert Shaw, editor of the Review of Reviews, *is often cited as evidence that he connived at the revolt. Does it provide good supporting evidence for that conclusion?*

My dear Dr. Shaw: I enclose you, purely for your own information, a copy of a letter of September 5th from our Minister to Colombia. I think it might interest you to see that there was absolutely not the slightest chance of securing by treaty any more than we endeavored to secure. The alternatives were to go to Nicaragua, against the advice of the great majority of competent engineers—some of the most competent saying that we had better have no canal at this time than go there—or else to take the territory by force without any attempt at getting a treaty.

I cast aside the proposition made at this time to foment the secession of Panama. Whatever other governments can do, the United States cannot go into the securing by such underhand means, the secession. Privately, I freely say to you that I should be delighted if Panama were an independent State, or if it made itself so at this moment; but for me to say so publicly would amount to an instigation of revolt, and therefore I cannot say it.

3. Official Connivance in Washington (1903)

The rebels in Panama, encouraged by Roosevelt's ill-concealed anger, revolted on November 3, 1903. Under the ancient treaty of 1846 with Colombia, the United States had guaranteed the neutrality of the isthmus, obviously against foreign invaders. In this case Roosevelt guaranteed the neutrality of the isthmus by having orders issued to the Nashville *and other U.S. naval units to prevent Colombian troops from landing and crossing from the Atlantic port of Colón to Panama City and crushing the rebellion. On November 4, 1903, Panama proclaimed its independence. A little more than an hour after receiving the news, Roosevelt hastily authorized de facto recognition, which was extended on November 6, 1903. This unseemly haste suggested improper connivance by Washington, and in response to a public demand Roosevelt sent the following official documents to Congress. They consist of interchanges between Acting Secretary of State Francis B. Loomis (Hay was then absent) and the U.S. vice-consul general at Panama City, Felix Ehrman. What do these documents suggest about U.S. complicity in the Panamanian revolution?*

[2]From *The Letters of Theodore Roosevelt* by E. E. Morrison, ed. Copyright © 1951 by the President and Fellows of Harvard College. Reprinted by permission of Harvard University Press.
[3]*Foreign Relations of the United States* (Washington, D.C.: Government Printing Office, 1903), p. 231.

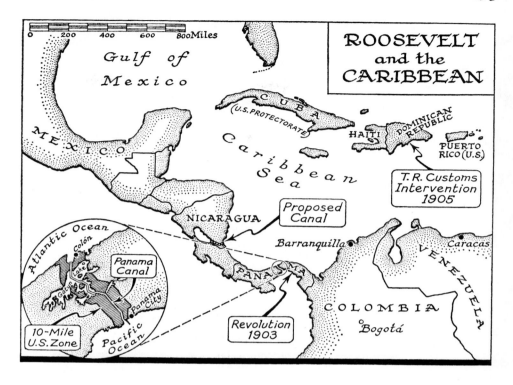

Mr. Loomis to Mr. Ehrman
Department of State
Washington, November 3, 1903
(Sent 3:40 P.M.)

Uprising on Isthmus reported. Keep Department promptly and fully informed.

Loomis, Acting

Mr. Ehrman to Mr. Hay
Panama, November 3, 1903
(Received 8:15 P.M.)

No uprising yet. Reported will be in the night. Situation is critical.

Ehrman

Mr. Ehrman to Mr. Hay
Panama, November 3, 1903
(Received 9:50 P.M.)

Uprising occurred [at Panama City] tonight, 6; no bloodshed. [Colombian] Army
and navy officials taken prisoners. Government will be organized tonight, consisting

three consuls, also cabinet. Soldiers changed. Supposed same movement will be effected in Colón. Order prevails so far. Situation serious. Four hundred [Colombian] soldiers landed Colón today [from] Barranquilla.

Ehrman

Mr. Loomis to Mr. Ehrman
Department of State
Washington, November 3, 1903
(Sent 11:18 P.M.)

Message sent to *Nashville* to Colón may not have been delivered. Accordingly see that following message is sent to *Nashville* immediately: *Nashville,* Colón:

In the interests of peace make every effort to prevent [Colombian] Government troops at Colón from proceeding to Panama. The transit of the Isthmus must be kept open and order maintained. Acknowledge.

(signed) *Darling,* Acting [Secretary of Navy]

Secure special train [to deliver message], if necessary. Act promptly.

Loomis, Acting

[Resolute action by Commander Hubbard of the Nashville, *in response to his instructions from Washington, forced the Colombian troops to sail away from Colón on November 5, two days after the revolutionists seized Panama City.]*

C. The Monroe Doctrine in the Caribbean

1. Roosevelt Launches a Corollary (1904)

The corrupt and bankrupt "banana republics" of the Caribbean were inclined to overborrow, and Roosevelt believed they could properly be "spanked" by European creditors. But the British-German spanking of Venezuela in 1902 resulted in the sinking of two Venezuelan gunboats and the bombardment of a fort and village. Such interventions foreshadowed a possibly permanent foothold and a consequent violation of the Monroe Doctrine. Sensing this danger, Roosevelt, in his annual message to Congress of 1904, sketched out his famous corollary to the Monroe Doctrine. Monroe had in effect warned the European powers in 1823, "Hands off." Roosevelt was now saying that since the United States would not permit the powers to lay their

---

[1]*A Compilation of the Messages and Papers of the Presidents* (New York: Bureau of National Literature, 1906) vol. 16 (December 6, 1904), pp. 7053–7054.

hands on, he had an obligation to do so himself. In short, he would intervene to keep them from intervening. In the statement embodied in his annual message, how does he justify this newly announced U.S. role, and what assurances does he give to the Latin American countries?

It is not true that the United States feels any land hunger or entertains any projects as regards the other nations of the Western Hemisphere, save such as are for their welfare. All that this country desires is to see the neighboring countries stable, orderly, and prosperous. Any country whose people conduct themselves well can count upon our hearty friendship. If a nation shows that it knows how to act with reasonable efficiency and decency in social and political matters, if it keeps order and pays its obligations, it need fear no interference from the United States.

Chronic wrongdoing, or an impotence which results in a general loosening of the ties of civilized society, may in America, as elsewhere, ultimately require intervention by some civilized nation, and in the Western Hemisphere the adherence of the United States to the Monroe Doctrine may force the United States, however reluctantly, in flagrant cases of such wrongdoing or impotence, to the exercise of an international police power. If every country washed by the Caribbean Sea would show the progress in stable and just civilization which, with the aid of the Platt amendment, Cuba has shown since our troops left the island, and which so many of the republics in both Americas are constantly and brilliantly showing, all question of interference by this Nation with their affairs would be at an end.

Our interests and those of our southern neighbors are in reality identical. They have great natural riches, and if within their borders the reign of law and justice obtains, prosperity is sure to come to them. While they thus obey the primary laws of civilized society, they may rest assured that they will be treated by us in a spirit of cordial and helpful sympathy. We would interfere with them only in the last resort, and then only if it became evident that their inability or unwillingness to do justice at home and abroad had violated the rights of the United States or had invited foreign aggression to the detriment of the entire body of American nations. It is a mere truism to say that every nation, whether in America or anywhere else, which desires to maintain its freedom, its independence, must ultimately realize that the right of such independence cannot be separated from the responsibility of making good use of it.

2. A Latin American Protests (1943)

Following up his new corollary to the Monroe Doctrine, Roosevelt arranged with the local authorities to take over and administer the customshouses of the bankrupt Santo Domingo. The European creditors then had no real excuse for interfering, for they received their regular payments. In his annual message of 1905, Roosevelt

---

[2]Luis Quintanilla, *A Latin American Speaks* (New York: The Macmillan Company 1943), pp. 125–126. By permission of the author.

added a refinement to his corollary to the Monroe Doctrine: to prevent European creditors from taking over customshouses (and perhaps staying), the United States had an obligation to take over the customshouses. In subsequent years, and pursuant to the Roosevelt corollary to the Monroe Doctrine, the marines landed and acted as international policemen, notably in Haiti, Santo Domingo, and Nicaragua. The Latin Americans, cherishing their sovereign right to revolution and disorder, bitterly resented this bayonet-enforced twisting of Monroe's protective dictum. Below, an outspoken Mexican diplomat, with a Ph.D. from Johns Hopkins University, expresses his wrath. It has been said that the Roosevelt corollary was so radically different from the original Monroe Doctrine (see Vol. I, p. 255) that the two should never have been associated. Was Roosevelt's corollary a logical extension or a radical revision of the Monroe Doctrine?

No document has proved more harmful to the prestige of the United States in the Western Hemisphere [than the Roosevelt corollary]. No White House policy could be more distasteful to Latin Americans—not even, perhaps, outspoken imperialism. Latin Americans are usually inclined to admire strength, force, a nation *muy hombre* [very manly]. This was imperialism without military glamour. . . . Moreover, it was a total distortion of the original Message. Monroe's Doctrine was defensive and negative: defensive, in that it was essentially an opposition to eventual aggression from Europe; negative, in that it simply told Europe what it should not do—not what the United States should do.

The Monroe Doctrine of later corollaries became aggressive and positive; aggressive, because, even without actual European attack, it urged United States "protection" of Latin America—and that was outright intervention; positive, because instead of telling Europe what not to do, it told the United States what it should do in the Western Hemisphere. From a case of America vs. Europe, the corollaries made of the Doctrine a case of the United States vs. America.

President Monroe had merely shaken his head, brandished his finger, and said to Europe, "Now, now, gentlemen, if you meddle with us, we will not love you any more," while Teddy Roosevelt, brandishing a big stick, had shouted, "Listen, you guys, don't muscle in—this territory is ours."

In still another corollary, enunciated to justify United States intervention [in Santo Domingo], the same Roosevelt said: "It is far better that this country should put through such an arrangement [enforcing fulfillment of financial obligations contracted by Latin American states] rather than to allow any foreign country to undertake it." To intervene in order to protect: to intervene in order to prevent others from so doing. It is the "Invasion for Protection" corollary, so much in the limelight recently, in other parts of the world.

[Latin American bitterness against this perversion of the Monroe Doctrine festered for nearly three decades. A sharp turn for the better came in 1933, when President Franklin D. Roosevelt, implementing a policy initiated by President Herbert Hoover, formally renounced the doctrine of intervention in Latin America. Thus what the first Roosevelt gave, the second Roosevelt took away.]

D. Roosevelt and Japan

1. President Roosevelt Anticipates Trouble (1905)

Secretary of State John Hay, attempting to halt European land-grabbing in China, had induced the reluctant powers to accept his famed Open Door policy in 1899–1900. But Russia's continued encroachments on China's Manchuria led to the exhausting Russo-Japanese War of 1904–1905, during which the underdog Japanese soundly thrashed the Russian army and navy. President Roosevelt, who was finally drafted as peace mediator, wrote the following letter to his close friend Senator Henry Cabot Lodge. Victory-drunk, Japan was becoming understandably cocky, while the race-conscious California legislature was preparing to erect barriers against Japanese immigrants. Why did Roosevelt regard the attitude of Californians as bigoted, foolish, and dangerous?

That Japan will have her head turned to some extent I do not in the least doubt, and I see clear symptoms of it in many ways. We should certainly as a nation have ours turned if we had performed such feats as the Japanese have in the past sixteen months; and the same is true of any European nation. Moreover, I have no doubt that some Japanese, and perhaps a great many of them, will behave badly to foreigners. They cannot behave worse than the State of California, through its Legislature, is now behaving toward the Japanese.

The feeling on the Pacific slope, taking it from several different standpoints, is as foolish as if conceived by the mind of a Hottentot. These Pacific Coast people wish grossly to insult the Japanese and to keep out the Japanese immigrants on the ground that they are an immoral, degraded, and worthless race; and at the same time that they desire to do this for the Japanese, and are already doing it for the Chinese, they expect to be given advantages in Oriental markets; and with besotted folly are indifferent to building up the navy while provoking this formidable new power—a power jealous, sensitive, and warlike, and which if irritated could at once take both the Philippines and Hawaii from us if she obtained the upper hand on the seas.

Most certainly the Japanese soldiers and sailors have shown themselves to be terrible foes. There can be none more dangerous in all the world. But our own navy, ship for ship, is I believe at least as efficient as theirs, although I am not certain that our torpedo boats would be handled as well as theirs. At present we are superior to them in number of ships, and this superiority will last for some time. It will of course come to an end if Hale* has his way, but not otherwise.

I hope that we can persuade our people on the one hand to act in a spirit of generous justice and genuine courtesy toward Japan, and on the other hand to keep the navy respectable in numbers and more than respectable in the efficiency of its units. If we act thus we need not fear the Japanese. But if, as Brooks Adams [a prominent historian, whose work *The Law of Civilization and Decay* (1895) deeply

---

[1]From *The Letters of Theodore Roosevelt* by E. E. Morrison, ed. Copyright © 1951 by the President and Fellows of Harvard College. Reprinted by permission of Harvard University Press.

*Maine Senator Eugene Hale, chairman of the Senate Naval Affairs Committee.

influenced Roosevelt] says, we show ourselves "opulent, aggressive, and unarmed," the Japanese may sometime work us an injury.

2. Japan Resents Discrimination (1906)

The San Francisco Board of Education precipitated a crisis in 1906 by ordering all Asian students to attend a specially segregated school. The sensitive Japanese rose in instant resentment against what they regarded as a deliberate and insulting act of discrimination. The Tokyo Mainichi Shimbun, *a reputable journal, reacted as follows. Where was Japanese national pride most deeply wounded?*

The whole world knows that the poorly equipped army and navy of the United States are no match for our efficient army and navy. It will be an easy work to awake the United States from her dream of obstinacy when one of our great admirals appears on the other side of the Pacific. . . . The present situation is such that the Japanese nation cannot rest easy by relying only upon the wisdom and statesmanship of President Roosevelt. The Japanese nation must have a firm determination to chastise at any time the obstinate Americans.

Stand up, Japanese nation! Our countrymen have been HUMILIATED on the other side of the Pacific. Our poor boys and girls have been expelled from the public schools by the rascals of the United States, cruel and merciless like demons.

At this time we should be ready to give a blow to the United States. Yes, we should be ready to strike the Devil's head with an iron hammer for the sake of the world's civilization. . . . Why do we not insist on sending [war]ships?

3. The Gentlemen's Agreement (1908)

The San Francisco school incident revealed anew that a municipality or a state could take legal action that might involve the entire nation in war. Roosevelt soothed the Japanese, but not the Californians, by adopting the Asians' side of the dispute. He publicly branded the action of the school board as a "wicked absurdity," and he brought that entire body to Washington, where he persuaded the members to come to terms. The San Franciscans agreed to readmit Japanese children to the public schools on condition that Roosevelt would arrange to shut off the influx of Japanese immigrants. This he did in the famous Gentlemen's Agreement, which consisted of an understanding growing out of an extensive exchange of diplomatic notes. These were officially summarized as follows in the annual report of the U.S. commissioner-general of immigration. In what ways did these agreements leave the fundamental issues unresolved?

In order that the best results might follow from an enforcement of the regulations, an understanding was reached with Japan that the existing policy of discouraging the emigration of its subjects of the laboring classes to continental United

---

[2]October 22, 1906, in T. A. Bailey, *Theodore Roosevelt and the Japanese-American Crises* (Stanford University Press, 1934), p. 50.

[3]*Annual Report of the Secretary of Commerce and Labor, 1908* (1908), pp. 221–222.

States should be continued and should, by cooperation of the governments, be made as effective as possible.

This understanding contemplates that the Japanese Government shall issue passports to continental United States only to such of its subjects as are non-laborers or are laborers who, in coming to the continent, seek to resume a formerly acquired domicile, to join a parent, wife, or children residing there, or to assume active control of an already possessed interest in a farming enterprise in this country; so that the three classes of laborers entitled to receive passports have come to be designated "former residents," "parents, wives, or children of residents," and "settled agriculturists."

With respect to Hawaii, the Japanese Government stated that, experimentally at least, the issuance of passports to members of the laboring classes proceeding thence would be limited to "former residents" and "parents, wives, or children of residents." The said government has also been exercising a careful supervision over the subject of the emigration of its laboring class to foreign contiguous territory [Mexico, Canada].

[The honor-system Gentlemen's Agreement worked reasonably well until 1924, when Congress in a fit of pique slammed the door completely in the faces of the Japanese. The resulting harvest of ill will had much to do with the tragic events that eventually led to Pearl Harbor and World War II.]

Thought Provokers

1. Critics said that although the Filipinos might not have been able to govern themselves, Americans were incapable of governing them if true to the "consent of the governed" philosophy of the Declaration of Independence. Comment.
2. Would it have been better to delay construction of the Panama Canal for ten years or so rather than have the scandal that attended the Panama coup? Was the scandal necessary?
3. With reference to Roosevelt's corollary to the Monroe Doctrine, are nations entitled to complete sovereignty if they fail to exercise it properly? When certain states of the United States defaulted on their debts to British creditors in the 1830s, Britain did not attempt to take over American customshouses. Why not? Are there different rules of international behavior for small nations and large nations?
4. Why did Japan especially resent California's discrimination in 1906, and why was the Gentlemen's Agreement better than exclusion by act of Congress?

29

Progressivism and the Republican Roosevelt, 1901–1912

Men with the muckrake are often indispensable to the well-being of society, but only if they know when to stop raking the muck.

Theodore Roosevelt, 1906

Prologue: A wave of political reform, known as the progressive movement, washed over the United States as the new century opened. Progressivism was inspired by muckraking journalists, who exposed corruption, the adulteration of food and drugs, and the exploitation of labor; by socialists, who called attention to the growing class divisions in the industrial United States; by ministers of the gospel alarmed at the grinding poverty in which many Americans lived; and by feminists who clamored for fair treatment for families, women, and children. Theodore Roosevelt embraced many of the tenets of progressivism when he became president in 1901. He fought to tame the big corporations and to protect consumers from dangerous products. Among his major achievements as a reformer was the invigoration of the campaign to conserve the nation's fast-disappearing natural resources, especially the forests. Other progressives championed the cause of women's suffrage, still a subject of hot controversy. When Roosevelt's handpicked successor, William Howard Taft, appeared to betray many of the principles of progressivism, Roosevelt determined to challenge him for the Republican presidential nomination in 1912.

A. The Heyday of Muckraking

1. Exposing the Meat Packers (1906)

In 1906 Upton Sinclair, the youthful and prolific socialist writer, published his novel The Jungle, *a damning exposure of conditions in the Chicago meat-packing plants.*

---

[1]*Congressional Record,* 59th Cong., 1st sess. (June 4, 1906), p. 7801.

Seeking to turn people to socialism, he succeeded in turning their stomachs. The up-roar that followed publication of his novel caused President Roosevelt to initiate an official investigation, and the following sober report was hardly less shocking than The Jungle. *It confirmed the essential truth of Sinclair's exposé, except for such lurid scenes as men falling into vats and emerging as lard. Which aspects of this official investigation revealed conditions most detrimental to the public health?*

. . . Meat scraps were also found being shoveled into receptacles from dirty floors, where they were left to lie until again shoveled into barrels or into machines for chopping. These floors, it must be noted, were in most cases damp and soggy, in dark, ill-ventilated rooms, and the employees in utter ignorance of cleanliness or danger to health expectorated at will upon them. In a word, we saw meat shoveled from filthy wooden floors, piled on tables rarely washed, pushed from room to room in rotten box carts, in all of which processes it was in the way of gathering dirt, splinters, floor filth, and the expectoration of tuberculous and other diseased workers.

Where comment was made to floor superintendents about these matters, it was always the reply that this meat would afterwards be cooked, and that this steriliza-tion would prevent any danger from its use. Even this, it may be pointed out in pass-ing, is not wholly true. A very considerable portion of the meat so handled is sent out as smoked products and in the form of sausages, which are prepared to be eaten without being cooked. . . .

As an extreme example of the entire disregard on the part of employees of any notion of cleanliness in handling dressed meat, we saw a hog that had just been killed, cleaned, washed, and started on its way to the cooling room fall from the slid-ing rail to a dirty wooden floor and slide part way into a filthy men's privy. It was picked up by two employees, placed upon a truck, carried into the cooling room and hung up with other carcasses, no effort being made to clean it. . . .

In one well-known establishment we came upon fresh meat being shoveled into barrels, and a regular proportion being added of stale scraps that had lain on a dirty floor in the corner of a room for some days previous. In another establishment, equally well known, a long table was noted covered with several hundred pounds of cooked scraps of beef and other meats. Some of these meat scraps were dry, leathery, and unfit to be eaten; and in the heap were found pieces of pigskin, and even some bits of rope strands and other rubbish. Inquiry evoked the frank admis-sion from the man in charge that this was to be ground up and used in making "pot-ted ham."

All of these canned products bear labels, of which the following is a sample:

ABATTOIR NO.—
THE CONTENTS OF THIS PACKAGE HAVE BEEN
INSPECTED ACCORDING TO THE ACT OF
CONGRESS OF MARCH 3, 1891.

[The agitation and investigation inspired by Sinclair's The Jungle *had much to do with bringing about the passage by Congress of the Meat Inspection Act and the Pure Food and Drug Act of 1906.]*

2. *Theodore Roosevelt Roasts Muckrakers (1906)*

President Roosevelt, though recognizing some unpalatable truths in Upton Sinclair's
The Jungle, *was critical. He wrote the author bluntly that Sinclair had said things that should not have been written unless backed up "with testimony that would satisfy an honest man of reasonable intelligence." Privately he declared that Sinclair had reflected unfairly on both honest and dishonest capitalism in Chicago. Finally, nauseated by excessive sensationalism, Roosevelt made the following famous attack (which gave rise to the term* muckraker) *in a Washington speech. What are the strengths and weaknesses of his argument that hysterical and indiscriminate muckraking was doing more harm than good?*

In Bunyan's *Pilgrim's Progress* you may recall the description of the Man with the Muck-rake [manure rake], the man who could look no way but downward, with the muck-rake in his hand; who was offered a celestial crown for his muck-rake, but who would neither look up nor regard the crown he was offered, but continued to rake himself the filth of the floor.

In *Pilgrim's Progress* the Man with the Muck-rake is set forth as the example of him whose vision is fixed on carnal instead of on spiritual things. Yet he also typifies the man who in this life consistently refuses to see aught that is lofty, and fixes his eyes with solemn intentness only on that which is vile and debasing.

Now it is very necessary that we should not flinch from seeing what is vile and debasing. There is filth on the floor, and it must be scraped up with the muck-rake: and there are times and places where this service is the most needed of all the services that can be performed. But the man who never does anything else, who never thinks or speaks or writes save of his feats with the muck-rake, speedily becomes, not a help to society, not an incitement to good, but one of the most potent forces for evil.

There are—in the body politic, economic, and social—many and grave evils, and there is urgent necessity for the sternest war upon them. There should be relentless exposure of and attack upon every evil man, whether politician or businessman; every evil practice, whether in politics, in business, or in social life. I hail as a benefactor every writer or speaker, every man who, on the platform, or in book, magazine, or newspaper, with merciless severity makes such attack, provided always that he in his turn remembers that the attack is of use only if it is absolutely truthful. The liar is no whit better than the thief, and if his mendacity takes the form of slander, he may be worse than most thieves. It puts a premium upon knavery untruthfully to attack an honest man, or even with hysterical exaggeration to assail a bad man with untruth. An epidemic of indiscriminate assault upon character does no good, but very great harm. The soul of every scoundrel is gladdened whenever an honest man is assailed, or even when a scoundrel is untruthfully assailed.

Now, it is easy to twist out of shape what I have just said. . . . Some persons are sincerely incapable of understanding that to denounce mudslinging does not mean the endorsement of whitewashing, and both the interested individuals who need

---

[2]Theodore Roosevelt, "The Man with the Muck-Rake," *Putnam's Monthly and the Critic* 1 (October 1906): 42–43.

whitewashing and those others who practice mudslinging like to encourage such confusion of ideas. One of the chief counts against those who make indiscriminate assault upon men in business or men in public life is that they invite a reaction which is sure to tell powerfully in favor of the unscrupulous scoundrel who really ought to be attacked, who ought to be exposed, who ought, if possible, to be put in the penitentiary. If Aristides is praised overmuch as just, people get tired of hearing it;* and overcensure of the unjust finally and from similar reasons results in their favor.

Any excess is almost sure to invite a reaction; and, unfortunately, the reaction, instead of taking the form of punishment of those guilty of the excess, is very apt to take the form either of punishment of the unoffending or of giving immunity, and even strength, to offenders. The effort to make financial or political profit out of the destruction of character can only result in public calamity. Gross and reckless assaults on character, whether on the stump or in newspaper, magazine, or book, create a morbid and vicious public sentiment, and at the same time act as a profound deterrent to able men of normal sensitiveness and tend to prevent them from entering the public service at any price.

[Roosevelt thus threw muck at the muckrakers. They resented his attack, claiming that even if they exaggerated, they were exposing evil conditions and promoting desirable legislation. (At the same time, they made money selling their magazine articles and books.) But Roosevelt was unconvinced. In 1911 he went so far as to write privately: "I think the muckrakers stand on a level of infamy with the corruptionists in politics. After all, there is no great difference between violation of the eighth [no stealing] and the ninth [no lying] commandments; and to sell one's vote for money is morally, I believe, hardly as reprehensible as to practice slanderous mendacity for hire" (Roosevelt Letters, vol. 7, p. 447). The truth is that he continued with intemperate muckraking himself, attacking "malefactors of great wealth," "nature fakers," and others. "You're the chief muckraker," Speaker Joseph G. Cannon told him flatly in 1906.]

B. Corruption in the Cities

1. Lincoln Steffens Bares Philadelphia Bossism (1904)

A California-born journalist, (Joseph) Lincoln Steffens, after serving as a "gentleman reporter" in New York, emerged as one of the first and most influential of the reforming muckrakers. Associated with McClure's Magazine, *the leading muckraking journal, he published a sensational series of articles on municipal graft, later collected in book form as* The Shame of the Cities *(1904). After the muckraking craze ended, Steffens became disillusioned, visited Russia, interviewed Lenin, and developed a warm admiration for the Soviet Union. In his famous exposé about conditions in Philadelphia, what is most ironic? What is most shocking? Who was responsible for the existence and continuation of these irregularities?*

---

*An allusion to Plutarch's story of the Athenian who voted for the banishment of Aristides (called "The Just") because he was tired of hearing everyone call him just.

[1]Lincoln Steffens, *The Shame of the Cities* (New York: McClure, Phillips & Co., 1904), pp. 193–201, passim.

Other American cities, no matter how bad their own condition may be, all point with scorn to Philadelphia as worse—"the worst-governed city in the country." St. Louis, Minneapolis, Pittsburgh submit with some patience to the jibes of any other community; the most friendly suggestion from Philadelphia is rejected with contempt. The Philadelphians are "supine," "asleep"; hopelessly ring-ruled, they are "complacent." "Politically benighted," Philadelphia is supposed to have no light to throw upon a state of things that is almost universal.

This is not fair. Philadelphia is, indeed, corrupt; but it is not without significance. Every city and town in the country can learn something from the typical political experience of this great representative city. New York is excused for many of its ills because it is the metropolis; Chicago, because of its forced development; Philadelphia is our "third largest" city and its growth has been gradual and natural.

Immigration has been blamed for our municipal conditions. Philadelphia, with 47 percent of its population native-born of native-born parents, is the most American of our greater cities.

It is "good," too, and intelligent. I don't know just how to measure the intelligence of a community, but a Pennsylvania college professor who declared to me his belief in education for the masses as a way out of political corruption, himself justified the "rake-off" of preferred contractors on public works on the ground of a "fair business profit."

Another plea we [Americans] have made is that we are too busy to attend to public business, and we have promised, when we come to wealth and leisure, to do better. Philadelphia has long enjoyed great and widely distributed prosperity. It is the city of homes. There is a dwelling house for every five persons—men, women, and children—of the population; and the people give one a sense of more leisure and repose than any community I ever dwelt in. Some Philadelphians account for their political state on the ground of their ease and comfort. . . .

Then we hear that we are a young people and that when we are older and "have traditions," like some of the old countries, we also will be honest. Philadelphia is one of the oldest of our cities and treasures for us scenes and relics of some of the noblest traditions of "our fair land." Yet I was told once, "for a joke," a party of boodlers [grafters] counted out the "divvy" [division] of their graft in unison with the ancient chime of Independence Hall. . . .

Philadelphia is proud; good people there defend corruption and boast of their machine. My college professor, with his philosophic view of "rake-offs," is one Philadelphia type. Another is the man who, driven to bay with his local pride, says: "At least you must admit that our machine is the best you have ever seen." . . .

Disgraceful? Other cities say so. But I say that if Philadelphia is a disgrace, it is a disgrace not to itself alone, nor to Pennsylvania, but to the United States and to American character. For this great city, so highly representative in other respects, is not behind in political experience, but ahead, with New York.

Philadelphia is a city that has had its reforms. . . . The present condition of Philadelphia, therefore, is not that which precedes, but that which follows reform, and in this distinction lies its startling general significance. What has happened . . . in Philadelphia may happen in any American city "after the reform is over."

For reform with us is usually revolt, not government, and is soon over. Our people do not seek, they avoid self-rule, and "reforms" are spasmodic efforts to punish bad rulers and get somebody that will give us good government or something that will make it. A self-acting form of government is an ancient superstition. We are an inventive people, and we all think that we shall devise some day a legal machine that will turn out good government automatically. The Philadelphians have treasured this belief longer than the rest of us and have tried it more often. . . .

The Philadelphia machine isn't the best. It isn't sound, and I doubt if it would stand in New York or Chicago. The enduring strength of the typical American political machine is that it is a natural growth—a sucker, but deep-rooted in the people. The New Yorkers vote for Tammany Hall. The Philadelphians do not vote; they are disfranchised, and their disfranchisement is one anchor of the foundation of the Philadelphia organization.

This is no figure of speech. The honest citizens of Philadelphia have no more rights at the polls than the Negroes down South. Nor do they fight very hard for this basic privilege. You can arouse their Republican ire by talking about the black Republican votes lost in the Southern states by white Democratic intimidation, but if you remind the average Philadelphian that he is in the same position, he will look startled, then say, "That's so, that's literally true, only I never thought of it in just that way." And it is literally true.

The machine controls the whole process of voting, and practices fraud at every stage. The [tax] assessor's list is the voting list, and the assessor is the machine's man. . . . The assessor pads the list with the names of dead dogs, children, and non-existent persons. One newspaper printed the picture of a dog, another that of a little four-year-old Negro boy, down on such a list. A "ring" orator, in a speech resenting sneers at his ward as "low down," reminded his hearers that that was the ward of Independence Hall, and, naming over the signers of the Declaration of Independence, he closed his highest flight of eloquence with the statement that "these men, the fathers of American liberty, voted down here once. And," he added with a catching grin, "they vote here yet."

Rudolph Blankenburg, a persistent fighter for the right and the use of the right to vote (and, by the way, an immigrant), sent out just before one election a registered letter to each voter on the rolls of a certain selected division. Sixty-three percent were returned marked "not at," "removed," "deceased," etc. . . .

The repeating [voting more than once] is done boldly, for the machine controls the election officers, often choosing them from among the fraudulent names; and when no one appears to serve, assigning the heeler [political hanger-on] ready for the expected vacancy. The police are forbidden by law to stand within thirty feet of the polls, but they are at the [ballot] box and they are there to see that the machine's orders are obeyed and that repeaters whom they help to furnish are permitted to vote without "intimidation" on the names they, the police, have supplied. . . .

The business proceeds with very few hitches; there is more jesting than fighting. Violence in the past has had its effect; and is not often necessary nowadays, but if it is needed the police are there to apply it. Several citizens told me that they had seen the police help to beat citizens or election officers who were trying to do their duty, then arrest the victim. . . .

2. George Washington Plunkitt Defends "Honest Graft" (1905)

Tammany Hall was the powerful and corrupt Democratic political machine that dominated New York City politics for many years. One of its cleverest officials, who became a millionaire through "honest graft," was George Washington (!) Plunkitt. According to his account, as here recorded by a newspaper reporter, he was above such dirty work as "shaking down" houses of prostitution ("disorderly houses"). Is his distinction between two kinds of graft legitimate? How did Tammany Hall sustain its power? Did it provide any valuable service?

Everybody is talkin' these days about Tammany men growin' rich on graft, but nobody thinks of drawin' the distinction between honest graft and dishonest graft. There's all the difference in the world between the two. Yes, many of our men have grown rich in politics. I have myself. I've made a big fortune out of the game, and I'm gettin' richer every day, but I've not gone in for dishonest graft—blackmailin' gamblers, saloon-keepers, disorderly people, etc.—and neither has any of the men who have made big fortunes in politics.

There's an honest graft, and I'm an example of how it works. I might sum up the whole thing by sayin': "I seen my opportunities and I took 'em."

Just let me explain by examples. My party's in power in the city, and it's goin' to undertake a lot of public improvements. Well, I'm tipped off, say, that they're goin' to lay out a new park at a certain place.

I see my opportunity and I take it. I go to that place and I buy up all the land I can in the neighborhood. Then the board of this or that makes its plan public, and there is a rush to get my land, which nobody cared particular for before.

Ain't it perfectly honest to charge a good price and make a profit on my investment and foresight? Of course it is. Well, that's honest graft.

Or, supposin' it's a new bridge they're goin' to build. I get tipped off and I buy as much property as I can that has to be taken for approaches. I sell at my own price later on and drop some more money in the bank.

Wouldn't you? It's just like lookin' ahead in Wall Street or in the coffee or cotton market. It's honest graft, and I'm lookin' for it every day in the year. I will tell you frankly that I've got a good lot of it, too.

I'll tell you of one case. They were goin' to fix up a big park, no matter where. I got on to it, and went lookin' about for land in that neighborhood.

I could get nothin' at a bargain but a big piece of swamp, but I took it fast enough and held on to it. What turned out was just what I counted on. They couldn't make the park complete without Plunkitt's swamp, and they had to pay a good price for it. Anything dishonest in that?

Up in the watershed I made some money, too. I bought up several bits of land there some years ago and made a pretty good guess that they would be bought up for water purposes later by the city.

Somehow, I always guessed about right, and shouldn't I enjoy the profit of my foresight? It was rather amusin' when the condemnation commissioners came along

---

[2]William L. Riordan, *Plunkitt of Tammany Hall* (1948 ed.), pp. 3–8.

and found piece after piece of the land in the name of George Plunkitt of the Fifteenth Assembly District, New York City. They wondered how I knew just what to buy. The answer is—I seen my opportunity and I took it. I haven't confined myself to land; anything that pays is in my line. . . .

I've told you how I got rich by honest graft. Now, let me tell you that most politicians who are accused of robbin' the city get rich the same way.

They didn't steal a dollar from the city treasury. They just seen their opportunities and took them. That is why, when a reform administration comes in and spends a half million dollars in tryin' to find the public robberies they talked about in the campaign, they don't find them.

The books are always all right. The money in the city treasury is all right. Everything is all right. All they can show is that the Tammany heads of departments looked after their friends, within the law, and gave them what opportunities they could to make honest graft. Now, let me tell you that's never goin' to hurt Tammany with the people. Ever good man looks after his friends, and any man who doesn't isn't likely to be popular. If I have a good thing to hand out in private life, I give it to a friend. Why shouldn't I do the same in public life? . . .

Tammany was beat in 1901 because the people were deceived into believin' that it worked dishonest graft. They didn't draw a distinction between dishonest and honest graft, but they saw that some Tammany men grew rich, and supposed they had been robbin' the city treasury or levyin' blackmail on disorderly houses, or workin' in with the gamblers and lawbreakers.

As a matter of policy, if nothing else, why should the Tammany leaders go into such dirty business when there is so much honest graft lyin' around when they are in power? Did you ever consider that?

Now, in conclusion, I want to say that I don't own a dishonest dollar. If my worst enemy was given the job of writin' my epitaph when I'm gone, he couldn't do more than write.

> "George W. Plunkitt.
> He Seen His Opportunities and He Took 'Em."

C. The Plight of Labor

1. From the Depths (1906)

Many observers in the progressive era saw poverty as proof of the moral weakness of the poor. For others, poverty and the glaring inequalities of wealth in America were evidence of the immorality of a society based on capitalism. What perspective does this famous image, by William Balfour Ker, entitled From the Depths, *convey? Why are the poor positioned under the floor and in the dark? Are their hands supporting the scene above or seeking to disrupt it?*

---

[1]*From the Depths,* by William Balfour Ker, 1906, courtesy of The Harvard College Library.

2. George Baer's Divine Right of Plutocrats (1902)

The anthracite coal miners of Pennsylvania, who were frightfully exploited and accident cursed, struck for higher wages in 1902. About 140,000 men were idled, and the chilled East was threatened with paralysis. George F. Baer, the multimillionaire spokesman for the owners, refused to permit intervention, arbitration, or even negotiation. He believed that mining was a "business," not a "religious, sentimental, or academic proposition." In response to a complaining letter from a Mr. W. F. Clark, he sent the following reply. What is the social philosophy of big business as here revealed?

17th July 1902

My dear Mr. Clark:—
I have your letter of the 16th instant.
I do not know who you are. I see that you are a religious man; but you are evidently biased in favor of the right of the working man to control a business in which he has no other interest than to secure fair wages for the work he does.
I beg of you not to be discouraged. The rights and interests of the laboring man will be protected and cared for—not by the labor agitators, but by the Christian men to whom God in His infinite wisdom has given the control of the property interests of the country, and upon the successful management of which so much depends.
Do not be discouraged. Pray earnestly that right may triumph, always remembering that the Lord God Omnipotent still reigns, and that His reign is one of law and order, and not of violence and crime.

Yours truly,
Geo. F. Baer
President

[When the Baer letter was published, the press assailed its "arrant hypocrisy," "egregious vanity," and "ghastly blasphemy." President Roosevelt nevertheless finally brought the disputants together late in 1902. Although he admittedly lost his temper and did not behave "like a gentleman," he had a large hand in working out the resulting compromise wage increase.]

3. Child Labor in the Coal Mines (1906)

The arrogant attitude of the coal operators seems even less excusable in the light of John Spargo's book The Bitter Cry of the Children—*another significant contribution to the muckraking movement. An English-born socialist, Spargo had come to America in 1901 at the age of twenty-five. He was especially stirred by the rickety children of the New York tenement districts. Their mothers had no time to prepare proper meals; needlework labor in the sweatshops ran from twelve to twenty hours a day, at*

---

[2]*Literary Digest* 25 (August 30, 1902): 258. A photostatic copy of the letter is in Caro Lloyd, *Henry Demarest Lloyd* (New York: Funk & Wagnalls Company, 1912), vol. 2, p. 190.
[3]John Spargo, *The Bitter Cry of the Children* (New York: Macmillan, 1906), pp. 163–165.

a wage ranging from ten cents to a cent and a half an hour. In Spargo's description of work in the coal mines, what were the various kinds of hazards involved?

Work in the coal breakers is exceedingly hard and dangerous. Crouched over the chutes, the boys sit hour after hour, picking out the pieces of slate and other refuse from the coal as it rushes past to the washers. From the cramped position they have to assume, most of them become more or less deformed and bent-backed like old men. When a boy has been working for some time and begins to get round-shouldered, his fellows say that "He's got his boy to carry round whenever he goes."

The coal is hard, and accidents to the hands, such as cut, broken, or crushed fingers, are common among the boys. Sometimes there is a worse accident: a terrified shriek is heard, and a boy is mangled and torn in the machinery, or disappears in the chute to be picked out later smothered and dead. Clouds of dust fill the breakers and are inhaled by the boys, laying the foundations for asthma and miners' consumption.

I once stood in a breaker for half an hour and tried to do the work a twelve-year-old boy was doing day after day, for ten hours at a stretch, for sixty cents a day. The gloom of the breaker appalled me. Outside the sun shone brightly, the air was pellucid, and the birds sang in chorus with the trees and the rivers. Within the breaker there was blackness, clouds of deadly dust enfolded everything, the harsh, grinding roar of the machinery and the ceaseless rushing of coal through the chutes filled the ears. I tried to pick out the pieces of slate from the hurrying stream of coal, often missing them; my hands were bruised and cut in a few minutes; I was covered from head to foot with coal dust, and for many hours afterwards I was expectorating some of the small particles of anthracite I had swallowed.

I could not do that work and live, but there were boys of ten and twelve years of age doing it for fifty and sixty cents a day. Some of them had never been inside of a school; few of them could read a child's primer. True, some of them attended the night schools, but after working ten hours in the breaker the educational results from attending school were practically nil. "We goes fer a good time, an' we keeps de guys wot's dere hoppin' all de time," said little Owen Jones, whose work I had been trying to do. . . .

As I stood in that breaker I thought of the reply of the small boy to Robert Owen [British social reformer]. Visiting an English coal mine one day, Owen asked a twelve-year-old lad if he knew God. The boy stared vacantly at his questioner: "God?" he said, "God? No, I don't. He must work in some other mine." It was hard to realize amid the danger and din and blackness of that Pennsylvania breaker that such a thing as belief in a great All-good God existed.

From the breakers the boys graduate to the mine depths, where they become door tenders, switch boys, or mule drivers. Here, far below the surface, work is still more dangerous. At fourteen or fifteen the boys assume the same risks as the men, and are surrounded by the same perils. Nor is it in Pennsylvania only that these conditions exist. In the bituminous mines of West Virginia, boys of nine or ten are frequently employed. I met one little fellow ten years old in Mt. Carbon, W. Va., last year, who was employed as a "trap boy." Think of what it means to be a trap boy at ten years of age. It means to sit alone in a dark mine passage hour after hour, with no human soul near; to see no living creature except the mules as they pass with their loads, or a rat or two seeking to share one's meal; to stand in water or mud that covers the ankles, chilled to the marrow by the cold draughts that rush in when you open the trap door for the mules to pass through; to work for fourteen hours—waiting—opening and shutting a door—then waiting again—for sixty cents; to reach the surface when all is wrapped in the mantle of night, and to fall to the earth exhausted and have to be carried away to the nearest "shack" to be revived before it is possible to walk to the farther shack called "home."

Boys twelve years of age may be *legally* employed in the mines of West Virginia, by day or by night, and for as many hours as the employers care to make them toil or their bodies will stand the strain. Where the disregard of child life is such that this may be done openly and with legal sanction, it is easy to believe what miners have again and again told me—that there are hundreds of little boys of nine and ten years of age employed in the coal mines of this state.

4. Sweatshop Hours for Bakers (1905)

The abuse of labor in dangerous or unhealthful occupations prompted an increasing number of state legislatures, exercising so-called police powers, to pass regulatory laws. In 1898 the Supreme Court upheld a Utah statute prohibiting miners from working more than eight hours a day, except in emergencies. In 1905, however, the Court, by a five-to-four decision in the case of Lochner v. *New York, overthrew a state law forbidding bakers to work more than ten hours a day. The majority held that the right of both employers and employees to make labor contracts was protected by the Fourteenth Amendment. How might one describe the social conscience of the majority of the Supreme Court in the light of this memorable decision written by Mr. Justice Rufus W. Peckham?*

The question whether this act is valid as a labor law, pure and simple, may be dismissed in a few words. There is no reasonable ground for interfering with the liberty of person or the right of free contract, by determining the hours of labor, in the occupation of a baker. There is no contention that bakers as a class are not equal in intelligence and capacity to men in other trades or manual occupations, or that they are not able to assert their rights and care for themselves without the protecting arm of the state interfering with their independence of judgment and of action. They are in no sense wards of the state.

Viewed in the light of a purely labor law, with no reference whatever to the question of health, we think that a law like the one before us involves neither the safety, the morals, nor the welfare of the public, and that the interest of the public is not in the slightest degree affected by such an act. The law must be upheld, if at all, as a law pertaining to the health of the individual engaged in the occupation of a baker. It does not affect any other portion of the public than those who are engaged in that occupation. Clean and wholesome bread does not depend upon whether the baker works but ten hours per day or only sixty hours a week. The limitation of the hours of labor does not come within the police power on that ground. . . .

---

[4]*198 U.S. Reports* 57, 59, 61.

We think that there can be no fair doubt that the trade of a baker, in and of itself, is not an unhealthy one to that degree which would authorize the legislature to interfere with the right to labor, and with the right of free contract on the part of the individual, either as employer or employee.

In looking through statistics regarding all trades and occupations, it may be true that the trade of baker does not appear to be as healthy as some other trades, and is also vastly more healthy than still others. To the common understanding the trade of a baker has never been regarded as an unhealthy one. Very likely physicians would not recommend the exercise of that or of any other trade as a remedy for ill health. Some occupations are more healthy than others, but we think there are none which might not come under the power of the legislature to supervise and control the hours of working therein, if the mere fact that the occupation is not absolutely and perfectly healthy is to confer that right upon the legislative department of the government. . . .

. . . We do not believe in the soundness of the views which uphold this law. On the contrary, we think that such a law as this, although passed in the assumed exercise of the police power, and as relating to the public health, or the health of the employees named, is not within that power, and is invalid. The act is not, within any fair meaning of the term, a health law, but is an illegal interference with the rights of individuals, both employers and employees, to make contracts regarding labor upon such terms as they may think best, or which they may agree upon with the other parties to such contracts.

Statutes of the nature of that under review, limiting the hours in which grown and intelligent men may labor to earn their living, are mere meddlesome interferences with the rights of the individual, and they are not saved from condemnation by the claim that they are passed in the exercise of the police power and upon the subject of the health of the individual whose rights are interfered with, unless there be some fair ground, reasonable in and of itself, to say that there is material danger to the public health, or to the health of the employees, if the hours of labor are not curtailed.

[Mr. Justice Holmes, the great dissenter, filed a famous protest in the bakers' case. He argued that a majority of the people of New York State evidently wanted the law and that the Court ought not to impose its own social philosophy. "The Fourteenth Amendment," he solemnly declared, referring to a famous work by an arch-conservative British social theorist, "does not enact Mr. Herbert Spencer's Social Statics." As for the right to work more than ten hours, the mayor of New York remarked, "There were no journeymen bakers that I know of clamoring for any such liberty." Possibly chastened by Holmes's vigorous views, the Court relented and in 1908 unanimously approved an Oregon statute prohibiting the employment of women in factories and other establishments more than ten hours in one day. In 1917 the Court upheld an Oregon ten-hour law for both men and women.]

5. The Triangle Shirtwaist Company Fire Claims 146 Lives (1911)

One of the most grisly catastrophes ever to befall American workers occurred at the Triangle Shirtwaist Company's New York City garment factory on March 25, 1911.

---

[5]*New York World*, March 26, 1911.

Trapped in a burning building in which many exit doors had been locked to discourage workers from taking unauthorized breaks, 146 laborers, mostly young women, perished. The resulting outrage encouraged the enactment of more stringent building codes and fed the growing movement for laws regulating working conditions, especially for women. (For more on women's labor laws, see the documents in Chapter 32, section D.) In the account of the fire that follows, what conditions seemed most responsible for the high loss of life? How might they have been remedied? How much of the public outrage about the fire owed to the fact that so many of the dead were young women?

At 4:35 o'clock yesterday afternoon fire springing from a source that may never be positively identified was discovered in the rear of the eighth floor of the ten-story building at the northwest corner of Washington Place and Greene Street, the first of three floors occupied as a factory of the Triangle Shirtwaist Company.

At 11:30 o'clock Chief Croker made this statement:

"Everybody has been removed. The number taken out, which includes those who jumped from windows, is 141 . . ."

At 2 o'clock this morning Chief Croker estimated the total dead as one hundred and fifty-four. He said further, "I expect something of this kind to happen in these so-called fire-proof buildings, which are without adequate protection as far as fire-escapes are concerned."

More than a third of those who lost their lives did so in jumping from windows. The firemen who answered the first of the four alarms turned in found 30 bodies on the pavements of Washington Place and Greene Street. Almost all of these were girls, as were the great majority of them all. . . .

Inspection by Acting Superintendent of Buildings Ludwig will be made the basis for charges of criminal negligence on the ground that the fire-proof doors leading to one of the inclosed tower stairways were locked. . . ."

It was the most appalling horror since the Slocum disaster and the Iroquois Theater fire in Chicago. Every available ambulance in Manhattan was called upon to cart the dead to the morgue—bodies charred to unrecognizable blackness or reddened to a sickly hue—as was to be seen by shoulders or limbs protruding through flame-eaten clothing. Men and women, boys and girls were of the dead that littered the street; that is actually the condition—the streets were littered.

The fire began in the eighth story. The flames licked and shot their way up through the other two stories. All three floors were occupied by the Triangle Waist Company. The estimate of the number of employees at work is made by Chief Croker at about 1,000. The proprietors of the company say 700 men and girls were in their place. . . .

Before smoke or flame gave signs from the windows, the loss of life was fully under way. The first signs that persons in the street knew that these three top stories had turned into red furnaces in which human creatures were being caught and incinerated was when screaming men and women and boys and girls crowded out on the many window ledges and threw themselves into the streets far below.

They jumped with their clothing ablaze. The hair of some of the girls streamed up aflame as they leaped. Thud after thud sounded on the pavements. It is a ghastly fact that on both the Greene Street and Washington Place sides of the building there grew mounds of the dead and dying.

And the worst horror of all was that in this heap of the dead now and then there stirred a limb or sounded a moan.

Within the three flaming floors it was as frightful. There flames enveloped many so that they died instantly. When Fire Chief Croker could make his way into these three floors, he found sights that utterly staggered him, that sent him, a man used to viewing horrors, back and down into the street with quivering lips.

The floors were black with smoke. And then he saw as the smoke drifted away bodies burned to bare bones. There were skeletons bending over sewing machines.

The elevator boys saved hundreds. They each made twenty trips from the time of the alarm until twenty minutes later when they could do no more. Fire was streaming into the shaft, flames biting at the cables. They fled for their own lives.

Some, about seventy, chose a successful avenue of escape. They clambered up a ladder to the roof. A few remembered the fire escape. Many may have thought of it but only as they uttered cries of dismay.

Wretchedly inadequate was this fire escape—a lone ladder running down to a rear narrow court, which was smoke filled as the fire raged, one narrow door giving access to the ladder. By the score they fought and struggled and breathed fire and died trying to make that needle-eye road to self-preservation. . . .

Shivering at the chasm below them, scorched by the fire behind, there were some that still held positions on the window sills when the first squad of firemen arrived.

The nets were spread below with all promptness. Citizens were commandeered into service, as the firemen necessarily gave their attention to the one engine and hose of the force that first arrived.

The catapult force that the bodies gathered in the long plunges made the nets utterly without avail. Screaming girls and men, as they fell, tore the nets from the grasp of the holders, and the bodies struck the sidewalks and lay just as they fell. Some of the bodies ripped big holes through the life-nets. . . .

Concentrated, the fire burned within. The flames caught all the flimsy lace stuff and linens that go into the making of spring and summer shirtwaists and fed eagerly upon the rolls of silk.

The cutting room was laden with the stuff on long tables. The employees were toiling over such material at the rows and rows of machines. Sinisterly the spring day gave aid to the fire. Many of the window panes facing south and east were drawn down. Draughts had full play.

The experts say that the three floors must each have become a whirlpool of fire. Whichever way the entrapped creatures fled they met a curving sweep of flame. Many swooned and died. Others fought their way to the windows or the elevator or fell fighting for a chance at the fire escape, the single fire escape leading into the blind court that was to be reached from the upper floors by clambering over a window sill!

On all of the three floors, at a narrow window, a crowd met death trying to get out to that one slender fire escape ladder.

It was a fireproof building in which this enormous tragedy occurred. Save for the three stories of blackened windows at the top, you would scarcely have been able to tell where the fire had happened. The walls stood firmly. A thin tongue of flame now and then licked around a window sash. . . .

D. The Conservation Crusade

1. Roosevelt Defends the Forests (1903)

Greedy or shortsighted Americans had long plundered the nation's forests with heedless rapacity. President Roosevelt, a one-time Dakota cattle rancher and an accomplished naturalist, provided the lagging conservation movement with dynamic leadership. Using the Forest Reserve Act of 1891, he set aside some 150 million acres of government-owned timberland as national forest reserves—more than three times as much as his three immediate predecessors had preserved. The large timber companies complained bitterly, though in fact the worst predators on the forests were the small-fry lumbermen who had neither the incentive nor the resources to adopt long-term, sustained-yield logging practices. In this speech at Stanford University, Roosevelt explained the basis of his forest policy. His argument clearly demonstrates that he was not a preservationist, pure and simple. What are the implications of the distinction he draws between "beauty" and "use"? What does he mean when he says that "the whole object of forest protection" is "the making and maintaining of prosperous homes"?

I want today, here in California, to make a special appeal to all of you, and to California as a whole, for work along a certain line—the line of preserving your great natural advantages alike from the standpoint of use and from the standpoint of beauty. If the students of this institution have not by the mere fact of their surroundings learned to appreciate beauty, then the fault is in you and not in the surroundings. Here in California you have some of the great wonders of the world. You have a singularly beautiful landscape, singularly beautiful and singularly majestic scenery, and it should certainly be your aim to try to preserve for those who are to come after you that beauty, to try to keep unmarred that majesty.

Closely entwined with keeping unmarred the beauty of your scenery, your great natural attractions, is the question of making use of, not for the moment merely, but for future time, of your great natural products. Yesterday I saw for the first time a grove of your great trees, a grove which it has taken the ages several thousands of years to build up; and I feel most emphatically that we should not turn into shingles a tree which was old when the first Egyptian conqueror penetrated to the valley of the Euphrates, which it has taken so many thousands of years to build up, and which can be put to better use.

That, you may say, is not looking at the matter from the practical standpoint. There is nothing more practical in the end than the preservation of beauty, than the preservation of anything that appeals to the higher emotions in mankind. But, furthermore, I appeal to you from the standpoint of use. A few big trees, of unusual size and beauty, should be preserved for their own sake; but the forests as a whole should be used for business purposes, only they should be used in a way that will preserve them as permanent sources of national wealth. In many parts of California

---

[1]From Theodore Roosevelt at Leland Stanford Junior University, Palo Alto, California, May 12, 1903, in *Theodore Roosevelt, Presidential Addresses and State Papers of Theodore Roosevelt,* Vol. 1, New York: P.F. Collier, 1905, pp. 383–390.

the whole future welfare of the state depends upon the way in which you are able to use your water supply; and the preservation of the forests and the preservation of the use of the water are inseparably connected.

I believe we are past the stage of national existence when we could look on complacently at the individual who skinned the land and was content, for the sake of three years' profit for himself, to leave a desert for the children of those who were to inherit the soil. I think we have passed that stage. We should handle, and I think we now do handle, all problems such as those of forestry and of the preservation and use of our waters from the standpoint of the permanent interests of the home maker in any region—the man who comes in not to take what he can out of the soil and leave, having exploited the country, but who comes to dwell therein, to bring up his children, and to leave them a heritage in the country not merely unimpaired, but if possible even improved. That is the sensible view of civic obligation, and the policy of the state and of the nation should be shaped in that direction. It should be shaped in the interest of the home maker, the actual resident, the man who is not only to be benefited himself, but whose children and children's children are to be benefited by what he has done.

California has for years, I am happy to say, taken a more sensible, a more intelligent interest in forest preservation than any other state. It early appointed a forest commission; later on some of the functions of that commission were replaced by the Sierra Club, a club which has done much on the Pacific coast to perpetuate the spirit of the explorer and the pioneer. Then I am happy to say a great business interest showed an intelligent and farsighted spirit which is of happy augury, for the Redwood Manufacturers of San Francisco were first among lumbermen's associations to give assistance to the cause of practical forestry. The study of the redwood which the action of this association made possible was the pioneer study in the cooperative work which is now being carried out between lumbermen all over the United States and the Federal Bureau of Forestry.

All of this kind of work is peculiarly the kind of work in which we have a right to expect not merely hearty cooperation from, but leadership in college men trained in the universities of this Pacific coast state; for the forests of this state stand alone in the world. There are none others like them anywhere. There are no other trees anywhere like the giant sequoias; nowhere else is there a more beautiful forest than that which clothes the western slope of the Sierra. Very early your forests attracted lumbermen from other states, and by the course of timber land investments some of the best of the big tree groves were threatened with destruction. Destruction came upon some of them, but the women of California rose to the emergency through the California Club, and later the Sempervirens Club took vigorous action. But the Calaveras grove is not yet safe, and there should be no rest until that safety is secured, by the action of private individuals, by the action of the state, by the action of the nation. The interest of California in forest protection was shown even more effectively by the purchase of the Big Basin Redwood Park, a superb forest property the possession of which should be a source of just pride to all citizens jealous of California's good name.

I appeal to you, as I say, to protect these mighty trees, these wonderful monuments of beauty. I appeal to you to protect them for the sake of their beauty, but I also make the appeal just as strongly on economic grounds; as I am well aware that in dealing with such questions a farsighted economic policy must be that to which alone in the long run one can safely appeal. The interests of California in forests depend directly of course upon the handling of her wood and water supplies and the supply of material from the lumber woods and the production of agricultural products on irrigated farms. The great valleys which stretch through the state between the Sierra Nevada and coast ranges must owe their future development as they owe their present prosperity to irrigation. Whatever tends to destroy the water supply of the Sacramento, the San Gabriel, and the other valleys strikes vitally at the welfare of California. The welfare of California depends in no small measure upon the preservation of water for the purposes of irrigation in those beautiful and fertile valleys which cannot grow crops by rainfall alone. The forest cover upon the drainage basins of streams used for irrigation purposes is of prime importance to the interests of the entire state.

Now keep in mind that the whole object of forest protection is, as I have said again and again, the making and maintaining of prosperous homes. I am not advocating forest protection from the aesthetic standpoint only. I do advocate the keeping of big trees, the great monarchs of the woods, for the sake of their beauty, but I advocate the preservation and wise use of the forests because I feel it essential to the interests of the actual settlers. I am asking that the forests be used wisely for the sake of the successors of the pioneers, for the sake of the settlers who dwell on the land and by doing so extend the borders of our civilization. I ask it for the sake of the man who makes his farm in the woods or lower down along the sides of the streams which have their rise in the mountains. . . .

Citizenship is the prime test in the welfare of the nation; but we need good laws; and above all we need good land laws throughout the West. We want to see the free farmer own his home. The best of the public lands are already in private hands, and yet the rate of their disposal is steadily increasing. More than six million acres were patented during the first three months of the present year. It is time for us to see that our remaining public lands are saved for the home maker to the utmost limit of his possible use. I say this to you of this university because we have a right to expect that the best-trained, the best-educated men on the Pacific Slope, the Rocky Mountains and Great Plains states will take the lead in the preservation and right use of the forests, in securing the right use of the waters, and in seeing to it that our land policy is not twisted from its original purpose, but is perpetuated by amendment, by change when such change is necessary in the line of that purpose, the purpose being to turn the public domain into farms each to be the property of the man who actually tills it and makes his home on it.

2. The West Protests Conservation (1907)

The new forest-reserve policies often worked a hardship on honest western settlers, who sometimes had to get permission from a federal official before they could lawfully cut a stick of firewood. The government, they charged, was more concerned with preserving trees than people. The governor of Colorado, disturbed by the large-

---

[2]*San Francisco Chronicle,* June 22, 1907.

scale withdrawals of western timber and coal lands by Washington, summoned a Public Lands Convention to meet in Denver in 1907. The deliberations of this body inspired the following editorial in a San Francisco newspaper. Did the West really oppose conservation? Was the East unfair in its demands?

The convention which has just adjourned at Denver is the first body of importance that has dealt with the subject of the disposal of the public lands of the United States. Considering the fact that the country has been in the real estate business for more than a century, and that during that period it has, by hook and crook, chiefly by crook, disposed of the major part of its holdings, it seems like a case of locking the stable door after nearly all of the horses have been stolen. The only question left to determine is whether the people who have permitted the theft of the horses, and who lent a hand in the stealing, shall be allowed to enjoy the most of the benefits which may accrue from taking good care of the steeds which still remain in the stalls.

The Far West, in which all the lands—coal-bearing, forest, pasture, and agricultural—still remaining in the possession of the government are to be found, has formally gone on record in this matter, and demands that the new states be treated with the same consideration as those commonwealths which have already divided their patrimony among their individual citizens. The Denver Convention in its resolutions recognizes the wisdom of treating the lands of the nation as a public trust, but it insisted that this trust should be administered for the benefit of the states wherein the lands still remaining are situated and not for the benefit of the people of the older states of the Union, who have no lands, forests, mines, or pastures that are not in the possession of private individuals.

Congress will be unable to resist the justice of this contention. As a rule, that body is not overswift to recognize the rights of those sections of the Union with a small representation in the Lower House, but the American people, when they understand the matter thoroughly, may be depended upon to prevent an injustice. Just now the popular impression at the East is that the Far West is opposed to the conservation of its forests, and that it supports the efforts of unscrupulous grabbers to steal the public domain. But the campaign of education inaugurated by the Public Lands Convention will soon convince it that all that is asked for is even justice for the new states, and that demands that the profits arising from the eleventh-hour reform shall not be absorbed by the states that have eaten their cake and now wish to share with those who have scarcely had a chance to nibble theirs.

3. Gifford Pinchot Advocates Damming the Hetch Hetchy Valley (1913)

The city of San Francisco's proposal to dam the Tuolumne River, creating a reservoir in the Hetch Hetchy Valley within the boundaries of Yosemite National Park, stirred passionate debate in the early twentieth century. The controversy vividly demonstrated the division of "conservationists" into utilitarians and preservationists. The

---

[3]U.S. Congress, House of Representatives, Committee on the Public Lands, Hearings, *Hetch Hetchy Dam Site,* 63d Cong., 1st Sess. (June 25–28, July 7, 1913), pp. 25ff.

issue came to a dramatic climax in 1913, when Congress passed the Raker Act, authorizing construction of the dam. In his testimony before the House Committee on the Public Lands, famed conservationist Gifford Pinchot (1865–1946), chief forester of the United States in the Theodore Roosevelt administrations, offered the following rationale for the construction of the Hetch Hetchy dam. What is Pinchot's chief justification for building the dam? In what ways does he deserve his title as one of the founding fathers of the modern conservation movement?

Mr. Pinchot. . . . So we come now face to face with the perfectly clean question of what is the best use to which this water that flows out of the Sierras can be put. As we all know, there is no use of water that is higher than the domestic use. Then, if there is, as the engineers tell us, no other source of supply that is anything like so reasonably available as this one; if this is the best, and, within reasonable limits of cost, the only means of supplying San Francisco with water, we come straight to the question of whether the advantage of leaving this valley in a state of nature is greater than the advantage of using it for the benefit of the city of San Francisco.

Now, the fundamental principle of the whole conservation policy is that of use, to take every part of the land and its resources and put it to that use in which it will best serve the most people, and I think there can be no question at all but that in this case we have an instance in which all weighty considerations demand the passage of the bill. . . .

. . . I believe if we had nothing else to consider than the delight of the few men and women who would yearly go into the Hetch Hetchy Valley, then it should be left in its natural condition. But the considerations on the other side of the question to my mind are simply overwhelming, and so much so that I have never been able to see that there was any reasonable argument against the use of this water supply by the city of San Francisco. . . .

Mr. Raker.[*] Taking the scenic beauty of the park as it now stands, and the fact that the valley is sometimes swamped along in June and July, is it not a fact that if a beautiful dam is put there, as is contemplated, and as the picture is given by the engineers, with the roads contemplated around the reservoir and with other trails, it will be more beautiful than it is now, and give more opportunity for the use of the park?

Mr. Pinchot. Whether it will be more beautiful, I doubt, but the use of the park will be enormously increased. I think there is no doubt about that.

Mr. Raker. In other words, to put it a different way, there will be more beauty accessible than there is now?

Mr. Pinchot. Much more beauty will be accessible than now.

Mr. Raker. And by putting in roads and trails the Government, as well as the citizens of the Government, will get more pleasure out of it than at the present time?

Mr. Pinchot. You might say from the standpoint of enjoyment of beauty and the greatest good to the greatest number, they will be conserved by the passage of this bill, and there will be a great deal more use of the beauty of the park than there is now.

---

*John E. Raker, representative from California.

Mr. Raker. Have you seen Mr. John Muir's* criticism of the bill? You know him?

Mr. Pinchot. Yes, sir; I know him very well. He is an old and a very good friend of mine. I have never been able to agree with him in his attitude toward the Sierras for the reason that my point of view has never appealed to him at all. When I became Forester and denied the right to exclude sheep and cows from the Sierras, Mr. Muir thought I had made a great mistake, because I allowed the use by an acquired right of a large number of people to interfere with what would have been the utmost beauty of the forest. In this case I think he has unduly given away to beauty as against use.

4. John Muir Damns the Hetch Hetchy Dam (1912)

John Muir (1838–1914), born in Scotland and raised in Wisconsin, arrived in California in 1868 and established himself as an eminent naturalist and passionate crusader for wilderness preservation. On what grounds does he disagree with Gifford Pinchot's position on the Hetch Hetchy dam? In what ways do their two arguments continue to resonate in debates today about the environment?

Yosemite is so wonderful that we are apt to regard it as an exceptional creation, the only valley of its kind in the world; but Nature is not so poor as to have only one of anything. Several other yosemites have been discovered in the Sierra that occupy the same relative positions on the range and were formed by the same forces in the same kind of granite. One of these, the Hetch Hetchy Valley, is in the Yosemite National Park about twenty miles from Yosemite. . . .

. . . [As] the Merced River flows through Yosemite, so does the Tuolumne through Hetch Hetchy. The walls of both are of gray granite, rise abruptly from the floor, are sculptured in the same style and in both every rock is a glacier monument. . . .

. . . Hetch Hetchy Valley, far from being a plain, common, rock-bound meadow, as many who have not seen it seem to suppose, is a grand landscape garden, one of Nature's rarest and most precious mountain temples. As in Yosemite, the sublime rocks of its walls seem to glow with life, whether leaning back in repose or standing erect in thoughtful attitudes, giving welcome to storms and calms alike, their brows in the sky, their feet set in the groves and gay flowery meadows, while birds, bees, and butterflies help the river and waterfalls to stir all the air into music—things frail and fleeting and types of permanence meeting here and blending, just as they do in Yosemite, to draw her lovers into close and confiding communion with her.

Sad to say, this most precious and sublime feature of the Yosemite National Park, one of the greatest of all our natural resources for the uplifting joy and peace and health of the people, is in danger of being dammed and made into a reservoir to help supply San Francisco with water and light, thus flooding it from wall to wall

---

*John Muir (1838–1914), a Scottish-born American naturalist, was a leading critic of the Hetch Hetchy dam proposal. See the next selection.

⁴John Muir, *The Yosemite* (Garden City, N.Y.: Doubleday and Co., 1962; originally published 1912), pp. 192–202.

and burying its gardens and groves one or two hundred feet deep. This grossly destructive commercial scheme has long been planned and urged (though water as pure and abundant can be got from sources outside of the people's park, in a dozen different places), because of the comparative cheapness of the dam and of the territory which it is sought to divert from the great uses to which it was dedicated in the Act of 1890 establishing the Yosemite National Park.

The making of gardens and parks goes on with civilization all over the world, and they increase both in size and number as their value is recognized. Everybody needs beauty as well as bread, places to play in and pray in, where Nature may heal and cheer and give strength to body and soul alike. This natural beauty-hunger is made manifest in the little window-sill gardens of the poor, though perhaps only a geranium slip in a broken cup, as well as in the carefully tended rose and lily gardens of the rich, the thousands of spacious city parks and botanical gardens, and in our magnificent National Parks—the Yellowstone, Yosemite, Sequoia, etc.—Nature's sublime wonderlands, the admiration and joy of the world. Nevertheless, like anything else worth while, from the very beginning, however well guarded, they have always been subject to attack by despoiling gain-seekers and mischief-makers of every degree from Satan to Senators, eagerly trying to make everything immediately and selfishly commercial, with schemes disguised in smug-smiling philanthropy, industriously, sham-piously crying, "Conservation, conservation, panutilization," that man and beast may be fed and the dear Nation made great. Thus long ago a few enterprising merchants utilized the Jerusalem temple as a place of business instead of a place of prayer, changing money, buying and selling cattle and sheep and doves. . . .

That anyone would try to destroy such a place seems incredible; but sad experience shows that there are people good enough and bad enough for anything. The proponents of the dam scheme bring forward a lot of bad arguments to prove that the only righteous thing to do with the people's parks is to destroy them bit by bit as they are able. Their arguments are curiously like those of the devil, devised for the destruction of the first garden—so much of the very best Eden fruit going to waste; so much of the best Tuolumne water and Tuolumne scenery going to waste. . . .

These temple destroyers, devotees of ravaging commercialism, seem to have a perfect contempt for Nature, and, instead of lifting their eyes to the God of the mountains, lift them to the Almighty Dollar.

Dam Hetch Hetchy! As well dam for water-tanks the people's cathedrals and churches, for no holier temple has ever been consecrated by the heart of man.

5. "Beauty as Against Use" (1920s)

When Gifford Pinchot used the phrase "beauty as against use" in his testimony before the House Committee on Public Lands in 1913, he succinctly summarized the terms of the debate about natural resources in the opening years of the century (see page 218). Conservationists like Pinchot, who advocated that national resources be

---

[5]Herbert Johnson, courtesy of The National Park Service Archives.

utilized efficiently, faced two enemies: on the one hand, commercial interests that exploited natural resources, and on the other hand, preservationists like John Muir who celebrated the beauty of nature and wanted to preserve it unspoiled for all time. The following images by Herbert Johnson, entitled National Park as the People Inherited It, *and* The Logical Finish If We Let Down the Bars *illustrate the starkly contrasting ways in which conservation issues were often posed. Why did conservationists and preservationists alike find it so difficult to combine beauty and use? If the artist had drawn a third, middle panel in this scene, what would it have looked like? If forced to choose, which of these images would Theodore Roosevelt have endorsed? Why?*

NATIONAL PARK
AS THE PEOPLE INHERITED IT

THE LOGICAL FINISH
IF WE LET DOWN THE BARS

Herbert Johnson

E. The Crusade for Women's Suffrage _____

1. Senator Robert Owen Supports Women (1910)

Wedded to the tried and true, President Howard Taft was no enthusiast for women's suffrage. He believed the issue was one that should be handled by the individual states. As late as 1912 he wrote privately, "I cannot change my view . . . just to suit the exigencies of the campaign, and if it is going to hurt me, I think it will have to hurt me." But the embattled women now had an increasingly strong argument. Rapid industrialization after the Civil War had lured millions of women from the home into the office and the factory, where they were competing with men. By 1910 four states—Wyoming, Colorado, Utah, and Idaho—had granted unrestricted suffrage to women, and the progressive upheaval of the era added great impetus to the reform. Senator Robert L. Owen of Oklahoma, who had earlier demanded citizenship for Native Americans, here makes a speech to a learned society favoring women's suffrage. What ideas about the nature of womanhood underlie his argument? What changes in society does he think women's suffrage will entail?

Women compose one-half of the human race. In the last forty years, women in gradually increasing numbers have been compelled to leave the home and enter the factory and workshop. Over seven million women are so employed, and the remainder of the sex are employed largely in domestic services. A full half of the work of the world is done by women. A careful study of the matter has demonstrated the vital fact that these working women receive a smaller wage for equal work than men do, and that the smaller wage and harder conditions imposed on the woman worker are due to the lack of the ballot.

Many women have a very hard time, and if the ballot would help them, even a little, I should like to see them have it. . . . Equal pay for equal work is the first great reason justifying this change of governmental policy.

There are other reasons which are persuasive: First, women, take it all in all, are the equals of men in intelligence, and no man has the hardihood to assert the contrary. . . .

The man is usually better informed with regard to state governent, but women are better informed about house government, and she can learn state government with as much facility as he can learn how to instruct children, properly feed and clothe the household, care for the sick, play on the piano, or make a house beautiful. . . .

The woman ballot will not revolutionize the world. Its results in Colorado, for example, might have been anticipated. First, it did give women better wages for equal work; second, it led immediately to a number of laws the women wanted, and the first laws they demanded were laws for the protection of the children of the state, making it a misdemeanor to contribute to the delinquency of a child; laws for the improved care of defective children; also, the Juvenile Court for the conservation of wayward boys and girls; the better care of the insane, the deaf, the dumb, the

_____

[1]*Annals of the American Academy of Political and Social Science* 35, Supplement (May 1910): 6–9, passim.

blind; the curfew bell to keep children off the streets at night; raising the age of consent for girls; improving the reformatories and prisons of the state; improving the hospital services of the state; improving the sanitary laws affecting the health of the homes of the state. Their [women's] interest in the public health is a matter of great importance. Above all, there resulted laws for improving the school system.

Several important results followed. Both political parties were induced to put up cleaner, better men, for the women would not stand a notoriously corrupt or unclean candidate. The headquarters of political parties became more decent, and the polling places became respectable. The bad women, enslaved by mercenary vice, do not vote, and good women do vote in as great proportion as men. Every evil prophecy against granting the suffrage has failed. The public men of Colorado, Wyoming, Utah, and Idaho give it a cordial support.

The testimony is universal:

First, it has not made women mannish; they still love their homes and children just the same as ever, and are better able to protect themselves and their children because of the ballot.

Second, they have not become office-seekers, nor pothouse politicians. They have not become swaggerers and insolent on the streets. They still teach good manners to men, as they always have done. It [suffrage] has made women broader and greatly increased the understanding of the community at large of the problems of good government; of proper sanitation, of pure food, or clean water, and all such matters in which intelligent women would naturally take an interest.

It has not absolutely regenerated society, but it has improved it. It has raised the educational qualification of the suffrage, and has elevated the moral standard of the suffrage, because there are more criminal men than criminal women. . . .

The great doctrine of the American Republic that "all governments derive their just powers from the consent of the governed" justifies the plea of one-half of the people, the women, to exercise the suffrage. The doctrine of the American Revolutionary War that taxation without representation is unendurable justifies women in exercising the suffrage.

2. A Woman Assails Women's Suffrage (1910)

As late as 1910 many women plainly did not want to shoulder the heavy civic responsibilities that would come with the ballot. One argument was that each sex was superior in its own sphere—women in the home, men in the outside world—and that a separation was best for all concerned. Agitators for women's suffrage feared that if their cause were submitted to a vote by all women, it would be defeated. The suffragists argued that the women who wanted the vote ought to have it. Mrs. Gilbert E. Jones, an opponent of votes for women, here pleads her case before a scholarly group. How do her views differ from those of Senator Owen, just given? Which of them esteemed women more highly? How do Jones's views compare with those of Jane Addams (see p. 127)?

---

[2]*Annals of the American Academy of Political and Social Science* 35, Supplement (May 1910): 16–21, passim.

The anti-suffragists are not organizing or rushing into committees, societies, or associations, and their doings are not being cried out from the house-tops. Yet they show by undeniable facts, easily verified, that woman suffrage bills and proposals have been defeated and turned down at the rate of once in every twenty-seven days in the state legislatures for the last twelve years. . . .

A great many states have granted to women school suffrage, but only a partisan or sectarian issue will bring out the woman's vote. In Massachusetts women have voted on school boards, and after thirty years' training, only 2 or 3 percent of the women register to vote. This hardly can be pronounced "success," or worth while. . . .

Taxation without representation is tyranny, but we must be very careful to define what we mean by the phrase. If we adopt the suffrage attitude, "I pay taxes, therefore I should vote," the natural conclusion is that everybody who pays taxes should vote, or we have a tyrannical form of government. Remember that this argument is used in an unqualified way. We have a "tyranny" here, we are told, because some women pay taxes, yet do not vote. If this is true without any qualification, it must be true not only of women, but of everybody. Accordingly, this government is tyrannical if corporations pay taxes, but do not vote; if aliens pay taxes, but do not vote; if minors pay taxes, but do not vote; if anybody pays taxes, but does not vote. The only correct conclusion is, not that women should vote because some of them pay taxes, but that every taxpayer should be given the privilege of the ballot. . . .

A very conscientious investigation by this League* cannot find that the ballot will help the wage-earning woman. Women must resort to organization, association, and trade unions, and then they can command and maintain a standard wage. Supply and demand will do the rest. Women are not well trained and often very deficient and unskilled in most of their occupations. They are generally only supplementary workers and drop their work when they marry. When married, and home and children are to be cared for, they are handicapped way beyond their strength. Married women should be kept out of industry, rather than urged into it, as scientists, physicians, and sociologists all state that as women enter into competitive industrial life with men, just so does the death rate of little children increase and the birth rate decrease.

Anti-suffragists deplore the fact that women are found in unsuitable occupations. But the suffragists glory in the fact that there are women blacksmiths, baggage masters, brakemen, undertakers, and women political "bosses" in Colorado.

The suffragists call this progress, independence, and emancipation of women. "Anti's" ask for more discrimination and better selection of industrial occupations for wage-earning women. Knowing that the average woman has half of the physical strength of the average man, and the price she must pay when in competition with him is too great for her ultimate health and her hope of motherhood, the "Anti's" ask for caution and extreme consideration before new activities are entered upon. . . .

The suffrage leaders say that a woman without the vote has no self-respect. We

---

*The National League for the Civic Education of Women, an antisuffrage group.

must then look to the suffrage states to find the fulfillment of the woman's true position, complete—worthy, exalted, and respected. But what do we find when we look at Utah! Women have voted there for forty years. Mormonism and woman suffrage were coincident. By the very nature of its teachings, as indicated by Brigham Young, the basis of the Mormon Church is woman—and the Mormon Church is the greatest political machine in the four suffrage States. . . .

The question of woman suffrage should be summed up in this way: Has granting the ballot to women in the two suffrage states where they have had it for forty years brought about any great reforms or great results? No—Wyoming has many more men than women, so the results cannot be measured. The Mormon women of Utah are not free American citizens. They are under the Elder's supreme power, and vote accordingly, and polygamy has been maintained by the woman's vote, and is still to be found, although forbidden, because women have political power.

Have the saloons been abolished in any of the suffrage states? No.

Do men still drink and gamble? Yes, without a doubt.

Have the slums been done away with? Indeed no.

Are the streets better cleaned in the states where women vote? No, they are quite as bad as in New York City and elsewhere.

Have the red-light districts been cleared away? Decidedly not, and they can be reckoned upon as a political factor, when they are really needed.

Have women purified politics? No, not in the least.

Have women voted voluntarily? Some do; but thousands are carried to the polls in autos and carriages; otherwise they would not vote.

Has pure food and pure milk been established by the woman's vote? Not at all.

Have women's wages been increased because women vote? No, indeed.

Have women equal pay for equal work? Not any more than in New York City.

Are there laws on the statute books that would give women equal pay for equal work? No, and never will be.

Are women treated with more respect in the four suffrage states than elsewhere? Not at all—certainly not in Utah. . . .

[The "anti's" also argued that women were adequately represented by their menfolk; that women already exercised a strong influence indirectly ("harem government"); that suffrage would end chivalry; that women were already overburdened in the home; that family quarrels over partisan issues would increase the divorce rate; that females were too emotional; and that women, if allowed to vote, would soon be serving on juries and forced to hear "indecent testimony." Despite such objections, some of them frivolous, nationwide women's suffrage finally triumphed with the passage of the Nineteenth Amendment in 1920.]

3. Images of the Suffrage Campaign (1900–1915)

Opponents of women's suffrage long argued that a woman's place was in the home, not in the public world of politics. But in the first years of the twentieth century, suffragists like Carrie Chapman Catt and Jane Addams began to turn that argument on its head. They stressed the roles that women already played outside the home, and argued further that modern women needed the vote precisely in order to fulfill their traditional duties as homemakers and mothers. What views of women's nature and social role are expressed in the following pro-suffrage cartoons? What arguments for women's suffrage do these images represent? Which do you think proved most persuasive?

But when the hounds of Starvation Wages, Broken Laws, Intolerable Hours, Cold, Hunger and Discouragement pursue her, where is her place and what is her protection?   1912

---

[3]p. 227, Lou Rogers, *New York Call,* May 1912, courtesy of The State Historical Society of Wisconsin; p. 228, Jessie Banks, *Woman Voter,* October 1915, courtesy of The Periodicals Division, Library of Congress; p. 229, Rose O'Neill, Stock Montage, Chicago.

Woman's Place Is at Home.   1915

Woman's Place Is in the Home. We're Going Home.   1915

Thought Provokers

1. In what ways did the muckrakers represent both the best and the worst features of a free press in the United States?
2. Was corruption a "natural" by-product of the adaptation of U.S. institutions to the new urban environment? Did it serve any useful civic purpose?
3. Was government protection necessary to improve the lot of the laborer in the industrializing United States? How justifiable were special laws to guard women and youthful workers?
4. What motives inspired Roosevelt's crusade for conservation? How different or similar is the attitude of the West today toward efforts at government control of the environment?
5. Were women powerless without the ballot? How has the suffrage changed the position of women? How has the nation's political agenda changed as a result of women's suffrage?

30

Wilsonian Progressivism at Home and Abroad, 1912–1916

We dare not turn from the principle that morality and not expediency is the thing that must guide us.

Woodrow Wilson, 1913

Prologue: The presidential election of 1912 was unusual in U.S. history. It featured three plausible candidates—William Howard Taft, Theodore Roosevelt, and Woodrow Wilson—and amounted to a referendum on which of the competing philosophies of progressivism would prevail. When Woodrow Wilson emerged the victor, he energetically set out to achieve landmark reforms in tariff policy, banking, and antitrust legislation. Triumphant at home, Wilson was soon embroiled in explosive diplomatic troubles abroad, beginning with Mexico in 1914. In that same year, war broke out in Europe, straining the United States' historic commitment to neutrality and testing all of Wilson's considerable political skills.

A. The Election of 1912

1. Theodore Roosevelt Proposes Government Regulation (1912)

Provoked by the failure of his successor, William Howard Taft, to pursue progressive policies, Theodore Roosevelt attempted to wrest the Republican presidential nomination from Taft in 1912. Having failed in that effort, Roosevelt became the candidate of one of the most vigorous third parties in U.S. history, the Progressive or Bull Moose party. In the ensuing election campaign, Roosevelt strenuously attacked the Democratic platform's call for strengthening the antitrust laws, and defended his own proposal for more extensive government regulation of the economy. In discussing the trust issue, however, Roosevelt went beyond the narrow technicalities of economic policy and raised fundamental questions of political philosophy. In the remarks excerpted here, what are Roosevelt's most telling arguments against antitrust? What

---

[1]*Theodore Roosevelt, Progressive Principles: Selections from Addresses Made During the Presidential Campaign of 1912,* Elmer H. Youngman, ed. (New York: Progressive National Service, 1913), pp. 141–152, 216–217.

was his underlying philosophy of government? Was that philosophy new in the context of the U.S. political tradition?

As construed by the Democratic platform, the Anti-Trust Law would, if it could be enforced, abolish all business of any size or any efficiency. The promise thus to apply and construe the law would undoubtedly be broken, but the mere fitful effort thus to apply it would do no good whatever, would accomplish widespread harm, and would bring all trust legislation into contempt. . . .

What is needed is . . . a National Industrial commission . . . which should have complete power to regulate and control all the great industrial concerns engaged in inter-State business—which practically means all of them in this country. This commission should exercise over these industrial concerns like powers to those exercised over the railways by the Inter-State Commerce Commission. . . .

Our proposal is to help honest business activity, however extensive, and to see that it is rewarded with fair returns so that there may be no oppression either of business men or of the common people. We propose to make it worth while for our business men to develop the most efficient business agencies for use in international trade; for it is to the interest of our whole people that we should do well in international business. . . .

We favor co-operation in business, and ask only that it be carried on in a spirit of honesty and fairness. We are against crooked business, big or little. We are in favor of honest business, big or little. We propose to penalize conduct and not size. But all very big business, even though honestly conducted, is fraught with such potentiality of menace that there should be thoroughgoing Governmental control over it, so that its efficiency in promoting prosperity at home and increasing the power of the Nation in international commerce may be maintained, and at the same time fair play insured to the wage-workers, the small business competitors, the investors, and the general public. Wherever it is practicable we propose to preserve competition; but where under modern conditions competition has been eliminated and cannot be successfully restored, then the Government must step in and itself supply the needed control on behalf of the people as a whole. . . .

The people of the United States have but one instrument which they can efficiently use against the colossal combinations of business—and that instrument is the Government of the United States (and of course in the several States the governments of the States where they can be utilized). Mr. Wilson's proposal* is that the people of the United States shall throw away this, the one great instrument, the one great weapon they have with which to secure themselves against wrong. He proposes to limit the governmental action of the people and therefore to leave unlimited and unchecked the action of the great corporations whose enormous power constitutes so serious a problem in modern industrial life. Remember that it is absolutely impossible to limit the power of these great corporations whose enormous power constitutes so serious a problem in modern industrial life except by extending the power of the Government. All that these great corporations ask is that the power of the Government shall be limited. No wonder they are supporting Mr. Wil-

---

*Roosevelt refers here to the "New Freedom" platform of presidential candidate Woodrow Wilson. See the next selection.

son, for he is advocating for them what they hardly dare venture to advocate for themselves. These great corporations rarely want anything from the Government except to be let alone and to be permitted to work their will unchecked by the Government. All that they really want is that governmental action shall be limited. In every great corporation suit the corporation lawyer will be found protesting against extension of governmental power. Every court decision favoring a corporation takes the form of declaring unconstitutional some extension of governmental power. Every corporation magnate in the country who is not dealing honestly and fairly by his fellows asks nothing better than that Mr. Wilson's programme be carried out and that there be stringent limitations of governmental power.

There once was a time in history when the limitation of governmental power meant increasing liberty for the people. In the present day the limitation of governmental power, of governmental action, means the enslavement of the people by the great corporations who can only be held in check through the extension of governmental power.

2. Woodrow Wilson Asks for "a Free Field and No Favor" (1912)

Two "progressive" candidates—Theodore Roosevelt and Woodrow Wilson—faced off in the crucial election of 1912. (William Howard Taft, the Republican candidate, finished a distant third.) The election amounted, in effect, to a referendum on which variant of progressivism would prevail. In Woodrow Wilson's remarks that follow, what are his principal differences from Theodore Roosevelt? What is the meaning of his distinction between "benevolence" and "justice"? Which of the two candidates' philosophies was more forward looking, and which more backward looking?

Mr. Roosevelt attached to his platform some very splendid suggestions as to noble enterprises which we ought to undertake for the uplift of the human race; but when I hear an ambitious platform put forth, I am very much more interested in the dynamics of it than in the rhetoric of it. . . . You know that Mr. Roosevelt long ago classified trusts for us as good and bad, and he said that he was afraid only of the bad ones. Now he does not desire that there should be any more bad ones, but proposes that they should all be made good by discipline, directly applied by a commission of executive appointment. All he explicitly complains of is lack of publicity and lack of fairness; not the exercise of power, for throughout that plank the power of the great corporations is accepted as the inevitable consequence of the modern organization of industry. All that it is proposed to do is to take them under control and regulation. . . .

If the government is to tell big business men how to run their business, then don't you see that big business men have to get closer to the government even than they are now? Don't you see that they must capture the government, in order not to be restrained too much by it? . . .

I don't care how benevolent the master is going to be, I will not live under a master. That is not what America was created for. America was created in order that

---

[2]Woodrow Wilson, *The New Freedom: A Call for the Emancipation of the Generous Energies of a People*, William Bayard Hale, ed. (Garden City, N.Y.: Doubleday, Page, 1913), pp. 191–222.

every man should have the same chance as every other man to exercise mastery over his own fortunes. . . . If you will but hold off the adversaries, if you will but see to it that the weak are protected, I will venture a wager with you that there are some men in the United States, now weak, economically weak, who have brains enough to compete with these gentlemen and who will presently come into the market and put these gentlemen on their mettle. . . .

I agree that as a nation we are now about to undertake what may be regarded as the most difficult part of our governmental enterprises. We have gone along so far without very much assistance from our government. We have felt, and felt more and more in recent months, that the American people were at a certain disadvantage as compared with the people of other countries, because of what the governments of other countries were doing for them and our government omitting to do for us.

It is perfectly clear to every man who has any vision of the immediate future, who can forecast any part of it from the indications of the present, that we are just upon the threshold of a time when the systematic life of this country will be sustained, or at least supplemented, at every point by governmental activity. And we have now to determine what kind of governmental activity it shall be; whether, in the first place, it shall be direct from the government itself, or whether it shall be indirect, through instrumentalities which have already constituted themselves and which stand ready to supersede the government.

I believe that the time has come when the governments of this country, both state and national, have to set the stage, and set it very minutely and carefully, for the doing of justice to men in every relationship of life. It has been free and easy with us so far; it has been go as you please; it has been every man look out for himself; and we have continued to assume, up to this year when every man is dealing, not with another man, in most cases, but with a body of men whom he has not seen, that the relationships of property are the same that they always were. We have great tasks before us, and we must enter on them as befits men charged with the responsibility of shaping a new era.

We have a great program of governmental assistance ahead of us in the cooperative life of the nation; but we dare not enter upon that program until we have freed the government. That is the point. Benevolence never developed a man or a nation. We do not want a benevolent government. We want a free and a just government. Every one of the great schemes of social uplift which are now so much debated by noble people amongst us is based, when rightly conceived, upon justice, not upon benevolence. It is based upon the right of men to breathe pure air, to live; upon the right of women to bear children, and not to be overburdened so that disease and breakdown will come upon them; upon the right of children to thrive and grow up and be strong; upon all these fundamental things which appeal, indeed, to our hearts, but which our minds perceive to be part of the fundamental justice of life.

Politics differs from philanthropy in this: that in philanthropy we sometimes do things through pity merely, while in politics we act always, if we are righteous men, on grounds of justice and large expediency for men in the mass. Sometimes in our pitiful sympathy with our fellow-men we must do things that are more than just. We must forgive men. We must help men who have gone wrong. We must sometimes help men who have gone criminally wrong. But the law does not forgive. It is its duty to equalize conditions, to make the path of right the path of safety and advantage, to see that every man has a fair chance to live and to serve himself, to see that injustice and wrong are not wrought upon any. . . .

The reason that America was set up was that she might be different from all the nations of the world in this: that the strong could not put the weak to the wall, that the strong could not prevent the weak from entering the race. America stands for opportunity. America stands for a free field and no favor. . . .

B. Campaigning for Monetary Reform

1. Louis Brandeis Indicts Interlocking Directorates (1914)

Populists, muckrakers, progressives, and Wilsonian Democrats alike had condemned the monopolistic "money trust." In 1912 the Democratic House of Representatives appointed the famed Pujo committee, which launched a searching investigation. The next year it released a sensational report stating that 341 directorships in 112 corporations controlled resources amounting to $22.245 billion. Many of these directorships, including the Wall Street House of Morgan, were interlocking. Louis D. Brandeis, a brilliant young liberal destined to be a Supreme Court justice, develops this aspect in the following partial summary of the Pujo committee's findings. What was the most objectionable feature of interlocking directorates from the standpoint of the public?

The practice of interlocking directorates is the root of many evils. It offends laws human and divine. Applied to rival corporations, it tends to the suppression of competition and to violation of the Sherman [antitrust] law. Applied to corporations which deal with each other, it tends to disloyalty and to violation of the fundamental law that no man can serve two masters. In either event it tends to inefficiency; for it removes incentive and destroys soundness of judgment. It is undemocratic, for it rejects the platform: "A fair field and no favors," substituting the pull of privilege for the push of manhood. It is the most potent instrument of the Money Trust. Break the control so exercised by the investment bankers over railroads, public-service and industrial corporations, over banks, life-insurance and trust companies, and a long step will have been taken toward attainment of the New Freedom.

The term "interlocking directorates" is here used in a broad sense as including all intertwined conflicting interests, whatever the form, and by whatever device effected. The objection extends alike to contracts of a corporation, whether with one of its directors individually, or with a firm of which he is a member, or with another corporation in which he is interested as an officer or director or stockholder. The objection extends likewise to men holding the inconsistent position of director in two potentially competing corporations, even if those corporations do not actually deal with each other.

---

[1]L. D. Brandeis, *Other People's Money* (1914), pp. 51–53.

A single example will illustrate the vicious circle of control—the endless chain—through which our financial oligarchy now operates:

J. P. Morgan (or a partner), a director of the New York, New Haven & Hartford Railroad, causes that company to sell to J. P. Morgan & Co. an issue of bonds. J. P. Morgan & Co. borrow the money with which to pay for the bonds from the Guaranty Trust Company, of which Mr. Morgan (or a partner) is a director. J. P. Morgan & Co. sell the bonds to the Penn Mutual Life Insurance Company, of which Mr. Morgan (or a partner) is a director. The New Haven spends the proceeds of the bonds in purchasing steel rails from the United States Steel Corporation, of which Mr. Morgan (or a partner) is a director. The United States Steel Corporation spends the proceeds of the rails in purchasing electrical supplies from the General Electric Company, of which Mr. Morgan (or a partner) is a director. The General Electric Company sells supplies to the Western Union Telegraph Company, a subsidiary of the American Telephone and Telegraph Company; and in both Mr. Morgan (or a partner) is a director.

2. J. P. Morgan Denies a Money Trust (1913)

J. Pierpont Morgan, bulbous-nosed but august, appeared before the Pujo committee with eight attorneys. (Their estimated fees for two days were $45,000.) He denied not only the existence of a money trust but even the possibility of its existence. Less convincing was his claim that he neither possessed nor desired great financial power. A subsequent letter from the House of Morgan to the Pujo committee summarized the influential financier's point of view. To what extent does this statement refute the charges against the bankers?

. . . There have been spread before your Committee elaborate tables of so-called interlocking directorates, from which exceedingly mistaken inferences have been publicly drawn. In these tables it is shown that 180 bankers and bank directors serve upon the boards of corporations having resources aggregating $25,000,000,000, and it is implied that this vast aggregate of the country's wealth is at the disposal of these 180 men.

But such an implication rests solely upon the untenable theory that these men, living in different parts of the country, in many cases personally unacquainted with each other, and in most cases associated only in occasional transactions, vote always for the same policies and control with united purpose the directorates of the 132 corporations on which they serve.

The testimony failed to establish any concerted policy or harmony of action binding these 180 men together, and, as a matter of fact, no such policy exists. The absurdity of the assumption of such control becomes more apparent when one considers that, on the average, these directors represent only one quarter of the memberships of their boards. It is preposterous to suppose that every "interlocking" director has full control in every organization with which he is connected, and that the majority of directors who are not "interlocking" are mere figureheads, subject to the will of a small minority of their boards.

---

²*Letter from Messrs. J. P. Morgan & Co. . . .* (privately printed, February 25, 1913), pp. 8–9, 12, 17–18.

Perhaps the greatest harm in the presentation referred to lay in the further unwarranted inference, to which has been given wide publicity, that the vast sum of $25,000,000,000 was in cash or liquid form, subject to the selfish use or abuse of individuals. Such an idea excites the public mind to demand the correction of a fancied situation which does not and, in our belief, never can exist. . . .

Such growth in the size of banks in New York and Chicago has frequently been erroneously designated before your Committee as "concentration," whereas we have hitherto pointed out [that] the growth of banking resources in New York City has been less rapid than that of the rest of the country. But increase of capital, and merger of two or more banks into one institution (with the same resources as the aggregate of the banks merging into it), has been frequent, especially since January 1, 1908.

These mergers, however, are a development due simply to the demand for larger banking facilities to care for the growth of the country's business. As our cities double and treble in size and importance, as railroads extend and industrial plants expand, not only is it natural, but it is necessary, that our banking institutions should grow in order to care for the increased demands put upon them. Perhaps it is not known as well as it should be that in New York City the largest banks are far inferior in size to banks in the commercial capitals of other and much smaller countries. . . .

For a private banker to sit upon . . . a directorate is in most instances a duty, not a privilege. Inquiry will readily develop the fact that the members of the leading banking houses in this country—and it was the leading houses only against which animad-versions were directed—are besought continually to act as directors in various corporations, whose securities they may handle, and that in general they enter only those boards which the opinion of the investing public requires them to enter, as an evidence of good faith that they are willing to have their names publicly associated with the management.

Yet, before your Committee, this natural and eminently desirable relationship was made to appear almost sinister, and no testimony whatever was adduced to show the actual working of such relationships.

3. William McAdoo Exposes the Bankers (c. 1913)

President Wilson, the foe of special privilege, was determined to break the so-called money monopoly. The need for a more flexible currency had been brought home to the nation by the disastrous "bankers' panic" of 1907. Wilson therefore threw the weight of his dynamic personality behind the Federal Reserve bill introduced in Congress in 1913. The big bankers, most of them conservative Republicans, fought it passionately. They favored a huge new central bank with themselves in control; they were forced, however, to accept a twelve-district Federal Reserve System, with a government-appointed Federal Reserve Board in control. Lanky, black-haired William G. McAdoo, Wilson's secretary of the treasury (and son-in-law), here describes the initial opposition of the bankers. In what respect were they most seriously wrong?

---

[3]From *Crowded Years* by William Gibbs McAdoo. Copyright 1931, © renewed 1959. Reprinted by permission of Houghton Mifflin Company. All rights reserved.

As time went by, we observed that the public generally—I mean the ordinary, average citizen—was in favor of the Federal Reserve Bill. The bankers in the larger money centers were almost to a man bitterly opposed to it, and many businessmen shared their views. Sentiment among the smaller banks was divided—those against the bill being largely in the majority.

At the national convention of the American Bankers' Association, held in Boston, October, 1913, only two delegates attempted to speak in favor of the legislation; each was howled down until the chairman managed to make himself heard, and begged the convention to give them the courtesy of attention.

Dr. Joseph French Johnson, professor of political economy at New York University, said at a dinner of the Academy of Political Science that the bill, if passed, would bring on a dangerous credit expansion and that it would cause "a collapse of the banking system." He added that "blacksmiths could not be expected to produce a Swiss watch." The blacksmiths were, in this case, I suppose, the Democrats, and the Federal Reserve Bill was the Swiss watch. So I infer, and I fancy that another meaning, to the effect that Professor Johnson himself was an excellent watchmaker, lurked in the background.

And from Chicago came reports of a speech of Senator Lawrence Y. Sherman, Republican member of the Senate from Illinois. In addressing the Illinois Bankers' Association he said: "I would support a law to wind a watch with a crowbar as cheerfully as I will support any such bill."

But James B. Forgan, banking magnate of Chicago, was more direct in his expression of opinion. He said nothing about crowbars and blacksmiths and Swiss watches. He declared that the bill was "unworkable, impractical, and fundamentally bad." It would bring about, he said, "the most damnable contraction of currency ever seen in any country."

Forgan's idea that the currency would be damnably contracted was not shared by all the opponents of the Glass-Owen [Federal Reserve] Bill. Many bankers and economists proved, to their own satisfaction by figures and diagrams, that the Federal Reserve System would produce an extraordinary inflation. These vast and irreconcilable differences of opinion between the various groups of our adversaries had the effect of lessening my respect for so-called banking experts. I found that they could take the same set of facts and reach two diametrically opposite conclusions.

For example, Forgan estimated that the currency would be contracted to the extent of $1,800,000,000, while Senator Elihu Root, using the same data, predicted an inflation of at least $1,800,000,000.

President Arthur T. Hadley, of Yale, who had a high reputation as an economist, believed that the bill, if passed, would lead to inflation on an unparalleled scale, with a consequent depreciation. He was so deeply moved that he wrote a personal letter to President Wilson on July 1, 1913, for the purpose of pointing out to the President that the Act would "involve the country in grave financial danger." Practically all of our gold would leave for Europe, he thought. He was greatly mistaken. There is now in the United States about 45 percent of all the gold in the world.

Frank A. Vanderlip, president of the National City Bank of New York, declared that the notes of the Federal Reserve Banks would be "fiat money," and James J. Hill, the famous railroad builder and financier, said the plan was "socialistic." James R. Mann, Republican leader of the House, condemned the bill as all wrong, badly conceived, and impossible as a practical measure. However, he added bitterly, it did not matter; the national banks would not go into the system, anyway. Most of them would become state banks, and the Federal Reserve would just lie down and die for lack of support. Saying this, he washed his hands of the whole affair.

[The Federal Reserve System, approved by Congress late in 1913, not only carried the nation triumphantly through World War I but remains the bulwark of the nation's financial structure. The sneers of the bankers gave way to cheers. Currency expansion to meet growing needs was abundantly provided by the issuance of Federal Reserve notes, backed in part by promissory notes and other assets held by the member banks. The national banks, authorized during the Civil War, were required to join the Federal Reserve System. Wall Street's grip on money and credit was thus weakened, and interlocking directorates were curbed the next year (1914) by the Clayton Anti-Trust Act.]

C. Moral Meddling in Mexico

1. Wilson Asks for War on General Huerta (1914)

The decade-long despotic rule of dictator Díaz in Mexico crumbled during the upheaval of 1910–1911. But the revolution took an ugly turn in 1913, when General Huerta—a full-blooded Indian who was an alcoholic and a drug addict—connived at the murder of the liberal President Madero and forthwith seized power. Wilson, whose heart went out to the oppressed masses of Mexico, refused to recognize this bloody-handed dictator, and thereby departed from the traditional U.S. policy of recognizing established regimes. Pursuing a plan of "watchful waiting," he modified the U.S. arms embargo to the advantage of Huerta's foes. The crisis came to a boil in April 1914, when Mexican officials seized two men from the U.S. Navy boat at Tampico. The local officials promptly tendered apologies. But Admiral Mayo, acting without specific authorization from Washington, demanded a twenty-one-gun salute to the American flag. When Huerta refused to comply, Wilson went before Congress to ask for authority (which he already had as commander in chief) to use force. How did he attempt to reconcile his friendship for the Mexican people with a request to fight them? What other inconsistencies emerge?

The [Tampico] incident cannot be regarded as a trivial one, especially as two of the men arrested were taken from the boat itself—that is to say, from the territory of the United States. But had it stood by itself, it might have been attributed to the ignorance or arrogance of a single officer. Unfortunately, it was not an isolated case. A series of incidents have recently occurred which cannot but create the impression that the representatives of General Huerta were willing to go out of their way to

---

[1]Arthur S. Link, ed., *The Papers of Woodrow Wilson* (Princeton: Princeton University Press, 1979), vol. 29, pp. 472–474.

show disregard for the dignity and rights of this Government,* and felt perfectly safe in doing what they pleased, making free to show in many ways their irritation and contempt. . . . So far as I can learn, such wrongs and annoyances have been suffered to occur only against representatives of the United States. . . .

The manifest danger of such a situation was that such offense might grow from bad to worse until something happened of so gross and intolerable a sort as to lead directly and inevitably to armed conflict. It was necessary that the apologies of General Huerta and his representatives should go much further; that they should be such as to attract the attention of the whole population to their significance, and such as to impress upon General Huerta himself the necessity of seeing to it that no further occasion for explanations and professed regrets should arise. I, therefore, felt it my duty to sustain Admiral Mayo in the whole of his demand, and to insist that the flag of the United States should be saluted in such a way as to indicate a new spirit and attitude on the part of the Huertistas.

Such a salute General Huerta has refused, and I have come to ask your approval and support in the course I now propose to pursue.

This Government can, I earnestly hope, in no circumstances be forced into war with the people of Mexico. Mexico is torn by civil strife. If we are to accept the tests of its own constitution, it has no government. General Huerta has set his power up in the City of Mexico, such as it is, without right and by methods for which there can be no justification. Only part of the country is under his control. If armed conflict should unhappily come as a result of his attitude of personal resentment toward this Government, we should be fighting only General Huerta and those who adhere to him and give him their support, and our object would be only to restore to the people of the distracted Republic the opportunity to set up again their own laws and their own government.

But I earnestly hope that war is not now in question. I believe that I speak for the American people when I say that we do not desire to control in any degree the affairs of our sister Republic. Our feeling for the people of Mexico is one of deep and genuine friendship, and everything that we have so far done or refrained from doing has proceeded from our desire to help them, not to hinder or embarrass them. We would not wish even to exercise the good offices of friendship without their welcome and consent. The people of Mexico are entitled to settle their own domestic affairs in their own way, and we sincerely desire to respect their right. The present situation need have none of the grave implications of interference if we deal with it promptly, firmly, and wisely.

No doubt I could do what is necessary in the circumstances to enforce respect for our Government without recourse to the Congress, and yet not exceed my constitutional powers as President. But I do not wish to act in a manner possibly of so grave consequence except in close conference and cooperation with both the Senate and House. I, therefore, come to ask your approval that I should use the armed forces of the United States in such ways and to such an extent as may be necessary to obtain from General Huerta and his adherents the fullest recognition of the rights

---

*Professor A. S. Link concludes that this statement misrepresents the facts; Huerta had shown "extraordinary concern" for U.S. interests (Wilson: *The New Freedom* [1956], p. 398).

and dignity of the United States, even amidst the distressing conditions now unhappily obtaining in Mexico.

There can in what we do be no thought of aggression or of selfish aggrandizement. We seek to maintain the dignity and authority of the United States, only because we wish always to keep our great influence unimpaired for the uses of liberty, both in the United States and wherever else it may be employed for the benefit of mankind.

2. A Republican Assails "Watchful Waiting" (1916)

A patriotic Congress promptly granted Wilson the authority to intervene in Mexico. A day earlier, however (April 21, 1914), U.S. forces, under emergency orders from the White House, had bombarded and occupied Vera Cruz in a vain attempt to prevent a German ship from landing munitions that might be used against U.S. troops. With a Louisville newspaper crying, "On to the Isthmus!" and with a full-blown war imminent, the "ABC" powers (Argentina, Brazil, and Chile) offered to mediate. Wilson gladly accepted this escape hatch, on April 25, 1914. Nearly three months later, Huerta was forced to abdicate, but U.S. businessmen clamored for full-dress intervention as U.S. citizens continued to lose both their property and their lives. When the European war erupted later in 1914, Republicans criticized Wilson for being "too proud to fight." They also condemned him for insisting that Americans leave the Mexican danger zone while he permitted others to sail through submarine-infested danger zones on the high seas. Here William E. Humphrey, a prominent congressman from Washington, voices typical Republican complaints. How effectively does he support his charges that Wilson's policy was meddling, vacillating, hypocritical, inconsistent, and futile?

The President's policy in Mexico is not based upon his party platform. It is characterized by weakness, uncertainty, vacillation, and uncontrollable desire to intermeddle in Mexican affairs. He has not had the courage to go into Mexico nor the courage to stay out.

The President has repeatedly declared that he would not interfere in Mexico nor permit others to do so. . . . At Columbus, Ohio, in his recent speech he said:

"The Mexicans may not know what to do with their government; but that is none of our business, and, so long as I have the power to prevent it, nobody shall 'butt in' to alter it for them."

At the notable talk in the White House not long ago to the Democratic National Committee, where he referred to other people "talking through their hat," if he is correctly reported, he declared "that the Mexicans can raise all the h——— they please; it is none of our business." Remember, the language I am using is not mine but the reported language of the President. Certainly their ability to raise what he so delicately described ought to satisfy even the President and that wing of the Democratic Party that believes in "watchful waiting."

But if the President had followed these declarations, however un-American and indefensible they may be, it would have been far better for us and probably for

[2]*Congressional Record,* 64th Cong., 1st sess. (January 27, 1916), pp. 1636–1638, passim.

Mexico. But his deeds have been strangers to his words. Instead of a policy of "hands off," it has been a policy of constant interference in Mexican affairs.

The President told Huerta that he must not be a candidate; that he would not be recognized. He talked about fair elections and constitutional government, and showed a strong desire not only to control Mexican politics but to go into Mexico and regulate the land system of that country. He sent his secret special agents to Mexico City and became involved in a personal quarrel with Huerta. This controversy reached its climax in the most grotesque and stupendous piece of folly in the history of civilized nations when the President appeared here before Congress and virtually asked that the United States declare war against Huerta, the individual. And, what was even more ridiculous and absurd, it was done. And for what reason? Who today will tell us the cause of that action? Americans had been driven from Mexico; American property had been destroyed in Mexico; American men had been murdered in Mexico; American women had been outraged in Mexico. But all these did not disturb the serenity of "watchful waiting," or recall to the mind of the President the Democratic platform declarations about protecting life and property of American citizens along the border and on foreign soil.

We were told that Huerta was a murderer, an assassin, a usurper, and a traitor, and a man that we would never under any circumstances recognize. But Huerta, the individual, not representing Mexico but himself, had refused to salute the American flag on a gasoline launch in a place where it had no right to be; or, to be exact, for the sake of history, Huerta agreed to fire six guns in salute, while the President, as I recall, demanded twenty-one.*

This insult from an assassin and a murderer that we would not in any way recognize was more than this administration, too proud to fight, could endure. Our magnificent battleship squadron was hurried to Mexican waters, although at that time the Mexican Navy consisted of one old antiquated gunboat. The Army was sent to Mexico, and, after Vera Cruz was bombarded by our Navy, it was landed on Mexican soil. Seventeen [nineteen] of our own soldiers lost their lives and more than a hundred Mexicans were killed. We seized the customhouse and carried away more than a million dollars.

And all this for what purpose? Why did we go to Mexico and what did we accomplish and why did we return? We were told that a German vessel was about to land a cargo of guns and ammunition, and this was the reason for hurrying our Navy to Mexican waters. But that same German vessel landed its cargo in Mexico. We are told that our Army and Navy went to Mexico to make Huerta apologize. Has anyone read that apology? We are told that our Army and Navy went to Mexico to make Huerta salute the flag. Has anyone heard that salute? . . .

Our policy in Mexico has earned us the contempt of the world, and beyond question has greatly influenced the warring nations of Europe in their present attitude toward us. . . .

We make a tremendous bluster about the killing of American citizens upon the high seas and fill the air with tumult and the noise of many typewriters, although the killing is only accidental and undoubtedly really regretted by those who did the act.

---

*Huerta had agreed to a twenty-one-gun salute if it was returned on a gun-for-gun basis, but this condition was unacceptable to Wilson.

But so far we have looked with equanimity undisturbed while hundreds of Americans have been purposely foully murdered in Mexico in a most cruel and fiendish manner. . . .

Speaking for myself, but believing that I voice the sentiment of the American people, there are some things that I would do in regard to Mexico if upon me rested the responsibility. I would either go into Mexico and pacify the country or I would keep my hands entirely out of Mexico. If we are too proud to fight, we should be too proud to quarrel. I would not choose between murderers. I would not permit either side to procure guns or ammunition in this country that may hereafter be used to murder Americans. I would not depend upon secret personal agents for my information. I would deal openly and in the light of day with the Mexican situation. I would practice pitiless publicity as well as preach it. I would give the American people the facts. I would let them know the truth, and if that is done the American people will quickly decide what shall be done.

And, above all, I would do this—the thing that should have been done more than three years ago, and if it had been done, the letting of American blood in Mexico would not have occurred: I would serve notice upon all factions that no longer would any of them be permitted, under any pretense whatever, to destroy American property, or to murder American men, or to ravish American women, and back of that notice I would place the power of this great Republic.

D. Acquiescing in the British Blockade

1. Lord Bryce's Propaganda Report (1915)

The American people were so deeply shocked by Germany's brutal invasion of Belgium that they uncritically swallowed large doses of Allied propaganda. British propagandists stressed the medically preposterous stories of Belgian babies (still living) with their hands hacked off and the alleged German practice of converting battlefield corpses into fertilizer and soap. The Germans, much less persuasively, charged that the Allies gouged out the eyes of prisoners, that French soldiers put cholera germs in wells used by Germans, and that a Belgian priest had placed a machine gun behind his altar and mowed down German Catholic soldiers who came to Mass. Lord Bryce, admired in the United States for his sympathetic two-volume The American Commonwealth, *served his country by lending his name to a sensational report on atrocities in Belgium.* In the following account (one of many alleging German arson, rape, mayhem, and murder), what part is least worthy of belief? What was the probable effect of the Bryce report in predisposing the American people to accept British infractions of neutral rights?*

---

[1]Viscount Bryce, *Report on the Committee on Alleged German Outrages* (London: H. M. Stationery Office, 1915), p. 51.

*Many of the incidents in the Bryce report were later proved to have been grossly exaggerated or completely fabricated.

The [German] officer spoke Flemish. He knocked at the door; the peasant did not come. The officer ordered the soldiers to break down the door, which two of them did. The peasant came and asked what they were doing. The officer said he did not come quickly enough, and that they had "trained up" [disciplined] plenty of others. His hands were tied behind his back, and he was shot at once without a moment's delay.

The wife came out with a little sucking child. She put the child down and sprang at the Germans like a lioness. She clawed their faces. One of the Germans took a rifle and struck her a tremendous blow with the butt on the head. Another took his bayonet and fixed it and thrust it through the child. He then put his rifle on his shoulder with the child up it, its little arms stretched out once or twice.

The officers ordered the houses to be set on fire, and straw was obtained, and it was done. The man and his wife and the child were thrown on the top of the straw. There were about forty other peasant prisoners there also, and the officer said: "I am doing this as a lesson and example to you. When a German tells you to do something next time you must move more quickly." The regiment of Germans was a regiment of Hussars, with crossbones and a death's-head on the cap.

2. Walter Page Plays Britain's Game (c. 1915)

The British, with their powerful navy, undertook to starve Germany into submission with a blockade. But the ancient practice of stationing warships off the three-mile line proved hazardous, primarily because of new long-range guns and lurking submarines. The British therefore took liberties with international law. They mined the North Sea and forced neutral ships into their ports to be searched for munitions and other contraband of war. They arbitrarily broadened the normal contraband lists to include such necessities as food and cotton. They halted the slippage of supplies into Germany through neighboring neutrals like Denmark by limiting these small countries to their prewar imports. Even though London paid for many of the intercepted cargoes, Washington protested against these disagreeable practices as violations of international law. Foreign Secretary Sir Edward Grey here tells how he dealt with Ambassador Walter Hines Page, the ex-journalist who became Wilson's ardently pro-British representative in London. Did Page behave appropriately as the spokesman in London for the U.S. government?

We got a list of absolute contraband that was not seriously challenged. But there was much more difficulty to come. We were now entitled to seize such things as copper and rubber in any ship on the high seas, if they were consigned to a German port. This alone was of little use. Germany could import goods as easily through Dutch, Danish, or Swedish ports as through her own, and in Sweden especially there were people disposed to make Sweden a source of supply for Germany. It was therefore as essential to Britain and the Allies to seize copper or rubber going to a Swedish or neutral port as when going to a German port.

---

[2]Viscount Grey, *Twenty-Five Years* volume 2, 1925, pp. 109–110.

It was on this point that controversy arose with the United States. The very fact that the United States was, in a sense, the trustee for the right of weaker neutrals made its Government disposed to champion those rights. Was a peaceful Swede desiring copper for innocent purposes to have it stopped? On the other hand, was the British Navy to let copper pass under its very guns to a Swede who was importing it for the German Government, and going to send it straight to Germany to be made into munitions to kill British soldiers?

The argument between these two opposite points of view was long, voluminous, and extensive. It was published, and anyone who has enough curiosity and time may read it.

The Navy acted and the Foreign Office had to find the argument to support the action; it was anxious work. British action provoked American argument; that was met by British counter-argument. British action preceded British argument; the risk was that action might follow American argument. In all this [Ambassador] Page's advice and suggestion were of the greatest value in warning us when to be careful or encouraging us when we could safely be firm.

One incident in particular remains in my memory. Page came to see me at the Foreign Office one day, and produced a long despatch from Washington contesting our claim to act as we were doing in stopping contraband going to neutral ports. "I am instructed," he said, "to read this despatch to you." He read, and I listened. He then said: "I have now read the despatch, but I do not agree with it; let us consider how it should be answered!"

3. Robert Lansing's Pro-Ally Tactics (c. 1916)

International law required a blockading power to stop and search all merchant ships before seizing or sinking them. If they were unresisting enemy merchantmen, they could lawfully be destroyed only if proper provision was made for the safety of passengers and crew. The blockading British, because of the menace of new weapons, were taking "liberties" with the old rules. The Germans, unable to sustain an orthodox blockade of the British Isles with fragile submarines vulnerable to ramming or gunfire, began to sink enemy merchantmen without warning. Berlin argued that Germany was forced to take such "liberties" because Allied merchant ships had first sunk German submarines attempting to stop them. Secretary of State Lansing, a fussily precise legalist who was warmly pro-Ally at heart, here explains his reactions. Why did the United States turn against Germany rather than Britain?

Sifted down to the bare facts the position was this: Great Britain insisted that Germany should conform her conduct of naval [submarine] warfare to the strict letter of the rules of international law, and resented even a suggestion that there should be any variation of the rules to make them reasonably applicable to new conditions. On the other hand, Great Britain was herself repeatedly departing from the rules of international law, on the plea that new conditions compelled her to do

---

[3] *War Memoirs of Robert Lansing* (1935), pp. 110–12. Copyright 1935 by the Bobbs-Merrill Company, Inc. Used by permission of the publisher.

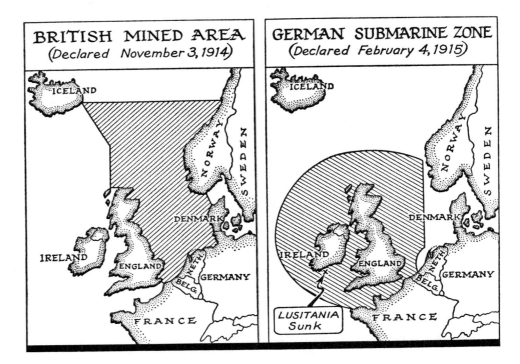

so, and even showed resentment because the United States refused to recognize her right to ignore or modify the rules whenever she thought it necessary to do so.

Briefly, the British Government wished international law enforced when they believed that it worked to the advantage of Great Britain, and wished the law modified when the change would benefit Great Britain.

There is no doubt that the good relations between the United States and Great Britain would have been seriously jeopardized by this unreasonable attitude, which seems unworthy of British statesmanship, except for the fact that the British violations of law affected American property, while the German violations affected American lives. Nothing else saved our relations with Great Britain from becoming strained to the breaking point. Even as it was, there were many Americans, both in public and in private life, who considered that we were unjust, or at least unfair, because we differentiated between the illegal acts of the belligerents on the basis of their results.

These complaints against the conduct of the British were increasing in the United States, were gaining more and more converts in Congress, and were exerting more and more pressure upon the government to adopt vigorous measures to compel Great Britain to cease her illegal practices, when the Germans, with their genius for always doing the wrong thing in the wrong way and at the wrong time, perpetrated new crimes in their submarine campaign. These events made the complaints against the British seem insignificant and ill-timed, and aroused anew the indignation of the American people toward the ruthless commanders of Germany's undersea corsairs.

The British have only the stupidity of the Germans to thank for saving them from having a very serious situation develop in their relations with this country in the spring of 1916. It was luck on their part and nothing more. They had done everything that they could to make the position of this government difficult; and the worst of it was that they did not appear to realize it, for which our Embassy at London, it must be admitted, was by no means blameless.

Sympathetic as I felt toward the Allies and convinced that we would in the end join with them against the autocratic governments of the Central Empires, I saw with apprehension the tide of resentment against Great Britain rising higher and higher in this country. It was becoming increasingly difficult to avoid bringing the controversies between our two governments to a head, and to keep from assuming positions which went beyond the field of discussion.

I did all that I could to prolong the disputes by preparing, or having prepared, long and detailed replies, and introducing technical and controversial matters in the hope that, before the extended interchange of arguments came to an end, something would happen to change the current of American public opinion, or to make the American people perceive that German absolutism was a menace to their liberties and to democratic institutions everywhere.

Fortunately, this hope and effort were not in vain. Germany did the very thing which she should not have done. The tide of sentiment in the United States turned, and it was possible to prevent a widespread demand being made that the Allied Powers be "brought to book" without further delay for their illegal treatment of our commerce.

Thought Provokers

1. What elements of conservatism can be found in Roosevelt's and Wilson's "progressive" philosophies? In what ways did their proposals foreshadow later U.S. political developments?
2. What were the good and bad features of interlocking directorates? Should private bankers have been permitted to write the Federal Reserve Act? To what extent did Wilson's tariff and banking legislation conform to the political philosophy defined in his campaign of 1912?
3. Would the prestige of the United States have been better served by a disavowal of Admiral Mayo's unauthorized demand than by the bombardment of Vera Cruz? Should the president of the United States sit in moral judgment of foreign governments?
4. Was the United States, before it became a belligerent in 1917, truly neutral with respect to the Great War that broke out in Europe in 1914?

31

The War to End War, 1917–1918

It is a fearful thing to lead this great peaceful people into war.

Woodrow Wilson, War Message, April 2, 1917

Prologue: The United States maintained a shaky neutrality for more than two years after war engulfed Europe in the summer of 1914. In practice, however, U.S. policies favored the Allies (chiefly Britain and France) against Germany and Austria-Hungary (the Central Powers). Facing ultimate starvation, the Germans finally proclaimed a desperate all-out campaign of submarine warfare in January 1917. As U.S. merchant ships were torpedoed on the high seas, Wilson reluctantly asked for a declaration of war. With a substantial minority dissenting, Congress agreed. War mobilization proceeded in the United States with unprecedented emotional fervor, deliberately cultivated by the government. Civil liberties were endangered, and "pacifists" were harassed. Wilson eventually rallied public opinion with his fourteen-point peace proposal, and U.S. troops made a significant military contribution in the final days of fighting. But Wilson proved incapable of securing congressional approval of the peace treaty he had helped to negotiate.

A. War with Germany

1. President Wilson Breaks Diplomatic Relations (1917)

After stern warnings from President Wilson, Germany generally avoided sinking unresisting passenger ships without warning. But in March 1916 a German submarine torpedoed a French liner, the Sussex, *and caused some eighty casualties, including injuries to several Americans. Wilson indignantly presented an ultimatum to Berlin threatening a severance of diplomatic relations—an almost certain prelude to war—unless Germany discontinued these inhumane tactics. The Germans reluctantly acquiesced. Finally, however, driven to the wall by the British blockade, they dramatically announced, on January 31, 1917, the opening of unrestricted submarine warfare on virtually all ships plying the war zone, including U.S. vessels. Wilson, whose hand had now been called, went sorrowfully before Congress to*

---

[1]*Congressional Record*, 64th Cong., 2d sess. (February 3, 1917), pp. 2578–2579.

deliver this speech. Was he naive or idealistic? Was he hasty in accepting the German U-boat challenge?

I think that you will agree with me that, in view of this [submarine] declaration . . . this Government has no alternative, consistent with the dignity and honor of the United States, but to take the course which . . . it announced that it would take. . . .

I have, therefore, directed the Secretary of State to announce to His Excellency the German Ambassador that all diplomatic relations between the United States and the German Empire are severed. . . .

Notwithstanding this unexpected action of the German Government, this sudden and deeply deplorable renunciation of its assurances, given this Government at one of the most critical moments of tension in the relations of the two governments, I refuse to believe that it is the intention of the German authorities to do in fact what they have warned us they will feel at liberty to do. I cannot bring myself to believe that they will indeed pay no regard to the ancient friendship between their people and our own, or to the solemn obligations which have been exchanged between them, and destroy American ships and take the lives of American citizens in the willful prosecution of the ruthless naval program they have announced their intention to adopt. Only actual overt acts on their part can make me believe it even now.

If this inveterate confidence on my part in the sobriety and prudent foresight of their purpose should unhappily prove unfounded—if American ships and American lives should in fact be sacrificed by their naval commanders in heedless contravention of the just and reasonable understandings of international law and the obvious dictates of humanity—I shall take the liberty of coming again before the Congress, to ask that authority be given me to use any means that may be necessary for the protection of our seamen and our people in the prosecution of their peaceful and legitimate errands on the high seas. I can do nothing less. I take it for granted that all neutral governments will take the same course.

We do not desire any hostile conflict with the Imperial German Government. We are the sincere friends of the German people, and earnestly desire to remain at peace with the Government which speaks for them. We shall not believe that they are hostile to us unless and until we are obliged to believe it; and we purpose nothing more than the reasonable defense of the undoubted rights of our people.

We wish to serve no selfish ends. We seek merely to stand true alike in thought and in action to the immemorial principles of our people which I sought to express in my address to the Senate only two weeks ago—seek merely to vindicate our right to liberty and justice and an unmolested life. These are the bases of peace, not war. God grant we may not be challenged to defend them by acts of willful injustice on the part of the Government of Germany!

[Wilson first undertook to arm U.S. merchantmen against the submarines ("armed neutrality"). When this tactic failed and German U-boats began to sink U.S. vessels, he again went before Congress, on April 2, 1917. Referring principally to these sinkings, he asked for a formal resolution acknowledging the fact that Germany had "thrust" war on the United States. "We have no quarrel with the German people," he declared—only with their government. With militaristic forces rampant, "there can be no assured security for the democratic governments of the world."

Hence, "The world must be made safe for democracy." War is "terrible." "But the right is more precious than peace, and we shall fight for the things which we have always carried nearest our hearts—for democracy, for the right of those who submit to authority to have a voice in their own governments, for the rights and liberties of small nations, for a universal dominion of right by such a concert of free peoples as shall bring peace and safety to all nations and make the world itself at last free."]

2. Representative Claude Kitchin Assails the War Resolution (1917)

Congress responded promptly to Wilson's request for a war resolution. But the lopsided though far-from-unanimous vote—82 to 6 in the Senate and 373 to 50 in the House—revealed a widespread opposition to hostilities, especially in the German-American areas. A flaming antiwar speech came from the lips of Claude Kitchin of North Carolina, an eloquent and beloved string-tie congressman, whose outburst produced a deluge of unflattering letters and telegrams. "Go to Germany," demanded one detractor. "They need fertilizer!" Ascertain what truth there was in Kitchin's allegation that Wilson's inconsistent and unneutral policies were taking the nation into war. Did Kitchin deserve to be called pro-German?

Great Britain every day, every hour, for two years has violated American rights on the seas. We have persistently protested. She has denied us not only entrance into the ports of the Central Powers but has closed to us by force the ports of neutrals. She has unlawfully seized our ships and our cargoes. She has rifled our mails. She has declared a war zone sufficiently large to cover all the ports of her enemy. She made the entire North Sea a military area—strewed it with hidden mines and told the neutral nations of the world to stay out or be blown up. We protested.* No American ship was sunk, no American life was destroyed, because we submitted and did not go in. We kept out of war. We sacrificed no honor. We surrendered permanently no essential rights. We knew that these acts of Great Britain, though in plain violation of international law and of our rights on the seas, were not aimed at us. They were directed at her enemy. They were inspired by military necessity. Rather than plunge this country into war, we were willing to forgo for the time our rights. I approved that course then; I approve it now.

Germany declares a war zone sufficiently large to cover the ports of her enemy. She infests it with submarines and warns the neutral world to stay out, though in plain violation of our rights and of international law. We know that these acts are aimed not directly at us but intended to injure and cripple her enemy, with which she is in a death struggle.

We refuse to yield; we refuse to forgo our rights for the time. We insist upon going in.

In my judgment, we could keep out of the war with Germany as we kept out of the war with Great Britain, by keeping our ships and our citizens out of the war

---

[2]*Congressional Record*, 65th Cong., 1st sess. (April 5, 1917), pp. 332–333.

*Kitchin was mistaken. The United States did not formally protest against the British mined zone; more than two years later, it merely reserved its rights.

zone of Germany as we did out of the war zone of Great Britain. And we would sacrifice no more honor, surrender no more rights, in the one case than in the other. Or we could resort to armed neutrality, which the President recently urged and for which I voted on March 1.

But we are told that Germany has destroyed American lives while Great Britain destroyed only property. Great Britain destroyed no American lives because this nation kept her ships and her citizens out of her war zone which she sowed with hidden mines.

But are we quite sure that the real reason for war with Germany is the destruction of lives as distinguished from property, that to avenge the killing of innocent Americans and to protect American lives war becomes a duty?

Mexican bandits raided American towns, shot to death sleeping men, women, and children in their own homes. We did not go to war* to avenge these deaths. . . .

We were willing to forgo our rights rather than plunge this country into war while half the world was in conflagration. I approved that course then; I approve it now.

Why can we not, why should we not, forgo for the time being the violation of our rights by Germany, and do as we did with Great Britain, do as we did with Mexico, and thus save the universe from being wrapped in the flames of war?

I have hoped and prayed that God would forbid our country going into war with another for doing that which perhaps under the same circumstances we ourselves would do.

B. The War for the American Mind

1. Un-Christlike Preachers (1918)

Ministers of the gospel, swallowing Allied propaganda and falling prey to the wartime hysteria, engaged in un-Christian excesses. "It is religious to hate the Kaiser," declared the Reverend James R. Day, chancellor of Syracuse University, "because the Bible teaches us to hate the Devil and all his works." Less elegantly, a prominent Baptist pastor in Cleveland cried, "To hell with the Kaiser!" Here a prominent Methodist bishop and author, Dr. William A. Quayle, pays his disrespects to Germany in a magazine article. Did he accept Wilson's view that the United States was fighting only Germany's rulers?

Let us set down sternly that we are at war with the Germans, not the Junkers [German aristocrats], not autocracy, not Prussianism, not the Kaiser. . . . The German people is what we war with. The German people is committing the unspeakable horrors which set the whole world aghast. The German people is not and has not been conducting war. It is and has been conducting murder. Hold fast to that. The Supreme Court of New York declared the sinking of the *Lusitania* an act of piracy. Piracy is not war. All decencies, honors, humanities, international agreements, and

---

*Technically, the United States did not go to war, but Wilson sent General Pershing into Mexico in 1916–1917 to pursue the bandit Villa.

[1]*Northwestern Christian Advocate,* quoted in *Literary Digest* 59 (October 19, 1918): 28.

laws have been smashed by them day and night from the first rape of Belgium to now. The new atrocity which appeared this week was spraying prisoners with burning oil. This is Germany's most recent jest. It makes them laugh so!

They have violated every treaty with the United States; they have lied from start to finish and to everybody. A treaty was a scrap of paper.* . . .

Germany has ravished the women of Belgium, Servia, Roumania, Poland, Armenia. Germany murdered the passengers of the *Lusitania* and struck a medal to celebrate that German triumph, dating it two days before the horrible occurrence. Germany had ruined cathedrals and cities in sheer wanton fury, in such fashion as has not been done in all the wars waged in Europe since the days of the building of the cathedrals. Germany has poisoned wells, crucified inhabitants and soldiers, burned people in their houses, and this by system. Germany has denatured men and boys, has wantonly defaced the living and the dying and the dead. An eye-witness tells of seeing women dead at a table with their tongues nailed to the table and left to die.

Germany has stolen things little and big: playthings from children, finery from women, pictures of incalculable worth, bank-deposits, railroads, factories. Germany has sunk hospital-ships, has bombed hospitals and Red Cross camps. Germany has disclosed neither decency nor honor from the day it started war, nor has a single voice in Germany to date been lifted up against the orgies of ruthlessness which turn the soul sick and which constitute the chief barbarity of history. Germany remains unblushing and unconscious of its indecency. Germany's egotism still struts like a Kaiser. And to climax its horrid crimes, Germany has inflicted compulsory polygamy on the virgins of its own land.

[If such tales were given currency by well-educated clergymen schooled in Christian forbearance, one can hardly blame rank-and-file Americans for believing the same accounts. Actually there were cases of rape and violence affecting civilians on both sides; the Germans were involved to a greater extent because they fought almost the entire war on enemy territory. The Lusitania *medal was struck off after the sinking; the story of the "crucified Canadian" was a complete hoax; the French cathedral at Rheims was damaged after the towers had been used for military observation. The rest of this account reflects an uncritical belief in the thoroughly unreliable stories in the Bryce report in Chapter 30.]*

2. Abusing the Pro-Germans (1918)

The several million enemy aliens in the United States were under suspicion, especially those who did not buy Liberty Bonds. One of them was Robert Paul Prager, a young German residing in Illinois. He had tried to enlist in the navy but was rejected because he had lost an eye. After he had spoken out for socialism, he was seized by a drunken mob in 1918, stripped of his clothes, wrapped in an American

---

*The phrase "scrap of paper" became one of the great propaganda weapons of the war. The German chancellor, Bethmann-Hollweg, had defended Germany's invasion of Belgium in 1914 by referring to the treaty of 1839 guaranteeing Belgian neutrality as a "scrap of paper."

[2]Frederick Palmer, *Newton D. Baker* (1931), vol. 2, pp. 162–163.

flag, and hanged. A patriotic jury acquitted the ringleaders. This was the worst outrage of its kind, but another almost occurred, as Secretary of War N. D. Baker related in the following letter. What does it reveal of the American state of mind at this time? Why was such an incident much less likely to occur in World War II?

The spirit of the country seems unusually good, but there is a growing frenzy of suspicion and hostility toward disloyalty. I am afraid we are going to have a good many instances of people roughly treated on very slight evidence of disloyalty. Already a number of men and some women have been "tarred and feathered," and a portion of the press is urging with great vehemence more strenuous efforts at detection and punishment. This usually takes the form of advocating "drum-head courts-martial"* and "being stood up against a wall and shot," which are perhaps none too bad for real traitors, but are very suggestive of summary discipline to arouse mob spirit, which unhappily does not take time to weigh evidence.

In Cleveland a few days ago a foreign-looking man got into a street car and, taking a seat, noticed pasted in the window next to him a Liberty Loan poster, which he immediately tore down, tore into small bits, and stamped under his feet. The people in the car surged around him with the demand that he be lynched, when a Secret Service man showed his badge and placed him under arrest, taking him in a car to the police station, where he was searched and found to have two Liberty Bonds in his pocket and to be a non-English Pole. When an interpreter was procured, it was discovered that the circular which he had destroyed had had on it a picture of the German Emperor, which had so infuriated the fellow that he destroyed the circular to show his vehement hatred of the common enemy. As he was unable to speak a single word of English, he would undoubtedly have been hanged but for the intervention and entirely accidental presence of the Secret Service agent.

I am afraid the grave danger in this sort of thing, apart from its injustice, is that the German Government will adopt retaliatory measures. While the government of the United States is not only not responsible for these things, but very zealously trying to prevent them, the German Government draws no fine distinctions.

3. Robert La Follette Demands His Rights (1917)

Senator Robert M. La Follette of Wisconsin—undersized, pompadoured, and fiery—was one of the most eloquent reformers of his generation. Representing a state with a heavy concentration of German-Americans, he had spoken out vehemently against war with Germany and had voted against it. He and his five dissenting colleagues were pilloried in the press as traitors for voting their consciences. On October 6, 1917, La Follette rose and quoted (from the press) a charge to a federal grand jury in Texas by a district judge. The jurist reportedly had said that these six senators ought to be convicted of treason and shot. "I wish I could pay for the ammunition," he continued. "I would like to attend the execution, and if I were in the firing squad I would not want to be the marksman who had the blank shell." La Follette then went on to present this classic defense of free speech. Why was free speech so severely threatened in this particular war?

---

*Originally a hasty court-martial in the field, around a drum as a table.
[3]*Congressional Record,* 65th Cong., 1st sess. (October 6, 1917) pp. 7878–7879.

But, sir, it is not alone Members of Congress that the war party in this country has sought to intimidate. The mandate seems to have gone forth to the sovereign people of this country that they must be silent while those things are being done by their Government which most vitally concern their well-being, their happiness, and their lives.

Today—for weeks past—honest and law-abiding citizens of this country are being terrorized and outraged in their rights by those sworn to uphold the laws and protect the rights of the people. I have in my possession numerous affidavits establishing the fact that people are being unlawfully arrested, thrown into jail, held incommunicado for days, only to be eventually discharged without ever having been taken into court, because they have committed no crime. Private residences are being invaded, loyal citizens of undoubted integrity and probity arrested, cross-examined, and the most sacred constitutional rights guaranteed to every American citizen are being violated.

It appears to be the purpose of those conducting this campaign to throw the country into a state of terror, to coerce public opinion, to stifle criticism, and suppress discussion of the great issues involved in this war.

I think all men recognize that in time of war the citizen must surrender some rights for the common good which he is entitled to enjoy in time of peace. *But, sir, the right to control their own Government, according to constitutional forms, is not one of the rights that the citizens of this country are called upon to surrender in time of war.*

Rather, in time of war, the citizen must be more alert to the preservation of his right to control his Government. He must be most watchful of the encroachment of the military upon the civil power. He must beware of those precedents in support of arbitrary action by administrative officials which, excused on the plea of necessity in wartime, become the fixed rule when the necessity has passed and normal conditions have been restored.

More than all, the citizen and his representative in Congress in time of war must maintain his right of free speech. More than in times of peace, it is necessary that the channels for free public discussion of governmental policies shall be open and unclogged.

I believe, Mr. President, that I am now touching upon the most important question in this country today—and that is the right of the citizens of this country and their representatives in Congress to discuss in an orderly way, frankly and publicly and without fear, from the platform and through the press, every important phase of this war; its causes, the manner in which it should be conducted, and the terms upon which peace should be made. . . .

I am contending for this right, because the exercise of it is necessary to the welfare, to the existence, of this Government, to the successful conduct of this war, and to a peace which shall be enduring and for the best interest of this country. . . .

Mr. President, our Government, above all others, is founded on the right of the people freely to discuss all matters pertaining to their Government, in war not less than in peace. . . . How can that popular will express itself between elections except by meetings, by speeches, by publications, by petitions, and by addresses to the representatives of the people?

Any man who seeks to set a limit upon those rights, whether in war or peace, aims a blow at the most vital part of our Government. And then as the time for election approaches, and the official is called to account for his stewardship—not a day, not a week, not a month, before the election, but a year or more before it, if the people choose—they must have the right to the freest possible discussion of every question upon which their representative has acted, of the merits of every measure he has supported or opposed, of every vote he has cast and every speech that he has made. And before this great fundamental right every other must, if necessary, give way, for in no other manner can representative government be preserved.

4. Zechariah Chafee Upholds Free Speech (1919)

The socialists, many of whom were antiwar, ran afoul of the Espionage Act of 1917. Prominent among them was Rose Pastor Stokes, a Russian-born Jew who had worked in the United States as a cigarmaker and who became a prominent social worker and propagandist for socialism. Referring to U.S. soldiers, she remarked that they were "not fighting for democracy but for the protection and safeguarding of Morgan's millions." In a letter to the Kansas City Star *she wrote: "No government which is for the profiteers can also be for the people, and I am for the people, while the Government is for the profiteers." She was sentenced to ten years in prison, although a higher court later reversed the decision. President Wilson approved of her original conviction. Professor Zechariah Chafee, Jr., of the Harvard Law School, a prominent liberal, made the following comments on these espionage cases shortly after the war ended. How did he support his assumption that the suppression of free speech can be self-defeating and dangerous in the long run?*

Never in the history of our country, since the Alien and Sedition Laws of 1798, has the meaning of free speech been the subject of such sharp controversy as today. Over two hundred prosecutions and other judicial proceedings during the war, involving speeches, newspaper articles, pamphlets, and books, have been followed since the armistice by a widespread legislative consideration of bills punishing the advocacy of extreme radicalism. . . .

The courts have treated opinions as statements of fact, and then condemned them as false because they differed from the President's speech or the resolution of Congress declaring war. They have made it impossible for an opponent of the war to write an article or even a letter in a newspaper of general circulation, because it will be read in some training camp where it might cause insubordination, or interfere with military success. He cannot address a large audience, because it is liable to include a few men in uniform; and some judges have held him punishable if it contains men between eighteen and forty-five; while Judge Van Valkenburgh, in *United States* v. *Rose Pastor Stokes,* would not even require that, because what is said to mothers, sisters, and sweethearts may lessen their enthusiasm for the war, and "our armies in the field and our navies upon the seas can operate and succeed only so far as they are supported and maintained by the folks at home." . . .

Although we have not gone so far as Great Britain in disregarding constitutional guarantees, we have gone much farther than in any other war, even in the Civil War, with the enemy at our gates. Undoubtedly some utterances had to be suppressed.

---

[4]*Harvard Law Review* 32 (June 1919): 923–933, 965, 971–973.

We have passed through a period of danger, and have reasonably supposed the danger to be greater than it actually was, but the prosecutions in Great Britain during a similar period of peril in the French Revolution have not since been regarded with pride.

Action in proportion to the emergency was justified, but we have censored and punished speech which was very far from direct and dangerous interference with the conduct of the war. The chief responsibility for this must rest, not upon Congress, which was content for a long period with the moderate language of the Espionage Act of 1917, but upon the officials of the Department of Justice and the Post Office, who turned that statute into a drag-net for pacifists, and upon the judges who upheld and approved this distortion of law.

It may be questioned, too, how much has actually been gained. Men have been imprisoned, but their words have not ceased to spread. The poetry in *The Masses* was excluded from the mails only to be given a far wider circulation in two issues of the *Federal Reporter*. The mere publication of Mrs. Stokes' statement in the Kansas City *Star*, "I am for the people and the Government is for the profiteers," was considered so dangerous to the morale of the training camps that she was sentenced to ten years in prison, and yet it was repeated by every important newspaper in the country during the trial. There is an unconscious irony in all suppression. . . .

Those who gave their lives for freedom would be the last to thank us for throwing aside so lightly the great traditions of our race. Not satisfied to have justice and almost all the people with our cause, we insisted on an artificial unanimity of opinion behind the war. Keen intellectual grasp of the President's aims by the nation at large was very difficult when the opponents of his idealism ranged unchecked, while the men who urged greater idealism went to prison. In our efforts to silence those who advocated peace without victory, we prevented at the very start that vigorous threshing out of fundamentals which might to-day have saved us from a victory without peace.

C. The Propaganda Front

1. George Creel Spreads Fear Propaganda (c. 1918)

George Creel—a young, dynamic, but tactless journalist—headed the nation's great propaganda engine, the Committee on Public Information. He not only prepared documentary movies and unleashed tens of thousands of orators but also issued some 75 million copies of pamphlets. He also employed a galaxy of distinguished historians and other scholars to prepare these propaganda booklets, many of them in paper covers of red, white, and blue. One title, How the War Came to America, *enjoyed a fantastic distribution of 7 million copies. Professor J. S. P. Tatlock, a Chaucer specialist at Stanford University, wrote the following highly imaginative account, in-*

[1]J. S. P. Tatlock, *Why America Fights Germany,* War Information Series no. 15, Cantonment Edition (U.S. Committee on Public Information, March 1918), pp. 9–10.

spired in part by Allied propaganda like the Bryce report (see Chapter 30). Distributed as a part of a pamphlet entitled Why America Fights Germany, *it boasted a circulation of about 750,000 copies. To what emotions does it appeal most strongly?*

Now let us picture what a sudden invasion of the United States by these Germans would mean; sudden, because their settled way is always to attack suddenly.

First, they set themselves to capture New York City. While their fleet blockades the harbor and shells the city and the forts from far at sea, their troops land somewhere near and advance toward the city in order to cut its rail communications, starve it into surrender, and then plunder it.

One body of from 50,000 to 100,000 men lands, let us suppose, at Barnegat Bay, New Jersey, and advances without meeting resistance, for the brave but small American army is scattered elsewhere. They pass through Lakewood, a station on the Central Railroad of New Jersey. They first demand wine for the officers and beer for the men. Angered to find an American town does not contain large quantities of either, they pillage and burn the post office and most of the hotels and stores. Then they demand $1,000,000 from the residents. One feeble old woman tries to conceal $20 which she has been hoarding in her desk drawer; she is taken out and hanged (to save a cartridge). Some of the teachers in two district schools meet a fate which makes them envy her. The Catholic priest and Methodist minister are thrown into a pig-sty, while the German soldiers look on and laugh. Some of the officers quarter themselves in a handsome house on the edge of the town, insult the ladies of the family, and destroy and defile the contents of the house.

By this time some of the soldiers have managed to get drunk; one of them discharges his gun accidentally, the cry goes up that the residents are firing on the troops, and then hell breaks loose. Robbery, murder, and outrage run riot. Fifty leading citizens are lined up against the First National Bank Building, and shot. Most of the town and the beautiful pinewoods are burned, and then the troops move on to treat New Brunswick in the same way—if they get there.

This is not just a snappy story. It is not fancy. The general plan of campaign against America has been announced repeatedly by German military men. *And every horrible detail is just what the German troops have done in Belgium and France.*

2. Woodrow Wilson Versus Theodore Roosevelt on the Fourteen Points (1918)

President Wilson's war-aims speeches were lofty and eloquent but rather vague and long-winded. An American journalist in Russia suggested that he compress his views into crisp, placard-like paragraphs. This he did in his famed Fourteen Points address to Congress on January 8, 1918. By promising independence (self-determination) to minority groups under enemy rule and by raising up hopes everywhere for a better tomorrow, the Fourteen Points undermined the foe's will to resist while simultane-

---

[2]*Congressional Record,* 65th Cong., 2d sess. (January 8, 1918), p. 691 and *Kansas City Star,* October 30, 1918. The full text may also be found in Ralph Stout, ed., *Roosevelt in the Kansas City "Star"* (1921), pp. 241–242, 243–246.

ously inspiring the Allies. George Creel's propaganda machine broadcast the Points in leaflet form throughout the world, while Allied rockets and shells showered them over enemy lines. German desertions multiplied. Form some judgment as to whether Wilson's aims were completely clear and consistent. Determine which ones would be most likely to weaken the resistance of Germany and Austria-Hungary. The frustrated Colonel Roosevelt fulminated against the Fourteen Points in the Kansas City Star. *Given that before 1917 he had been anti-Wilson, pro-tariff, anti-German, pro-Ally, and internationalist-minded, what are the most important inconsistencies in his position?*

Wilson's Points

I. Open covenants of peace, openly arrived at, after which there shall be no private international understandings of any kind, but diplomacy shall proceed always frankly and in the public view.

[Wilson finally meant secret *negotiations but* public *commitments. He had earlier laid himself open to criticism by landing the marines in Haiti and Santo Domingo in 1915 and 1916 to restore order.]*

II. Absolute freedom of navigation upon the seas, outside territorial waters, alike in peace and in war, except as the seas may be closed in whole or in part by international action [of the League of Nations] for the enforcement of international covenants.

[Big-navy Britain, fearing to blunt its blockade weapon, refused to accept this point.]

III. The removal, so far as possible, of all economic barriers, and the establishment of an equality of trade conditions among all the nations consenting to the peace, and associating themselves [in the League of Nations] for its maintenance.

[This meant, although not too clearly put, that the United States could still maintain tariffs but could not discriminate among fellow members of the League of Nations. Any commercial

Roosevelt's Complaints

The President has recently waged war on Haiti and San Domingo, and rendered democracy within these two small former republics not merely unsafe, but non-existent. He has kept all that he has done in the matter absolutely secret. If he means what he says, he will at once announce what open covenant of peace he has openly arrived at with these two little republics, which he has deprived of their right of self-determination.

It makes no distinction between freeing the seas from murder, like that continually practiced by Germany, and freeing them from blockade of contraband merchandise, which is the practice of a right universally enjoyed by belligerents, and at this moment practiced by the United States. Either this proposal is meaningless, or it is a mischievous concession to Germany.

The third point promises free trade among all the nations, unless the words are designedly used to conceal President Wilson's true meaning. This would deny to our country the right to make a tariff to protect its citizens, and especially its workingmen, against Germany or China or any other country. Apparently this is desired on the ground that the incidental domestic disaster to this country will prevent other countries from feeling hostile to

Wilson's Points

favors granted to one fellow member would automatically be extended to all.]

IV. Adequate guarantees given and taken that national armaments will be reduced to the lowest point consistent with domestic safety.

[This meant a force no larger than necessary to control domestic disorders and prevent foreign invasion.]

V. A free, open-minded, and absolutely impartial adjustment of all [wartime] colonial claims, based upon a strict observance of the principle that, in determining all such questions of sovereignty, the interests of the populations concerned must have equal weight with the equitable claims of the Government whose title is to be determined.

[German colonies captured by Britain and Japan might be returned, if this course seemed "equitable."]

VI. The evacuation of all Russian territory [inhabited by Russians], and such a settlement of all questions affecting Russia as will secure the best and freest cooperation of the other nations of the world in obtaining for her an unhampered and unembarrassed opportunity for the independent determination of her own political development and national policy, and assure her of a sincere welcome into the society of free nations, under institutions of her own choosing; and, more than a welcome, assistance also of every kind. . . .

[Wilson had in mind having the German invader evacuate Russian territory, and helping the Russian Poles and other non-Russian nationalities to

Roosevelt's Complaints

us. The supposition is foolish. England practiced free trade and yet Germany hated England particularly. . . .

Either this is language deliberately used to deceive, or else it means that we are to scrap our army and navy, and prevent riot by means of a national constabulary, like the state constabulary of New York or Pennsylvania.

Unless the language is deliberately used to deceive, this means that we are to restore to our brutal enemy the colonies taken by our allies while they were defending us from this enemy. The proposition is probably meaningless. If it is not, it is monstrous.

Point VI deals with Russia. It probably means nothing, but if it means anything, it provides that America shall share on equal terms with other nations, including Germany, Austria, and Turkey [the Central Powers], in giving Russia assistance. The whole proposition would not be particularly out of place in a college sophomore's exercise in rhetoric.

Wilson's Points

achieve self-determination. He would also lend a helping hand to the new Bolshevik government.]

VII. Belgium, the whole world will agree, must be evacuated and restored, without any attempt to limit the sovereignty which she enjoys in common with all other free nations. No other single act will serve as this will serve to restore confidence among the nations in the laws which they have themselves set and determined for the government of their relations with one another. Without this healing act the whole structure and validity of international law is forever impaired.

[Germany, disregarding a neutrality treaty of 1839, had struck through Belgium at France in 1914. The war-minded Roosevelt at first approved this act as one of military necessity, but he soon changed his views. The word "restored" in Point VII implied that the Germans would be assessed an indemnity for the damage they had done.]

VIII. All French territory should be freed and the invaded portions restored, and the wrong done to France by Prussia in 1871 in the matter of Alsace-Lorraine, which has unsettled the peace of the world for nearly fifty years, should be righted, in order that peace may once more be made secure in the interest of all.

[Wilson intended that Alsace-Lorraine, seized by Prussia (Germany) in 1871, should be returned to France.]

IX. A readjustment of the frontiers of Italy should be effected along clearly recognizable lines of nationality.

[Wilson would extend "self-determination" to nearby Italian peoples not under the Italian flag.]

Roosevelt's Complaints

Point VII deals with Belgium and is entirely proper and commonplace.

Point VIII deals with Alsace-Lorraine and is couched in language which betrays Mr. Wilson's besetting sin—his inability to speak in a straightforward manner. He may mean that Alsace and Lorraine must be restored to France, in which case he is right. He may mean that a plebiscite must be held, in which case he is playing Germany's evil game.

Point IX deals with Italy, and is right.

Wilson's Points	Roosevelt's Complaints

Wilson's Points

X. The peoples of Austria-Hungary, whose place among the nations we wish to see safeguarded and assured, should be accorded the freest opportunity of autonomous development.

[This point raised difficulties because of the quarreling minorities of the "succession states" that rose from the ruins of Austria-Hungary.]

XI. Rumania, Serbia, and Montenegro should be evacuated; occupied territories restored; Serbia accorded free and secure access to the sea; and the relations of the several Balkan states to one another determined by friendly counsel along historically established lines of allegiance and nationality; and international guarantees of the political and economic independence and territorial integrity of the several Balkan states should be entered into.

[This point was also invalidated by the "succession states," including Yugoslavia, which embraced Serbia.]

XII. The Turkish portions of the present Ottoman Empire should be assured a secure sovereignty, but the other nationalities which are now under Turkish rule should be assured an undoubted security of life and an absolutely unmolested opportunity of autonomous development, and the Dardanelles should be permanently opened as a free passage to the ships and commerce of all nations under international guarantees.

[Wilson's ideal was self-determination for the Greeks, Armenians, Arabs, and other non-Turks in the Turkish empire, much of whose land became mandates of France and Britain under the League of Nations.]

Roosevelt's Complaints

Point X deals with the Austro-Hungarian Empire, and is so foolish that even President Wilson has abandoned it.

[Wilson later stressed independence rather than local autonomy.]

Point XI proposes that we, together with other nations, including apparently Germany, Austria, and Hungary, shall guarantee justice in the Balkan Peninsula. As this would also guarantee our being from time to time engaged in war over matters in which we had no interest whatever, it is worth while inquiring whether President Wilson proposes that we wage these wars with the national constabulary to which he desired to reduce our armed forces.

Point XII proposes to perpetuate the infamy of Turkish rule in Europe, and as a sop to the conscience of humanity proposes to give the subject races autonomy, a slippery word which in a case like this is useful only for rhetorical purposes.

Wilson's Points

XIII. An independent Polish state should be erected which should include the territories inhabited by indisputably Polish populations, which should be assured a free and secure access to the sea, and whose political and economic independence and territorial integrity should be guaranteed by international covenant.

[Poland was to be restored from the territory of Germany, Russia, and Austria-Hungary, despite injustices to German and other minorities.]

XIV. A general association [League] of nations must be formed under specific covenants for the purpose of affording mutual guarantees of political independence and territorial integrity to great and small states alike.

In regard to these essential rectifications of wrong and assertions of right, we feel ourselves to be intimate partners of all the governments and peoples associated together against the Imperialists. We cannot be separated in interest or divided in purpose. We stand together until the end.

Roosevelt's Complaints

Point XIII proposes an independent Poland, which is right; and then proposes that we guarantee its integrity in the event of future war, which is preposterous unless we intend to become a military nation more fit for overseas warfare than Germany is at present.

In its essence Mr. Wilson's proposition for a League of Nations seems to be akin to the Holy Alliance of the nations of Europe a century ago, which worked such mischief that the Monroe Doctrine was called into being especially to combat it. If it is designed to do away with nationalism, it will work nothing but mischief. If it is devised in sane fashion as an addition to nationalism and as an addition to preparing our own strength for our own defense, it may do a small amount of good. But it will certainly accomplish nothing if more than a moderate amount is attempted, and probably the best first step would be to make the existing league of the Allies a going concern.

D. The Face of War

1. General John Pershing Defines American Fighting Tactics (1917–1918)

Generals, it has often been said, have a habit of fighting the previous war—a maxim to which jut-jawed General John J. Pershing, commander of the American Expeditionary Force, was no exception. Pershing had studied Civil War tactics at West Point in the late nineteenth century and saw no reason why they should not be ap-

---

[1]John J. Pershing, *My Experiences in the World War* (New York: Frederick A. Stokes Company, 1931), vol. 1, pp. 150–154; vol. 2, p. 358.

plied in France in the twentieth century. He expressed criticism bordering on contempt for the French and British fascination with fixed, entrenched warfare. Pershing insisted, therefore, that U.S. troops be trained in battle techniques different from those offered to European troops. This approach contributed to appallingly high U.S. casualty rates when the American soldiers, or "doughboys," eventually entered combat. How does Pershing here defend his tactical preferences? What factors might have motivated him to adopt them?

The most important question that confronted us in the preparation of our forces of citizen soldiery for efficient service was training. Except for the Spanish-American War, nearly twenty years before, actual combat experience of the Regular Army had been limited to the independent action of minor commands in the Philippines and to two expeditions into Mexico, each with forces smaller than a modern American division. The World War involved the handling of masses where even a division was relatively a small unit. It was one thing to call one or two million men to the colors, and quite another thing to transform them into an organized, instructed army capable of meeting and holding its own in the battle against the best trained force in Europe with three years of actual war experience to its credit.

Few people can realize what a stupendous undertaking it was to teach these vast numbers their various duties when such a large percentage of them were ignorant of practically everything pertaining to the business of the soldier in war. First of all, most of the officer personnel available had little or no military experience, and had to be trained in the manifold duties of commanders. They had to learn the interior economy of their units—messing, housing, clothing, and, in general, caring for their men—as well as methods of instruction and the art of leading them in battle. This great task was, of course, under the direction of the War Department. . . .

The British methods of teaching trench warfare appealed to me very strongly. They taught their men to be aggressive and undertook to perfect them in hand-to-hand fighting with bayonet, grenade and dagger. A certain amount of this kind of training was necessary to prepare the troops for trench warfare. Moreover it served to stimulate their morale by giving them confidence in their own personal prowess. Through the kindness of Sir Douglas Haig [commander in chief of the British army in France], we were fortunate early in our experience to have assigned to us Lieutenant General R. H. K. Butler and other officers of the British Army in addition to French officers to assist in this individual training. Later, several French and British officers also came to lecture at a number of our schools.

We found difficulty, however, in using these Allied instructors, in that the French and, to a large extent, the British, had practically settled down to the conviction that developments since 1914 had changed the principles of warfare. Both held that new conditions imposed by trench fighting had rendered previous conceptions of training more or less obsolete and that preparation for open warfare was no longer necessary. . . .

If the French doctrine had prevailed our instruction would have been limited to a brief period of training for trench fighting. A new army brought up entirely on such principles would have been seriously handicapped without the protection of the trenches. It would probably have lacked the aggressiveness to break through the enemy's lines and the knowledge of how to carry on thereafter. It was my opinion that the victory could not be won by the costly process of attrition, but it must be won by driving the enemy out into the open and engaging him in a war of movement. Instruction in this kind of warfare was based upon individual and group initiative, resourcefulness and tactical judgment, which were also of great advantage in trench warfare. Therefore, we took decided issue with the Allies and, without neglecting thorough preparation for trench fighting, undertook to train mainly for open combat, with the object from the start of vigorously forcing the offensive. . . .

For the purpose of impressing our own doctrine upon officers, a training program was issued which laid great stress on open warfare methods and offensive action. The following is a pertinent extract from my instructions on this point:

> The above methods to be employed must remain and become distinctly our own. All instruction must contemplate the assumption of a vigorous offensive. This purpose will be emphasized in every phase of training until it becomes a settled habit of thought.

Intimately connected with the question of training for open warfare was the matter of rifle practice. The earliest of my cablegrams on this subject was in August, in which it was urged that thorough instruction in rifle practice should be carried on at home because of the difficulty of giving it in France:

> Study here shows value and desirability of retaining our existing small arms target practice course. In view of great difficulty in securing ranges in France due to density of the population and cultivation. Recommend as far as practicable the complete course be given in the United States before troops embark. Special emphasis should be placed on rapid fire.

The armies on the Western Front in the recent battles that I had witnessed had all but given up the use of the rifle. Machine guns, grenades, Stokes mortars, and one-pounders had become the main reliance of the average Allied soldier. These were all valuable weapons for specific purposes but they could not replace the combination of an efficient soldier and his rifle. Numerous instances were reported in the Allied armies of men chasing an individual enemy throwing grenades at him instead of using the rifle. Such was the effect of association that continuous effort was necessary to counteract this tendency among our own officers and men and inspire them with confidence in the efficacy of rifle fire. . . .

My view was that the rifle and bayonet still remained the essential weapons of the infantry, and my cables, stressing the fact that the basic principles of warfare had not changed, were sent in an endeavor to influence the courses of training at home. Unfortunately, however, no fixed policy of instruction in the various arms, under a single authority, was ever carried out there. Unresponsive to my advice, the inclination was to accept the views of French specialists and to limit training to the narrow field of trench warfare. Therefore, in large measure, the fundamentals so thoroughly taught at West Point for a century were more or less neglected. The responsibility for the failure at home to take positive action on my recommendations in such matters must fall upon the War Department General Staff.

There were other causes . . . that led to confusion and irregularity in training to such an extent that we were often compelled during the last stages of the war to send men into battle with little knowledge of warfare and sometimes with no rifle practice at all. . . .

[On September 5, 1918, Pershing issued the following instructions to his army, then preparing for its first major battle at St. Mihiel.]

Combat Instructions (Extract)

From a tactical point of view, the method of combat in trench warfare presents a marked contrast to that employed in open warfare, and the attempt by assaulting infantry to use trench warfare methods in an open warfare combat will be successful only at great cost. Trench warfare is marked by uniform formations, the regulation of space and time by higher commands down to the smallest details . . . fixed distances and intervals between units and individuals . . . little initiative. . . . Open warfare is marked by . . . irregularity of formations, comparatively little regulation of space and time by higher commanders, the greatest possible use of the infantry's own fire power to enable it to get forward, variable distances and intervals between units and individuals . . . brief orders and the greatest possible use of individual initiative by all troops engaged in the action. . . . The infantry commander must oppose machine guns by fire from his rifles, his automatics and his rifle grenades and must close with their crews under cover of this fire and of ground beyond their flanks. . . . The success of every unit from the platoon to the division must be exploited to the fullest extent. Where strong resistance is encountered, reënforcements must not be thrown in to make a frontal attack at this point, but must be pushed through gaps created by successful units, to attack these strong points in the flank or rear.

2. A "Doughboy" Describes the Fighting Front (1918)

Of the 2 million young American men who served in the American Expeditionary Force, about half saw combat. Many of these troops had been raised on heroic stories about grandfathers and uncles who had fought in the Civil War, and they expected the war in France to provide the same kind of opportunities for glory that their forebears had found at Antietam and Shiloh, Bull Run and Fredericksburg. For the most part, they were bitterly disappointed when they discovered that modern warfare was a decidedly unheroic, dirty, impersonal, and bloody business. The following passages, taken from the battlefield diary of a thirty-one-year-old draftee from upstate New York who was assigned to an engineering company, vividly convey one soldier's reactions to his baptism of fire. What aspects of combat did he find most remarkable? How does his description of warfare fit with General Pershing's expectations about the role of the individual rifleman and the tactics of mobility and "open warfare"?

Thursday, September 12, 1918. Hiked through dark woods. No lights allowed, guided by holding on the pack of the man ahead. Stumbled through underbrush for about half mile into an open field where we waited in soaking rain until about 10:00 P.M. We then started on our hike to the St. Mihiel [France] front, arriving on the crest of a hill at 1:00 A.M. I saw a sight which I shall never forget. It was the zero hour and in one instant the entire front as far as the eye could reach in either direction was a sheet of flame, while the heavy artillery made the earth quake. The barrage was so intense that for a time we could not make out whether the Americans or Germans

---

[2]From the diary of Eugene Kennedy. Courtesy of Eugene Kennedy Collection, Hoover Institution on War, Revolution, and Peace, Stanford University.

were putting it over. After timing the interval between flash and report we knew that the heaviest artillery was less than a mile away and consequently it was ours. We waded through pools and mud across open lots into a woods on a hill and had to pitch tents in mud. Blankets all wet and we are soaked to the skin. Have carried full pack from 10:00 P.M. to 2:00 A.M., without a rest. . . . Despite the cannonading I slept until 8:00 A.M. and awoke to find every discharge of 14-inch artillery shaking our tent like a leaf. Remarkable how we could sleep. No breakfast. . . . The doughboys had gone over the top at 5:00 A.M. and the French were shelling the back areas toward Metz. . . . Firing is incessant, so is rain. See an air battle just before turning in.

Friday, September 13, 1918. Called at 3:00 A.M. Struck tents and started to hike at 5:00 A.M. with full packs and a pick. Put on gas mask at alert position and hiked about five miles to St. Jean, where we unslung full packs and went on about four miles further with short packs and picks. Passed several batteries and saw many dead horses who gave out at start of push. Our doughboys are still shoving and "Jerry" [the Germans] is dropping so many shells on road into no man's land that we stayed back in field and made no effort to repair shell-torn road. Plenty of German prisoners being brought back. . . . Guns booming all the time.

Saturday, September 14, 1918. Hiked up to same road again with rifle, belt, helmet, gas-mask, and pick. . . . First time under shell fire. Major Judge's horse killed. Gibbs has a finger knocked off each hand [by a sniper's bullet] while burying some of our men killed in opening drive. Clothing, bandages, equipment of all sorts, dead horses and every kind of debris strewn all over. . . .

Tuesday, September 17, 1918. Rolled packs and hiked with them up to road. Worked near town that is reduced to heap of stone. Trenches are 20 feet deep and in some places 15 feet across. The wire entanglement is beyond description. Several traps left by Germans. Man in our division had his arm blown off picking up a crucifix.

[Along with thousands of other doughboys, Kennedy was soon shifted from the St. Mihiel engagement to the major American battleground a few miles to the north, in the Argonne forest between the Meuse and Aire rivers. Here he describes his role in this, the largest U.S. action of the war.]

Thursday, October 17, 1918. Struck tents at 8:00 A.M. and moved about four miles to Chatel. Pitched tents on a side hill so steep that we had to cut steps to ascend. Worked like hell to shovel out a spot to pitch tent on. Just across the valley in front of us about two hundred yards distant, there had occurred an explosion due to a mine planted by the "Bosche" [Germans] and set with a time fuse. It had blown two men (French), two horses, and the wagon into fragments. . . . Arriving on the scene we found Quinn ransacking the wagon. It was full of grub. We each loaded a burlap bag with cans of condensed milk, peas, lobster, salmon, and bread. I started back . . . when suddenly another mine exploded, the biggest I ever saw. Rocks and dirt flew sky high. Quinn was hit in the knee and had to go to hospital. . . . At 6:00 P.M. each of our four platoons left camp in units to go up front and throw three foot and one artillery bridge across the Aire River. On way to river we were heavily shelled and gassed. . . . We put a bridge across 75-foot span. . . . Third platoon men had to get into water and swim or stand in water to their necks. The toughest job we had so far.

Friday, October 18, 1918. Bright but cool. Men of third platoon who swam river are drying their clothes. . . . Waiting for night to work under cover of darkness.

Started up front at 6:00 P.M.. . . . Worked one half hour when "Jerry" shelled us so strong that we had to leave job. We could hear snipers' bullets sing past us and had to make our way back carefully along railroad track bank dodging shells every few steps. Gas so thick that masks had to be kept on, adding to the burden of carrying a rifle, pick, shovel, and hand saw. Had to run from one dug-out to another until it let up somewhat, when we made a break for road and hiked to camp about 3 kilometers, gas masks on most of the way, shells bursting both sides of road.

Monday, October 21, 1918. Fragment from shell struck mess-kit on my back. . . . Equipment, both American and German, thrown everywhere, especially Hun helmets and belts of machine gunners. . . . Went scouting . . . for narrow-gauge rails to replace the ones "Jerry" spoiled before evacuating. Negro engineers working on railroad same as at St. Mihiel, that's all they are good for. . . .

Friday, November 1, 1918. Started out at 4:00 A.M. The drive is on. Fritz is coming back at us. Machine guns cracking, flares and Verry lights, artillery from both sides. A real war and we are walking right into the zone, ducking shells all the way. The artillery is nerve racking and we don't know from which angle "Jerry" will fire next. Halted behind shelter of railroad track just outside of Grand Pre after being forced back off main road by shell fire. Trees splintered like toothpicks. Machine gunners on top of railroad bank. . . . "Jerry" drove Ewell and me into a two-by-four shell hole, snipers' bullets close.

Sunday, November 3, 1918. Many dead Germans along the road. One heap on a manure pile. . . . Devastation everywhere. Our barrage has rooted up the entire territory like a ploughed field. Dead horses galore, many of them have a hind quarter cut off—the Huns need food. Dead men here and there. The sight I enjoy better than a dead German is to see heaps of them. Rain again. Couldn't keep rain out of our faces and it was pouring hard. Got up at midnight and drove stakes to secure shelter-half over us, pulled our wet blankets out of mud and made the bed all over again. Slept like a log with all my equipment in the open. One hundred forty-two planes sighted in evening.

Sunday, November 10, 1918. First day off in over two months. . . . Took a bath and we were issued new underwear but the cooties [lice] got there first. . . . The papers show a picture of the Kaiser entitled "William the Lost," and stating that he had abdicated. Had a good dinner. Rumor at night that armistice was signed. Some fellows discharged their arms in the courtyard, but most of us were too well pleased with dry bunk to get up.

E. The Struggle over the Peace Treaty

I. The Text of Article X (1919)

Wilson regarded the League of Nations as the backbone of the Treaty of Versailles, and Article X of the League Covenant, which he had partly authored, as the heart of the League. He envisaged the members of the League constituting a kind of police

---

[1]*Senate Executive Documents,* 67th Cong., 4th sess. (1923), vol. 8, no. 348, p. 3339.

force to prevent aggression. What weaknesses are contained in the wording of this article?

The Members of the League undertake to respect and preserve, as against external aggression, the territorial integrity and existing political independence of all Members of the League. In case of any such aggression, or in case of any threat or danger of such aggression, the Council shall advise upon the means by which the obligation shall be fulfilled.

[All member nations were represented in the Assembly of the League of Nations; only the great powers (originally Britain, France, Italy, and Japan) were represented in the Council. The same general scheme was adopted by the United Nations in 1945.]

2. Wilson Testifies for Article X (1919)

The already ominous mood of the Senate had grown uglier when Wilson conspicuously snubbed that body in framing the peace. The Republican majority was led by the aristocratic Senator Henry Cabot Lodge of Massachusetts, who was also chairman of the potent Committee on Foreign Relations. He was determined to Republicanize and Americanize the pact by adding reservations that would adequately safeguard U.S. interests. To avert such a watering down, Wilson met with the entire Foreign Relations Committee at the White House on August 19, 1919, and underwent about three and a half hours of grilling. Much of the discussion revolved about Article X. How persuasive is Wilson's defense?

[The President.] Article X is in no respect of doubtful meaning, when read in the light of the Covenant as a whole. The Council of the League can only "advise upon" the means by which the obligations of that great article are to be given effect to. Unless the United States is a party to the policy or action in question, her own affirmative vote in the Council is necessary before any advice can be given, for a unanimous vote of the Council is required. If she is a party, the trouble is hers anyhow. And the unanimous vote of the Council is only advice in any case. Each Government is free to reject it if it pleases.

Nothing could have been made more clear to the [Paris] conference than the right of our Congress under our Constitution to exercise its independent judgment in all matters of peace and war. No attempt was made to question or limit that right.

The United States will, indeed, undertake under Article X to "respect and preserve as against external aggression the territorial integrity and existing political independence of all members of the League," and that engagement constitutes a very grave and solemn moral obligation. But it is a moral, not a legal, obligation, and leaves our Congress absolutely free to put its own interpretation upon it in all cases that call for action. It is binding in conscience only, not in law.

Article X seems to me to constitute the very backbone of the whole Covenant. Without it the League would be hardly more than an influential debating society. . . .

---

[2]*Senate Documents,* no. 76, 66th Cong., 1st sess. (August 19, 1919), vol. 13, pp. 6, 19.

Senator [Warren G.] Harding. Right there, Mr. President, if there is nothing more than a moral obligation on the part of any member of the League, what avail Articles X and XI?

The President. Why, Senator, it is surprising that the question should be asked. If we undertake an obligation we are bound in the most solemn way to carry it out. . . . There is a national good conscience in such a matter. . . .

When I speak of a legal obligation, I mean one that specifically binds you to do a particular thing under certain sanctions. That is a legal obligation. Now a moral obligation is of course superior to a legal obligation, and, if I may say so, has a greater binding force. . . .

[Never too respectful of the "bungalow-minded" members of the Senate, Wilson remarked several days later that Senator Harding, destined to be his successor, "had a disturbingly dull mind, and that it seemed impossible to get any explanation to lodge in it."]

3. The Lodge-Hitchcock Reservations (1919)

Wilson finally agreed to accept mildly interpretative Senate reservations that the other powers would not have to approve. He balked, however, at the more restrictive terms of the fourteen Lodge reservations. These were made a part of the resolution of ratification and would require the assent of three of the four other major powers (Britain, France, Italy, Japan). To Wilson, such a course was unmanly and humiliating; besides, he detested Senator Lodge. He insisted that the Republican Lodge reservations, notably the one on Article X, devitalized the entire treaty. In the following, on the left, appears the Lodge reservation to Article X, which Wilson resentfully rejected. On the right appears the Democratic interpretative reservation, which Senator Hitchcock (the Senate minority leader) had drafted after consulting Wilson.* This version Wilson was willing to accept. What are the main differences between the two versions? Are those differences substantial enough to justify Wilson's refusal to accept the Lodge reservation?

<table>
<tr><td>

Lodge Reservation to Article X (November 1919)

The United States assumes no obligation to preserve the territorial integrity or political independence of any other country or to interfere in controversies between nations—whether members of the League or not—under the provisions of Article X, or to employ the military or naval forces of the United States under any article of the

</td><td>

Hitchcock Reservation to Article X (November 1919)

That the advice mentioned in Article X of the covenant of the League which the Council may give to the member nations as to the employment of their naval and military forces is merely advice which each member nation is free to accept or reject according to the conscience and judgment of its then existing Government, and in

</td></tr>
</table>

[3]Reprinted with the permission of Simon & Schuster, Inc. from *Woodrow Wilson and the Great Betrayal* by Thomas A. Bailey. Copyright © 1945 by Thomas A. Bailey, copyright renewed © 1973.

*The Hitchcock reservation follows almost verbatim a reservation that Wilson had himself secretly drafted in September 1919 and on which Hitchcock had based his. Ibid., p. 393.

Lodge Reservation to Article X (November 1919)	Hitchcock Reservation to Article X (November 1919)
treaty for any purpose, unless in any particular case the Congress, which, under the Constitution, has the sole power to declare war or authorize the employment of the military or naval forces of the United States, shall by act or joint resolution so provide.	the United States this advice can only be accepted by action of the Congress at the time in being, Congress alone under the Constitution of the United States having the power to declare war.

4. The Aborted Lodge Compromise (1919)

Colonel Edward House, Wilson's onetime intimate adviser, had fallen ill and was confined to his bed in New York. He turned to Stephen Bonsal, a distinguished newspaper correspondent who had been attached to the U.S. peace mission in Paris. Bonsal was instructed to go to Washington, confer with Lodge, and ascertain the senator's minimum terms for compromise. The meeting took place late in October 1919, and on November 16 Bonsal recorded the following account of the conference. In what respects does this account qualify the traditional concept of Lodge as a vindictive and uncompromising former Harvard student who was locking horns with Woodrow Wilson, the former professor from Princeton?

The Senator and I went over the [League] Covenant, Article by Article. Here are some of the details. In our final session there was an official copy of the Treaty on the library table, also one of the so-called Lodge Reservations before the Senate but, so far as I can remember, we did not once refer to them. It was on the printed copy of the Covenant that I brought with me that the Senator made the changes and inserted the interlineations which, if accepted, he thought would smooth the way to ratification.

The changes ran to about forty words, the "inserts" to about fifty. It seemed to me they were more concerned with verbiage than with the object and the intent of the instrument. In my judgment, they were complementary to, rather than limiting, any substantial purpose of the Covenant. In this they differed sharply from the Reservations Lodge had introduced into the Senate and which are now blocking the path to ratification.

The Senator, frankly and repeatedly, stated that his interest, or, as he put it several times, his anxiety, centered around Article X, which the President often refers to as the "heart of the Covenant," and his suggestion, indeed his demand, was to the effect that none of the obligations or commitments incurred under this provision should be undertaken without the approval of the Senate and the concurrence of the House.

When Lodge had finished what he had to say, I expressed my pleasure at the helpful collaboration of the chairman of the Committee, and with reason, I think. What he asked for now was decidedly milder than the reservations before the Senate, but there was, I ventured to point out, one drawback to any change, even if merely of verbiage, because, in this case, the document would have to be referred

---

[4]Excerpt from *Unfinished Business* by Stephen Bonsal (New York: Doubleday and Company, 1944), pp. 274–275.

back to all the co-signers of the Covenant, and this might open the gates to other changes and would certainly result in delay.

I also ventured to say that the clarification of Article X which he urged was implicit in the Article itself. I argued "it goes without saying," for a variety of obvious reasons, that the sanction of the Senate and the approval of the House, which alone can furnish the money, would have to be forthcoming before aggressive or even defensive action against an aggressor nation could be undertaken.

"If it goes without saying," commented the Senator somewhat tartly, "there is no harm in saying it—and much advantage."

Good-naturedly the Senator now chaffed me about the expression I had used, "it goes without saying," which he thought was a "barbarism." He then went on to express his opinion of the language in which the world charter was drawn, and it was a poor one.

"As an English production it does not rank high." Then, more in chaff than in earnest, he said: "It might get by at Princeton but certainly not at Harvard."

[With high hopes, Colonel House dispatched the new Lodge concessions to the White House. But on October 2, Wilson had suffered a devastating stroke. He was now virtually incapacitated, while his wife, Edith Bolling Galt Wilson, struggled to protect him from further stress. The president therefore offered no reply, no acknowledgment. Perhaps Mrs. Wilson thought the memorandum unimportant—or too important. Wilson might be upset and suffer a relapse. Or Wilson may have decided merely to treat Lodge's proffered hand with the contempt that he felt for the senator. Rebuffed and perhaps humiliated, Lodge now fought even more adamantly for his Fourteen Reservations.]

5. Wilson Defeats Henry Cabot Lodge's Reservations (1919)

The debate in the Senate ended in November 1919, and Lodge was ready for a vote on the Treaty of Versailles with his Fourteen Reservations attached. In general, these reaffirmed the United States' traditional or constitutional safeguards. But Wilson believed that if the odious Lodge reservations were voted down, the treaty would then be approved without "crippling" reservations. Yet the Democrats, now a minority, could not muster a simple majority, much less the two-thirds vote needed to approve a treaty. The naturally stubborn Wilson, shielded from disagreeable realities by his anxious wife, believed that the great body of public opinion was behind him and would prevail. He evidently had not been told, or would not believe, that public opinion was shifting around in favor of reservations. When the Democratic Senator Hitchcock suggested compromise, Wilson sternly replied, "Let Lodge compromise." Mrs. Wilson tells the story. How does she describe the president's basic position?

All this time the fight for the reservations to the Covenant of the League was being pressed in the Senate. Deprived of Executive leadership because of the illness of my husband, friends of the Treaty were on the defensive. The ground gained on the Western tour had been gradually lost until things were worse than when he

---

[5]Edith B. Wilson, *My Memoir* (1939), pp. 296–297. Copyright 1938, 1939 by Edith Bolling Wilson.

started. Friends, including such a valued and persuasive friend as Mr. Bernard M. Baruch, begged Mr. Wilson to accept a compromise, saying "half a loaf is better than no bread." I cannot be unsympathetic with them, for in a moment of weakness I did the same. In my anxiety for the one I loved best in the world, the long-drawn-out fight was eating into my very soul, and I felt nothing mattered but to get the Treaty ratified, even with those reservations.

On November 19th the Senate was to vote on the reservations. Senator Hitchcock came to tell me that unless the Administration forces accepted them, the Treaty would be beaten—the struggle having narrowed down to a personal fight against the President by Lodge and his supporters. In desperation I went to my husband. "For my sake," I said, "won't you accept these reservations and get this awful thing settled?"

He turned his head on the pillow and stretching out his hand to take mine answered in a voice I shall never forget: "Little girl, don't you desert me; that I cannot stand. Can't you see that I have no moral right to accept any change in a paper I have signed without giving to every other signatory, even the Germans, the right to do the same thing? It is not I that will not accept; it is the Nation's honor that is at stake."

His eyes looked luminous as he spoke, and I knew that he was right. He went on quietly: "Better a thousand times to go down fighting than to dip your colours to dishonorable compromise."

I felt like one of his betrayers to have ever doubted. Rejoining Senator Hitchcock outside, I told him that for the first time I had seen the thing clearly and I would never ask my husband again to do what would be manifestly dishonorable. When I went back to the President's room, he dictated a letter to Senator Hitchcock, saying: "In my opinion the resolution in that form [embodying the reservations] does not provide for ratification but rather for nullification of the Treaty. . . . I trust that all true friends of the Treaty will refuse to support the Lodge resolution."

That same day the Senate voted. The Administration forces, voting against ratification *with* the Lodge reservations, defeated it. The vote was then on the ratification of the Treaty without reservations—the Treaty as Mr. Wilson had brought it from France. The result was defeat.

When the word came from the Capitol, I felt I could not bear it and that the shock might be serious for my husband. I went to his bedside and told him the fatal news. For a few moments he was silent, and then he said: "All the more reason I must get well and try again to bring this country to a sense of its great opportunity and greater responsibility."

6. Lodge Blames Wilson (1919)

The crucial vote had come in the Senate on November 19, 1919, when the treaty with the Lodge reservations commanded only 39 yeas to 55 nays. The bulk of the Democrats, heeding Wilson's plea, voted against it. The vote for the treaty without any reservations was 38 yeas to 53 nays. The bulk of the Republicans voted against it. Lodge wrote in bitterness as follows to his friend, former Secretary of State Elihu Root. Was he correct in his assessment of the blame?

---

[6]J. A. Garraty, *Henry Cabot Lodge* (New York: Alfred A. Knopf, Inc., 1953), p. 379.

If Wilson had not written his letter to the Democratic caucus, calling on them to kill the treaty rather than accept the reservations, the treaty would have been ratified on the 19th of November. There would have been enough Democrats voting with us to have done it. It was killed by Wilson. He has been the marplot from the beginning. All the delays and all the troubles have been made by him. . . . We have worked for more than two months over those reservations, and they represent an amount of labor and modification and concession that it would take me a long time to explain to you. He can have the treaty ratified at any moment if he will accept the reservations, and if he declines to do so we are not in the least afraid to meet him at the polls on that issue.

[A shocked public forced the Senate to reconsider the treaty, which now emerged with fifteen revamped Lodge reservations tacked on. Wilson, refusing to budge an inch from his previous position, sent another stern letter to the Democrats in the Senate urging them to vote down the odious package. Lodge, no less stubborn, made it clear that the Senate would have to gag down the treaty with his reservations or there would be no treaty. Faced with naked realities, twenty-one Democrats deserted Wilson and supported ratification. The final vote, on March 19, 1920, was 49 yeas to 35 nays, or 7 votes short of the necessary two-thirds. A total of 23 loyal Democrats voted "nay." Senator Ashurst of Arizona, a "disloyal" Democrat, declared bitterly, "As a friend of the President, as one who has loyally followed him, I solemnly declare to him this morning: If you want to kill your own child because the Senate straightens out its crooked limbs, you must take the responsibility and accept the verdict of history" (Congressional Record, 66th Cong., 2d sess. (March 19, 1920), p. 4164).]

Thought Provokers

1. To what extent were Wilson's own policies to blame for the United States' entry into the war? Could—or should—the confrontation with Germany have been avoided?
2. Why was there more antienemy hysteria in the United States in 1917–1918 than during World War II, when the nation was in graver danger? Why did conscientious objectors fare so badly? Why did the government mount such a vigorous propaganda effort?
3. What were Wilson's purposes in announcing the Fourteen Points? Why did the announcement come so late in the war (in January 1918, nine months after U.S. entry)?
4. Were the doughboys well prepared for the war they found in France? What was most surprising about the conditions they encountered?
5. Would the world have been different if the United States had accepted Article X and signed the Treaty of Versailles? In the last analysis, who was more responsible for keeping the United States out of the League of Nations, Wilson or Lodge?

32

American Life in the "Roaring Twenties", 1919–1929

> You are all a lost generation.
>
> *Attributed by Ernest Hemingway to*
> *Gertrude Stein, 1926*

Prologue: Disappointed at the results of their intervention in the European war, Americans turned inward in the postwar decade. They repudiated all things allegedly "foreign," including radical political ideas and, especially, immigrants. The witch-hunting, frenzied "red scare" that rocked the country in the immediate postwar months was capped by the arrest and eventual execution of the Italian anarchists Sacco and Vanzetti. A revived Ku Klux Klan vented its hatred on Catholic and Jewish newcomers, as well as on blacks. Three centuries of virtually unrestricted immigration to the United States came to a halt with the passage of the restrictive Immigration Act of 1924. The prohibition "experiment" divided "wets" from "drys." In religion, fundamentalists warred against modernists, most famously in the Scopes "monkey trial" in Tennessee. "Flappers" flamboyantly flaunted the new freedom of young women, one of whose champions was Margaret Sanger, pioneer of the birth-control movement. Meanwhile, a high-mass-consumption economy began to flower fully, typified by the booming automobile industry and the emergence of advertising and the huge entertainment industries of radio and the movies. A literary renaissance blossomed, led by F. Scott Fitzgerald, William Faulkner, Sherwood Anderson, Eugene O'Neill, Sinclair Lewis, and Ernest Hemingway. Many of these writers sharply criticized the materialist culture of the decade, symbolized by rampant speculation on the stock market, which crashed in 1929.

A. The Revival of Antiforeignism

1. William A. White Condemns Deportations (1922)

Russian bolshevism inspired a wave of hysteria, which swept the United States after World War I and continued into 1920–1921. Strikes, bomb explosions, and other

---

[1]*Emporia* (Kansas) *Gazette,* January 8, 1920.

acts of violence were branded the work of alien "reds," scores of whom were rounded up and deported. In 1919, 249 undesirables were loaded onto a ship known as the "Soviet ark" and bundled off to the Russian "paradise." Guy Empey, a popular American wartime author who achieved celebrity by writing of his experiences in the British army, applauded the "deportation delirium," by writing: "My motto for the Reds is S.O.S.—ship or shoot. I believe we should place them all on a ship of stone, with sails of lead, and that their first stopping place should be hell." By early 1920 newspaper editor William Allen White was calling for sanity. In this excerpt, does he call for absolute freedom of speech? What does he think is the greatest harm done by the indiscriminate persecution of "radicals"?

The Attorney General seems to be seeing red. He is rounding up every manner of radical in the country; every man who hopes for a better world is in danger of deportation by the Attorney General. The whole business is un-American. There are certain rules fundamental which should govern in the treason cases.

First, it should be agreed that a man should believe what he chooses.

Second, it should be agreed that when he preaches violence he is disturbing the peace and should be put in jail. Whether he preaches violence in politics, business, or religion, whether he advocates murder and arson and pillage for gain or for political ends, he is violating the common law and should be squelched—jailed until he is willing to quit advocating force in a democracy.

Third, he should be allowed to say what he pleases so long as he advocates legal constitutional methods of procedure. Just because a man does not believe this government is good is no reason why he should be deported.

Abraham Lincoln did not believe this government was all right seventy-five years ago. He advocated changes, but he advocated constitutional means, and he had a war with those who advocated force to maintain the government as it was.

Ten years ago [Theodore] Roosevelt advocated great changes in our American life—in our Constitution, in our social and economic life. Most of the changes he advocated have been made, but they were made in the regular legal way. He preached no force. And if a man desires to preach any doctrine under the shining sun, and to advocate the realization of his vision by lawful, orderly, constitutional means—let him alone. If he is Socialist, anarchist, or Mormon, and merely preaches his creed and does not preach violence, he can do no harm. For the folly of his doctrine will be its answer.

The deportation business is going to make martyrs of a lot of idiots whose cause is not worth it.

2. Bartolomeo Vanzetti Condemns Judge Thayer (1927)

The most notorious case associated with the red scare involved Nicola Sacco, a shoemaker, and Bartolomeo Vanzetti, a fish peddler. They were convicted of the 1920 murder of a paymaster and his guard at South Braintree, Massachusetts. When

---

[2]*The Sacco-Vanzetti Case; Transcript of the Record of the Trial . . . and Subsequent Proceedings, 1920–27* (5 vols.) (New York, 1928–1929), pp. 4898–4899, 4904.

arrested, both men were carrying revolvers, and both told numerous lies. Moreover, they were both aliens (Italians), atheists, conscientious objectors ("draft dodgers"), and radicals. Their conviction by a jury in the anti-red atmosphere of the time, despite serious flaws in the evidence, raised grave doubts about the fairness of the trial and the presiding judge, Webster Thayer. Many critics believed that the accused had been found guilty of radicalism rather than murder—that they were martyrs in the "class struggle." Numerous demonstrations in their favor were staged by radical groups in foreign countries. After six years of fruitless appeal, the conviction of Sacco and Vanzetti was upheld, and they were condemned to death in the electric chair. Vanzetti's defiant words to Judge Thayer upon being sentenced are classic. Why, in his view, was he being executed?

You see, it is seven years that we are in jail. What we have suffered during these seven years no human tongue can say; and yet you see me before you, not trembling, you see me looking you in your eyes straight, not blushing, nor changing color, not ashamed or in fear.

Eugene Debs [the Socialist] say that not even a dog—something like that—not even a dog that kill the chickens would have been found guilty by American jury with the evidence that the Commonwealth have produced against us. I say that not even a leprous dog would have his appeal refused two times by the Supreme Court of Massachusetts—not even a leprous dog. . . .

We have proved that there could not have been another Judge on the face of the earth more prejudiced and more cruel than you [Thayer] have been against us. We have proven that. Still they refuse the new trial. We know, and you know in your heart, that you have been against us from the very beginning, before you see us. Before you see us you already know that we were radicals, that we were underdogs, that we were the enemy of the institution that you can believe in good faith in their goodness—I don't want to condemn that—and that it was easy on the time of the first trial to get a verdict of guiltiness.

We know that you have spoke yourself and have spoke your hostility against us, and your despisement against us with friends of yours on the train, at the University Club of Boston, on the Golf Club of Worcester, Massachusetts. I am sure that if the people who know all what you say against us would have the civil courage to take the stand, maybe your Honor—I am sorry to say this because you are an old man, and I have an old father—but maybe you would be beside us in good justice at this time. . . .

This is what I say: I would not wish to a dog or to a snake, to the most low and misfortunate creature of the earth—I would not wish to any of them what I have had to suffer for things that I am not guilty of. But my conviction is that I have suffered for things that I am guilty of. I am suffering because I am a radical and indeed I am a radical; I have suffered because I was an Italian, and indeed I am an Italian; I have suffered more for my family and for my beloved than for myself; but I am so convinced to be right that if you could execute me two times, and if I could be reborn two other times, I would live again to do what I have done already.

[A later investigation, using ballistic tests and other evidence, concluded that Vanzetti probably was innocent but that Sacco may have been guilty. See Francis Rus-

sell, "Sacco Guilty, Vanzetti Innocent?" American Heritage *13 (June 1962): 5–9, 107–111; also the same author's* Tragedy in Dedham *(New York: McGraw-Hill, 1962)].*

3. Walter Lippmann Pleads for Sacco and Vanzetti (1927)

Four days before the execution, scheduled for August 23, 1927, the militant New York World *ran a full-page editorial, written by its chief editorial writer, pundit Walter Lippmann, pleading for a stay of execution. On what grounds did Lippmann base his appeal?*

We recognize perfectly well that no government can with self-respect yield to the clamor of ignorance and sentimentality and partisanship. We realize perfectly well how much more difficult it is for the Governor to commute these sentences in the face of organized threats and of sporadic outrages. It will take greatness of mind and heart for the Governor and his Council to choose the wiser course. . . .

If Governor Fuller commutes these sentences, the Communists and Anarchists will shout that they coerced him. They will make the most of it for a day, a week, a month. The extremists on the other side will call him a weakling, and sneer. They will make the most of it for a day, a week, a month. But in the meantime moderate and disinterested opinion, which is never very talkative, will mobilize behind him and will recognize that he did a wise and a brave thing. . . .

Therefore we plead with the Governor to see this matter in the light, not of to-day and to-morrow, but of years to come. We plead with him to stay the execution because it will defeat the only purpose for which the death penalty can be exacted. We plead with him to remember that, however certain he may be in his own mind that the two men are guilty, no such certainty exists in the minds of his fellow-citizens. . . .

The Sacco-Vanzetti case is clouded and obscure. It is full of doubt. The fairness of the trial raises doubt. The evidence raises doubt. The inadequate review of the evidence raises doubt. The Governor's inquiry has not appeased these doubts. The report of his Advisory Committee has not settled these doubts. Everywhere there is doubt so deep, so pervasive, so unsettling, that it cannot be denied and it cannot be ignored. No man, we submit, should be put to death where so much doubt exists.

The real solution of this case would be a new trial before a new judge under new conditions. Fervently we hope that the Supreme Judicial Court of Massachusetts will decide that under the law such a new trial can be held. But if it does not, then to the Governor, to his Council, and to the friends of justice in Massachusetts we make this plea:

Stay the execution. Wait. The honor of an American Commonwealth is in your hands. Listen, and do not put an irrevocable end upon a case that is so full of doubt. It is human to err, and it is possible in the sight of God that the whole truth is not yet known. [Emphasis in original.]

---

[3]*New York World*, August 19, 1927. A longer extract appears in R. P. Weeks, ed., *Commonwealth vs. Sacco and Vanzetti* (1958), pp. 240–246.

[As the condemned men were being prepared for execution, mobs stoned U.S. embassies in European and South American capitals, and aroused workers went on strike in Italy, France, and the United States. As Sacco was strapped to the electric chair, he cried out in Italian, "Long live anarchy!" Some five months earlier a reporter for the New York World *had visited Vanzetti in his cell and recorded the following remarks by the prisoner, which were published in the* World *on May 13, 1927, and which have become famous:*

"If it had not been for these thing, I might have live out my life, talking at street corners to scorning men. I might have die, unmarked, unknown, a failure. Now we are not a failure. This is our career and our triumph. Never in our full life can we hope to do such work for tolerance, for joostice, for man's onderstanding of man, as now we do by an accident.

"Our word—our lives—our pains—nothing! The taking of our lives—lives of a good shoemaker and a poor fish peddler—all! That last moment belong to us—that agony is our triumph!"]

B. The Reconstituted Ku Klux Klan

1. Tar-Bucket Terror in Texas (1921)

The hysterical atmosphere of the red scare was also partly responsible for the revival of the Ku Klux Klan in the 1920s. The bed sheets, hoods, and lashes were old, but the principles, aside from hatred of blacks, were new. The revamped Klan was antiforeign, anti-Catholic, anti-Jewish, and anticommunist. It professed to uphold Christianity, the Bible, prohibition, clean movies, the law, the Constitution, the public schools, the home, marriage vows. It undertook to persuade unchaste people, especially women, to mend their ways by giving them a dose of the lash and a coat of tar and feathers. The press reported in 1921 that an African-American bellboy had been branded on the forehead with the letters KKK; that in Florida an Episcopal archdeacon had been whipped, tarred, and feathered; and that there had been forty-three tar-bucket parties in Texas in six months. The Houston Chronicle *here addresses a protest to the Klan members. Does it register any sympathy for the Klan? What does it see as the Klan's greatest outrages?*

Boys, you'd better disband. You'd better take your sheets, your banners, your masks, your regalia, and make one fine bonfire.

Without pausing to argue over the objects you have in mind, it is sufficient to say that your methods are hopelessly wrong. Every tradition of social progress is against them. They are opposed to every principle on which this Government is founded. They are out of keeping with civilized life.

You seem to forget that the chief advantage of democracy is to let in the daylight, to prevent secret punishment, to insure a fair hearing for every person, to make impossible that kind of tyranny which can only flourish in the dark.

The newspapers of last Sunday were disgraced with the account of four illegal,

---

[1]*Houston Chronicle,* quoted in *Literary Digest* 70 (August 27, 1921): 12.

unnecessary, and wholly ineffectual outrages. Without assuming that your organization was directly responsible for any or all of them, it was, in large measure, indirectly responsible. Your organization has made the thought of secretly organized violence fashionable.

It matters not who can get into your organization or who is kept out; any group of men can ape your disguise, your methods, and your practices. If outrages occur for which you are not accountable—and they will—you have no way of clearing yourselves, except by throwing off your disguise and invoking that publicity you have sought to deny. Your role of masked violence, of purification by stealth, of reform by terrorism is an impossible one. Your position is such that you must accept responsibility for every offense which smacks of disguised tyranny. . . .

Who was responsible for the Tenaha case, where a woman was stripped naked and then covered with tar and feathers? Has there ever been any crime committed in this state so horrible or one that brought such shame on Texas? Is there any member of the Ku Klux Klan in Texas so pure and holy that he can condemn even the vilest woman to such disgrace and torture? Masked men did it, and the world was told in press dispatches that they were the hooded Klansmen of Texas.

If that outrage was done by Ku Klux Klansmen, then every decent man who was inveigled into the order should resign immediately. If it was not the work of the real order, its members should disband because of this one act, if for no other reason.

The Ku Klux Klan, as recently rejuvenated, serves no useful purpose. On the other hand, it makes room for innumerable abuses. The community—meaning the whole nation—is against it, and the community will grow more resolutely against it as time goes on. Those who brought it into being, no matter what their intentions, would better bring about its dissolution before the storm breaks.

2. A Methodist Editor Clears the Klan (1923)

The brutal excesses of the Ku Klux Klan (or its imitators) brought it into disrepute, and by the mid-1920s it was rapidly disintegrating. For several years, however, with its hundreds of thousands of members, it remained a potent political force. The Reverend Bob Shuler (Methodist), editor of Shuler's Magazine *and the fundamentalist pastor of a large Los Angeles church, published the following advertisement in the* Eugene (Oregon) Register. *What biases formed the basis of his pro-Klan views? Is vigilantism ever justified? How valid is the author's comparison of the Klan with the Knights of Columbus, an American Roman Catholic society for men, founded in 1882?*

This editor has repeatedly affirmed privately and publicly that he is not a member of the Ku Klux or any other secret organization. But when it comes to secret societies, he sees no difference absolutely between the Ku Klux and many others, the Knights of Columbus, for instance. The Knights of Columbus has an oath, just as binding, or more so, than the Ku Klux oath. Moreover, the Knights of Columbus' oath is not one-half so American as the Ku Klux. If you charge that the Ku Klux has put over mobs, I answer that the Knights of Columbus has put over two mobs to where any other secret organization on earth has ever put over one.

---

[2]*Eugene Register,* quoted in *Literary Digest* 76 (January 20, 1923): 18–19.

This editor has been favored recently by being permitted to look over documentary evidence as to the tenets, principles, and aims of the Ku Klux Klan. He finds that this organization stands with positive emphasis for Americanism as opposed to foreign idealism; for the principles of the Christian religion as opposed to Roman Catholicism and infidelity; for the American public schools and for the placing of the Holy Bible in the schoolrooms of this nation; for the enforcement of the laws upon the statute books and for a wholesome respect for the Constitution of the United States; for the maintenance of virtue among American women, sobriety and honor among American men, and for the eradication of all agencies and influences that would threaten the character of our children. So the principles of the Klan are not so damnable as pictured, it would seem.

This organization is opposing the most cunning, deceitful, and persistent enemy that Americanism and Protestant Christianity have ever had—the Jesuits. Speaking of "invisible empires," of forces that creep through the night and do their dirty work under cover, influences that are set going in the secret places of darkness, the Jesuits are the finished product. They have burned, killed, defamed, blackmailed, and ruined their enemies by the hundreds. History reeks with it. Though I disagree with the logic of the Klan, the members of that organization declare that they can only fight such a foe by using his own fire.

As to the charge that the Ku Klux Klan has functioned in mob violence in their efforts to correct conditions, I have this to say: I am convinced that most of the mobs reported have not been ordered and directed by the Klan as an organization. I am moreover convinced that many of them have been put over by forces opposed to the Klan and for the purpose of seeking to place the guilt for mob rule upon the Klan. The most of these mobs have been, according to investigation, not Ku Klux mobs at all, but gatherings of indignant citizens, bent on correcting conditions that the officers of the law refused to correct. The way to cause the Ku Klux to retire from the field is for the officers of the law to take that field and occupy it.

The Ku Klux has the same right to exist so long as it obeys the law that any other organization has. We have not heard of any investigation of the Knights of Columbus, although their un-American oaths are historic and their mob activities have been repeatedly published and heralded from platforms far and near.

C. The Wets Versus the Drys

1. A German Observes Bootlegging (1928)

Before the end of World War I most of the states had decreed the prohibition of alcoholic beverages. Nationwide prohibition, authorized by the Eighteenth Amendment in 1919, resulted largely from the spirit of self-sacrifice aroused by the war. A militant majority was thus able to force its will upon a large and vocal minority, especially in the big cities, where the foreign-born population was accustomed to the

---

[1]From *This Was America,* ed. by Oscar Handlin (Cambridge, Mass.: Harvard University Press, 1949), pp. 495–496. Used by permission of the author.

regular consumption of alcohol. The "Sea Devil" Felix von Luckner, a German naval hero who had destroyed some $25 million worth of Allied commerce with his raider the Seeadler (Sea Eagle) *during World War I, visited the United States as a lecturer and recorded his curious experiences with alcohol. What did he see as the good and bad features of prohibition? What conditions made enforcement peculiarly difficult?*

My first experience with the ways of prohibition came while we were being entertained by friends in New York. It was bitterly cold. My wife and I rode in the rumble seat of the car, while the American and his wife, bundled in furs, sat in front. Having wrapped my companion in pillows and blankets so thoroughly that only her nose showed, I came across another cushion that seemed to hang uselessly on the side. "Well," I thought, "this is a fine pillow; since everyone else is so warm and cozy, I might as well do something for my own comfort. This certainly does no one any good hanging on the wall." Sitting on it, I gradually noticed a dampness in the neighborhood that soon mounted to a veritable flood. The odor of fine brandy told me I had burst my host's peculiar liquor flask.

In time, I learned that not everything in America was what it seemed to be. I discovered, for instance, that a spare tire could be filled with substances other than air, that one must not look deeply into certain binoculars, and that the Teddy Bears that suddenly acquired tremendous popularity among the ladies very often had hollow metal stomachs.

"But," it might be asked, "where do all these people get the liquor?" Very simple. Prohibition has created a new, a universally respected, a well-beloved, and a very profitable occupation, that of the bootlegger who takes care of the importation of the forbidden liquor. Everyone know this, even the powers of government. But this profession is beloved because it is essential, and it is respected because its pursuit is clothed with an element of danger and with a sporting risk. . . .

Yet it is undeniable that prohibition has in some respects been signally successful. The filthy saloons, the gin mills which formerly flourished on every corner and in which the laborer once drank off half his wages, have disappeared. Now he can instead buy his own car, and ride off for a weekend or a few days with his wife and children in the country or at the sea. But, on the other hand, a great deal of poison and methyl alcohol has taken the place of the good old pure whiskey. The number of crimes and misdemeanors that originated in drunkenness has declined. But by contrast, a large part of the population has become accustomed to disregard and to violate the law without thinking. The worst is that, precisely as a consequence of the law, the taste for alcohol has spread ever more widely among the youth. The sporting attraction of the forbidden and the dangerous leads to violations. My observations have convinced me that many fewer would drink were it not illegal.

2. Fiorello La Guardia Pillories Prohibition (1926)

Wholesale violations of the prohibition law became so notorious that in 1926, a Senate judiciary subcommittee held extended hearings. It uncovered shocking conditions.

---

[2]*Hearings before the Subcommittee of the Committee on the Judiciary, U.S. Senate, Sixty-ninth Congress, First Session* (April 5–24, 1926), *on . . . Bills to Amend the National Prohibition Act,* vol. 1, pp. 649–651.

Stubby, turbulent, fiery Fiorello ("The Little Flower") La Guardia, then a congressman from New York and later to be the controversial reform mayor of New York City, expressed characteristically vigorous views. Which of his statistics seem least susceptible of proof? Which of his arguments would probably carry the most weight with the average taxpayer?

It is impossible to tell whether prohibition is a good thing or a bad thing. It has never been enforced in this country.

There may not be as much liquor in quantity consumed to-day as there was before prohibition, but there is just as much alcohol.

At least 1,000,000 quarts of liquor is consumed each day in the United States. In my opinion such an enormous traffic in liquor could not be carried on without the knowledge, if not the connivance, of the officials entrusted with the enforcement of the law.

I am for temperance; that is why I am for modification.

I believe that the percentage of whisky drinkers in the United States now is greater than in any other country of the world. Prohibition is responsible for that. . . .

At least $1,000,000,000 a year is lost to the National Government and the several states and counties in excise taxes. The liquor traffic is going on just the same. This amount goes into the pockets of bootleggers and into the pockets of the public officials in the shape of graft. . . .

I will concede that the saloon was odious, but now we have delicatessen stores, pool rooms, drug stores, millinery shops, private parlors, and 57 other varieties of speakeasies selling liquor and flourishing.

I have heard of $2,000 a year prohibition agents who run their own cars with liveried chauffeurs.

It is common talk in my part of the country that from $7.50 to $12 a case is paid in graft from the time the liquor leaves the 12-mile limit until it reaches the ultimate consumer. There seems to be a varying market price for this service created by the degree of vigilance or the degree of greed of the public officials in charge.

It is my calculation that at least $1,000,000 a day is paid in graft and corruption to Federal, state, and local officers. Such a condition is not only intolerable, but it is demoralizing and dangerous to organized government. . . .

The Prohibition Enforcement Unit has entirely broken down. It is discredited; it has become a joke. Liquor is sold in every large city. . . .

Only a few days ago I charged on the floor of the House that 350 cases of liquor of a seizure of 1,500 made by Federal officials and stored in the Federal building at Indianapolis, Ind., had been removed. The Department of Justice, under date of April 9, 1926, confirmed my charge. The Attorney General admits that since this liquor was in the possession of the Federal authorities in the Federal building at Indianapolis, 330 cases are missing. If bootleggers can enter Federal buildings to get liquor, the rest can be easily imagined. . . .

I have been in public office for a great many years. I have had the opportunity to observe first the making of the present prohibition laws as a member of Congress, and later as president of the Board of Aldermen of the largest city in this country its attempted enforcement. In order to enforce prohibition in New York City

I estimated at the time would require a police force of 250,000 men and a force of 200,000 men to police the police.

3. The WCTU Upholds Prohibition (1926)

Mrs. Ella A. Boole, president of the National Woman's Christian Temperance Union (WCTU), appeared before the same Senate judiciary subcommittee. Hailing from the same metropolitan area as La Guardia, Boole was a member of the Daughters of the American Revolution (DAR), held a Ph.D. from the University of Wooster, and was a Presbyterian. She had run unsuccessfully for the U.S. Senate on the Prohibition ticket in 1920. What values underlay her insistence on enforcing unpopular laws, despite widespread flouting?

You have listened to testimony of shocking conditions due to corruption of officials, and lack of enforcement, some of which suggested no remedy except a surrender to those who violate the law, while the propaganda of all these organizations is encouraging continued violation. Permit me to show another side of the picture, and propose that instead of lowering our standards we urge that the law be strengthened, and in that way notice be served on law violators that America expects her laws to be enforced and to be obeyed. . . .

Enforcement has never had a fair trial. Political patronage, leakage through the permit system, connivance at the violation of law, and spread of the propaganda that it is not obligatory to obey a law unless you believe in it, and to the effect that the responsibility for the enforcement of law rested with the officers alone, when it should be shared by the individual citizen, have materially hindered the work of enforcement—all this with the result that the United States has not derived from prohibition what it would have derived had all the people observed the law and had there been hearty cooperation of the press and the people. . . .

It is not easy to get at the facts about the effect of prohibition on health, morals, and economic [life] because they are interwoven with other causes, and partial statistics may be misleading. But the elimination of a preventable cause of poverty, crime, tuberculosis, the diseases of middle life, unhappy homes, and financial depression brings results insofar as the law is observed and enforced. . . .

The closing of the open saloon with its doors swinging both ways, an ever-present invitation for all to drink—men, women, and boys—is an outstanding fact, and no one wants it to return. It has resulted in better national health, children are born under better conditions, homes are better, and the mother is delivered from the fear of a drunken husband. There is better food. Savings-banks deposits have increased, and many a man has a bank account to-day who had none in the days of the saloon.

The increase in home owning is another evidence that money wasted in drink is now used for the benefit of the family. Improved living conditions are noticeable in our former slum districts. The Bowery and Hell's Kitchen* are transformed.

---

[3]*Hearings before the Subcommittee of the Committee on the Judiciary, U.S. Senate, Sixty-ninth Congress, First Session* (April 5–24, 1926), *on . . . Bills to Amend the National Prohibition Act,* vol. 1, pp. 1068–1071.
*The Bowery and Hell's Kitchen were two notorious immigrant ghettos in turn-of-the-century New York.

Safety-first campaigns on railroads and in the presence of the increasing number of automobiles are greatly strengthened by prohibition.

The prohibition law is not the only law that is violated. Traffic laws, anti-smuggling laws, as well as the Volstead [prohibition] Act, are held in contempt. It is the spirit of the age.

Life-insurance companies have long known that drinkers were poor risks, but they recognize the fact that prohibition has removed a preventable cause of great financial loss to them.

The wonderful advances in mechanics in the application of electricity and in transportation demand brains free from the fumes of alcohol, hence law enforcement and law observance contribute to this progress. . . .

Your attention has been called to the failures. We claim these have been the result of lax enforcement. The machinery of enforcement should be strengthened.

[The federal enforcement machinery finally broke down, and the Eighteenth Amendment was repealed in 1933. Prohibition had done much good but at a staggering cost. In addition to the evils already noted, gangsterism was flourishing, and the courts and jails were clogged. With repeal, the control of liquor went back to state and local governments.]

D. New Goals for Women

1. Margaret Sanger Campaigns for Birth Control (1920)

Few other feminists could rival Margaret Sanger's energy, daring, and genius for organization and publicity. Prosecuted in 1914 for publishing a radical journal, The Woman Rebel, *she fled to England, where she made the acquaintance of the noted sexual theorist Havelock Ellis. She returned to the United States in 1915 and launched herself on a lifelong crusade for birth control. Despite being arrested several more times in subsequent years, she persevered in founding the American Birth Control League (later Planned Parenthood) in 1921. For the next decade and more, Sanger tirelessly championed her cause. What arguments does she emphasize here in favor of contraception? What was her view of women? of men? of the relation between the sexes? Critics sometimes accused her of drinking too deeply from the well of racism and nativism that seemed to overflow in the 1920s. Do the remarks that follow offer any evidence in support of such a charge?*

The most far-reaching social development of modern times is the revolt of woman against sex servitude. The most important force in the remaking of the world is a free motherhood. Beside this force, the elaborate international programmes of modern statesmen are weak and superficial. . . .

---

[1]Margaret Sanger, *Woman and the New Race* (New York: Brentano's, 1920), passim.

Only in recent years has woman's position as the gentler and weaker half of the human family been emphatically and generally questioned. Men assumed that this was woman's place; woman herself accepted it. It seldom occurred to anyone to ask whether she would go on occupying it forever. . . .

Caught in this "vicious circle," woman has, through her reproductive ability, founded and perpetuated the tyrannies of the Earth. Whether it was the tyranny of a monarchy, an oligarchy or a republic, the one indispensable factor of its existence was, as it is now, hordes of human beings—human beings so plentiful as to be cheap, and so cheap that ignorance was their natural lot. . . .

The creators of over-population are the women, who, while wringing their hands over each fresh horror, submit anew to their task of producing the multitudes who will bring about the *next* tragedy of civilization.

While unknowingly laying the foundations of tyrannies and providing the human tinder for racial conflagrations, woman was also unknowingly creating slums, filling asylums with insane, and institutions with other defectives. She was replenishing the ranks of the prostitutes, furnishing grist for the criminal courts and inmates for prisons. Had she planned deliberately to achieve this tragic total of human waste and misery, she could hardly have done it more effectively. . . .

It is true that, obeying the inner urge of their natures, some women revolted. They went even to the extreme of infanticide and abortion. Usually their revolts were not general enough. They fought as individuals, not as a mass. . . .

To-day, however, woman is rising in fundamental revolt. Even her efforts at mere reform are, as we shall see later, steps in that direction. Underneath each of them is the feminine urge to complete freedom. Millions of women are asserting their right to voluntary motherhood. They are determined to decide for themselves whether they shall become mothers, under what conditions and when. This is the fundamental revolt referred to. It is for woman the key to the temple of liberty.

Even as birth control is the means by which woman attains basic freedom, so it is the means by which she must and will uproot the evil she has wrought through her submission. . . .

Two chief obstacles hinder the discharge of this tremendous obligation. The first and the lesser is the legal barrier. Dark-Age laws would still deny to her the knowledge of her reproductive nature. Such knowledge is indispensable to intelligent motherhood and she must achieve it, despite absurd statutes and equally absurd moral canons.

The second and more serious barrier is her own ignorance of the extent and effect of her submission. Until she knows the evil her subjection has wrought to herself, to her progeny and to the world at large, she cannot wipe out that evil. . . .

What effect will the practice of birth control have upon woman's moral development? . . . It will break her bonds. It will free her to understand the cravings and soul needs of herself and other women. It will enable her to develop her love nature separate from and independent of her maternal nature.

It goes without saying that the woman whose children are desired and are of such number that she can not only give them adequate care but keep herself mentally and spiritually alive, as well as physically fit, can discharge her duties to her children much better than the overworked, broken and querulous mother of a large, unwanted family. . . .

To achieve this she must have a knowledge of birth control. She must also assert and maintain her right to refuse the marital embrace except when urged by her inner nature. . . .

What can we expect of offspring that are the result of "accidents"—who are brought into being undesired and in fear? What can we hope for from a morality that surrounds each physical union, for the woman, with an atmosphere of submission and shame? What can we say for a morality that leaves the husband at liberty to communicate to his wife a venereal disease?

Subversion of the sex urge to ulterior purposes has dragged it to the level of the gutter. Recognition of its true nature and purpose must lift the race to spiritual freedom. Out of our growing knowledge we are evolving new and saner ideas of life in general. Out of our increasing sex knowledge we shall evolve new ideals of sex. These ideals will spring from the innermost needs of women. They will serve these needs and express them. They will be the foundation of a moral code that will tend to make fruitful the impulse which is the source, the soul and the crowning glory of our sexual natures.

When mothers have raised the standards of sex ideals and purged the human mind of its unclean conception of sex, the fountain of the race will have been cleansed. Mothers will bring forth, in purity and in joy, a race that is morally and spiritually free. . . .

Birth control itself, often denounced as a violation of natural law, is nothing more or less than the facilitation of the process of weeding out the unfit, of preventing the birth of defectives or of those who will become defectives. So, in compliance with nature's working plan, we must permit womanhood its full development before we can expect of it efficient motherhood. If we are to make racial progress, this development of womanhood must precede motherhood in every individual woman. Then and then only can the mother cease to be an incubator and be a mother indeed. Then only can she transmit to her sons and daughters the qualities which make strong individuals and, collectively, a strong race. . . .

2. The Lynds Discover Changes in the Middle-American Home (1929)

In 1924 the sociologists Robert S. Lynd and Helen Merrell Lynd arrived in Muncie, Indiana, with a team of researchers. They spent the next eighteen months studying the pattern and texture of life in Muncie, and in 1929 they published the results of their research in Middletown: A Study in Modern American Culture. *Middletown has ever since been recognized as a classic work of American scholarship, perhaps the most detailed, thoughtful portrait ever drawn of life in an American community. The Lynds described the changes in the lives of ordinary, "average" people since the 1890s. Their research revealed that the pace of change was faster among "business-class" people than among the "working class." (One of the most striking changes they*

---

[2]Excerpt from "Food, Clothing, and Housework" in *Middletown: A Study in American Culture* by Robert S. Lynd and Helen M. Lynd, copyright 1929 by Harcourt, Inc. and renewed 1957 by Robert S. and Helen M. Lynd, reprinted by permission of the publisher.

found was that the traditional prohibition on discussing sexual matters, including birth control, was weakening. Among the more prosperous segments of Middletown's population, most women by 1924 not only discussed birth control but practiced it. The practice was much less widespread among the poorer elements of the populace.) In the following selection about housework, what are the major differences between the lives of women in the 1890s and the 1920s? How did the lives of women in the two social classes differ? What were the effects on family life of the emergence of a high-mass-consumption economy in the 1920s?

At no point can one approach the home life of Middletown without becoming aware of the shift taking place in the traditional activities of male and female. This is especially marked in the complex of activities known as "housework," which have always been almost exclusively performed by the wife, with more or less help from her daughters. In the growing number of working class families in which the wife helps to earn the family living, the husband is beginning to share directly in housework. Even in families of the business class the manual activities of the wife in making a home are being more and more replaced by goods and services produced or performed by other agencies in return for a money price, thus throwing ever greater emphasis upon the money-getting activities of the husband. . . .

The rhythm of the day's activities varies according to whether a family is of the working or business class, most of the former starting the day at six or earlier and the latter somewhat later. . . .

Dorothy Dix catches the traditional situation in her remark, "Marriage brings a woman a life sentence of hard labor in her home. Her work is the most monotonous in the world and she has no escape from it." Many working class housewives, struggling to commute this sentence for their daughters if not for themselves, voiced in some form the wish of one mother, "I've always wanted my girls to do something other than housework; I don't want *them* to be house drudges like me!" And both groups are being borne along on the wave of material changes toward a somewhat lighter sentence to household servitude. Of the ninety-one working class wives who gave data on the amount of time their mothers spent on housework as compared with themselves, sixty-six (nearly three-fourths) said that their mothers spent more time, ten approximately the same, and fifteen less time. Of the thirty-seven wives of the business group interviewed who gave similar data, seventeen said that their mothers spent more time, eight about the same, and twelve less time.

The fact that the difference between the women of this business group and their mothers is less marked than that between the working class women and their mothers is traceable in part to the decrease in the amount of paid help in the homes of the business class. It is apparently about half as frequent for Middletown housewives to hire full-time servant girls to do their housework today as in 1890. The thirty-nine wives of the business group answering on this point reported almost precisely half as many full-time servants as their mothers in 1890, and this ratio is supported by Federal Census figures; thirteen of the thirty-nine have full-time servants, only two of them more than one. But if the women of the business class have fewer servants than their mothers, they are still markedly more served than the working class. One hundred and twelve out of 118 working class women had no paid help at all during the year preceding the interview, while only four of the thirty-nine women of the business group interviewed had had no help; one of the former group and twenty-five of the latter group had the equivalent of one or more days a week. Both groups of housewives have been affected by the reduction in the number of "old maid" sisters and daughters performing the same duties as domestic servants but without receiving a fixed compensation. Prominent among the factors involved in this diminution of full-time servants are the increased opportunities for women to get a living in other kinds of work; the greater cost of a "hired girl," ten to fifteen dollars a week as against three dollars in 1890; and increased attention to child-rearing, making mothers more careful about the kind of servants they employ. "Every one has the same problem today," said one thoughtful mother. "It is easy to get good girls by the hour but very difficult to get any one good to stay all the time. Then, too, the best type of girl, with whom I feel safe to leave the children, wants to eat with the family." The result is a fortification of the tendency to spend time on the children and transfer other things to service agencies outside the home. A common substitute for a full-time servant today is the woman who "comes in" one or two days a week. A single day's labor of this sort today costs approximately what the housewife's mother paid for a week's work.

Smaller houses, easier to "keep up," labor-saving devices, canned goods, baker's bread, less heavy meals, and ready-made clothing are among the places where the lack of servants is being compensated for and time saved today. Working class housewives repeatedly speak, also, of the use of running water, the shift from wood to coal fires, and the use of linoleum on floors as time-savers. Wives of the business class stress certain non-material changes as well. "I am not as particular as my mother," said many of these housewives, or "I sometimes leave my supper dishes until morning, which my mother would never have thought of doing. She used to do a much more elaborate fall and spring cleaning, which lasted a week or two. I consider time for reading and clubs and my children more important than such careful housework and I just don't do it." These women, on the other hand, mention numerous factors making their work harder than their mothers'. "The constant soot and cinders in this soft-coal city and the hard, alkaline water make up for all you save by new conveniences." A number feel that while the actual physical labor of housework is less and one is less particular about many details, rising standards in other respects use up the saved time. "People are more particular about diet today. They care more about having things nicely served and dressing for dinner. So many things our mothers didn't know about we feel that we ought to do for our children."

Most important among these various factors affecting women's work is the increased use of labor-saving devices. Just as the advent of the Owens machine in one of Middletown's largest plants has unseated a glass-blowing process that had come down largely unchanged from the days of the early Egyptians, so in the homes of Middletown certain primitive hand skills have been shifted overnight to modern machines. The oil lamp, the gas flare, the broom, the pump, the water bucket, the washboard, the flatiron, the cook stove, all only slightly modified forms of some of man's most primitive tools, dominated Middletown housework in the nineties. In 1924, as noted above, all but 1 per cent. of Middletown's houses were wired for electricity. Between March, 1920, and February, 1924, there was an average increase of 25 per cent. in the K.W.H. [kilowatt hours] of current used by each local family. How this additional current is being used may be inferred from the following record of sales of electrical appliances by five local electrical shops, a prominent drug store, and the local electric power company for the only items it sells, irons and toasters, over the six-month period from May first to October thirty-first, 1923: curlers sold, 1,173; irons, 1,114; vacuum cleaners, 709; toasters, 463; washing machines, 371; heaters, 114; heating pads, 18; electric refrigerators, 11; electric ranges, 3; electric ironers, 1. The manager of the local electric power company estimates that nearly 90 per cent. of Middletown homes have electric irons.

It is in part by compelling advertising couched in terms of certain of women's greatest values that use of these material tools is being so widely diffused:

"Isn't Bobby more important than his clothes?" demands an advertisement of the "Power Laundries" in a Middletown paper.

The advertisement of an electrical company reads:

This is the test of a successful mother—she puts first things first. She does not give to sweeping the time that belongs to her children. . . . Men are judged successful according to their power to delegate work. Similarly the wise woman delegates to electricity all that electricity can do. She cannot delegate the one task more important. Human lives are in her keeping; their future is molded by her hands and heart.

Another laundry advertisement beckons:

Time for sale! Will you buy? Where can you buy back a single yesterday? Nowhere, of course. Yet, right in your city, you can purchase tomorrows. Time for youth and beauty! Time for club work, for church and community activities. Time for books and plays and concerts. Time for home and children. . . .

3. The Supreme Court Declares That Women Are Different from Men (1908)

When a Portland, Oregon, laundry violated an Oregon statute limiting the number of hours that women could work in a day, the laundry owner was convicted and fined ten dollars. The owner, Curt Muller, appealed his conviction all the way to the U.S. Supreme Court, which affirmed his guilt in the case of Muller v. Oregon *in 1908. On what grounds did the Court rest its decision? Could feminists in the early twentieth century support the Court's reasoning in this case?*

On February 19, 1903, the legislature of the State of Oregon passed an act (Session Laws, 1903, p. 148), the first section of which is in these words:

"Sec. 1. That no female (shall) be employed in any mechanical establishment, or factory, or laundry in this State more than ten hours during any one day. The hours of work may be so arranged as to permit the employment of females at any time so that they shall not work more than ten hours during the twenty-four hours of any one day."

Section 3 made a violation of the provisions of the prior sections a misdemeanor, subject to a fine of not less than $10 nor more than $25. On September 18, 1905, an information was filed in the Circuit Court of the State for the county of

---

[3]*Muller* v. *Oregon* (208 U.S. 412), pp. 416–423.

Multnomah, charging that the defendant "on the 4th day of September, A.D. 1905, in the county of Multnomah and State of Oregon, then and there being the owner of a laundry, known as the Grand Laundry, in the city of Portland, and the employer of females therein, did then and there unlawfully permit and suffer one Joe Haselbock, he, the said Joe Haselbock, then and there being an overseer, superintendent and agent of said Curt Muller, in the said Grand Laundry, to require a female, to wit, one Mrs. E. Gotcher, to work more than ten hours in said laundry on said 4th day of September, A.D. 1905, contrary to the statutes in such cases made and provided, and against the peace and dignity of the State of Oregon."

A trial resulted in a verdict against the defendant, who was sentenced to pay a fine of $10. The Supreme Court of the State affirmed the conviction, *State* v. *Muller,* 48 Oregon, 252, whereupon the case was brought here on writ of error.

The single question is the constitutionality of the statute under which the defendant was convicted so far as it affects the work of a female in a laundry. . . .

That woman's physical structure and the performance of maternal functions place her at a disadvantage in the struggle for subsistence is obvious. This is especially true when the burdens of motherhood are upon her. Even when they are not, by abundant testimony of the medical fraternity continuance for a long time on her feet at work, repeating this from day to day, tends to injurious effects upon the body, and as healthy mothers are essential to vigorous offspring, the physical well-being of woman becomes an object of public interest and care in order to preserve the strength and vigor of the race.

Still again, history discloses the fact that woman has always been dependent upon man. He established his control at the outset by superior physical strength, and this control in various forms, with diminishing intensity, has continued to the present. As minors, though not to the same extent, she has been looked upon in the courts as needing especial care that her rights may be preserved. Education was long denied her, and while now the doors of the school room are opened and her opportunities for acquiring knowledge are great, yet even with that and the consequent increase of capacity for business affairs it is still true that in the struggle for subsistence she is not an equal competitor with her brother. Though limitations upon personal and contractual rights may be removed by legislation, there is that in her disposition and habits of life which will operate against a full assertion of those rights. She will still be where some legislation to protect her seems necessary to secure a real equality of right. Doubtless there are individual exceptions, and there are many respects in which she has an advantage over him; but looking at it from the viewpoint of the effort to maintain an independent position in life, she is not upon an equality. Differentiated by these matters from the other sex, she is properly placed in a class by herself, and legislation designed for her protection may be sustained, even when like legislation is not necessary for men and could not be sustained. It is impossible to close one's eyes to the fact that she still looks to her brother and depends upon him. Even though all restrictions on political, personal and contractual rights were taken away, and she stood, so far as statutes are concerned, upon an absolutely equal plane with him, it would still be true that she is so constituted that she will rest upon and look to him for protection; that her physical structure and a proper discharge of her maternal functions—having in view not merely her own health, but the well-being of the race—justify legislation to protect her from the greed as well as the passion of man. The limitations which this statute places upon her contractual powers, upon her right to agree with her employer as to the time she shall labor, are not imposed solely for her benefit, but also largely for the benefit of all. Many words cannot make this plainer. The two sexes differ in structure of body, in the functions to be performed by each, in the amount of physical strength, in the capacity for long-continued labor, particularly when done standing, the influence of vigorous health upon the future well-being of the race, the self-reliance which enables one to assert full rights, and in the capacity to maintain the struggle for subsistence. This difference justifies a difference in legislation and upholds that which is designed to compensate for some of the burdens which rest upon her. . . .

For these reasons, . . . we are of the opinion that it cannot be adjudged that the act in question is in conflict with the Federal Constitution, so far as it respects the work of a female in a laundry, and the judgment of the Supreme Court of Oregon is *Affirmed.*

4. The Supreme Court Declares That Men and Women Are Equal (1923)

Fifteen years after the Muller *case—and three years after passage of the Nineteenth Amendment, which enfranchised women—the Supreme Court reversed its ruling in* Muller *and declared in the case of* Adkins v. Children's Hospital *that sexual inequalities were rapidly disappearing. The case involved a federal statute regulating women's wages in Washington, D.C. Justice George Sutherland, speaking for the Court majority, invalidated the regulation in the following decision. How does his reasoning differ from that of the Court majority in the* Muller *case? Justice Oliver Wendell Holmes, Jr., dissented from Sutherland's opinion, declaring that it would take more than the Nineteenth Amendment to convince him that there were no differences between men and women. Does Sutherland's or Holmes's position provide the superior foundation for legislation regarding women? Why might feminists have disagreed over the* Adkins *case?*

The question presented for determination by these appeals is the constitutionality of the Act of September 19, 1918, providing for the fixing of minimum wages for women and children in the District of Columbia. . . .

In the *Muller Case* the validity of an Oregon statute, forbidding the employment of any female in certain industries more than ten hours during any one day was upheld. The decision proceeded upon the theory that the difference between the sexes may justify a different rule respecting hours of labor in the case of women than in the case of men. It is pointed out that these consist in differences of physical structure, especially in respect of the maternal functions, and also in the fact that historically woman has always been dependent upon man, who has established his control by superior physical strength. . . . But the ancient inequality of the sexes, otherwise than physical, as suggested in the *Muller Case* has continued "with diminishing intensity." In view of the great—not to say revolutionary—changes which

---

[4]*Adkins* v. *Children's Hospital* (261 U.S. 525), pp. 539–562.

have taken place since that utterance, in the contractual, political and civil status of women, culminating in the Nineteenth Amendment, it is not unreasonable to say that these differences have now come almost, if not quite, to the vanishing point. In this aspect of the matter, while the physical differences must be recognized in appropriate cases, and legislation fixing hours or conditions of work may properly take them into account, we cannot accept the doctrine that women of mature age, *sui juris,* require or may be subjected to restrictions upon their liberty of contract which could not lawfully be imposed in the case of men under similar circumstances. To do so would be to ignore all the implications to be drawn from the present day trend of legislation, as well as that of common thought and usage, by which woman is accorded emancipation from the old doctrine that she must be given special protection or be subjected to special restraint in her contractual and civil relationships. In passing, it may be noted that the instant statute applies in the case of a woman employer contracting with a woman employee as it does when the former is a man. . . .

Thought Provokers

1. Why did antiforeignism flare up so viciously in the postwar years? Could the United States have continued indefinitely to allow unlimited immigration? Were Sacco and Vanzetti villains or scapegoats?
2. What was the relation of the revived Ku Klux Klan in the 1920s to the original Klan of Reconstruction days? Why does the United States periodically spawn violent vigilante-style movements?
3. Was prohibition a typically American "experiment"? Under what circumstances does the government have a right to regulate personal behavior, such as drinking alcoholic beverages or using narcotic drugs?
4. In what ways was the urbanized economic order of the 1920s a new frontier for women? How did the spreading practice of birth control reflect changes in the values and styles of family life? Does an emphasis on gender difference or on gender equality form a better basis for public policy?

33

The Politics
of Boom and Bust,
1920–1932

The country is in the midst of an era of prosperity
more extensive and of peace more permanent than it
has ever before experienced.

President Calvin Coolidge, 1928

Prologue: In 1920 Warren G. Harding, campaigning on a promise to return to
"normalcy" in the nation's war-strained affairs, won the presidency by a landslide vote. As president, Harding soon turned his back on the United States' recent
comrades-in-arms and made a separate peace with recent enemies. But he responded to pressures from League of Nations advocates and called the Washington
Conference on the Limitation of Armament (1921–1922). There the United States secured agreement on limited naval disarmament by making what proved to be costly
concessions in the Pacific. Harding was spared the worst embarrassments of his
scandal-ridden administration by his death in 1923. Puritanical and tight-lipped
Calvin Coolidge succeeded him. Coolidge tried to force the now-unpopular Allies to
pay a substantial part of their war debt to the United States, thus aggravating postwar international economic dislocations. Onetime Progressive Herbert Hoover defeated earthy New York Democrat Al Smith for the presidency in 1928, but his
administration was almost immediately engulfed by the steepest and deepest economic downturn in U.S. history.

A. Warren Harding and the Washington Conference

1. President Harding Hates His Job (c. 1922)

*The Old Guard Republicans nominated President Harding largely because he was a
second-rater whom they could easily manage. The times, one of them said, did not
demand "first-raters." Harding, according to Alice Roosevelt, "was not a bad man.
He was just a slob." In beyond his depth, Harding privately moaned that the job was
too big for him. William Allen White, the peppery Kansas journalist, visited the White*

---

[1]W. A. White, *Autobiography* (1946), p. 616. By permission of The Macmillan Company.

House and talked with the president's secretary, Jud Welliver, an old friend, who (as White remembered it) burst out with the following monologue. What does he identify as Harding's most serious disqualifications for the presidency?

"Lord, Lord, man! You can't know what the President is going through. You see he doesn't understand it; he just doesn't know a thousand things that he ought to know. And he realizes his ignorance, and he is afraid. He has no idea where to turn.

"Not long ago, when the first big tax bill came up, you remember there were two theories of taxation combating for the administration's support. He would listen for an hour to one side, become convinced; and then the other side would get him and overwhelm him with its contentions. Some good friend would walk into the White House all cocked and primed with facts and figures to support one side, and another man who he thought perhaps ought to know would reach him with a counter argument which would brush his friend's theory aside.

"I remember he came in here late one afternoon after a long conference, in which both sides appeared, talked at each other, wrangled over him. He was weary and confused and heartsick, for the man really wants to do the right and honest thing. But I tell you, he doesn't know. That afternoon he stood at my desk and looked at me for a moment and began talking out loud:

" 'Jud,' he cried, 'you have a college education, haven't you? I don't know what to do or where to turn in this taxation matter. Somewhere there must be a book that tells all about it, where I could go to straighten it out in my mind. But I don't know where the book is, and maybe I couldn't read it if I found it! And there must be a man in the country somewhere who could weigh both sides and know the truth. Probably he is in some college or other. But I don't know where to find him. I don't know who he is, and I don't know how to get him. My God, but this is a hell of a place for a man like me to be!' "

2. William Randolph Hearst Blasts Disarmament at Washington (1922)

The infant League of Nations was designed in part to bring about disarmament. But with the powerful United States not a cooperating member, a feverish naval race was clattering forward. Rich Uncle Sam, though still slightly behind Britain, could outstrip all others. The U.S. taxpayers balked, however, and a popular clamor forced Harding to summon a multipower conference at Washington for arms limitation. After prolonged wrangling, the conferees agreed that certain capital ships of the major powers—the United States, Britain, Japan, France, Italy—were to be scrapped and the remainder pegged at a tonnage ratio of 5–5–3–1.7–1.7. The sensitive Japanese were induced to accept an inferior ratio after receiving pledges from the United States and Britain not to fortify further their Far Eastern bases, including the Philippines and Guam. The surrender of potential (but expensive) naval supremacy by "Uncle Sap" aroused much criticism in the United States. The influential Hearst newspapers, traditionally anti-Japanese and anti-British, protested vehemently, as

---

[2]*Selections from the Writings and Speeches of William Randolph Hearst* (1948), pp. 193–194.

follows. In what ways does this selection reflect the mood of the age, as revealed in the preceding chapter?

Great Britain and Japan are the ones who gain in this Conference, the ones who are going home satisfied.

England, a naval empire, and Japan, a militaristic empire, have won all the points at the expense of the Republic of France, the Republic of China, the Republic of Russia, and the United States. . . .

We have surrendered Guam and the fortifications of our island possessions, so that the American Navy would have no bases for naval operations in case war should ever be forced upon us.

We have surrendered the naval supremacy that lay within our grasp, and which would always have protected us from any attack by overseas nations. . . .

We have surrendered the adequate development of our merchant marine, and not even the battleships to be put out of commission by the decision of this Conference can be transformed into merchant vessels.

The United States, the one first-class Power of the world, in wealth, in potential strength, in strategic position and condition, has been transformed into distinctly a second-class Power by the subordinate position it has voluntarily taken with regard to England and Japan.

But worst of all is the fact that Japan, by the recognition formally accorded it in this Conference, has been made the dominant nation among the yellow nations of the world, the militaristic leader of a thousand million racial enemies of the white peoples.

Not only the people of the United States but the peoples of Europe, the white race throughout the world, will pay dearly for this act of criminal folly in times to come.

3. Japan Resents the Washington Setback (1922)

*If the Japanese had won a great diplomatic victory at Washington, they were unaware of it. A Tokyo newspaper (*Yorodzu*) lamented that Uncle Sam, a "hateful and haughty" "international boor," though professing to work for peace, had invited the nations to Washington where he had "tricked them one and all." Indignant mass meetings were held at various places in Japan. The consensus of the Japanese press was that Britain had gained the most, whereas Japan had lost the most. Japan was forced to junk the formidable Anglo-Japanese military alliance, which seemed to menace the United States, and accept for the Pacific a weak four-power consultative pact (the United States, Britain, Japan, and France). "We have discarded whiskey and accepted water," moaned one Japanese diplomat. What aspect of the conference results rankled the Japanese most deeply?*

Our Navy will not have more than 60 percent of the American naval strength hereafter. We must think of some way of improving our relations with America.

---

[3]*Tokyo Kokumin,* quoted in *Literary Digest* 72 (January 28, 1922): 18.

Our Government and delegates have brought forth a quadruple agreement [Four Power Pact], replacing the Anglo-Japanese Alliance. It now becomes clear that Japan's claims will not be granted in future without a judgment by the four Powers. Although there are four nations, England is now in a state so that she cannot oppose the will of America. Any decision in a trial of the court of four Powers will be rendered as America sees fit.

Under the circumstances, no Japanese, however optimistic, will have the heart to be optimistic of Japan's future. No one will be able to deny that Japan has [had] her hands and feet cut off in Washington.

We do not advocate pessimistic views by choice. If there be any material by which we can be optimistic, we [should] like to know what it is. If Japan's position has been improved in any way by the Washington Conference, we [should] like to be informed of it. Reflecting upon Japan, which was thus reduced to a state of blockade on all sides, we cannot but deeply sigh with despair. . . .

American public opinion makes it believed that benefits have been conferred upon Japan. Japan was in a position wherein she was obliged to abandon the Anglo-Japanese Alliance. In place of the Alliance, a quadruple agreement was given to Japan. Thus America has saved Japan's face, American public opinion claims.

By virtue of the quadruple entente, Japan decided not to make an issue out of a race discrimination in America. Our Government and delegates are so magnanimous that they would not raise an issue out of the race discrimination which is insulting to the Japanese race. Nay, our governing classes are never magnanimous. They have never been magnanimous to our countrymen. They are magnanimous to Western peoples. Because they are afraid of Western peoples, they feign to be magnanimous. While being governed by such weak-kneed statesmen, the Japanese race cannot expect to rise above water.

B. The Depression Descends

1. The Plague of Plenty (1932)

In his acceptance speech of 1928, delivered in the Stanford University football stadium, Hoover optimistically envisioned the day when poverty would be banished from the United States. A popular Republican slogan was "a chicken in every pot, a car in every garage." The next year the stock market collapsed and depression descended. Hoover, a "rugged individualist" who had pulled himself up by his own bootstraps, was unwilling to turn Washington into a gigantic soup kitchen for the unemployed. He struggled desperately to halt the depression, but in general his efforts were too little and too late. To boost morale, he issued a number of cheery statements to the effect that prosperity was just around the corner. The following testimony of a newspaper editor, Oscar Ameringer of Oklahoma City, was given in 1932 before a House committee. What is particularly paradoxical about the situation he describes?

---

[1]*Unemployment in the United States. Hearings before a Subcommittee of the Committee on Labor, House of Representatives, Seventy-second Congress, First Session, on H.R. 206 . . . (1932), pp. 98–99.*

During the last three months I have visited, as I have said, some twenty states of this wonderfully rich and beautiful country. Here are some of the things I heard and saw:

In the state of Washington I was told that the forest fires raging in that region all summer and fall were caused by unemployed timber workers and bankrupt farmers in an endeavor to earn a few honest dollars as firefighters. The last thing I saw on the night I left Seattle was numbers of women searching for scraps of food in the refuse piles of the principal market of that city. A number of Montana citizens told me of thousands of bushels of wheat left in the fields uncut on account of its low price that hardly paid for the harvesting. In Oregon I saw thousands of bushels of apples rotting in the orchards. Only absolute[ly] flawless apples were still salable, at from 40 to 50 cents a box containing 200 apples. At the same time, there are millions of children who, on account of the poverty of their parents, will not eat one apple this winter.

While I was in Oregon the Portland *Oregonian* bemoaned the fact that thousands of ewes were killed by the sheep raisers because they did not bring enough in the market to pay the freight on them. And while Oregon sheep raisers fed mutton to the buzzards, I saw men picking for meat scraps in the garbage cans in the cities of New York and Chicago. I talked to one man in a restaurant in Chicago. He told me of his experience in raising sheep. He said that he had killed 3,000 sheep this fall and thrown them down the canyon, because it cost $1.10 to ship a sheep, and then he would get less than a dollar for it. He said he could not afford to feed the sheep, and he would not let them starve, so he just cut their throats and threw them down the canyon.

The roads of the West and Southwest teem with hungry hitchhikers. The camp fires of the homeless are seen along every railroad track. I saw men, women, and children walking over the hard roads. Most of them were tenant farmers who had lost their all in the late slump in wheat and cotton. Between Clarksville and Russellville, Ark., I picked up a family. The woman was hugging a dead chicken under a ragged coat. When I asked her where she had procured the fowl, first she told me she had found it dead in the road, and then added in grim humor, "They promised me a chicken in the pot, and now I got mine."

In Oklahoma, Texas, Arkansas, and Louisiana I saw untold bales of cotton rotting in the fields because the cotton pickers could not keep body and soul together on 35 cents paid for picking 100 pounds. . . .

As a result of this appalling overproduction on the one side and the staggering underconsumption on the other side, 70 per cent of the farmers of Oklahoma were unable to pay the interests on their mortgages. Last week one of the largest and oldest mortgage companies in that state went into the hands of the receiver. In that and other states we have now the interesting spectacle of farmers losing their farms by foreclosure and mortgage companies losing their recouped holdings by tax sales.

The farmers are being pauperized by the poverty of industrial populations, and the industrial populations are being pauperized by the poverty of the farmers. Neither has the money to buy the product of the other, hence we have overproduction and underconsumption at the same time and in the same country.

I have not come here to stir you in a recital of the necessity for relief for our suffering fellow citizens. However, unless something is done for them and done soon, you will have a revolution on hand. And when that revolution comes it will not come from Moscow, it will not be made by the poor Communists whom our police are heading up regularly and efficiently. When the revolution comes it will bear the label "Laid in the U.S.A." and its chief promoters will be the people of American stock.

2. Distress in the South (1932)

As the depression deepened, "Hooverville" shantytowns sprang up, and millions of footsore men sought nonexistent jobs. Some sold apples on wind-swept street corners. Hoover, in his Memoirs, *advances the improbable thesis that these people were exploited by the apple producers and that "many persons left their jobs for the more profitable one of selling apples." Blacks—the last hired and the first fired—were especially hard hit, but the white sharecroppers in the South were scarcely better off. Hoover's policy was that "no one shall starve in this country," but he was criticized for being more willing to use federal funds to supply seed for farmers and feed for animals than food for human beings. Congressman George Huddleston of Alabama thus described conditions in his state before a Senate committee. What kinds of physical and psychic scars were inflicted by the conditions he describes?*

We have a great many tenant farmers there [Alabama]. We have a great many Negro farmers, and practically all of them are tenants. Their ability to survive, to eat, to have a shelter, depends upon the ability of the landlord to supply them with the necessaries of life. They have a system under which they make a contract with the landlord to cultivate his land for the next year, and in the meantime he feeds them through the winter; and at the end of the year they gather their crops and pay for their supplies and rent, if they are able to do so. Conditions in agriculture have been such for several years that the landlords have been gradually impoverished, and their farms are mortgaged to the farm-loan system and to the mortgage companies in a multitude of instances.

In a very large percentage [of cases] the landlord is now unable to finance these tenants for another year. He is unable to get the supplies. He has no security and no money with which to feed and clothe his tenants until they can make another crop. . . .

Many of these people, especially the Negro tenants, are now in the middle of a winter, practically without food and without clothes, and without anything else, and how are they going to live? Many of these local counties have no charitable organizations. They are poor people and impoverished. They have no county funds. There is no place to turn, nobody that has any money that they can turn to and ask for help.

Many white people are in the same kind of a situation. They beg around among their neighbors. The neighbors are poor and they have no means of helping them. They stray here and there.

---

[2]*Unemployment Relief. Hearings before a Subcommittee of the Committee on Manufactures, United States Senate, Seventy-second Congress, First Session, on S. 174 . . .* (1932), pp. 244–245.

Any thought that there has been no starvation, that no man has starved, and no man will starve, is the rankest nonsense. Men are actually starving by the thousands today, not merely in the general sections that I refer to, but throughout this country as a whole, and in my own district. I do not mean to say that they are sitting down and not getting a bite of food until they actually die, but they are living such a scrambling, precarious existence, with suffering from lack of clothing, fuel, and nourishment, until they are subject to be swept away at any time, and many are now being swept away.

The situation has possibilities of epidemics of various kinds. Its consequences will be felt many years. The children are being stunted by lack of food. Old people are having their lives cut short. The physical effects of the privations that they are forced to endure will not pass away within fifty years, and when the social and civic effects will pass away, only God knows. That is something that no man can estimate.

3. Rumbles of Revolution (1932)

Franklin Roosevelt was later acclaimed as the Messiah whose New Deal saved the United States for capitalism by averting armed revolution. He was quoted as saying that if he failed he would be not the worst but the last president of the United States. Certainly in 1932 the signs were ominous. Hundreds of midwestern farmers were picketing the highways to keep their underpriced produce from reaching market, overturning milk trucks, overpowering armed deputies, releasing prisoners from jail. With increasing millions of desperate people out of work and with thousands defying the police, the worst might have happened. The testimony in the following selection of Oscar Ameringer, the Oklahoma newspaperman, is impressive. Does it confirm that the talk of revolution was to be taken seriously?

Some time ago a cowman came into my office in Oklahoma City. He was one of these double-fisted gentlemen, with the gallon hat and all. He said, "You do not know me from Adam's ox."

I said: "No; I do not believe I know you." . . .

He said, "I came to this country without a cent, but, knowing my onions, and by tending strictly to business, I finally accumulated two sections of land and a fine herd of white-faced Hereford cattle. I was independent."

I remarked that anybody could do that if he worked hard and did not gamble and used good management.

He said, "After the war, cattle began to drop, and I was feeding them corn, and by the time I got them to Chicago the price of cattle, considering the price of corn I had fed them, was not enough to even pay my expenses. I could not pay anything."

Continuing, he said, "I mortgaged my two sections of land, and to-day I am cleaned out; by God, I am not going to stand for it."

I asked him what he was going to do about it, and he said, "We have got to have a revolution here like they had in Russia and clean them up."

I finally asked him, "Who is going to make the revolution?"

---

[3]*Unemployment in the United States, Hearings before a Subcommittee of the Committee on Labor, House of Representatives, Seventy-second Congress, First Session, on H.R. 206* . . . (1932), pp. 100–101.

He said, "I just want to tell you I am going to be one of them, and I am going to do my share in it."

I asked what his share was and he said, "I will capture a certain fort. I know I can get in with twenty of my boys," meaning his cowboys, "because I know the inside and outside of it, and I [will] capture that with my men."

I rejoined, "Then what?"

He said, "We will have 400 machine guns, so many batteries of artillery, tractors, and munitions and rifles, and everything else needed to supply a pretty good army."

Then I asked, "What then?"

He said, "If there are enough fellows with guts in this country to do like us, we will march eastward and we will cut the East off. We will cut the East off from the West. We have got the granaries; we have the hogs, the cattle, the corn; the East has nothing but mortgages on our places. We will show them what we can do."

That man may be very foolish, and I think he is, but he is in dead earnest; he is a hard-shelled Baptist and a hard-shelled Democrat, not a Socialist or a Communist, but just a plain American cattleman whose ancestors went from Carolina to Tennessee, then to Arkansas, and then to Oklahoma. I have heard much of this talk from serious-minded prosperous men of other days.

As you know, talk is always a mental preparation for action. Nothing is done until people talk and talk and talk it, and they finally get the notion that they will do it.

I do not say we are going to have a revolution on hand within the next year or two, perhaps never. I hope we may not have such; but the danger is here. That is the feeling of our people—as reflected in the letters I have read. I have met these people virtually every day all over the country. There is a feeling among the masses generally that something is radically wrong. They are despairing of political action. They say the only thing you do in Washington is to take money from the pockets of the poor and put it into the pockets of the rich. They say that this Government is a conspiracy against the common people to enrich the already rich. I hear such remarks every day.

I never pass a hitchhiker without inviting him in and talking to him. Bankers even are talking about that. They are talking in irrational tones. You have more Bolshevism among the bankers to-day than the hod carriers, I think. It is a terrible situation, and I think something should be done and done immediately.

C. Herbert Hoover Clashes with Franklin Roosevelt

1. On Public Versus Private Power

a. Hoover Upholds Free Enterprise (1932)

President Hoover, the wealthy conservative, instinctively shied away from anything suggesting socialism. In 1931 he emphatically vetoed the Muscle Shoals bill, which would have put the federal government in the electric power business on the Tennessee River. (An expanded version later created the Tennessee Valley Authority

---

[1a]*New York Times,* November 1, 1932 (speech at Madison Square Garden, New York, October 31, 1932).

[TVA] under President Roosevelt.) Hoover ringingly reaffirmed his basic position in a speech during the Hoover-Roosevelt presidential campaign of 1932. Why was he so strongly opposed to federally owned electric power? Why would he have found local community ownership more acceptable?

I have stated unceasingly that I am opposed to the Federal Government going into the power business. I have insisted upon rigid regulation. The Democratic candidate has declared that under the same conditions which may make local action of this character desirable, he is prepared to put the Federal Government into the power business. He is being actively supported by a score of Senators in this campaign, many of whose expenses are being paid by the Democratic National Committee, who are pledged to Federal Government development and operation of electrical power.

I find in the instructions to campaign speakers issued by the Democratic National Committee that they are instructed to criticize my action in the veto of the bill which would have put the Government permanently into the operation of power at Muscle Shoals, with a capital from the Federal Treasury of over $100,000,000. In fact thirty-one Democratic Senators, being all except three, voted to override that veto.

In that bill was the flat issue of the Federal Government permanently in competitive business. I vetoed it because of principle and not because it especially applied to power business. In that veto, I stated that I was firmly opposed to the Federal Government entering into any business, the major purpose of which is competition with our citizens. . . .

From their utterances in this campaign and elsewhere it appears to me that we are justified in the conclusion that our opponents propose to put the Federal Government in the power business.

b. Roosevelt Pushes Public Power (1932)

Franklin Roosevelt, who as governor of New York had shown much concern for the Niagara–St. Lawrence River power resources, had already locked horns with the private utility magnates. As president, he later had a large hand in launching the TVA project, which also involved fertilizer, flood control, and improved navigation. He presented his views on public power as follows during the campaign of 1932. Are his arguments more convincing than Hoover's?

I therefore lay down the following principle: That where a community—a city or county or a district—is not satisfied with the service rendered or the rates charged by the private utility, it has the undeniable basic right, as one of its functions of government, one of its functions of home rule, to set up, after a fair referendum to its voters has been had, its own governmentally owned and operated service. . . .

My distinguished opponent is against giving the Federal Government, in any case, the right to operate its own power business. I favor giving the people this right

---

[1b]*Roosevelt's Public Papers,* vol. 1, pp. 738, 741–742 (speech at Portland, Oregon, September 21, 1932).

where and when it is essential to protect them against inefficient service or exorbitant charges.

As an important part of this policy, the natural hydro-electric power resources belonging to the people of the United States, or the several States, shall remain forever in their possession.

To the people of this country I have but one answer on this subject. Judge me by the enemies I have made. Judge me by the selfish purposes of these utility leaders who have talked of radicalism while they were selling watered stock to the people, and using our schools to deceive the coming generation.

My friends, my policy is as radical as American liberty. My policy is as radical as the Constitution of the United States.

I promise you this: Never shall the Federal Government part with its sovereignty or with its control over its power resources, while I am President of the United States.

2. On Government in Business

a. Hoover Assails Federal Intervention (1932)

Hoover's conservative nature recoiled from the prospect of government in business, especially on the scale envisaged by the TVA. Annoyed by Democratic charges that he was a complete reactionary, he struck back in a major campaign speech at Madison Square Garden. Laboriously written by himself (he was the last president to scorn ghostwriters), it was perhaps the best conceived of his campaign. "Every time the Federal Government extends its arm," he declared, "531 Senators and Congressmen become actual boards of directors of that business." What truth is there in his charge that government in business invites a species of servitude?

There is one thing I can say without any question of doubt—that is, that the spirit of liberalism is to create free men. It is not the regimentation of men. It is not the extension of bureaucracy. I have said in this city [New York] before now that you cannot extend the mastery of government over the daily life of a people without somewhere making it master of people's souls and thoughts.

Expansion of government in business means that the Government, in order to protect itself from the political consequences of its errors, is driven irresistibly, without peace, to greater and greater control of the Nation's press and platform. Free speech does not live many hours after free industry and free commerce die.

It is a false liberalism that interprets itself into Government operation of business. Every step in that direction poisons the very roots of liberalism. It poisons political equality, free speech, free press, and equality of opportunity. It is the road not to liberty but to less liberty. True liberalism is found not in striving to spread bureaucracy, but in striving to set bounds to it. . . .

Even if the Government conduct of business could give us the maximum of efficiency instead of least efficiency, it would be purchased at the cost of freedom. It

---

[2a]*New York Times,* November 1, 1932 (speech at Madison Square Garden, New York, October 31, 1932).

would increase rather than decrease abuse and corruption, stifle initiative and invention, undermine development of leadership, cripple mental and spiritual energies of our people, extinguish equality of opportunity, and dry up the spirit of liberty and progress.

Men who are going about this country announcing that they are liberals because of their promises to extend the Government in business are not liberals; they are reactionaries of the United States.

b. Roosevelt Attacks Business in Government (1932)

The Reconstruction Finance Corporation (RFC), established late in the Hoover administration, was designed primarily to bail out hard-pressed banks and other big businesses—"a bread line for bankers." Charles G. Dawes, former vice president of the United States, hastily resigned as the head of the RFC so that his Chicago bank might secure an emergency loan of $80 million to stave off bankruptcy. The Democrats, who argued that loans to ordinary citizens were no less imperative, attacked this presumed favoritism. How well does Roosevelt, in the following campaign speech, refute the Republican philosophy of separating government and business?

Some of my friends tell me that they do not want the Government in business. With this I agree, but I wonder whether they realize the implications of the past. For while it has been American doctrine that the Government must not go into business in competition with private enterprises, still it has been traditional, particularly in Republican administrations, for business urgently to ask the Government to put at private disposal all kinds of Government assistance.

The same man who tells you that he does not want to see the Government interfere in business—and he means it, and has plenty of good reasons for saying so—is the first to go to Washington and ask the Government for a prohibitory tariff on his product. When things get just bad enough, as they did two years ago, he will go with equal speed to the United States Government and ask for a loan; and the Reconstruction Finance Corporation is the outcome of it.

Each group has sought protection from the government for its own special interests, without realizing that the function of Government must be to favor no small group at the expense of its duty to protect the rights of personal freedom and of private property of all its citizens.

3. On Balancing the Budget

a. Hoover Stresses Economy (1932)

Hoover, the Iowa orphan, was dedicated to strict economy, a sound dollar, and the balanced budget. He was alarmed by proposals in the Democratic House to unbalance the budget further by voting huge sums to provide jobs for the unemployed. One proposed public works scheme called for the construction of 2,300 new post offices.

[2b]*Roosevelt's Public Papers,* vol. 1, p. 748 (Commonwealth Club speech, San Francisco, September 23, 1932).

[3a]*New York Times,* May 28, 1932 (Washington press conference of May 27, 1932).

The upkeep and interest charges on these would cost $14 million a year, whereas, he noted, "the upkeep and rent of buildings at present in use amounts to less than $3,000,000." Hoover unburdened himself as follows at a press conference. In the light of subsequent developments, did he overemphasize the effects of an unbalanced budget in relation to uneconomical public works? (Since 1932 the federal Treasury has more often than not shown an annual deficit.)

The urgent question today is the prompt balancing of the Budget. When that is accomplished, I propose to support adequate measures for relief of distress and unemployment.

In the meantime, it is essential that there should be an understanding of the character of the draft bill made public yesterday in the House of Representatives for this purpose. That draft bill supports some proposals we have already made in aid to unemployment, through the use of the Reconstruction Finance Corporation, to make loans for projects which have been in abeyance and which proposal makes no drain on the taxpayer. But in addition it proposes to expend about $900,000,000 for Federal public works.

I believe the American people will grasp the economic fact that such action would require appropriations to be made to the Federal Departments, thus creating a deficit in the Budget that could only be met with more taxes and more Federal bond issues. That makes balancing of the Budget hopeless.

The country also understands that an unbalanced budget means the loss of confidence of our own people and of other nations in the credit and stability of the Government, and that the consequences are national demoralization and the loss of ten times as many jobs as would be created by this program, even if it could be physically put into action. . . .

This is not unemployment relief. It is the most gigantic pork barrel ever proposed to the American Congress. It is an unexampled raid on the public Treasury.

b. Roosevelt Stresses Humanity (1932)

The Democratic platform of 1932, which assailed Republican extravagance and deficits, had come out squarely for a balanced budget. A favorite slogan of the Democrats was, "Throw the spenders out." When Roosevelt died thirteen years later, the national debt (including war costs) had risen some $19 billion to $258 billion. During the campaign of 1932, Roosevelt expressed his views on a balanced budget as follows. In the light of these views, did his later record constitute a breach of faith with the voters?

Let us have the courage to stop borrowing to meet continuing deficits. Stop the deficits! Let us have equal courage to reverse the policy of the Republican leaders and insist on a sound currency. . . .

This dilemma can be met by saving in one place what we would spend in others, or by acquiring the necessary revenue through taxation. Revenues must cover

---

[3b]*Roosevelt's Public Papers,* vol. 1, pp. 662, 663, 810. (The first two paragraphs are taken from a radio address from Albany, July 30, 1932; the last paragraph is taken from a speech at Pittsburgh, October 19, 1932.)

expenditures by one means or another. Any Government, like any family, can for a year spend a little more than it earns. But you and I know that a continuation of that habit means the poorhouse. . . .

The above two categorical statements are aimed at a definite balancing of the budget. At the same time, let me repeat from now to election day so that every man, woman, and child in the United States will know what I mean: If starvation and dire need on the part of any of our citizens make necessary the appropriation of additional funds which would keep the budget out of balance, I shall not hesitate to tell the American people the full truth and ask them to authorize the expenditure of that additional amount.

4. On Restricted Opportunity

a. Roosevelt Urges Welfare Statism (1932)

"Why change?" cried Republicans in the campaign of 1932. "Things could be worse." A slight business upturn did occur in the summer, but a sag soon followed—resulting, claimed Hoover, from fear of a Rooseveltian revolution. Roosevelt himself jeered that the "no change" argument was like saying, "Do not swap toboggans while you are sliding downhill." He set forth his own concept of change in his memorable Commonwealth Club speech in San Francisco. Was his argument regarding the overbuilding of the United States' industrial plant sound in the light of subsequent history?

A glance at the situation today only too clearly indicates that equality of opportunity, as we have known it, no longer exists. Our industrial plant is built; the problem just now is whether under existing conditions it is not overbuilt.

Our last frontier has long since been reached, and there is practically no more free land. More than half of our people do not live on the farms or on lands, and cannot derive a living by cultivating their own property. There is no safety valve in the form of a Western prairie, to which those thrown out of work by the Eastern economic machines can go for a new start.* We are not able to invite the immigration from Europe to share our endless plenty. We are now providing a drab living for our own people. . . .

Recently a careful study was made of the concentration of business in the United States. It showed that our economic life was dominated by some six hundred odd corporations, who controlled two-thirds of American industry. Ten million small business men divided the other third. More striking still, it appeared that if the process of concentration goes on at the same rate, at the end of another century we shall have all American industry controlled by a dozen corporations, and run by perhaps a hundred men. Put plainly, we are steering a steady course toward economic oligarchy, if we are not there already.

Clearly, all this calls for a re-appraisal of values. A mere builder of more industrial plants, a creator of more railroad systems, an organizer of more corporations, is

---

4a*Roosevelt's Public Papers,* vol. 1, pp. 750–753 (speech of September 23, 1932).
*For the safety-valve notion, see note, p. 147.

as likely to be a danger as a help. The day of the great promoter or the financial Titan, to whom we granted anything if only he would build, or develop, is over.

Our task now is not discovery or exploitation of natural resources, or necessarily producing more goods. It is the soberer, less dramatic business of administering resources and plants already in hand, of seeking to re-establish foreign markets for our surplus production, of meeting the problem of underconsumption, of adjusting production to consumption, of distributing wealth and products more equitably, of adapting existing economic organizations to the service of the people. The day of enlightened administration has come.

b. Hoover Calls for New Frontiers (1932)

Roosevelt's annoying vagueness prompted Hoover to refer to "a chameleon on plaid." Smarting from the New Dealish overtones of the Commonwealth Club speech, Hoover struck back in his Madison Square Garden speech. Did he interpret the United States' past and future with greater accuracy than Roosevelt did?

But I do challenge the whole idea that we have ended the advance of America, that this country has reached the zenith of its power, the height of its development. That is the counsel of despair for the future of America. That is not the spirit by which we shall emerge from this depression. That is not the spirit that made this country. If it is true, every American must abandon the road of countless progress and unlimited opportunity. I deny that the promise of American life has been fulfilled, for that means we have begun the decline and fall. No nation can cease to move forward without degeneration of spirit.

I could quote from gentlemen who have emitted this same note of pessimism in economic depressions going back for a hundred years. What Governor Roosevelt has overlooked is the fact that we are yet but on the frontiers of development of science, and of invention. I have only to remind you that discoveries in electricity, the internal-combustion engine, the radio—all of which have sprung into being since our land was settled—have in themselves represented the greatest advances in America.

The philosophy upon which the Governor of New York proposes to conduct the Presidency of the United States is the philosophy of stagnation, of despair. It is the end of hope. The destinies of this country should not be dominated by that spirit in action. It would be the end of the American system.

D. An Appraisal of Hoover

1. Hoover Defends His Record (1932)

Hoover smarted under charges that he had not fought the "Hoover depression" with every ounce of energy for the benefit of all the people. Such accusations, he asserted,

---

[4b]*New York Times,* November 1, 1932 (speech at Madison Square Garden, New York, October 31, 1932).
[1]*New York Times,* October 5, 1932 (speech of October 4, 1932).

were "deliberate, intolerable falsehoods." At times he put in an eighteen-hour day, remarking that his office was a "compound hell." When he spoke wearily at St. Paul during the last stages of the 1932 campaign, a man was stationed behind him ready to thrust forward an empty chair if he collapsed. In a major speech at Des Moines, Iowa, he thus refuted charges that he was a "see-nothing, do-nothing president." What is the least convincing part of this recital?

We have fought an unending war against the effect of these calamities upon our people. This is no time to recount the battles on a thousand fronts. We have fought the good fight to protect our people in a thousand cities from hunger and cold.

We have carried on an unceasing campaign to protect the Nation from that un-healing class bitterness which arises from strikes and lockouts and industrial conflict. We have accomplished this through the willing agreement of employer and labor, which placed humanity before money through the sacrifice of profits and dividends before wages.

We have defended millions from the tragic result of droughts.

We have mobilized a vast expansion of public construction to make work for the unemployed.

We [have] fought the battle to balance the Budget.

We have defended the country from being forced off the gold standard, with its crushing effect upon all who are in debt.

We have battled to provide a supply of credits to merchants and farmers and industries.

We have fought to retard falling prices.

We have struggled to save homes and farms from foreclosure of mortgages; battled to save millions of depositors and borrowers from the ruin caused by the failure of banks; fought to assure the safety of millions of policyholders from failure of their insurance companies; and fought to save commerce and employment from the failure of railways.

We have fought to secure disarmament and maintain the peace of the world; fought for stability of other countries whose failure would inevitably injure us. And, above all, we have fought to preserve the safety, the principles, and ideals of American life. We have builded the foundations of recovery. . . .

Thousands of our people in their bitter distress and losses today are saying that "things could not be worse." No person who has any remote understanding of the forces which confronted this country during these last eighteen months ever utters that remark. Had it not been for the immediate and unprecedented actions of our government, things would be infinitely worse today.

2. Roosevelt Indicts Hoover (1932)

Roosevelt did not use kid gloves in his ghostwritten campaign speeches. (The one at Topeka represented his own efforts and those of some twenty-five assistants.) Though crediting Hoover with "unremitting efforts," he assailed him for having claimed credit for prosperity while disclaiming responsibility for the depression; for having

---

[2]*Roosevelt's Public Papers,* vol. 1, p. 677 (speech of August 20, 1932).

placed the blame for the depression on wicked foreigners instead of on shortsighted Republican economic policies; for having marked time and issued airily optimistic statements when he should have grasped the bull by the horns. At Pittsburgh, Roosevelt cried, "I do indict this Administration for wrong action, for delayed action, for lack of frankness and for lack of courage." At Columbus, Ohio, he presented the following bill of particulars. What is the unfairest part of his indictment?

Finally, when facts could no longer be ignored and excuses had to be found, Washington discovered that the depression came from abroad. In October of last year, the official policy came to us as follows: "The depression has been deepened by events from abroad which are beyond the control either of our citizens or our Government"—an excuse, note well, my friends, which the President still maintained in his acceptance speech last week.

Not for partisan purposes, but in order to set forth history aright, that excuse ought to be quietly considered. The records of the civilized Nations of the world prove two facts: first, that the economic structure of other Nations was affected by our own tide of speculation, and the curtailment of our lending helped to bring on their distress; second, that the bubble burst in the land of its origin—the United States.

The major collapse in other countries followed. It was not simultaneous with ours. Moreover, further curtailment of our loans, plus the continual stagnation in trade caused by the Grundy [Hawley-Smoot] tariff, has continued the depression throughout international affairs.

So I sum up the history of the present Administration in four sentences:

First, it encouraged speculation and overproduction, through its false economic policies.

Second, it attempted to minimize the [1929 stock market] crash and misled the people as to its gravity.

Third, it erroneously charged the cause to other Nations of the world.

And finally, it refused to recognize and correct the evils at home which had brought it forth; it delayed relief; it forgot reform.

Thought Provokers

1. What lessons does the Washington disarmament conference of 1921–1922 hold for arms-control negotiations?
2. What puzzled people most about the impact of the Great Depression? Who was hardest hit? Why was there not more radicalism in the depression-era United States?
3. Hoover was a former associate of Woodrow Wilson, as was Franklin Roosevelt. In what ways might they both be considered "Wilsonians"? What were the sharpest differences between them?
4. No other man in the United States had a higher reputation than Hoover in the 1920s, and none rated lower in public esteem in the early 1930s. Was this reversal of public opinion justified? Should Hoover be admired for the constancy of his beliefs, even under severe criticism?

34

The Great Depression and the New Deal, 1933–1939

I pledge you, I pledge myself, to a new deal for the American people.

Franklin D. Roosevelt, Accepting Nomination of Democratic National Convention, 1932

Prologue: The Depression lay heavily upon the land as Roosevelt boldly set up numerous New Deal agencies designed to provide relief, recovery, and reform. He presided over one of the most active periods of political innovation in the Republic's history. His programs forever changed the structure of U.S. social and economic life, although they never did fully defeat the devastating Great Depression. Roosevelt ignored campaign pledges to reduce government expenses, balance the budget, prune the bureaucracy, maintain a sound currency, and eliminate the improper use of money in politics. But he honored other promises, directly or indirectly, in the reciprocal tariff program, the repeal of prohibition, the insurance of bank deposits, and the encouragement of labor unions. Roosevelt, a knowledgeable naturalist, also initiated several environmental programs, including enormous construction projects aimed at taming the great rivers of the Tennessee, Missouri, Columbia, and Colorado. On the left, critics complained that the New Deal was not radical enough. Yet conservative critics of the New Deal cried that Roosevelt promoted class hatred by setting the poor against the rich. New Dealers retorted that they were merely putting need above greed. The voters endorsed Roosevelt so resoundingly at the polls in 1934 and 1936 that he was emboldened to unveil his scheme for "packing" the Supreme Court in 1937. Though soundly rebuffed, he won an unprecedented third-term election in 1940, with a strong assist from the crisis in Europe and a new war-born prosperity.

A. The Face of the Great Depression

1. Cesar Chavez Gets Tractored off the Land (1936)

Cesar Chavez, born in Arizona in 1927, became famous in the 1960s as the president of the United Farm Workers of America, a labor union organized to protect

---

[1]From Edwin G. Hill, *In the Shadow of the Mountain: The Spirit of the CCC*, p. 175. Copyright © 1990. Reprinted by permission from Washington State University. All rights reserved.

309

migratory farmworkers, mostly Mexican and Mexican-American, who harvested many of the crops in the American West. Here he tells of his eviction from his boyhood home near Yuma, Arizona, in the depths of the Great Depression. How did he assess the Depression's impact on his father and the rest of his family? In what ways might the experience of the Depression have contributed to his later commitment to organizing the farmworkers?

Oh, I remember having to move out of our house. My father had brought in a team of horses and wagon. We had always lived in that house, and we couldn't understand why we were moving out. When we got to the other house, it was a worse house, a poor house. That must have been around 1934. I was about six years old.

It's known as the North Gila Valley, about fifty miles north of Yuma. My dad was being turned out of his small plot of land. He had inherited this from his father, who had homesteaded it. I saw my two, three other uncles also moving out. And for the same reason. The bank had foreclosed on the loan.

If the local bank approved, the Government would guarantee the loan and small farmers like my father would continue in business. It so happened the president of the bank was the guy who most wanted our land. We were surrounded by him: he owned all the land around us. Of course, he wouldn't pass the loan.

One morning a giant tractor came in, like we had never seen before. My daddy used to do all his work with horses. So this huge tractor came in and began to knock down this corral, this small corral where my father kept his horses. We didn't understand why. In the matter of a week, the whole face of the land was changed. Ditches were dug, and it was different. I didn't like it as much.

We all of us climbed into an old Chevy that my dad had. And then we were in California, and migratory workers. There were five kids—a small family by those standards. It must have been around '36. I was about eight. Well, it was a strange life. We had been poor, but we knew every night there was a bed *there,* and that *this* was our room. There was a kitchen. It was sort of a settled life, and we had chickens and hogs, eggs and all those things. But that all of a sudden changed. When you're small you can't figure these things out. You know something's not right and you don't like it, but you don't question it and you don't let that get you down. You sort of just continue to move.

But this had quite an impact on my father. He had been used to owning the land and all of a sudden there was no more land. What I heard . . . what I made out of conversations between my mother and my father—things like, we'll work this season and then we'll get enough money and we'll go and buy a piece of land in Arizona. Things like that. Became like a habit. He never gave up hope that some day he would come back and get a little piece of land.

I can understand very, very well this feeling. These conversations were sort of melancholy. I guess my brothers and my sisters could also see this very sad look on my father's face.

2. A Salesman Goes on Relief (1930s)

Ben Isaacs was a door-to-door clothing salesman when the Depression hit. His weekly income suddenly plummeted from $400 to $10, and then to nothing. Eventually he had to go on relief. What was the most difficult part of his experience? What does he think about the surge of post–World War II prosperity?

I was in business for myself, selling clothing on credit, house to house. And collecting by the week. Up to that time, people were buying very good and paying very good. But they start to speculate, and I felt it. My business was dropping from the beginning of 1928. They were mostly middle-class people. They weren't too rich, and they weren't too poor.

All of a sudden, in the afternoon, October, 1929 . . . I was going on my business and I heard the newspaper boys calling, running all around the streets and giving news and news: stock market crashed, stock market crashed. It came out just like lightning. . . .

We lost everything. It was the time I would collect four, five hundred dollars a week. After that, I couldn't collect fifteen, ten dollars a week. I was going around trying to collect enough money to keep my family going. It was impossible. Very few people could pay you. Maybe a dollar if they would feel sorry for you or what.

We tried to struggle along living day by day. Then I couldn't pay the rent. I had a little car, but I couldn't pay no license for it. I left it parked against the court. I sold it for $15 in order to buy some food for the family. I had three little children. It was a time when I didn't even have money to buy a pack of cigarettes, and I was a smoker. I didn't have a nickel in my pocket.

Finally people started to talk me into going into the relief. They had open soup kitchens. Al Capone,* he had open soup kitchens somewhere downtown, where people were standing in line. And you had to go two blocks, stand there, around the corner, to get a bowl of soup.

Lotta people committed suicide, pushed themselves out of buildings and killed themselves, 'cause they couldn't face the disgrace. Finally, the same thing with me.

I was so downcasted that I couldn't think of anything. Where can I go? What to face? Age that I can't get no job. I have no trade, except selling is my trade, that's all. I went around trying to find a job as a salesman. They wouldn't hire me on account of my age. I was just like dried up. Every door was closed on me, every avenue. Even when I was putting my hand on gold, it would turn into dust. It looked like bad luck had set its hand on my shoulder. Whatever I tried, I would fail. Even my money.

I had two hundred dollar in my pocket. I was going to buy a taxi. You had to have your own car to drive a taxi, those days. The man said: You have to buy your car from us. Checker Cab Company. So I took the two hundred dollar to the office, to make a down payment on the taxi. I took the money out—he said the kind of car we haven't got, maybe next week. So I left the office, I don't know what happened.

---

[2]From *Hard Times* by Studs Terkel. Copyright © 1970 by Studs Terkel. Reprinted by permission of Pantheon Books, a division of Random House, Inc.
*Al Capone was a notorious Chicago gangster.

The two hundred dollar went away, just like that. I called back: Did you find any money on the table? He said no, no money.

Things were going so bad with me, I couldn't think straight. Ordinarily, I won't lose any money. But that time, I was worrying about my family, about this and that. I was walking the street just like the easy person, but I didn't know whether I was coming or going.

I didn't want to go on relief. Believe me, when I was forced to go to the office of the relief, the tears were running out of my eyes. I couldn't bear myself to take money from anybody for nothing. If it wasn't for those kids—I tell you the truth—many a time it came to my mind to go commit suicide. Than go ask for relief. But somebody has to take care of those kids. . . .

I went to the relief and they, after a lotta red tape and investigation, they gave me $45 a month. Out of that $45 we had to pay rent, we had to buy food and clothing for the children. So how long can that $45 go? I was paying $30 on the rent. I went and find another a cheaper flat, stove heat, for $15 a month. I'm telling you, today a dog wouldn't live in that type of a place. Such a dirty, filthy, dark place.

I couldn't buy maybe once a week a couple of pounds of meat that was for Saturday. The rest of the days, we had to live on a half a pound of baloney. I would spend a quarter for half a pound of baloney. It was too cold for the kids, too unhealthy. I found a six-room apartment for $25 a month. It was supposed to be steam heat and hot water. Right after we move in there, they couldn't find no hot water. It wasn't warm enough for anybody to take a bath. We had to heat water on the stove. Maybe the landlord was having trouble with the boiler. But it was nothing like that. The landlord had abandoned the building. About two months later, all of a sudden—no water. The city closed it for the non-payment of the water bill.

My wife used to carry two pails of water from the next-door neighbors and bring it up for us to wash the kids and to flush the toilet with it, and then wash our hands and face with it, or make tea or something, with that two pails of water. We lived without water for almost two months.

Wherever I went to get a job, I couldn't get no job. I went around selling razor blades and shoe laces. There was a day I would go over all the streets and come home with fifty cents, making a sale. That kept going until 1940, practically. 1939 the war started. Things start to get a little better. My wife found a job in a restaurant for $20 a week. Right away, I sent a letter to the relief people: I don't think I would need their help any more. I was disgusted with relief, so ashamed. I couldn't face it any more.

My next-door neighbor found me a job in the factory where he was working. That time I was around fifty. The man said, "We can't use you." They wouldn't hire nobody over forty-five. Two weeks later, this same man said, "Go tell Bill (the name of the foreman) I sent you. He'll hire you." They hire me. They give me sixty cents an hour. Twenty-year-old boys, they were paying seventy, seventy-five cents an hour. They were shortage of hand, that's why they hire me. . . .

But in those days, we were all on relief and they were going around selling razor blades and shoe laces.

We were going to each other's. That was the only way we could drown our sorrow. We were all living within a block of each other. We'd come to each other's house and sit and talk and josh around and try to make a little cheerfulness.

Today we live far away from the rest of our friends. Depression days, that time, we were all poor. After things got better and people became richer and everyone had their own property at different neighborhoods, we fall apart from each other.

3. A Boy in Chicago Writes to President Roosevelt (1936)

In an unprecedented outpouring, tens of thousands of Americans in the Depression wrote directly to the president about their plight. Their letters, often written in rough English, nevertheless provide eloquent testimony about the personal bond that many people felt with the president and with his wife, Eleanor, and they offer vivid glimpses of the predicaments in which millions of Americans found themselves. The following letter was written by a twelve-year-old boy in Chicago in February 1936. What does he think is the Depression's worst impact on his family?

Mr. and Mrs. Roosevelt.
Wash. D. C.
Dear Mr. President:

I'm a boy of 12 years. I want to tell you about my family. My father hasn't worked for 5 months. He went plenty times to relief, he filled out application. They won't give us anything. I don't know why. Please you do something. We haven't paid 4 months rent, Everyday the landlord rings the door bell, we don't open the door for him. We are afraid that will be put out, been put out before, and don't want to happen again. We haven't paid the gas bill, and the electric bill, haven't paid grocery bill for 3 months. My brother goes to Lane Tech. High School. he's eighteen years old, hasn't gone to school for 2 weeks because he got no carfare. I have a sister she's twenty years, she can't find work. My father he staying home. All the time he's crying because he can't find work. I told him why are you crying daddy, and daddy said why shouldn't I cry when there is nothing in the house. I feel sorry for him. That night I couldn't sleep. The next morning I wrote this letter to you. in my room. Were American citizens and were born in Chicago, Ill. and I don't know why they don't help us Please answer right away because we need it. will starve Thank you.

God bless you.

[Anonymous]
Chicago, Ill.

4. Hard Times in a North Carolina Cotton Mill (1938–1939)

Sam T. Mayhew was a black North Carolinian who worked in a cotton mill. The cotton textile industry was among the economic sectors hardest hit by the Great Depression, and Mayhew, along with thousands of other mill workers, lost his job. How did he survive? What is his attitude toward welfare?

---

[3]From *Down and Out in the Great Depression: Letters from the Forgotten Man,* by Robert S. McElvaine. Copyright © 1983 by the University of North Carolina Press. Used by permission of the publisher.

[4]From *Such as Us: Southern Voices of the Thirties,* edited by Tom E. Terrill and Jerrold Hirsch. Copyright © 1978 by the University of North Carolina Press. Used by permission of the publisher.

"At present I belong to the ranks of the unemployed. I have regular employment only four months of the annum, and sometimes that is just part-time." Sam T. Mayhew throws away the end of a fat cigar and settles back comfortably to be interviewed. The black expanse of face above hefty shoulders is interrupted by an impressive black mustache, which presents itself before the discontent in the big black eyes registers.

"The past year it was just part-time. We worked at the gin [cotton mill] a few days the first of September and then were laid off till the middle, when the gin started running again. The gin shut down for the year on December 24, which gave me around 78 working days, 26 days to the month, for the year. I am paid $2 a day at the gin. So my income this year was 2 times 78—$156, I believe it is. I've got it all figured out and set down here in this little book. Now, to get an estimate of how much my family of seven has to live on, divide $156 by 12. I've figured it out; it's less than 50 cents a week, 7 and a fraction cents a day apiece for us, with everything we eat and wear coming out of the store. It's [wrong] . . . to say folks can't live that cheap; they can and do when they have to, such living as it is.

"Since February, I've been getting a little relief help from the government. Everything they've give since my first trip to Jackson I've set down in this little book; it starts out with 24 pounds of flour, 5 pounds of butter, 3 pounds of prunes and beans and ends up with 17 grapefruits and 3 pounds of butter, which is all they give me last week. I've figured up what the government has give me since February—counting flour at 75 cents, butter at 30 and so forth—and it comes to exactly $14.60. I've estimated that is just one-fourth of what we ought to have to live on, to eat. Several times I've asked for clothes the women make at the sewing room, but each time those have been denied.

"There's three grown folks and four children at my house, but what these children really ought to eat is more expensive than what we could manage on. I read considerably about the diet children ought to have—milk, butter, eggs, cereals, and fruits—but I can't stretch my income to provide it. I'm particular concerned into diets and meals, because at my house I have to do practically all the cooking since my wife has been physically and mentally incapacitated. My mother always taught her boys as well as girls to do every kind of work that came to hand, from cooking to washing, and it's well she did. The way I start the day is this: first, I make a fire in the stove, heat some lard in my frying pan, cut up an onion in the hot grease, then sift some flour and pepper and salt in the pan, and when the mixture is brown add a little water. This is the main dish for breakfast. Sometimes I stir up some egg bread with a spoon to serve with this onion gravy, sometimes biscuits.

"After breakfast the children get off to school and are gone till three-thirty in the afternoon. By time they get home, I try to have them a hot dish of dried peas or beans and some prunes or canned fruit if we have any. When there's meat, I season the beans with a little slice which I cut up into six pieces—I can't eat hog meat myself on account of high blood pressure—but when meat's out, I put a spoonful of lard in the pot for seasoning. Lunch? We don't have any lunch; two meals a day is all we have winter and summer. The children don't get very hungry, because they're used to it; sometimes when they see other children at school with candy and cakes, it's right hard on them. But they know I don't have so much as a nickel extra to give them to buy an apple or orange, and they don't complain.

"Sam Junior is in the eighth grade at school. He is the *Virginian-Pilot* paper boy and makes eighty cents a week, which only about takes care of his school supplies and book rentals. I don't know what Sam Junior wants to be yet; sometimes I think I ought to talk to him and help him decide. Then I'm afraid I won't be able to help him reach his achievement, which would make him more disappointed than if he had never planned anything. So, I'm just waiting, not saying yet what I'd like to see him do. . . .

"No, I never thought about settling up North. There's no such hard distinction about color there, though. Four or five years ago, when I was trying without success to get the welfare to buy me a new artificial limb, I wrote to President Roosevelt asking him to interefere in my behalf, stating my circumstances and needs. In a short while here came a letter from the president, assuring me that the matter would be attended to through the proper agencies at once. I know it wasn't long before the welfare office at Jackson ordered me a new limb! My typewriter* already had more than paid for itself—the limb was around $125—in what it has done for me personally and toward the advancement of education among our race, not to mention the pleasure it is to conduct business matters in a businesslike way." . . .

B. An Enigma in the White House

I. The Agreeable FDR (1949)

The smiling, wisecracking Franklin Roosevelt could occasionally be brutal when he "got his Dutch up," but ordinarily he recoiled from hurting people's feelings. Senator Huey Long complained, "I wonder if he says 'Fine!' to everybody." This trait of ultra-agreeableness led visitors to suspect a lack of candor and truthfulness. In the following account from Mrs. Roosevelt's memoirs, note particularly why the president was often misunderstood.

The few books that have already been written about Franklin show quite plainly that everyone writes from his own point of view, and that a man like my husband, who was particularly susceptible to people, took color from whomever he was with, giving to each one something different of himself. Because he disliked being disagreeable, he made an effort to give each person who came in contact with him the feeling that he understood what his particular interest was. . . .

Often people have told me that they were misled by Franklin. Even when they have not said it in so many words, I have sometimes felt that he left them, after an interview, with the idea that he was in entire agreement with them. I would know quite well, however, that he was not, and that they would be very much surprised when later his actions were in complete contradiction to what they thought his attitude would be.

This misunderstanding not only arose from his dislike of being disagreeable, but from the interest that he always had in somebody else's point of view and his

---

*The typewriter had been purchased earlier out of Mayhew's meager savings.
[1]Eleanor Roosevelt, *This I Remember* (1949), p. 2.

willingness to listen to it. If he thought it was well expressed and clear, he nodded his head and frequently said, "I see," or something of the sort. This did not mean that he was convinced of the truth of the arguments, or even that he entirely understood them, but only that he appreciated the way in which they were presented.

2. Coffee for the Veterans (1933)

In 1932, during Herbert Hoover's last year as president, some thirty thousand unemployed veterans had descended on Washington to obtain advance bonus payments from Congress. They occupied vacant buildings, erected makeshift camps without proper sanitation, and posed a threat to the public health and safety. A fearful Hoover, having doubled the White House guard, finally gave orders that resulted in their eviction by federal troops with bayonets, tear gas, and torches. A second, smaller bonus army came early in the Roosevelt administration, and Secretary of Labor Frances Perkins (the first female cabinet member) describes how Roosevelt welcomed them. How do Roosevelt's political instincts compare with those of Hoover?

Like other kindhearted, liberal people, Roosevelt had been shocked by President Hoover's orders to drive veterans of World War I out of Anacostia Flats in Washington and to burn their encampment when they had marched there in protest in 1931 [1932]. He had been shocked that the President should fear his fellow citizens. His instinct had cried out that veterans in an illegal encampment in Washington, even if difficult and undesirable, must all be faced in a human and decent way. He had said little, had just shaken his head and shuddered, when the incident took place.

When the veterans came to Washington in March 1933, in a similar, if smaller, march on the capital followed by an encampment, Roosevelt drove out and showed himself, waving his hat at them. He asked Mrs. Roosevelt and Louis Howe* to go. "Above all," he said to them, "be sure there is plenty of good coffee. No questions asked. Just let free coffee flow all the time. There is nothing like it to make people feel better and feel welcome."

After the veterans in 1933 had the free coffee and a visit from Mrs. Roosevelt, they were willing to send a committee to talk with Howe. Gradually they began to go home, and relief funds were found to help them start back.

[This was the last demonstration of its kind during these years.]

3. FDR the Administrative "Artist" (1948)

The numerous and overlapping agencies of the New Deal created an atmosphere of indescribable confusion. Roosevelt was generally reputed to be a wretchedly bad

---

[2]From *The Roosevelt I Knew* by Frances Perkins. Copyright 1946 by Frances Perkins; © renewed 1974 by Susanna W. Coggeshall. Used by permission of Viking Penguin, a division of Penguin Putnam, Inc.

*A former newspaperman, Howe was a key Roosevelt aide and speechwriter.

[3]From *Roosevelt and Hopkins: An Intimate History*. Copyright © 1948, 1950 by Robert E. Sherwood. Copyright renewed © 1976, 1978 by Madeline H. Sherwood. Reprinted by permission of Brandt & Brandt Literary Agents, Inc.

administrator. Rather than face a disagreeable scene by dismissing an incompetent subordinate, he would set up a competing agency. Robert E. Sherwood, playwright and winner of three Pulitzer Prizes, served with a government agency (the Office of War Information) during World War II. He was forced to discharge one of his employees, and here he tells what happened when he reported this unpleasant incident to the president. In what sense was Roosevelt both a poor administrator and a superior one?

Roosevelt now had an expression of open amazement and said, "I can't believe it. I can't believe you had the courage to fire anybody. I thought you were a complete softy—like me."

That scrap of highly unimportant conversation can indicate why those who knew Roosevelt well could never imagine him assuming the role of dictator. He could be and was ruthless and implacable with those whom he considered guilty of disloyalty; but with those in his Administration who were inefficient or even recalcitrant or hopelessly inept, but loyal, he was "a complete softy." He wasted precious hours of time and incalculable quantities of energy and ingenuity trying to find face-saving jobs—or "kicking upstairs" methods—for incompetents who should have been thrown out unceremoniously.

Roosevelt's methods of administration—typified in his handling of the work relief organization—were, to say the least, unorthodox. They filled some practical-minded observers with apprehension and dismay, and some with disgust; they filled others with awe and wonder. I am sure that no final appraisal of them can be made for a long time to come; but there is one thing that can be said about these methods—whether they were good or bad, sensible or insane, they *worked*.

While preparing this book I interviewed Harold Smith, who was Director of the Budget from 1939 to 1946. Smith was a modest, methodical, precise man, temperamentally far removed from Roosevelt and Hopkins. But I know of no one whose judgment and integrity and downright common sense the President trusted more completely. In the course of a long conversation, Smith said to me:

"A few months ago, on the first anniversary of Roosevelt's death, a magazine asked me to write an article on Roosevelt as an administrator. I thought it over and decided I was not ready to make such an appraisal. I've been thinking about it ever since. When I worked with Roosevelt—for six years—I thought, as did many others, that he was a very erratic administrator. But now, when I look back, I can really begin to see the size of his programs. They were by far the largest and most complex programs that any President ever put through. People like me who had the responsibility of watching the pennies could only see the five or six or seven per cent of the programs that went wrong, through inefficient organization or direction. But now I can see in perspective the ninety-three or -four or -five per cent that went right—including the winning of the biggest war in history—because of unbelievably skillful organization and direction. And if I were to write that article now, I think I'd say that Roosevelt must have been one of the greatest geniuses as an administrator that ever lived. What we couldn't appreciate at the time was the fact that he was a real *artist* in government."

That word "artist" was happily chosen, for it suggests the quality of Roosevelt's extraordinary creative imagination. I think that he would have resented the application of the word as implying that he was an impractical dreamer; he loved to represent himself as a prestidigitator who could amaze and amuse the audience by "pulling another rabbit out of a hat." But he was an artist and no canvas was too big for him.

C. Voices of Protest

1. Senator Huey P. Long Wants Every Man to Be a King (1934)

Senator Huey P. Long of Louisiana (1893–1935) helped Franklin Roosevelt win the Democratic party's nomination for the presidency in 1932. But Long quickly made himself a thorn in Roosevelt's flesh, especially with his demands for radical redistribution of the nation's income. Roosevelt worried that Long might emerge as a rival for leadership of the Democratic party and might even be elected president in 1940, but Long's career was cut short by an assassin's bullet in 1935. Long was a flamboyant personality and a sulfurous speaker. His radio audiences included millions of spellbound and supposedly sympathetic listeners. In the excerpt from his radio address of February 23, 1934, given here, what appear to be the main sources of his popular appeal? How responsible were his proposals? In what ways did he represent an alternative to Roosevelt's New Deal?

Now, we have organized a society, and we call it share-our-wealth society, a society with the motto "Every man a king."

Every man a king, so there would be no such thing as a man or woman who did not have the necessities of life, who would not be dependent upon the whims and caprices and ipsi dixit of the financial martyrs for a living. What do we propose by this society? We propose to limit the wealth of big men in the country. There is an average of $15,000 in wealth to every family in America. That is right here today.

We do not propose to divide it up equally. We do not propose a division of wealth, but we propose to limit poverty that we will allow to be inflicted upon any man's family. We will not say we are going to try to guarantee any equality, or $15,000 to families. No; but we do say that one third of the average is low enough for any one family to hold, that there should be a guaranty of a family wealth of around $5,000; enough for a home, an automobile, a radio, and the ordinary conveniences, and the opportunity to educate their children; a fair share of the income of this land thereafter to that family so there will be no such thing as merely the select to have those things, and so there will be no such thing as a family living in poverty and distress.

We have to limit fortunes. Our present plan is that we will allow no one man to own more than $50 million. We think that with that limit we will be able to carry out the balance of the program. It may be necessary that we limit it to less than $50

---

[1]Senator Huey P. Long, "Every Man a King," *Congressional Record,* March 1, 1934.

million. It may be necessary, in working out of the plans, that no man's fortune would be more than $10 million or $15 million. But be that as it may, it will still be more than any one man, or any one man and his children and their children, will be able to spend in their lifetimes; and it is not necessary or reasonable to have wealth piled up beyond that point where we cannot prevent poverty among the masses.

Another thing we propose is [an] old-age pension of $30 a month for anyone that is 60 years old. Now, we do not give this pension to a man making $1,000 a year, and we do not give it to him if he has $10,000 in property, but outside of that we do.

We will limit hours of work. There is not any necessity of having overproduction. I think all you have got to do, ladies and gentlemen, is just limit the hours of work to such an extent as people will work only so long as is necessary to produce enough for all of the people to have what they need. Why, ladies and gentlemen, let us say that all of these labor-saving devices reduce hours down to where you do not have to work but four hours a day; that is enough for these people, and then praise be the name of the Lord, if it gets that good. Let it be good and not a curse, and then we will have 5 hours a day and five days a week, or even less than that, and we might give a man a whole month off during a year, or give him two months; and we might do what other countries have seen fit to do, and what I did in Louisiana, by having schools by which adults could go back and learn the things that have been discovered since they went to school.

We will not have any trouble taking care of the agricultural situation. All you have to do is balance your production with your consumption. You simply have to abandon a particular crop that you have too much of, and all you have to do is store the surplus for the next year, and the Government will take it over. When you have good crops in the area in which the crops that have been planted are sufficient for another year, put in your public works in the particular year when you do not need to raise any more, and by that means you get everybody employed. When the Government has enough of any particular crop to take care of all of the people, that will be all that is necessary; and in order to do all of this, our taxation is going to be to take the billion-dollar fortunes and strip them down to frying size, not to exceed $50 million and if it is necessary to come to $10 million, we will come to $10 million. We have worked the proposition out to guarantee a limit upon property (and no man will own less than one third the average), and guarantee a reduction of fortunes and a reduction of hours to spread wealth throughout this country. We would care for the old people above 60 and take them away from this thriving industry and give them a chance to enjoy the necessities and live in ease, and thereby lift from the market the labor which would probably create a surplus of commodities.

Those are the things we propose to do. "Every man a king." Every man to eat when there is something to eat; all to wear something when there is something to wear. That makes us all a sovereign.

You cannot solve these things through these various and sundry alphabetical codes. You can have the NRA and PWA and CWA and the UUG and GIN and any other kind of "dadgummed" lettered code. You can wait until doomsday and see twenty-five more alphabets, but that is not going to solve this proposition. Why hide? Why quibble? You know what the trouble is. The man that says he does not know what the trouble is is just hiding his face to keep from seeing the sunlight.

God told you what the trouble was. The philosophers told you what the trouble was; and when you have a country where one man owns more than 100,000 people, or a million people, and when you have a country where there are four men, as in America, that have got more control over things than all the 130 million people together, you know what the trouble is.

We had these great incomes in this country; but the farmer, who plowed from sunup to sundown, who labored here from sunup to sundown for six days a week, wound up at the end of the time with practically nothing. . . .

Get together in your community tonight or tomorrow and organize one of our share-our-wealth societies. If you do not understand it, write me and let me send you the platform; let me give you the proof of it.

This is Huey P. Long talking, United States Senator, Washington, D.C. Write me and let me send you the data on this proposition. Enroll with us. Let us make known to the people what we are going to do. I will send you a button, if I have got enough of them left. We have got a little button that some of our friends designed, with our message around the rim of the button, and in the center "Every man a king." Many thousands of them are meeting through the United States, and every day we are getting hundreds and hundreds of letters. Share-our-wealth societies are now being organized, and people have it within their power to relieve themselves from this terrible situation. . . .

2. Father Coughlin Demands "Social Justice" (1934, 1935)

Father Charles E. Coughlin (1891–1979), a Canadian-born Roman Catholic priest, was a master of the new medium of the radio, rivaled perhaps only by Franklin Roosevelt. Speaking from the pulpit of his parish church in the modest working-class community of Royal Oak, Michigan, he commanded audiences of millions of listeners for his weekly broadcasts in the 1930s. It was said that a stroller could walk through certain neighborhoods on a summer Sunday afternoon and not miss a word of Father Coughlin's sermon as his voice wafted from radios through parlor windows into the streets. At first, Coughlin supported the New Deal, but he grew more critical and more viciously antisemitic, as well as passionately isolationist, as time went on. In the portions of his radio addresses reprinted here, to what social groups does he seem primarily to be speaking? What does he mean by "social justice"? How much of an alternative to the New Deal did he represent?

. . . , These shall be the principles of social justice towards the realization of which we must strive:

1. I believe in liberty of conscience and liberty of education, not permitting the state to dictate either my worship to my God or my chosen avocation in life.

---

[2]The Rev. Chas. E. Coughlin, *A Series of Lectures on Social Justice* (Royal Oak, Mich.: Radio League of the Little Flower, 1935), pp. 16–19, 232–236.

2. I believe that every citizen willing to work and capable of working shall receive a just, living, annual wage which will enable him both to maintain and educate his family according to the standards of American decency.

3. I believe in nationalizing those public resources which by their very nature are too important to be held in the control of private individuals.

4. I believe in private ownership of all other property.

5. I believe in upholding the right to private property but in controlling it for the public good.

6. I believe in the abolition of the privately owned Federal Reserve Banking system and in the establishment of a Government owned Central Bank.

7. I believe in rescuing from the hands of private owners the right to coin and regulate the value of money, which right must be restored to Congress where it belongs.

8. I believe that one of the chief duties of this Government owned Central Bank is to maintain the cost of living on an even keel and arrange for the repayment of dollar debts with equal value dollars.

9. I believe in the cost of production plus a fair profit for the farmer.

10. I believe not only in the right of the laboring man to organize in unions but also in the duty of the Government, which that laboring man supports, to protect these organizations against the vested interests of wealth and of intellect.

11. I believe in the recall of all non-productive bonds and therefore in the alleviation of taxation.

12. I believe in the abolition of tax-exempt bonds.

13. I believe in broadening the base of taxation according to the principles of ownership and the capacity to pay.

14. I believe in the simplification of government and the further lifting of crushing taxation from the slender revenues of the laboring class.

15. I believe that in the event of a war for the defense of our nation and its liberties, there shall be a conscription of wealth as well as a conscription of men.

16. I believe in preferring the sanctity of human rights to the sanctity of property rights; for the chief concern of government shall be for the poor because, as it is witnessed, the rich have ample means of their own to care for themselves.

These are my beliefs. These are the fundamentals of the organization which I present to you under the name of the NATIONAL UNION FOR SOCIAL JUSTICE. It is your privilege to reject or to accept my beliefs; to follow me or to repudiate me.

Hitherto you have been merely an audience. Today, in accepting the challenge of your letters, I call upon everyone of you who is weary of drinking the bitter vinegar of sordid capitalism and upon everyone who is fearsome of being nailed to the cross of communism to join this Union which, if it is to succeed, must rise above the concept of an audience and become a living, vibrant, united, active organization, superior to politics and politicians in principle, and independent of them in power.

This work cannot be accomplished in one week or two weeks or in three months, perchance. But it must begin today, at this moment. It shall be a Union for the employed and the unemployed, for the old and the young, for the rich and the poor, independent of race, color or creed. It is my answer to the challenge received from the youth of the nation; my answer to those who have dared me to act!

All I ask of you today is that you voluntarily subscribe your name to this Union. In addressing your letter to me, please be careful to note well the county in which you live as well as the State. Information will be sent to you for your organization within your own county and your own district. . . .

Pursuing our principles in the program for social justice, permit me to refer to the attitude of the National Union towards public and private property. In diagnosing the economic ills of America we are convinced that there is a growing tendency to diminish the ownership of private property. In one sense, there is too little of private ownership. This is caused, first, by an economic system which persistently tends to concentrate wealth in the hands of a few, and, second, by an obnoxious system of taxation which discourages private ownership.

On the other hand, there are some things which, by their nature, should be owned nationally or publicly. Among these things there are listed the Central Bank which will have the sole right of issuing, coining and regulating the value of money be it currency or credit. In no sense does the National Union propose to nationalize any other bank. The local banking system must be kept intact. Its functions of safeguarding depositors' money and of extending local loans upon a reasonable basis must not be destroyed. It is regrettable that more than $773-million, or 23 per cent of the capital stock of these banks is now owned by the government. It would be a benediction, however, if the government nationalized the Federal Reserve Bank, whose capital stock is valued at approximately $140-million.

Then there are the natural resources scattered throughout the nation. The ownership and development of Niagara Falls, of the St. Lawrence Waterway, which is capable of generating one million two hundred thousand horsepower, of Boulder Dam, of the Tennessee Valley project, of the Grand Coulee on the Colorado—these and other natural resources should be owned and developed by the nation. In no sense should they be farmed out for private exploitation. The National Union further subscribes in its principles to a permanent public works program of reforestation, of land reclamation, of slum clearance, of national highway building and of other public activities whereat the idle factory workers may be employed during slack industrial seasons.

Relative to the many public utilities, the National Union regards the great majority of their holding companies as economic maladies. In many cases these holding companies were born in iniquity. By their nature they deceived the investing public. By their desire for greedy gain, oftentimes they marked up their values three, four and five times the tangible value of their physical properties. On this false basis they sold their securities to an unsuspecting public.

However, the National Union is not convinced that the ownership and the operation of public utilities should be nationalized. We prescribe that these should be kept in private hands subject to governmental supervision. At all times we must avoid the communistic tendency to sovietize industry or public service enterprises. Two extremes confront us: The one is advocating the national ownership of those things which should be retained in private hands; the other is advocating and supporting the private ownership of those things which should be owned in public.

Thus, while we cling to this twofold principle of ownership—one public, the other, private—let it also be noted that even private ownership must be subject to public regulation for the public good.

Relying upon that principle, the theory is sustained that, for the public welfare, the government may enact salutary laws to regulate not only personal liberties but also property and industrial liberties. Private ownership must be protected against corporate ownership. Small business must be safeguarded reasonably against monopolistic business. Were we to permit private ownership and small business gradually to be assimilated by corporate and monopolistic creations, then we are only preparing the way either for state capitalism or for communism.

3. Norman Thomas Proposes Socialism (1934)

Norman Thomas (1884–1968), a Princeton University graduate and ordained Presbyterian minister, succeeded Eugene Debs as head of the Socialist party and was several times the party's presidential candidate, but he always polled fewer than 1 million popular votes, and he never won a single electoral vote. Here he lays out the Socialist program for coping with the Depression. What are his main criticisms of the New Deal? Why did socialism not establish more of a foothold in Depression America?

All that I have said implies an importance in America of an immediate program of social insurance, unemployment relief, agricultural aid, and the guarantee of civil liberty, including the right of all workers to organize. It certainly implies that immediate concern for peace and an immediate program for preserving it, such as we have already discussed. But the essential feature of any immediate program for Socialism which is of value, and the one thing which will make an immediate program a sound beginning of the transitional period, is a redistribution of the national income on a basis that will give to workers collectively the fruits of their labor. Without this there is no cure for unemployment, bitter poverty, recurring crises and ultimate collapse. Now a kind of patchwork job of limited redistribution of income can be done, as everybody knows, by a program of high taxation on the rich and various social benefits for the poor. But this can never reach to the heart of our problem. Redistribution of the national income should not be a process of intervention by government to restore to the robbed a small portion of what has been taken from them. It should be a process of ending exploitation and establishing a scheme of things in which production is naturally and logically for use rather than for the private profit of an owning class. There is no such scheme of things which does not require social ownership. It follows that the immediate and essential objective of any desirable program must be the socialization and proper management of key industries. Socialization is not identical with nationalization. Increasingly it must be on an international scale. Immediately it may include ownership and operation by bona fide consumers' coöperatives. But practically the next steps toward socialization will require a process by which the national government will take over ownership. Such nationalization will fall short of socialization if, for instance, railroads should be taken over for military purposes, or banks in order to make a state capitalism more efficient. True socialization can never lose sight of the great purpose of shared abundance. . . .

. . . On March 4, 1933, a Socialist administration ought to have begun with the socialization of banking. In rapid succession it would have taken over railroads, coal mines, and the power and oil industries. Then, as I have already indicated, it would have turned its attention to other monopolies. Any worthwhile agricultural program will compel the government to set up socialized marketing agencies and to take over and run as a public non-profit-making organization the dairy trust and probably the packing houses. In some cases it might not be necessary or desirable for the government to acquire all the existing property of, let us say, the power corporations or the dairy trust. It might condemn those facilities necessary for building up a great and economical system in conjunction with resources and facilities already in possession of governmental agencies, federal, state, and local.

This brief discussion of the necessity for capturing political power brings us face to face with the most challenging of all our American failures. That is, our failure to organize any strong party which consciously represents the great masses of workers who look toward the coöperative commonwealth. The debates on philosophy and tactics carried on with so much bitterness by our working-class parties and sects leave the masses almost untouched. Neither their discontent nor their rising hopes have yet found expression in a mighty and militant party. . . .

4. Dr. Francis E. Townsend Promotes Old-Age Pensions (1933)

Dr. Francis E. Townsend (1867–1960) was an obscure sixty-six-year-old physician in 1933 when he penned a letter to his local newspaper in Long Beach, California, that set off a tidal wave of enthusiasm for his old-age pension plan. Within weeks, "Townsend Clubs" sprouted up all over the country to promote Dr. Townsend's proposal, and by the following year the clubs claimed to have over 2 million members. What were the main features of Townsend's idea? How practical was it? To what extent did the Social Security Act of 1935 owe to pressure from the Townsendites?

It is estimated that the population of the age of 60 and above in the United States is somewhere between nine and twelve millions. I suggest that the national government retire all who reach that age on a monthly pension of $200 a month or more, on condition that they spend the money as they get it. This will insure an even distribution throughout the nation of two or three billions of fresh money each month. Thereby assuring a healthy and brisk state of business, comparable to that we enjoyed during war times.

Where is the money to come from? More taxes? Certainly. We have nothing in this world we do not pay taxes to enjoy. But do not overlook the fact that we are already paying a large proportion of the amount required for these pensions in the form of life insurance policies, poor farms, aid societies, insane asylums and prisons. The inmates of the last two mentioned institutions would undoubtedly be greatly lessened when it once became assured that old age meant security from want and care. A sales tax sufficiently high to insure the pensions at a figure adequate to maintain the business of the country in a healthy condition would be the easiest tax

---

[4]Dr. Francis E. Townsend, *New Horizons (An Autobiography)* (New York: J. L. Stewart, 1943), pp. 137–140.

in the world to collect, for all would realize that the tax was a provision for their own future, as well as the assurance of good business now.

Would not a sales tax of sufficient size to maintain a pension system of such magnitude exhaust our taxability from our sources?, I am asked. By no means—income and inheritance taxes would still remain to us, and would prove far more fertile sources of Government income than they are today. Property taxes could be greatly reduced and would not constitute a penalty upon industry and enterprise.

Our attitude toward Government is wrong. We look upon Government as something entirely foreign to ourselves; as something over which we have no control, and which we cannot expect to do us a great deal of good. We do not realize that it can do us infinite harm, except when we pay our taxes. But the fact is, we must learn to expect and demand that the central Government assume the duty of regulating business activity. When business begins to slow down and capital shows signs of timidity, stimulus must be provided by the National Government in the form of additional capital. When times are good and begin to show signs of a speculative debauch such as we saw in 1929, the brakes must be applied through a reduction of the circulation medium. This function of the Government could be easily established and maintained through the pension system for the aged.

D. The Struggle to Organize Labor

1. Tom Girdler Girds for Battle (1937)

The New Dealers, with their strong appeal to the low-waged voter, encouraged the unionization of labor, notably through the Wagner Act of 1935. "Big steel" (including the U.S. Steel Corporation) reluctantly accepted unionization by the CIO (Committee for Industrial Organization). "Little steel," led by the tough-fisted but mild-appearing Tom Girdler, who became a hero to conservatives, struck back. At his Republic Steel Company's plant in Chicago on Memorial Day 1937, the police fired upon and killed ten strikers, while wounding many others. Several additional lives were lost in Ohio cities. Girdler, before a Senate committee, here justifies his opposition. Are the tactics of the CIO defensible (if correctly reported)? Are the accusations regarding communism convincing?

First of all let me make it clear that the fundamental issue in this strike is not one involving wages, hours, or working conditions in Republic [Steel Company] plants. This is not a strike in the sense that a large body of our employees quit work because of grievances against the company. What has happened is that an invading army descended upon our plants and forced many of our employees from their jobs.

Fully 23,000 of our employees have remained at work throughout the strike despite threats and violence, and many additional thousands have been kept from work against their will.

---

[1]"Delivery or Non-Delivery of Mail in Industrial Strife Areas," Senate Committee on Post Offices, *Hearings,* 75th Cong., 1st sess. (1937), pp. 207–210.

The basic issue of this strike is the right of American citizens to work, free from molestation, violence, coercion, and intimidation by a labor organization whose apparent policy is either to rule or to ruin American industry. . . .

The difficulties in the present dispute arise from the fact that the company will not enter into a contract, oral or written, with an irresponsible party; and the C.I.O., as presently constituted, is wholly irresponsible. . . .

The irresponsibility of the C.I.O. is well established by the fact that 200 strikes and walk-outs have taken place in the plants of the General Motors Corporation since that corporation signed an agreement with the C.I.O. which called for an end of strikes during the period of the agreement. . . .

Further evidence of the irresponsible character of the C.I.O. is to be seen in the lawless and terroristic conduct of its members since the beginning of the present strike. Republic plants have been surrounded by armed crowds who call themselves pickets and who, by force and violence, have imprisoned in the plants thousands of employees who refused to heed the strike call and remained at work. These men have been prevented from returning to their families when their work is done, and other employees who want to work have been prevented from getting into the plants.

Airplanes delivering food to workers besieged in the plants have been fired upon by armed mobs about the gates. The delivery of the United States mails has been interfered with. Railroad tracks have been dynamited. Families of men who are at work in the plants in certain communities have been threatened, coerced, and stoned. Defiance of law and order has been so flagrant that in some communities law enforcement has completely collapsed.

These illegal practices have not been peculiar to the Republic strike. They have characterized C.I.O. methods since the beginning of its organization drive in many industries. They have more than confirmed the conclusion reached by this company before the present strike ever started that the C.I.O. was and is an irresponsible and dangerous force in America. . . .

We believe that the C.I.O. with its terroristic methods and Communistic technique of picketing constitutes the most dangerous threat to the preservation of democracy in the United States. . . .

Now, let me state a few fundamental conclusions which I have reached about the C.I.O.

First. The C.I.O. has denied to free American citizens who refuse to pay tribute to it the right to work.

Second. The C.I.O. encourages and promotes violence and disregard of law. If this is done under instructions and approval of its leaders, it amounts to a confession on their part that they are deliberately adopting the methods of force and terrorism which have proved so successful for the dictators of Europe. If this is done without their approval and occurs because they cannot control their own men, it is a confession that the C.I.O. is an irresponsible party and that a contract with it would not be worth the paper upon which it is written.

Third. The C.I.O. is associated with Communism. Many of its leaders and organizers are avowed Communists. The *Daily Worker,* the official newspaper of the Communist Party of the United States, gives the C.I.O. its full support. Can any organization which welcomes the support of the International Communist Party still claim that it adheres to the principles of democracy?

2. John Lewis Lambastes Girdler (1937)

John L. Lewis—gruff, domineering, shaggy-browed—had risen from the depths of the coal mines to the head of the potent United Mine Workers of America. Seeking new worlds to conquer, he undertook to unionize mass-production industries through his Committee for Industrial Organization (CIO). The clash between him and Tom Girdler—both strong-minded men—became so noisy that FDR himself burst out, "A plague on both your houses." Four years later, in 1941, Girdler's "little steel" was forced to accept unionization. In this impassioned speech over a radio hookup, Lewis betrayed his anger. What was his loudest complaint? Why did he regard people like Girdler as more dangerous than communists?

Five of the corporations in the steel industry elected to resist collective bargaining and undertook to destroy the steel-workers' union. These companies filled their plants with industrial spies, assembled depots of guns and gas bombs, established barricades, controlled their communities with armed thugs, leased the police power of cities, and mobilized the military power of a state to guard them against the intrusion of collective bargaining within their plants.

During this strike eighteen steel workers were either shot to death or had their brains clubbed out by police, or armed thugs in the pay of the steel companies. . . .

The steel workers have now buried their dead, while the widows weep and watch their orphaned children become objects of public charity. The murder of these unarmed men has never been publicly rebuked by any authoritative officer of the state or federal government. Some of them, in extenuation, plead lack of jurisdiction, but murder as a crime against the moral code can always be rebuked without regard to the niceties of legalistic jurisdiction by those who profess to be the keepers of the public conscience.

[Tom] Girdler, of Republic Steel, in the quiet of his bedchamber, doubtless shrills his psychopathic cackles as he files notches on his corporate gun and views in retrospect the ruthless work of his mercenary killers. . . .

The United States Chamber of Commerce, the National Association of Manufacturers, and similar groups representing industry and financial interests are rendering a disservice to the American people in their attempts to frustrate the organization of labor and in their refusal to accept collective bargaining as one of our economic institutions.

These groups are encouraging a systematic organization of vigilante groups to fight unionization under the sham pretext of local interests. They equip these vigilantes with tin hats, wooden clubs, gas masks, and lethal weapons, and train them in the arts of brutality and oppression. They bring in snoops, finks [strikebreakers], hatchet gangs, and Chowderhead Cohens to infest their plants and disturb the communities.

Fascist organizations have been launched and financed under the shabby pretext that the C.I.O. movement is Communistic. The real breeders of discontent and alien doctrines of government and philosophies subversive of good citizenship are such as these who take the law into their own hands. No tin-hat brigade of goose-

---

[2]*Vital Speeches* 3 (September 15, 1937): 731 (speech of September 3, 1937).

stepping vigilantes or bibble-babbling mob of blackguarding and corporation-paid scoundrels will prevent the onward march of labor, or divert its purpose to play its natural and rational part in the development of the economic, political, and social life of our nation. . . .

Do those who have hatched this foolish cry of Communism in the C.I.O. fear the increased influence of labor in our democracy? Do they fear its influence will be cast on the side of shorter hours, a better system of distributed employment, better homes for the underprivileged, social security for the aged, a fairer distribution of the national income?

Certainly the workers that are being organized want a voice in the determination of these objectives of social justice.

E. Conservation in the New Deal

1. Back-Country Poets Reflect on the Civilian Conservation Corps (1934, 1935)

The Civilian Conservation Corps (CCC) was one of the most popular of New Deal programs. From its inception in 1933 to its demise in 1942, more than 3 million young men served in the CCC, for periods ranging from six months to two years. Each received bed and board and a monthly salary of $30, of which he was required to send $25 home to his family. The CCC built trails in the national parks and forests, fought wildfires, helped to erect dams and bridges, and planted millions of trees in the nation's denuded forestlands. The CCC provided more than much-needed income to Depression-pinched young men and their families. It also acquainted millions of city dwellers with the outdoors, many for the first time in their lives, and helped to spread the ideals of conservation. In these two specimens of barracks poetry from CCC enlistees, published in the CCC national newspaper, Happy Days, *what do they identify as the most positive and the most negative aspects of their service? How might the attitudes shaped by CCC service have carried over into the World War II and postwar eras?*

What Might Have Been
(To Mr. Roosevelt)
By Raymond Kraus
Co. 1232, Olympia, Wash.

A pauper's life we might have led,
And died revolting for our bread;
We might have shed each other's blood,
And died face down within the mud.

---

[1]From Edwin G. Hill, *In the Shadow of the Mountain. The Spirit of the CCC*, p. 175. Copyright ©1990. Reprinted by permission from Washington State University. All rights reserved.

But all because we have this man,
Whose only words are there: "I can!"
Our nation shall evolve on high,
And we shall see a brighter sky.

He gave to us the chance to say,
I've earned my bread and keep today,
The chance to smile, to toil, to sweat,
This damn depression thus forget.

The Wail of a Spike Camper
By R. F. McMahon, Co. 1744
Avery, Idaho

I joined a brand new outfit
They called it the CCC
They issued me my clothing
And put three shots in me.
They sent me out to a spike camp
Put a cot beneath my frame
They gave me a thousand-pound hammer
And a pick to go with same.
They fed me mush and eggs and bacon
I never got to town
It looks to me like I'm a sucker
Until my time runs down.

2. A Daughter of the Plains Struggles with Dust Storms (1934)

Mother Nature and carelessly exploitative farming practices combined in the 1930s to lay waste much of the Great Plains from the Dakotas to Texas. The "Dust Bowl," a region around the Texas and Oklahoma panhandles, was so cruelly blighted by enormous dust storms during the Depression years that it came to stand as a symbol of the accumulated devastation of centuries of unbridled development. The great dust storms helped to spur a renewed conservation effort in the New Deal era. Ann Marie Low, who lived in North Dakota, recorded in her diary some of the storms' worst ravages. What were the major hardships that she had to endure?

[*April 25, 1934, Wednesday*] Last weekend was the worst dust storm we ever had. We've been having quite a bit of blowing dirt every year since the drouth started, not only here, but all over the Great Plains. Many days this spring the air is just full of dirt coming, literally, for hundreds of miles. It sifts into everything. After we wash the dishes and put them away, so much dust sifts into the cupboards we must wash them again before the next meal. Clothes in the closets are covered with dust.

---

[2]Reprinted from *Dust Bowl Diary* by Ann Marie Low by permission of the University of Nebraska Press. Copyright © 1984 by the University of Nebraska Press.

Last weekend no one was taking an automobile out for fear of ruining the motor. I rode Roany to Frank's place to return a gear. To find my way I had to ride right beside the fence, scarcely able to see from one fence post to the next.

Newspapers say the deaths of many babies and old people are attributed to breathing in so much dirt.

[*May 7, 1934, Monday*] The dirt is still blowing. Last weekend Bud [her brother] and I helped with the cattle and had fun gathering weeds. Weeds give us greens for salad long before anything in the garden is ready. We use dandelions, lamb's quarter, and sheep sorrel. I like sheep sorrel best. Also, the leaves of sheep sorrel, pounded and boiled down to a paste, make a good salve.

Still no job. I'm trying to persuade Dad I should apply for rural school #3 out here where we went to school. I don't see a chance of getting a job in a high school when so many experienced teachers are out of work.

He argues that the pay is only $60.00 a month out here, while even in a grade school in town I might get $75.00. Extra expenses in town would probably eat up that extra $15.00. Miss Eston, the practice teaching supervisor, told me her salary has been cut to $75.00 after all the years she has been teaching in Jamestown. She wants to get married. School boards will not hire married women teachers in these hard times because they have husbands to support them. Her fiancé is the sole support of his widowed mother and can't support a wife, too. So she is just stuck in her job, hoping she won't get another salary cut because she can scarcely live on what she makes and dress the way she is expected to.

Dad argues the patrons always stir up so much trouble for a teacher at #3 some teachers have quit in mid-term. The teacher is also the janitor, so the hours are long.

I figure I can handle the work, kids, and patrons. My argument is that by teaching here I can work for my room and board at home, would not need new clothes, and so could send most of my pay to Ethel [her sister] and Bud.

In April, Ethel had quit college, saying she did not feel well.

[*May 21, 1934, Monday*] Ethel has been having stomach trouble. Dad has been taking her to doctors though suspecting her trouble is the fact that she often goes on a diet that may affect her health. The local doctor said he thought it might be chronic appendicitis, so Mama took Ethel by train to Valley City last week to have a surgeon there remove her appendix.

Saturday Dad, Bud, and I planted an acre of potatoes. There was so much dirt in the air I couldn't see Bud only a few feet in front of me. Even the air in the house was just a haze. In the evening the wind died down, and Cap came to take me to the movie. We joked about how hard it is to get cleaned up enough to go anywhere.

The newspapers report that on May 10 there was such a strong wind the experts in Chicago estimated 12,000,000 tons of Plains soil was dumped on that city. By the next day the sun was obscured in Washington, D.C., and ships 300 miles out at sea reported dust settling on their decks.

Sunday the dust wasn't so bad. Dad and I drove cattle to the Big Pasture. Then I churned butter and baked a ham, bread, and cookies for the men, as no telling when Mama will be back.

[*May 30, 1934, Wednesday*] Ethel got along fine, so Mama left her at the hospital and came to Jamestown by train Friday. Dad took us both home.

The mess was incredible! Dirt had blown into the house all week and lay inches deep on everything. Every towel and curtain was just black. There wasn't a clean dish or cooking utensil. There was no food. Oh, there were eggs and milk and one loaf left of the bread I baked the weekend before. I looked in the cooler box down the well (our refrigerator) and found a little ham and butter. It was late, so Mama and I cooked some ham and eggs for the men's supper because that was all we could fix in a hurry. It turned out they had been living on ham and eggs for two days.

Mama was very tired. After she had fixed starter for bread, I insisted she go to bed and I'd do all the dishes.

It took until 10 o'clock to wash all the dirty dishes. That's not wiping them—just washing them. The cupboards had to be washed out to have a clean place to put them.

3. Franklin Roosevelt Creates the Tennessee Valley Authority (1933)

During the famed "Hundred Days" that marked the beginning of his first adminis-tration in 1933, Franklin Roosevelt took one especially bold initiative with huge en-vironmental implications: the creation of the Tennessee Valley Authority (TVA), designed as a comprehensive program for the planned development of the Tennessee River watershed. Beginning at Muscle Shoals, Alabama, a dam site that the govern-ment had controlled since World War I but had never utilized, the TVA built dams to control flooding and to generate electrical power, and it encouraged modern, scien-tific farming practices in the Upper South region it served. It also displaced thou-sands of people whose land was destined to be drowned by the huge reservoirs that built up behind the dams, and it provoked the bitter opposition of privately owned power companies. In this message to Congress calling for the creation of the TVA, how does Roosevelt justify this extraordinary undertaking? Roosevelt later proposed similar programs for other major river systems, but almost none came to fruition. Why did the TVA approach prove so limited in its application elsewhere?

[The White House] *April 10, 1933*

To the Congress: The continued idleness of a great national investment in the Tennessee Valley leads me to ask the Congress for legislation neccessary to enlist this project in the service of the people.

It is clear that the Muscle Shoals development is but a small part of the poten-tial public usefulness of the entire Tennessee River. Such use, if envisioned in its en-tirety, transcends mere power development: it enters the wide fields of flood control, soil erosion, afforestation, elimination from agricultural use of marginal lands, and distribution and diversification of industry. In short, this power develop-ment of war days leads logically to national planning for a complete river watershed

---

[3]From Edgar B. Nixon, ed., *Franklin D. Roosevelt and Conservation, 1911–1945,* pp. 151–152. Copyright © 1957 by the U.S. Government Printing Office.

involving many States and the future lives and welfare of millions. It touches and gives life to all forms of human concerns.

I, therefore, suggest to the Congress legislation to create a Tennessee Valley Authority—a corporation clothed with the power of government but possessed of the flexibility and initiative of a private enterprise. It should be charged with the broadest duty of planning for the proper use, conservation and development of the natural resources of the Tennessee River drainage basin and its adjoining territory for the general social and economic welfare of the nation. This Authority should also be clothed with the necessary power to carry these plans into effect. Its duty should be the rehabilitation of the Muscle Shoals development and the coordination of it with the wider plan.

Many hard lessons have taught us the human waste that results from lack of planning. Here and there a few wise cities and counties have looked ahead and planned. But our nation has "just grown." It is time to extend planning to a wider field, in this instance comprehending in one great project many States directly concerned with the basin of one of our greatest rivers.

This in a true sense is a return to the spirit and vision of the pioneer. If we are successful here we can march on, step by step, in a like development of other great natural territorial units within our borders.

4. Roosevelt Promotes Natural Resources Planning (1935)

At his ancestral estate in Hyde Park, New York, Roosevelt had long taken a special interest in studying and adopting techniques of sound ecological management, and he became a quite knowledgeable arborist. In 1935, he advocated a national program of comprehensive resource planning and environmental management. He explained his objectives in the message to Congress that follows. What are his principal concerns? How do his ideas about natural resources management compare with those of his distant cousin, Theodore Roosevelt, as given at pp. 215? Did the two Roosevelts share a common understanding of "Nature"?

Jan. 24, 1935

To the Congress: During the three or four centuries of white man on the American Continent, we find a continuous striving of civilization against Nature. It is only in recent years that we have learned how greatly by these processes we have harmed Nature and Nature in turn has harmed us.

We should not too largely blame our ancestors, for they found such teeming riches in woods and soil and water—such abundance above the earth and beneath it—such freedom in the taking, that they gave small heed to the results that would follow the filling of their own immediate needs. Most of them, it is true, had come from many peopled lands where neccessity had invoked the preserving of the bounties of Nature. But they had come here for the obtaining of a greater freedom, and it was natural that freedom of conscience and freedom of government should

---

[4] From Edgar B. Nixon, ed., *Franklin D. Roosevelt and Conservation, 1911–1945*, pp. 341–344. Copyright © 1957 by the U.S. Government Printing Office.

extend itself in their minds to the unrestricted enjoyment of the free use of land and water.

Furthermore, it is only within our own generation that the development of science, leaping forward, has taught us where and how we violated nature's immutable laws and where and how we can commence to repair such havoc as man has wrought.

In recent years little groups of earnest men and women have told us of this havoc; of the cutting of our last stands of virgin timber; of the increasing floods, of the washing away of millions of acres of our top soils, of the lowering of our water-tables, of the dangers of one crop farming, of the depletion of our minerals—in short the evils that we have brought upon ourselves today and the even greater evils that will attend our children unless we act.

Such is the condition that attends the exploitation of our natural resources if we continue our planless course.

But another element enters in. Men and Nature must work hand in hand. The throwing out of balance of the resources of Nature throws out of balance also the lives of men. We find millions of our citizens stranded in village and on farm—stranded there because Nature can not support them in the livelihood they had sought to gain through her. We find other millions gravitated to centers of population so vast that the laws of natural economics have broken down.

If the misuse of natural resources alone were concerned, we should consider our problem only in terms of land and water. It is because misuse extends to what men and women are doing with their occupations and to their many mistakes in herding themselves together that I have chosen, in addressing the Congress, to use the broader term "National Resources."

For the first time in our national history we have made an inventory of our national assets and the problems relating to them. For the first time we have drawn together the foresight of the various planning agencies of the Federal Government and suggested a method and a policy for the future.

I am sending you herewith the report of the National Resources Board, appointed by me on June 30, 1934 to prepare the comprehensive survey which so many of us have sought so long. I transmit also the report made by the Mississippi Valley Committee of the Public Works Administration, which Committee has also acted as the Water Planning Committee in the larger report.

These documents constitute a remarkable foundation for what I hope will be a permanent policy of orderly development in every part of the United States. It is a large subject but it is a great and inspiring subject. May I commend to each and every one of you, who constitute the Congress of the United States, a careful reading of the reports.

In this inventory of our national wealth we follow the custom of prudent people toward their own private property. We as a Nation take stock of what we as a Nation own. We consider the uses to which it can be put. We plan these uses in the light of what we want to be, and what we want to accomplish as a people. We think of our land and water and human resources not as static and sterile possessions but as life-giving assets to be directed by wise provision for future days. We seek to use our natural resources not as a thing apart but as something that is interwoven with industry, labor, finance, taxation, agriculture, homes, recreation, good citizenship.

The result of this interweaving will have a greater influence on the future American standard of living than all the rest of our economics put together.

For the coming eighteen months I have asked the Congress for four billion dollars for public projects. A substantial portion of this sum will be used for objectives suggested in this report. As years pass the Government should plan to spend each year a reasonable and continuing sum in the development of this program. It is my hope, for example, that after the immediate crisis of unemployment begins to mend, we can afford to appropriate approximately five hundred million dollars each year for this purpose. Eventually this appropriation should replace all such appropriations given in the past without planning.

A permanent National Resource Board, towards the establishment of which we should be looking forward, would recommend yearly to the President and the Congress priority of projects in the national plan. This will give to the Congress, as is entirely proper, the final determination in relation to the projects and the appropriations involved.

As I have already stated, it is only because of the current emergency of unemployment and because of the physical impossibility of surveying, weighing and testing each and every project that a segregation of items is clearly impossible at the moment.

For the same reason the constituting of fixed and permanent administrative machinery would retard the immediate employment objective.

Our goal must be a national one. Achievements in the arts of communication, of transportation, of mechanized production, of agriculture, of mining and of power, do not minimize the rights of State Governments but they go far beyond the economics of State boundaries.

Only through the growth of thought and action in terms of national economics, can we best serve individual lives in individual localities.

It is, as Reports point out, an error to say that we have "conquered Nature." We must, rather, start to shape our lives in more harmonious relationship with Nature. This is a mile-stone in our progress toward that end. The future of every American family everywhere will be affected by the action we take.

5. Roosevelt Dedicates Boulder (Hoover) Dam (1935)

Work on Boulder Dam began during the Hoover administration in the 1920s, and the dam was later renamed in honor of Roosevelt's immediate predecessor. Hoover Dam was probably the federal government's largest public works project to date when it was completed in 1935. Ever since, the dam has generated electricity and shaped water management in ways that have profoundly influenced the development of the southwestern region of the United States. Some modern-day environmentalists have attacked Hoover Dam and the other large-scale "reclamation" projects in the West—such as Shasta Dam in California, Fort Peck Dam in Montana, and the several dams on the Columbia River in Washington State—as having inflicted unjustifiable environmental damage on the entire region. On the basis of his

---

[5]From Edgar B. Nixon, ed., *Franklin D. Roosevelt and Conservation, 1911–1945*, pp. 489–491. Copyright © 1957 by the U.S. Government Printing Office.

remarks reprinted here, made on the occasion of Boulder Dam's dedication, how might Roosevelt have replied to such critics?

Senator [Key] Pittman, Secretary [of the Interior, Harold] Ickes, Governors of the Colorado's States, and you especially who have built Boulder Dam: This morning I came, I saw and I was conquered, as everyone would be who sees for the first time this great feat of mankind.

Ten years ago the place where we gathered was an unpeopled, forbidding desert. In the bottom of the gloomy canyon whose precipitous walls rose to a height of more than a thousand feet, flowed a turbulent, dangerous river. The mountains on either side of the canyon were difficult of access with neither road nor trail, and their rocks were protected by neither trees nor grass from the blazing heat of the sun. The site of Boulder City was a cactus-covered waste. And the transformation wrought here in these years is a twentieth century marvel.

We are here to celebrate the completion of the greatest dam in the world, rising 726 feet above the bedrock of the river and altering the geography of a whole region; we are here to see the creation of the largest artificial lake in the world—115 miles long, holding enough water, for example, to cover the whole State of Connecticut to a depth of ten feet; and we are here to see nearing completion a power house which will contain the largest generators and turbines yet installed in this country, machinery that can continuously supply nearly two million horsepower of electric energy. All of these dimensions are superlative. They represent and embody the accumulated engineering knowledge and experience of centuries, and when we behold them it is fitting that we pay tribute to the genius of their designers. We recognize also the energy, the resourcefulness and the zeal of the builders, who, under the greatest physical obstacles, have pushed this work forward to completion two years in advance of contract requirements. But especially, my friends, we express our gratitude to the thousands of workers who gave brain and brawn in this great work of construction.

Beautiful and great as this structure is, it must also be considered in its relationship to the agricultural and industrial development and in its contribution to the health and comfort of the people of America who live in the Southwest.

To divert and distribute the waters of an arid region so that there shall be security of rights and efficiency in service, is one of the greatest problems of law and of administration to be found in any government. The farms, the cities, the people who live along the many thousands of miles of this river and its tributaries all of them depend for their permanence in value upon the conservation, regulation, and the equitable and fair division of its ever-changing water supply. What has been accomplished on the Colorado in working out such a scheme of distribution is inspiring to the whole country. Through the cooperation of the States whose people depend upon this river, and of the Federal Government which is concerned in the general welfare, there is being constructed a system of distributive works and of laws and practices which will insure to the millions of people who now dwell in this basin, and to the millions of others who will come to dwell here in future generations, a safe, just, and permanent system of water rights. In devising these policies and the means of putting them into practice the Bureau of Reclamation of the Federal Government has taken and is destined to take in the future, a leading and helpful part. The Bureau has been the instrument which gave effect to the legislation introduced into the Congress by Senator Hiram Johnson and Congressman Philip Swing.

When in flood the river was a threatening torrent. In the dry months of the year it shrank to a trickling stream. For a generation the people of Imperial Valley had lived in the shadow of disaster from this river which provided their livelihood, and which is the foundation of their hopes for themselves and their children. Every spring they awaited with dread the coming of a flood, and at the end of every summer they feared a shortage of water would destroy their crops.

The gates of these great diversion tunnels were closed here at Boulder Dam last February and in June a great flood came down the river. It came roaring down the canyons of the Colorado, through Grand Canyon, Iceberg and Boulder Canyons, but it was caught, it was caught and held safely behind Boulder Dam.

Last year a drought of unprecedented severity was visited upon the west. The watershed of this Colorado River did not escape. In July the canals of the Imperial Valley went dry. Crop losses in that Valley alone totaled $10,000,000 that summer. Had Boulder Dam been completed one year earlier, this loss would have been prevented, because the spring flood would have been stored to furnish a steady water supply for the long dry summer and fall.

Across the San Jacinto mountains southwest of Boulder Dam the cities of Southern California are constructing an aqueduct to cost $200,000,000, which they have raised, for the purpose of carrying the regulated waters of the River to the Pacific Coast 250 miles away.

And across the desert and mountains to the west and south run great electric transmission lines by which factory motors, street and household lights and irrigation pumps can be operated in Southern Arizona and California. Part of this power will be used in pumping the water through the aqueduct to supplement the domestic supplies of Los Angeles and surrounding cities.

Navigation of the river from Boulder Dam to the Grand Canyon has been made possible, a 115-mile stretch that had been traversed less than half a dozen times in all history. An immense new park has been created for the enjoyment of all of our people. And that is why, my friends, those of you who are not here today but can hear my voice, I tell you—come to Boulder Dam and see it with your own eyes.

F. The Supreme Court Fight and After

1. Harold Ickes Defends His Chief (1937)

The ultraconservative Supreme Court had repeatedly overthrown crucial New Deal measures for economic and social reform. Roosevelt, intoxicated by his heady majorities of 1932, 1934, and 1936, concluded that in a true democracy the "horse-and-buggy" Court ought to catch up with the will of the people. Two weeks after his

---

[1]Reprinted with permission of Simon & Schuster from *The Secret Diary of Harold L. Ickes, Vol. II: The Inside Struggle, 1936–1939* by Harold L. Ickes. Copyright © 1954 by Simon & Schuster, Inc. Copyright renewed © 1982 by Simon & Schuster.

second inauguration, he sprang his clever Supreme Court scheme on a surprised Congress and nation. Among other changes, he proposed increasing the membership of the Court from nine to fifteen by appointing additional (New Deal) justices to off-set those aged seventy or more who were unwilling to retire. Critics cried that this was "packing" the Court; supporters replied that this was "unpacking" the Court by offsetting reactionaries. "Honest Harold" Ickes, the acid-tongued secretary of the interior, here tells how he defended Roosevelt before an audience of Texans. Given that the Court scheme had not received mention in the Democratic platform or in Roosevelt's speeches during the recent campaign of 1936, how persuasive is Ickes's argument regarding a popular mandate?

Then I switched to a discussion of the constitutional situation, with special reference to the recent proposal of the President to change the judiciary system. I could hear a gasp go up as I disclosed my purpose to discuss this issue. A week or ten days ago the Texas State Senate, with only three or four votes opposing, had gone on record as being against the President's proposal. The House decided neither to approve nor disapprove.

I waded right into the constitutional issue with both feet. In my first sentence I asked where had the Supreme Court gotten its supposed power to pass upon the constitutionality of acts of Congress. I read the Tenth Amendment and then I said that this power had been usurped.*

I then went on to discuss the supposed checks and balances in our tripartite Federal system, pointing out that while there were ample checks and balances with respect to the legislative and executive branches, there wasn't a single check on the judiciary except that of impeachment, which was slow and cumbersome and of doubtful efficacy when it came to a court of nine men. I remarked in passing that one could not be impeached for being too old, that that was not a crime but merely a misfortune.

I argued that the people had given the President a mandate at the last election to provide them with such social and economic legislation as is implicit in the term "New Deal." I said that he would be recreant to his trust if he didn't do all within his power to give the people what he had promised them and what they had shown so unmistakably that they wanted.

I expressed the opinion that the people wanted the benefits of the New Deal now. I pointed out that while those who are opposing the President pretend to do it on the basis that a constitutional amendment is the proper procedure, it would take all of twenty years to get such an amendment through.

With respect to an act or acts of Congress limiting the powers of the Supreme Court so as to provide, for instance, that no law could be held to be unconstitutional except on a two-thirds or three-quarters majority, I ventured to predict that any such law would be declared unconstitutional by the Supreme Court and therefore would be ineffective.

---

*The Tenth Amendment reserved undelegated powers to the states, but the function of judicial review, "usurped" by the Supreme Court, is generally regarded as implicit in the views of the Founding Fathers and in the Constitution.

2. Dorothy Thompson Dissents (1937)

As the battle over the Supreme Court mounted, critics accused Roosevelt of perverting the Constitution by destroying the delicate checks and balances, of undermining the integrity and independence of the judiciary, and of grooming himself for dictatorship. Even many New Dealers preferred an unhurried constitutional amendment to a hurried act of Congress. Perhaps most damaging was the suggestion of "slickness," together with Roosevelt's argument, based on false information, that the aged justices were behind in their work. Dorothy Thompson, a noted and respected columnist, sounded the following clarion call. How sound is her view that the people must be protected against fickle majorities and that haste is not necessary?

If the American people accept this last audacity of the President without letting out a yell to high heaven, they have ceased to be jealous of their liberties and are ripe for ruin.

This is the beginning of pure personal government. Do you want it? Do you like it? Look around about the world—there are plenty of examples [e.g., Hitler]—and make up your mind.

The Executive is already powerful by reason of his overwhelming victory in November, and will be strengthened even more if the reorganization plan for the administration, presented some weeks ago, is adopted. We have, to all intents and purposes, a one-party Congress, dominated by the President. Although nearly 40 percent of the voters repudiated the New Deal at the polls, they have less than 20 percent representation in both houses of Congress. And now the Supreme Court is to have a majority determined by the President and by a Senate which he dominates.

When that happens we will have a one-man Government. It will all be constitutional. So, he claims, is Herr Hitler.

Leave the personality and the intentions of the President out of the picture. They are not the crux of this issue. He may be as wise as Solon, lofty as Plato, and pure as Parsifal. He may have the liberties of the American people deeply at heart. But he will have a successor who may be none of these things. There have been benevolent dictatorships and benevolent tyrannies. They have even, at times in history, worked for the popular welfare. But that is not the welfare which, up to now, the American people have chosen.

And let us not be confused by the words "liberal" and "conservative" or misled into thinking that the expressed will of the majority is the essence of democracy. By that definition Hitler, Stalin, and Mussolini are all great democratic leaders. The essence of democracy is the protection of minorities.

Nor has a majority of this generation the right to mortgage a majority of the next. In the Constitution of the United States are incorporated the rights of the people, rights enjoyed by every American citizen in perpetuity, which cannot be voted away by any majority, ever.

Majorities are temporary things. The Supreme Court is there to protect the fun-

---

[2] *Washington Star,* February 10, 1937, quoted in *Congressional Digest* 16 (March 1937): 96.

damental law even against the momentary "will of the people." That is its function. And it is precisely because nine men can walk out and say: "You can't do that!" that our liberties are protected against the mob urge that occasionally overcomes democracies. That is why the Supreme Court has been traditionally divorced from momentary majorities. . . .

The Constitution can be changed. There are ways provided for doing so. To change it will require much deliberation, debate, time. And what is wrong with deliberation and debate and time? What is the hurry? Under what threat are we living at this instant?

This is no proposal to change the Constitution. This is no proposal to limit the powers of the Supreme Court. This is a proposal to capture the Supreme Court. . . .

If, of the six men over 70, four had been "liberals" and two "conservatives," instead of the other way around, do you think that this program would have been proposed? . . .

Don't talk of liberalism! The liberal does not believe that the end justifies the means. Long experience has taught him that the means usually determine the end. No human being can believe in the sincerity of this proposal. It is clever, in a world sick of cleverness and longing for plain talk and simple honesty. Must we begin to examine every message from the President to see whether there is a trick in it somewhere?

[Roosevelt threw all his weight behind the Supreme Court reform but suffered his most severe political setback when he lost out on the packing feature. He underestimated popular reverence for the Court. But he did win certain other judicial reforms, the Supreme Court did shift to a more liberal position, and within four years he had filled seven vacancies with younger men. He lost a battle but in the end won the war. Yet he lost essential legislative support in Congress.]

3. Republicans Roast Roosevelt (1940)

The Roosevelt-Willkie presidential campaign of 1940 generated new bitterness. Roosevelt's challenge to the third-term tradition, combined with his unsuccessful attempt to pack the Supreme Court and purge certain members of Congress hostile to him, accentuated fears of dictatorship. The Democrats argued that Roosevelt had saved capitalism by averting, whatever the monetary cost and confusion, a revolutionary uprising. The Republican platform, invoking the Preamble to the Constitution, found the New Deal wanting on many counts. In the light of subsequent developments, which is the more valid accusation?

Instead of leading us into More Perfect Union, the Administration has deliberately fanned the flames of class hatred.

Instead of the Establishment of Justice the Administration has sought the subjection of the Judiciary to Executive discipline and domination.

---

[3]K. H. Porter and D. B. Johnson, eds., *National Party Platforms,* 1840–1956 (Urbana, Ill.: University of Illinois Press, 1961).

Instead of insuring Domestic Tranquillity, the Administration has made impossible the normal friendly relation between employers and employees, and has even succeeded in alienating both the great divisions of Organized Labor.

Instead of Providing for the Common Defense, the Administration, notwithstanding the expenditure of billions of our dollars, has left the Nation unprepared to resist foreign attack.

Instead of promoting the General Welfare, the Administration has Domesticated the Deficit, Doubled the Debt, Imposed Taxes where they do the greatest economic harm, and used public money for partisan political advantage.

Instead of the Blessings of Liberty, the Administration has imposed upon us a Regime of Regimentation which has deprived the individual of his freedom and has made of America a shackled giant.

Wholly ignoring these great objectives, as solemnly declared by the people of the United States [in the Constitution], the New Deal Administration has for seven long years whirled in a turmoil of shifting, contradictory, and overlapping administrations and policies. Confusion has reigned supreme. The only steady undeviating characteristic has been the relentless expansion of the power of the Federal government over the everyday life of the farmer, the industrial worker, and the businessman. The emergency demands organization—not confusion. It demands free and intelligent cooperation—not incompetent domination. It demands a change.

The New Deal Administration has failed America.

It has failed by seducing our people to become continuously dependent upon government, thus weakening their morale and quenching the traditional American spirit.

4. Assessing the New Deal (1935, 1936)

That most newspaper publishers in the 1930s were critical of the New Deal may help explain why many newspaper cartoonists took a dim view of Roosevelt and his reform program. The first print below, by Herbert Johnson of the Saturday Evening Post, *is a typical example of traditional conservative criticism of the New Deal. It is worth noting that John T. McCutcheon, the cartoonist who produced the second image, refused to support the anti–New Deal views of his publisher at the* Chicago Tribune. *Would the "forgotten man" in the second print be likely to see himself as the "taxpayer" in the first image? Why or why not? Which image had a greater political appeal in the 1930s? How did Franklin Roosevelt work to counter the opposition of the press-lords of his day?*

"Yes, You Remembered Me"

Thought Provokers

1. Compare and contrast the presidential leadership of Hoover and Roosevelt. Temperamentally, could Roosevelt ever have been a true dictator?

2. What probably would have happened if the federal government had refused to provide relief for the millions of unemployed, as well as for the impoverished farmers? Was planned scarcity immoral?

3. What were the greatest hardships Americans suffered during the Great Depression? Why was there not more radical protest against "hard times"?

4. To what extent did Roosevelt's critics offer realistic alternatives to the New Deal? How did Roosevelt outmaneuver his opponents?

5. Is the right to work without first joining a union a basic right? Why did the CIO call management fascist, and why did management call the CIO communist?

6. Why did Roosevelt's Supreme Court proposal stir up such a hornets' nest? Was Roosevelt justified in breaking his platform promises regarding economy and a balanced budget? Did the New Deal change the basic character of the American people? of the federal government?

7. Were the New Deal's natural resource and conservation policies on balance helpful or harmful to the environment? How should environmental concerns be balanced with other human needs?

35

Franklin D. Roosevelt and the Shadow of War, 1933–1941

> The epidemic of world lawlessness is spreading. . . .
> There must be positive endeavors to preserve peace.
>
> *Franklin D. Roosevelt, 1937*

Prologue: The same depression that generated the New Deal at home accelerated the rise of power-hungry dictators abroad: Hitler, Mussolini, and the Japanese warlords. Congress tried to insulate the nation from the imminent world war by arms embargoes and other presumed safeguards. But when Hitler attacked Poland in 1939, the American people found themselves torn between two desires: they wanted to avoid involvement, but they feared for their future security if they did not get involved to the extent of bolstering the democracies. Under Roosevelt's prodding, Congress repealed the arms embargo in 1939, and the administration gradually took a series of steps that removed any pretense of neutrality. Most Americans—except the diehard isolationists—were willing to risk hostilities in an effort to help the democracies and halt the aggressors. Roosevelt took the gamble but lost when a shooting war developed with Germany in the Atlantic and when Japan struck a devastating aerial blow at Pearl Harbor.

A. The Struggle Against Isolationism

1. Two Views of Isolationism (1936, 1938)

As Europe and Asia moved toward a new world war in the 1930s, Americans remembered with great bitterness and regret their country's involvement in World War I. Revisionist histories and congressional investigations of the World War I–era munitions industry reinforced the idea that America's involvement in the Great War of 1914–1918 had been a terrible mistake. Many Americans, especially in the arch-

---

[1]p. 345, © C. D. Batchelor, *New York Daily News,* 1936; p. 346, © AP Hirschfeld. Art reproduced by special arrangement with Hirschfeld's exclusive representative, the Margo Feiden Galleries Limited, New York.

isolationist Midwest, resolved never again to allow their country to be drawn into a foreign war. Yet other Americans, particularly in the great cities of the eastern seaboard, argued that the United States could not safely ignore the threat posed by Nazi Germany and militaristic Japan. These internationally minded Americans accused their isolationist countrymen of being hopelessly naive about the dangers their country faced. The first cartoon below, by C. D. Batchelor of the Daily News, *makes the pro-isolationist case; the second, by Albert Hirschfeld of the* New Masses, *makes the pro-internationalist case. Which is more persuasive as propaganda? Were the two images aimed at the same sectors of the American public?*

"*Come on in, I'll treat you right. I used to know your daddy.*"

The Isolationist

2. Roosevelt Pleads for Repeal of the Arms Embargo (1939)

The arms-embargoing Neutrality Acts of 1935 and 1937 made no distinction between aggressor and victim. When Hitler wantonly launched World War II in September 1939, the United States could not legally sell munitions to the unprepared democracies, although U.S. sentiment and self-interest both cried aloud for aid to Britain and France. A worried Roosevelt summoned Congress into special session and made the following dramatic appeal. He was wrong on two counts. First, the arms embargo, as purely domestic legislation, was not a departure from long-established international law. Second, the Jeffersonian embargo and nonintercourse acts did not cause the War of 1812; they came within a few days of averting it. What does this excerpt suggest

---

[2]*Congressional Record,* 76th Cong., 2d sess. (September 21, 1939), pp. 10–11.

about Roosevelt's technique as a politician? What did he see as the most dangerous loophole in the existing legislation?

Beginning with the foundation of our constitutional Government in the year 1789, the American policy in respect to belligerent nations, with one notable exception, has been based on international law. . . .

The single exception was the policy adopted by this nation during the Napoleonic Wars, when, seeking to avoid involvement, we acted for some years under the so-called Embargo and Non-Intercourse Acts. That policy turned out to be a disastrous failure—first, because it brought our own nation close to ruin, and, second, because it was the major cause of bringing us into active participation in European wars in our own War of 1812. It is merely reciting history to recall to you that one of the results of the policy of embargo and non-intercourse was the burning in 1814 of part of this Capitol in which we are assembled.

Our next deviation by statute from the sound principles of neutrality, and peace through international law, did not come for 130 years. It was the so-called Neutrality Act of 1935—only 4 years ago—an Act continued in force by the Joint Resolution of May 1, 1937, despite grave doubts expressed as to its wisdom by many Senators and Representatives and by officials charged with the conduct of our foreign relations, including myself.

I regret that the Congress passed that Act. I regret equally that I signed that Act.

On July 14th of this year, I asked the Congress, in the cause of peace and in the interest of real American neutrality and security, to take action to change that Act.

I now ask again that such action be taken in respect to that part of the Act which is wholly inconsistent with ancient precepts of the law of nations—the [arms] embargo provisions. I ask it because they are, in my opinion, most vitally dangerous to American neutrality, American security, and American peace.

These embargo provisions, as they exist today, prevent the sale to a belligerent by an American factory of any completed implements of war, but they allow the sale of many types of uncompleted implements of war, as well as all kinds of general material and supplies. They, furthermore, allow such products of industry [e.g., copper] and agriculture [e.g., cotton] to be taken in American-flag ships to belligerent nations. There in itself—under the present law—lies definite danger to our neutrality and our peace.

3. Senator Arthur Vandenberg Fights Repeal (1939)

Senator Arthur H. Vandenberg of Michigan—voluble orator, long-time newspaperman, and author of books on Alexander Hamilton—was a leader of the Republican isolationists and a serious contender for the presidential nomination in 1940. Later,

---

[3]*Congressional Record,* 76th Cong., 2d sess. (October 4, 1939), p. 95.

in 1945, he underwent a spectacular conversion to internationalism and rose to heights of statesmanship in supporting the Marshall Plan for the rehabilitation of postwar Europe. While fighting against the repeal of the arms embargo in 1939, he wrote in his diary that he deplored Roosevelt's "treacherous" and "cowardly" idea that the United States could be "half in and half out of this war." Hating Hitlerism, he felt that the honorable course would be to go in or to stay out—and he much preferred to stay out. In this speech in the Senate against the repeal of the arms embargo, what does he regard as both unneutral and unethical?

Mr. President, I believe this debate symbolically involves the most momentous decision, in the eyes of America and of the World, that the United States Senate has confronted in a generation.

In the midst of foreign war and the alarms of other wars, we are asked to depart basically from the neutrality which the American Congress has twice told the world, since 1935, would be our rule of conduct in such an event. We are particularly asked to depart from it through the repeal of existing neutrality law establishing an embargo on arms, ammunition, and implements of war. We are asked to depart from it in violation of our own officially asserted doctrine, during the [first] World War, that the rules of a neutral cannot be prejudicially altered in the midst of a war.

We are asked to depart from international law itself, as we ourselves have officially declared it to exist. Consciously or otherwise, but mostly consciously, we are asked to depart from it in behalf of one belligerent whom our personal sympathies largely favor, and against another belligerent whom our personal feelings largely condemn. In my opinion, this is the road that may lead us to war, and I will not voluntarily take it. . . .

The proponents of the change vehemently insist that their steadfast purpose, like ours, is to keep America out of the war, and their sincere assurances are presented to our people. But the motive is obvious, and the inevitable interpretation of the change, inevitably invited by the circumstances, will be that we have officially taken sides.

Somebody will be fooled—either the America which is assured that the change is wholly pacific, or the foreigners who believe it is the casting of our die. Either of these disillusionments would be intolerable. Each is ominous. Yet someone will be fooled—either those at home who expect too much, or those abroad who will get too little.

There is no such hazard, at least to our own America, in preserving neutrality in the existing law precisely as we almost unanimously notified the world was our intention as recently as 1935 and 1937. There is no such jeopardy, at least to our own America, in maintaining the arms embargo as it is. No menace, no jeopardy, to us can thus be persuasively conjured.

Therefore millions of Americans and many members of the Congress can see no reason for the change, but infinite reason to the contrary, if neutral detachment is our sole objective. I am one who deeply holds this view. If I err, I want to err on America's side.

[Despite such pleas, the arms embargo was repealed early in November 1939. The vote was 55 to 24 in the Senate, 243 to 172 in the House.]

4. Charles Lindbergh Argues for Isolation (1941)

After France fell to Hitler in 1940, the embattled British stood alone. U.S. interventionists called for a helping hand to Britain; the isolationists called for hands off. The isolationist America First group proclaimed, "We have nothing to fear from a Nazi-European victory." Boyish-faced, curly-haired Colonel Charles A. Lindbergh, who had narrowed the Atlantic with his historic solo flight in 1927, stressed the width of the ocean in his new role as a leading isolationist orator. After inspecting Germany's aircraft facilities in 1938, he stoutly maintained that Hitler (who decorated him) could never be conquered in the air. If Lindbergh proved so wrong in an area in which he was a specialist, form some judgment about the assessment of the U.S. strategic position that he made in this speech before a New York mass meeting in April 1941. To what extent is interventionism undemocratic, assuming that Lindbergh's figures were correct? Is his analysis of public opinion trustworthy?

We have weakened ourselves for many months, and still worse, we have divided our own people, by this dabbling in Europe's wars. While we should have been concentrating on American defense, we have been forced to argue over foreign quarrels. We must turn our eyes and our faith back to our own country before it is too late. And when we do this, a different vista opens before us.

Practically every difficulty we would face in invading Europe becomes an asset to us in defending America. Our enemy, and not we, would then have the problem of transporting millions of troops across the ocean and landing them on a hostile shore. They, and not we, would have to furnish the convoys to transport guns and trucks and munitions and fuel across three thousand miles of water. Our battleships and our submarines would then be fighting close to their home bases. We would then do the bombing from the air and the torpedoing at sea. And if any part of an enemy convoy should ever pass our navy and our air force, they would still be faced with the guns of our coast artillery, and behind them the divisions of our Army.

The United States is better situated from a military standpoint than any other nation in the world. Even in our present condition of unpreparedness no foreign power is in a position to invade us today. If we concentrate on our own defenses and build the strength that this nation should maintain, no foreign army will ever attempt to land on American shores.

War is not inevitable for this country. Such a claim is defeatism in the true sense. No one can make us fight abroad unless we ourselves are willing to do so. No one will attempt to fight us here if we arm ourselves as a great nation should be armed. Over a hundred million people in this nation are opposed to entering the war. If the principles of democracy mean anything at all, that is reason enough for us to stay out. If we are forced into a war against the wishes of an overwhelming majority of our people, we will have proved democracy such a failure at home that there will be little use fighting for it abroad.

The time has come when those of us who believe in an independent American destiny must band together and organize for strength. We have been led toward war

---

[4]*New York Times,* April 24, 1941, p. 12.

by a minority of our people. This minority has power. It has influence. It has a loud voice. But it does not represent the American people. During the last several years I have traveled over this country from one end to the other. I have talked to many hundreds of men and women, and I have letters from tens of thousands more, who feel the same way as you and I.

[Public opinion polls during these months showed contradictory desires. A strong majority of the American people wanted to stay out of war, but a strong majority favored helping Britain even at the risk of war. The Lend-Lease Act of 1941 received about two-to-one support in the public opinion polls and more than that in congressional voting.]

5. The New York Times *Rejects Isolationism (1941)*

The New York Times *challenged Lindbergh's views in a lengthy and well-reasoned editorial that brilliantly set forth the case for intervention. What are its principal points?*

Those who tell us now that the sea is still our certain bulwark, and that the tremendous forces sweeping the Old World threaten no danger to the New, give the lie to their own words in the precautions they would have us take.

To a man they favor an enormous strengthening of our defenses. Why? Against what danger would they have us arm if none exists? To what purpose would they have us spend these almost incredible billions upon billions for ships and planes, for tanks and guns, if there is no immediate threat to the security of the United States? Why are we training the youth of the country to bear arms? Under pressure of what fear are we racing against time to double and quadruple our industrial production?

No man in his senses will say that we are arming against Canada or our Latin-American neighbors to the south, against Britain or the captive states of Europe. We are arming solely for one reason. We are arming against Hitler's Germany—a great predatory Power in alliance with Japan.

It has been said, times without number, that if Hitler cannot cross the English Channel he cannot cross three thousand miles of sea. But there is only one reason why he had not crossed the English Channel. That is because forty-five million determined Britons, in a heroic resistance, have converted their island into an armed base, from which proceeds a steady stream of sea and air power. As Secretary [of State Cordell] Hull has said: "It is not the water that bars the way. It is the resolute determination of British arms. Were the control of the seas by Britain lost, the Atlantic would no longer be an obstacle—rather, it would become a broad highway for a conqueror moving westward."

That conqueror does not need to attempt at once an invasion of continental United States in order to place this country in deadly danger. We shall be in deadly

---

danger the moment British sea power fails; the moment the eastern gates of the Atlantic are open to the aggressor; the moment we are compelled to divide our one-ocean Navy between two oceans simultaneously.

The combined Axis fleets [German, Italian, Japanese] outmatch our own: they are superior in numbers to our fleet in every category of vessel, from warships and aircraft-carriers to destroyers and submarines.* The combined Axis air strength will be much greater than our own if Hitler strikes in time—and when has he failed to strike in time? The master of Europe will have at his command shipways that can outbuild us, the resources of twenty conquered nations to furnish his materials, the oil of the Middle East to stoke his engines, the slave labor of a continent—bound by no union rules, and not working on a forty-hour week—to turn out his production.

Grant Hitler the gigantic prestige of a victory over Britain, and who can doubt that the first result, on our side of the ocean, would be the prompt appearance of imitation Nazi regimes in a half-dozen Latin-American nations, forced to be on the winning side, begging favors, clamoring for admission to the Axis? What shall we do then? Make war upon these neighbors, send armies to fight in the jungles of Central or South America; run the risk of outraging native sentiment and turning the whole continent against us? Or shall we sit tight while the area of Nazi influence draws ever closer to the Panama Canal, and a spreading checkerboard of Nazi airfields provides ports of call for German planes that may choose to bomb our cities?

But even if Hitler gave us time, what kind of "time" would we have at our disposal?

There are moral and spiritual dangers for this country as well as physical dangers in a Hitler victory. There are dangers to the mind and heart as well as to the body and the land.

Victorious in Europe, dominating Africa and Asia through his Axis partners, Hitler could not afford to permit the United States to live an untroubled and successful life, even if he wished to. We are the arch-enemy of all he stands for: the very citadel of that "pluto-democracy" which he hates and scorns. As long as liberty and freedom prevailed in the United States there would be constant risk for Hitler that our ideas and our example might infect the conquered countries which he was bending to his will. In his own interest he would be forced to harry us at every turn.

Who can doubt that our lives would be poisoned every day by challenges and insults from Nazi politicians; that Nazi agents would stir up anti-American feeling in every country they controlled; that Nazi spies would overrun us here; that Hitler would produce a continual series of lightning diplomatic strokes—alliances and "non-aggression pacts" to break our will; in short, that a continuous war of nerves, if nothing worse, would be waged against us?

And who can doubt that, in response, we should have to turn our own nation into an armed camp, with all our traditional values of culture, education, social reform, democracy and liberty subordinated to the single, all-embracing aim of self-preservation? In this case we should indeed experience "regimentation." Every item of foreign trade, every transaction in domestic commerce, every present prerogative

---

*Three foreign fleets are not necessarily equal to the sum of all their parts. There are different languages and signals, different-caliber guns and ammunition, different types of maneuvers, and so forth.

of labor, every civil liberty we cherish, would necessarily be regulated in the interest of defense.

B. The Lend-Lease Controversy

1. FDR Drops the Dollar Sign (1940)

A serious student of history, Roosevelt was determined to avoid the blunders of World War I. The postwar quarrel with the Allies over debts lingered in his memory as he groped for some means of bolstering the hard-pressed British without getting involved in a repayment wrangle. Keeping his new brainstorm under his hat until his triumphant reelection over Wendell Willkie—he might have lost if he had revealed it before then—he outlined his scheme at one of his breezy, off-the-cuff press conferences. How did he propose to eliminate the root of the debt difficulty?

It is possible—I will put it that way—for the United States to take over British [war] orders, and, because they are essentially the same kind of munitions that we use ourselves, turn them into American orders. We have got enough money to do it. And thereupon, as to such portion of them as the military events of the future determine to be right and proper for us to allow to go to the other side, either lease or sell the materials, subject to mortgage, to the people on the other side. That would be on the general theory that it may still prove true that the best defense of Great Britain is the best defense of the United States, and therefore that these materials would be more useful to the defense of the United States if they were used in Great Britain than if they were kept in storage here.

Now, what I am trying to do is to eliminate the dollar sign. That is something brand new in the thoughts of practically everybody in this room, I think—get rid of the silly, foolish old dollar sign.

Well, let me give you an illustration: Suppose my neighbor's home catches fire, and I have a length of garden hose four or five hundred feet away. If he can take my garden hose and connect it up with his hydrant, I may help him to put out his fire. Now, what do I do? I don't say to him before that operation, "Neighbor, my garden hose cost me $15; you have got to pay me $15 for it." What is the transaction that goes on? I don't want $15—I want my garden hose back after the fire is over. All right. If it goes through the fire all right, intact, without any damage to it, he gives it back to me and thanks me very much for the use of it. But suppose it gets smashed up—holes in it—during the fire; we don't have to have too much formality about it, but I say to him, "I was glad to lend you that hose; I see I can't use it any more, it's all smashed up." He says, "How many feet of it were there?" I tell him, "There were 150 feet of it." He says, "All right, I will replace it." Now, if I get a nice garden hose back, I am in pretty good shape.

---

[1] *The Public Papers and Addresses of Franklin D. Roosevelt, 1940 Volume* (1941), pp. 606–608.

In other words, if you lend certain munitions and get the munitions back at the end of the war, if they are intact—haven't been hurt—you are all right. If they have been damaged or have deteriorated or have been lost completely, it seems to me you come out pretty well if you have them replaced by the fellow to whom you have lent them.

[After the United States entered the war, supplies provided by foreign countries to U.S. forces were credited to their account as reverse lend-lease. The total value of U.S. lend-lease was over $50 billion, less some $7 billion in reverse lend-lease. Some cash was involved in the final settlement of accounts.]

2. Senator Burton Wheeler Assails Lend-Lease (1941)

Like the interventionists, Roosevelt believed that the salvation of Britain through large-scale military aid was crucial for the defense of the United States. But so strong was isolationist opposition that the proposed lend-lease act could not be entitled "An Act to Intervene in World War II for the Defense of Britain." The official title was "An Act Further to Promote the Defense of the United States." As finally passed, the new law virtually pledged the United States to the full extent of its economic resources to provide military supplies for those who were fighting aggression. Fiery Senator Burton K. Wheeler of Montana, "a born prosecutor" who had run for vice president on the left-wing La Follette Progressive ticket of 1924, was one of the most vehement isolationists. In the following radio speech, how prophetic is he?

The lend-lease policy, translated into legislative form, stunned a Congress and a nation wholly sympathetic to the cause of Great Britain. . . . It warranted my worst fears for the future of America, and it definitely stamps the President as war-minded.

The lend-lease-give program is the New Deal's Triple-A foreign policy; it will plow under every fourth American boy.

Never before have the American people been asked or compelled to give so bounteously and so completely of their tax dollars to any foreign nation. Never before has the Congress of the United States been asked by any President to violate international law. Never before has this Nation resorted to duplicity in the conduct of its foreign affairs. Never before has the United States given to one man the power to strip this Nation of its defenses. Never before has a Congress coldly and flatly been asked to abdicate.

If the American people want a dictatorship—if they want a totalitarian form of government and if they want war—this bill should be steamrollered through Congress, as is the wont of President Roosevelt.

Approval of this legislation means war, open and complete warfare. I, therefore, ask the American people before they supinely accept it, Was the last World War worth while?

---

[2]Reprinted in *Congressional Record,* 77th Cong., 1st sess. (speech of January 12, 1941), Appendix, pp. 178–179.

If it were, then we should lend and lease war materials. If it were, then we should lend and lease American boys. President Roosevelt has said we would be repaid by England. We will be. We will be repaid, just as England repaid her war debts of the first World War—repaid those dollars wrung from the sweat of labor and the toil of farmers with cries of "Uncle Shylock." Our boys will be returned—returned in caskets, maybe; returned with bodies maimed; returned with minds warped and twisted by sights of horrors and the scream and shriek of high-powered shells.

Considered on its merits and stripped of its emotional appeal to our sympathies, the lend-lease-give bill is both ruinous and ridiculous. . . .

It gives to one man—responsible to no one—the power to denude our shores of every warship. It gives to one individual the dictatorial power to strip the American Army of our every tank, cannon, rifle, or anti-aircraft gun. No one would deny that the lend-lease-give bill contains provisions that would enable one man to render the United States defenseless, but they will tell you, "The President would never do it." To this I say, "Why does he ask the power if he does not intend to use it?" Why not, I say, place some check on American donations to a foreign nation? . . .

I say in the kind of language used by the President—shame on those who ask the powers—and shame on those who would grant them.

[Talk of "plowing under every fourth American boy" spurred Roosevelt into declaring at his press conference of January 14, 1941, that this was "the most untruthful, the most dastardly, unpatriotic thing that has ever been said. Quote me on that. That really is the rottenest thing that has been said in public life in my generation." What measure of truth was there in Wheeler's charge?]

3. William Randolph Hearst Denounces Aid to the Soviet Union (1941)

The fateful lend-lease bill became law in March 1941. Three months later, Hitler treacherously attacked Stalin, his co-conspirator in the nonaggression pact of 1939. Isolationists rejoiced that the two arch-menaces would now bleed each other white and thus reduce the danger of U.S. involvement. Catholics expressed relief at the weakening of the atheistic menace of Soviet Russia. Roosevelt, however, fearful that the Russians could not stem Hitler's mechanized might, promised them lend-lease aid and ultimately delivered supplies worth $11 billion. The Hearst press here expresses distaste for "Bloody Joe" Stalin as a bedfellow. To what extent were its apprehensions justified by events?

If we are fighting totalitarianism as a foul principle and oppressive policy, why in the name of high heaven should we not desire to see the two totalitarian powers exterminate each other and destroy not only the principle but the practice of despotic government?

If we are citizens—or subjects—of a genuine democracy and if we are devoted to the ideals of democracy, and honestly desirous of preserving and perpetuating those ideals, why should we not desire to see the enemies of democracy destroy each other? . . .

---

[3]*New York Journal-American,* September 5, 1941.

Is our free country piling up deficits, bleeding its citizens white with confiscatory taxation, rushing headlong into national bankruptcy, shoveling out our wealth abroad, and shipping our war materials to alien nations to bolster up Bolshevism in Russia to spread it over all of Europe, including Britain, and to breed it and broadcast it in our own America?

We may not think that this is what we want to do, but this is exactly what we are doing with our Bolshevist alliance, and no smoke screen of fine phrases can obscure that outstanding fact.

No country which fights for Russia can claim to be honestly opposed to tyranny, since Bolshevism is the basest and bloodiest tyranny that has disgraced the supposed civilization of Europe since the time of Ivan the Terrible.

No country can truthfully claim to be crusading for democracy and the four freedoms when it is supporting a tyranny which is the most evil enemy of democracy—a tyranny where all the four freedoms have been brutally suppressed—a tyranny with no liberty, no opportunity, no morality, and no God.

C. War in the Atlantic

1. Framing the Atlantic Charter (1941)

Roosevelt finally met with Prime Minister Winston Churchill in deepest secrecy off the coast of Newfoundland in August 1941. Major items of discussion were lend-lease shipments, common defense, and the halting of Japanese aggression. Churchill later wrote that for Roosevelt—the head of a technically neutral state—to meet in this way with the prime minister of a belligerent state was "astonishing" and amounted to "warlike action." The most spectacular offspring of the conference was the unofficial Atlantic Charter, which in 1942 became the cornerstone of Allied war aims. An admixture of the old Wilson Fourteen Points (see p. 257) and the New Deal, it held out seductive hope to the victims of the dictators. What aspects of the Atlantic Charter come closest to "warlike action"?

. . . The President of the United States of America and the Prime Minister, Mr. Churchill, representing His Majesty's Government in the United Kingdom, being met together, deem it right to make known certain common principles in the national policies of their respective countries on which they base their hopes for a better future for the world.

First, their countries seek no aggrandizement, territorial or other;

Second, they desire to see no territorial changes that do not accord with the freely expressed wishes of the peoples concerned [self-determination, one of Wilson's Fourteen Points; in part Points V and XII of the fourteen];

Third, they respect the right of all peoples to choose the form of government under which they will live; and they wish to see sovereign rights and self-government

---

[1]*Department of State Bulletin* 5 (August 14, 1941): 125–126.

restored to those who have been forcibly deprived of them [territorial restoration, Points VI, VII, VIII, XI of the fourteen];

Fourth, they will endeavor, with due respect for their existing obligations, to further the enjoyment by all states, great or small, victor or vanquished, of access, on equal terms, to the trade and to the raw materials of the world which are needed for their economic prosperity [Point III of the fourteen];

Fifth, they desire to bring about the fullest collaboration between all nations in the economic field with the object of securing, for all, improved labor standards, economic advancement, and social security [a combination of the objectives of the League of Nations and the New Deal];

Sixth, after the final destruction of the Nazi tyranny, they hope to see established a peace which will afford to all nations the means of dwelling in safety within their own boundaries, and which will afford assurance that all the men in all the lands may live out their lives in freedom from fear and want;

Seventh, such a peace should enable all men to traverse the high seas and oceans without hindrance [freedom of the seas, Point II of the fourteen];

Eighth, they believe that all of the nations of the world, for realistic as well as spiritual reasons, must come to the abandonment of the use of force. Since no future peace can be maintained if land, sea, or air armaments continue to be employed by nations which threaten, or may threaten, aggression outside of their frontiers, they believe, pending the establishment of a wider and permanent system of general security [the United Nations, replacing the League of Nations], that the disarmament of such nations is essential. They will likewise aid and encourage all other practicable measures which will lighten for peace-loving peoples the crushing burden of armaments [Point IV of the fourteen].

2. The Chicago Tribune *Is Outraged (1941)*

A highly influential mouthpiece of midwestern isolationism was the Chicago Tribune, *self-elected "The World's Greatest Newspaper." Violently anti-Roosevelt and anti-intervention, it resorted to extreme measures, including the publication of Washington's secret war plans three days before Pearl Harbor. To what extent does the* Tribune's *editorial on the Atlantic Conference confirm Churchill's later observation that the deliberations amounted to "warlike action"?*

Mr. Roosevelt's dangerous ambition always to do what no other President ever did, and to be the man who shakes the world, led him to meet Mr. Churchill, as is now disclosed, at sea. There, he, the head of a nation which is not at war, and the head of the British empire, which is at war, signed their names to an eight-point war and peace program, as if both countries not only were fighting side by side but saw their way to victory. . . .

---

[2]Editorial against Atlantic Charter (August 15, 1941) as quoted in *A Century of Tribune Editorials* (1947), pp. 129–130. Reprinted by permission of the *Chicago Tribune*.

For Mr. Churchill the event would be, he could hope, that last step which would bring him what he has awaited as his salvation—the final delivery on Mr. Roosevelt's commitments, the delivery of the United States with all its man power into the war at all points. Mr. Churchill would appreciate that Mr. Roosevelt in the eyes of the world became his full ally. . . .

Mr. Roosevelt himself had that end in view. As head of a nation at peace he had no right to discuss war aims with the ruler of a country at war. He had no right to take a chair at such a conference. He had no regard for his constitutional duties or his oath of office when he did so. He not only likes to shatter traditions, he likes to shatter the checks and restraints which were put on his office. He is thoro[ugh]ly un-American. His ancestry is constantly emerging. He is the true descendant of that James Roosevelt, his great-grandfather, who was a Tory in New York during the Revolution and took the oath of allegiance to the British king.* . . .

He comes of a stock that has never fought for the country and he now betrays it, altho[ugh] it has repudiated his program and him with it. . . .

The American people can rest assured that Mr. Churchill was paying little attention to the rehash of the Wilsonian futilities, to the freedom of the seas and the freedom of peoples such as the [British-ruled] people of India, for instance. What he wanted to know of Mr. Roosevelt was: When are you coming across? And it is the answer to that question that concerns the American people, who have voted 4 to 1 that they are not going across at all unless their government drags them in against their will.

One phrase in the statement would have Mr. Churchill's complete approval—"after final destruction of the Nazi tyranny." To that he committed the President of the United States in circumstances as spectacular and theatrical as could be arranged. Mr. Roosevelt pledged himself to the destruction of Hitler and the Nazis. In the circumstances in which this was done Mr. Churchill would insist that it was the pledge of a government, binding upon the country.

The country repudiates it. Mr. Roosevelt had no authority and can find none for making such a pledge. He was more than outside the country. He was outside his office. The spectacle was one of two autocratic rulers, one of them determining the destiny of his country in the matter of war or peace absolutely in his own will, as if his subjects were without voice.

The country rejects that idea of its government.

3. FDR Proclaims Shoot-at-Sight (1941)

Lend-lease carried an implied commitment that the United States would guarantee delivery of arms, although the law specifically forbade "convoying vessels by naval vessels of the United States." Roosevelt got around this restriction by setting up a

---

*James Roosevelt, only fifteen years old when the fighting began, was a student at Princeton from 1776 to 1780. His father, a staunch patriot, was forced to flee New York City. There is no evidence that young James took the alleged oath; the probabilities are strong that he did not. (Information provided by Elizabeth B. Drewry, director of the Franklin D. Roosevelt Library.)

³*Department of State Bulletin* 5 (September 13, 1941): 193, 195, 197.

system of patrols by U.S. warships working in collaboration with the British. On September 4, 1941, the U.S. destroyer Greer *in Icelandic waters trailed a German submarine for three and one-half hours while radioing its position to nearby British aircraft. The U-boat finally fired two torpedoes (which missed), whereupon the* Greer *retaliated with depth bombs (which also missed). Seven days later, after presumably taking time to verify the facts, Roosevelt went on the radio with this sensational shoot-at-sight speech. What liberties did he take with the truth? Did the crisis justify his doing so?*

The Navy Department of the United States has reported to me that, on the morning of September fourth, the United States destroyer *Greer,* proceeding in full daylight toward Iceland, had reached a point southeast of Greenland. She was carrying American mail to Iceland. She was flying the American flag. Her identity as an American ship was unmistakable.

She was then and there attacked by a submarine. Germany admits that it was a German submarine. The submarine deliberately fired a torpedo at the *Greer,* followed later by another torpedo attack. In spite of what Hitler's propaganda bureau has invented, and in spite of what any American obstructionist organization may prefer to believe, I tell you the blunt fact that the German submarine fired first upon this American destroyer without warning, and with deliberate design to sink her.

Our destroyer, at the time, was in waters which the Government of the United States has declared to be waters of self-defense—surrounding outposts of American protection in the Atlantic.

In the north, outposts have been established by us in Iceland, Greenland, Labrador, and Newfoundland. Through these waters there pass many ships of many flags. They bear food and other supplies to civilians; and they bear [lend-lease] matériel of war, for which the people of the United States are spending billions of dollars, and which, by Congressional action, they have declared to be essential for the defense of our own land.

The United States destroyer, when attacked, was proceeding on a legitimate mission. . . .

Generation after generation, America has battled for the general policy of the freedom of the seas.* That policy is a very simple one—but a basic, fundamental one. It means that no nation has the right to make the broad oceans of the world, at great distances from the actual theater of land war, unsafe for the commerce of others. . . .

It is no act of war on our part when we decide to protect the seas which are vital to American defense. The aggression is not ours. Ours is solely defense.

But let this warning be clear. From now on, if German or Italian vessels of war enter the waters, the protection of which is necessary for American defense, they do so at their own peril.

---

*The traditional American concept of freedom of the seas did not include the armed convoying of gift lend-lease munitions through German-proclaimed war zones to the enemies of Germany.

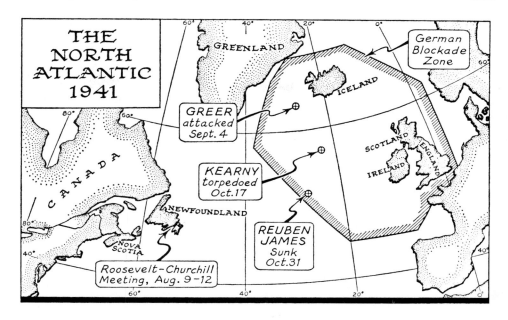

THE NORTH ATLANTIC 1941

GREENLAND

German Blockade Zone

ICELAND

GREER attacked Sept. 4

CANADA

SCOTLAND

ENGLAND

IRELAND

KEARNY torpedoed Oct. 17

NEWFOUNDLAND

REUBEN JAMES Sunk Oct. 31

NOVA SCOTIA

Roosevelt–Churchill Meeting, Aug. 9–12

[Patrolling led to convoying by presidential edict, despite the express terms of the Lend-Lease Act, and convoying led to shooting. In October 1941 the U.S. destroyer Kearny *suffered torpedo damage and a loss of eleven lives in a battle with German submarines southwest of Iceland. Later that month, the U.S. destroyer* Reuben James *was torpedoed and sunk while on convoy duty. An undeclared shooting war with Hitler was now being waged in the Atlantic.]*

D. Blowup in the Pacific

1. Harold Ickes Prepares to "Raise Hell" (1941)

New Japanese aggression in south Indochina, despite warnings from Washington, finally prompted Roosevelt to clamp down a complete embargo on shipments going to Japan when he froze all Japanese assets in the United States on July 25, 1941. Faced with the loss of critical oil supplies, the Tokyo warlords were confronted with agonizing alternatives: yielding some of the fruits of their aggression in the Far East or fighting the United States and its allies. The United States was by no means ready for war in the vast Pacific, and the administration seriously considered a three-month truce; Roosevelt favored six months. But this proposal was never formally presented to Japan. The outspoken secretary of the interior, Harold Ickes, recorded in his secret

---

[1]Reprinted with permission of Simon & Schuster from *The Secret Diary of Harold L. Ickes, Vol. III: The Lowering Clouds, 1939–1941* by Harold L. Ickes. Copyright © 1954 by Simon & Schuster, Inc. Copyright renewed © 1982 by Simon & Schuster.

diary the story as he heard it. What does this account (written on November 30) reveal of the inner workings of the federal government? Why did the truce scheme fail?

Our State Department has been negotiating for several days with Saburo Kurusu, the special envoy sent over from Japan, and with Ambassador Kichisaburo Nomura. I have had a suspicion for a long time that the State Department would resume a policy of appeasement toward Japan, if it could get away with it.

Our State Department, according to a story that I have heard, had actually proposed what it called a "truce" for three months with Japan. We were to resume shipments of cotton and other commodities, but the most important item on the list was gasoline for "civilian" purposes. Now anyone who knows anything about Japan and about the situation there knows that there is very little, if any, civilian use of gasoline. . . . Then a strong protest came in from General Chiang Kai-shek to the effect that to do this would destroy the morale of the Chinese. It was the intention of the State Department to crowd the thing through without even giving Halifax [British ambassador] a chance to refer it to Churchill. However, the British fought for and obtained a sufficient delay to consult Churchill, and he was strongly opposed.

The strong opposition of China and Britain caused the appeasers of the State Department to pause. They went to the White House, and in the end the President refused to go through with the deal.

If it had not been for the strenuous intervention of Churchill and Chiang Kai-shek, the appeasers in the State Department, with the support of the President, would have resumed at least a partial commercial relationship with Japan, as the result of which we would have sent Japan cotton and gasoline and other commodities. . . .

If this negotiation with Japan had been consummated, I would have promptly resigned from the Cabinet with a ringing statement attacking the arrangement and raising hell generally with the State Department and its policy of appeasement. I have no doubt that the country would have reacted violently. As a matter of fact, some of the newspapers indicated that they were uneasy and printed editorials deprecating any attempt at even a partial resumption of relationship with Japan. I believe that the President would have lost the country on this issue and that hell would have been to pay generally.

Now matters are very tense indeed so far as Japan is concerned. The morning papers carry headlines announcing that Japan has solemnly declared her determination "to purge American and British influence from East Asia for the honor and pride of mankind." So it may be, after all, that there will be a clash in the Pacific.

2. Tōgō Blames the United States (1952)

Instead of appeasement, Secretary of State Hull presented stern terms to the two Japanese envoys in his note of November 26, 1941. Japan would have to withdraw its armed forces from China, after four years of aggression, and from Indochina as well. In return, the United States would unfreeze Japanese assets and make some

---

[2]Reprinted with the permission of Simon & Schuster, Inc. from *Cause of Japan* by Shigenori Tōgō. Copyright © 1956 by Simon & Schuster, Inc. Copyright © renewed by Fumihiko Tōgō.

other secondary concessions. Such loss of face was so abhorrent to the Japanese war-lords that Hull had little hope that the terms would be accepted. The next day he told Secretary of War Stimson, "I have washed my hands of it, and it is now in the hands of you and [Secretary of the Navy] Knox—the Army and Navy." Here, the reaction of Japan is described by the then foreign minister, Tōgō Shigenori, who later died in prison while serving a twenty-year sentence as a war criminal. Where did he lay the blame for the breakdown of negotiations?

Ambassador Grew, then in Tokyo, later said that when the note of 26 November was sent, the button which set off the war had been pushed.

On the 26th and 27th Secretary Hull held special press conferences at which he gave a full account of the Japanese-American negotiations; the American press responded by reporting almost unanimously that it was Japan's choice whether to accept the Hull Note or go to war. Later—in wartime—an American chronicler wrote that even a Monaco or a Luxemburg would have taken up arms against the United States if it had been handed such a memorandum as that which the State Department presented to the Japanese government. . . .

It is therefore no longer arguable at this time of day that the American authorities, having made all necessary preparations in the expectation that the negotiations would break down and a war ensue, delivered the Hull Note anticipating that Japan would reject it, thus compelling her to elect between total surrender and war. Indeed, remembering that the question of how to insure that Japan should fire the first shot had been in the forefront in the War Cabinet's discussions in Washington, it seems not unwarrantable to construe the note as going beyond the forcing of a choice—it is not too much to say that it was the throwing down of a challenge to Japan, or at the least constituted an ultimatum without time limit.

This we knew in Tokyo—though we could not then know of the words and acts of the high American officials which confirmed our deduction—from the drastic terms of the note and the inclusion among them of conditions never theretofore suggested. Our interpretation was confirmed by the reaction to Hull's disclosures by the American press—which played up, as if at the urging of the governmental authorities, the choice between the terms of the Hull Note and war—and by the plainly visible tightening of the encirclement of Japan.

So far as concerns my own state of mind upon receipt of the Hull Note, I can never forget the despair which overpowered me. I had fought and worked unflaggingly until that moment; but I could feel no enthusiasm for the fight thereafter. I tried as it were to close my eyes and swallow the Hull Note whole, as the alternative to war, but it stuck in the craw. In contrast to my dejection, many of the military men were elated at the uncompromising attitude of the United States, as if to say, "Didn't we tell you so?"—they were by no means easy to be patient with.

[The Japanese later argued that they were forced to break out of the economic encirclement resulting from Roosevelt's embargo-freezing order of July 25, 1941. This view found surprising support in 1944 from one U.S. ally, Captain Oliver Lyttleton, British minister of production. In a London speech he declared, "Japan was provoked into attacking the Americans at Pearl Harbor. It is a travesty on history ever to say that America was forced into the war. . . . It is incorrect to say that America was

ever truly neutral." The subsequent uproar in the United States forced Lyttleton hastily to soften his remarks. (New York Times, June 21, 22, 1944.)]

3. Cordell Hull Justifies His Stand (1948)

Isolationist Senator Vandenberg, writing in his diary just after Pearl Harbor, felt that the United States would have had to yield "relatively little" to pacify Japan, and feared that "we may have driven her needlessly into hostilities through our dogmatic diplomatic attitudes." "We 'asked for it,'" he added, "and we 'got it.'" Secretary of State Hull, the soft-spoken Tennessean, here outlines three possible alternatives in his Memoirs. *Assuming that the ultimate security of the United States required the halting of the Japanese, and knowing that the U.S. Navy was not ready for Japan, form conclusions regarding the wisdom of Hull's choice among the three possibilities. Were other courses open?*

There were three methods to meet the danger from Japan. One was by a preventive attack. But democracies do not engage in preventive attacks except with greatest difficulty. Had I suggested to the President that he go to Congress and ask for a declaration of war against Japan at some time after the invasion of southern Indo-China, he could have made a good case concerning the dangers to us inherent in Japan's course of aggression. But, remembering the fact that on August 13, 1941, only three weeks after Japan invaded southern Indo-China, the House of Representatives sustained the Selective Service Act by a majority of just one vote, it seems most unlikely that the President could have obtained a declaration.

Nor would the military and naval authorities have been ready for a preventive attack. The fact that they pleaded for more time solely to prepare our defenses in the Pacific was proof in itself that they were not prepared to take the offensive.

A preventive attack, moreover, would have run counter to our determination to pursue the course of peace to the end, with the hope, however microscopic, that even at the last hour the Japanese might have a change of heart.

The second method to meet the danger was to agree to Japan's demands. This would have given us peace—that is, until Japan, after strengthening herself through the concessions we should have made, was ready to move again. But it would have denied all the principles of right living among nations which we had supported; it would have betrayed the countries [China, Britain] that later became our allies; and it would have given us an infamous place in history.

When we realize that Japan was ruthlessly invading peaceful countries, that the United States had pleaded with her from the beginning to cease her course of military conquest in partnership with Hitler, and that all problems in the Pacific would have practically settled themselves if Japan had adopted a policy of peace, it is evident that Japan had no right to make demands upon us. Japan negotiated as if we, too, were an aggressor, as if both countries had to balance their aggressions. Japan

---

[3]From Cordell Hull, *Memoirs of Cordell Hull, Vol. II.* Copyright © 1948. Reprinted by permission of the Estate of Cordell Hull.

had no more right to make demands upon us than an individual gangster has to make demands upon his intended victim.

The third method was simply to continue discussions with Japan, to convince her that her aggressions cost her more than they were worth, to point out to her that her partnership with Hitler could be as dangerous to her as it was to the rest of the world, to lay before her proposal after proposal which in the long run would have given her in peace the prosperity her military leaders were seeking in conquest.

It was this third that we chose. Of the three, it was the only American method.

[The Tokyo warlords claimed that they had only two choices: surrender or war. Actually they had a third choice: accommodation. Considerable loss of face would have been better than loss of the war. The argument that Hull's note of November 26 provoked the Japanese into an attack is weakened by two facts. First, the naval force that attacked Pearl Harbor had left its rendezvous in Japan twenty-four hours earlier. Second, early in November the imperial conference had unanimously decided on war, provided that diplomacy had not produced a satisfactory accord by December 1.]

E. The Blame for Pearl Harbor

1. War Warnings from Washington (1941)

The military officials in Washington had cracked Tokyo's secret code. They knew from intercepted messages, especially after Secretary Hull's final note of November 26, that Japan was about to attack. But they could only guess where. The following war warnings were dispatched to Pacific commanders, including General MacArthur, who was caught with his planes down in the Philippines some eight hours after the Pearl Harbor attack on December 7, 1941. The messages from Washington did not mention Hawaii, evidently because of the belief, fortified by reports of massed ship movements, that the Japanese were about to strike in Southeast Asia. The surprised U.S. commanders later complained that they had not been properly warned. Comment critically in the light of these warnings. What grounds existed for the assumption that the attack would not come at Pearl Harbor?

[Navy Department to Pacific Commanders, November 24, 1941]

Chances of favorable outcome of negotiations with Japan very doubtful. This situation, coupled with statements of Japanese Government and movements their naval and military forces, indicates in our opinion that a surprise aggressive movement in any direction, including attack on Philippines or Guam, is a possibility. Chief of Staff has seen this dispatch; concurs and requests action [by the respective addresses] to inform senior Army officers their areas. Utmost secrecy necessary in order not to complicate an already tense situation or precipitate Japanese action.

---

[1]*Pearl Harbor Attack; Hearings before the Joint Committee on the Investigation of the Pearl Harbor Attack,* 79th Cong. 1st sess. (1946), pt. xiv, pp. 1405, 1406.

[Navy Department to Asiatic and Pacific Fleets, November 27, 1941]

This dispatch is to be considered a war warning. Negotiations with Japan looking toward stabilization of conditions in the Pacific have ceased, and an aggressive move by Japan is expected within the next few days. The number and equipment of Japanese troops, and the organization of naval task forces, indicates an amphibious expedition against either the Philippines, Thai [Siam] or Kra [Malay] peninsula, or possibly Borneo [Dutch East Indies]. . . .

2. Admiral H. E. Kimmel Defends Himself (1946)

In 1942, after carrier-based Japanese bombers had crippled the U.S. fleet at Pearl Harbor on that fateful Sunday morning, the special Roberts commission found Admiral H. E. Kimmel and General W. C. Short, respectively the navy and army commanders in Hawaii at the time of the attack on Pearl Harbor, guilty of "dereliction of duty." But the army and navy conducted their own investigations and concluded that there were no grounds for a court-martial. After the war a full-dress joint congressional investigation (10 million words) elicited the following testimony from Admiral Kimmel, who must be judged in the light of three points. First, as early as 1932 the navy had staged a successful mock (Japanese) raid on Pearl Harbor on a Sunday morning with carrier-based aircraft. Second, the attacking Japanese carriers had been lost to U.S. naval intelligence for some days. Third, four hours and thirteen minutes before the surprise attack the navy sighted an enemy submarine off the mouth of Pearl Harbor; an hour and ten minutes before the strike the navy fired upon and sank a Japanese submarine off the mouth of Pearl Harbor. What were the strengths and weaknesses of Kimmel's defense?

The so-called "war warning" dispatch of November 27 did not warn the Pacific Fleet of an attack in the Hawaiian area. It did not state expressly or by implication that an attack in the Hawaiian area was imminent or probable. It did not repeal or modify the advice previously given me by the Navy Department that no move against Pearl Harbor was imminent or planned by Japan.

The phrase "war warning" cannot be made a catch-all for all the contingencies hindsight may suggest. It is a characterization of the specific information which the dispatch contained. . . .

In brief, on November 27, the Navy Department suggested that I send from the immediate vicinity of Pearl Harbor the carriers of the fleet, which constituted the fleet's main striking defense against an air attack.*

On November 27, the War and Navy Departments suggested that we send from the island of Oahu [site of Pearl Harbor] 50 percent of the Army's resources in pursuit planes.

These proposals came to us on the very same day of the so-called "war warning."

In these circumstances no reasonable man in my position would consider that

---

[2]*Pearl Harbor Attack*, pt. VI, pp. 2518, 2520, 2521.

*Fortunately for the United States, the three great carriers were not at Pearl Harbor when the attack came.

the "war warning" was intended to suggest the likelihood of an attack in the Hawaiian area.

From November 27 to the time of the attack, all the information which I had from the Navy Department or from any other source, confirmed, and was consistent with, the Japanese movement in southeast Asia described in the dispatch of November 27. . . .

In short, all indications of the movements of Japanese military and naval forces which came to my attention confirmed the information in the dispatch of 27 November—that the Japanese were on the move against Thailand or the Kra [Malay] Peninsula in southeast Asia.

3. Secretary Henry Stimson Charges Negligence (1946)

General Short complained that the warnings from Washington were not specific enough regarding a possible Japanese attack. He felt that he should have been advised that Washington, using a top-secret code-breaking device called "Magic," was intercepting Japanese coded messages (despite the need for secrecy in using these Magic intercepts). Yet on November 30—a week early—the Honolulu Advertiser *had headlined a story "*JAPANESE MAY STRIKE OVER WEEKEND.*" Newly installed army radar actually picked up the attacking Japanese planes fifty-three minutes in advance, but this evidence stirred no defense action. Secretary of War Stimson, who had served in three presidential cabinets, here defends his office before the joint congressional committee. Is his analogy to a sentinel convincing?*

Many of the discussions on this subject indicated a failure to grasp the fundamental difference between the duties of an outpost command and those of the commander in chief of an army or nation and his military advisers.

The outpost commander is like a sentinel on duty in the face of the enemy. His fundamental duties are clear and precise. He must assume that the enemy will attack at his particular post; and that the enemy will attack at the time and in the way in which it will be most difficult to defeat him. It is not the duty of the outpost commander to speculate or rely on the possibilities of the enemy attacking at some other outpost instead of his own. It is his duty to meet him at his post at any time, and to make the best possible fight that can be made against him with the weapons with which he has been supplied.

On the other hand, the Commander in Chief of the Nation (and his advisers) . . . has much more difficult and complex duties to fulfill. Unlike the outpost commander, he must constantly watch, study, and estimate where the principal or most dangerous attack is most likely to come, in order that he may most effectively distribute his insufficient forces and munitions to meet it. He knows that his outposts are not all equally supplied or fortified, and that they are not all equally capable of defense. He knows also that from time to time they are of greatly varying importance to the grand strategy of the war. . . .

---

[3]*Pearl Harbor Attack,* pt. XI, pp. 5428–5429.

From the foregoing I believe that it was inevitable and proper that a far greater number of items of information coming through our Intelligence should be collected and considered and appraised by the General Staff at Washington than those which were transmitted to the commander of an outpost.

General Short had been told the two essential facts: (1) A war with Japan is threatening. (2) Hostile action by Japan is possible at any moment. Given those two facts, both of which were stated without equivocation in the message of November 27, the outpost commander should be on the alert to make his fight.

Even without any such message, the outpost commander should have been on the alert. If he did not know that the relations between Japan and the United States were strained and might be broken at any time, he must have been almost the only man in Hawaii who did not know it, for the radio and the newspapers were blazoning out those facts daily, and he had a chief of staff and an intelligence officer to tell him so. And if he did not know that the Japanese were likely to strike without warning, he could not have read his history of Japan or known the lessons taught in Army schools in respect to such matters.*

Under these circumstances, which were of general knowledge and which he must have known, to cluster his airplanes in such groups and positions that in an emergency they could not take to the air for several hours, and to keep his anti-aircraft ammunition so stored that it could not be promptly and immediately available, and to use his best reconnaissance system, the radar, only for a very small fraction of the day and night, in my opinion betrayed a misconception of his real duty which was almost beyond belief.

[The joint congressional committee investigating Pearl Harbor was a partisan body that submitted two reports. The majority (six Democrats, joined by two Republicans) generally absolved the Democratic Roosevelt administration of responsibility for the surprise attack, while finding the Hawaii commanders guilty of "errors of judgment and not derelictions of duty." Two Republican senators filed a minority report highly critical of the Roosevelt administration.]

4. Franklin Roosevelt Awaits the Blow (1941)

On the evening of December 6—the day before Pearl Harbor—U.S. naval intelligence intercepted and decoded the bulk of Tokyo's warlike reply to Secretary Hull's last "tough" note (November 26). Commander Lester Schultz, a naval aide at the White House, promptly delivered these intercepts to the White House. Five years later he testified before the joint congressional committee concerning the president's reaction. Certain critics of Roosevelt claim that he now knew of the Japanese plan to strike Pearl Harbor the next day and that he deliberately exposed the fleet in order to lure the Japanese into an act of aggression that would unify American opinion. What light does Commander Schultz's testimony shed on this interpretation?

---

*Attacking without warning had been a feudal practice in Japan. The Japanese attacked the Chinese without warning in 1894 and 1931 and the Russians in 1904. In the age of Hitler, attacks without warning were commonplace, as indeed they have been throughout history.

4*Pearl Harbor Attack,* pt. X, pp. 4662–4663.

Commander Schultz. The President read the papers, which took perhaps ten minutes. Then he handed them to [long-time Roosevelt adviser] Mr. [Harry] Hopkins. . . . Mr. Hopkins then read the papers and handed them back to the President. The President then turned toward Mr. Hopkins and said in substance . . . "This means war." Mr. Hopkins agreed, and they discussed then, for perhaps five minutes, the situation of the Japanese forces, that is, their deployment and—

Mr. Richardson [committee counsel]. Can you recall what either of them said?

Commander Schultz. In substance I can. . . . Mr. Hopkins . . . expressed a view that since war was undoubtedly going to come at the convenience of the Japanese, it was too bad that we could not strike the first blow and prevent any sort of surprise. The President nodded and then said in effect, "No, we can't do that. We are a democracy and a peaceful people." Then he raised his voice, and this much I remember definitely. He said, "But we have a good record."

The impression that I got was that we would have to stand on that record; we could not make the first overt move. We would have to wait until it came.

During this discussion there was no mention of Pearl Harbor. The only geographic name I recall was Indochina. The time at which war might begin was not discussed, but from the manner of the discussion there was no indication that tomorrow was necessarily the day.

Thought Provokers

1. What would have been the outcome of World War II in Europe (or in Asia) if the United States had been truly neutral? Would the results have been to the nation's best interests?

2. Have events since 1945 given support to the view that a democratic United States could exist as a kind of fortified island?

3. Lend-lease was designed to defend the United States by helping others fight the United States' potential enemies with U.S. weapons. Was there an element of immorality in this policy? Would the United States have kept out of the war if the Lend-Lease Act had not been passed?

4. Assuming that the Atlantic Charter was a warlike step, was it justified? Roosevelt believed that a Hitler victory would be ruinous for the United States, and to combat isolationist pressures he repeatedly misrepresented facts (*Greer* case) or usurped powers (convoying). Was he justified in using such methods to arouse the American people to an awareness of their danger?

5. With regard to the diplomatic breakdown preceding Pearl Harbor, it has been said that both Japan and the United States were right if one conceded their major premises. Explain fully, and form a conclusion.

6. Why were the defenders at Pearl Harbor caught by surprise? Who deserves the most blame for the surprise?

36

America in World War II, 1941–1945

No matter how long it may take us to overcome this premeditated invasion [Pearl Harbor], the American people in their righteous might will win through to absolute victory.

Franklin D. Roosevelt, War Message, 1941

Prologue: The nation was plunged into war by the worst military disaster in its history—the Japanese surprise attack at Pearl Harbor, Hawaii, on December 7, 1941. Caught flatfooted, the United States quickly whipped itself into fighting shape. War production revived the depression-drugged economy, stimulating the growth of numerous "boom towns," many of them in the South and West. A panicky government interned some 110,000 Japanese-Americans in so-called relocation centers, and a few race riots involving blacks and Chicanos blotted the wartime record, but for the most part the United States' many racial and ethnic minorities were willing and welcome partners in the war effort. Millions of new defense-related jobs created unprecedented employment opportunities for women. As the mighty U.S. economic machine went into high gear, the tide of battle slowly began to turn. U.S. troops fought their way agonizingly up the chains of Pacific islands from New Guinea toward Japan. In Europe the hard-pressed and ever-suspicious Soviet Union, eager to have the Western allies share equally in the bloodletting, clamored ceaselessly for a second front. After frustrating postponements, the Western allies at last invaded the north French coast on D-Day, June 6, 1944. After Germany was hammered into inglorious defeat in May 1945, Japan was atom-bombed into submission in August 1945. World War II ended as the nuclear age dawned, ushered in by an ominous mushroom-shaped cloud.

A. War and American Society

1. The War Transforms the Economy (1943)

As war orders flooded the nation's factories, the decade-old blight of depression was banished, and the face of the United States was transformed. Millions of workers

---

[1]Merlo J. Pusey, "Revolution at Home," *South Atlantic Quarterly* 42 (July 1943): 207–219, published by Duke University Press.

pulled up stakes and moved to the bustling war production centers. Older cities were bursting with war workers, many of them desperate for housing. New towns appeared almost overnight, especially in the wide-open West. The billions of dollars of war contracts financed a virtual revolution in the U.S. economy, conferring enormous advantages on certain businesses and regions. In the selection that follows, which changes are deemed most beneficial and which most harmful? What factors most shaped the decisions about where and how to spend defense dollars? Which economic effects of the war proved most lasting? Which of the author's predictions turned out to be most accurate?

While big industry, fed by government capital and war orders, is growing bigger every day, small industry is being wrecked by the withholding of priorities and materials. The problem is clearly stated by investigators for the Senate Committee on Education and Labor:

> Throughout the first two and a half years of our effort one hundred of America's largest corporations have received 75 per cent of all war contracts by dollar volume. To them has gone the bulk of new plants built at Government expense, over fourteen billions of dollars. To them are flowing in increasing numbers the workers seeking jobs in war industry. America, a land of giant corporations before the war, will emerge from this war with a larger share of its vastly expanded economy controlled by a smaller number of firms.
>
> This situation . . . has been accompanied by the destruction of one small community after another through the shutting down of its factories and the migration of its people. The face of America is already greatly changed. If we continue destroying America's small business and uprooting smaller communities, and many of our large ones as well, we shall not recognize postwar America.

. . . Certain advantages will undoubtedly accrue from this new emphasis on bigness. In the housing industry, for example, inefficient contractors operating on a shoestring are being replaced by large companies building two hundred to a thousand dwelling units at one time. To keep under the $6,000 ceiling on private homes built for war workers and at the same time make a profit, large-scale operations become imperative. Modern building methods are employed out of necessity. More important, large companies are learning that there are big opportunities in building houses which wage earners can afford to rent or buy. Here we have the nucleus of what may become a vast postwar industry capable of immeasurably improving the environment in which millions of our people live. . . .

We have built an enormous portion of our vast war plant within close range of big industries where expert management and skilled labor were at hand. Baltimore, Indianapolis, Buffalo, Hartford, St. Louis, Detroit, Los Angeles, Portland, Seattle, and numerous other cities find their manufacturing plants expanding at a rate that seemed impossible in peacetime. Detroit has sucked into its voracious mills enough manpower to make a new city much larger than Denver. Its satellite cities—Flint, Saginaw, Lansing, and Jackson—appear to have duplicated that feat on a smaller scale.

Of course, the lightning of war did not strike all the big cities with equal intensity. New York is suffering from a wave of unemployment because its consumer-goods industries are not readily adjustable to the making of tanks, airplanes, or ammunition. The jewelry industry in Providence is quietly starving for metal. But at near-by Hartford, where typewriters have given way to pistols and machine-tool makers are enjoying their golden age, every foot of space and every ounce of energy is at a premium. War is pushing Hartford ahead as ruthlessly as it is shoving New York behind. . . .

One exception to the general trend stands out in striking contrast. That is the sudden spurt of industrialization in the West. Great Salt Lake and Utah valleys, for example, are undergoing the most profound changes they have experienced since Brigham Young's pioneers broke their parched soil nearly a hundred years ago. Great military establishments have taken the place of quiet farms. Peaceful landscapes have given way to smoke-belching behemoths of industry. Aluminum, radio parts, coke, steel, and other strategic products are beginning to pour out of an area that has heretofore been noted chiefly for the exportation of Mormonism. . . .

Taken as a unit, the West is feeling the stimulus of war industry more keenly than either the North or the South. In 1940 the West had only 10.5 per cent of the country's population. But more than 13 per cent of the government's war-plant fund is being spent there, chiefly for permanent assets. One explanation is the pull of power. Southern California, the beneficiary of Boulder Dam power, has become a seething caldron of war industry. San Diego was until recently known as the "hottest spot" in the whole national picture of wartime dislocations. Los Angeles has eclipsed even the fantastic peacetime records of that city. The Golden State as a whole is getting more than $390,000,000 in Federal money for war plants. That gives it a sizable lead on the great industrial state of New York, and puts it far ahead of all New England in the wartime expansion of industrial capacity.

In the Northwest, Seattle is the hub of an amazing workshop for war. Grand Coulee and Bonneville dams are doing for the Northwest what Boulder Dam has done for Southern California and Nevada. Their great resources of power attract war industries as certainly as a bag of oats attracts a mule. The investment of Federal funds in war plants in the state of Washington will equal $80 per capita (1940 census). That outpouring of funds added to previous investments in power has given the Columbia River Valley and Puget Sound region great opportunity to raid neighboring states for manpower. And they are making the most of it. War has thus thrown into double-quick pace the industrial revolution that was already under way in the West.

The meaning of these social and economic upheavals is plain. "The hand that signs the war contract," as a Senate committee said recently, "is the hand that shapes the future." Metal-ribbed Nevada has acquired new government-financed plants costing the equivalent of nearly $600 for every resident. The agricultural Dakotas have no new war plants. In each case the consequences will be far-reaching. For in this nationwide mobilization there is no chance to maintain the status quo. If strategy and geography do not thrust a community into the maelstrom of war activity, its resources will be drained into other areas where they can better serve the national interest. So the whole pattern of our economic and social life is undergoing kaleidoscopic changes, without so much as a bomb being dropped on our shores.

2. A Japanese-American Is Convicted (1943)

Fearing Japanese invasion and possible sabotage, the secretary of war in early 1942 ordered the removal of Japanese-Americans from Arizona, California, Oregon, and Washington. Though later upheld by the Supreme Court, the constitutionality of the removal order was questioned at the time and has been hotly debated ever since. One young Japanese-American citizen, Gordon K. Hirabayashi, refused to register for deportation and deliberately violated an 8:00 P.M. curfew imposed on Japanese-Americans in his native city of Seattle. He was tried and convicted for both offenses, and the Supreme Court, in the decision excerpted here, upheld his conviction. What were Hirabayashi's principal reasons for denying the military orders? How does the Court justify the government's actions? Are the Court's arguments convincing? (In early 1985 a federal court in San Francisco overturned Hirabayashi's conviction of forty-three years earlier.)

Appellant asserted that the indictment should be dismissed because he was an American citizen who had never been a subject of and had never borne allegiance to the Empire of Japan, and also because the Act of March 21, 1942, was an unconstitutional delegation of Congressional power. On the trial to a jury it appeared that appellant was born in Seattle in 1918, of Japanese parents who had come from Japan to the United States, and who had never afterward returned to Japan; that he was educated in the Washington public schools and at the time of his arrest was a senior in the University of Washington; that he had never been in Japan or had any association with Japanese residing there.

The evidence showed that appellant had failed to report to the Civil Control Station on May 11 or May 12, 1942, as directed, to register for evacuation from the military area. He admitted failure to do so, and stated it had at all times been his belief that he would be waiving his rights as an American citizen by so doing. The evidence also showed that for like reason he was away from his place of residence after 8:00 P.M. on May 9, 1942. The jury returned a verdict of guilty on both counts and appellant was sentenced to imprisonment for a term of three months on each, the sentences to run concurrently. . . .

Appellant does not deny that he knowingly failed to obey the curfew order as charged in the second count of the indictment, or that the order was authorized by the terms of Executive Order No. 9066, or that the challenged Act of Congress purports to punish with criminal penalties disobedience of such an order. His contentions are only that Congress unconstitutionally delegated its legislative power to the military commander by authorizing him to impose the challenged regulation, and that, even if the regulation were in other respects lawfully authorized, the Fifth Amendment prohibits the discrimination made between citizens of Japanese descent and those of other ancestry. . . .

The war power of the national government is "the power to wage war successfully." It extends to every matter and activity so related to war as substantially to affect its conduct and progress. The power is not restricted to the winning of victories

---
[2]*Hirabayashi* v. *United States,* 320 U.S. 83 (1943).

in the field and the repulse of enemy forces. It embraces every phase of the national defense, including the protection of war materials and the members of the armed forces from injury and from the dangers which attend the rise, prosecution and progress of war. . . .

The actions taken must be appraised in the light of the conditions with which the President and Congress were confronted in the early months of 1942. . . .

The challenged orders were defense measures for the avowed purpose of safeguarding the military area in question, at a time of threatened air raids and invasion by the Japanese forces, from the danger of sabotage and espionage. As the curfew was made applicable to citizens residing in the area only if they were of Japanese ancestry, our inquiry must be whether in the light of all the facts and circumstances there was any substantial basis for the conclusion, in which Congress and the military commander united, that the curfew as applied was a protective measure necessary to meet the threat of sabotage and espionage which would substantially affect the war effort and which might reasonably be expected to aid a threatened enemy invasion. The alternative which appellant insists must be accepted is for the military authorities to impose the curfew on all citizens within the military area, or on none. In a case of threatened danger requiring prompt action, it is a choice between inflicting obviously needless hardship on the many, or sitting passive and unresisting in the presence of the threat. We think that constitutional government, in time of war, is not so powerless and does not compel so hard a choice if those charged with the responsibility of our national defense have reasonable ground for believing that the threat is real. . . . At a time of threatened Japanese attack upon this country, the nature of our inhabitants' attachments to the Japanese enemy was consequently a matter of grave concern. Of the 126,000 persons of Japanese descent in the United States, citizens and noncitizens, approximately 112,000 resided in California, Oregon and Washington at the time of the adoption of the military regulations. Of these approximately two-thirds are citizens because born in the United States. Not only did the great majority of such persons reside within the Pacific Coast states but they were concentrated in or near three of the large cities, Seattle, Portland and Los Angeles, all in Military Area No. 1.

There is support for the view that social, economic and political conditions which have prevailed since the close of the last century, when the Japanese began to come to this country in substantial numbers, have intensified their solidarity and have in large measure prevented their assimilation as an integral part of the white population. In addition, large numbers of children of Japanese parentage are sent to Japanese language schools outside the regular hours of public schools in the locality. Some of these schools are generally believed to be sources of Japanese nationalistic propaganda, cultivating allegiance to Japan. Considerable numbers, estimated to be approximately 10,000, of American-born children of Japanese parentage have been sent to Japan for all or a part of their education.

Congress and the Executive, including the military commander, could have attributed special significance, in its bearing on the loyalties of persons of Japanese descent, to the maintenance of Japan by its system of dual citizenship. Children born in the United States of Japanese alien parents, and especially those children born before December 1, 1924, are under many circumstances deemed, by Japanese law, to be citizens of Japan. No official census of those whom Japan regards as having thus retained Japanese citizenship is available, but there is ground for the belief that the number is large.

The large number of resident alien Japanese, approximately one-third of all Japanese inhabitants of the country, are of mature years and occupy positions of influence in Japanese communities. The association of influential Japanese residents with Japanese Consulates has been deemed a ready means for the dissemination of propaganda and for the maintenance of the influence of the Japanese Government with the Japanese population in this country.

As a result of all these conditions affecting the life of the Japanese, both aliens and citizens, in the Pacific Coast area, there has been relatively little social intercourse between them and the white population. The restrictions, both practical and legal, affecting the privileges and opportunities afforded to persons of Japanese extraction residing in the United States, have been sources of irritation and may well have tended to increase their isolation, and in many instances their attachments to Japan and its institutions.

Viewing these data in all their aspects, Congress and the Executive could reasonably have concluded that these conditions have encouraged the continued attachment of members of this group to Japan and Japanese institutions. These are only some of the many considerations which those charged with the responsibility for the national defense could take into account in determining the nature and extent of the danger of espionage and sabotage, in the event of invasion or air raid attack. The extent of that danger could be definitely known only after the event and after it was too late to meet it. Whatever views we may entertain regarding the loyalty to this country of the citizens of Japanese ancestry, we cannot reject as unfounded the judgment of the military authorities and of Congress that there were disloyal members of that population, whose number and strength could not be precisely and quickly ascertained. We cannot say that the war-making branches of the Government did not have ground for believing that in a critical hour such persons could not readily be isolated and separately dealt with, and constituted a menace to the national defense and safety, which demanded that prompt and adequate measures be taken to guard against it.

Appellant does not deny that, given the danger, a curfew was an appropriate measure against sabotage. It is an obvious protection against the perpetration of sabotage most readily committed during the hours of darkness. If it was an appropriate exercise of the war power its validity is not impaired because it has restricted the citizen's liberty. Like every military control of the population of a dangerous zone in wartime, it necessarily involves some infringement of individual liberty, just as does the police establishment of fire lines during a fire, or the confinement of people to their houses during an air raid alarm—neither of which could be thought to be an infringement of constitutional right. Like them, the validity of the restraints of the curfew order depends on all the conditions which obtain at the time the curfew is imposed and which support the order imposing it.

But appellant insists that the exercise of the power is inappropriate and unconstitutional because it discriminates against citizens of Japanese ancestry, in violation of the Fifth Amendment. The Fifth Amendment contains no equal protection clause and it restrains only such discriminatory legislation by Congress as amounts to a denial of due process. . . . Congress may hit a particular danger where it is seen, without providing for others which are not so evident or so urgent. . . . Distinctions between citizens solely because of their ancestry are by their very nature odious to a free people whose institutions are founded upon the doctrine of equality. For that reason, legislative classification or discrimination based on race alone has often been held to be a denial of equal protection. . . . We may assume that these considerations would be controlling here were it not for the fact that the danger of espionage and sabotage, in time of war and of threatened invasion, calls upon the military authorities to scrutinize every relevant fact bearing on the loyalty of populations in the danger areas. Because racial discriminations are in most circumstances irrelevant and therefore prohibited, it by no means follows that, in dealing with the perils of war, Congress and the Executive are wholly precluded from taking into account those facts and circumstances which are relevant to measures for our national defense and for the successful prosecution of the war, and which may in fact place citizens of one ancestry in a different category from others. "We must never forget, that it is *a constitution* we are expounding," "a constitution intended to endure for ages to come, and, consequently, to be adapted to the various *crises* of human affairs."* The adoption by Government, in the crisis of war and of threatened invasion, of measures for the public safety, based upon the recognition of facts and circumstances which indicate that a group of one national extraction may menace that safety more than others, is not wholly beyond the limits of the Constitution and is not to be condemned merely because in other and in most circumstances racial distinctions are irrelevant. . . .

3. A Black American Ponders the War's Meaning (1942)

Blacks had bitter memories of World War I, when they had clamored in vain to play a major role in the "war to make the world safe for democracy." Despite urgent manpower needs, in 1917–1918 African-Americans had been deemed unfit for combat assignments and relegated mostly to "labor battalions" in the army. At home they won only limited access to war-related jobs and were the victims of several bloody race riots at war's end. In the light of this sorry record, it was an open question whether blacks would support the Allied cause in World War II. Japanese propagandists tried to exploit the United States' vexed history of race relations by claiming brotherhood with African-Americans as another "people of color" oppressed by white rule. On what grounds did the black author of the following essay decide to support the war? Was he being realistic? Might he have been disillusioned or pleased with the course of the civil rights movement after the war?

War had no heroic traditions for me. Wars were white folks'. All wars in historical memory. The last war, and the Spanish-American War before that, and the Civil War. I had been brought up in a way that admitted of no heroics. I think my parents were right. Life for them was a fierce, bitter, soul-searching war of spiritual and eco-

---

*The quotation is from John Marshall's decision in *McCulloch* v. *Maryland* (1819). See Vol. 1, p. 216.
[3]J. Saunders Redding, "A Negro Looks at This War," from *American Mercury* 55 (November 1942): 585–592.

nomic attrition; they fought it without heroics, but with stubborn heroism. Their heroism was screwed up to a pitch of idealism so intense that it found a safety valve in cynicism about the heroics of white folks' war. This cynicism went back at least as far as my paternal grandmother, whose fierce eyes used to lash the faces of her five grandchildren as she said, "An' he done som'pin big an' brave away down dere to Chickymorgy an' dey made a iron image of him 'cause he got his head blowed off an' his stomick blowed out fightin' to keep his slaves." I cannot convey the scorn and the cynicism she put into her picture of that hero-son of her slave-master, but I have never forgotten.

I was nearly ten when we entered the last war in 1917. The European fighting, and the sinking of the *Lusitania,* had seemed as remote, as distantly meaningless to us, as the Battle of Hastings. Then we went in and suddenly the city was flag-draped, slogan-plastered, and as riotously gay as on circus half-holidays. I remember one fine Sunday we came upon an immense new billboard with a new slogan: GIVE! TO MAKE THE WORLD SAFE FOR DEMOCRACY. My brother, who was the oldest of us, asked what making the world safe for democracy meant. My father frowned, but before he could answer, my mother broke in.

"It's just something to say, like . . ."—and then she was stuck until she hit upon one of the family's old jokes—"like 'Let's make a million dollars.'" We all laughed, but the bitter core of her meaning lay revealed, even for the youngest of us, like the stone in a halved peach. . . .

And so, since I have reached maturity and thought a man's thoughts and had a man's—a Negro man's—experiences, I have thought that I could never believe in war again. Yet I believe in this one.

There are many things about this war that I do not like, just as there are many things about "practical" Christianity that I do not like. But I believe in Christianity, and if I accept the shoddy and unfulfilling in the conduct of this war, I do it as voluntarily and as purposefully as I accept the trash in the workings of "practical" Christianity. I do not like the odor of political pandering that arises from some groups. I do not like these "race incidents" in the camps. I do not like the world's not knowing officially that there were Negro soldiers on Bataan with General Wainwright.* I do not like the constant references to the Japs as "yellow bastards," "yellow bellies," and "yellow monkeys," as if color had something to do with treachery, as if color were the issue and the thing we are fighting rather than oppression, slavery, and a way of life hateful and nauseating. These and other things I do not like, yet I believe in the war. . . .

This is a war to keep men free. The struggle to broaden and lengthen the road of freedom—our own private and important war to enlarge freedom here in America—will come later. That this private, intra-American war will be carried on and won is the only real reason we Negroes have to fight. We must keep the road open. Did we not believe in a victory in that intra-American war, we could not believe in nor stomach the compulsion of this. If we could not believe in the realization of democratic freedom for ourselves, certainly no one could ask us to die for the preservation of that ideal for others. But to broaden and lengthen the road of freedom

---

*Bataan was an area in the Philippines through which Jonathan Wainwright's captured American garrison was cruelly forced to march to prisoner-of-war camps in May 1942—the "Bataan Death March."

is different from preserving it. And our first duty is to keep the road of freedom open. It must be done continuously. It is the duty of the whole people to do this. Our next duty (and this, too, is the whole people's) is to broaden the road so that more people can travel it without snarling traffic. To die in these duties is to die for something. . . .

I believe in this war, finally, because I believe in the ultimate vindication of the wisdom of the brotherhood of man. This is not foggy idealism. I think that the growing manifestations of the interdependence of all men is an argument for the wisdom of brotherhood. I think that the shrunk compass of the world is an argument. I think that the talk of united nations and of planned interdependence is an argument.

More immediately, I believe in this war because I believe in America. I believe in what America professes to stand for. Nor is this, I think, whistling in the dark. There are a great many things wrong here. There are only a few men of good will. I do not lose sight of that. I know the inequalities, the outraged hopes and faith, the inbred hate; and I know that there are people who wish merely to lay these by in the closet of the national mind until the crisis is over. But it would be equally foolish for me to lose sight of the advances that are made, the barriers that are leveled, the privileges that grow. Foolish, too, to remain blind to the distinction that exists between simple race prejudice, already growing moribund under the impact of this war, and theories of racial superiority as a basic tenet of a societal system—theories that at bottom are the avowed justification for suppression, defilement and murder.

I will take this that I have here. I will take the democratic theory. The bit of road of freedom that stretches through America is worth fighting to preserve. The very fact that I, a Negro in America, can fight against the evils in America is worth fighting for. This open fighting against the wrongs one hates is the mark and the hope of democratic freedom. I do not underestimate the struggle. I know the learning that must take place, the evils that must be broken, the depths that must be climbed. But I am free to help in doing these things. I count. I am free (though only a little as yet) to pound blows at the huge body of my American world until, like a chastened mother, she gives me nurture with the rest.

4. A Woman Remembers the War (1984)

With millions of men in the armed forces and the nation's factories straining to keep them supplied, women were drawn by the millions into nontraditional jobs. For many of those women, the war represented not simply a bloody conflict of global proportions, but also an unanticipated opportunity for economic freedom and personal growth. In the following selection, one war worker looks back on her experience in a plant in California. What does she remember most and least fondly about her wartime job? What aspects of it challenged her most? What was most fulfilling about it? What were the war's principal effects on her?

---

[4]From Mark Jonathan Harris, Franklin D. Mitchell, and Steven J. Schecter, *The Homefront: America During World War II*, pp. 126–129. Copyright © 1984. Reprinted by permission of Mark Jonathan Harris.

When the war started I was twenty-six, unmarried, and working as a cosmetics clerk in a drugstore in Los Angeles. I was running the whole department, handling the inventory and all that. It seemed asinine, though, to be selling lipstick when the country was at war. I felt that I was capable of doing something more than that toward the war effort.

There was also a big difference between my salary and those in defense work. I was making something like twenty-two, twenty-four dollars a week in the drug-store. You could earn a much greater amount of money for your labor in defense plants. Also it interested me. There was a certain curiosity about meeting that kind of challenge, and here was an opportunity to do that, for there were more and more openings for women.

So I went to two or three plants and took their tests. And they all told me I had absolutely no mechanical ability. I said, "I don't believe that." So I went to another plant, A.D.E.L. I was interviewed and got the job. This particular plant made the hydraulic-valve system for the B-17. And where did they put women? In the burr room. You sat at a workbench, which was essentially like a picnic table, with a bunch of other women, and you worked grinding and sanding machine parts to make them smooth. That's what you did all day long. It was very mechanical and it was very bor-ing. There were about thirty women in the burr room, and it was like being in a beauty shop every day. I couldn't stand the inane talk. So when they asked me if I would like to work someplace else in the shop, I said I very much would.

They started training me. I went to a blueprint class and learned how to use a micrometer and how to draw tools out of the tool crib and everything else. Then one day they said, "Okay, how would you like to go into the machine shop?"

I said, "Terrific."

And they said, "Now, Adele, it's going to be a real challenge, because you'll be the only woman in the machine shop." I thought to myself, Well, that's going to be fun, all those guys and Adele in the machine shop. So the foreman took me over there. It was a big room, with a high ceiling and fluorescent lights, and it was very noisy. I walked in there, in my overalls, and suddenly all the machines stopped and every guy in the shop just turned around and looked at me. It took, I think, two weeks before anyone even talked to me. The discrimination was indescribable. They wanted to kill me.

My attitude was, "Okay, you bastards, I'm going to prove to you I can do any-thing you can do, and maybe better than some of you." And that's exactly the way it turned out. I used to do the rework on the pieces that the guy on the shift before me had screwed up. I finally got assigned to nothing but rework.

Later they taught me to run an automatic screwing machine. It's a big mother, and it took a lot of strength just to throw that thing into gear. They probably thought I wasn't going to be able to do it. But I was determined to succeed. As a matter of fact, I developed the most fantastic biceps from throwing that machine into gear. Even today I still have a little of that muscle left.

Anyway, eventually some of the men became very friendly, particularly the older ones, the ones in their late forties or fifties. They were journeymen tool and die makers and were so skilled that they could work anywhere at very high salaries. They were sort of fatherly, protective. They weren't threatened by me. The younger men, I think, were.

Our plant was an open shop, and the International Association of Machinists was trying to unionize the workers. I joined them and worked to try to get the union in the plant. I proselytized for the union during lunch hour, and I had a big altercation with the management over that. The employers and my lead man and foreman called me into the office and said, "We have a right to fire you."

I said, "On what basis? I work as well or better than anybody else in the shop except the journeymen."

They said, "No, not because of that. Because you're talking for the union on company property. You're not allowed to do that."

I said, "Well, that's just too bad, because I can't get off the grounds here. You won't allow us to leave the grounds during lunch hour. And you don't pay me for my lunch hour, so that time doesn't belong to you, so you can't tell me what to do." And they backed down.

I had one experience at the plant that really made me work for the union. One day while I was burring I had an accident and ripped some cartilage out of my hand. It wasn't serious, but it looked kind of messy. They had to take me over to the industrial hospital to get my hand sutured. I came back and couldn't work for a day or two because my hand was all bandaged. It wasn't serious, but it was awkward. When I got my paycheck, I saw that they had docked me for time that I was in the industrial hospital. When I saw that I was really mad.

It's ironic that when the union finally got into the plant, they had me transferred out. They were anxious to get rid of me because after we got them in I went to a few meetings and complained about it being a Jim Crow union. So they arranged for me to have a higher rating instead of a worker's rating. This allowed me to make twenty-five cents an hour more, and I got transferred to another plant. By this time I was married. When I became pregnant I worked for about three months more, then I quit.

For me defense work was the beginning of my emancipation as a woman. For the first time in my life I found out that I could do something with my hands besides bake a pie. I found out that I had manual dexterity and the mentality to read blueprints and gauges, and to be inquisitive enough about things to develop skills other than the conventional roles that women had at that time. I had the consciousness-raising experience of being the only woman in this machine shop and having the mantle of challenge laid down by the men, which stimulated my competitiveness and forced me to prove myself. This, plus working in the union, gave me a lot of self-confidence.

B. The Second Front Controversy

1. Eisenhower Urges the Earliest Possible Second Front (1942)

The German "Blitzkrieg" invasion of the Soviet Union was six months old by the time the United States entered World War II in December 1941, and by that date the Soviets had already suffered hundreds of thousands of casualties. From the outset, the Soviet leader, Joseph Stalin, emphasized that what he most urgently needed from his British

---

[1]Eisenhower, Dwight D., *The Papers of Dwight David Eisenhower: The War Years, Vol. I,* p. 151, copyright © 1970 The Johns Hopkins University Press.

and American allies was for them to open a second front in western Europe that would help to reduce the ferocious German pressure on the Soviets in the East. American military planners agreed, though political considerations, logistical bottlenecks, and strategic disagreements with the British combined to delay a full-scale second front for two and one-half more years, until D-Day, June 6, 1944—just eleven months before the conclusion of the war in Europe. The simmering controversy over the second front exacerbated Soviet suspicions of the West and significantly soured U.S.-Soviet relations, helping to set the stage for the Cold War that followed. In the following document from February 28, 1942, Dwight D. Eisenhower, then the head of the Army's War Plans Division and soon to become Supreme Allied Commander in Europe (and later president of the United States), laid out the strategic case for the earliest possible second front. What are his chief points? What are his principal worries about the Soviet Union?

. . . The task of keeping Russia in the war involves, in the opinion of the War Plans Division, immediate and definite action. It is not sufficient to urge upon the Russians the indirect advantages that will accrue to them from Allied operations in distant parts of the world, although these operations may be designed to free our forces for a later offensive against Germany, or to keep Japan from immediately attacking Siberia. Russia's problem is to sustain herself during the coming summer, and she must not be permitted to reach such a precarious position that she will accept a negotiated peace, no matter how unfavorable to herself, in preference to a continuation of the fight.

There are two important ways in which this result can probably be brought about. The first is by direct aid through lease-lend; the second is through the early initiation of operations that will draw off from the Russian front sizable portions of the German Army, both air and ground. Such an operation must be so conceived, and so presented to the Russians, that they will recognize the importance of the support rendered. Air, possibly ground, attack from England is indicated. Air operations can be initiated long before a sizable land attack could be staged. . . .

2. Churchill Explains to Stalin That There Will Be No Second Front in 1942 (1942)

Stalin sent his foreign minister, Vaycheslav Molotov, to London and Washington, D.C., in May 1942 to secure agreement on an early second front. Winston Churchill tried to dampen Soviet hopes, but Roosevelt assured Molotov that the Americans would open such a front in 1942—a promise that Churchill almost immediately persuaded Roosevelt to break. It fell to Churchill to carry that discouraging news to Stalin. The British prime minister wrote that his mission to Moscow was "like carrying a large lump of ice to the North Pole." Churchill later reported to Roosevelt on his meeting with the Soviet leader in August 1942. How does he characterize Stalin's reaction? What seem to be Churchill's underlying anxieties about the British-American-Soviet alliance?

---

[2]From *Roosevelt and Churchill* by Francis Lowenheim and Manfred Jonas and Harold D. Langley, editors, copyright © 1975 by Francis L. Lowenheim, Harold D. Langley and Manfred Jonas. Used by permission of Dutton, a division of Penguin Putnam, Inc.

. . . [W]e all repaired to the Kremlin at eleven P.M. and were received only by Stalin and Molotov with the interpreter. Then began a most unpleasant discussion. Stalin handed me the enclosed document to which see also my reply. When it was translated I said I would answer it in writing and that he must understand we have made up our minds upon the course to be pursued and that reproaches were vain. Thereafter we argued for about two hours, during which he said many disagreeable things, especially about our being too much afraid of fighting the Germans, and if we tried it like the Russians we should find it not so bad, that we had broken our promise about Sledgehammer [a proposed Allied invasion of Nazi-occupied France, planned for 1942], that we had failed in delivering the supplies promised to Russia and only sent remnants after we had taken all we needed for ourselves. Apparently these complaints were addressed as much to the United States as to Britain.

I repulsed all his contentions squarely but without taunts of any kind. I suppose he is not used to being contradicted repeatedly but he did not become at all angry or even animated. On one occasion I said, "I pardon that remark only on account of the bravery of the Russian troops." Finally he said we could carry it no further. He must accept our decision and abruptly invited us to dinner at eight o'clock tonight.

Accepted the invitation [but] said I would leave by plane at dawn the next morning, i.e., fifteenth. Joe seemed somewhat concerned at this and asked could I not stay longer. I said certainly, if there was any good to be done, and that I would wait one more day anyhow. I then exclaimed there was no ring of comradeship in his attitude. I had travelled far to establish good working relations. We had done our utmost to help Russia and would continue to do so. We had been left entirely alone for a year against Germany and Italy. Now that the three great nations were allied, victory was certain provided we did not fall apart, and so forth. I was somewhat animated in this passage and before it could be translated he made the remark that he liked the temperament or spirit of my utterance. Thereafter the talk began again in a somewhat less tense atmosphere.

He plunged into a long discussion of two Russian trench mortar-firing rockets which he declared were devastating in their effects and which he offered to demonstrate to our experts if they could wait. He said he would let us have all information about them, but should there not be something in return. Should there not be an agreement to exchange information of inventions. I said that we would give them everything without any bargaining except only those devices which, if carried in aeroplanes over the enemy lines and shot down, would make our bombing of Germany more difficult. He accepted this. He also agreed that his military authorities should meet our generals and this was arranged for three o'clock this afternoon. . . . All this part of the talk was easier, but when [special American emissary to the Soviet Union Averell] Harriman asked about the plans for bringing American aircraft across Siberia, to which the Russians have only recently consented after long American pressing, he replied, curtly, "Wars are not won with plans." Harriman backed me up throughout and we neither of us yielded an inch nor spoke a bitter word. . . .

It is my considered opinion that in his heart so far as he has one Stalin knows we are right and that six divisions on Sledgehammer would do him no good this year. Moreover I am certain that his sure-footed and quick military judgement makes him a strong supporter of Torch. I think it not impossible that he will make amends. In that hope I persevere. Anyhow I am sure it was better to have it out this way than any other. There was never at any time the slightest suggestion of their not fighting on and I think myself that Stalin has good confidence that he will win. . . .

3. Stalin Resents the Delay of the Second Front (1943)

At their meeting in Casablanca, Morocco, in January 1943, Roosevelt and Churchill announced their intention to invade Italy later that year, thus postponing the planned major attack across the English Channel until 1944. As the second front continued to be delayed, Stalin grew increasingly embittered. In this secret message to Churchill on June 24, 1943, he gave full vent to his anger. From the viewpoint of the Western Allies, what part of Stalin's attitude might have been most alarming?

. . . When you now write that "it would be no help to Russia if we threw away a hundred thousand men in a disastrous cross-Channel attack," all I can do is remind you of the following.

First, your own Aide-Mémoire of June 1942, in which you declared that preparations were under way for an invasion, not by a hundred thousand, but by an Anglo-American force exceeding one million men at the very start of the operation.

Second, your February [1943] message, which mentioned extensive measures preparatory to the invasion of Western Europe in August or September 1943, which, apparently, envisaged an operation, not by a hundred thousand men, but by an adequate force.

So when you now declare: "I cannot see how a great British defeat and slaughter would aid the Soviet armies," is it not clear that a statement of this kind in relation to the Soviet Union is utterly groundless and directly contradicts your previous and responsible decisions, listed above, about extensive and vigorous measures by the British and Americans to organize the invasion this year, measures on which the complete success of the operation should hinge?

I shall not enlarge on the fact that this responsible decision, revoking your previous decisions on the invasion of Western Europe, was reached by you and the President without Soviet participation and without inviting its representatives to the Washington conference, although you cannot but be aware that the Soviet Union's role in the war against Germany and its interest in the problems of the second front are great enough.

There is no need to say that the Soviet Government cannot become reconciled to this disregard of vital Soviet interests in the war against the common enemy.

You say that you "quite understand" my disappointment. I must tell you that the point here is not just the disappointment of the Soviet Government, but the preservation of its confidence in its Allies, a confidence which is being subjected to severe stress. One should not forget that it is a question of saving millions of lives in the occupied areas of Western Europe and Russia, and of reducing the enormous sacrifices of the Soviet armies, compared with which the sacrifices of the Anglo-American armies are insignificant.

---

[3]Ministry of Foreign Affairs of the USSR, *Correspondence between the Chairman of the Council of Ministers of the USSR and the Presidents of the USA and the Prime Ministers of Great Britain during the Great Patriotic War of 1941–1945* (1957), vol. 2, pp. 75–76.

4. Roosevelt and Stalin Meet Face-to-Face (1943)

At the Iranian capital of Teheran, Roosevelt and Stalin met face to face at last in November 1943, for the first of just two such occasions (the other was at Yalta, in the Soviet Crimea, in early 1945). Talk of the second front dominated much of the discussion among Churchill, Roosevelt, and Stalin. In the following exchange, how does the second-front question reveal the tensions in the "Grand Alliance"? How does the second-front issue foreshadow U.S.-Soviet problems in the postwar era?

Second Plenary Meeting, November 29, 1943, 4 P.M.
Conference Room, Soviet Embassy

Present

United States	United Kingdom	Soviet Union
President Roosevelt	Prime Minister Churchill	Marshal Stalin
Mr. Hopkins	Foreign Secretary Eden	Foreign Commissar
Mr. Harriman	Sir Archibald Clark Kerr	Molotov
Admiral Leahy	Field Marshal Dill	Marshal Voroshilov
General Marshall	General Brooke	Mr. Pavlov
Admiral King	Admiral of the Fleet	Mr. Berezhkov
General Arnold	Cunningham	
Major General Deane	Air Chief Marshal Portal	
Captain Royal	Lieutenant General Ismay	
Captain Ware	Lieutenant General Martel	
Mr. Bohlen	Major Birse	

Bohlen Collection

Bohlen Minutes

Secret

The President said that since there was no agenda for the conference he thought it would be a good idea to have a report from the military staffs who had met this morning, and if there was no objection they might hear from General Brooke, Marshal Voroshilov and General Marshall.

General Brooke said that the committee had not finished its work and had merely made a survey of the various operations mentioned, and had also examined the operation Overlord [code name for the Allied invasion of northern France that eventually took place on "D-Day," June 6, 1944], taking into account the period of time which must elapse before Overlord was put into effect. He said that the committee considered the fact that if active operations were not undertaken in the Mediterranean during this period it would provide the Germans with an opportunity to remove their forces from that area either for the Soviet front or for the defense against Overlord. The committee also examined the advantages of continuing the operations up the leg of Italy until they had brought the Germans to a decisive battle. The committee briefly reviewed the question of providing the Partisans in Yu-

---
[4]*Foreign Relations of the United States, 1943* (Washington D.C.: Government Printing Office), pp. 533–539.

goslavia with aid and supplies in order to assist them in containing German forces. The advantages of Turkey's participation in the war from the point of view of opening up the Dardanelles, the supply route to Russia and its effect on the Balkans was [were] also considered. The possibility of an operation in southern France in connection with Overlord was also briefly discussed. The effect of the air attacks on Germany was outlined to the committee by Air Marshal Portal, and General Marshall provided the figures of the United States build-up in England, and General Brooke himself had described the change-over from the defense to offensive preparations in England. General Brooke concluded that Marshal Voroshilov had put forth a number of questions and had received answers.

General Marshall said he had little to add to what General Brooke had said and he did not intend to go into any detail. He said that the chief problems were landing craft and suitable airfields to afford fighter protection for any operation. He emphasized that the question of adequate landing craft came first in importance, and added that by landing craft he meant those capable of carrying 40 tanks. He said that he had endeavored to make clear to the committee the manner in which preparations for Overlord were proceeding; that the flow of troops from the United States were [was] on schedule and that one million tons of material had already been shipped to England. He repeated that the variable factor was production of landing craft and that the schedule of production had been stepped up. He said that some veteran divisions had already been transferred from the Italian theater to England.

Marshal Voroshilov said that the answers which he had received to his questions at the committee meeting had been confirmed here at the conference by General Brooke and General Marshall. He added that the questions of Yugoslavia and Turkey mentioned by General Brooke had not been considered in detail.

Marshal Stalin then inquired who will command Overlord.

The President replied that it had not yet been decided.

Marshall Stalin said that nothing would come out of the operation unless one man was made responsible not only for the preparation but for the execution of the operation.

The Prime Minister said that General Morgan had been in charge of the preparatory work for some time but that the actual Commander had not yet been appointed. He said the British Government was willing to have a United States General in command in view of the fact that from the United States would come the bulk of the troops, and that possibly the Commander-in-Chief in the Mediterranean would be a British General. He suggested that the question of who should command Overlord had best be discussed between the three of them rather than in the large meeting.

The President said that the decisions taken here will affect the choice of the particular officer to command Overlord.

Marshall Stalin stated that the Russians do not expect to have a voice in the selection of the Commander-in-Chief; they merely want to know who he is to be and to have him appointed as soon as possible.

The Prime Minister expressed agreement and said that he thought the appointment could be announced within a fortnight. He then went on to say that he was a little concerned at the number and complexity of the problems which were before the conference. He said many hundreds of millions of people are watching this conference, and he hoped that it would not break up until an agreement had been reached on big military, political and moral questions. He said that the British Staff and himself had given prolonged thought to the Mediterranean theater and that they were most anxious to have the armies there fight against the enemy and not have them stripped of essential elements. He stated that their Soviet allies had now had an opportunity to survey the scene and that he would appreciate learning their views as to the best [use?] which could be made of the British forces in the Mediterranean area. He said the question of what help could be given from the Mediterranean theater to Overlord and the scale and timing of such help was of great importance. The operation into southern France from northern Italy had been mentioned but not studied and should, therefore, be explored more fully between the United States and British Staffs. Mr. Churchill said that Marshal Stalin had correctly stressed the value of pincers movement but that the time element was important and a premature subsidiary attack might be wiped out. He went on to say that personally all he wanted was landing craft for two divisions in the Mediterranean and that with such a force many operations would be feasible, for example, it could be used to facilitate the operations in Italy or to take the island of Rhodes if Turkey will enter the war, and could be used for these purposes for at least six months and then employed in support of Overlord. He pointed out that this force of landing craft could not be supplied for the forces in the Mediterranean without either delaying Overlord six to eight weeks or without withdrawing forces from the Indian theater. That is the dilemma. He said he would appreciate the views of Marshal Stalin and his military aides on the general strategy. The Prime Minister continued that the questions of Yugoslavia and Turkey were more political than military. He said that there are now in the Balkans 21 German Divisions and 21 Bulgarian Divisions, a total of 42. He added that there were 54,000 Germans scattered around the Aegean islands which would be an easy prey. If Turkey came in, the nine Bulgarian Divisions from [in?] Yugoslavia and Greece would be withdrawn, thus endangering the remaining German Divisions. No important operations were envisaged for the Balkans but merely supply and commando raids to assist Tito and his forces to contain the German forces there. Mr. Churchill added that Great Britain had no ambitious interests in the Balkans but merely wanted to pin down the German Divisions there. With regard to Turkey Mr. Churchill said that the British Government as allies of Turkey had accepted the responsibility to persuade or force Turkey to enter the war. He would need, and he hoped to obtain, help from the President and Marshal Stalin in his task in accordance with the agreement reached at Moscow. He added that the British Government would go far in pointing out to the Turks that their failure to respond to the invitation of our three great powers would have very serious political and territorial consequences for Turkey particularly in regard to the future status of the straits. He said this morning the military committee had discussed briefly the question of aid to Turkey, but it appeared to be more political than military, and there was no thought of using a major army, and that at the most two Divisions apart from the air and antiaircraft forces would be sent to Turkey. Mr. Churchill proposed that the two foreign secretaries and the representative of the President meet to discuss the political aspects of the Turkish question as well as other political questions involving the Balkans area. Mr. Churchill said that he had asked some questions yesterday regarding Bulgaria, in particular if Bulgaria attacked Turkey would the Soviet Government consider Bulgaria as a foe. The Prime Minister concluded that if Turkey declared war on Germany it would be a terrible blow to German morale, would neutralize Bulgaria and would directly affect Rumania which even now was seeking someone to surrender unconditionally to. Hungary likewise would be immediately affected. He said that now is the time to reap the crop if we will pay the small price of the reaping. He summed up the task before the conference as: (1) to survey the whole field of the Mediterranean, and (2), how to relieve Russia, and (3), how to help Overlord.

Marshall Stalin said that Mr. Churchill need have no worry about the Soviet attitude toward Bulgaria; that if Turkey entered the war the Soviet Union would go to war with Bulgaria, but even so he did not think Turkey would come in. He continued that there was no difference of opinion as to the importance of helping the Partisans, but that he must say that from the Russian point of view the question of Turkey, the Partisans and even the occupation of Rome were not really important operations. He said that Overlord was the most important and nothing should be done to distract attention from that operation. He felt that a directive should be given to the military staffs, and proposed the following one:

> (1). In order that Russian help might be given from the east to the execution of Overlord, a date should be set and the operation should not be postponed. (2). If possible the attack in southern France should precede Overlord by two months, but if that is impossible, then simultaneously or even a little after Overlord. An operation in southern France would be a supporting operation as contrasted with diversionary operations in Rome or in the Balkans, and would assure the success of Overlord. (3). The appointment of a Commander-in-Chief for Overlord as soon as possible. Until that is done the Overlord operation cannot be considered as really in progress. Marshall Stalin added that the appointment of the Commander-in-Chief was the business of the President and Mr. Churchill but that it would be advantageous to have the appointment made here.

The President then said he had been most interested in hearing the various angles discussed from Overlord to Turkey. He attached great importance to the question of logistics and timing. He said it is clear that we are all agreed as to the importance of Overlord and the only question was one of when. He said the question was whether to carry out Overlord at the appointed time or possibly postpone it for the sake of other operations in the Mediterranean. He felt that the danger of an expedition in the eastern Mediterranean might be that if not immediately successful it might draw away effectives which would delay Overlord. He said that in regard to the Balkans, the Partisans and other questions are pinning down some 40 Axis Divisions and it was therefore his thought that supplies and commando raids be increased to that area to insure these Divisions remaining there. The President then said he was in favor of adhering to the original date for Overlord set at Quebec, namely, the first part of May.

Marshal Stalin said he would like to see Overlord undertaken during the month of May; that he did not care whether it was the 1st, 15th or 20th, but that a definite date was important.

The Prime Minister said it did not appear that the points of view were as far apart as it seemed. The British Government was anxious to begin Overlord as soon as possible but did not desire to neglect the great possibilities in the Mediterranean merely for the sake of avoiding a delay of a month or two.

Marshal Stalin said that the operations in the Mediterranean have a value but they are really only diversions.

The Prime Minister said in the British view the large British forces in the Mediterranean should not stand idle but should be pressing the enemy with vigor. He added that to break off the campaign in Italy where the allied forces were holding a German army would be impossible.

Marshall Stalin said it looked as though Mr. Churchill thought that the Russians were suggesting that the British armies do nothing.

The Prime Minister said that if landing craft is [are] taken from the Mediterranean theater there will be no action. He added that at Moscow the conditions under which the British Government considered Overlord could be launched had been fully explained, and these were that there should not be more than 12 mobile German divisions behind the coastal troops and that German reinforcements for sixty days should not exceed 15 Divisions. He added that to fulfill these conditions it was necessary in the intervening period to press the enemy from all directions. He said that the Divisions now facing the allies in Italy had come from the most part in France [*for the most part from France?*], and to break off the action in Italy would only mean that they would return to France to oppose Overlord. Turning again to the question of Turkey, The Prime Minister said that all were agreed on the question of Turkey's entrance into the war. If she refused, then that was the end of it. If she does enter, the military needs will be slight, and it will give us the use of Turkish bases in Anatolia, and the taking of the island of Rhodes which he felt could be done with one assault Division. Once Rhodes was taken the other Aegean islands could be starved out and they way opened to the Dardanelles. Mr. Churchill pointed out that the operation against Rhodes was a limited operation and would not absorb more effectives, and that in any case the troops for this purpose would come from those now used for the defense of Egypt. Once Rhodes was taken these forces from Egypt could proceed forward against the enemy. All he wanted was a small quantity of landing craft. He then said that he accepted Marshal Stalin's suggestion that terms of reference be drawn up for the military staffs.

Marshal Stalin interposed to ask how many French Divisions were being trained in North Africa.

General Marshall replied that for the present there were five Divisions ready and four in training, and that one of these five was in Italy with the American Fifth Army and another was en route. He said that from the battle experience gained it would be possible to decide how best to utilize the other French Divisions.

The President then proposed that instead of three directives to the three Staffs that one directive be agreed upon here. He then proposed a joint directive as follows: (1). That the military staffs should assume that Overlord is the dominating operation. (2). That the Staffs make recommendations in regard to other operations in the Mediterranean area, having carefully in mind the possibility of causing a delay in Overlord.

Marshal Stalin said he saw no need for any military committee here, that the questions involved should be decided at the conference. He also saw no need for any political sub-committee. Marshal Stalin then said he wished to ask Mr. Churchill an indiscreet question, namely, do the British really believe in Overlord or are they only saying so to reassure the Russians. . . .

5. Roosevelt Seeks to Mollify "Uncle Joe" (1943)

Roosevelt was especially concerned at Teheran to temper the Soviet leader's frustration with the failure of the British and the Americans to play a larger role in the war. Having at this point few other resources at his disposal (the Americans were still not prepared to undertake the large-scale invasion of western Europe for which Stalin was clamoring), the president was obliged to rely on personal charm. "I can handle that old buzzard," Roosevelt allegedly boasted in private. Roosevelt later reported his experience at Teheran to his secretary of labor, Frances Perkins. How effective were Roosevelt's tactics on this occasion? What might Churchill's reaction have been?

"You know [reported Roosevelt], the Russians are interesting people. For the first three days I made absolutely no progress. I couldn't get any personal connection with Stalin, although I had done everything he asked me to do. I had stayed at his Embassy, gone to his dinners, been introduced to his ministers and generals. He was correct, stiff, solemn, not smiling, nothing human to get hold of. I felt pretty discouraged. If it was all going to be official paper work, there was no sense in my having made this long journey which the Russians had wanted. They couldn't come to America or any place in Europe for it. I had come there to accommodate Stalin. I felt pretty discouraged because I thought I was making no personal headway. What we were doing could have been done by the foreign ministers.

"I thought it over all night and made up my mind I had to do something desperate. I couldn't stay in Teheran forever. I had to cut through this icy surface so that later I could talk by telephone or letter in a personal way. I had scarcely seen Churchill alone during the conference. I had a feeling that the Russians did not feel right about seeing us conferring together in a language which we understood and they didn't.

"On my way to the conference room that morning we caught up with Winston [Churchill] and I had just a moment to say to him, 'Winston, I hope you won't be sore at me for what I am going to do.'

"Winston just shifted his cigar and grunted. I must say he behaved very decently afterward.

"I began almost as soon as we got into the conference room. I talked privately with Stalin. I didn't say anything that I hadn't said before, but it appeared quite chummy and confidential, enough so that the other Russians joined us to listen. Still no smile.

"Then I said, lifting my hand up to cover a whisper (which of course had to be interpreted), 'Winston is cranky this morning, he got up on the wrong side of the bed.'

"A vague smile passed over Stalin's eyes, and I decided I was on the right track. As soon as I sat down at the conference table, I began to tease Churchill about his Britishness, about John Bull, about his cigars, about his [drinking?] habits. It began to register with Stalin. Winston got red and scowled, and the more he did so, the more Stalin smiled. Finally Stalin broke out into a deep, hearty guffaw, and for the first time in three days I saw light. I kept it up until Stalin was laughing with me, and it

---

[5]From *The Roosevelt I Knew* by Frances Perkins. Copyright 1946 by Frances Perkins; © renewed 1974 by Susanna W. Coggeshall. Used by permission of Viking Penguin, a division of Penguin Putnam, Inc.

was then that I called him 'Uncle Joe.' He would have thought me fresh the day before, but that day he laughed and came over and shook my hand.

"From that time on our relations were personal, and Stalin himself indulged in an occasional witticism. The ice was broken and we talked like men and brothers.

"You know . . . he was deeply touched by the presentation of the sword which Churchill brought him from the British people."

[Relations between Roosevelt and Stalin remained friendly until several weeks before Roosevelt's death in April 1945. Then Stalin abusively charged bad faith in connection with the surrender of German troops in Italy, and Roosevelt came back with protests against Stalin's violations of his Yalta pledges, notably in connection with Poland.]

C. The "Unconditional Surrender" Controversy

1. Robert Sherwood Defends FDR (1948)

Late in 1942 the Allies launched a side-issue invasion of French North Africa, but Stalin refused to recognize it as a genuine second front. Shortly after Roosevelt flew to Casablanca, in French Morocco, for a conference with Prime Minister Churchill, his eighth cousin once removed. Roosevelt knew that the embittered Stalin was deeply suspicious of a possible deal between Hitler and the Allies. The Soviet Union might even make a separate peace with the Germans, as it had done, with disastrous effect, in 1918. At Roosevelt's instigation, the Casablanca conference proclaimed a policy of "unconditional surrender"—that is, the unconditional surrender of the Axis regimes but not "the destruction of the German populace, nor of the Italian or Japanese populace." Robert E. Sherwood, the ghostwriter associate of Roosevelt, here gives his version. Note how many different objectives the president had in view. Why can one argue that "unconditional surrender" did not prolong German resistance?

There were many propaganda experts, both British and American, who believed that the utterance of these words ["unconditional surrender"] would put the iron of desperate resistance into the Germans, Japanese, and Italians and thereby needlessly prolong the war and increase its cost; there are some who still believe that it did so. These critics were not necessarily opposed to the principle of total defeat—but they considered it a disastrous mistake for the President to announce it publicly. . . .

I wrote Winston Churchill asking him if he had discussed the unconditional surrender statement with Roosevelt before the press conference at Casablanca, and his reply was as follows: "I heard the words 'Unconditional Surrender' for the first time from the President's lips at the Conference. It must be remembered that at that

---

[1]From *Roosevelt and Hopkins: An Intimate History*. Copyright © 1948, 1950 by Robert E. Sherwood. Copyright renewed © 1976, 1978 by Madeline H. Sherwood. Reprinted by permission of Brandt & Brandt Literary Agents, Inc.

moment no one had a right to proclaim that Victory was assured. Therefore, Defiance was the note. I would not myself have used these words, but I immediately stood by the President and have frequently defended the decision. It is false to suggest that it prolonged the war. Negotiation with Hitler was impossible. He was a maniac with supreme power to play his hand out to the end, which he did; and so did we."

Roosevelt himself absolved Churchill with all responsibility for the statement. Indeed, he suggested that it was an unpremeditated one on his own part. He said, "We had so much trouble getting those two French generals together that I thought to myself that this was as difficult as arranging the meeting of Grant and Lee—and then suddenly the press conference was on, and Winston and I had had no time to prepare for it, and the thought popped into my mind that they had called Grant 'Old Unconditional Surrender' and the next thing I knew, I had said it."

Roosevelt, for some reason, often liked to picture himself as a rather frivolous fellow who did not give sufficient attention to the consequences of chance remarks. In this explanation, indicating a spur-of-the-moment slip of the tongue, he certainly did considerably less than justice to himself. For this announcement of unconditional surrender was very deeply deliberated. Whether it was wise or foolish, whether it prolonged the war or shortened it—or even if it had no effect whatsoever on the duration (which seems possible)—it was a true statement of Roosevelt's considered policy and he refused all suggestions that he retract the statement or soften it and continued refusal to the day of his death. In fact, he restated it a great many times. . . .

What Roosevelt was saying was that there would be no negotiated peace, no compromise with Nazism and Fascism, no "escape clauses" provided by another Fourteen Points which could lead to another Hitler. (The Ghost of Woodrow Wilson was again at his shoulder.) Roosevelt wanted this uncompromising purpose to be brought home to the American people and the Russians and the Chinese, and to the people of France and other occupied nations, and he wanted it brought home to the Germans—that neither by continuance of force nor by contrivance of a new spirit of sweet reasonableness could their present leaders gain for them a soft peace. He wanted to ensure that when the war was won it would stay won.

2. Cordell Hull Opposes Unconditional Surrender (1948)

"Unconditional surrender" had its warm supporters. In addition to the advantages already indicated, it would hearten German-conquered peoples like the Poles; it would key the Allies up for greater sacrifices; it would postpone disruptive arguments among the Allies over surrender terms; it would avert a quarrel like that with Germany after 1918 over the armistice terms. Yet critics like Senator Burton Wheeler of Montana branded "unconditional surrender" as "brutal" and "asinine." It was vague and easily misinterpreted; it would provide ammunition for enemy propagandists; it would close the door to negotiations with Germany; it would pave the

---

[2]From Cordell Hull, *Memoirs of Cordell Hull, Vol. II.* Copyright © 1948. Reprinted by permission of the Estate of Cordell Hull.

way for Soviet ascendancy in Eastern Europe. Secretary of State Hull, somewhat miffed, advanced additional arguments in his Memoirs. *Notice what he reveals about relations between the president and the State Department. Would the alternative policy that he suggests have made more sense?*

The principle of unconditional surrender overshadowed our policy toward the Axis and their satellites and our planning for their future.

Originally this principle had not formed part of the State Department's thinking. We were as much surprised as Mr. Churchill when, for the first time, the President, in the Prime Minister's presence, stated it suddenly to a press conference during the Casablanca Conference in January, 1943. I was told that the Prime Minister was dumbfounded.

Basically, I was opposed to the principle for two reasons, as were many of my associates. One was that it might prolong the war by solidifying Axis resistance into one of desperation. The people of the Axis countries, by believing they had nothing to look forward to but unconditional surrender to the will of their conquerors, might go on fighting long after calmer judgment had convinced them that their fight was hopeless.

The President himself had qualified his unconditional surrender phrase by stating at Casablanca that this did not mean the destruction of the people of Germany, Japan, and Italy, but the ending of a philosophy based on conquest and subjugation of other peoples. Nevertheless the phrase itself spread more widely than the qualification, and it became a weapon in the hands of Nazi propagandists.

The second reason was that the principle logically required the victor nations to be ready to take over every phase of the national and local Governments of the conquered countries, and to operate all governmental activities and properties. We and our Allies were in no way prepared to undertake this vast obligation.

I thought that our principle of surrender should be flexible. In some cases the most severe terms should be imposed. I had Germany and Japan in mind in this connection. In other cases we would have preliminary informal conversations that would result in substantial adjustments away from the terms of unconditional surrender. Here I had in mind Italy and the Axis satellite states, Rumania, Hungary, Bulgaria, and Finland.

In our postwar-planning discussions in the State Department, which had begun more than three years prior to the Casablanca Conference, we had not embraced the idea of unconditional surrender. In the United Nations Declaration of January 1, 1942, each Government simply pledged itself not to make a separate armistice or peace with the enemies. Nevertheless, after the President had stated the principle so emphatically at Casablanca, there was nothing we could do except to follow it at least in form. It was to rise on numerous occasions to plague us and to require explanation.

[Ironically, Japan did not surrender unconditionally in 1945 but held out for the retention of the emperor.]

D. Dropping the Atomic Bomb

1. Japan's Horrified Reaction (1945)

With Germany knocked out of the war, President Truman journeyed to Potsdam, near Berlin, in July 1945, to concert plans with Stalin and the British leaders. He was there informed that U.S. scientists had experimentally detonated the first atomic bomb in history. The conferees now called on the Japanese to surrender or be destroyed, although the Potsdam ultimatum made no reference, as perhaps it should have, to the existence of the fantastic new weapon. When Tokyo brushed aside the demand for surrender, Truman ordered the dropping of atomic bombs (the only two the United States then had)* on Hiroshima (August 6) and Nagasaki (August 9). The horrified reaction of the Nippon Times *is herewith given. Determine whether there was force in the Japanese charge of hypocrisy, and whether there is any moral difference between atomic bombing and large-scale incendiary bombing of civilian centers. (The Japanese had already bombed civilian centers, beginning with Shanghai in 1932.) Did the Japanese refusal to respond to the Potsdam ultimatum justify the bombing?*

How can a human being with any claim to a sense of moral responsibility deliberately let loose an instrument of destruction which can at one stroke annihilate an appalling segment of mankind? This is not war; this is not even murder; this is pure nihilism. This is a crime against God and humanity which strikes at the very basis of moral existence. What meaning is there in any international law, in any rule of human conduct, in any concept of right and wrong, if the very foundations of morality are to be overthrown as the use of this instrument of total destruction threatens to do?

The crime of the Americans stands out in ghastly repulsiveness all the more for the ironic contradiction it affords to their lying pretensions. For in their noisy statements, they have always claimed to be the champions of fairness and humanitarianism. In the early days of the China Affair [beginning in 1937], the United States repeatedly protested against the bombing operations of the Japanese forces, notwithstanding the fact that the Japanese operations were conducted on a limited scale against strictly military objectives. But where its own actions are concerned, the United States seems to see no inconsistency in committing on an unimaginably vast scale the very same crime it had falsely accused others of committing.

This hypocritical character of the Americans had already been amply demonstrated in the previous bombings of Japanese cities. Strewing explosives and fire bombs indiscriminately over an extensive area, hitting large cities and small towns without distinction, wiping out vast districts which could not be mistaken as being anything but strictly residential in character, burning or blasting to death countless thousands of helpless women and children, and machine-gunning fleeing refugees,

---

[1]*Nippon Times* (Tokyo), August 10, 1945.

*The third bomb was not scheduled to be ready until about August 24, two weeks after the dropping of the second one.

the American raiders had already shown how completely they violate in their actual deeds the principles of humanity which they mouth in conspicuous pretense.

But now beside the latest technique of total destruction which the Americans have adopted, their earliest crimes pale into relative insignificance. What more barbarous atrocity can there be than to wipe out at one stroke the population of a whole city without distinction*—men, women, and children; the aged, the weak, the infirm; those in positions of authority, and those with no power at all; all snuffed out without being given a chance of lifting even a finger in either defense or defiance!

The United States may claim, in a lame attempt to raise a pretext in justification of its latest action, that a policy of utter annihilation is necessitated by Japan's failure to heed the recent demand for unconditional surrender. But the question of surrendering or not surrendering certainly can have not the slightest relevance to the question of whether it is justifiable to use a method which under any circumstance is strictly condemned alike by the principles of international law and of morality. For this American outrage against the fundamental moral sense of mankind, Japan must proclaim to the world its protest against the United States, which has made itself the archenemy of humanity.

2. The Christian Century *Deplores the Bombing (1945)*

The use of the atomic bomb was reluctantly but overwhelmingly recommended by Truman's large corps of expert advisers. Some of the scientists at first proposed test demonstrations in an uninhabited place, but the United States had only two bombs, and they might prove to be humiliating duds. They could not wreak much damage in desert areas and might leave the Japanese unimpressed. If the cities to be bombed were warned in advance, the Japanese might move American prisoners of war to them and at the same time ambush the U.S. bombers. Japan was reeling, but it perhaps had enough suicide resistance left to exact a million casualties, while losing more than a million of its own people. The atomic bomb, indicating that awesome forces were working against the Japanese, might stun them into a quick surrender— as it did. (A dry-run demonstration would have weakened this effect.) The cost was perhaps 150,000 Japanese lives, as against 2 million—Japanese, American, and British. The Christian Century, *a prominent Protestant journal published in Chicago, did not accept the philosophy of a "mercy bombing." Which, if any, of its suggestions would have strengthened the moral position of the United States?*

Something like a moral earthquake has followed the dropping of atomic bombs on two Japanese cities. Its continued tremors throughout the world have diverted attention even from the military victory itself. . . . It is our belief that the use made of the atomic bomb has placed our nation in an indefensible moral position.

---

*At Hiroshima about 150,000 people were killed and wounded out of a total population of some 350,000. The firebomb raid on Tokyo of March 10, 1945, killed an estimated 83,000 people.

[2]"America's Atomic Atrocity." Copyright 1945 Christian Century Foundation. Reprinted by permission from the August 29, 1945, issue of *The Christian Century*.

We do not propose to debate the issue of military necessity, though the facts are clearly on one side of this issue. The atomic bomb was used at a time when Japan's navy was sunk, her air force virtually destroyed, her homeland surrounded, her supplies cut off, and our forces poised for the final stroke. Recognition of her imminent defeat could be read between the lines of every Japanese communiqué. Neither do we intend to challenge Mr. Churchill's highly speculative assertion that the use of the bomb saved the lives of more than one million American and 250,000 British soldiers.

We believe, however, that these lives could have been saved had our government followed a different course, more honorable and more humane. Our leaders seem not to have weighed the moral considerations involved. No sooner was the bomb ready than it was rushed to the front and dropped on two helpless cities, destroying more lives than the United States has lost in the entire war.

Perhaps it was inevitable that the bomb would ultimately be employed to bring Japan to the point of surrender. . . . But there was no military advantage in hurling the bomb upon Japan without warning. The least we might have done was to announce to our foe that we possessed the atomic bomb; that its destructive power was beyond anything known in warfare; and that its terrible effectiveness had been experimentally demonstrated in this country. We could thus have warned Japan of what was in store for her unless she surrendered immediately. If she doubted the good faith of our representations, it would have been a simple matter to select a demonstration target in the enemy's own country at a place where the loss of human life would be at a minimum.

If, despite such warning, Japan had still held out, we would have been in a far less questionable position had we then dropped the bombs on Hiroshima and Nagasaki. At least our record of deliberation and ample warning would have been clear. Instead, with brutal disregard of any principle of humanity, we "demonstrated" the bomb on two great cities, utterly extinguishing them.* This course has placed the United States in a bad light throughout the world. What the use of poison gas did to the reputation of Germany in World War I, the use of the atomic bomb has done for the reputation of the United States in World War II. Our future security is menaced by our own act, and our influence for justice and humanity in international affairs has been sadly crippled.

3. Harry Truman Justifies the Bombing (1945)

German scientists were known to be working on an atomic bomb, and Roosevelt was persuaded to push forward with an ultrasecret competing project that ultimately cost some $2.5 billion. The charge was made—without proof—that Truman had to use the new weapon or face an investigation of squandered money. More probable was his desire to end the Far Eastern war speedily, before the bothersome Russians came in. The evidence is strong that they hurried up their six-day participation following

---

*Hiroshima was about three-fourths devastated; Nagasaki, one-third.

[3]*Memoirs of Harry S. Truman*, vol. 1: *Years of Decisions*. Doubleday & Co., Inc. Copyright © 1955 by Time Inc., renewed 1983 by Margaret Truman Daniel. Reprinted by permission of Margaret Truman Daniel.

*the dropping of the first bomb. At all events, President Truman accepted full respon-
sibility for his decision and later defended it in his* Memoirs, *as excerpted here. Did
he make the decision by himself? Did he try to use the bomb as a lawful weapon?
In the light of conditions at the time, rather than hindsight, was he justified in his
action?*

My own knowledge of these [atomic] developments had come about only after
I became President, when Secretary [of War] Stimson had given me the full story. He
had told me at that time that the project was nearing completion, and that a bomb
could be expected within another four months. It was at his suggestion, too, that I
had then set up a committee of top men and had asked them to study with great
care the implications the new weapon might have for us. . . .

It was their recommendation that the bomb be used against the enemy as soon
as it could be done. They recommended further that it should be used without specific warning, and against a target that would clearly show its devastating strength. I
had realized, of course, that an atomic bomb explosion would inflict damage and
casualties beyond imagination. On the other hand, the scientific advisers of the committee reported, "We can propose no technical demonstration likely to bring an end
to the war; we see no acceptable alternative to direct military use." It was their conclusion that no technical demonstration they might propose, such as over a deserted
island, would be likely to bring the war to an end. It had to be used against an
enemy target.

The final decision of where and when to use the atomic bomb was up to me.
Let there be no mistake about it. I regarded the bomb as a military weapon, and
never had any doubt that it should be used. The top military advisers to the President recommended its use, and when I talked to Churchill, he unhesitatingly told
me that he favored the use of the atomic bomb if it might aid to end the war.

In deciding to use this bomb I wanted to make sure that it would be used as a
weapon of war in the manner prescribed by the laws of war. That meant that I
wanted it dropped on a military target. I had told Stimson that the bomb should be
dropped as nearly as possibly upon a war production center of prime military importance. . . .

Four cities were finally recommended as targets: Hiroshima, Kokura, Niigata,
and Nagasaki. They were listed in that order as targets for the first attack. The order
of selection was in accordance with the military importance of these cities, but allowance would be given for weather conditions at the time of the bombing.

*[The devastating impact of the atomic bomb, together with the Soviet Union's
sudden entry into the war against Japan, undoubtedly forced the Japanese surrender sooner than would otherwise have been possible. Even so, the fanatical military
men in Tokyo almost won out for a last-ditch stand.*

*In 1959, during interchanges with the students of Columbia University, former
president Truman vigorously justified his action. He noted that "when we asked
them to surrender at Potsdam, they gave us a very snotty answer. That is what I
got. . . . They told me to go to hell, words to that effect." Mr. Truman insisted that the
dropping of the bomb was "just a military maneuver, that is all," because "we were
destroying the factories that were making more munitions." He then concluded: "All*

this uproar about what we did and what could have been stopped—should we take these wonderful Monday morning quarterbacks, the experts who are supposed to be right? They don't know what they are talking about. I was there. I did it. I would do it again." (Truman Speaks *[New York: Columbia University Press, 1960], pp. 73–74.]*

Thought Provokers

1. It has been said that the four years of World War II did more to transform U.S. society than twelve years of the Great Depression and eight years of the New Deal. Comment.
2. If the situation had been reversed, would Stalin have been more willing than the other Allies to open a second front? Explain.
3. Wilsonian propaganda in 1917–1918 drove a wedge between the German people and their government. Why was this technique less effective in World War II? On balance, and with the benefit of hindsight, was the policy of unconditional surrender "perhaps the biggest political mistake of the war" (Hanson W. Baldwin)?
4. Does the probability that the Germans or the Japanese would have used the atomic bomb against the United States, if they had developed it first, strengthen the moral position of the United States? If Truman had announced at Potsdam that the United States had the atomic bomb, would the Japanese have been likely to surrender at once? Was the United States shortsighted in establishing a precedent that might one day be used against it? Comment on Secretary Stimson's view that the dropping of the bomb would prove war to be so horrible that there could never be another.

37

The Cold War Begins, 1945–1952

> I have been asked whether I have any regrets about
> any of the major decisions I had to make as President.
> I have none.
>
> *Harry S Truman, 1960*

Prologue: The United States stood triumphant at the end of World War II. Americans had been spared the worst ravages of the global conflict. In contrast to the plight of other combatants, their homeland had not been scorched by fighting, they had lost relatively few fighting men, and their economy was snapped out of depression and whipped into robust trim as a result of the war effort. Confident of the future, Americans immediately after the war launched a baby boom that added some 50 million persons to the nation's population over the next decade and a half. The beginnings of vast changes in family life and especially in the role of women were apparent as Americans moved en masse to the burgeoning suburbs.

Meanwhile, the end of World War II provided only short-lived relief to an aching world, for a new "Cold War" contest between the Soviet Union and the United States began to take shape. Many observers traced the origins of the Cold War conspicuously to the "Big Three" meeting at Yalta.

In February 1945, while Germany was still fighting desperately and Japan was far from finished, an ailing Roosevelt arrived at Yalta in the Russian Crimea. There, in collaboration with Prime Minister Churchill, he thrashed out final agreements with Stalin. Nine weeks later Roosevelt was dead. The ultimate communist takeover of the satellite governments of Central Europe, which appeared to contradict Stalin's pledges at Yalta, deepened U.S. fears. In 1947 President Truman proclaimed the Truman Doctrine, designed in the short run to shore up communist-threatened Greece and Turkey, but aimed in the long run at defining a global policy of "containment" of communist expansionism.

In 1948, Truman implemented the Marshall Plan, designed to rehabilitate wartorn Western Europe. The Marshall Plan proved conspicuously successful in attaining its objectives. But continuing fear of the Soviet Union forced the United States, despite its ancient antialliance tradition, to negotiate in 1949 an epochal military defense alliance in the form of the North Atlantic Treaty Organization (NATO). The "containment" policy suffered a severe blow in 1949, when communists emerged the victors in China's civil war. The "fall" of China touched off bitter political warfare between Republicans and Democrats in the United States and contributed to the rise of McCarthyism—fanatical and often irresponsible pursuit of alleged communist "traitors" in the United States. The outbreak of a shooting war in Korea in 1950 seemed to confirm the worst fears about communist intentions and provided the opportunity for a massive U.S. military buildup.

A. The New Shape of Postwar Society

1. Dr. Benjamin Spock Advises the Parents of the Baby-Boom Generation (1957)

The post–World War II baby boom exploded in a U.S. society that was fast moving and fragmented. Parents could no longer assume, as they once had, that their children would grow up to inhabit a world much like the one the older generation had known. Moreover, the remarkable geographical mobility of Americans in the postwar era meant that many families now faced the responsibilities of child rearing without the traditional support and advice of grandparents and other relatives, who were now likely to live hundreds of miles away. Confronted with these uncertainties, Americans turned to books for guidance, especially to Dr. Benjamin Spock's The Common Sense Book of Baby and Child Care, *first published in 1945, and possibly the most widely used advice book in U.S. history. What historical factors does Spock see as unique to the modern era? He has been accused of opposing the women's movement. What is his view of the mother's role?*

The Working Mother

To work or not to work? Some mothers *have* to work to make a living. Usually their children turn out all right, because some reasonably good arrangement is made for their care. But others grow up neglected and maladjusted. It would save money in the end if the government paid a comfortable allowance to all mothers of young children who would otherwise be compelled to work. You can think of it this way: useful, well-adjusted citizens are the most valuable possessions a country has, and good mother care during early childhood is the surest way to produce them. It doesn't make sense to let mothers go to work making dresses in a factory or tapping typewriters in an office, and have them pay other people to do a poorer job of bringing up their children.

A few mothers, particularly those with professional training, feel that they must work because they wouldn't be happy otherwise. I wouldn't disagree if a mother felt strongly about it, provided she had an ideal arrangement for her children's care. After all, an unhappy mother can't bring up very happy children.

What about the mothers who don't absolutely have to work but would prefer to, either to supplement the family income or because they think they will be more satisfied and therefore get along better at home? That's harder to answer.

The important thing for a mother to realize is that the younger the child the more necessary it is for him to have a steady, loving person taking care of him. In

---

most cases, the mother is the best one to give him this feeling of "belonging," safely and surely. She doesn't quit on the job, she doesn't turn against him, she isn't indifferent to him, she takes care of him always in the same familiar house. If a mother realizes clearly how vital this kind of care is to a small child, it may make it easier for her to decide that the extra money she might earn, or the satisfaction she might receive from an outside job, is not so important, after all.

What children need most from parents or substitutes. The things that are most vital in the care of a child are a little bit different at different age periods. During the first year, a baby needs a lot of motherly care. He has to be fed everything he eats, he eats often, and his food is usually different from the adults'. He makes a great deal of laundry work. In cities he usually has to be pushed in his carriage for outings. For his spirit to grow normally, he needs someone to dote on him, to think he's the most wonderful baby in the world, to make noises and baby talk at him, to hug him and smile at him, to keep him company during wakeful periods.

A day nursery or a "baby farm" is no good for an infant. There's nowhere near enough attention or affection to go around. In many cases, what care there is is matter-of-fact or mechanical rather than warm-hearted. Besides, there's too much risk of epidemics of colds and diarrhea.

Individual care at least until three. The infant whose mother can't take care of him during the daytime needs *individual* care, whether it's in his own home or someone else's. It may be a relative, neighbor, or friend whom the mother knows and has confidence in. If a new maid or nurse is to come into the home, the mother should know her well before she leaves the baby in her care. Or the mother may decide to leave him in a foster home for "foster day care," that is to say, in the care of a woman who makes a profession of caring for children. But the foster mother should be doing it more because she loves children than for the income it brings. The only safe way to choose a foster home is through a first-rate, conscientious child-placing agency that investigates and supervises the individual homes it recommends. But whoever the mother chooses should be a woman who is gentle and loving, and who is not trying to take care of more than two or, at the very most, three babies or small children.

Between the ages of 1 and 3, the care of a child requires a little less time but a lot more understanding. It's good for him to have other children around. He's a person now, with ideas of his own. He needs more and more opportunity to be independent, has to be steered tactfully. An adult who is too bossy makes him balky and frantic. One who lacks self-confidence may be helpless to control him. One who smothers him with too much attention hampers his development. Furthermore, this is the age when he comes to depend for security on one or two familiar, devoted people, and is upset if they disappear or keep changing. This is the least advisable period for the mother who has always taken care of him to go off to work for the first time, or to make changes in the person who takes her place. Many day nurseries do not have enough nurses or attendants to give each child the feeling of really belonging to someone. And the staff may not have had the expert training in understanding small children to be able to foster their fullest development, spiritually, socially, and physically.

So if you have to go off to work when your baby is about a year old, the best solution is individual care, just as it is for the younger infant. But for this age it is particularly important to find a person who has the ability to understand a child and get along with him easily, and who is not likely to quit the job in a few months.

2. A Working Mother Lauds the New "Two-Income Family" (1951)

Dr. Spock might have advised mothers to stay at home, but even as he wrote, a quiet revolution in women's status was grinding inexorably forward as more and more women—including mothers—took up wage-labor jobs. In the 1960s the women's movement would burst noisily into public consciousness, and women would storm all kinds of previously male bastions in the workplace and elsewhere; but in the 1940s and 1950s the issue of working women was still controversial. When the following article appeared in Harper's Magazine *in 1951, one reader wrote to the editor that she was "violently agitated" by it. Another wrote that he and his wife were "singing hallelujahs that the days of financial necessity which compelled for a time two-income living have passed." Still another lamented that the spectacle of women trading home and hearth for factory and office "is contrary to all standards, ethics, etc. which Western civilization has practiced and protected. . . . Woe to Western civilization and especially to the family unit as we know it—for it is the hub around which our civilization revolves, and when that is gone, everything is gone—if such thoughts as are expressed, and evidently supported, by Mrs. Mavity [author of the article] ever become universally accepted by society." In her article that follows, what does Nancy Barr Mavity see as the root cause driving women into the workplace? What role does she assign to the Great Depression and World War II?*

I am a wife, a mother, and a grandmother, and I have been a continuous job-holder since I graduated from college. Besides all that, I am a dodo.

I never used to think of myself as a dodo, but it has been brought home to me by my married daughter and her contemporaries that I most certainly am. These young people have perpetrated a revolution right under the noses of my generation. There have been no parades, no crusading arguments or lectures or legislative lobbying. They did not fight for a revolution—they simply are one.

The whole argument of marriage versus a career which burned like a roaring fire when I was my daughter's age is now as dead as wet ashes. The revolution that we were so vociferous about as a matter of principle has taken place unobtrusively as a matter of hard necessity.

My daughter and her friends and the young married women who work in my office do not call themselves career women. They do not harangue about the right to develop their individual capacities. They do not discuss the primary function of woman as a homemaker. They do not argue the propriety of muscling in on the labor market. They just plain work. . . .

Under present circumstances, a single pay envelope will not meet the needs of a white-collar-class family. It is as simple as that. . . .

---

[2]"The Two-Income Family," by Nancy Barr Mavity. Copyright © 1951 by *Harper's Magazine*. All rights reserved. Reprinted from the December issue by special permission.

Through a good many years of my life I heard men say, "I'd be ashamed to let my wife work." The standard of a man's success in America was—and to some extent still is—his earning capacity. It was a symbol of his masculine prowess and an extension of his virility. To maintain his social, his economic, and his psychological position as titular head of the family by virtue of being its source of supply, he often had to relinquish long-term goals for temporary advantages and to sacrifice his natural aptitudes to the demands of an immediate and steady job. No wonder Thoreau said that "most men lead lives of quiet desperation."

No wonder, then, that men jealously guarded their prerogatives. To be a "good provider" was one of the chief criteria—and in the eyes of many was *the* criterion—of man's achievement. Every woman of my generation who worked in what was called a "man's job" knew what it was to walk on eggs. With a diplomacy that would make Machiavelli look like a coal-heaver in a conference of foreign ministers the masculine ego had to be protected from the slightest scratch in both marital and occupational relations.

This often made the women of my generation hopping mad. What we did not realize was that the restrictions foisted on us by the masculine ego were not prompted by innate sex cussedness. They were imposed by a cultural code which men dared not flout under penalty of losing face, and which they would keep women from flouting, if they could, for the same reason. But something has happened to alter this code, something that has convinced men as well as women that the rigid demarcation of their spheres of action made them both the losers. . . .

These young people were children during the great depression of the thirties. They learned the facts of economic life by experiencing or observing the collapse of financial security. They were married either just before or during or after the late war, and when their husbands were called into the armed forces the young wives had to learn to stand alone in a practical as well as an emotional sense.

Once the war was over and husbands returned, few of them had had a chance to accumulate any savings. The allotments they received from the government were insufficient to support their families in accordance with middle-class standards of living. Wives with or without children either had to produce income or throw themselves on the mercy of relatives who had problems of their own. . . .

How does a two-income family cope with the problem of bringing up young children? Not so long ago a woman of proved vocational ability was adjured to divide her life into two—or, more rarely, three—periods. She might work until she produced a baby, but then she must either bury her vocation altogether, exchanging it for that of housewife-and-mother, or else lay it away for long years with the rather feeble hope of resuscitating it after the children were grown. That picture has now changed out of all recognition. Indeed, one hears wives arguing that children, instead of constituting the unanswerable argument against the two-income family, are strong arguments in its favor.

"If it weren't for the children," said one wife to me, "I'd be tempted to try to get along on one salary, even if it meant skimping. But we need two incomes to enable us to have a house with a yard that the children can play in; to live in a neighborhood where I don't have to worry about their playmates; to provide a guitar for the musical one and dancing lessons for the one who needs to improve her muscular coordination—not to mention teeth-straightening and medical insurance and the bonds we are stowing away for their education. . . ."

The depression years, the war years, and the postwar years have cracked the old economic-social family mold. These were forces outside the control of individual women, but they have learned a lesson from circumstances. The working wives of 1951 have learned to recognize the mistakes of my generation, and are determined not to repeat them. . . .

3. The Move to Suburbia (1954)

Americans by the millions abandoned the cities and joined the exodus to suburbia in the 1940s and 1950s. Most migrating Americans were young married couples just beginning to form families and have children. They took up residence in spanking-new neighborhoods that they obviously preferred to the crowded, and expensive, turmoil of the cities. Yet countless observers found much to criticize in the new suburban way of life that was quickly becoming an American norm. What aspects of that lifestyle does the following article criticize? How persuasive is the criticism? If life in the suburbs was really as thin and conformist as the author claims, why did all those millions of people keep moving to suburbia? How was the raw, historyless character of suburban life any different from life on the thinly populated frontier?

A young man who had attended an exclusive preparatory school and an Ivy League college felt that his horizon had been restricted because, during the years of his education he had met only the sons of bankers, brokers, executives, lawyers and doctors. He determined that, when the time came, *his* children would go to public school.

The time came. The young man and his wife moved out to the suburbs where their children could get fresh air and play space, go to public school and grow up with children of all kinds. "And whom do my children meet?" he asks. "The children of bankers, brokers, executives, lawyers and doctors!"

Despite the drawback that depressed this particular parent, the suburb into which he moved had certain things in its favor, besides the obvious attraction of lebensraum.* It was a town, one of the older suburbs. It had grown up gradually over the years with its own schools, churches and deepening civic consciousness until it had developed into a real *community* with traditions of its own.

New Suburbia is something else again. Around every major city from the Atlantic to the Pacific the new suburbs have been springing up like mushrooms in a damp season. They are sometimes created by dividing large estates—as on Long Island, in Westchester County and in areas around Chicago, Detroit and Los Angeles. More often the new suburbs are built on what had been until recently empty acreage. Whether in California or New Jersey they are typically "prefabricated" in all their details and the parts are suddenly assembled on the spot. Unlike towns and

---

³"Homogenized Children of New Suburbia," by Sidonie M. Gruenberg, *New York Times Magazine,* Sept. 19, 1954. Copyright © 1954 by The New York Times Co. Reprinted by permission.
*A German word meaning space required for life, growth, or activity.

cities and the suburbs of the past, they do not evolve gradually but emerge full-blown. They are designed and constructed by corporations or real estate operators who work on mass-production principles. A hundred or a thousand houses open their doors almost simultaneously, ready for occupancy. . . .

. . .The new suburbanites take what they can afford and can get. And they pay a subtle psychological price. For one thing, the new suburb is a community only in the sense that it is an aggregate of dwellings—often identical houses. It may in time become a community, but not yet. No one has grown up in it; it has no traditions. We really don't know what effect it will ultimately have on children; we can only conjecture.

The families of New Suburbia consist typically of a young couple with one or two children, or perhaps one child and another on the way. The child living here sees no elderly people, no teenagers. Except on weekends and holidays he sees only mothers and other children of his own age. This dearth of weekday variety was remarked on by a woman who had moved to a new suburb and returned after some months to visit friends in her former city neighborhood. "Though I have lived in the city most of my life," she said, "I was actually startled to see such a variety of people, of every type and age. It seemed so long since I had seen old people and school kids, since I had seen men around in the daytime!"

If Old Suburbia is lacking in a variety of work going on that boys and girls can watch or actively share in, it at least has a garage, a movie theatre, a shoe repair shop. In New Suburbia there is often nothing but a supermarket and a gasoline station. In Old Suburbia children grow up seeing people of all ages and playing with children older than themselves—from whom each child normally learns the ways and customs appropriate to the age into which he matures day by day. In New Suburbia the children are likely to be nearly of the same age. In Old Suburbia the fathers take the train to the city each day, leaving the car with the mothers. In New Suburbia there is often no railroad station, so the fathers drive to work in their own cars or by "car pool." The mothers remain—with the house and yard and children.

The children growing up in New Suburbia run the danger of becoming "homogenized." In many of the new suburbs the white child never sees a Negro. In others the Jewish child never plays with any but Jewish children. Some of these suburbs are virtually all Catholic. In others there are no Catholics. Even without racial and religious segregation—and in these new developments groups tend to segregate themselves to an alarming degree—the pressure to conform is intense, and stultifying. . . .

Moreover, in this atmosphere children are likely to picture the good life in terms of uniform, standardized patterns; and that tends to block invention and experiment. Because nothing out of the way ever happens in these quiet, sanitary and standardized surroundings, one wonders what will arouse the imagination of these children. What spiritual equivalent will they find for the challenge and inspiration that an older generation found during childhood in city streets, on farms, in market towns? . . .

Many of the mothers in these new suburbs have had considerable training in offices or shops and some have a degree of executive ability. In New Suburbia they find no outlets for their talents and energies and they tend to focus all their efforts upon their children. Everything that the mothers do, all the little chores, tend to take on disproportionate significance, so that the children feel the pressures while the mothers cannot help feeling frustrated and discontented. This does not mean that they are unhappy with their homes and their children, for they have, essentially, what every woman wants; but they are confused and often feel that there is something lacking in the lives they lead. At the same time, their children cannot help but get a picture of adults as being constantly concerned with trivialities.

Some of the other obvious shortcomings of the new suburbs are incidental to their very newness. In time, a church will be built, perhaps several. A meeting place or assembly hall will rise. In some new suburbs the school from the very first offers a meeting place for parents. But the important question, it seems to me, is how the parents can keep the benefits of New Suburbia without paying too heavy a price. . . .

B. The Yalta Agreements

1. Franklin Roosevelt "Betrays" China and Japan (1945)

One of President Roosevelt's primary objectives at the Yalta Conference was to coordinate with Stalin the final blows of the war. The American people were eager to induce the Soviet Union to enter the conflict against Japan so as to reduce their anticipated losses in the final stages of the assault. The Soviets had already suffered millions of casualties in fighting Hitler, and Stalin told Roosevelt that he would have to receive concessions if he were to justify another war to his war-weary people. The following, one of the top-secret Yalta agreements hammered out between Roosevelt and Stalin, was not made public until exactly a year later. The basic reason for secrecy was that the Soviet Union and Japan were not then at war, and publication or even leakage of the terms might prompt a Japanese attack before the Soviet Union was ready. A need for the utmost secrecy was the excuse given for not then notifying China, an ally of the United States, that its rights were being bartered away in Outer Mongolia and in Manchuria (the Manchurian railroads and the ports of Dairen and Port Arthur). In what ways did the deal "betray" China? Was Roosevelt justified in agreeing to these terms?

The leaders of the three Great Powers—the Soviet Union, the United States of America, and Great Britain—have agreed that in two or three months* after Germany has surrendered and the war in Europe was terminated, the Soviet Union shall enter into the war against Japan on the side of the Allies on condition that:

---

[1]*Foreign Relations of the United States: The Conferences at Malta and Yalta, 1945* (Washington, D.C.: Government Printing Office, 1955), p. 984.

*The Soviet Union entered the Far Eastern war exactly three months after Germany surrendered. Some scholars have argued that the U.S. decision to drop the two atomic bombs on Japan was hastened by the desire to conclude the fighting before the Soviet Union could fully enter the war and play a major role. Of course, at the time of Yalta, Roosevelt could not know when—or even if—the bombs would be available.

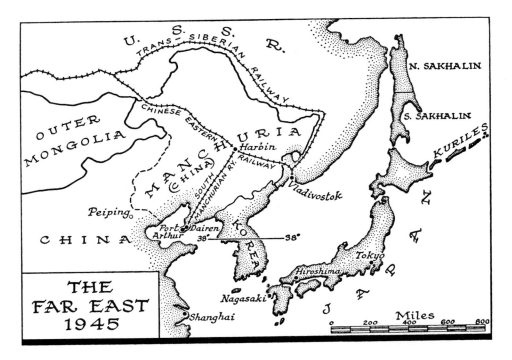

1. The status quo in Outer Mongolia (the Mongolian People's Republic) shall be preserved; [*This area, twice the size of Texas, had been under China's sway until 1912; it had become a Soviet satellite in 1924.*]

2. The former rights of Russia violated by the treacherous attack of Japan in 1904 shall be restored, viz.:

a) The southern part of Sakhalin, as well as all the islands adjacent to it, shall be returned to the Soviet Union. [*Japan and Russia had shared control until 1905, when Japan secured South Sakhalin.*]

b) The commercial port of [China's] Dairen shall be internationalized, the pre-eminent interests of the Soviet Union in this port being safeguarded, and the lease of [China's] Port Arthur as a naval base of the USSR restored. [*FDR here recognized Russia's age-old need for an ice-free port. Dairen was internationalized, and the Port Arthur naval base was leased to the Soviet Union. Both were ultimately restored to communist China.*]

c) The Chinese Eastern Railroad and the South Manchurian Railroad, which provides an outlet to Dairen, shall be jointly operated by the establishment of a joint Soviet-Chinese Company, it being understood that the preeminent interests of the Soviet Union shall be safeguarded and that China shall retain full sovereignty in Manchuria; [*The Yalta agreement ensured the Soviet Union temporary control of these two key railroads in China's Manchuria.*]

3. The Kurile Islands [of Japan] shall be handed over to the Soviet Union. [*Though colonized by both Russians and Japanese, these islands had become a Japanese possession in 1875. Giving away the territory of enemy Japan raised little protest at the time.*]

It is understood that the agreement concerning Outer Mongolia, and the ports and railroads referred to above, will require concurrence of Generalissimo Chiang Kai-shek [*Jiang Jieshi*]. The President will take measures in order to obtain this concurrence on advice from Marshal Stalin.

The Heads of the three Great Powers have agreed that these claims of the Soviet Union shall be unquestionably fulfilled after Japan has been defeated [*that is, whether China consented or not*].

For its part, the Soviet Union expresses its readiness to conclude with the National Government of China a pact of friendship and alliance between the USSR and China in order to render assistance to China with its armed forces for the purpose of liberating China from the Japanese yoke. [*The pact of friendship was concluded after some demur by the Chinese on August 14, 1945, six days after the Soviet Union opened war on Japan. Following the dropping of the atomic bomb, the Russians could not wait for China's acquiescence.*]

I. [J.] Stalin
Franklin D. Roosevelt
Winston S. Churchill

2. The Freeman's *Bill of Indictment (1953)*

Roosevelt left Yalta pleased with the victory for Allied unity. He had secured Stalin's consent to a conference at San Francisco to frame the United Nations Charter, and he had won a concession from him limiting the use of the veto. But Roosevelt and Churchill had been forced to agree to Soviet retention of eastern Poland, with compensating western territory to be given to the Poles at the expense of Germany. All this did violence to the rights of millions of Poles and Germans, as well as to the plain terms of the Atlantic Charter of 1941. On the other hand, Stalin had promised free elections for dismembered Poland and for the other satellite nations of Central Europe—a pledge he later flouted. Critics have charged that Roosevelt should have known by this time that the Soviet Union did not honor agreements that it found inconvenient and that he should have stood firm for principle.* The Freeman, *a critical journal, published the following attack eight years later. How balanced is its appraisal?*

Yalta was the most cynical and immoral international transaction to which the United States was ever a partner. It was a repudiation of all the ideals for which the war against Nazism was supposedly being fought. America came very close to losing its soul at Yalta. What was even more ominous than the provisions of the agreement was the absence, at the time of its publication, of any loud or audible outcry

---

[2]*Freeman* (New York) 3 (March 9, 1953): 403. By permission of The Foundation for Economic Education.
*Admiral Leahy reported in 1950 that at Yalta he had complained to Roosevelt about the vagueness of the agreement regarding a free Poland: "'Mr. President, this is so elastic that the Russians can stretch it all the way from Yalta to Washington without ever technically breaking it.' The President replied, 'I know, Bill—I know it. But it's the best I can do for Poland at this time.'" W. D. Leahy, *I Was There* (New York: Whittlesey House, 1950), pp. 315–316.

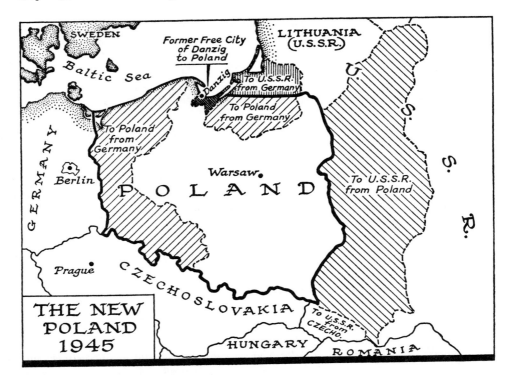

of protest.* It would seem that the normal American ability to distinguish between right and wrong, freedom and slavery, had been badly blurred.

From the practical standpoint, most of our serious international difficulties at the present time can be traced back to a deal which gave Stalin the keys to Eastern Europe and East Asia in exchange for paper promises which, as anyone with reasonable knowledge of the Soviet record and Soviet psychology could have anticipated, were broken almost as soon as the ink on the Yalta document was dry.

The principle of self-determination for all peoples, spelled out in the first three clauses of the Atlantic Charter [see p. 355], was completely scrapped at Yalta, although there were hypocritical professions of respect for Atlantic Charter principles in the pact. The Soviet annexation of eastern Poland, definitely sanctioned, and the Polish annexation of large slices of ethnic German territory, foreshadowed in the agreement, were obviously against the will of the vast majority of the peoples concerned. There was no pretense of an honest plebiscite. These decisions have created millions of destitute, embittered refugees and have drawn frontier lines which are a very probable cause of future conflict.

Both the freedom and the territorial independence of Poland were offered as sacrifices on the altar of appeasement. The treatment of Poland, carved up territorially and made ripe for a foreign dictatorship, its fate determined by outsiders with-

---

*Polish-Americans did protest vigorously at the time; the unpublished secret agreements came out piecemeal later.

out even the presence of a Polish spokesman, was similar in many ways to the treatment of Czechoslovakia at Munich. . . .

Two features of the Yalta agreement represent endorsement by the United States of the legitimacy of human slavery—scarcely fit news for the birthday of Abraham Lincoln. There was recognition that German labor could be used as a source of "reparations," which could be invoked as justification for the detention at forced labor of large numbers of German war prisoners in the Soviet Union and also in France and Great Britain. And there was a self-assumed obligation by the United States and Great Britain to repatriate all Soviet citizens in their zones of occupation. So long as this was carried out (it has now, fortunately, long been stopped), there were tragic scenes of actual and attempted suicide on the part of Soviet citizens who feared above everything else to return to their homeland of concentration camps.

Finally, the secret clauses of the Yalta agreement, which offered Stalin extensive territorial and economic concessions in the Far East at the expense of China and Japan, were immoral, unnecessary, and unwise. They were immoral because they gave away the rights and interests of an ally, the Nationalist government of China, without consulting or even informing Chiang Kai-shek. They were unnecessary, because Stalin's eagerness to be in at the kill in the Far East was beyond serious doubt or question.

[The Freeman *was more sympathetic toward Germans than were most other Americans. Putting Germans under Polish rule and using German slave labor in the Soviet Union for reparations did not seem immoral to many Americans in 1945, especially in view of Hitler's diabolical slaughter of some 6 million Jews. As for returning tens of thousands of anticommunist refugees to Soviet tyranny, many Americans felt that this was not an unreasonable request to grant to their good Soviet ally. Eight years later, perspectives had radically changed with respect to both Germany and the Soviet Union.]*

3. Secretary Edward Stettinius Defends Yalta (1949)

Handsome Secretary of State Stettinius—with his prematurely white hair and flashing white teeth—replaced the aged and ailing Secretary Cordell Hull late in 1944. Without political influence or diplomatic experience, he was expected to be a kind of errand boy for President Roosevelt, who took him along to Yalta. Stettinius here presents a spirited defense of the controversial agreements. What conditions existing at the time caused the Yalta decisions to appear in a less sinister light than was later cast upon them?

What did the Soviet Union gain in eastern Europe which she did not already have as the result of the smashing victories of the Red Army? Great Britain and the United States secured pledges at Yalta, unfortunately not honored, which did promise free elections and democratic governments.

[3]From *Roosevelt and the Russians: The Yalta Conference* by E. R. Stettinius, 1949, pp. 303–306. Copyright 1949 by Stettinius Foundation, Inc. Used by Permission of Harold Ober Associates Incorporated.

What, too, with the possible exception of the Kuriles, did the Soviet Union receive at Yalta which she might not have taken without any agreement? If there had been no agreement, the Soviet Union could have swept into North China, and the United States and the Chinese would have been in no real position to prevent it.

It must never be forgotten that, while the Crimea Conference was taking place, President Roosevelt had just been told by his military advisers that the surrender of Japan might not occur until 1947, and some predicted even later. The President was told that without Russia it might cost the United States a million casualties to conquer Japan.

It must be remembered, too, that at the time of the Yalta Conference it was still uncertain whether the atomic bomb could be perfected and that, since the Battle of the Bulge had set us back in Europe, it was uncertain how long it might take for Germany to crack. There had been immense optimism in the autumn of 1944, as Allied troops raced through France, that the war was nearly over. Then came the Battle of the Bulge, which was more than a military reversal. It cast a deep gloom over the confident expectation that the German war would end soon. In Washington, for instance, the procurement agencies of the armed services immediately began placing orders on the basis of a longer war in Europe than had been estimated.

With hindsight, it can be said that the widespread pessimism was unwarranted. The significant fact is not, however, this hindsight but the effect of this thinking on the strategy and agreements made in the Crimea. It was important to bring the Soviet Union into the united sphere of action. Russian co-operation in the Japanese war ran parallel to their co-operation in the world organization and to united action in Europe.

Furthermore, critics of the Far Eastern agreement have tended to overlook the fact that in the agreement the Soviet Union pledged that China was to retain "full sovereignty in Manchuria" and that the Soviet Union would conclude a pact of friendship with the Chinese Nationalist Government.

It is my understanding that the American military leaders felt that the war had to be concluded as soon as possible. There was the fear that heavy casualties in Japan or the possible lack of continuous victories would have an unfortunate effect on the attitude of the American people.

President Roosevelt had great faith in his Army and Navy staffs, and he relied wholeheartedly upon them. Their insistent advice was that the Soviet Union had to be brought into the Far Eastern war soon after Germany's collapse. The President, therefore, in signing the Far Eastern agreement, acted upon the advice of his military advisers. He did not approve the agreement from any desire to appease Stalin and the Soviet Union.

It is apparently the belief of some critics of the Yalta Conference that it would have been better to have made no agreements with the Soviet Union. Yet if we had made no agreements at Yalta, the Russians still would have been in full possession of the territory in Europe that President Roosevelt is alleged to have given them. The failure to agree would have been a serious blow to the morale of the Allied world, already suffering from five years of war; it would have meant the prolongation of the German and Japanese wars; it would have prevented the establishment of the United Nations; and it would probably have led to other consequences incalculable in their tragedy for the world.

[The legend has taken root that an ailing Roosevelt, advised by the sickly Harry Hopkins and the communist-employed Alger Hiss (whose role has been exaggerated), was sold a gold brick by crafty "Uncle Joe" Stalin. The secret intelligence reports concerning Japan's powers of resistance were faulty, but Roosevelt had to rely on the information that was given him. And if he was sick, what of the hale and hearty Churchill, who signed the agreements? Five months after Yalta, President Truman journeyed to Potsdam, where one of his primary purposes was to hold Stalin to his promise to enter the war against Japan. Truman was not sick, and he had further information about Japanese powers of resistance. When the Soviet Union finally entered the war six days before its end, great was the rejoicing in the United States. As for the charge that the United States "lost" China because of the Yalta agreements, the fact is that China was never the United States' to lose. The "salvation" of Nationalist China would probably have involved large numbers of U.S. troops, and public opinion was unwilling to provide them. As for Japan, there was little opposition at the time of Yalta to depriving a savage enemy of the Kurile Islands and handing them over to a resolute ally.]

C. The Truman Doctrine

1. George Kennan Proposes Containment (1946)

As the Grand Alliance crumbled in the postwar months, U.S. policymakers groped for ways to understand the Soviet Union and to respond to Soviet provocations. On February 22, 1946, the scholarly chargé d'affaires at the U.S. embassy in Moscow, George F. Kennan, sent his famous "Long Telegram" to the State Department, giving his views of the sources of Soviet conduct. A later version of this message was published anonymously in Foreign Affairs *(July 1947). Kennan's ideas proved immensely influential in defining the so-called containment doctrine that dominated U.S. strategic thinking for the next two decades or more of the Cold War. Kennan argued that the Soviet Union regarded itself as encircled by hostile capitalist countries. In Soviet eyes, capitalist governments hoped to avert economic conflict among themselves by seeking war against the socialist world. Kennan denied the accuracy of these Soviet perceptions but insisted that they nonetheless motivated Soviet behavior. Painting the Soviet leaders as insecure, fearful, and cynical, he wrote: "In the name of Marxism they sacrificed every single ethical value in their methods and tactics. Today they cannot dispense with it. It is fig leaf of their moral and intellectual respectability. Without it they would stand before history, at best, as only the last of that long succession of cruel and wasteful Russian rulers who have relentlessly forced their country on to ever new heights of military power in order to guarantee the external security of their internally weak regimes. That is why Soviet purposes must always be solemnly clothed in trappings of Marxism, why no one should underrate importance of dogma in Soviet affairs." Kennan then went on to analyze the practical implications of this diagnosis and to recommend U.S. countermeasures. How prophetic was he? In his memoirs many years later, Kennan pleaded that he had*

---

[1]*Foreign Relations of the United States, 1946,* vol. 6 (Washington, D.C.: Government Printing Office).

never meant to suggest the kind of massive U.S. military buildup that the contain-ment doctrine was later used to justify. Was he in fact misunderstood? If so, why?

In general, all Soviet efforts on unofficial international plane will be negative and destructive in character, designed to tear down sources of strength beyond reach of Soviet control. This is only in line with basic Soviet instinct that there can be no compromise with rival power and that constructive work can start only when communist power is dominant. But behind all this will be applied insistent, unceas-ing pressure for penetration and command of key positions in administration and especially in police apparatus of foreign countries. The Soviet regime is a police regime par excellence, reared in the dim half world of Tsarist police intrigue, accus-tomed to think primarily in terms of police power. This should never be lost sight of in gauging Soviet motives.

In summary, we have here a political force committed fanatically to the belief that with US there can be no permanent modus vivendi, that it is desirable and nec-essary that the internal harmony of our society be disrupted, our traditional way of life be destroyed, the international authority of our state be broken, if Soviet power is to be secure. This political force has complete power of disposition over energies of one of world's greatest peoples and resources of world's richest national territory, and is borne along by deep and powerful currents of Russian nationalism. In addi-tion, it has an elaborate and far flung apparatus for exertion of its influence in other countries, an apparatus of amazing flexibility and versatility, managed by people whose experience and skill in underground methods are presumably without paral-lel in history. Finally, it is seemingly inaccessible to considerations of reality in its basic reactions. For it, the vast fund of objective fact about human society is not, as with us, the measure against which outlook is constantly being tested and re-formed, but a grab bag from which individual items are selected arbitrarily and ten-dentiously to bolster an outlook already preconceived. This is admittedly not a pleasant picture. Problem of how to cope with this force is undoubtedly greatest task our diplomacy has ever faced and probably greatest it will ever have to face. It should be point of departure from which our political general staff work at present juncture should proceed. It should be approached with same thoroughness and care as solution of major strategic problem in war, and if necessary, with no smaller out-lay in planning effort. I cannot attempt to suggest all answers here. But I would like to record my conviction that problem is within our power to solve—and that with-out recourse to any general military conflict. And in support of this conviction there are certain observations of a more encouraging nature I should like to make:

(One) Soviet power, unlike that of Hitlerite Germany, is neither schematic nor adventuristic. It does not work by fixed plans. It does not take unnecessary risks. Im-pervious to logic of reason, and it is highly sensitive to logic of force. For this reason it can easily withdraw—and usually does—when strong resistance is encountered at any point. Thus, if the adversary has sufficient force and makes clear his readiness to use it, he rarely has to do so. If situations are properly handled there need be no prestige engaging showdowns.

(Two) Gauged against western world as a whole, Soviets are still by far the weaker force. Thus, their success will really depend on degree of cohesion, firmness and vigor which western world can muster. And this is factor which it is within our power to influence.

(Three) Success of Soviet system, as form of internal power, is not yet finally proven. It has yet to be demonstrated that it can survive supreme test of successive transfer of power from one individual or group to another. Lenin's death was first such transfer, and its effects wracked Soviet state for 15 years after. Stalin's death or retirement will be second. But even this will not be final test. Soviet internal system will now be subjected, by virtue of recent territorial expansions, to series of additional strains which once proved severe tax on Tsardom. We here are convinced that never since termination of civil war have mass of Russian people been emotionally farther removed from doctrines of communist party than they are today. In Russia, party has now become a great and—for the moment—highly successful apparatus of dictatorial administration, but it has ceased to be a source of emotional inspiration. Thus, internal soundness and permanence of movement need not yet be regarded as assured.

(Four) All Soviet propaganda beyond Soviet security sphere is basically negative and destructive. It should therefore be relatively easy to combat it by any intelligent and really constructive program.

For these reasons I think we may approach calmly and with good heart problem of how to deal with Russia. As to how this approach should be made, I only wish to advance, by way of conclusion, following comments:

(One) Our first step must be to apprehend, and recognize for what it is, the nature of the movement with which we are dealing. We must study it with same courage, detachment, objectivity, and same determination not to be emotionally provoked or unseated by it, with which doctor studies unruly and unreasonable individual.

(Two) We must see that our public is educated to realities of Russian situation. I cannot over-emphasize importance of this. Press cannot do this alone. It must be done mainly by government, which is necessarily more experienced and better informed on practical problems involved. In this we need not be deterred by [ugliness] of picture. I am convinced that there would be far less hysterical anti-Sovietism in our country today if realities of this situation were better understood by our people. There is nothing as dangerous or as terrifying as the unknown. It may also be argued that to reveal more information on our difficulties with Russia would reflect unfavorably on Russian American relations. I feel that if there is any real risk here involved, it is one which we should have courage to face, and sooner the better. But I cannot see what we would be risking. Our stake in this country, even coming on heels of tremendous demonstrations of our friendship for Russian people, is remarkably small. We have here no investments to guard, no actual trade to lose, virtually no citizens to protect, few cultural contacts to preserve. Our only stake lies in what we hope rather than what we have; and I am convinced we have better chance of realizing those hopes if our public is enlightened and if our dealings with Russians are placed entirely on realistic and matter of fact basis.

(Three) Much depends on health and vigor of our own society. World communism is like malignant parasite which feeds only on diseased tissue. This is point at which domestic and foreign policies meet. Every courageous and incisive measure to solve internal problems of our own society, to improve self-confidence, discipline, morale and community spirit of our own people, is a diplomatic victory over Moscow worth a thousand diplomatic notes and joint communiqués. If we cannot abandon fatalism and indifference in face of deficiencies of our own society, Moscow will profit—Moscow cannot help profiting by them in its foreign policies.

(Four) We must formulate and put forward for other nations a much more positive and constructive picture of sort of world we would like to see than we have put forward in past. It is not enough to urge people to develop political processes similar to our own. Many foreign peoples, in Europe at least, are tired and frightened by experiences of past, and are less interested in abstract freedom than in security. They are seeking guidance rather than responsibilities. We should be better able than Russians to give them this. And unless we do, Russians certainly will.

(Five) Finally we must have courage and self-confidence to cling to our own methods and conceptions of human society. After all, the greatest danger that can befall us in coping with this problem of Soviet Communism, is that we shall allow ourselves to become like those with whom we are coping.

2. Harry Truman Appeals to Congress (1947)

A crisis developed early in 1947 when the bankrupt British served notice on Washington that they could no longer afford to support the "rightist" government of Greece against Communist guerrillas. If Greece fell, Turkey and all the eastern Mediterranean countries would presumably collapse, like falling dominoes. After hurried consultations in Washington, President Truman boldly went before Congress to ask for $400 million to provide military and economic assistance to Greece and Turkey. This was a great deal of money, he conceded, but a trifling sum compared with the more than a third of a trillion dollars already expended in the recent war to guarantee freedom. On what grounds did he base his appeal? Were there any dangers in this approach?

I am fully aware of the broad implications involved if the United States extends assistance to Greece and Turkey, and I shall discuss these implications with you at this time.

One of the primary objectives of the foreign policy of the United States is the creation of conditions in which we and other nations will be able to work out a way of life free from coercion. This was a fundamental issue in the war with Germany and Japan. Our victory was won over countries which sought to impose their will, and their way of life, upon other nations.

To insure the peaceful development of nations, free from coercion, the United States has taken a leading part in establishing the United Nations. The United Nations is designed to make possible lasting freedom and independence for all its members. We shall not realize our objectives, however, unless we are willing to help free peoples to maintain their free institutions and their national integrity against ag-

---

[2]*Congressional Record*, 80th Cong., 1st sess. (March 12, 1947), p. 1981.

gressive movements that seek to impose upon them totalitarian regimes. [Applause.] This is no more than a frank recognition that totalitarian regimes imposed upon free peoples, by direct or indirect aggression, undermine the foundations of international peace and hence the security of the United States.

The peoples of a number of countries of the world have recently had totalitarian regimes forced upon them against their will. The Government of the United States has made frequent protests against coercion and intimidation, in violation of the Yalta Agreement, in Poland, Rumania, and Bulgaria. I must also state that in a number of other countries there have been similar developments. . . .

I believe that it must be the policy of the United States to support free peoples who are resisting attempted subjugation by armed minorities or by outside pressures.

I believe that we must assist free peoples to work out their own destiny in their own way.

I believe that our help should be primarily through economic and financial aid, which is essential to economic stability and orderly political processes.

The world is not static and the status quo is not sacred. But we cannot allow changes in the status quo in violation of the Charter of the United Nations by such methods as coercion, or by such subterfuge as political infiltration. In helping free and independent nations to maintain their freedom, the United States will be giving effect to the principles of the Charter of the United Nations. . . .

This is a serious course upon which we embark. I would not recommend it except that the alternative is much more serious. [Applause.] . . .

The free peoples of the world look to us for support in maintaining their freedoms.

If we falter in our leadership, we may endanger the peace of the world—and we shall surely endanger the welfare of our own Nation.

Great responsibilities have been placed upon us by the swift movement of events.

I am confident that the Congress will face these responsibilities squarely. [Applause, the members rising.]

3. The Chicago Tribune *Dissents (1947)*

The nation was momentarily stunned by Truman's bombshell. Critics complained that the initial appropriation would be but a drop in the bucket (as it was), that the Soviet Union (though not mentioned by name) would be gravely offended, and that the United Nations was being rudely bypassed. (Speed was of the essence, and the administration concluded that the Soviets would paralyze action in the United Nations.) The Chicago Tribune, *a powerful isolationist newspaper, was vehemently anti-British, anticommunist, and anti-Roosevelt. Which of its arguments against the Truman Doctrine are persuasive?*

---

[3]Editorial against Truman doctrine (March 13, 1947). Reprinted by permission of the Chicago Tribune Company.

Mr. Truman made as cold a war speech yesterday against Russia as any President has ever made except on the occasion of going before Congress to ask for a declaration of war. . . .

The outcome will inevitably be war. It probably will not come this year or next year, but the issue is already drawn. The declaration of implacable hostility between this country and Russia is one which cannot be tempered or withdrawn. . . .

Mr. Truman's statement constituted a complete confession of the bankruptcy of American policy as formulated by Mr. Roosevelt and pursued by himself. We have just emerged from a great war which was dedicated to the extinction of the three nations [Germany, Italy, Japan] which were as vocally opposed to Russia as Mr. Truman proclaims himself to be now. If communism was the real danger all along, why did Mr. Roosevelt and Mr. Truman adopt Russia as an ally, and why, at Teheran, Yalta, and Potsdam, did they build up Russia's power by making her one concession after another?

The Truman speech also leaves the United Nations as a meaningless relic of mistaken intentions. The world league to insure a lasting peace is a fraud and a sham, so impotent that Mr. Truman proposes that the United States ignore it and seek peace by force and threat of force—the very means which U.N. was intended to exclude in international dealings.

The one hope that is left is Congress, but even its peremptory refusal to follow Truman into his anti-communist crusade will not wholly undo the damage which the President has already done. His words cannot be unsaid, nor can their effect upon Russia be canceled out. Already, as witness Moscow's recall of the Soviet Ambassador from Washington, the nations are engaging in the usual preliminaries to war.

When the country views the terrible predicament in which it now finds itself, it cannot avoid the conclusion that wisdom at all times counseled the United States to follow Americanism only, to dedicate itself to the pursuit of its own interests, and to let Europe's wars alone. We have fought two of them without avail, and Mr. Truman is calling upon us to fight a third.

We were drawn into these wars primarily at the behest of Britain, and that nation, by dumping the Greek and Turkish problems into Mr. Truman's lap, is summoning us to the struggle again. If the United States can be induced to crush Russia, Britain again will rise to a station of security and comparative eminence, for it will be the only other surviving major nation.

For 10 years the United States has been dominated by alien interests. These interests, primarily financial, have bought up every newspaper, radio station, columnist, and commentator, and every so-called organization of public opinion that could be purchased. It has killed our sons by the hundreds of thousands and brought the nation to bankruptcy. It will use whatever tactics seem best to rush into World War III. It will coerce the timid and fool the stupid.

Congress must cease being a catspaw for this movement and think of America's interest first—even exclusively.

[The dangers involved in the Truman Doctrine were great, but the dangers of drifting seemed greater. Congress, by better than a two-to-one vote in both houses, finally approved the initial appropriation early in 1948.]

4. The World Through Soviet Eyes (1946)

As the Cold War came to an end in the late 1980s and early 1990s, Russian and American scholars for the first time gained open access to Soviet archives. Among the documents that came to light in 1990 was the following telegram sent to the Soviet foreign ministry in Moscow by Soviet Ambassador to the United States Nikolai Novikov on September 27, 1946. It is in many ways a companion piece to George Kennan's famous "Long Telegram" from Moscow in February of the same year, reprinted in part earlier in this section (p. 409). Like Kennan, who tried to explain the sources of Soviet conduct to his superiors in Washington, Novikov attempted to identify the taproots of U.S. foreign policy and the outlines of U.S. international strategy. In what ways does his analysis confirm Kennan's appraisal of the ways in which the Soviets viewed the rest of the world? In what ways does Novikov's portrait of American policy constitute a mirror image of Kennan's rendering of Soviet policy? How accurate are Novikov's assessments?

The foreign policy of the United States, which reflects the imperialist tendencies of American monopolistic capital, is characterized in the postwar period by a striving for world supremacy. This is the real meaning of the many statements by President Truman and other representatives of American ruling circles: that the United States has the right to lead the world. All the forces of American diplomacy—the army, the air force, the navy, industry, and science—are enlisted in the service of this foreign policy. For this purpose broad plans for expansion have been developed and are being implemented through diplomacy and the establishment of a system of naval and air bases stretching far beyond the boundaries of the United States, through the arms race, and through the creation of ever newer types of weapons. . . .

Obvious indications of the U.S. effort to establish world dominance are . . . to be found in the increase in military potential in peacetime and in the establishment of a large number of naval and air bases both in the United States and beyond its borders.

In the summer of 1946, for the first time in the history of the country, Congress passed a law on the establishment of a peacetime army, not on a volunteer basis but on the basis of universal military service. The size of the army, which is supposed to amount to about one million persons as of July 1, 1947, was also increased significantly. The size of the navy at the conclusion of the war decreased quite insignificantly in comparison with wartime. At the present time, the American navy occupies first place in the world, leaving England's navy far behind, to say nothing of those of other countries.

Expenditures on the army and navy have risen colossally, amounting to 13 billion dollars according to the budget for 1946-47 (about 40 percent of the total budget of 36 billion dollars). This is more than ten times greater than corresponding expenditures in the budget for 1938, which did not amount to even one billion dollars.

---

[4]Nikolai Novikov, "U.S. Foreign Policy in the Post War Period," September 27, 1946. Archives of the Soviet Foreign Ministry: AVPSSSR, f.06, op.8, p. 45, d.759. Reprinted from United States Institute of Peace, *Origins of the Cold War* (Washington, D.C., 1991), pp. 3–16.

Along with maintaining a large army, navy, and air force, the budget provides that these enormous amounts also will be spent on establishing a very extensive system of naval and air bases in the Atlantic and Pacific oceans. According to existing official plans, in the course of the next few years 228 bases, points of support, and radio stations are to be constructed in the Atlantic Ocean and 258 in the Pacific. A large number of these bases and points of support are located outside the boundaries of the United States. In the Atlantic Ocean bases exist or are under construction in the following foreign island territories: Newfoundland, Iceland, Cuba, Trinidad, Bermuda, the Bahamas, the Azores, and many others; in the Pacific Ocean: former Japanese mandated territories—the Marianas, Caroline and Marshall Islands, Bonin, Ryukyu, Philippines, and the Galapagos Islands (they belong to Ecuador).

The establishment of American bases on islands that are often 10,000 to 12,000 kilometers from the territory of the United States and are on the other side of the Atlantic and Pacific oceans clearly indicates the offensive nature of the strategic concepts of the commands of the U.S. army and navy. This interpretation is also confirmed by the fact that the American navy is intensively studying the naval approaches to the boundaries of Europe. For this purpose, American naval vessels in the course of 1946 visited the ports of Norway, Denmark, Sweden, Turkey, and Greece. In addition, the American navy is constantly operating in the Mediterranean Sea.

All of these facts show clearly that a decisive role in the realization of plans for world dominance by the United States is played by its armed forces. . . .

The "hard-line" policy with regard to the USSR announced by [Secretary of State James] Byrnes after the rapprochement of the reactionary Democrats with the Republicans is at present the main obstacle on the road to cooperation of the Great Powers. It consists mainly of the fact that in the postwar period the United States no longer follows a policy of strengthening cooperation among the Big Three (or Four) but rather has striven to undermine the unity of these countries. The objective has been to impose the will of other countries on the Soviet Union. This is precisely the tenor of the policy of certain countries, which is being carried out with the blessing of the United States, to undermine or completely abolish the principle of the veto in the Security Council of the United Nations. This would give the United States opportunities to form among the Great Powers narrow groupings and blocs directed primarily against the Soviet Union, and thus to split the United Nations. Rejection of the veto by the Great Powers would transform the United Nations into an Anglo-Saxon domain in which the United States would play the leading role.

The present policy of the American government with regard to the USSR is also directed at limiting or dislodging the influence of the Soviet Union from neighboring countries. In implementing this policy in former enemy or Allied countries adjacent to the USSR, the United States attempts, at various international conferences or directly in these countries themselves, to support reactionary forces with the purpose of creating obstacles to the process of democratization of these countries. In so doing, it also attempts to secure positions for the penetration of American capital into their economies. Such a policy is intended to weaken and overthrow the democratic governments in power there, which are friendly toward the USSR, and replace them in the future with new governments that would obediently carry out a policy dictated from the United States. In this policy, the United States receives full support from English diplomacy. . . .

The numerous and extremely hostile statements by American government, political, and military figures with regard to the Soviet Union and its foreign policy are very characteristic of the current relationship between the ruling circles of the United States and the USSR. These statements are echoed in an even more unrestrained tone by the overwhelming majority of the American press organs. Talk about a "third war," meaning a war against the Soviet Union, and even a direct call for this war—with the threat of using the atomic bomb—such is the content of the statements on relations with the Soviet Union by reactionaries at public meetings and in the press. At the present time, preaching war against the Soviet Union is not a monopoly of the far-right, yellow American press represented by the newspaper associations of Hearst and McCormick. This anti-Soviet campaign also has been joined by the "reputable" and "respectable" organs of the conservative press, such as the *New York Times* and *New York Herald Tribune*. Indicative in this respect are the numerous articles by Walter Lippmann in which he almost undisguisedly calls on the United States to launch a strike against the Soviet Union in the most vulnerable areas of the south and southeast of the USSR.

The basic goal of this anti-Soviet campaign of American "public opinion" is to exert political pressure on the Soviet Union and compel it to make concessions. Another, no less important goal of the campaign is the attempt to create an atmosphere of war psychosis among the masses, who are weary of war, thus making it easier for the U.S. government to carry out measures for the maintenance of high military potential. It was in this very atmosphere that the law on universal military service in peacetime was passed by Congress, that the huge military budget was adopted, and that plans are being worked out for the construction of an extensive system of naval and air bases.

Of course, all of these measures for maintaining a high military potential are not goals in themselves. They are only intended to prepare the conditions for winning world supremacy in a new war, the date for which, to be sure, cannot be determined now by anyone, but which is contemplated by the most bellicose circles of American imperialism.

Careful note should be taken of the fact that the preparation by the United States for a future war is being conducted with the prospect of war against the Soviet Union, which in the eyes of American imperialists is the main obstacle in the path of the United States to world domination. This is indicated by facts such as the tactical training of the American army for war with the Soviet Union as the future opponent, the siting of American strategic bases in regions from which it is possible to launch strikes on Soviet territory, intensified training and strengthening of Arctic regions as close approaches to the USSR, and attempts to prepare Germany and Japan to use those countries in a war against the USSR.

D. The Marshall Plan

1. Secretary George Marshall Speaks at Harvard (1947)

By June 1947 it was painfully evident that the Truman Doctrine was merely a child on an adult's errand. The hunger and economic prostration produced by the war were providing an alarming hotbed for the propagation of communism in Europe, especially in Italy and France. A communist takeover of all Western Europe appeared to be a distinct (and depressing) possibility. At this critical juncture the secretary of state, General George C. Marshall, speaking at the Harvard University commencement exercises, made the following breathtaking proposal. To what extent is it both selfish and unselfish? What is its relation to the Truman Doctrine?

The truth of the matter is that Europe's requirements for the next three or four years of foreign food and other essential products—principally from America—are so much greater than her present ability to pay that she must have substantial additional help or face economic, social, and political deterioration of a very grave character. . . .

Aside from the demoralizing effect on the world at large and the possibilities of disturbances arising as a result of the desperation of the people concerned, the consequences to the economy of the United States should be apparent to all. It is logical that the United States should do whatever it is able to do to assist in the return of normal economic health in the world, without which there can be no political stability and no assured peace. Our policy is directed not against any country or doctrine but against hunger, poverty, desperation, and chaos. Its purpose should be the revival of a working economy in the world so as to permit the emergence of political and social conditions in which free institutions can exist.

Such assistance, I am convinced, must not be on a piecemeal basis as various crises develop. Any assistance that this Government may render in the future should provide a cure rather than a mere palliative. Any government that is willing to assist in the task of recovery will find full cooperation, I am sure, on the part of the United States Government. Any government which maneuvers to block the recovery of other countries cannot expect help from us. Furthermore, governments, political parties, or groups which seek to perpetuate human misery in order to profit therefrom politically or otherwise will encounter the opposition of the United States.

It is already evident that, before the United States Government can proceed much further in its efforts to alleviate the situation and help start the European world on its way to recovery, there must be some agreement among the countries of Europe as to the requirements of the situation and the part those countries themselves will take in order to give proper effect to whatever action might be undertaken by this Government.

---

[1]*Department of State Bulletin* 16 (June 15, 1947; speech of June 5, 1947): 1159–1160.

It would be neither fitting nor efficacious for this Government to undertake to draw up unilaterally a program designed to place Europe on its feet economically. This is the business of the Europeans. The initiative, I think, must come from Europe. The role of this country should consist of friendly aid in the drafting of a European program and of later support of such a program so far as it may be practical for us to do so. The program should be a joint one, agreed to by a number, if not all, European nations.

2. Senator Arthur Vandenberg Is Favorable (1947, 1948)

Tax-burdened Americans, having spent billions in World War II, were reluctant to pour more treasure down the "European rathole." Eloquent Senator Vandenberg of Michigan (see p. 347), a recent convert from isolationism to internationalism, was one of the foremost champions in Congress of the Marshall Plan. In the following excerpts from letters to his constituents, what are his arguments for the Marshall Plan? In what ways does he see the plan as serving the self-interest of the United States?

I have no illusions about this so-called "Marshall Plan." . . . Furthermore, I certainly do not take it for granted that American public opinion is ready for any such burdens as would be involved unless and until it is far more effectively demonstrated to the American people that this (1) is within the latitudes of their own available resources and (2) serves their own intelligent self-interest.

. . . I am entirely willing to admit that America herself cannot prosper in a broken world. But it is equally true that if America ever sags, the world's hopes for peace will sag with her. Meanwhile, however, there are some very realistic problems which we must face—including the basic fact that even our friends in Western Europe will soon be totally devoid of dollar exchange and therefore unable to buy commodities from us which are indispensible to their own self-rehabilitation. I must confess that this poses a tough conundrum in international economics entirely aside from considerations of "charity" or "communism." . . .

So we have no alternative but to do the best we can, in the absence of certified knowledge, and to balance one "calculated risk" against another. . . .

You are entirely right that an "international WPA"* can't save Europe from communism or anything else. Is somebody proposing one? I hadn't heard about it. The so-called "Marshall Plan" is the exact opposite, if it runs true to form—and it's our business to see that it does. It is a program geared to self-help. It requires beneficiary countries to proceed specifically to do the things for themselves which will put them on their own feet (and off ours) by 1951—and our aid is progressively contingent upon concurrent results.

---

[2]From *The Private Papers of Senator Vandenberg* by Arthur H. Vandenberg, Jr. Copyright 1952 by Arthur Vandenberg, Jr. Copyright © renewed 1980. Reprinted by permission of Houghton Mifflin Co. All rights reserved.

*Works Progress Administration—a New Deal agency designed to provide employment on public works.

. . . I respectfully submit that we do "know enough" to know what will happen if it, or something like it, doesn't work. We know that independent governments, whatever their character otherwise, will disappear from Western Europe; that aggressive communism will be spurred throughout the world; and that our concept of free men, free government, and a relatively free international economy will come up against accumulated hazards which can put our own, precious "American way of life" in the greatest, kindred hazard since Pearl Harbor. . . .

Let's be equally frank in our "calculations" as to what happens if the iron curtain reaches the Atlantic; if peace and justice are at the mercy of expanding, hostile totalitarian aggression, and if the greatest creditor and capitalist nation on earth should find itself substantially isolated in a communist world where the competition would force us into complete regimentation of ourselves beyond anything we have ever experienced.

This question of "what the Bill will cost" is a very interesting one. Unfortunately, the critics of the Bill have nothing to say about what the failure to pass the Bill will cost. You can get some direct and specific idea on this latter point by reading the testimony before our Senate Foreign Relations Committee by Secretary of Defense Forrestal and Secretary of the Army Royall, who both assert that without legislation of this character they would find it necessary immediately to ask for heavily increased appropriations for military defense. Why? Because it is infinitely cheaper to defend ourselves by economic means.

In other words, in the final analysis, peace is cheaper than war. War has no bargains. Peace does. There is no guarantee that this European Recovery Plan will "work." But certainly there is an even chance that it can succeed. In my opinion, we cannot afford not to take that chance.

3. Moscow's Misrepresentations (c. 1947)

The Marshall Plan certainly would not have received congressional approval if the American people had not been convinced that their security depended on preventing Western Europe from falling under the sway of Soviet communism. Humanitarian instincts, gratitude to former allies, the creation of prosperous customers for surplus goods—all these points were argued, but security was unquestionably paramount. U.S. critics of the Marshall Plan charged that the poor people of the United States needed help, and that Washington should not subsidize socialism (in Britain and elsewhere). The following description of the Marshall Plan was prepared by Soviet propagandists for a children's magazine. How accurate is it?

The American papers immediately raised a great noise about this [Marshall] plan. In different terms, they emphasized "the magnanimity" of America which had decided to help war-stricken Europe.

However, actually, this cunning plan pursued entirely different aims. The American capitalists want to use the help of the Marshall Plan to overwhelm Europe and bring it into subjection to themselves. The government of the Soviet Union at once

---

[3]Pages 198–200 from *My Three Years in Moscow* by Walter Bedell Smith. Copyright 1949 by Walter Bedell Smith. Reprinted by permission of HarperCollins Publishers, Inc.

recognized the real meaning of the Marshall Plan, and definitely refused to take part in setting it up. So also did the governments of the other democratic lands—Poland, Czechoslovakia, Bulgaria, Yugoslavia, Rumania, Hungary, and also Finland.* But sixteen European states adopted the Marshall Plan against the wishes of their peoples.

Let us see now how the U.S.A. is preparing to carry out the Marshall Plan, and what it promises the European countries which have fallen for the American bait.

Representatives of these sixteen European states met together and calculated that they had to receive from the U.S.A. 29 billion dollars to restore their economies. The Americans answered that this sum was too high, and asked for its reduction to 20-22 billion dollars.

The Americans, moreover, attached the following condition: they themselves will dictate to each European country what branch of economy it must develop and what it must curtail. For example, they say to Britain: "You Britishers, build fewer ships for yourselves; you will buy ships from us in America." They propose to the French a reduction in the production of automobiles—American factories can make automobiles for France.

It goes without saying that this was very useful for American capitalists. In America everybody is fearfully awaiting "the economic crisis," i.e., the time when many factories and industries suddenly close and millions of people are left without work. At that time it will be difficult for the manufacturers to get rid of their output. A man out of work has nothing with which to buy them. So the American capitalists are greatly concerned how to sell profitably their output in Europe. Further, the European countries inevitably will become dependent on America: once they make a few machines, tools, and automobiles, it means that willy-nilly they must defer to the Americans.

According to the Marshall Plan, the American capitalists want to restore all the great factories of Western Germany. In other countries they are hastening to close many factories, while in Germany, on the contrary, they are opening them up. Their purpose there, too, is quite understandable: clearly, the U.S.A. considers Western Germany as its colony. By controlling the big industries there which can also make armaments, it will be easy for the Americans to frighten the European countries dependent on them.

The American capitalists counted on using the Marshall Plan to stir up trouble between the peoples of the democratic countries and the Soviet Union. The Americans proposed to these countries as follows: "We will give you dollars if only you will abandon your friendship with the Soviet Union. But if you don't, we won't give you anything." But the peoples of these countries did not fall for the American capitalists' trick. They answered the Americans: "We will not exchange our freedom and independence for dollars." . . .

But this isn't all. The American capitalists have still another dastardly aim. After using the Marshall Plan to reduce the European countries, they want to unite them in a military alliance for a future war against the democratic states.

The Marshall Plan is highly profitable to the United States. For the European countries it brings only poverty. Any land which wants to receive "aid" by means of this plan will be entirely dependent on America. Its economy will not be assisted: on the contrary, it will fall into greater ruin because the country will have to close many

---

*Soviet pressures on these satellite countries kept them from accepting the Marshall Plan.

of its industries and plants, and hundreds of thousands of people will be out of work. That is why both in America itself and in all other lands progressive people are opposing the Marshall Plan with all their strength.

E. The China Tangle

1. Secretary Dean Acheson Drops Jiang Jieshi (1949)

Jiang Jieshi's (Chiang Kai-shek) Nationalist China was creaking at the joints when its eight-year war with Japan ended in 1945. Washington continued to provide Jiang with arms to fight the Chinese communists, but many of these supplies were corruptly sold or abjectly surrendered. President Truman finally dispatched the highly respected General George Marshall in a fruitless attempt to persuade the Nationalists to form a coalition government with the communists. After Washington had cut back the flow of arms to Nationalist China, the corruption-riddled regime collapsed; Jiang fled with the remnants of his army to the offshore island of Formosa (Taiwan). Secretary of State Acheson, whose keen intellect and toplofty manner irritated members of Congress, defended the administration in the following official letter. What part seems least candid? What was Acheson's ability as a prophet? Should the historic policy have been reversed? Would U.S. public opinion have tolerated such a reversal?

A realistic appraisal of conditions in China, past and present, leads to the conclusion that the only alternative open to the United States was full-scale intervention in behalf of a Government which had lost the confidence of its own troops and its own people. Such intervention would have required the expenditure of even greater sums than have been fruitlessly spent thus far, the command of Nationalist armies by American officers, and the probable participation of American armed forces—land, sea, and air—in the resulting war.

Intervention of such a scope and magnitude would have been resented by the mass of the Chinese people, would have diametrically reversed our historic policy, and would have been condemned by the American people. . . .

The unfortunate but inescapable fact is that the ominous result of the civil war in China was beyond the control of the government of the United States. Nothing that this country did or could have done within the reasonable limits of its capabilities could have changed that result; nothing that was left undone by this country has contributed to it. It was the product of internal Chinese forces, forces which this country tried to influence but could not. A decision was arrived at within China, if only a decision by default.

And now it is abundantly clear that we must face the situation as it exists in fact. We will not help the Chinese or ourselves by basing our policy on wishful thinking. We continue to believe that, however tragic may be the immediate future of China, and however ruthlessly a major portion of this great people may be exploited by a

---

[1]*United States Relations with China, with Special Reference to the Period 1944–1949* (1949), pp. xv–xvi.

[Communist] party in the interest of foreign imperialism, ultimately the profound civilization and the democratic individualism of China will reassert themselves, and she will throw off the foreign yoke. I consider that we should encourage all developments in China which now and in the future work toward this end.

2. Senator Joseph McCarthy Blasts "Traitors" (1952)

The loss of a half-billion or so Chinese to the communists was a staggering blow to U.S. policy. Scapegoats had to be found. The violently anticommunist Republican senator Joseph R. McCarthy leaped into the fray, flinging accusations wildly and indiscriminately. In his view, Secretary Acheson and General Marshall, themselves allegedly "soft" on communism and advised by communist "traitors" in the State Department, had deliberately and treasonably allowed China to go down the drain. Senator McCarthy asked himself the following questions—and answered them—in a book published in 1952. Which of his charges seem the most convincing? the most overdrawn? Did he prove that more arms for China would have averted the communist takeover? Do you think Acheson realized he was following the Communist party line in Asia?

Either he knew what he was doing or he was incompetent beyond words. As late as November, 1945, William Z. Foster, head of the Communist Party of the United States, notified the world that China was the prime target of the Soviet Union. He said: "On the international scale, the key task . . . is to stop American intervention in China. . . . The war in China is the key of all problems on the international front."

Less than a month after this Communist proclamation, Marshall embarked upon the "Marshall Mission to China." The testimony before the Russell Committee was that this mission was an Acheson-Marshall-Vincent* project. Before Marshall went to China the Communists occupied a very small portion of China. Their Army numbered less than 300,000 badly equipped troops. When Marshall returned from China to be rewarded by Truman with an appointment as Secretary of State, the Communist-controlled area had greatly increased and the Communist Army had grown from 300,000 badly equipped troops to an Army of over 2,000,000 relatively well-equipped soldiers.

What about the State Department's excuse that we withdrew aid from Chiang Kai-shek [Jiang Jieshi] because his government was corrupt?

Chiang Kai-shek had been engaged in conflict and warfare since 1927—first with the Communists, then with Japan, then simultaneously with the Communists and Japan, and after Japan's defeat, again with the Communists. During that time, all the disruption of war beset Chiang's Government. Under the circumstances it would be a miracle if there were no corruption or incompetence in his government.

But if corruption and incompetence are grounds for turning an administration over to the Communists, then Earl Browder should be President of the United States,

---

[2]Quoted from Senator Joseph McCarthy, *McCarthyism: The Fight for America* (New York: Devin-Adair Company, 1952), pp. 37–40.

*John C. Vincent was a foreign service officer allegedly "soft" on communism.

Harry Bridges should be Secretary of Labor, and Alger Hiss* should be Secretary of Defense.

What about Acheson's claim that we gave Chiang Kai-shek every help which he could utilize, including $2 billion worth of aid since the end of World War II?

That is untrue. Acheson made this claim in a letter to Senator Pat McCarran on March 14, 1949, in arguing against any further aid to anti-Communist China, which according to Acheson "would almost surely be catastrophic."

Of the phony $2 billion figure, $335,800,000 was for repatriating Japanese soldiers in China and transporting Chinese Nationalist armed forces to accept the surrender of the Japanese. Even President Truman declared that those expenditures should properly have been charged to World War II. . . .

Is it true that Marshall, under State Department instructions, signed an order cutting off not only arms to our friends in China, but also all ammunition so that the arms they had would be useless?

Yes. The embargo on all arms and ammunition to China began in 1946 and continued into 1947.

Those were crucial years, and China's plight was so bad that even the New York *Times* reported on June 22, 1947, that the guns of the anti-Communists were so worn and burned out that "bullets fell through them to the ground."

The Communists, on the other hand, were kept well supplied by the Russians. Admiral Cooke has so testified before the McCarran Committee. . . . [a Senate committee, chaired by Nevada democrat Patrick McCarran, that investigated alleged communist subversion]

Do you claim that General Marshall, who has long worked with Acheson, was knowingly working for the Communist cause in China?

As I stated in my book, *The Story of General George Marshall—America's Retreat from Victory,* I cannot delve into the mind of Marshall. I can only present the facts to the American people. Whether Marshall knowingly betrayed China or whether he honestly thought that he was helping China, the results are equally disastrous for America. . . .

Since the fall of China has Acheson ever admitted that his China policy was a failure?

No. There is no indication that Acheson considers the loss of China to Communism a "failure." Instead, he hailed it as "a new day which has dawned in Asia."

[The United States supplied Jiang's Nationalists with vastly more arms than the Soviet Union sent to the Chinese communists, although departing Soviet troops did abandon large quantities of Japanese munitions to the communists. The Americans also abandoned comparable supplies of their own to the Nationalists. The tale about bullets falling out of worn-out guns came from an unnamed Chinese correspondent's report (New York Times, *June 22, 1947, p. 38) that "some machine gun barrels were so burned that bullets fell through them to the ground." Machine guns can be so badly worn as to fire inaccurately, but the bullets are firmly lodged in the cartridges, and the cartridges are either clipped or belted together.*

---

*Alger Hiss was a former State Department official convicted in 1950 of perjury in connection with passing secrets on to the Soviets. Harry Bridges was a Pacific Coast labor leader accused of Communist party affiliation. Earl Browder was twice a candidate for the presidency on the Communist party ticket.

> *General Barr, a U.S. military observer, reported to the Department of the Army on November 16, 1948: "I am convinced that the military situation has deteriorated to the point where only the active participation of United States troops could effect a remedy. . . . Military matériel and economic aid in my opinion is less important to the salvation of China than other factors. No battle has been lost since my arrival due to lack of ammunition or equipment. Their military debacles in my opinion can all be attributed to the world's worst leadership and many other morale-destroying factors that lead to a complete loss of will to fight. The complete ineptness of high military leaders and the widespread corruption and dishonesty throughout the Armed Forces could, in some measure, have been controlled and directed had the above authority and facilities been available. Chinese leaders completely lack the moral courage to issue and enforce an unpopular decision."* (United States Relations with China, with Special Reference to the Period 1944–1949 [1949], p. 358.)]

F. The Korean Crisis and the NSC-68

1. Senator Tom Connally Writes Off Korea (1950)

Secretary Acheson compounded his China felony, in McCarthyite eyes, by making a memorable speech to the National Press Club of Washington early in 1950. He outlined the United States' "defensive perimeter" in the Far East but conspicuously omitted from it the Republic of South Korea and Jiang's last-hope Formosa. He stated that the areas thus excluded would have to depend on themselves for defense and on "the commitments of the entire civilized world under the Charter of the United Nations." Some three months later Senator Connally, chairman of the powerful Senate Foreign Relations Committee, gave the following interview. Critics of the Truman administration later charged that the Acheson and Connally statements were open invitations to the Soviet-backed North Korean communists to invade South Korea, as they did in June 1950. Was this inference fair?

Question. Do you think the suggestion that we abandon South Korea is going to be seriously considered?

Answer. I am afraid it is going to be seriously considered because I'm afraid it's going to happen, whether we want it to or not. I'm for Korea. We're trying to help her—we're appropriating money now to help her. But South Korea is cut right across by this line—north of it are the Communists, with access to the mainland—and Russia is over there on the mainland. So that whenever she takes a notion, she can just overrun Korea, just like she probably will overrun Formosa when she gets ready to do it. I hope not, of course.

Question. But isn't Korea an essential part of the defense strategy?

---

[1]Reprinted from *U.S. News and World Report* 28 (May 5, 1950): 30. Copyright 1950, U.S. News and World Report.

Answer. No. Of course, any position like that is of some strategic importance. But I don't think it is very greatly important. It has been testified before us that Japan, Okinawa, and the Philippines make the chain of defense which is absolutely necessary. And, of course, any additional territory along in that area would be that much more, but it's not absolutely essential.

2. Truman Accepts the Korean Challenge (1950)

President Truman was forced to make a series of agonizing decisions: the Truman Doctrine (1947), the Marshall Plan (1947), the Berlin airlift (1948), the North At-lantic Pact (1949), the Korean intervention (1950). Speaking later (1959) at Co-lumbia University, he was asked, "Mr. President, what was the most complicated, the one single, most difficult decision you had to make?" Unhesitatingly he replied: "Korea. The reason for that was the fact that the policies of our allies and the mem-bers of the United Nations were at stake at the same time as ours." Here in his Mem-oirs *he explains more fully the reasons for intervening with armed forces to support the South Korean republic, a special ward of the United Nations. Remembering that the League of Nations had collapsed in the 1930s because it failed to act resolutely, assess the validity of Truman's view that his intervention in Korea averted World War III.*

On Saturday, June 24, 1950, I was in Independence, Missouri, to spend the weekend with my family and to attend to some personal family business.

It was a little after ten in the evening, and we were sitting in the library of our home on North Delaware Street when the telephone rang. It was the Secretary of State calling from his home in Maryland.

"Mr. President," said Dean Acheson, "I have very serious news. The North Kore-ans have invaded South Korea."

My first reaction was that I must get back to the capital, and I told Acheson so. . . .

The plane left the Kansas City Municipal Airport at two o'clock, and it took just a little over three hours to make the trip to Washington. I had time to think aboard the plane. In my generation, this was not the first occasion when the strong had at-tacked the weak. I recalled some earlier instances: [Japan in] Manchuria, [Italy in] Ethiopia, [Germany in] Austria. I remembered how each time that the democracies failed to act it had encouraged the aggressors to keep going ahead.

Communism was acting in Korea just as Hitler, Mussolini, and the Japanese had acted ten, fifteen, and twenty years earlier. I felt certain that if South Korea was al-lowed to fall, Communist leaders would be emboldened to override nations closer to our own shores. If the Communists were permitted to force their way into the Re-public of Korea without opposition from the free world, no small nation would have the courage to resist threats and aggression by stronger Communist neighbors. If this was allowed to go unchallenged it would mean a third world war, just as simi-lar incidents had brought on the second world war. It was also clear to me that the

---

[2]*Memoirs by Harry S. Truman: Years of Trial and Hope* (1956), vol. 2, pp. 331–333. Published by Double-day and Company. Copyright © 1956 by Time, Inc. Reprinted by permission of Margaret Truman Daniel.

foundations and the principles of the United Nations were at stake unless this unprovoked attack on Korea could be stopped.

3. NSC-68 Offers a Blueprint for the Cold War (1950)

Jolted by the communist success in China and the Soviet development of an atomic bomb, President Truman in early 1950 ordered a far-reaching reassessment of U.S. Cold War policies. The result was a lengthy secret document, declassified only a quarter of a century later, known as National Security Council Memorandum Number 68 (NSC-68). The memorandum assessed the balance of Soviet and U.S. power in the world and made sweeping recommendations for a vigorous U.S. military buildup. It laid out, in effect, a blueprint for U.S. foreign policy for the next two decades. It advised against negotiating with the Soviet Union until the United States had time "to build up strength," although it conceded that some discussions with the Soviets were probably necessary "to gain public support for the [buildup] and to minimize the immediate risks of war." NSC-68 also advocated the development of hydrogen bombs and the expansion of conventional military forces, and it frankly

---

[3]*Foreign Relations of the United States, 1950* (Washington, D.C.: Government Printing Office), pp. 237–238, 272–286.

acknowledged that substantial tax increases would be necessary to finance this effort. On what premises about the state of the world and the character of the Soviet Union does NSC-68 build its argument? Are those premises justifiable? What policy choices does the memorandum present? Why does it choose the particular policies it recommends? What does it see as the United States' strengths and liabilities in the confrontation with the Soviet Union? What obstacles to developing those strengths does it identify?

I. Background of the Present Crisis

Within the past thirty-five years the world has experienced two global wars of tremendous violence. It has witnessed two revolutions—the Russian and the Chinese—of extreme scope and intensity. It has also seen the collapse of five empires—the Ottoman, the Austro-Hungarian, German, Italian and Japanese—and the drastic decline of two major imperial systems, the British and the French. During the span of one generation, the international distribution of power has been fundamentally altered. For several centuries it had proved impossible for any one nation to gain such preponderant strength that a coalition of other nations could not in time face it with greater strength. The international scene was marked by recurring periods of violence and war, but a system of sovereign and independent states was maintained, over which no state was able to achieve hegemony.

Two complex sets of factors have now basically altered this historical distribution of power. First, the defeat of Germany and Japan and the decline of the British and French Empires have interacted with the development of the United States and the Soviet Union in such a way that power has increasingly gravitated to these two centers. Second, the Soviet Union, unlike previous aspirants to hegemony, is animated by a new fanatic faith, antithetical to our own, and seeks to impose its absolute authority over the rest of the world. Conflict has, therefore, become endemic and is waged, on the part of the Soviet Union, by violent or non-violent methods in accordance with the dictates of expediency. With the development of increasingly terrifying weapons of mass destruction, every individual faces the ever-present possibility of annihilation should the conflict enter the phase of total war. . . .

The issues that face us are momentous, involving the fulfillment or destruction not only of this Republic but of civilization itself. They are issues which will not await our deliberations. With conscience and resolution this Government and the people it represents must now make new and fateful decisions. . . .

Four possible courses of action by the United States in the present situation can be distinguished. They are:

a. Continuation of current policies, with current and currently projected programs for carrying out these policies;

b. Isolation;

c. War; and

d. A more rapid building up of the political, economic, and military strength of the free world than provided under *a,* with the purpose of reaching, if possible, a tolerable state of order among nations without war and of preparing to defend ourselves in the event that the free world is attacked. . . .

On the basis of current programs, the United States has a large potential military capability but an actual capability which, though improving, is declining relative to the U.S.S.R., particularly in light of its probable fission bomb capability and possible thermonuclear bomb capability. The same holds true for the free world as a whole relative to the Soviet world as a whole. If war breaks out in 1950 or in the next few years, the United States and its allies, apart from a powerful atomic blow, will be compelled to conduct delaying actions, while building up their strength for a general offensive. . . .

There are some who advocate a deliberate decision to isolate ourselves. Superficially, this has some attractiveness as a course of action, for it appears to bring our commitments and capabilities into harmony by reducing the former and by concentrating our present, or perhaps even reduced, military expenditures on the defense of the United States.

This argument overlooks the relativity of capabilities. With the United States in an isolated position, we would have to face the probability that the Soviet Union would quickly dominate most of Eurasia, probably without meeting armed resistance. It would thus acquire a potential far superior to our own, and would promptly proceed to develop this potential with the purpose of eliminating our power, which would, even in isolation, remain as a challenge to it and as an obstacle to the imposition of its kind of order in the world. There is no way to make ourselves inoffensive to the Kremlin except by complete submission to its will. Therefore isolation would in the end condemn us to capitulate or to fight alone and on the defensive, with drastically limited offensive and retaliatory capabilities in comparison with the Soviet Union. (These are the only possibilities, unless we are prepared to risk the future on the hazard that the Soviet Empire, because of overextension or other reasons, will spontaneously destroy itself from within.). . . .

Some Americans favor a deliberate decision to go to war against the Soviet Union in the near future. It goes without saying that the idea of "preventive" war—in the sense of a military attack not provoked by a military attack upon us or our allies—is generally unacceptable to Americans. . . .

The ability of the United States to launch effective offensive operations is now limited to attack with atomic weapons. A powerful blow could be delivered upon the Soviet Union, but it is estimated that these operations alone would not force or induce the Kremlin to capitulate and that the Kremlin would still be able to use the forces under its control to dominate most or all of Eurasia. This would probably mean a long and difficult struggle during which the free institutions of Western Europe and many freedom-loving people would be destroyed and the regenerative capacity of Western Europe dealt a crippling blow.

Apart from this, however, a surprise attack upon the Soviet Union, despite the provocativeness of recent Soviet behavior, would be repugnant to many Americans. Although the American people would probably rally in support of the war effort, the shock of responsibility for a surprise attack would be morally corrosive. Many would doubt that it was a "just war" and that all reasonable possibilities for a peaceful settlement had been explored in good faith. Many more, proportionately, would hold such views in other countries, particularly in Western Europe and particularly after Soviet occupation, if only because the Soviet Union would liquidate articulate opponents. It would, therefore, be difficult after such a war to create a satisfactory international order among nations. Victory in such a war would have brought us little if at all closer to victory in the fundamental ideological conflict. . . .

A program for rapidly building up strength and improving political and economic conditions will place heavy demands on our courage and intelligence; it will be costly; it will be dangerous. But half-measures will be more costly and more dangerous, for they will be inadequate to prevent and may actually invite war. Budgetary considerations will need to be subordinated to the stark fact that our very independence as a nation may be at stake. . . .

The United States is currently devoting about 22 percent of its gross national product ($255 billion in 1949) to military expenditures (6 percent), foreign assistance (2 percent), and investment (14 percent), little of which is in war-supporting industries. . . .

From the point of view of the economy as a whole, the program might not result in a real decrease in the standard of living, for the economic effects of the program might be to increase the gross national product by more than the amount being absorbed for additional military and foreign assistance purposes. One of the most significant lessons of our World War II experience was that the American economy, when it operates at a level approaching full efficiency, can provide enormous resources for purposes other than civilian consumption while simultaneously providing a high standard of living. After allowing for price changes, personal consumption expenditures rose by about one-fifth between 1939 and 1944, even though the economy had in the meantime increased the amount of resources going into Government use by $60-$65 billion (in 1939 prices). . . .

4. Secretary Acheson Defends NSC-68 (1969)

Many government officials criticized NSC-68 as too simplistic in its view of the world and too rigid and aggressive in its definition of U.S. policies. But its leading architect, Secretary of State Dean Acheson, stoutly defended the recommendations of NSC-68. In the passage from his memoirs that follows, what are his views on the relation of public opinion to foreign policy? How should one judge his admission that he and his colleagues "made our points clearer than truth"? What were the major obstacles to acceptance of NSC-68's recommendations? How were those obstacles overcome?

The purpose of NSC-68 was to so bludgeon the mass mind of "top government" that not only could the President make a decision but that the decision could be carried out. Even so, it is doubtful whether anything like what happened in the next few years could have been done had not the Russians been stupid enough to have instigated the attack against South Korea and opened the "hate America" campaign. . . .

The task of a public officer seeking to explain and gain support for a major policy is not that of the writer of a doctoral thesis. Qualification must give way to simplicity of statement, nicety and nuance to bluntness, almost brutality, in carrying home a point. It is better to carry the hearer or reader into the quadrant of one's thought than merely to make a noise or to mislead him utterly. In the State Depart-

---

[4]From *Present at the Creation: My Years in the State Department,* by Dean Acheson. Copyright © 1969 by Dean Acheson. Used by permission of W. W. Norton & Company, Inc.

ment we used to discuss how much time that mythical "average American citizen" put in each day listening, reading, and arguing about the world outside his own country. Assuming a man or woman with a fair education, a family, and a job in or out of the house, it seemed to us that ten minutes a day would be a high average. If this were anywhere near right, points to be understandable had to be clear. If we made our points clearer than truth, we did not differ from most other educators and could hardly do otherwise. . . .

Such an analysis was decried by some liberals and some Kremlinologists. The real threat, they said, lay in the weakness of the Western European social, economic, and political structure. Correct that and the Russian danger would disappear. This I did not believe. The threat to Western Europe seemed to me singularly like that which Islam had posed centuries before, with its combination of ideological zeal and fighting power. Then it had taken the same combination to meet it: Germanic power in the east and Frankish in Spain, both energized by a great outburst of military power and social organization in Europe. This time it would need the added power and energy of America, for the drama was now played on a world stage.

If these were the intentions of the Kremlin, what were its capabilities for realizing and ours for frustrating them? Ours was demonstrably the potentially stronger society, but did it have the strength now, and would it have it in the future, to frustrate the Kremlin design? At the end of the war we were the most powerful nation on earth, with the greatest army, navy, and air force, a monopoly of the most destructive weapon, and all supported by the most productive industry and agriculture. But now our army had been demobilized, our navy put in mothballs, and our air force no longer had a monopoly of atomic weapons. In three or four years at the most we could be threatened with devastating damage, against which no sure protection appeared. Surely we produced far more aluminum, for instance, than the Soviet Union; but while we splashed it over the front of automobiles, in Russia more went into military aircraft than here. On the other hand, our almost minute army cost many times what theirs did. A brief comparison of the pay, care, and equipment of private soldiers showed why. Half the total effort of their rival society went into creating military power, which in a short time at present rates could top ours. What relation did these facts have to foreign policy, national security, the existence of a spacious environment for free societies? How much of our national product would we need to divert, as sensible insurance, to an arms effort we loathed? The paper recommended specific measures for a large and immediate improvement of military forces and weapons, and of the economic and morale factors which underlay our own and our allies' ability to influence the conduct of other societies. . . .

In explaining to the nation the course it recommended, I made clear, also—in an address in Dallas on June 13, 1950—those it would not recommend. We should not pull down the blinds, I said, and sit in the parlor with a loaded shotgun, waiting. Isolation was not a realistic course of action. It did not work and it had not been cheap. Appeasement of Soviet ambitions was, in fact, only an alternative form of isolation. It would lead to a final struggle for survival with both our moral and military positions weakened. A third course, euphemistically called preventive war, adopted with disastrous results in other times by other types of people and governments than ours, would take the form of nuclear attack on the Soviet Union. It would not solve problems; it would multiply them. Then as now nothing seemed to me more depressing in the history of our own country than the speeches of the 1850s about "the irrepressible conflict." War is not inevitable. But talk of war's inevitability had, in the past, helped to make it occur.

While NSC-68 did not contain cost estimates, that did not mean we had not discussed them. To carry through the sort of rearmament and rehabilitation-of-forces program that we recommended, at the rate we thought necessary, for ourselves and with help for our allies, would require, our group estimated, a military budget of the magnitude of about fifty billion dollars per annum. This was a very rough guess, but, as the existing ceiling was thirteen and a half billion, the proposal—or rather the situation out of which it grew—required considerable readjustment of thinking. It seemed better to begin this process by facing the broad facts, trends, and probabilities before getting lost in budgetary intricacies. If that begins before an administration has decided what it *wants* to do, or made what diplomats used to call a decision "in principle"—in essence—the mice in the Budget Bureau will nibble to death the will to decide. . . .

[The enormous cost of NSC-68's recommendations, which called for a fourfold jump in military spending, to about $50 billion, or more than 13 percent of the United States' gross national product, posed a formidable barrier to its implementation. In mid-1950 the document remained, in historian Walter LaFeber's words, "a policy in search of an opportunity." The needed opportunity soon appeared in the form of the Korean War, which, Acheson later admitted, "saved us" from persisting with an insufficiently aggressive foreign policy and an underfinanced military establishment. The Defense Department budget quadrupled during the Korean War and stayed at that high level even after the conclusion of hostilities, as the United States in the 1950s pursued the biggest peacetime military buildup in its history.]

G. The Sacking of General Douglas MacArthur

1. Truman Asserts Civil Supremacy (1951)

General Douglas MacArthur—handsome, proud, dramatic—served brilliantly as United Nations commander in Korea, until rocked back on his heels by the unexpected descent of hordes of Chinese "volunteers." He urged on Washington a blockade of the Chinese coast, a bombing of supply bases in China, and the use of Jiang's Formosan troops in Korea. The Soviet Union had a treaty of alliance (1950) with China, and both the Truman administration and its U.N. allies were anxious to avoid a general war in the Far East while the Soviet menace loomed large in Europe. MacArthur, who sharply disagreed with the policy of Washington, ruined Truman's proposed peace negotiations by delivering an ultimatum to the enemy (March 24, 1951). Peppery Harry Truman, who had been an army captain in World War I, would brook no such insubordination. He here expresses his views in

[1]*Memoirs by Harry S. Truman: Years of Trial and Hope* (1956), vol. 2, pp. 444–445. Published by Doubleday and Company. Copyright © 1956 by Time, Inc. Reprinted by permission of Margaret Truman Daniel.

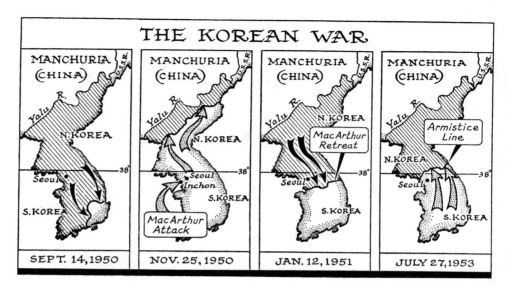

his Memoirs. *How does he defend the view that the military must be subordinate to civil authority?*

If there is one basic element in our Constitution, it is civilian control of the military. Policies are to be made by the elected political officials, not by generals or admirals. Yet time and again General MacArthur had shown that he was unwilling to accept the policies of the administration. By his repeated public statements he was not only confusing our allies as to the true course of our policies but, in fact, was also setting his policy against the President's.

I have always had, and I have to this day, the greatest respect for General MacArthur, the soldier. Nothing I could do, I knew, could change his stature as one of the outstanding military figures of our time—and I had no desire to diminish his stature. I had hoped, and I had tried to convince him, that the policy he was asked to follow was right. He had disagreed. He had been openly critical. Now, at last, his actions [in issuing an ultimatum] had frustrated a political course decided upon, in conjunction with its allies, by the government he was sworn to serve. If I allowed him to defy the civil authorities in this manner, I myself would be violating my oath to uphold and defend the Constitution.

I have always believed that civilian control of the military is one of the strongest foundations of our system of free government. Many of our people are descended from men and women who fled their native countries to escape the oppression of militarism. We in America have sometimes failed to give the soldier and the sailor their due, and it has hurt us. But we have always jealously guarded the constitutional provision that prevents the military from taking over the government from the authorities, elected by the people, in whom the power resides.

It has often been pointed out that the American people have a tendency to choose military heroes for the highest office in the land, but I think the statement is misleading. . . . We have chosen men who, in time of war, had made their mark, but until 1952 we had never elevated to the White House any man whose entire life had been dedicated to the military.*

One reason that we have been so careful to keep the military within its own preserve is that the very nature of the service hierarchy gives military commanders little, if any, opportunity to learn the humility that is needed for good public service. The elected official will never forget—unless he is a fool—that others as well or better qualified might have been chosen, and that millions remained unconvinced that the last choice made was the best one possible. . . .

These are things a military officer is not likely to learn in the course of his profession. The words that dominate his thinking are "command" and "obedience," and the military definitions of these words are not definitions for use in a republic.

That is why our Constitution embodies the principle of civilian control of the military. This was the principle that General MacArthur threatened. I do not believe that he purposefully decided to challenge civilian control of the military, but the result of his behavior was that this fundamental principle of free government was in danger.

It was my duty to act.

2. MacArthur Calls for Victory (1951)

Joseph W. Martin, Republican House minority leader, had written to General MacArthur in March 1951, complaining about the folly of not using Jiang's several hundred thousand orphaned Chinese troops in Korea. (They were needed for the defense of Formosa; they might have defected; they would have been resented by the South Koreans.) Martin solicited MacArthur's views. The outspoken general, without labeling his reply as confidential, wrote as follows. On April 5, 1951, Martin read the letter to the House. Truman had already made up his mind to remove MacArthur, and this indiscreet statement strengthened his determination. What part of the letter reveals most clearly the military man rather than the statesman?

I am most grateful for your note of the eighth forwarding me a copy of your address of February 12. The latter I have read with much interest, and find that with the passage of years you have certainly lost none of your old-time punch.

My views and recommendations with respect to the situation created by Red China's entry into war against us in Korea have been submitted to Washington in most complete detail. Generally these views are well known and clearly understood, as they follow the conventional pattern of meeting force with maximum counter-force, as we have never failed to do in the past. Your view with respect to the utilization of the Chinese forces on Formosa is in conflict with neither logic nor this tradition.

It seems strangely difficult for some to realize that here in Asia is where the Communist conspirators have elected to make their play for global conquest, and

---

*Truman neglected to say that General Eisenhower had been president of Columbia University for four years.

[2]*Congressional Record,* 82d Cong., 1st sess. (April 5, 1951), p. 3380.

that we have joined the issue thus raised on the battlefield; that here we fight Europe's war with arms while the diplomats there still fight it with words; that if we lose the war to Communism in Asia the fall of Europe is inevitable; win it, and Europe most probably would avoid war and yet preserve freedom.

As you point out, we must win. There is no substitute for victory.

3. Truman Looks Beyond Victory (1951)

An angered Truman abruptly dismissed MacArthur from his Far Eastern commands (April 11, 1951), but circumstances conspired to make the general's removal unduly brutal. The five-star general, "fired by a two-bit president," returned home to receive a hero's welcome. He delivered a dramatic speech before Congress in which he repeated the no-substitute-for-victory formula and then, with tear-inducing pathos, recited the lines of the old barracks ballad: "Old soldiers never die; they just fade away." The excitement faded away, even though the general did not, and a stalemate truce came to Korea in 1953. A cocksure Truman delivered this rebuttal in his Memoirs, *taking as his text the indiscreet MacArthur letter to Congressman Martin. Why, in Truman's view, was the kind of victory that the general proposed the wrong kind of victory?*

Of course the third paragraph of MacArthur's letter was the real "clincher." I do not know through what channels of information the general learned that the Communists had chosen to concentrate their efforts on Asia—and more specifically on his command. . . . Actually, of course, my letter of January 13 [to MacArthur] had made it clear that Communism was capable of attacking not only in Asia but also in Europe, and that this was one reason why we could not afford to extend the conflict in Korea. But then MacArthur added a belittling comment about our diplomatic efforts, and reached his climax with the pronouncement that "there is no substitute for victory."

But there is a right kind and a wrong kind of victory, just as there are wars for the right thing and wars that are wrong from every standpoint.

As General Bradley later said: "To have extended the fighting to the mainland of Asia would have been the wrong war, at the wrong time and in the wrong place."

The kind of victory MacArthur had in mind—victory by the bombing of Chinese cities, victory by expanding the conflict to all of China—would have been the wrong kind of victory.

To some professional military men, victory—success on the battlefield alone—becomes something of an end in itself. Napoleon, during his ill-fated Moscow campaign, said, "I beat them in every battle, but it does not get me anywhere."

The time had come to draw the line. MacArthur's letter to Congressman Martin showed that the general was not only in disagreement with the policy of the government but was challenging this policy in open insubordination to his Commander in Chief.

---

[3]*Memoirs by Harry S. Truman: Years of Trial and Hope* (1956), vol. 2, 446–447. Published by Doubleday and Company. Copyright © 1956 by Time, Inc. Reprinted by permission of Margaret Truman Daniel.

Thought Provokers

1. Did the baby-boom generation have a unique upbringing and thus a historically unique set of values? What was distinctive about the condition of the American family in the early Cold War era? What forces worked most powerfully to change the role of women?

2. What choices did Roosevelt have at Yalta? Was he justified in making the concessions that he did to the Soviet Union?

3. Why did George Kennan's views of Soviet behavior prove so influential? What is the role of ideas in the formulation of foreign policy? Was the Truman Doctrine a balanced, proportionate response to the crisis that President Truman faced in the 1940s? To what extent did the Cold War proceed from each side's misperception of the other?

4. To what extent was the Marshall Plan an act of altruism? of self-interest?

5. Is it proper to speak of the communist takeover in China as the "fall" of China? Why did Senator McCarthy use the China issue so viciously against the Democrats? Would a different U.S. policy have produced a different outcome in China?

6. NSC-68 has been called perhaps the single most important document of the Cold War. Comment. What difference might it have made if NSC-68 had been published in 1950 and publicly discussed?

7. Was Korea a necessary war for the United States? What would have happened if the Americans had stayed out?

8. Was Truman wise to fire General MacArthur? When is a military officer justified in disobeying orders? MacArthur believed that there was "no substitute for victory." Would his policies have brought victory or simply more bloodshed in Korea?

38

The Eisenhower Era,
1952–1960

We must guard against the acquisition of
unwarranted influence, whether sought or
unsought, by the military-industrial complex.

Dwight D. Eisenhower, 1961

Prologue: War hero Dwight D. Eisenhower ascended triumphantly to the White
House in 1953. Worried about the budget-busting implications of President Harry
Truman's military buildup, Eisenhower and Secretary of State John Foster Dulles tried
to define a new strategic doctrine. It emphasized "massive retaliation" with nuclear
weapons against the Soviets if they dared to break the peace. At the same time,
Eisenhower took some hesitant steps toward promoting nuclear disarmament, although he proved unable to thaw the Cold War with Russia. After Stalin's death in
1953, the more subtle Nikita Khrushchev emerged as the undisputed Soviet leader.
The Soviet Union matched the U.S. hydrogen bomb in 1953, and tensions further
heightened in 1956 when the Soviets crushed an uprising in Hungary and backed
President Nasser of Egypt during the Suez explosion. The Soviets jolted the Americans in 1957 by shooting two satellites—Sputniks—into earth orbit. Eisenhower's
administration, like Truman's, was badgered and embarrassed by the anticommunist
crusade of Senator Joe McCarthy. McCarthyism cruelly wounded many individuals
and left scars on the body politic that took decades to heal. The Supreme Court in
1954 ordered the desegregation of schools, notably in the South. The white South at
first resisted massively, but the Court's decision imparted momentum to the rising
wave of the civil rights movement, which was to crest in the 1960s. Americans knew
unprecedented prosperity in the 1950s, but affluence had its critics. Many of them
came to power when the New Frontier arrived with the election of Senator John
F. Kennedy to the presidency in 1960.

A. A New Look in Foreign Policy

1. Secretary John Foster Dulles Warns
of Massive Retaliation (1954)

*In 1950, NSC-68 (see p. 427) had proposed an enormous, and enormously costly,
program of U.S. military expansion to support a tougher foreign policy in the Cold*

---

[1]*State Department Bulletin* 30 (January 25, 1954): 107–110.

War. Although Republican critics admired the toughness of Truman's and Acheson's policies, they choked on the price tag. Accordingly, the new secretary of state, John Foster Dulles, announced in 1954 that the United States would henceforward rely less on conventional military forces and more on "massive retaliation" with nuclear bombs to support its international policies. In fact, the policy of massive retaliation proved scarcely less expensive and considerably less practical than reliance on an array of conventional military means. (It was impossible, for example, to imagine incinerating Moscow with atomic bombs in order to induce the Soviet Union to halt the invasion of Hungary in 1956.) Dulles announced the new doctrine in the following speech of January 12, 1954. What were his chief criticisms of the foreign policy of his predecessors? What did he see as the advantages of the massive retaliation doctrine? In the light of history, how successful was "massive retaliation" in the examples that Dulles cites—in Korea, Indochina, Germany, and Austria? Was the arms race actually accelerated by the desire to buy security on the cheap?

It is now nearly a year since the Eisenhower administration took office. During that year I have often spoken of various parts of our foreign policies. Tonight I should like to present an overall view of those policies which relate to our security.

First of all, let us recognize that many of the preceding foreign policies were good. Aid to Greece and Turkey had checked the Communist drive to the Mediterranean. The European Recovery Program had helped the peoples of Western Europe to pull out of the postwar morass. The Western powers were steadfast in Berlin and overcame the blockade with their airlift. As a loyal member of the United Nations, we had reacted with force to repel the Communist attack in Korea. When that effort exposed our military weakness, we rebuilt rapidly our military establishment. We also sought a quick buildup of armed strength in Western Europe.

These were the acts of a nation which saw the danger of Soviet communism; which realized that its own safety was tied up with that of others; which was capable of responding boldly and promptly to emergencies. These are precious values to be acclaimed. Also, we can pay tribute to congressional bipartisanship which puts the nation above politics.

But we need to recall that what we did was in the main emergency action, imposed on us by our enemies.

Let me illustrate.

1. We did not send our army into Korea because we judged in advance that it was sound military strategy to commit our Army to fight land battles in Asia. Our decision had been to pull out of Korea. It was Soviet-inspired action that pulled us back.

2. We did not decide in advance that it was wise to grant billions annually as foreign economic aid. We adopted that policy in response to the Communist efforts to sabotage the free economies of Western Europe.

3. We did not build up our military establishment at a rate which involved huge budget deficits, a depreciating currency, and a feverish economy because this seemed, in advance, a good policy. Indeed, we decided otherwise until the Soviet military threat was clearly revealed.

We live in a world where emergencies are always possible and our survival may depend upon our capacity to meet emergencies. Let us pray that we shall always have that capacity. But, having said that, it is necessary also to say that emergency measures—however good for the emergency—do not necessarily make good permanent policies. Emergency measures are costly; they are superficial; and they imply that the enemy has the initiative. They cannot be depended on to serve our long-time interests.

This "long time" factor is of critical importance.

The Soviet Communists are planning for what they call "an entire historical era," and we should do the same. They seek, through many types of maneuvers, gradually to divide and weaken the free nations by overextending them in efforts which, as Lenin put it, are "beyond their strength, so that they come to practical bankruptcy." Then, said Lenin, "our victory is assured." Then, said Stalin, will be "the moment for the decisive blow."

In the face of this strategy, measures cannot be judged adequate merely because they ward off an immediate danger. It is essential to do this, but it is also essential to do so without exhausting ourselves.

When the Eisenhower administration applied this test, we felt that some transformations were needed.

It is not sound military strategy permanently to commit U.S. land forces to Asia to a degree that leaves us no strategic reserves.

It is not sound economics, or good foreign policy, to support permanently other countries; for in the long run, that creates as much ill will as good will.

Also, it is not sound to become permanently committed to military expenditures so vast that they lead to "practical bankruptcy." . . .

What the Eisenhower administration seeks is a . . . maximum deterrent at a bearable cost. . . .

The total cost of our security efforts, at home and abroad, was over $50 billion per annum, and involved, for 1953, a projected budgetary deficit of $9 billion; and $11 billion for 1954. This was on top of taxes comparable to wartime taxes; and the dollar was depreciating in effective value. Our allies were similarly weighed down. This could not be continued for long without grave budgetary, economic, and social consequences.

But before military planning could be changed, the President and his advisers, as represented by the National Security Council, had to take some basic policy decisions. This has been done. The basic decision was to depend primarily upon a great capacity to retaliate, instantly, by means and at places of our choosing. Now the Department of Defense and the Joint Chiefs of Staff can shape our military establishment to fit what is *our* policy, instead of having to try to be ready to meet the enemy's many choices. That permits of a selection of military means instead of a multiplication of means. As a result, it is now possible to get, and share, more basic security at less cost.

Let us now see how this concept has been applied to foreign policy, taking first the Far East.

In Korea this administration effected a major transformation. The fighting has been stopped on honorable terms. That was possible because the aggressor, already thrown back to and behind his place of beginning, was faced with the possibility that the fighting might, to his own great peril, soon spread beyond the limits and methods which he had selected. . . .

I have said in relation to Indochina that, if there were open Red Chinese army aggression there, that would have "grave consequences which might not be confined to Indochina."

I expressed last month the intention of the United States to maintain its position in Okinawa. This is needed to insure adequate striking power to implement the collective security concept which I describe. . . .

We have persisted, with our allies, in seeking the unification of Germany and the liberation of Austria. Now the Soviet rulers have agreed to discuss these questions. We expect to meet them soon in Berlin. I hope they will come with sincerity which will equal our own.

We have sought a conference to unify Korea and relieve it of foreign troops. So far, our persistence is unrewarded; but we have not given up.

These efforts at negotiation are normal initiatives that breathe the spirit of freedom. They involve no plan for a partnership division of world power with those who suppress freedom. . . .

2. President Eisenhower Calls for "Open Skies" (1955)

The end of hostilities in Korea in 1953, Stalin's death in the same year, and the withdrawal of Soviet occupation forces from Austria in early 1955 brought a welcome thaw to the Cold War. Trying to take advantage of this period of apparently relaxed tensions, President Eisenhower agreed to a summit meeting with Soviet leaders in July 1955 at Geneva. There he proposed a straightforward first step toward the ultimate goal of reducing the size of military arsenals, especially the fearsome stockpiles of nuclear weapons. How realistic was Eisenhower's plan? Why did the Soviets not agree to it? What other approaches might have been tried?

Disarmament is one of the most important subjects on our agenda. It is also extremely difficult. In recent years the scientists have discovered methods of making weapons many, many times more destructive of opposing armed forces—but also of homes, and industries and lives—than ever known or even imagined before. These same scientific discoveries have made much more complex the problems of limitation and control and reduction of armament. . . .

The United States government is prepared to enter into a sound and reliable agreement making possible the reduction of armament. I have directed that an intensive and thorough study of this subject be made within our own government. . . .

No sound and reliable agreement can be made unless it is completely covered by an inspection and reporting system adequate to support every portion of the agreement.

The lessons of history teach us that disarmament agreements without adequate reciprocal inspection increase the dangers of war and do not brighten the prospects of peace.

---

[2]*The Public Papers of the Presidents: Dwight D. Eisenhower, 1955* (Washington, D.C.: National Archives and Records Service, 1956), pp. 713–716.

Thus it is my view that the priority attention of our combined study of disarmament should be upon the subject of inspection and reporting. . . .

Gentlemen, since I have been working on this memorandum to present to this Conference, I have been searching my heart and mind for something that I could say here that could convince everyone of the great sincerity of the United States in approaching this problem of disarmament.

I should address myself for a moment principally to the delegates from the Soviet Union, because our two great countries admittedly possess new and terrible weapons in quantities which do give rise in other parts of the world, or reciprocally, to the fears and dangers of surprise attack.

I propose, therefore, that we take a practical step, that we begin an arrangement, very quickly, as between ourselves—immediately. These steps would include:

To give to each other a complete blueprint of our military establishments, from beginning to end, from one end of our countries to the other; lay out the establishments and provide the blueprints to each other.

Next, to provide within our countries facilities for aerial photography to the other country—we to provide you the facilities within our country, ample facilities for aerial reconnaissance, where you can make all the pictures you choose and take them to your own country to study, you to provide exactly the same facilities for us and we to make these examinations, and by this step to convince the world that we are providing as between ourselves against the possibility of great surprise attack, thus lessening danger and relaxing tension. Likewise we will make more easily attainable a comprehensive and effective system of inspection and disarmament, because what I propose, I assure you, would be but a beginning. . . .

B. The McCarthy Hysteria

1. Joseph McCarthy Upholds Guilt by Association (1952)

Senator Joseph R. McCarthy of Wisconsin, hitherto unknown to fame, rocketed into the headlines in 1950 when he declared in a political speech that there were scores of known communists in the State Department.* The collapse of Jiang's China and the bloodily indecisive Korean War gave point to his charges, while accelerating the hunt for scapegoats. A few "pinks" and communist sympathizers were exposed and driven out of government. But persons with liberal or nonconformist ideas were indiscriminately branded as communists, with a subsequent loss of reputation and jobs. In McCarthy's view, birds that waddled like ducks, quacked like ducks, and

---

[1]Quoted from Senator Joseph McCarthy, *McCarthyism: The Fight for America* (New York: Devin-Adair Company, 1952), pp. 7, 79–80.

**Webster's Third International Dictionary* (1961) defines McCarthyism as "a political attitude of the mid-twentieth century closely allied to know-nothingism, and characterized chiefly by opposition to elements held to be subversive, and by the use of tactics involving personal attacks on individuals by means of widely publicized indiscriminate allegations, especially on the basis of unsubstantiated charges."

associated with ducks were presumed to be ducks. Anti-McCarthyites cited the axiom that it was better to let ten guilty men escape than to condemn one innocent man. McCarthy here defends his tactics. How convincing is he?

One of the safest and most popular sports engaged in today by every politician and office seeker is to "agree with McCarthy's aim of getting rid of Communists in government," but at the same time to "condemn his irresponsible charges and shot-gun technique." It is a completely safe position to take. The Communist Party and their camp followers in press and radio do not strike back as long as you merely condemn Communism in general terms. It is only when one adopts an effective method of digging out and exposing the under-cover dangerous, "sacred cow" Communists that all of the venom and smear of the Party is loosed upon him.

I suggest to you, therefore, that when a politician mounts the speaker's rostrum and makes the statement that he "agrees with McCarthy's aims but not his methods," that you ask him what methods he himself has used against Communists. I suggest you ask him to name a single Communist or camp follower that he has forced out of the government by his methods. . . .

Is not a person presumed innocent until proven guilty?

Yes.

Why do you condemn people like Acheson, Jessup, Lattimore, Service, Vincent,* and others who have never been convicted of any crime?

The fact that these people have not been convicted of treason or of violating some of our espionage laws is no more a valid argument that they are fit to represent this country in its fight against Communism than the argument that a person who has a reputation of consorting with criminals, hoodlums, gamblers, and kidnappers is fit to act as your baby sitter because he has never been convicted of a crime.

A government job is a privilege, not a right. There is no reason why men who chum with Communists, who refuse to turn their backs upon traitors† and who are consistently found at the time and place where disaster strikes America and success comes to international Communism, should be given positions of power in government. . . .

I have not urged that those whom I have named be put in jail. Once they are exposed so the American people know what they are, they can do but little damage. . . .

Strangely enough, those who scream the loudest about what they call guilt by association are the first to endorse innocence by association.

For example, those who object most strongly to my showing Jessup's affinity for Communist causes, the Communist money used to support the publication over which he had control, and his close friendship and defense of a Communist spy [Hiss], also argue Hiss' innocence by association. The argument is that Hiss was

---

*Professors Philip C. Jessup and Owen Lattimore were prominent officials or advisers who were allegedly "soft" on communism; John S. Service and John C. Vincent were foreign service officers similarly branded by McCarthy.

†After State Department official Alger Hiss was convicted of perjury in connection with Soviet espionage, his friend Secretary of State Acheson loyally but indiscreetly declared, "I do not intend to turn my back [on him]."

innocent because Justices Frankfurter and Reed testified they were friends of his, because Acheson chummed and walked with him each morning, because Hiss was the top planner at the United Nations conference and helped to draft the Yalta agreement.

We are not concerned with GUILT by association because here we are not concerned with convicting any individual of any crime. We are concerned with the question of whether the individual who associates with those who are trying to destroy this nation, should be admitted to the high councils of those planning the policies of this nation: whether they should be given access to top secret material to which even Senators and Congressmen are not given access.

2. A Senator Speaks Up (1950)

The infiltration of a few communists into government was perhaps inevitable, but the embarrassed Truman administration played into the hands of the McCarthyites by its cover-up tactics. In the interests of free debate, the Constitution exempts from libel suits anything that may be said on the floor of Congress. Senator McCarthy clearly abused this privilege. At a time when he was riding high and many Republicans regarded him as a political asset, the tall and gray-haired Republican Margaret Chase Smith of Maine, the only female U.S. senator, courageously spoke out against his excesses.* (Later McCarthy vindictively invaded Maine in an unsuccessful effort to defeat her for reelection.) Why does she believe that McCarthy's tactics, whatever his aims, are contrary to the Constitution and basically un-American?

I think that it is high time for the United States Senate and its Members to do some real soul searching, and to weigh out consciences as to the manner in which we are performing our duty to the people of America, and the manner in which we are using or abusing our individual powers and privileges.

I think it is high time that we remembered that we have sworn to uphold and defend the Constitution. I think it is high time that we remembered that the Constitution, as amended, speaks not only of the freedom of speech but also of trial by jury instead of trial by accusation.

Whether it be a criminal prosecution in court or a character prosecution in the Senate, there is little practical distinction when the life of a person has been ruined.

Those of us who shout the loudest about Americanism in making character assassinations are all too frequently those who, by our own words and acts, ignore some of the basic principles of Americanism—

The right to criticize.

The right to hold unpopular beliefs.

The right to protest.

The right of independent thought.

The exercise of these rights should not cost one single American citizen his reputation or his right to a livelihood, nor should he be in danger of losing his

---

[2]*Congressional Record,* 81st Cong., 2d sess. (June 1, 1950), pp. 7894–7895.

*Senator Smith simultaneously presented "a Declaration of Conscience" signed by six fellow senators.

reputation or livelihood merely because he happens to know someone who holds unpopular beliefs. Who of us does not? Otherwise none of us could call our souls our own. Otherwise thought control would have set in.

The American people are sick and tired of being afraid to speak their minds lest they be politically smeared as Communists or Fascists by their opponents. Freedom of speech is not what it used to be in America. It has been so abused by some that it is not exercised by others.

The American people are sick and tired of seeing innocent people smeared and guilty people whitewashed. But there have been enough proved cases, such as the *Amerasia* case, the Hiss case, the Coplon case, the Gold case,* to cause nation-wide distrust and strong suspicion that there may be something to the unproved, sensational accusations. . . .

Today our country is being psychologically divided by the confusion and the suspicions that are bred in the United States Senate to spread like cancerous tentacles of "know nothing, suspect everything" attitudes. . . .

As a United States Senator, I am not proud of the way in which the Senate has been made a publicity platform for irresponsible sensationalism. I am not proud of the reckless abandon in which unproved charges have been hurled from this [Republican] side of the aisle. I am not proud of the obviously staged, undignified countercharges which have been attempted in retaliation from the other [Democratic] side of the aisle.

I do not like the way the Senate has been made a rendezvous for vilification, for selfish political gain at the sacrifice of individual reputations and national unity. I am not proud of the way we smear outsiders from the floor of the Senate and hide behind the cloak of congressional immunity, and still place ourselves beyond criticism on the floor of the Senate.

As an American, I am shocked at the way Republicans and Democrats alike are playing directly into the Communist design of "confuse, divide, and conquer." As an American, I do not want a Democratic administration whitewash or cover-up any more than I want a Republican smear or witch hunt.

As an American, I condemn a Republican Fascist just as much as I condemn a Democratic Communist. I condemn a Democratic Fascist just as much as I condemn a Republican Communist. They are equally dangerous to you and me and to our country. As an American, I want to see our Nation recapture the strength and unity it once had when we fought the enemy instead of ourselves.

3. McCarthy Inspires Fear at Harvard (1954)

Senator McCarthy overplayed his hand, notably in the televised investigation of the army. To millions of viewers he exposed his vindictiveness, arrogance, and intellectual

---

Amerasia was a communist-tainted magazine that acquired confidential government documents. Judith Coplon, a Justice Department employee, and Harry Gold, a Philadelphia biochemist, were both convicted in 1950 of spying for the Soviet Union.

[3]Cited in *Congressional Record*, 83d Cong., 2d sess., p. A5909. Reprinted by permission of the Harvard *Crimson*. The letters appeared in the issues of November 24 and 30, 1954. The Richardson letter ended in the *Crimson* with four dots after "crowd"; the five missing lines are published in the *Congressional Record*.

dishonesty. Apologists claimed that his anticommunist zeal, whether sincere or not, destroyed all sense of fair play. His bubble burst when the Senate "condemned" him in 1954 by a formal vote—not, curiously enough, for his abuses of U.S. citizens but for his contemptuous attitude toward the Senate itself. A petition urging the censure of McCarthy was circulated at Harvard University, and two undergraduates who refused to sign it gave their reasons in the first of the following letters to the Harvard Crimson. *An English-born student named J. C. P. Richardson, who was backing the petition, took sharp issue with them in the second letter. Who had the sounder position?*

To the Editors of the *Crimson:*

This afternoon my roommate and I were asked to sign a petition advocating the censure of Senator Joseph R. McCarthy. We both refused. And yet, we both hope that the censure motion is adopted.

Discussing our actions, we came to the conclusion that we did not sign because we were afraid that sometime in the future McCarthy will point to us as having signed the petition, and, as he had done to others, question our loyalty.

We are afraid that of the thousands of petition signers, one will be proved a Communist, and as a result, McCarthy, or someone like him, will say, because we were both co-signers and classmates of the Communist, that we, too, are Reds.

The fact that two college students and others like us will not sign a petition for fear of reprisal indicates only too clearly that our democracy is in danger. It is clear that McCarthy is suppressing free speech and free actions by thrusting fear into the hearts of innocent citizens.

Let us hope that the Senators of the United States are not victims of the same fear that has infected us.

K. W. L. '58
M. F. G. '58

To the Editors of the *Crimson:*

The letter sent to you by two Harvard students and published yesterday can safely be said to represent the viewpoint of about one half of those who did not sign the anti-McCarthy petition.

The position taken by the authors is common and understandable, but it is by no means justifiable. In a free society, when opinions become unpopular and dangerous, it is most important that they be expressed. To yield to the climate of fear, to become a scared liberal, is to strengthen the very forces which one opposes. Courage must complement conviction, for otherwise each man will become a rubber-stamp, content to spend the rest of his life echoing popular beliefs, never daring to dissent, never having enough courage to say what he thinks, and never living as an individual, but only as part of the crowd.

Yes, our democracy is in danger, but as long as men are not afraid to express their view in spite of the consequences, it shall flourish. Only when fear is allowed to limit dissension does democracy falter.

The blame for America's present intellectual intolerance rests as heavily on those who have bowed to it as it does on those who encourage it.

Sincerely,
J. C. Peter Richardson '56

C. The Supreme Court and the Black Revolution

1. The Court Rejects Segregation (1954)

The Fourteenth Amendment (1868) had made African-Americans citizens and assured them "the equal protection of the laws." The southern states established "separate but equal" facilities in the schools, public toilets, and transportation. In many instances, however, the facilities for blacks, though "separate," were not "equal" to those for whites. In 1892 a Louisianan by the name of Plessy, of one-eighth African descent, was jailed for insisting on sitting in a railroad car reserved for whites. The case was appealed to the Supreme Court, where Plessy lost by a seven-to-one vote (see p. 57). The Court held that separate but equal public conveyances did not violate the Fourteenth Amendment. This principle was applied to educational facilities until May 17, 1954, when the Supreme Court, by a nine-to-zero vote, reversed its basic policy and decreed that separate educational facilities were not equal within the meaning of the Fourteenth Amendment. In the heart of the decision given here, what ground is there for the white southern complaint that this was a sociological rather than a legal decision? Are separateness and inequality inseparable?

In approaching this problem, we cannot turn the clock back to 1868 when the [Fourteenth] Amendment was adopted, or even to 1896 when *Plessy* v. *Ferguson* was written. We must consider public education in the light of its full development and its present place in American life throughout the Nation. Only in this way can it be determined if segregation in public schools deprives the plaintiffs of the equal protection of the laws.

Today, education is perhaps the most important function of state and local governments. Compulsory school attendance laws and the great expenditures for education both demonstrate our recognition of the importance of education to our democratic society. It is required in the performance of our most basic public responsibilities, even service in the armed forces. It is the very foundation of good citizenship. Today it is a principal instrument in awakening the child to cultural values, in preparing him for later professional training, and in helping him to adjust normally to his environment. In these days, it is doubtful that any child may reasonably be expected to succeed in life if he is denied the opportunity of an education. Such an opportunity, where the state has undertaken to provide it, is a right which must be made available to all on equal terms.

We come then to the question presented: Does segregation of children in public schools solely on the basis of race, even though the physical facilities and other "tangible" factors may be equal, deprive the children of the minority group of equal educational opportunities? We believe that it does. . . .

Such considerations apply with added force to children in grade and high schools. To separate them from others of similar age and qualifications, solely because of their race, generates a feeling of inferiority as to their status in the community that may affect their hearts and minds in a way unlikely ever to be undone. The

---

[1]*Brown* v. *Board of Education of Topeka,* 347 U.S. 492–495 (1954).

effect of this separation on their educational opportunities was well stated by a finding in the Kansas case by a court which nevertheless felt compelled to rule against the Negro plaintiffs:

"Segregation of white and colored children in public schools has a detrimental effect upon the colored children. The impact is greater when it has the sanction of the law; for the policy of separating the races is usually interpreted as denoting the inferiority of the Negro group. A sense of inferiority affects the motivation of a child to learn. Segregation with the sanction of law, therefore, has a tendency to [retard] the educational and mental development of Negro children, and to deprive them of some of the benefits they would receive in a racial[ly] integrated school system."

Whatever may have been the extent of psychological knowledge at the time of *Plessy* v. *Ferguson,* this finding is amply supported by modern authority. Any language in *Plessy* v. *Ferguson* contrary to this finding is rejected.

We conclude that in the field of public education the doctrine of "separate but equal" has no place. Separate educational facilities are inherently unequal. Therefore, we hold that the plaintiffs and others similarly situated for whom the actions have been brought are, by reason of the segregation complained of, deprived of the equal protection of the laws guaranteed by the Fourteenth Amendment.

2. One Hundred Representatives Dissent (1956)

Chief Justice Earl Warren, a gray-haired, open-faced California governor turned judge, had already come under some fire for his liberal views. Bitter was the outcry of white southerners against the "Earl Warren Communist Court." Although the desegregation decision called for gradual implementation, the social upheaval that it foreshadowed was enormous. One hundred southern members of Congress—nineteen senators and eighty-one House members—issued the following manifesto in 1956. The first part of it declared that since the Constitution does not mention education, the schools are solely the concern of the states under reserved powers (Tenth Amendment). How persuasive is the manifesto's contention that the Court's decision would worsen, rather than improve, race relations?

In the case of *Plessy* v. *Ferguson,* in 1896, the Supreme Court expressly declared that under the Fourteenth Amendment no person was denied any of his rights if the states provided separate but equal public facilities. This decision has been followed in many other cases. It is notable that the Supreme Court, speaking through Chief Justice Taft, a former President of the United States, unanimously declared in 1927 in *Lum* v. *Rice* that the "separate but equal" principle is ". . . within the discretion of the state in regulating its public schools and does not conflict with the Fourteenth Amendment."

This interpretation, restated time and time again, became a part of the life of the people of many of the states and confirmed their habits, customs, traditions, and way of life. It is founded on elemental humanity and common sense, for parents

---

[2]*Congressional Record,* 84th Cong., 2d sess. (March 12, 1956), pp. 4515–4516.

should not be deprived by Government of the right to direct the lives and education of their own children.

Though there has been no constitutional amendment or act of Congress changing their established legal principle almost a century old, the Supreme Court of the United States, with no legal basis for such action, undertook to exercise their naked judicial power and substituted their personal political and social ideas for the established law of the land.

This unwarranted exercise of power by the court, contrary to the Constitution, is creating chaos and confusion in the states principally affected. It is destroying the amicable relations between the white and Negro races that have been created through ninety years of patient effort by the good people of both races. It has planted hatred and suspicion where there has been heretofore friendship and understanding.

Without regard to the consent of the governed, outside agitators are threatening immediate and revolutionary changes in our public school systems. If done, this is certain to destroy the system of public education in some of the states.

With the gravest concern for the explosive and dangerous conditions created by this decision and inflamed by outside meddlers:

We reaffirm our reliance on the Constitution as the fundamental law of the land.

We decry the Supreme Court's encroachments on rights reserved to the states and to the people, contrary to established law and to the Constitution.

We commend the motives of those states which have declared the intention to resist forced integration by any lawful means.

We appeal to the states and people who are not directly affected by these decisions to consider the constitutional principles involved against the time when they too, on issues vital to them, may be the victims of judicial encroachment.

Even though we constitute a minority in the present Congress, we have full faith that a majority of the American people believe in the dual system of government which has enabled us to achieve our greatness and will in time demand that the reserved rights of the states and of the people be made secure against judicial usurpation.

We pledge ourselves to use all lawful means to bring about a reversal of this decision, which is contrary to the Constitution, and to prevent the use of force in its implementation.

In this trying period, as we all seek to right this wrong, we appeal to our people not to be provoked by the agitators and troublemakers invading our states and to scrupulously refrain from disorder and lawless acts.

3. Eisenhower Sends Federal Troops (1957)

Following the school-desegregation decision of the "Earl Warren Court," southern white resistance mounted. A showdown occurred in the autumn of 1957, when angry mobs in Little Rock, Arkansas, prevented nine black pupils from attending the all-white Central High School. When the governor of the state refused to provide proper protection, President Eisenhower backed up the federal court by sending in

---

[3]*Vital Speeches,* vol. 24, pp. 11–12 (October 15, 1957; address of September 24, 1957).

federal troops. Under their protective bayonets the African-American pupils attended the school, despite disagreeable incidents. The ugly episode became a hot issue in the Cold War. Little Rock rapidly became the best-known U.S. city as communist propagandists had a field day, ignoring the fact that the federal government was trying to help the blacks. President Eisenhower addressed the American people on a nationwide radio and television hookup, explaining why he had regretfully resorted to drastic action. Was he on sound legal ground? Why was he concerned about the foreign implications of the affair?

For a few minutes this evening I want to talk to you about the serious situation that has arisen in Little Rock. To make this talk I have come to the President's office in the White House. I could have spoken from Rhode Island, where I have been staying recently, but I felt that, in speaking from the house of Lincoln, of Jackson, and of Wilson, my words would better convey both the sadness I feel in the action I was compelled today to take and the firmness with which I intend to pursue this course until the orders of the Federal Court at Little Rock can be executed without unlawful interference.

In that city, under the leadership of demagogic extremists, disorderly mobs have deliberately prevented the carrying out of proper orders from a Federal Court. Local authorities have not eliminated that violent opposition and, under the law, I yesterday issued a Proclamation calling upon the mob to disperse.

This morning the mob again gathered in front of the Central High School of Little Rock, obviously for the purpose of again preventing the carrying out of the Court's order relating to the admission of Negro children to that school.

Whenever normal agencies prove inadequate to the task and it becomes necessary for the Executive Branch of the Federal Government to use its powers and authority to uphold Federal Courts, the President's responsibility is inescapable.

In accordance with that responsibility, I have today issued an Executive Order directing the use of troops under Federal authority to aid in the execution of Federal law at Little Rock, Arkansas. This became necessary when my Proclamation of yesterday was not observed, and the obstruction of justice still continues. . . .

Our personal opinions about the decision have no bearing on the matter of enforcement; the responsibility and authority of the Supreme Court to interpret the Constitution are very clear. . . .

Mob rule cannot be allowed to override the decisions of our courts.

Now, let me make it very clear that Federal troops are not being used to relieve local and state authorities of their primary duty to preserve the peace and order of the community. Nor are the troops there for the purpose of taking over the responsibility of the School Board and the other responsible local officials in running Central High School. The running of our school system and the maintenance of peace and order in each of our states are strictly local affairs, and the Federal Government does not interfere, except in very special cases and when requested by one of the several states. In the present case the troops are there, pursuant to law, solely for the purpose of preventing interference with the orders of the Court. . . .

In the South, as elsewhere, citizens are keenly aware of the tremendous disservice that has been done to the people of Arkansas in the eyes of the nation, and that has been done to the nation in the eyes of the world.

At a time when we face grave situations abroad because of the hatred that Communism bears toward a system of government based on human rights, it would be difficult to exaggerate the harm that is being done to the prestige and influence and, indeed, to the safety of our nation and the world.

Our enemies are gloating over this incident and using it everywhere to misrepresent our whole nation. We are portrayed as a violator of those standards of conduct which the peoples of the world united to proclaim in the Charter of the United Nations. There they affirmed "faith in fundamental human rights" and "in the dignity and worth of the human person," and they did so "without distinction as to race, sex, language, or religion."

And so, with deep confidence, I call upon citizens of the State of Arkansas to assist in bringing to an immediate end all interference with the law and its processes. If resistance to the Federal Court order ceases at once, the further presence of Federal troops will be unnecessary and the city of Little Rock will return to its normal habits of peace and order—and a blot upon the fair name and high honor of our nation will be removed.

Thus will be restored the image of America and of all its parts as one nation, indivisible, with liberty and justice for all.

4. The *Arkansas Democrat* Protests (1958)

Occupying federal troops—the first in the South since 1877—remained eight months, until the nine African-American pupils could attend the high school without serious molestation. Many white southerners who were resigned to gradual integration of the schools bitterly resented President Eisenhower's armed intervention. In the light of the following article in a Little Rock newspaper, explain why. Where is the editor on the weakest ground? the strongest ground?

Little Rock's Central High School is still under military occupation. The troops are still there—on the campus, in the building.

The troops are still there, despite the fact that their presence is resented by the big majority of the students, the parents, and the people in general throughout the South.

The troops continue to stand guard during school hours, on the grounds and within the corridors and classrooms, despite the fact that there is no law or precedent—Federal or State—that permits them to do so.

There is not even an order, or so much as a sanction, from the U.S. Supreme Court that makes its own "laws" on mixing of races in the public schools.

Federal troops continue to occupy Central High—in defiance of the Constitution, law, and precedent—while the Congress of the United States sits out the sessions and does nothing.

Never before in the history of America has any area of our so-called Free Republic been so shamefully treated.

---

[4]"Editorial—Anti–Little Rock Intervention" by Karr Shannon in *Arkansas Democrat* (March 10, 1958). Reprinted by permission.

When two sections of this country were at war with each other, no troops ever patrolled the public school buildings and grounds from day to day. After the South had been beaten down, Federal forces kept the vanquished under the iron heel for the duration of the "Reconstruction" period. But not once did they molest the public schools with troop occupation.

Education, or attempted education, under the scrutiny of armed troops is un-American, un-Godly.

It is not even Communistic. Russia, in all her cruelty, has never bothered school children in occupied territory by stationing armed soldiers on the grounds and in the buildings. Germany never did it.

No other nation, however barbaric and cruel and relentless, ever—in the history of the human race—resorted to such tactics—only the United States, which sets itself up as a world example of peace, freedom, and democracy, forces the military upon a free school.

How much longer will Congress sit idly by and let such brazen violation of American principle and law continue on and on and on?

5. A Black Newspaper Praises Courage (1958)

The conduct of the nine African-American pupils at Central High School, in the face of the sneers, jeers, jostling, spitting, and other insults, evoked praise in varied places. A black newspaper in Chicago paid them the following tribute. What parts of their ordeal must have taken the most courage?

Few incidents in recent American history can match the courage shown by the nine teen-age Negroes of Little Rock. They risked their lives for the sake of establishing a principle: the right to attend an integrated high school. They did it in the face of ugly and determined opposition; they did it under circumstances that would have caused many stout-hearted grownups to withdraw behind the protective shield of their own homes.

This was the most severe test of the law. The Federal courts paved the way; Federal troops held the angry mob at bay. But the nine Negro pupils did not have to march through the guardsmen to enter Little Rock's Central High School. They could have waited until public indignation had subsided; or they could have decided to attend a nearby Negro school rather than avail themselves of their legal rights. They didn't. Instead they went ahead, despite jeers and bitter invectives.

How many of us would have had the fortitude to do what these youngsters have done? How often have we failed to take advantage of victories won for us? It is therefore the more remarkable that these young Negroes, living in the Deep South, fearlessly implemented the Court's action by their daily presence at Central High School.

Though their lot was not a happy one even inside the high school building, though they were pushed around, insulted, and beaten by some of the white students, the Negro pupils held their ground. The Supreme Court's integration ruling

---

[5]*Chicago Daily Defender,* May 28, 1958.

would have been meaningless had these Negro boys and girls failed to follow the course mapped out for them by the law. They should be applauded by all of us.

6. Martin Luther King, Jr., Asks for the Ballot (1957)

While the Supreme Court adjudicated, African-Americans were meanwhile taking the struggle for civil rights into their own hands. The first mass protest against the detested segregation laws erupted in Montgomery, Alabama. On December 1, 1955, a dignified black woman named Rosa Parks refused to move out of the "whites only" seating section of a city bus. For this, she was arrested; at that moment, "somewhere in the universe," one black leader later commented, "a gear in the machinery had shifted." Her arrest sparked a hugely successful boycott of the bus system by Montgomery's African-Americans and catapulted into prominence a young black minister of the gospel, the Reverend Martin Luther King, Jr., who assumed a conspicuous leadership role in the boycott. He swiftly emerged as the nation's premier black spokesman and until his murder in 1968 led a civil rights crusade that changed the face of American society. As early as 1957 he identified political rights as the key to improving the condition of African-Americans in the South—where in some states fewer than 5 percent of eligible black voters were casting their ballots in the 1950s. In the speech reprinted here, what benefits does King think will flow from enfranchisement? What does he see as the federal government's role in securing black rights? Was his faith in the power of the ballot misplaced?

Three years ago the Supreme Court of this nation rendered in simple, eloquent and unequivocal language a decision which will long be stenciled on the mental sheets of succeeding generations. For all men of good will, this May 17 decision came as a joyous daybreak to end the long night of enforced segregation. It came as a great beacon light of hope to millions of distinguished people throughout the world who had dared only to dream of freedom. It came as a legal and sociological deathblow to the old Pessy doctrine of "separate-but-equal." It came as a reaffirmation of the good old American doctrine of freedom and equality for all people.

Unfortunately, this noble and sublime decision has not gone without opposition. This opposition has often risen to ominous proportions. Many states have risen up in open defiance. The legislative halls of the South ring loud with such words as "interposition" and "nullification." Methods of defiance range from crippling economic reprisals to the tragic reign of violence and terror. All of these forces have conjoined to make for massive resistance.

But, even more, all types of conniving methods are still being used to prevent Negroes from becoming registered voters. The denial of this sacred right is a tragic betrayal of the highest mandates of our democratic traditions and it is democracy turned upside down.

So long as I do not firmly and irrevocably possess the right to vote I do not possess myself. I cannot make up my mind—it is made up for me. I cannot live as a democratic citizen, observing the laws I have helped to enact—I can only submit to the edict of others.

So our most urgent request to the President of the United States and every member of Congress is to give us the right to vote.

Give us the ballot and we will no longer have to worry the federal government about our basic rights.

Give us the ballot and we will no longer plead to the federal government for passage of an antilynching law; we will by the power of our vote write the law on the statute books of the Southern states and bring an end to the dastardly acts of the hooded perpetrators of violence.

Give us the ballot and we will transform the salient misdeeds of bloodthirsty mobs into the calculated good deeds of orderly citizens.

Give us the ballot and we will fill our legislative halls with men of good will, and send to the sacred halls of Congress men who will not sign a Southern Manifesto,* because of their devotion to the manifesto of justice.

Give us the ballot and we will place judges on the benches of the South who will "do justly and love mercy," and we will place at the head of the Southern states governors who have felt not only the tang of the human, but the glow of the divine.

Give us the ballot and we will quietly and nonviolently, without rancor or bitterness, implement the Supreme Court's decision on May 17, 1954.

In this junction of our nation's history there is an urgent need for dedicated and courageous leadership. If we are to solve the problems ahead and make racial justice a reality, this leadership must be fourfold.

First, there is need for a strong, aggressive leadership from the federal government. So far, only the judicial branch of the government has evinced this quality of leadership. If the executive and legislative branches of the government were as concerned about the protection of our citizenship rights as the federal courts have been, then the transition from a segregated to an integrated society would be infinitely smoother. But we so often look to Washington in vain for this concern.

In the midst of the tragic breakdown of law and order, the executive branch of the government is all too silent and apathetic. In the midst of the desperate need for civil-rights legislation, the legislative branch of the government is all too stagnant and hypocritical.

This dearth of positive leadership from the federal government is not confined to one particular political party. Both parties have betrayed the cause of justice. The Democrats have betrayed it by capitulating to the prejudices and undemocratic practices of the Southern Dixiecrats. The Republicans have betrayed it by capitulating to the blatant hypocrisy of right-wing, reactionary Northerners. These men so often have a high blood pressure of words and an anemia of deeds.

In the midst of these prevailing conditions, we come to Washington today pleading with the President and the members of Congress to provide a strong, moral and courageous leadership for a situation that cannot permanently be evaded. We

---

*In March, 1956, more than ninety southerners, led by Senator Walter George, presented in Congress their "Declaration of Constitutional Principles," commonly known as the "Southern Manifesto." The document condemned the Supreme Court decision on segregation in education as a usurpation of the powers of the states and encouraged the use of "every lawful means" to resist its implementation.

come humbly to say to the men in the forefront of our government that the civil-rights issue is not an ephemeral, evanescent domestic issue that can be kicked about by reactionary guardians of the status quo; it is rather an eternal moral issue which may well determine the destiny of our nation in the ideological struggle with Communism. The hour is late. The clock of destiny is ticking out. We must act now, before it is too late.

A second area in which there is need for strong leadership is from the white Northern liberals. There is a dire need today for a liberalism which is truly liberal. What we are witnessing today in so many Northern communities is a sort of quasi liberalism which is based on the principle of looking sympathetically at all sides. It is a liberalism so bent on seeing all sides that it fails to become committed to either side. It is a liberalism that is so objectively analytical that it is not subjectively committed. It is a liberalism which is neither hot nor cold, but lukewarm.

We call for a liberalism from the North which we will be thoroughly committed to the ideal of racial justice and will not be deterred by the propaganda and subtle words of those who say, "Slow up for a while; you are pushing too fast."

A third area that we must look to for strong membership is from the moderates of the white South. It is unfortunate, indeed, that at this time the leadership of the white South stems from the closed-minded reactionaries. These persons gain prominence and power by the dissemination of false ideas, and by deliberately appealing to the deepest hate responses within the human mind. It is my firm belief that this closed-minded, reactionary, recalcitrant group constitutes a numerical minority. There are in the white South more open-minded moderates than appears on the surface. These persons are silent today because of fear of social, political and economic reprisals. God grant that the white moderates of the South will rise up courageously, without fear, and take up the leadership in this tense period of transition.

I cannot close without stressing the urgent need for strong, courageous and intelligent leadership from the Negro community. We need leadership that is calm and yet positive. This is no day for the rabble-rouser, whether he be Negro or white. We must realize that we are grappling with the most weighty social problem of this nation, and in grappling with such a complex problem there is no place for misguided emotionalism. We must work passionately and unrelentingly for the goal of freedom, but we must be sure that our hands are clean in the struggle. We must never struggle with falsehood, hate or malice. Let us never become bitter.

There is another warning signal. We talk a great deal about our rights, and rightly so. We proudly proclaim that three fourths of the peoples of the world are colored. We have the privilege of noticing in our generation the great drama of freedom and independence as it unfolds in Asia and Africa. All of these things are in line with the unfolding work of providence.

But we must be sure that we accept them in the right spirit. We must not seek to use our emerging freedom and our growing power to do the same thing to the white minority that has been done to us for so many centuries. We must not become victimized with a philosophy of "black supremacy." Our aim must never be to defeat or to humiliate the white man, but to win his friendship and understanding, and thereby create a society in which all men will be able to live together as brothers.

We must also avoid the temptation of being victimized with a psychology of victors. In our nation, under the guidance of the superb legal staff of the N.A.A.C.P. [National Association for the Advancement of Colored People], we have been able, through the courts, to remove the legal basis of segregation. This is by far one of the most marvelous achievements of our generation. Every person of good will is profoundly indebted to the N.A.A.C.P. for its noble work. We must not, however, remain satisfied with a court "victory" over our white brothers.

We must respond to every decision with an understanding of those who have opposed us and with an appreciation of the difficult adjustments that the court orders pose for them.

We must act in such a way as to make possible a coming-together of white people and colored people on the basis of a real harmony of interest and understanding. We must seek an integration based on mutual respect.

I conclude by saying that each of us must keep faith in the future. Let us realize that as we struggle alone, God struggles with us. He is leading us out of a bewildering Egypt, through a bleak and desolate wilderness, toward a bright and glittering promised land. Let us go forth into the glorious future with the words of James Weldon Johnson resounding in our souls:

> God of our weary years,
> God of our silent tears,
> Thou who has brought us thus far on the way;
> Thou who has by thy might,
> Led us into the light,
> Keep us forever in the path, we pray.
> Lest our feet stray from the places, our God,
>   where we met thee.
> Lest our hearts, drunk with the wine of the world
>   we forget thee;
> Shadowed beneath thy hand, may we forever stand
> True to our God, true to our native land.*

D. The Promise and Problems of a Consumer Society

1. The Editors of Fortune Celebrate American Affluence (1955)

No other nation had ever enjoyed a surge of prosperity as dazzling and as widely shared as Americans experienced in the two decades after World War II. In the selection below, the editors of the business magazine Fortune *describe America's postwar affluence and some of its implications. What do they see as historically unprecedented in the postwar American economy? How well placed was their faith in future prosperity?*

---

*"Lift Every Voice and Sing" from *Saint Peter Relates an Incident* by James Weldon Johnson. Copyright 1917, 1921, 1935 by James Weldon Johnson, copyright renewed © 1963 by Grace Nail Johnson. Used by permission of Viking Penguin, a division of Penguin Books USA, Inc.

[1]From the editors of *Fortune,* "The Changing American Market" (Garden City, NY: Hanover House, 1955), pp. 13–18, 73–74, 249–250. © 1955 Time, Inc. All rights reserved.

All history can show no more portentous economic phenomenon than today's American market. It is colossal, soaking up half the world's steel and oil, and three-fourths of its cars and appliances. The whole world fears it and is baffled by it. Let U.S. industry slip 5 per cent, and waves of apprehension sweep through foreign chancelleries. Let U.S. consumer spending lag even half as much, and the most eminent economists anxiously read the omens. The whole world also marvels at and envies this market. It is enabling Americans to raise their standard of living every year while other countries have trouble in maintaining theirs. And of course the whole world wants to get in on it. For it still can punish the incompetent and inefficient, and still reward handsomely the skillful, efficient, and daring.

The American market is all this mainly because it is a changed and always changing market. The underlying reason for the American market's growth and changeability is the nation's rising productivity, or output per man-hour—that cachet of efficiency without which no nation today is civilized or even modern. American productivity is of course the world's highest. For years it has been increasing unevenly but incessantly at an average rate of about 2 per cent a year, and it has done even better since 1947. And because productivity is rising so swiftly, the market is expanding much faster than the population. For rising productivity, in the long run, ends up as rising purchasing power, and the standard of living rises, palpably if not uniformly. People who could buy x amount of goods five years ago may buy x plus 8 or 10 or 15 per cent today, and x plus 16 or 20 or 30 per cent five years from now. Such is the dynamism that gives the American Dream its economic substance.

There is another important reason for the market's changeability. The market, after all, is the people. Their energy, efficiency, taste, and capacity for change at bottom are responsible for the American market's pitfalls and prizes. Most of the basic American characteristics are well understood—the restless, enthusiastic energy, the lack of traditional impedimenta, the almost dogmatic optimism, and the special delight in the brand-new. . . .

The most important change of the past few years, by all odds, is the rise of the great mass into a new moneyed middle class—a rapidly growing market that seems bound, sooner or later, to become *the* American market. It is like no other middle class in history, either abroad or at home. When the world thinks of the American middle class, it still thinks in terms of the characters in the novels of Sinclair Lewis, who in the 1920s made literary (and financial) capital out of his ability to portray the "typical" bourgeois American.

To the extent that his characters embodied universal and enduring human traits, they are still true to life. But to the extent that they were based on economic types then prevalent, they are all but archaic. For in those days marketing men divided all consumers into two groups, the "class" and the "mass" market. The "class" market consisted of the very wealthy and somewhat less wealthy who could buy almost offhandedly all the comforts and luxuries of life, including the time of numerous menials; the "mass" market consisted of the remainder, some of whom were just beginning to buy the durables that are now commonplace.

So late as 1929, the high-water market of that gaudy but optimistic era that hoped to abolish poverty altogether, the mass-and-class pattern, was disconcertingly evident. In 1929, *Fortune* estimates, 36 million family units got a total of $118 billion in cash, in 1953 dollars, after taxes. To see just where the mass market was, let us break the $118 billion down into three groups:

At the top were a million family units* (3 per cent of them all) with more than $10,000, who together received $24 billion or 20 per cent of the total income. Just under them was the smaller $7,500-to-$10,000 group getting $11 billion or 9 per cent of the total.

In the middle were 5,500,000 family units (15 per cent of them all) with between $4,000 and $7,500, who together received $30 billion or 25 per cent of total income.

At the bottom were 29 million family units (80 per cent of them all) with less than $4,000, who together received a total of $53 billion or 46 per cent of total income.

The bottom group constituted the mass market of 1929. None of its members had a spendable income of more than $4,000 or about $2,500 in 1929 dollars. Few of them, manifestly, were in the market for many luxuries, or even much more than essentials. A lot of them, it is true, managed to buy cars. A new 1929 Ford sedan, without trimmings, listed for only $500. But the cost of buying and maintaining even so modest a machine put them out of the market for other and even more necessary things. It was the top and middle groups that were able to keep up with the improvements and innovations in consumer durables. And together those groups accounted for only 21 per cent of all family units.

See how all that has changed. There were in 1953 in the U.S., *Fortune* estimates, a total of 51 million family units, 42 per cent more than in 1929, who got $222 billion, or 87 per cent more than in 1929. Plainly, the nation as a whole had gained enormously. But look at how this has pushed families above the $4,000 level, where, economists agree, "discretionary" buying power becomes significant:

The $4,000-to-$7,500 group in 1953 contained 18 million family units or 35 per cent of the total. *And they got $93 billion or 42 per cent of total income.* Since 1929, in other words, this group has more then trebled in both numbers and income.

Furthermore, this new middle market has enjoyed its greatest growth since 1947. Between 1941 and 1947, *Fortune* estimates, the number of family units in it increased by only 13 per cent, and their total income by 14 per cent. But since 1947 the number of family units in it has increased by *40 per cent,* and their total income by *36 per cent.* The last few years obviously have made the new middle market. . . .

Now look at the bottom group. In 1929, remember, 80 per cent of family units got less than $4,000, and together they got less than half of the total income. Today, by contrast, about half the family units get less than $4,000, and they account for a little more than a quarter of the income. The $4,000-and-under group, moreover, is now much better off, with a much smaller per centage of family units under $1,000 and $2,000:

Fewer than 10 per cent of family units got less than $1,000 in 1953—against 16 per cent in 1929.

Only 23 per cent got less than $2,000—against 43 per cent in 1929.

---

*Family units include (1) families consisting of related persons residing together and (2) unrelated individuals—whether residing alone or with others.

Only 38 per cent got less than $3,000, against nearly 66 per cent in 1929.

And now 17 per cent get $3,000 to $4,000, against 11 per cent in 1929. Many of these, of course, are farmers or live in small towns or suburbs and have their gardens and other equivalents of income. They probably enjoy a *real* standard of living equal to or better than that of many in higher income groups. And the chances are good that many will soon move to a higher level.

All in all, 58 per cent of family units today have a real income of $3,000 to $10,000, against 31 per cent in 1929.

Such has been the evolution of the "class" and "mass" market of George Babbitt's day* in what might be called the new All-American market, this *growing* middle group fringed with what is left of the top "class" and old "mass" markets. Although the income range may seem fairly wide, the needs and buying power of the members of this group are remarkably homogeneous. Some spend more money on this thing, and some on the other, but essentially they buy the same things—the same staples, the same appliances, the same cars, the same furniture, and much the same recreation. The lesson is obvious. The marketer who designs his product to appeal to the whole group has hit the new mass market.

All this adds up to one of the swiftest and most thorough-going changes in economic history—and yet a relatively easy one for almost everybody. There are two forces behind it. One is a pervasive, complex rearrangement or redistribution of incomes; the other a sharp increase in the country's real per capita income. . . .

In 1907, when transatlantic immigration reached its peak, 1,200,000 Europeans landed in the U.S. In recent years an average of about 1,200,000 Americans moved to the suburbs every year. Suburbia's population, by *Fortune*'s count, numbered about 30 million in 1953 and has grown by about one-half since 1947. The American market as a whole, thanks to the economy's steadily increasing productivity, is expanding much faster than the American population. But the suburban market, thanks to the migration, is growing much faster even than the American market.

What is more, Suburbia is the exemplification of the new and growing moneyed middle class, which *Fortune* described as a market that seems bound, sooner or later, to become *the* American market. The average family-unit income of Suburbia is $6,500, which is 70 per cent higher than that of the rest of the nation. Since 1940, real, spendable income of U.S. customers, in 1953 dollars, has increased by nearly two-thirds, and most of this increase has gone to expand the numbers and incomes of family units with more than $4,000 a year. Not only are about a third of these families concentrated in the suburbs, the $4,000-and-over group makes up two-thirds of the suburbs. Suburbia is already the cream of the market.

The middle-class Suburbia, rapidly growing larger and more affluent, is developing a way of life that seems eventually bound to become dominant in America. It has been a major force in the phenomenal rise in the nation's birth rate. It has centered its customs and conventions on the needs of children and geared its buying habits to them. It has made the "ranch house" nationally popular. It has kept whole industries busy making equipment for outdoor living. It has helped double the sale

---

*George Babbit was the protagonist in Sinclair Lewis's 1922 novel, *Babbit*. This character gave rise to the term *Babbitry* to describe the smug, provincial, materialistic middle class that many social critics reviled in the 1920s and again in the 1950s.

of raiment woven of once lowly denim, and caused the sales of sports shirts to overtake the sales of "dress shirts. . . ."

[O]n the whole people seem more inclined to spend than they ever have been. Social security, pensions, and other fringe benefits, which doubtless hastened the decline in the savings rate, should accelerate the decline still further. The "readjustments" [recessions] of 1949 and 1954, which were short-lived mainly because consumers did not stop spending, have suggested that the nation is, or is pretty close to being, depression-proof. This will generate more confidence and more spending.

Moreover, the dynamic projection involves a tremendous expansion of the economy. The question is not whether the economy will expand, but how much it will expand. The shortfalls, in the projections, to repeat, are examples of the fact that projections based on past trends cannot accurately forecast a market as changeable and changing as the U.S. consumer market.

For U.S. business always has been and always will be coming up with products whose impact on the market cannot be assessed beforehand. Thus, there are no allowances in the projections for helicopters or two-way wrist-radios or heat-pump air conditioning on a mass scale, and this despite the fact that most of the shortfall is in durable goods. But there is no reason why there should be. The trend of the consumer market today is not toward the development of new and startling products but the improvement, variation, and adornment of the old products. Thus people are spending 25 per cent more for food *per capita* (in 1953 dollars) than they were before the war, buying about 25 per cent more per car, perhaps 25 per cent more units (not value) of clothes, and so on. The challenge to business is to keep up with the market's potentialities not only by making and selling more of everything, but by improving, varying, and adorning everything—by blurring still further the already blurred line that distinguishes Americans' luxuries and Americans' necessities.

2. John Kenneth Galbraith Criticizes the Affluent Society (1958)

America knew fabulous prosperity in the postwar era—or did it? In an influential book first published in the late 1950s, Harvard economist John Kenneth Galbraith probingly questioned the implications of the United States' apparent affluence. His ideas contributed significantly to discussion among policymakers about the kinds of social reforms that later were enacted as the Great Society programs. What is the distinction that Galbraith draws between the private and the public realms? How convincing is his argument? What does the relationship between private and public goods suggest about the character of American values?

The final problem of the productive society is what it produces. This manifests itself in an implacable tendency to provide an opulent supply of some things and a niggardly yield of others. This disparity carries to the point where it is a cause of social discomfort and social unhealth. The line which divides our area of wealth from

---

[2]Excerpt from *The Affluent Society,* Fourth Edition, by John Kenneth Galbraith. Copyright © 1958, 1969, 1976, 1984 by John Kenneth Galbraith. Reprinted by permission of Houghton Mifflin Company. All rights reserved.

our area of poverty is roughly that which divides privately produced and marketed goods and services from publicly rendered services. Our wealth in the first is not only in startling contrast with the meagerness of the latter, but our wealth in privately produced goods is, to a marked degree, the cause of crisis in the supply of public services. For we have failed to see the importance, indeed the urgent need, of maintaining a balance between the two.

This disparity between our flow of private and public goods and services is no matter of subjective judgment. On the contrary, it is the source of the most extensive comment which only stops short of the direct contrast being made here. In the years following World War II, the papers of any major city—those of New York were an excellent example—told daily of the shortages and shortcomings in the elementary municipal and metropolitan services. The schools were old and overcrowded. The police force was under strength and underpaid. The parks and playgrounds were insufficient. Streets and empty lots were filthy, and the sanitation staff was underequipped and in need of men. Access to the city by those who work there was uncertain and painful and becoming more so. Internal transportation was overcrowded, unhealthful and dirty. So was the air. Parking on the streets should have been prohibited, but there was no space elsewhere. These deficiencies were not in new and novel services but in old and established ones. Cities have long swept their streets, helped their people move around, educated them, kept order, and provided horse rails for equipages which sought to pause. That their residents should have a nontoxic supply of air suggests no revolutionary dalliance with socialism.

The discussion of this public poverty competed, on the whole successfully, with the stories of ever-increasing opulence in privately produced goods. The Gross National Product was rising. So were retail sales. So was personal income. Labor productivity had also advanced. The automobiles that could not be parked were being produced at an expanded rate. The children, though without schools, subject in the playgrounds to the affectionate interest of adults with odd tastes, and disposed to increasingly imaginative forms of delinquency, were admirably equipped with television sets. We had difficulty finding storage space for the great surpluses of food despite a national disposition to obesity. Food was grown and packaged under private auspices. The care and refreshment of the mind, in contrast with the stomach, was principally in the public domain. Our colleges and universities were often severely overcrowded and underprovided, and the same was even more often true of the mental hospitals.

The contrast was and remains evident not alone to those who read. The family which takes its mauve and cerise, airconditioned, power-steered and power-braked automobile out for a tour passes through cities that are badly paved, made hideous by litter, blighted buildings, billboards and posts for wires that should long since have been put underground. They pass on into a countryside that has been rendered largely invisible by commercial art. (The goods which the latter advertise have an absolute priority in our value system. Such aesthetic considerations as a view of the countryside accordingly come second. On such matters, we are consistent.) They picnic on exquisitely packaged food from a portable icebox by a polluted stream and go on to spend the night at a park which is a menace to public health and morals. Just before dozing off on an air mattress, beneath a nylon tent, amid the stench of decaying refuse, they may reflect vaguely on the curious unevenness of their blessings. Is this, indeed, the American genius? . . .

A feature of the years immediately following World War II was a remarkable attack on the notion of expanding and improving public services. During the depression years, such services had been elaborated and improved partly in order to fill some small part of the vacuum left by the shrinkage of private production. During the war years, the role of government was vastly expanded. After that came the reaction. Much of it, unquestionably, was motivated by a desire to rehabilitate the prestige of private production and therewith of producers. No doubt some who joined the attack hoped, at least tacitly, that it might be possible to sidestep the truce on taxation vis-à-vis equality by having less taxation of all kinds. For a time, the notion that our public services had somehow become inflated and excessive was all but axiomatic. Even liberal politicians did not seriously protest. They found it necessary to aver that they were in favor of public economy too.

In this discussion, a certain mystique was attributed to the satisfaction of privately supplied wants. A community decision to have a new school means that the individual surrenders the necessary amount, willy-nilly, in his taxes. But if he is left with that income, he is a free man. He can decide between a better car or a television set. This was advanced with some solemnity as an argument for the TV set. The difficulty is that this argument leaves the community with no way of preferring the school. All private wants, where the individual can choose, are inherently superior to all public desires which must be paid for by taxation and with an inevitable component of compulsion.

The cost of public services was also held to be a desolating burden on private production, although this was at a time when the private production was burgeoning. Urgent warnings were issued on the unfavorable effects of taxation on investment. . . .

Finally, it was argued, with no little vigor, that expanding government posed a grave threat to individual liberties. . . .

With time, this attack on public services has subsided. The disorder associated with social imbalance has become visible even if the need for balance between private and public services is still imperfectly appreciated. . . .

Nonetheless, the postwar onslaught on the public services left a lasting imprint. To suggest that we canvass our public wants to see where happiness can be improved by more and better services has a sharply radical tone. Even public services to avoid disorder must be defended. By contrast, the man who devises a nostrum for a nonexistent need and then successfully promotes both remains one of nature's noblemen.

3. Newton Minow Criticizes the "Vast Wasteland" of Television (1961)

Newton N. Minow, chairman of the Federal Communications Commission in the John F. Kennedy administration, delivered the following address to the National

---

[3]Newton N. Minow, "Program Control: The Broadcasters are Public Trustees," *Vital Speeches of the Day* 27, no. 17 (June 15, 1961), pp. 533–535.

Association of Broadcasters in 1961. Delivered, ironically, in what some observers regard as the "golden age" of television programming, his remarks have become a classic indictment of the cultural vapidity of television—called a medium, some have said, because so little of it is rare or well done. How fair is Minow's critique? What might explain the dismal situation that Minow describes? Has programming changed substantially in the intervening years?

It may . . . come as a surprise to some of you, but I want you to know that you have my admiration and respect. Yours is a most honorable profession. Anyone who is in the broadcasting business has a tough row to hoe. You earn your bread by using public property. When you work in broadcasting you volunteer for public service, public pressure, and public regulation. You must compete with other attractions and other investments, and the only way you can do it is to prove to us every three years that you should have been in business in the first place.

I can think of easier ways to make a living.

But I cannot think of more satisfying ways.

I admire your courage—but that doesn't mean I would make life any easier for you. Your license lets you use the public's airwaves as Trustees for 180,000,000 Americans. The public is your beneficiary. If you want to stay on as Trustees, you must deliver a decent return to the public—not only to your stockholders. So, as a representative of the public, your health and your product are among my chief concerns. . . .

I have confidence in your health.

But not in your product. . . .

[In] today's world, with chaos in Laos and the Congo aflame, with Communist tyranny on our Caribbean doorstep and relentless pressure on our Atlantic alliance, with social and economic problems at home of the gravest nature, yes, and with technological knowledge that makes it possible, as our President has said, not only to destroy our world but to destroy poverty around the world—in a time of peril and opportunity, the old complacent, unbalanced fare of Action-Adventure and Situation Comedies is simply not good enough.

Your industry possesses the most powerful voice in America. It has an inescapable duty to make that voice ring with intelligence and with leadership. In a few years, this exciting industry has grown from a novelty to an instrument of overwhelming impact on the American people. It should be making ready for the kind of leadership that newspapers and magazines assumed years ago, to make our people aware of their world.

Ours has been called the jet age, the atomic age, the space age. It is also, I submit, the television age. And just as history will decide whether the leaders of today's world employed the atom to destroy the world or rebuild it for mankind's benefit, so will history decide whether today's broadcasters employed their powerful voice to enrich the people or debase them. . . .

Like everybody, I wear more than one hat. I am the Chairman of the FCC. I am also a television viewer and the husband and father of other television viewers. . . . I invite you to sit down in front of your television set when your station goes on the air and stay there without a book, magazine, newspaper, profit and loss sheet or rating book to distract you—and keep your eyes glued to that set until the station signs off. I can assure you that you will observe a vast wasteland.

You will see a procession of game shows, violence, audience participation shows, formula comedies about totally unbelievable families, blood and thunder, mayhem, violence, sadism, murder, western badmen, western good men, private eyes, gangsters, more violence, and cartoons. And, endlessly, commercials—many screaming, cajoling, and offending. And most of all, boredom. True, you will see a few things you will enjoy. But they will be very, very few. And if you think I exaggerate, try it. . . .

I do not accept the idea that the present over-all programming is aimed accurately at the public taste. The ratings tell us only that some people have their television sets turned on and of that number, so many are tuned to one channel and so many to another. They don't tell us what the public might watch if they were offered half a dozen additional choices. A rating, at best, is an indication of how many people saw what you gave them. Unfortunately, it does not reveal the depth of the penetration, or the intensity of reaction, and it never reveals what the acceptance would have been if what you gave them had been better—if all the forces of art and creativity and daring and imagination had been unleashed. I believe in the people's good sense and good taste, and I am not convinced that the people's taste is as low as some of you assume. . . .

Certainly, I hope you will agree that ratings should have little influence where children are concerned. The best estimates indicate that during the hours of 5 to 6 P.M. 60% of your audience is composed of children under 12. And most young children today, believe it or not, spend as much time watching television as they do in the schoolroom. I repeat—let that sink in—most young children today spend as much time watching television as they do in the schoolroom. It used to be said that there were three great influences on a child: home, school, and church. Today, there is a fourth great influence, and you ladies and gentlemen control it.

If parents, teachers, and ministers conducted their responsibilities by following the ratings, children would have a steady diet of ice cream, school holidays, and no Sunday School. What about your responsibilities? Is there no room on television to teach, to inform, to uplift, to stretch, to enlarge the capacities of our children? Is there no room for programs deepening their understanding of children in other lands? Is there no room for a children's news show explaining something about the world to them at their level of understanding? Is there no room for reading the great literature of the past, teaching them the great traditions of freedom? There are some fine children's shows, but they are drowned out in the massive doses of cartoons, violence, and more violence. Must these be your trademarks? Search your consciences and see if you cannot offer more to your young beneficiaries whose future you guide so many hours each and every day. . . .

E. Eisenhower Says Farewell (1961)

Dwight Eisenhower, the war hero, presided over nearly eight years of peaceful U.S. relations with the rest of the world. Yet Eisenhower also presided over the largest

From *Public Papers of the President: Dwight D. Eisenhower, 1960–1961* (Washington, D.C.: National Archives and Records Service, 1961), pp. 1036–1039.

peacetime buildup of armaments in U.S. history up to that time. In his final message to the American people as president, the popular ex-soldier sounded a surprising warning about the economic, political, and social consequences of the garrison state that the United States was apparently becoming. His speech is justly remembered as one of the most telling criticisms of the domestic consequences of the Cold War. What are the most worrisome aspects of the "military-industrial complex" that Eisenhower described? Why did he wait until he was on his way out of office to express his alarm?

Good evening, my fellow Americans:

First, let me express my gratitude to the radio and television networks for the opportunity to express myself to you during these past eight years and tonight.

Three days from now, after half a century in the service of our country, I shall lay down the responsibilities of office as, in traditional solemn ceremony, the authority of the President is vested in my successor.

This evening I come to you with a message of leave-taking and farewell, and to share a few final thoughts with you, my countrymen. . . .

We now stand ten years past the midpoint of a century that has witnessed four major wars among great nations. Three of these involved our own country. Despite these holocausts America is today the strongest, the most influential, and most productive nation in the world. Understandably proud of this pre-eminence, we yet realize that America's leadership and prestige depend, not merely upon our unmatched material progress, riches, and material strength, but on how we use our power in the interests of world peace and human betterment. . . .

Crises there will continue to be. In meeting them, whether foreign or domestic, great or small, there is a recurring temptation to feel that some spectacular and costly action could become the miraculous solution to all current difficulties. A huge increase in newer elements of our defense; development of unrealistic programs to cure every ill in agriculture; a dramatic expansion in basic and applied research— these and many other possibilities, each possibly promising in itself, may be suggested as the only way to the road we wish to travel.

But each proposal must be weighed in the light of a broader consideration: the need to maintain balance in and among national problems—balance between the private and the public economy, balance between cost and hoped for advantage— balance between the clearly necessary and the comfortably desirable; balance between our essential requirements as a nation and the duties imposed by the nation upon the individual; balance between actions of the moment and the national welfare of the future. Good judgment seeks balance and progress; lack of it eventually finds imbalance and frustration.

The record of many decades stands as proof that our people and their government have, in the main, understood these truths and have responded to them well, in the face of stress and threat. But threats, new in kind or degree, constantly arise. I mention two only.

A vital element in keeping the peace is our military establishment. Our arms must be mighty, ready for instant action, so that no potential aggressor may be tempted to risk his own destruction.

Our military organization today bears little relation to that known by any of my predecessors in peacetime, or indeed by the fighting men in World War II or Korea.

Until the latest of our world conflicts, the United States had no armaments industry. American makers of plowshares could, with time and as required, make swords as well. But now we can no longer risk emergency improvision of national defense; we have been compelled to create a permanent armaments industry of vast proportions. Added to this, three and a half million men and women are directly engaged in the defense establishment. We annually spend on military security more than the net income of all United States corporations.

This conjunction of an immense military establishment and a large arms industry is new in American experience. The total influence—economic, political, even spiritual—is felt in every city, every state house, every office of the federal government. We recognize the imperative need for this development. Yet we must not fail to comprehend its grave implications. Our toil, resources and livelihood are all involved; so is the very structure of our society.

In the councils of government, we must guard against the acquisition of unwarranted influence, whether sought or unsought, by the military-industrial complex. The potential for the disastrous rise of misplaced power exists and will persist.

We must never let the weight of this combination endanger our liberties or democratic processes. We should take nothing for granted. Only an alert and knowledgeable citizenry can compel the proper meshing of the huge industrial and military machinery of defense with our peaceful methods and goals, so that security and liberty may prosper together.

Akin to, and largely responsible for the sweeping changes in our industrial-military posture, has been the technological revolution during recent decades.

In this revolution, research has become central; it also becomes more formalized, complex, and costly. A steadily increasing share is conducted for, by, or at the direction of, the federal government.

Today, the solitary inventor, tinkering in his shop, has been overshadowed by task forces of scientists in laboratories and testing fields. In the same fashion, the free university, historically the fountainhead of free ideas and scientific discovery, has experienced a revolution in the conduct of research. Partly because of the huge costs involved, a government contract becomes virtually a substitute for intellectual curiosity. For every old blackboard there are now hundreds of new electronic computers.

The prospect of domination of the nation's scholars by federal employment, project allocations, and the power of money is ever present and is gravely to be regarded.

Yet, in holding scientific research and discovery in respect, as we should, we must also be alert to the equal and opposite danger that public policy could itself become the captive of a scientific-technological elite.

It is the task of statesmanship to mold, to balance, and to integrate these and other forces, new and old, within the principles of our democratic system—ever aiming toward the supreme goals of our free society.

Thought Provokers

1. What were the advantages and disadvantages of the "massive retaliation" doctrine? Did Eisenhower's foreign policies ease or intensify Cold War tensions?

2. Did Senator McCarthy help or hinder the cause of anticommunism? Is U.S. society peculiarly vulnerable to his kind of demagoguery? What finally stopped McCarthy? Did McCarthyism perish with Joseph McCarthy?

3. Progressives and liberals have historically argued that the courts should take a hands-off policy toward legislation in the economic realm, yet they applauded the Supreme Court's activist role in civil rights matters. Were they being inconsistent? What were the greatest obstacles to the success of the civil rights movement? What were its greatest assets?

4. What, if anything, was new about the sources and character of American prosperity in the 1950s? Could the economy of the Eisenhower era provide a model for later economic policymakers—or *should* it? Does the Public Broadcasting System (PBS) provide an attractive alternative to the "sins" of the commercial broadcasters as described by Newton Minow?

5. How prophetic was Eisenhower's warning about the "military-industrial complex"? Is that complex more or less powerful now than in Eisenhower's day? To what extent was it an inevitable product of the Cold War?

39

The Stormy Sixties, 1960–1968

And so, my fellow Americans: ask not what your country can do for you—ask what you can do for your country.

President John F. Kennedy, 1961

Prologue: Youthful President John F. Kennedy launched his administration with high hopes and great vigor. Young people seemed particularly attracted to the tough-minded yet idealistic style of Kennedy's presidency. Yet Kennedy's record in office, before his tragic assassination in 1963, was spotty. He presided over a botched invasion of Cuba in 1961 and in the same year took the first fateful steps into the Vietnam quagmire. In 1962 he emerged victorious from a tense standoff with the Russians over the emplacement of Soviet missiles in Cuba. Sobered by this brush with the prospect of nuclear holocaust, Kennedy initiated a new policy of realistic accommodation with the Soviets—while the Soviets, determined never again to be so humiliated, began a massive military buildup. At home, the black revolution, led most conspicuously by Martin Luther King, Jr., exploded. Lyndon Johnson, ascending to the presidency after Kennedy's death, won election in his own right in 1964 and promptly threw his support behind the cause of civil rights. In a remarkable burst of political leadership, Johnson persuaded the Congress to pass a vast array of social welfare legislation, known collectively as the Great Society programs. But Johnson's dreams for a happier America were blasted by the mounting unpopularity of the war in Vietnam, which had drawn half a million U.S. troops by the mid-1960s. Bedeviled by the Vietnam problem, Johnson withdrew from the 1968 presidential race, paving the way for the election of Richard Nixon.

A. The Cuban Missile Crisis

1. President Kennedy Proclaims a "Quarantine" (1962)

After the abortive Bay of Pigs invasion in 1961, the United States watched Castro's Cuba for further trouble. Officials in Washington knew that the Soviet Union was

[1]*Public Papers of the President of the United States, John F. Kennedy: 1962* (Washington, D.C.: National Archives and Records Service, 1963), pp. 807–808 (October 22, 1962).

sending Castro immense quantities of weapons, which Moscow repeatedly claimed were defensive.* In mid-October 1962, high-flying U.S. spy planes returned with startling photographic evidence that Soviet technicians were installing about forty nuclear missiles with a striking range of about 2,200 miles. Rather than forewarn Premier Nikita Khrushchev in Moscow, Kennedy quietly consulted with members of Congress and then went on radio and television with a bombshell address that caught the Soviets off-guard. In this excerpt, what options did he leave for himself if the initial "quarantine" should fail? What were the risks in Kennedy's strategy? Were they worth it?

Acting, therefore, in the defense of our own security and of the entire Western Hemisphere, . . . I have directed that the following *initial* steps be taken immediately:

First: To halt this offensive buildup, a strict quarantine on all offensive military equipment under shipment to Cuba is being initiated. All ships of any kind bound for Cuba from whatever nation or port will, if found to contain cargoes of offensive weapons, be turned back. This quarantine will be extended, if needed, to other types of cargo and carriers. We are not at this time, however, denying the necessities of life, as the Soviets attempted to do in their Berlin blockade of 1948.

Second: I have directed the continued and increased close [aerial] surveillance of Cuba and its military buildup. . . .

Third: It shall be the policy of this Nation to regard any nuclear missile launched from Cuba against any nation in the Western Hemisphere as an attack by the Soviet Union on the United States, requiring a full retaliatory response upon the Soviet Union.

Fourth: As a necessary military precaution, I have reinforced our base at Guantanamo [Cuba], evacuated today the dependents of our personnel there, and ordered additional military units to be on a standby alert basis.

Fifth: We are calling tonight for an immediate meeting of the Organ of Consultation under the Organization of American States, to consider this threat to hemispheric security and to invoke Articles 6 and 8 of the Rio Treaty in support of all necessary action. . . . Our other allies around the world have also been alerted.

Sixth: Under the Charter of the United Nations, we are asking tonight that an emergency meeting of the Security Council be convoked without delay to take action against this latest Soviet threat to world peace. Our resolution will call for the prompt dismantling and withdrawal of all offensive weapons in Cuba, under the supervision of U.N. observers, before the quarantine can be lifted.

Seventh and finally: I call upon Chairman Khrushchev to halt and eliminate this clandestine, reckless, and provocative threat to world peace and to stable relations between our two nations. I call upon him further to abandon this course of world domination, and to join in an historic effort to end the perilous arms race and to transform the history of man.

---

*The Soviets were correct in the sense that so-called offensive weapons aimed at the United States were defensive in that they would deter an invasion of Cuba.

2. Premier Khrushchev Proposes a Swap (1962)

During the tense six days after Kennedy's proclamation of a "quarantine," Soviet technicians in Cuba worked feverishly to emplace the missiles. A number of approaching Soviet merchant ships, presumably loaded with "offensive" weapons, turned back. Several, not carrying such cargoes, were allowed to reach Cuba. Premier Khrushchev, at first disposed to give some ground in a letter of October 26 to Kennedy, took a tougher stand in the following message of October 27 and proposed a swap. The U.S. missiles in Turkey were so obsolete that two months earlier President Kennedy had given orders for their withdrawal, but they were still there. He and his advisers felt that to remove them, as Khrushchev asked, on an exchange basis would weaken the morale of Turkey, the eastern anchor of the North Atlantic Treaty Organization (NATO). Was Kennedy right to risk nuclear incineration for the sake of Turkey? How much plausibility was there in Khrushchev's proposal?

Our purpose has been and is to help Cuba, and no one can challenge the humanity of our motives aimed at allowing Cuba to live peacefully and develop as its people desire. You want to relieve your country from danger and this is understandable. However, Cuba also wants this. All countries want to relieve themselves from danger.

But how can we, the Soviet Union and our government, assess your actions which, in effect, mean that you have surrounded the Soviet Union with military bases, surrounded our allies with military bases, set up military bases literally around our country, and stationed your rocket weapons at them? This is no secret. High-placed American officials demonstratively declare this. Your rockets are stationed in Britain and in Italy and pointed at us. Your rockets are stationed in Turkey.

You are worried over Cuba. You say that it worries you because it lies at a distance of 90 miles across the sea from the shores of the United States. However, Turkey lies next to us. Our sentinels are pacing up and down and watching each other. Do you believe that you have a right to demand security for your country and the removal of such weapons that you qualify as offensive, while not recognizing this right for us? . . .

That is why I make this proposal: We agree to remove those weapons from Cuba which you regard as offensive weapons. We agree to do this and to state this commitment in the United Nations. Your representatives will make a statement to the effect that the United States, on its part, bearing in mind the anxiety and concern of the Soviet state, will evacuate its analogous weapons from Turkey. Let us reach an understanding on what time you and we need to put this into effect.

After this, representatives of the U.N. Security Council could control on-the-spot the fulfillment of these commitments.

---

[2]*Department of State Bulletin* 47 (November 12, 1962): 742.

3. Kennedy Advances a Solution (1962)

President Kennedy skillfully avoided an argument over a missile swap by ignoring his opponent's suggestion. Referring to Khrushchev's more promising letter of the previous day, he advanced the following proposals on October 27. The tension was building up, and an air strike against Cuba was scheduled for three days later, before the nuclear missiles could become fully operative. In this letter, what restrictions was Kennedy prepared to place on the United States?

Dear Mr. Chairman:

I have read your letter of October 26th with great care and welcomed the statement of your desire to seek a prompt solution to the problem. The first thing that needs to be done, however, is for work to cease on offensive missile bases in Cuba and for all weapons systems in Cuba capable of offensive use to be rendered inoperable, under effective United Nations arrangements.

Assuming this is done promptly, I have given my representatives in New York instructions that will permit them to work out this weekend—in cooperation with the Acting Secretary General and your representative—an arrangement for a permanent solution to the Cuban problem along the lines suggested in your letter of October 26th. As I read your letter, the key elements of your proposals—which seem generally acceptable as I understand them—are as follows:

1) You would agree to remove these weapons systems from Cuba under appropriate United Nations observation and supervision; and undertake, with suitable safeguards, to halt the further introduction of such weapons systems into Cuba.

2) We, on our part, would agree—upon the establishment of adequate arrangements through the United Nations to ensure the carrying out and continuation of these commitments—(a) to remove promptly the quarantine measures now in effect and (b) to give assurances against an invasion of Cuba. I am confident that other nations of the Western Hemisphere would be prepared to do likewise.

If you will give your representative similar instructions, there is no reason why we should not be able to complete these arrangements and announce them to the world within a couple of days.

[The next day, October 28, 1962, Khrushchev consented to Kennedy's terms, and a great sense of relief swept over the world. Kennedy himself had privately reckoned that the odds in favor of a nuclear blowup ran as high as fifty-fifty.]

4. The Soviets Save Face (1962)

The Soviets, claiming that they had achieved their objective of preventing an invasion of Cuba, gathered up and (ostensibly) shipped home their forty-two nuclear missiles. The United States in truth had won only a partial diplomatic victory. Thou-

---

[3]*Department of State Bulletin* 47 (November 12, 1962): 743.

[4]Translation copyright 1962 by *The Current Digest of the Soviet Press,* published weekly at The Ohio State University.

sands of Soviet workers stayed behind, and Castro remained defiant with Soviet weapons and backing. In the following selection, the official Soviet newspaper Izvestia *put the best possible face it could on the diplomatic setback. What gains for Soviet diplomacy did it claim were achieved?*

The threat to peace was created by hostile, adventurist schemes aimed at the very existence of the Cuban Republic. The Soviet Union could not disregard Cuba's predicament in the face of the imperialistic provocations. Our country, fulfilling its international duty, came to the fraternal assistance of the Cuban people, and in these troubled days of the provocational aggravation . . . it has stood, stands, and will continue to stand firmly with Cuba.

The contemplated scheme of aggression against Cuba was built upon a very shaky foundation, but the danger with which Cuba was threatened was not thereby diminished. The pretext that was advanced in the U.S.A. for action against Cuba was the presence of Soviet weapons in Cuba that the United States termed "offensive." These weapons were depicted as representing a "threat" to America and the whole Western Hemisphere, although neither Cuba nor the Soviet Union was threatening the United States with its actions, while at the same time extremist, militant circles in the U.S. revealed . . . a desire to end the independence of the Cuban Republic.

In that tense moment the Soviet government, which had displayed the utmost self-control, calm and firmness, took speedy and efficient action to prevent the outbreak of the imminent conflict and thereby preserve universal peace.

The progression of events showed that the far-seeing, wise course of the Soviet government was the only correct one in the situation that had developed and led in a short time to the start of the normalization of the situation and the creation of conditions in which the interests of universal peace and of the . . . integrity of the Cuban Republic will be assured.

The decisive step of the Soviet Union—which foiled the aggressive plans of an attack on Cuba and deprived the authors of these plans of a reason and pretext for military action—was the indication that appropriate measures were being taken to stop the build-up in Cuba of objectives depicted by the United States as threatening American security, to dismantle these objectives and return them to the Soviet Union.

This step by the Soviet government was made possible as a result of the statement made by U.S. President Kennedy in his message of Oct. 27 to N. S. Khrushchev. The message states that there will be no attacks on Cuba, no invasion, not only on the part of the United States but on the part of the other countries of the Western Hemisphere as well, if the weapons termed "offensive" by the U.S.A. are shipped out of Cuba.

Thus reason and wisdom prevailed. At present, all conditions exist for the total elimination of the conflict and for further efforts toward the strengthening of peace and security. All honest people, anxious over the fate of peace, render their due to our Communist Party, to the Soviet government and to Nikita Sergeyevich Khrushchev for the fact that the forces of aggression and war have been restrained and reason in international relations has prevailed over folly.

These days telegrams are being received in Moscow, in the Kremlin, from all corners of the globe. They express the impassioned voices of people of good will, conveying their support of the peace-loving position of the Soviet Union. . . .

B. President Johnson's Great Society

I. Michael Harrington Discovers Another America (1962)

Some books shape the course of history. Michael Harrington's The Other America, *published in 1962, was such a book. It shook middle-class Americans out of their complacent assumption that the problem of poverty had been solved in their country. With reasoned yet passionate argument, Harrington forcefully documented the existence of an "invisible" America populated by hopelessly impoverished people. The book's millions of readers—many of them idealistic young people—helped form the political constituency that made possible the Johnson administration's war on poverty in the late 1960s. Who are the poor people Harrington describes? Why are they "invisible"? What does Harrington identify as historically new about their condition? Are the problems he describes now resolved?*

There is a familiar America. It is celebrated in speeches and advertised on television and in the magazines. It has the highest mass standard of living the world has ever known.

In the 1950's this America worried about itself, yet even its anxieties were products of abundance. The title of a brilliant book was widely misinterpreted, and the familiar America began to call itself "the affluent society."* There was introspection about Madison Avenue and tail fins; there was discussion of the emotional suffering taking place in the suburbs. In all this, there was an implicit assumption that the basic grinding economic problems had been solved in the United States. In this theory the nation's problems were no longer a matter of basic human needs, of food, shelter, and clothing. Now they were seen as qualitative, a question of learning to live decently amid luxury.

While this discussion was carried on, there existed another America. In it dwelt somewhere between 40,000,000 and 50,000,000 citizens of this land. They were poor. They still are. . . .

The millions who are poor in the United States tend to become increasingly invisible. Here is a great mass of people, yet it takes an effort of the intellect and will even to see them. . . .

There are perennial reasons that make the other America an invisible land.

Poverty is often off the beaten track. It always has been. The ordinary tourist never left the main highway, and today he rides interstate turnpikes. He does not go into the valleys of Pennsylvania where the towns look like movie sets of Wales in

---

[1]Reprinted with the permission of Scribner, a Division of Simon & Schuster Inc. from *The Other America: Poverty in the United States* by Michael Harrington. Copyright © 1962, 1969, 1981 by Michael Harrington.

*See the selection by John Kenneth Galbraith on pages 459–461.

the thirties. He does not see the company houses in rows, the rutted roads (the poor always have bad roads whether they live in the city, in towns, or on farms), and everything is black and dirty. And even if he were to pass through such a place by accident, the tourist would not meet the unemployed men in the bar or the women coming home from a runaway sweatshop.

Then, too, beauty and myths are perennial masks of poverty. The traveler comes to the Appalachians in the lovely season. He sees the hills, the streams, the foliage— but not the poor. Or perhaps he looks at a run-down mountain house and, remembering Rousseau rather than seeing with his eyes, decides that "those people" are truly fortunate to be living the way they are and that they are lucky to be exempt from the strains and tensions of the middle class. The only problem is that "those people," the quaint inhabitants of those hills, are undereducated, underprivileged, lack medical care, and are in the process of being forced from the land into a life in the cities, where they are misfits. . . .

Now the American city has been transformed. The poor still inhabit the miserable housing in the central area, but they are increasingly isolated from contact with, or sight of, anybody else. Middle-class women coming in from Suburbia on a rare trip may catch the merest glimpse of the other America on the way to an evening at the theater, but their children are segregated in suburban schools. The business or professional man may drive along the fringes of slums in a car or bus, but it is not an important experience to him. The failures, the unskilled, the disabled, the aged, and the minorities are right there, across the tracks, where they have always been. But hardly anyone else is.

In short, the very development of the American city has removed poverty from the living, emotional experience of millions upon millions of middle-class Americans. Living out in the suburbs, it is easy to assume that ours is, indeed, an affluent society. . . .

It is a blow to reform and the political hopes of the poor that the middle class no longer understands that poverty exists. But, perhaps more important, the poor are losing their links with the great world. If statistics and sociology can measure a feeling as delicate as loneliness . . . , the other America is becoming increasingly populated by those who do not belong to anybody or anything. They are no longer participants in an ethnic culture from the old country; they are less and less religious; they do not belong to unions or clubs. They are not seen, and because of that they themselves cannot see. Their horizon has become more and more restricted; they see one another, and that means they see little reason to hope. . . .

Here is the most familiar version of social blindness: "The poor are that way because they are afraid of work. And anyway they all have big cars. If they were like me (or my father or my grandfather), they could pay their own way. But they prefer to live on the dole and cheat the taxpayers."

This theory, usually thought of as a virtuous and moral statement, is one of the means of making it impossible for the poor ever to pay their way. There are, one must assume, citizens of the other America who choose impoverishment out of fear of work (though, writing it down, I really do not believe it). But the real explanation of why the poor are where they are is that they made the mistake of being born to the wrong parents, in the wrong section of the country, in the wrong industry, or in the wrong racial or ethnic group. Once that mistake has been made, they could have been paragons of will and morality, but most of them would never even have had a chance to get out of the other America.

There are two important ways of saying this: The poor are caught in a vicious circle; or, The poor live in a culture of poverty.

In a sense, one might define the contemporary poor in the United States as those who, for reasons beyond their control, cannot help themselves. All the most decisive factors making for opportunity and advance are against them. They are born going downward, and most of them stay down. They are victims whose lives are endlessly blown round and round the other America.

Here is one of the most familiar forms of the vicious circle of poverty. The poor get sick more than anyone else in the society. That is because they live in slums, jammed together under unhygienic conditions; they have inadequate diets, and cannot get decent medical care. When they become sick, they are sick longer than any other group in society. Because they are sick more often and longer than anyone else, they lose wages and work, and find it difficult to hold a steady job. And because of this, they cannot pay for good housing, for a nutritious diet, for doctors. At any given point in the circle, particularly when there is a major illness, their prospect is to move to an even lower level and to begin the cycle, round and round, toward even more suffering. . . .

What shall we tell the American poor, once we have seen them? Shall we say to them that they are better off than the Indian poor, the Italian poor, the Russian poor? That is one answer, but it is heartless. I should put it another way. I want to tell every well-fed and optimistic American that it is intolerable that so many millions should be maimed in body and in spirit when it is not necessary that they should be. My standard of comparison is not how much worse things used to be. It is how much better they could be if only we were stirred. . . .

These, then, are the strangest poor in the history of mankind.

They exist within the most powerful and rich society the world has ever known. Their misery has continued while the majority of the nation talked of itself as being "affluent" and worried about neuroses in the suburbs. In this way tens of millions of human beings became invisible. They dropped out of sight and out of mind; they were without their own political voice.

Yet this need not be. The means are at hand to fulfill the age-old dream: poverty can now be abolished. How long shall we ignore this underdeveloped nation in our midst? How long shall we look the other way while our fellow human beings suffer? How long?

2. President Johnson Declares War on Poverty (1964)

The United States in the 1960s continued to present appalling contrasts in wealth. An official government report in 1964 declared that one-fifth of the families in the country—9.3 million in all—"enjoyed" annual incomes of less than $3,000. Under

---

[2]*Public Papers of the Presidents of the United States: Lyndon B. Johnson, 1963–1964* (Washington, D.C.: National Archives and Records Service, 1965), vol. 1, pp. 376–377 (March 16, 1964).

President Kennedy, Congress made a modest beginning at relieving poverty by passing several laws providing for self-help and job retraining. President Johnson threw his full weight behind the Economic Opportunity Act of 1964, which a Democratic Congress approved and implemented with an initial appropriation of $947.5 million. This legislation included provisions for a Job Corps that would provide training for unskilled young men and women, aid for education, and a domestic Peace Corps to work with Native Americans and other disadvantaged groups. In a part of his message to Congress the president made the following plea. Was he convincing in his argument that these heavy outlays would in the long run help the taxpayer?

I have called for a national war on poverty. Our objective: total victory.

There are millions of Americans—one fifth of our people—who have not shared in the abundance which has been granted to most of us, and on whom the gates of opportunity have been closed.

What does this poverty mean to those who endure it?

It means a daily struggle to secure the necessities for even a meager existence. It means that the abundance, the comforts, the opportunities they see all around them are beyond their grasp.

Worst of all, it means hopelessness for the young.

The young man or woman who grows up without a decent education, in a broken home, in a hostile and squalid environment, in ill health or in the face of racial injustice—that young man or woman is often trapped in a life of poverty.

He does not have the skills demanded by a complex society. He does not know how to acquire those skills. He faces a mounting sense of despair which drains initiative and ambition and energy. . . .

The war on poverty is not a struggle simply to support people, to make them dependent on the generosity of others.

It is a struggle to give people a chance.

It is an effort to allow them to develop and use their capacities, as we have been allowed to develop and use ours, so that they can share, as others share, in the promise of this nation.

We do this, first of all, because it is right that we should.

From the establishment of public education and land grant colleges through agricultural extension and encouragement to industry, we have pursued the goal of a nation with full and increasing opportunities for all its citizens.

The war on poverty is a further step in that pursuit.

We do it also because helping some will increase the prosperity of all.

Our fight against poverty will be an investment in the most valuable of our resources—the skills and strength of our people.

And in the future, as in the past, this investment will return its cost many fold to our entire economy.

If we can raise the annual earnings of 10 million among the poor by only $1,000 we will have added 14 billion dollars a year to our national output. In addition we can make important reductions in public assistance payments which now cost us 4 billion dollars a year, and in the large costs of fighting crime and delinquency, disease and hunger.

This is only part of the story.

Our history has proved that each time we broaden the base of abundance, giving more people the chance to produce and consume, we create new industry, higher production, increased earnings and better income for all.

Giving new opportunity to those who have little will enrich the lives of all the rest.

Because it is right, because it is wise, and because, for the first time in our history, it is possible to conquer poverty, I submit, for the consideration of the Congress and the country, the Economic Opportunity Act of 1964.

The Act does not merely expand old programs or improve what is already being done.

It charts a new course.

It strikes at the causes, not just the consequences of poverty.

It can be a milestone in our one-hundred-eighty year search for a better life for our people.

3. War on the Antipoverty War (1964)

President Johnson's antipoverty scheme aroused the dogs of criticism, especially among conservatives. They declared that it was contrived to catch votes; that it would undermine individual initiative; that it would inject big government into private affairs; that it was socialistic; that it was a revival of Franklin Roosevelt's Civilian Conservation Corps; and that it would burden the taxpayers. In truth, the cost of keeping a high school dropout in one of the fresh-air training camps was estimated to be about three times that of keeping a student in Harvard University. The executive editor of the Cleveland Plain Dealer *here speaks out plainly against some of the weaknesses of the scheme. What are his most telling points?*

The political astuteness of President Johnson is nowhere better illustrated than by his proposal described as the "antipoverty program" or the "war on poverty." It has more than a faint odor of hokum about it, but its implications are that anyone bold enough to question or peer deeply into it must be in favor of poverty—and that's politically and socially disastrous.

The present level of extravagance in the American uppercrust, affluence in the middle class, and considerable comfort even in the lower pay brackets is so widely taken for granted these days that a campaigner against poverty has to hunt around for groups and areas to help. . . .

But there are increasingly large numbers of Negro dropouts from high school and teenage unemployment. And small farmers who can't seem to get ahead. And inhabitants of "Appalachia," the mountains where coal mining has gone to pot. These are areas with average incomes of $3,000 a year or under. They've got to be saved from themselves by the Federal Government. Hence, the "war on poverty," a colorful phrase much favored by newspapers, TV, and radio.

There's really no war on anything. The Johnson proposal is an attempt to sop up some unemployed teens by giving them jobs in conservation camps, to lend

---

[3]"A Poke at Poverty Hokum" by Philip W. Porter, *Cleveland Plain Dealer,* March 28, 1964, reprinted by permission.

some money to the hardscrabble farmers, to produce some loan help for college students—and, just as important, add some new bureaucrats to the payroll.

The objective is good, particularly the movement of dropouts from the street corner to the forest. But the only way to solve the Appalachia problem is to transplant whole families and villages to places where there are jobs—but they won't leave. And lending money to marginal farmers is fruitless; the quicker they give up small uneconomical "family" units, and try to earn money elsewhere, the better off they'll be.

Some individuals will be helped, no doubt. The politicans have something new to promise. But eradicating all poverty is about as unlikely an attainment as entering the Kingdom of Heaven, which our grandmothers talked so much about.

The objective, though vague and built of goober feathers, is good. But will it work on those of low mentality who are not educable, or those who lack desire to improve themselves? And in reverse, is it really needed by the determined individual, the man already moonlighting to go to law school, or waiting tables to pay for college?

Has the Horatio Alger, Jr., concept, the bootblack who became a tycoon, vanished completely? Andrew Carnegie built a fortune from little. So did Henry Ford. Lyndon Johnson himself started from scratch. . . .

But today, the Federal Government has got to get into the act. And anyone who asks questions or objects is automatically a stinker.

[The war against poverty, although it improved the quality of life for many underprivileged Americans, fell far short of the roseate forecasts of its sponsors. The war in Vietnam began to siphon away billions of dollars, and the national budget could not fully support both wars. Bureaucratic bungling, political favoritism, and outright graft combined to bring the antipoverty program into considerable disrepute and to undermine its nobler purposes.]

C. The Black Revolution Erupts

1. Students Sit In for Equality (1960)

On February 1, 1960, four black college freshmen men sat down at the whites-only lunch counter at the Woolworth's store in Greensboro, North Carolina, and tried to order something to eat. The black waitress refused to serve them: "Fellows like you make our race look bad," she said. "That's why we can't get anyplace today, because of people like you, rabble-rousers, trouble-makers. . . . So why don't you go on out and stop making trouble?" But the students refused to move, and sat themselves into the history books. Though the Congress of Racial Equality (CORE) had used similar tactics against segregation since its founding in 1942, the students at Greensboro

---

[1]From *My Soul is Rested* by Howell Raines. Copyright © 1977 by Howell Raines. Used by permission of Penguin, a division of Penguin Putnam, Inc. Edward Rodman letter reprinted with the permission of Simon & Schuster from *Freedom Ride,* by James Peck. Copyright © 1962 by James Peck; copyright © renewed by The Executors of the Estate of James Peck.

had never heard of CORE's sit-ins; theirs was a spontaneous gesture, undertaken without formal leadership or preparation. Their example touched off a wave of similar protests against segregation across the South. In the selections that follow, two students recount their experiences as sitters-in. Franklin McCain was one of the four college freshmen in Greensboro; Edward Rodman was a high-school student in Portsmouth, Virginia. What motivated them? What were the greatest obstacles they faced? From whom did they receive support?

Franklin McCain

The planning process was on a Sunday night, I remember it quite well. I think it was Joseph [McNeil, one of the four students with McCain] who said, "It's time that we take some action now. We've been getting together, and we've been, up to this point, still like most people we've talked about for the past few weeks or so—that is, people who talk a lot but, in fact, make very little action." After selecting the technique, then we said, "Let's go down and just ask for service." It certainly wasn't titled a "sit-in" or "sit-down" at that time. "Let's just go down to Woolworth's tomorrow and ask for service, and the tactic is going to be simply this: we'll just stay there." We never anticipated being served, certainly, the first day anyway. "We'll stay until we get served." And I think Ezell [Blair, Jr., another of the students] said, "Well, you know that might be weeks, that might be months, that might be never." And I think it was the consensus of the group, we said, "Well, that's just the chance we'll have to take."

What's likely to happen? Now, I think that that was a question that all of us asked ourselves. . . . What's going to happen once we sit down? Of course, nobody had the answers. Even your wildest imagination couldn't lead you to believe what would, in fact, happen.

Why Woolworth's?

They advertise in public media, newspapers, radios, television, that sort of thing. They tell you to come in: "Yes, buy the toothpaste; yes, come in and buy the notebook paper. . . . No, we don't separate your money in this cash register, but no, please don't step down to the hot dog stand. . . ." The whole system, of course, was unjust, but that just seemed like insult added to injury. That was just like pouring salt into an open wound. That's inviting you to do something. . . .

Once getting there . . . we did make purchases of school supplies and took the patience and time to get receipts for our purchases, and Joseph and myself went over to the counter and asked to be served coffee and doughnuts. As anticipated, the reply was, "I'm sorry, we don't serve you here." And of course we said, "We just beg to disagree with you. We've in fact already been served; you've served us already and that's just not quite true." The attendant or waitress was a little bit dumbfounded, just didn't know what to say under circumstances like that. And we said, "We wonder why you'd invite us in to serve us at one counter and deny service at another. If this is a private club or private concern, then we believe you ought to sell membership cards and sell only to persons who have a membership card. If we don't have a card, then we'd know pretty well that we shouldn't come in or even attempt to come in." That didn't go over too well, simply because I don't really think she understood what we were talking about, and for the second reason, she had no logical response to a statement like that. And the only thing that an individual in her case or position could do is, of course, call the manager. [Laughs] Well, at this time, I think we were joined by Dave Richmond and Ezell Blair at the counter with us, after that dialogue.

Were you afraid at this point?

Oh, hell yes, no question about that. [Laughs] At that point there was a policeman who had walked in off the street, who was pacing the aisle . . . behind us, where we were seated, with his club in his hand, just sort of knocking it in his hand, and just looking mean and red and a little bit upset and a little bit disgusted. And you had the feeling that he didn't know what the hell to do. You had the feeling that this is the first time that this big bad man with the gun and the club has been pushed in a corner, and he's got absolutely no defense, and the thing that's killing him more than anything else—he doesn't know what he can or what he cannot do. He's defenseless. Usually his defense is offense, and we've provoked him, yes, but we haven't provoked him outwardly enough for him to resort to violence. And I think this is just killing him; you can see it all over him.

People in the store were—we got mixed reactions from people in the store. A couple of old ladies . . . came up to pat us on the back sort of and say, "Ah, you should have done it ten years ago. It's a good thing I think you're doing."

These were black ladies.

No, these are white ladies.

Really?

Yes, and by the same token, we had some white ladies and white men to come up and say to us, "Nasty, dirty niggers, you know you don't belong here at the lunch counter. There's a counter—" There was, in fact, a counter downstairs in the Woolworth store, a stand-up type counter where they sold hot dogs. . . .

But at any rate, there were expressions of support from white people that first day?

Absolutely right. Absolutely. And I think probably that was certainly some incentive for additional courage on the part of us. And the other thing that helped us psychologically quite a lot was seeing the policeman pace the aisle and not be able to do anything. I think that this probably gave us more strength, more encouragement, than anything else on that particular day, on day one. . . .

[B]y then we had the confidence, my goodness, of a Mack truck. And there was virtually nothing that could move us, there was virtually nothing probably at that point that could really frighten us off. . . . If it's possible to know what it means to have your soul cleansed—I felt pretty clean at that time. I probably felt better on that day than I've ever felt in my life. Seems like a lot of feelings of guilt or what-have-you suddenly left me, and I felt as though I had gained my manhood, so to speak, and not only gained it, but had developed quite a lot of respect for it. Not Franklin McCain only as an individual, but I felt as though the manhood of a number of other black persons had been restored and had gotten some respect from just that one day. . . .

. . . The individual who had probably most influence on us was Gandhi, more than any single individual. During the time that the Montgomery Bus Boycott was in effect, we were tots for the most part, and we barely heard of Martin Luther King. Yes, Martin Luther King's name was well-known when the sit-in movement was in effect, but to pick out Martin Luther King as a hero. . . . I don't want you to misunderstand what I'm about to say: Yes, Martin Luther King was a hero. . . . No, he was not the individual that we had upmost in mind when we started the sit-in movement. . . .

I'm told that the chamber of commerce wastes no time in letting prospective industry or businesses know that this is where the sit-in movement originated some fourteen, fifteen years ago, way back in 1960. This is another reason that we can call ourself the Gate City . . . the gateway to the New South. . . .

So, it's rather amusing the way they have . . . used it to their advantage, something that as a matter of fact they were staunchly against at that particular time. But I think that's only smart. It's only good business to do that. I'm sure if I were the chamber of commerce, I'd do the same thing.

Edward Rodman

Our story here in Portsmouth, Virginia, begins on February 12, Lincoln's Birthday. Several girls decided to observe the occasion by staging a sit-in, in sympathy with the students of North Carolina. So after school, the first sit-in of Portsmouth's history took place. There was no violence, but no one was served. We sat until the lunch counter at Rose's Variety Store closed.

Our group was a loosely knit collection of high school students, each with the same ideal: equality for all. Frankly speaking, that is about all we had in common. We were lacking organization, leadership, and planning.

By February 15, our numbers had increased considerably. We demonstrated at two stores at the Shopping Center. Again we met no obstruction—only a few hecklers, whose worst insults we passed off with a smile. Things were looking good. The newspaper and radio reporters were there getting our story.

Our spontaneous movement was gaining momentum quickly. We were without organization; we had no leader and no rules for conduct other than a vague understanding that we were not to fight back. We should have known the consequences, but we didn't.

I was late getting to the stores the following day, because of a meeting. It was almost four P.M. when I arrived. What I saw will stay in my memory for a long time. Instead of the peaceful, nonviolent sit-ins of the past few days, I saw before me a swelling, pushing mob of white and Negro students, news photographers, TV cameras, and only two policemen. Immediately, I tried to take the situation in hand. I did not know it at the time, but this day I became the sit-in leader.

I didn't waste time asking the obvious questions, "Who were these other Negro boys from the corner?" "Where did all the white hoods come from?" It was obvious. Something was going to break loose, and I wanted to stop it. First I asked all the girls to leave, then the hoods. But before I could finish, trouble started. A white boy shoved a Negro boy. The manager then grabbed the white boy to push him out and was shoved by the white boy. The crowd followed. Outside the boy stood in the middle of the street, daring any Negro to cross a certain line. He then pulled a car chain and claw hammer from his pocket and started swinging the chain in the air.

He stepped up his taunting with the encouragement of others. When we did not respond, he became so infuriated that he struck a Negro boy in the face with the chain. The boy kept walking. Then, in utter frustration, the white boy picked up a street sign and threw it at a Negro girl. It hit her and the fight began. The white boys, armed with chains, pipes, and hammers, cut off an escape through the street. Negro boys grabbed the chains and beat the white boys. The hammers they threw away. The white boys went running back to their hot rods. I tried to order a retreat.

During the fight I had been talking to the store manager and to some newspapermen. I did not apologize for our sit-in—only for unwanted fighters of both races and for their conduct. Going home, I was very dejected. I felt that this outbreak had killed our movement. I was not surprised the following day when a mob of three thousand people formed. The fire department, all of the police force, and police dogs were mobilized. The police turned the dogs loose on the Negroes—but not on the whites. Peaceful victory for us seemed distant.

Next day was rainy and I was thankful that at least no mob would form. At ten A.M. I received a telephone call that was to change our whole course of action. Mr. Hamilton, director of the YMCA, urged me to bring a few students from the original sit-in group to a meeting that afternoon. I did. That meeting was with Gordon Carey, a field secretary of CORE. We had seen his picture in the paper in connection with our recent campaign for integrated library facilities and we knew he was on our side. He had just left North Carolina where he had helped the student sit-ins. He told us about CORE and what CORE had done in similar situations elsewhere. I decided, along with the others, that Carey should help us organize a nonviolent, direct action group to continue our peaceful protests in Portsmouth. He suggested that an all-day workshop on nonviolence be held February 20.

Reverend Chambers organized an adult committee to support our efforts. At the workshop we first oriented ourselves to CORE and its nonviolent methods. I spoke on "Why Nonviolent Action?" exploring Gandhi's principles of passive resistance and Martin Luther King's methods in Alabama. We then staged a sociodrama acting out the right and wrong ways to handle various demonstration situations. During the lunch recess, we had a real-life demonstration downtown—the first since the fighting. With our new methods and disciplined organization, we were successful in deterring violence. The store manager closed the counter early. We returned to the workshop, evaluated the day's sit-in, and decided to continue in this manner. We established ourselves officially as the Student Movement for Racial Equality.

Since then, we have had no real trouble. Our struggle is not an easy one, but we know we are not alone and we plan to continue in accordance with our common ideal: equality for all through nonviolent action.

2. Riders for Freedom (1961)

In December 1960, in the case of Boynton v. Virginia *(364 U.S. 454), the U.S. Supreme Court declared that segregation in waiting rooms and restaurants serving interstate bus passengers was in violation of the Interstate Commerce Act. On this narrow but firm legal base, the Congress of Racial Equality (CORE) decided to*

---

[2]From *My Soul is Rested* by Howell Raines. Copyright © 1977 by Howell Raines. Used by permission of Penguin, a division of Penguin Putnam, Inc.

mount a dramatic protest against segregation: two racially mixed busloads of volunteers would travel from Washington, D.C., through the deepest South. "Our intention," CORE director James Farmer declared, "was to provoke the southern authorities into arresting us and thereby prod the Justice Department into enforcing the law of the land." On May 4, 1961, after graphic and realistic rehearsals of the harassment and beatings they expected to receive, seven blacks and six whites set out from Washington on their fateful "Freedom Ride." The two selections below describe what happened. The first statement is by CORE director James Farmer; the second is by Hank Thomas, one of the riders. Did the Freedom Riders achieve their objectives? Were their tactics justified? What was the federal government's role at this stage of the civil rights movement? Was the attitude of whites uniform throughout the South?

James Farmer

I was impressed by the fact that most of the activity thus far had been of local people working on their local problems—Greensborans sitting-in in Greensboro and Atlantans sitting-in in Atlanta—and the pressure of the opposition against having outsiders come was very, very great. If any outsiders came in . . . , "Get that outside agitator." . . . I thought that this was going to limit the growth of the Movement. . . . We somehow had to cut across states lines and establish the position that we were entitled to act any place in the country, no matter where we hung our hat and called home, because it was our country.

We also felt that one of the weaknesses of the student sit-in movement of the South had been that as soon as arrested, the kids bailed out. . . . This was not quite Gandhian and not the best tactic. A better tactic would be to remain in jail and to make the maintenance of segregation so expensive for the state and the city that they would hopefully come to the conclusion that they could no longer afford it. Fill up the jails, as Gandhi did in India, fill them to bursting if we had to. In other words, stay in without bail.

So those were the two things: cutting across state lines, putting the movement on wheels, so to speak, and remaining in jail, not only for its publicity value but for the financial pressure it would put upon the segregators. We decided that a good approach here would be to move away from restaurant lunch counters. That had been the Southern student sit-in movement, and anything we would do on that would be anticlimactic now. We would have to move into another area and so we decided to move into the transportation, interstate transportation. . . .

So we, following the Gandhian technique, wrote to Washington. We wrote to the Justice Department, to the FBI, and to the President, and wrote to Greyhound Bus Company and Trailways Bus Company, and told them that on May first or May fourth—whatever the date was,* I forget now—we were going to have a Freedom Ride. Blacks and whites were going to leave Washington, D.C., on Greyhound and Trailways, deliberately violating the segregated seating requirements and at each rest stop would violate the segregated use of facilities. And we would be nonviolent, absolutely nonviolent, throughout the campaign, and we would accept the consequences of our actions. This was a deliberate act of civil disobedience. . . .

We got no reply from Justice. Bobby Kennedy [U.S. attorney general] no reply.

---

*May 4.

We got no reply from the FBI. We got no reply from the White House, from President Kennedy. We got no reply from Greyhound or Trailways. *We got no replies.* [Laughs]. . . .

We had some of the group of thirteen sit at a simulated counter asking for coffee. Somebody else refused them service, and then we'd have others come in as white hoodlums to beat 'em up and knock them off the counter and club 'em around and kick 'em in the ribs and stomp 'em, and they were quite realistic, I must say. I thought they bent over backwards to be realistic. I was aching all over. [Laughs] And then we'd go into a discussion as to how the roles were played, whether there was something that the Freedom Riders did that they shouldn't have done, said that they shouldn't have said, something that they didn't say or do that they should have, and so on. Then we'd reverse roles and play it over and over again and have lengthy discussions of it.

I felt, by the way, that by the time that group left Washington, they were prepared for anything, even death, and this was a possibility, and we knew it, when we got to the Deep South.

Through Virginia we had no problem. In fact they had heard we were coming, Greyhound and Trailways, and they had taken down the For Colored and For Whites signs, and we rode right through. Yep. The same was true in North Carolina. Signs had come down just the previous day, blacks told us. And so the letters in advance did something.

In South Carolina it was a different story. . . . John Lewis* started into a white waiting room in some town in South Carolina† . . . and there were several young white hoodlums, leather jackets, ducktail haircuts, standing there smoking, and they blocked the door and said, "Nigger, you can't come in here." He said, "I have every right to enter this waiting room according to the Supreme Court of the United States in the Boynton case."‡

They said, "Shit on that." He tried to walk past, and they clubbed him, beat him, and knocked him down. One of the white Freedom Riders . . . Albert Bigelow,§ who had been a Navy captain during World War II, big, tall, strapping fellow, very impressive, from Connecticut—then stepped right between the hoodlums and John Lewis. Lewis had been absorbing more of the punishment. They then clubbed Bigelow and finally knocked him down, and that took some knocking because he was a pretty strapping fellow, and he didn't hit back at all. [They] knocked him down, and at this point police arrived and intervened. They didn't make any arrests. Intervened. . . .

Hank Thomas

The Freedom Ride didn't really get rough until we got down in the Deep South. Needless to say, Anniston, Alabama, I'm never gonna forget that, when I was on the bus that they threw some kind of incendiary device on.

---

*Later a U.S. congressman from Georgia.

†Rock Hill.

‡The 1960 Supreme Court case outlawing segregated facilities at bus terminals.

§Despite his military background, a Quaker pacifist. He was best known for sailing the yacht *Golden Rule* into an atomic testing area in the Pacific as a protest against nuclear warfare.

I got real scared then. You know, I was thinking—I'm looking out the window there, and people are out there yelling and screaming. They just about broke every window out of the bus. . . . I really thought that that was going to be the end of me.

They shot the tires out, and the bus driver was forced to stop. . . . He got off, and man, he took off like a rabbit, and might well have. I couldn't very well blame him there. And we were trapped on the bus. They tried to board. Well, we did have two FBI men aboard the bus. All they were there to do were to observe and gather facts, but the crowd apparently recognized them as FBI men, and they did not try to hurt them.

It wasn't until the thing was shot on the bus and the bus caught afire that everything got out of control, and . . . when the bus was burning, I figured . . . [pauses] . . . panic did get ahold of me. Needless to say, I couldn't survive that burning bus. There was a possibility I could have survived the mob, but I was just so afraid of the mob that I was gonna stay on that bus. I mean, I just got that much afraid. And when we got off the bus . . . first they closed the doors and wouldn't let us off. But then I'm pretty sure they realized, that somebody said, "Hey, the bus is gonna explode," because it had just gassed up, and so they started scattering then, and I guess that's the way we got off the bus.* Otherwise, we probably all would have been succumbed by the smoke, and not being able to get off, probably would have been burned alive or burned on there anyway. That's the only time I was really, really afraid. I got whacked over the head with a rock or I think some kind of a stick as I was coming off the bus.

We were taken to the hospital. The bus started exploding, and a lot of people were cut by flying glass. We were taken to the hospital, most of us, for smoke inhalation. . . . I think I was half out of it, half dazed, as a result of the smoke, and, gosh, I can still smell that stuff down in me now. You got to the point where you started having the dry heaves. Took us to the hospital, and it was incredible. The people at the hospital would not do anything for us. They would not. And I was saying, "You're *doctors,* you're medical personnel." They wouldn't. Governor Patterson got on statewide radio and said, "Any rioters in this state will not receive police protection." And then the crowd started forming outside the hospital, and the hospital told us to leave. And we said, "No, we're not going out there," and there we were. A caravan from Birmingham, about a fifteen-car caravan led by the Reverend Fred Shuttlesworth, came up from Birmingham to get us out. . . .

[E]very one of those cars had a shotgun in it. And Fred Shuttlesworth had got on the radio and said—you know Fred, he's very dramatic—"I'm going to get my people." [Laughs] He said, "I'm a nonviolent man, but I'm going to get my people." And apparently a hell of a lot of people believed in him. Man, they came there and they were a welcome sight. And each one of 'em got out with their guns and everything

---

*John Patterson, then governor of Alabama, maintains that he and his public safety director, Floyd Mann, were indirectly responsible for the Freedom Riders' getting off the burning bus: "Floyd recommended that we send a state plainclothes investigator to Atlanta to catch the bus and ride with the Freedom Riders, and we did. Now this has never been reported that I know of in any paper. . . . We sent a man named E. L. Cowling. . . . He went over to Atlanta and caught the bus, and he was on the bus when they came to Anniston. . . . So Cowling walked up to the door of the bus and drew his pistol and backed the crowd away from the bus and told them that if anybody touched anybody he'd kill them. And he got the Freedom Riders off the burning bus. That's true."

and the state police were there, but I think they all realized that this was not a time to say anything because, I'm pretty sure, there would have been a lot of people killed. . . .

Oh, we did have one girl, Genevieve Hughes, a white girl, who had a busted lip. I remember a nurse applying something to that, but other than that, nothing. Now that I look back on it, man, we had some vicious people down there, wouldn't even so much as *treat* you. But that's the way it was. But strangely enough, even those bad things then don't stick in my mind that much. Not that I'm full of love and goodwill for everybody in my heart, but I chalk it off to part of the things that I'm going to be able to sit on my front porch in my rocking chair and tell my young'uns about, my grandchildren about.

3. Martin Luther King, Jr., Writes from a Birmingham Jail (1963)

The year 1963 marked the one hundredth anniversary of the Emancipation Proclamation, yet millions of African-Americans remained enchained by racism. Although racial prejudice was a national curse, it worked most viciously in the South, the ancient homeland of slavery. Nearly a decade after the Supreme Court's desegregation order, fewer than 10 percent of black children in the South attended classes with white children. The problem was especially acute in Birmingham, Alabama, the most segregated big city in the United States. Segregation was the rule in schools, restaurants, rest rooms, ball parks, libraries, and taxicabs. Although African-Americans were nearly half the city's residents, they constituted fewer than 15 percent of the city's voters. More than fifty cross-burnings and eighteen racial bombings between 1957 and 1963 had earned the city the nickname of "Bombingham" among blacks. Thus Birmingham was a logical choice—and a courageous one—as the site of a mass protest by the Reverend Martin Luther King, Jr., and his Southern Christian Leadership Conference. Arrested during a protest demonstration on Good Friday, 1963, King penned the following letter from jail, writing on scraps of paper smuggled to him by a prison trusty. He was responding to criticism from eight white Alabama clergymen who had deplored his tactics as "unwise and untimely"—though King throughout his life preached the wisdom of nonviolence. Why does King believe that African-Americans could wait no longer for their civil rights? How does he view himself in relation to white "moderates" and black extremists?

Mr Dear Fellow Clergymen:

• • •

You deplore the demonstrations taking place in Birmingham. But your statement, I am sorry to say, fails to express a similar concern for the conditions that

---

brought about the demonstrations. I am sure that none of you would want to rest content with the superficial kind of social analysis that deals merely with effects and does not grapple with underlying causes. It is unfortunate that demonstrations are taking place in Birmingham, but it is even more unfortunate that the city's white power structure left the Negro community with no alternative. . . .

We know through painful experience that freedom is never voluntarily given by the oppressor; it must be demanded by the oppressed. Frankly, I have yet to engage in a direct-action campaign that was "well timed" in the view of those who have not suffered unduly from the disease of segregation. For years now I have heard the word "Wait!" It rings in the ear of every Negro with piercing familiarity. This "Wait" has almost always meant "Never." We must come to see, with one of our distinguished jurists, that "justice too long delayed is justice denied."

We have waited for more than 340 years for our constitutional and God-given rights. The nations of Asia and Africa are moving with jetlike speed toward gaining political independence, but we still creep at horse-and-buggy pace toward gaining a cup of coffee at a lunch counter. Perhaps it is easy for those who have never felt the stinging darts of segregation to say, "Wait." But when you have seen vicious mobs lynch your mothers and fathers at will and drown your sisters and brothers at whim; when you have seen hate-filled policemen curse, kick, and even kill your black brothers and sisters; when you see the vast majority of your twenty million Negro brothers smothering in an airtight cage of poverty in the midst of an affluent society; when you suddenly find your tongue twisted and your speech stammering as you seek to explain to your six-year-old daughter why she can't go to the public amusement park that has just been advertised on television, and see tears welling up in her eyes when she is told that Funtown is closed to colored children, and see ominous clouds of inferiority beginning to form in her little mental sky, and see her beginning to distort her personality by developing an unconscious bitterness toward white people; when you have to concoct an answer for a five-year-old son who is asking: "Daddy, why do white people treat colored people so mean?"; when you take a cross-country drive and find it necessary to sleep night after night in the uncomfortable corners of your automobile because no motel will accept you; when you are humiliated day in and day out by nagging signs reading "white" and "colored"; when your first name becomes "nigger," your middle name becomes "boy" (however old you are) and your last name becomes "John," and your wife and mother are never given the respected title "Mrs."; when you are harried by day and haunted by night by the fact that you are a Negro, living constantly at tiptoe stance, never quite knowing what to expect next, and are plagued with inner fears and outer resentments; when you are forever fighting a degenerating sense of "nobodiness"—then you will understand why we find it difficult to wait. There comes a time when the cup of endurance runs over, and men are no longer willing to be plunged into the abyss of despair. I hope, sirs, you can understand our legitimate and unavoidable impatience. . . .

You speak of our activity in Birmingham as extreme. At first I was rather disappointed that fellow clergymen would see my nonviolent efforts as those of an extremist. I began thinking about the fact that I stand in the middle of two opposing forces in the Negro community. One is a force of complacency, made up in part of Negroes who, as a result of long years of oppression, are so drained of self-respect and a sense of "somebodiness" that they have adjusted to segregation; and in part of a few middle-class Negroes who, because of a degree of academic and economic security and because in some ways they profit by segregation, have become insensitive to the problems of the masses. The other force is one of bitterness and hatred, and it comes perilously close to advocating violence. It is expressed in the various black nationalist groups that are springing up across the nation, the largest and best-known being Elijah Muhammad's Muslim movement. Nourished by the Negro's frustration over the continued existence of racial discrimination, this movement is made up of people who have lost faith in America, who have absolutely repudiated Christianity, and who have concluded that the white man is an incorrigible "devil."

I have tried to stand between these two forces, saying that we need emulate neither the "do-nothingism" of the complacent nor the hatred and despair of the black nationalist. For there is the more excellent way of love and nonviolent protest. I am grateful to God that, through the influence of the Negro church, the way of nonviolence became an integral part of our struggle.

If this philosophy had not emerged, by now many streets of the South would, I am convinced, be flowing with blood. And I am further convinced that if our white brothers dismiss as "rabble-rousers" and "outside agitators" those of us who employ nonviolent direct action, and if they refuse to support our nonviolent efforts, millions of Negroes will, out of frustration and despair, seek solace and security in black-nationalist ideologies—a development that would inevitably lead to a frightening racial nightmare. . . .

I wish you had commended the Negro sit-inners and demonstrators of Birmingham for their sublime courage, their willingness to suffer and their amazing discipline in the midst of great provocation. One day the South will recognize its real heroes. They will be the James Merediths,* with the noble sense of purpose that enables them to face jeering and hostile mobs, and with the agonizing loneliness that characterizes the life of the pioneer. They will be old, oppressed, battered Negro women, symbolized in a seventy-two-year-old woman in Montgomery, Alabama, who rose up with a sense of dignity and with her people decided not to ride segregated buses, and who responded with ungrammatical profundity to one who inquired about her weariness: "My feets is tired, but my soul is at rest." They will be the young high school and college students, the young ministers of the gospel and a host of their elders, courageously and nonviolently sitting in at lunch counters and willingly going to jail for conscience' sake. One day the South will know that when these disinherited children of God sat down at lunch counters, they were in reality standing up for what is best in the American dream and for the most sacred values in our Judaeo-Christian heritage, thereby bringing our nation back to those great wells of democracy which were dug deep by the founding fathers in their formulation of the Constitution and the Declaration of Independence. . . .

Yours for the cause of Peace and Brotherhood,
Martin Luther King, Jr.

---

*Escorted by 400 federal marshals and 3,000 federal troops, James Meredith was the first black student to enroll at the historically all-white University of Mississippi in 1962. Four years later, he was wounded by gunfire while leading a voter-registration drive in Mississippi.

4. President Johnson Supports Civil Rights (1965)

Prompted largely by the mass outpouring of sentiment inspired by Martin Luther King, Jr., Congress passed a major Civil Rights Act in 1964. It prohibited discrimination in most public places, forbade employers or unions to discriminate on the basis of race, and created an Equal Employment Opportunity Commission to provide enforcement. Yet King and other black leaders were determined not to rest until they had secured federal legislation protecting the right of African-Americans to vote. Once again, King chose Alabama as the stage for demonstrations designed to force the Johnson administration's hand. On March 7, 1965, demonstrators marching from Selma, Alabama, to the state capital at Montgomery were brutally beaten and dispersed by state troopers and hastily deputized "possemen." Millions of Americans witnessed the violent assault on television, and within days hundreds of clergy of all faiths had poured into Selma to aid Reverend King. One of them, a Boston Unitarian minister, died after having been clubbed by a gang of white hooligans. The pressure on Washington to act mounted to irresistible proportions, and on March 15 President Johnson addressed Congress and the nation, as follows, to plead for a voting rights bill. Although Johnson had in fact tried to discourage King from marching in Alabama, he now threw the full moral and legal weight of his office behind the cause of black voting rights. In what broader context does he try to see the civil rights movement? How do his personal feelings and experiences influence his political action?

Mr. Speaker, Mr. President, Members of the Congress:

I speak tonight for the dignity of man and the destiny of democracy.

I urge every member of both parties, Americans of all religions and of all colors, from every section of this country, to join me in that cause.

At times history and fate meet at a single time in a single place to shape a turning point in man's unending search for freedom. So it was at Lexington and Concord. So it was a century ago at Appomattox. So it was last week in Selma, Alabama.

There, long-suffering men and women peacefully protested the denial of their rights as Americans. Many were brutally assaulted. One good man, a man of God, was killed.

There is no cause for pride in what has happened in Selma. There is no cause for self-satisfaction in the long denial of equal rights of millions of Americans. But there is cause for hope and for faith in our democracy in what is happening here tonight.

For the cries of pain and the hymns and protests of oppressed people have summoned into convocation all the majesty of this great Government—the Government of the greatest Nation on earth.

Our mission is at once the oldest and the most basic of this country: to right wrong, to do justice, to serve man.

In our time we have come to live with moments of great crisis. Our lives have been marked with debate about great issues; issues of war and peace, issues of prosperity and depression. But rarely in any time does an issue lay bare the secret heart of America itself. Rarely are we met with a challenge, not to our growth or

---

[4]*Public Papers of the Presidents of the United States: Lyndon B. Johnson, 1965,* vol. 1 (Washington, D.C.: National Archives and Records Service, 1966), pp. 281–287.

abundance, our welfare or our security, but rather to the values and the purposes and the meaning of our beloved Nation.

The issue of equal rights for American Negroes is such an issue. And should we defeat every enemy, should we double our wealth and conquer the stars, and still be unequal to this issue, then we will have failed as a people and as a nation.

For with a country as with a person, "What is a man profited, if he shall gain the whole world, and lose his own soul?"

There is no Negro problem. There is no Southern problem. There is no Northern problem. There is only an American problem. And we are met here tonight as Americans—not as Democrats or Republicans—we are met here as Americans to solve that problem.

This was the first nation in the history of the world to be founded with a purpose. The great phrases of that purpose still sound in every American heart, North and South: "All men are created equal"—"government by consent of the governed"—"give me liberty or give me death." Well, those are not just clever words, or those are not just empty theories. In their name Americans have fought and died for two centuries, and tonight around the world they stand there as guardians of our liberty, risking their lives.

Those words are a promise to every citizen that he shall share in the dignity of man. This dignity cannot be found in a man's possessions; it cannot be found in his power, or in his position. It really rests on his right to be treated as a man equal in opportunity to all others. It says that he shall share in freedom, he shall choose his leaders, educate his children, and provide for his family according to his ability and his merits as a human being.

To apply any other test—to deny a man his hopes because of his color or race, his religion or the place of his birth—is not only to do injustice, it is to deny America and to dishonor the dead who gave their lives for American freedom.

The Right to Vote

Our fathers believed that if this noble view of the rights of man was to flourish, it must be rooted in democracy. The most basic right of all was the right to choose your own leaders. The history of this country, in large measure, is the history of the expansion of that right to all of our people.

Many of the issues of civil rights are very complex and most difficult. But about this there can and should be no argument. Every American citizen must have an equal right to vote. There is no reason which can excuse the denial of that right. There is no duty which weighs more heavily on us than the duty we have to ensure that right.

Yet the harsh fact is that in many places in this country men and women are kept from voting simply because they are Negroes.

Every device of which human ingenuity is capable has been used to deny this right. The Negro citizen may go to register only to be told that the day is wrong, or the hour is late, or the official in charge is absent. And if he persists, and if he manages to present himself to the registrar, he may be disqualified because he did not spell out his middle name or because he abbreviated a word on the application.

And if he manages to fill out an application he is given a test. The registrar is the sole judge of whether he passes this test. He may be asked to recite the entire Constitution, or explain the most complex provisions of State law. And even a college degree cannot be used to prove that he can read and write.

For the fact is that the only way to pass these barriers is to show a white skin.

Experience has clearly shown that the existing process of law cannot overcome systematic and ingenious discrimination. No law that we now have on the books—and I have helped to put three of them there—can ensure the right to vote when local officials are determined to deny it.

In such a case our duty must be clear to all of us. The Constitution says that no person shall be kept from voting because of his race or his color. We have all sworn an oath before God to support and to defend that Constitution. We must now act in obedience to that oath.

Guaranteeing the Right to Vote

Wednesday I will send to Congress a law designed to eliminate illegal barriers to the right to vote.

The broad principles of that bill will be in the hands of the Democratic and Republican leaders tomorrow. After they have reviewed it, it will come here formally as a bill. I am grateful for this opportunity to come here tonight at the invitation of the leadership to reason with my friends, to give them my views, and to visit with my former colleagues.

I have had prepared a more comprehensive analysis of the legislation which I had intended to transmit to the clerk tomorrow but which I will submit to the clerks tonight. But I want to really discuss with you now briefly the main proposals of this legislation.

This bill will strike down restrictions to voting in all elections—Federal, State, and local—which have been used to deny Negroes the right to vote.

This bill will establish a simple, uniform standard which cannot be used, however ingenious the effort, to flout our Constitution.

It will provide for citizens to be registered by officials of the United States Government if the State officials refuse to register them.

It will eliminate tedious, unnecessary lawsuits which delay the right to vote.

Finally, this legislation will ensure that properly registered individuals are not prohibited from voting.

I will welcome the suggestions from all of the Members of Congress—I have no doubt that I will get some—on ways and means to strengthen this law and to make it effective. But experience has plainly shown that this is the only path to carry out the command of the Constitution.

To those who seek to avoid action by their National Government in their own communities; who want to and who seek to maintain purely local control over elections, the answer is simple:

Open your polling places to all your people.

Allow men and women to register and vote whatever the color of their skin.

Extend the rights of citizenship to every citizen of this land.

The Need for Action

There is no constitutional issue here. The command of the Constitution is plain.

There is no moral issue. It is wrong—deadly wrong—to deny any of your fellow Americans the right to vote in this country.

There is no issue of States rights or national rights. There is only the struggle for human rights.

I have not the slightest doubt what will be your answer. . . .

This time, on this issue, there must be no delay, no hesitation and no compromise with our purpose.

We cannot, we must not, refuse to protect the right of every American to vote in every election that he may desire to participate in. And we ought not and we cannot and we must not wait another 8 months before we get a bill. We have already waited a hundred years and more, and the time for waiting is gone. . . .

We Shall Overcome

But even if we pass this bill, the battle will not be over. What happened in Selma is part of a far larger movement which reaches into every section and State of America. It is the effort of American Negroes to secure for themselves the full blessings of American life.

Their cause must be our cause too. Because it is not just Negroes, but really it is all of us, who must overcome the crippling legacy of bigotry and injustice.

And we shall overcome.

As a man whose roots go deeply into Southern soil I know how agonizing racial feelings are. I know how difficult it is to reshape the attitudes and the structure of our society.

But a century has passed, more than a hundred years, since the Negro was freed. And he is not fully free tonight.

It was more than a hundred years ago that Abraham Lincoln, a great President of another party, signed the Emancipation Proclamation, but emancipation is a proclamation and not a fact.

A century has passed, more than a hundred years, since equality was promised. And yet the Negro is not equal.

A century has passed since the day of promise. And the promise is unkept.

The time of justice has now come. I tell you that I believe sincerely that no force can hold it back. It is right in the eyes of man and God that it should come. And when it does, I think that day will brighten the lives of every American.

For Negroes are not the only victims. How many white children have gone uneducated, how many white families have lived in stark poverty, how many white lives have been scarred by fear, because we have wasted our energy and our substance to maintain the barriers of hatred and terror?

So I say to all of you here, and to all in the Nation tonight, that those who appeal to you to hold on to the past do so at the cost of denying you your future.

This great, rich, restless country can offer opportunity and education and hope to all: black and white, North and South, sharecropper and city dweller. These are the enemies: poverty, ignorance, disease. They are the enemies and not our fellow man, not our neighbor. And these enemies too, poverty, disease and ignorance, we shall overcome. . . .

The Purpose of This Government

My first job after college was as a teacher in Cotulla, Texas, in a small Mexican-American school. Few of them could speak English, and I couldn't speak much

Spanish. My students were poor and they often came to class without breakfast, hungry. They knew even in their youth the pain of prejudice. They never seemed to know why people disliked them. But they knew it was so, because I saw it in their eyes. I often walked home late in the afternoon, after the classes were finished, wishing there was more that I could do. But all I knew was to teach them the little that I knew, hoping that it might help them against the hardships that lay ahead.

Somehow you never forget what poverty and hatred can do when you see its scars on the hopeful face of a young child.

I never thought then, in 1928, that I would be standing here in 1965. It never even occurred to me in my fondest dreams that I might have the chance to help the sons and daughters of those students and to help people like them all over this country.

But now I do have that chance—and I'll let you in on a secret—I mean to use it. And I hope that you will use it with me. . . .

5. A Conservative Denounces Black Rioters (1965)

With the passage of the Voting Rights Act in the summer of 1965, the civil rights movement seemed to stand triumphant, and the Johnson administration seemed at last to have fulfilled the promises of emancipation made a century earlier. But the moment of satisfaction was brief. Just five days after President Johnson signed the Voting Rights Act, a rampaging riot swept through the black Los Angeles ghetto of Watts, leaving some thirty-four persons dead. Moderates were shocked and disillusioned; conservatives were angry. They turned their rage on African-American leaders like Martin Luther King. In the following selection Dr. Will Herberg, a noted conservative intellectual of the day, denounces the Watts rioters and blames King for their actions. Is his assessment of King's role fair?

The country is still reeling from the shock of what happened in Los Angeles. Six days of "racial" rioting, of violence uncontrolled and uncontrollable. Thousands of Negroes running wild, burning, destroying, looting, spreading from the Negro section outward, on a scale that made a senior officer of the National Guard, which finally quelled the rioting, describe it as veritable insurrection.

The fury of hatred and violence revealed in these six dreadful days has engendered a profound uneasiness through every part of the country. How could it have happened? After all, Los Angeles is not the Congo—or is it?

Of course, the politicians and the professional bleeding hearts immediately began to mumble the tired old phrases about "poverty" and "frustration," as though nobody was, or ever had been, poor or frustrated except the Los Angeles Negroes. (The living standards and conditions of life of the Negroes in Los Angeles, bad as they are, would have seemed something near to heaven to most of the immigrants who came to this country in earlier years.) . . .

Internal order is the first necessity of every society. Even justice is secondary to order, because without order there can be no society and no justice, however partial and fragmentary. . . .

---

[5]*National Review* 17 (September 7, 1965): 769–770. 150 E. 35th Street, New York, N.Y. 10016. By permission.

But the internal order of a community, which is so primary and precious to it, is always precarious. . . .

It is preserved by force—by the naked force of police . . . but more immediately by the force of custom and respect for constituted authority. It is these two—custom and respect for constituted authority—that do the everyday work of maintaining order and security. When these are weakened or destroyed, hell breaks loose—whether it is in the Congo or in Los Angeles, whether it is Negroes or whites who do the devil's work. . . .

This internal order is now in jeopardy; and it is in jeopardy because of the doings of such highminded, self-righteous "children of light" as the Rev. Dr. Martin Luther King and his associates in the leadership of the "civil rights" movement. If you are looking for those ultimately responsible for the murder, arson, and looting in Los Angeles, look to them: they are the guilty ones, these apostles of "nonviolence."

For years now, the Rev. Dr. Martin Luther King and his associates have been deliberately undermining the foundations of internal order in this country. With their rabble-rousing demagoguery, they have been cracking the "cake of custom" that holds us together. With their doctrine of "civil disobedience," they have been teaching hundreds of thousands of Negroes—particularly the adolescents and the children—that it is perfectly all right to break the law and defy constituted authority if you are a Negro-with-a-grievance; in protest against injustice. And they have done more than talk. They have on occasion after occasion, in almost every part of the country, called out their mobs on the streets, promoted "school strikes," sit-ins, lie-ins, in explicit violation of the law and in explicit defiance of the public authority. They have taught anarchy and chaos by word and deed—and, no doubt, with the best intentions—and they have found apt pupils everywhere, with intentions not of the best. Sow the wind, and reap the whirlwind. But it is not they alone who reap it, but we as well; the entire nation.

It is worth noting that the worst victims of these high-minded rabble-rousers are not so much the hated whites, but the great mass of the Negro people themselves. The great mass of the Negro people cannot be blamed for the lawlessness and violence in Harlem, Chicago, Los Angeles, or elsewhere. All they want to do is what decent people everywhere want to do: make a living, raise a family, bring up their children as good citizens, with better advantages than they themselves ever had. The "civil rights" movement and the consequent lawlessness has well nigh shattered these hopes; not only because of the physical violence and insecurity, but above all because of the corruption and demoralization of the children, who have been lured away from the steady path of decency and self-government to the more exhilarating road of "demonstrating"—and rioting. An old friend of mine from Harlem put it to me after the riots last year: "For more than fifteen years we've worked our heads off to make something out of these boys. Now look at them—they're turning into punks and hoodlums roaming the streets."

Shall we wreak our wrath upon such "punks" and "hoodlums," the actual rioters, and allow those ultimately responsible, the Martin Luther Kings, the inciters to law-defiance in the name of "conscience," to go immune in their self-righteousness? They stand horrified at the rioting and violence. But isn't it all the handiwork of the demons they themselves raised? They are the guilty ones—despite the best intentions.

If they have any conscience left besides that which they use as justification for the violation of law, let them search it now.

D. Vietnam Troubles

1. The Joint Chiefs of Staff Propose a Wider War (1964)

U.S. involvement in Vietnam went back at least as far as 1950, when President Truman began aiding the French in their effort to suppress a nationalist insurgency in their Indochinese colony. Despite U.S. help, the French forces collapsed in 1954. An international conference in Geneva, Switzerland, in 1954 divided Vietnam at the 17th parallel, and called for elections in all of Vietnam in 1956. The elections were never held, primarily because the government in South Vietnam, encouraged by the United States, feared that the communists in the North, led by Ho Chi Minh, would score a massive victory. President Eisenhower pledged in 1954 to provide military assistance to the government of South Vietnam, and by the end of Eisenhower's term in office about seven hundred U.S. "advisers" were helping to bolster the Vietnamese military. President Kennedy thus inherited a risky but limited commitment to South Vietnam. Meanwhile, communist-led nationalist forces, abetted by the communist regime in North Vietnam, were stepping up the pressure on the shaky South Vietnamese government in Saigon. A bloody military coup in late 1963 brought a new, apparently tougher, government to Saigon, setting the stage for increasing U.S. involvement. A few months later, General Maxwell D. Taylor, the chairman of the Joint Chiefs of Staff, sent the following memorandum to Secretary of Defense Robert S. McNamara, proposing intensified U.S. military actions in Vietnam. What reasons does he offer for such actions? How persuasive are his reasons?

1. National Security Action Memorandum No. 273 [NSAM 273] makes clear the resolve of the President to ensure victory over the externally directed and supported communist insurgency in South Vietnam. In order to achieve that victory, the Joint Chiefs of Staff are of the opinion that the United States must be prepared to put aside many of the self-imposed restrictions which now limit our efforts, and to undertake bolder actions which may embody greater risks.

2. The Joint Chiefs of Staff are increasingly mindful that our fortunes in South Vietnam are an accurate barometer of our fortunes in all of Southeast Asia. It is our view that if the U.S. program succeeds in South Vietnam it will go far toward stabilizing the total Southeast Asia situation. Conversely, a loss of South Vietnam to the communists will presage an early erosion of the remainder of our position in that subcontinent.

3. Laos, existing on a most fragile foundation now, would not be able to endure the establishment of a communist—or pseudo neutralist—state on its eastern flank. Thailand, less strong today than a month ago by virtue of the loss of Prime Minister

---

[1]*The Pentagon Papers,* New York Times edition (1971), pp. 274–277.

Sarit would probably be unable to withstand the pressures of infiltration from the north should Laos collapse to the communists in its turn. Cambodia apparently has estimated that our prospects in South Vietnam are not promising and, encouraged by the actions of the French, appears already to be seeking an accommodation with the communists. Should we actually suffer defeat in South Vietnam, there is little reason to believe that Cambodia would maintain even a pretense of neutrality.

4. In a broader sense, the failure of our programs in South Vietnam would have heavy influence on the judgments of Burma, India, Indonesia, Malaysia, Japan, Taiwan, the Republic of Korea, and the Republic of the Philippines with respect to U.S. durability, resolution, and trustworthiness. Finally, this being the first real test of our determination to defeat the communist wars of national liberation formula, it is not unreasonable to conclude that there would be a corresponding unfavorable effect upon our image in Africa and in Latin America.

5. All of this underscores the pivotal position now occupied by South Vietnam in our world-wide confrontation with the communists and the essentiality that the conflict there would be brought to a favorable end as soon as possible. . . .

6. The Joint Chiefs of Staff are convinced that, in keeping with the guidance in NSAM 273, the United States must make plain to the enemy our determination to see the Vietnam campaign through to a favorable conclusion. . . .

7. Our considerations, furthermore, cannot be confined entirely to South Vietnam. Our experience in the war thus far leads us to conclude that, in this respect, we are not now giving sufficient attention to the broader area problems of Southeast Asia. The Joint Chiefs of Staff believe that our position in Cambodia, our attitude toward Laos, our actions in Thailand, and our great effort in South Vietnam do not comprise a compatible and integrated U.S. policy for Southeast Asia. U.S. objectives in Southeast Asia cannot be achieved by either economic, political, or military measures alone. All three fields must be integrated into a single, broad U.S. program for Southeast Asia. The measures recommended in this memorandum are a partial contribution to such a program.

8. Currently we and the South Vietnamese are fighting the war on the enemy's terms. He has determined the locale, the timing, and the tactics of the battle while our actions are essentially reactive. One reason for this is the fact that we have obliged ourselves to labor under self-imposed restrictions with respect to impeding external aid to the Viet Cong. These restrictions include keeping the war within the boundaries of South Vietnam, avoiding the direct use of U.S. combat forces, and limiting U.S. direction of the campaign to rendering advice to the government of Vietnam. These restrictions, while they may make our international position more readily defensible, all tend to make the task in Vietnam more complex, time-consuming, and in the end, more costly. In addition to complicating our own problem, these self-imposed restrictions may well now be conveying signals of irresolution to our enemies—encouraging them to higher levels of vigor and greater risks. A reversal of attitude and the adoption of a more aggressive program would enhance greatly our ability to control the degree to which escalation will occur. It appears probable that the economic and agricultural disappointments suffered by Communist China, plus the current rift with the Soviets, could cause the communists to think twice about undertaking a large-scale military adventure in Southeast Asia.

9. . . . It is our conviction that if support of the insurgency from outside South

Vietnam in terms of operational direction, personnel, and material were stopped completely, the character of the war in South Vietnam would be substantially and favorably altered. Because of this conviction, we are wholly in favor of executing the covert actions against North Vietnam which you have recently proposed to the President. . . .

10. Accordingly, the Joint Chiefs of Staff consider that the United States must make ready to conduct increasingly bolder actions in Southeast Asia; specifically as to Vietnam to:

a. Assign to the U.S. military commander responsibilities for the total U.S. program in Vietnam.

b. Induce the Government of Vietnam to turn over to the United States military commander, temporarily, the actual tactical direction of the war.

c. Charge the United States military commander with complete responsibility for conduct of the program against North Vietnam.

d. Overfly Laos and Cambodia to whatever extent is necessary for acquisition of operational intelligence.

e. Induce the Government of Vietnam to conduct overt ground operations in Laos of sufficient scope to impede the flow of personnel and material southward.

f. Arm, equip, advise, and support the Government of Vietnam in its conduct of aerial bombing of critical targets in North Vietnam and in mining the sea approaches to that country.

g. Advise and support the Government of Vietnam in its conduct of large-scale commando raids against critical targets in North Vietnam.

h. Conduct aerial bombing of key North Vietnam targets, using U.S. resources under Vietnamese cover, and with the Vietnamese openly assuming responsibility for the actions.

i. Commit additional U.S. forces, as necessary, in support of the combat action within South Vietnam.

j. Commit U.S. forces as necessary in direct actions against North Vietnam. . . .

2. President Johnson Asserts His War Aims (1965)

On August 2–4, 1964, two U.S. destroyers in the Gulf of Tonkin were reportedly fired on by North Vietnamese torpedo boats. President Johnson, concealing the fact that the destroyers had been engaging in provocative raids on North Vietnam, used the incident to secure from Congress a sweeping mandate for U.S. military intervention (the Gulf of Tonkin Resolution). Then, in February 1965, Viet Cong guerrillas attacked a U.S. base at Pleiku, South Vietnam, and Johnson seized the occasion to begin an enormous escalation of the U.S. military presence in Southeast Asia. He ordered virtually continuous bombing of North Vietnam and sharply increased the number of U.S. troops in South Vietnam (to nearly 200,000 by the end of 1965). On April 7, 1965, in a major address at Johns Hopkins University, Johnson set forth his reasons for the increasing U.S. commitment. Just two weeks earlier, the assistant secretary of defense for international security affairs had noted in a private memorandum that

---

[2]*Public Papers of the Presidents of the United States: Lyndon B. Johnson* (Washington, D.C.: National Archives and Records Service, 1966), p. 395.

U.S. war aims were "70%—to avoid a humiliating U.S. defeat (to our reputation as a guarantor), 20%—to keep South Vietnam (and the adjacent) territory from Chinese hands, 10%—to permit the people of South Vietnam to enjoy a better, freer way of life. Also—to emerge from crisis without unacceptable taint from methods used. Not—to 'help a friend.'" Was Johnson's speech consistent with that thinking?

. . . Why are we in South Viet-Nam?

We are there because we have a promise to keep. Since 1954 every American President has offered support to the people of South Viet-Nam. We have helped to build, and we have helped to defend. Thus, over many years, we have made a national pledge to help South Viet-Nam defend its independence.

And I intend to keep that promise.

To dishonor that pledge, to abandon this small and brave nation to its enemies, and to the terror that must follow, would be an unforgivable wrong.

We are also there to strengthen world order. Around the globe from Berlin to Thailand are people whose well being rests in part on the belief that they can count on us [to honor some forty defensive alliances] if they are attacked. To leave Viet-Nam to its fate would shake the confidence of all these people in the value of an American commitment and in the value of America's word. The result would be increased unrest and instability, and even wider war.

We are also there because there are great stakes in the balance. Let no one think for a moment that retreat from Viet-Nam would bring an end to conflict. The battle would be renewed in one country and then another. The central lesson of our time is that the appetite of aggression is never satisfied. . . .

Our objective is the independence of South Viet-Nam and its freedom from attack. We want nothing for ourselves—only that the people of South Viet-Nam be allowed to guide their own country in their own way.

We will do everything necessary to reach that objective and we will do only what is absolutely necessary.

3. The British Prime Minister Criticizes U.S. Bombing (1965)

Operation Rolling Thunder—large-scale bombing raids on North Vietnam—evoked worldwide criticism in 1965. Even U.S. allies grew restive. On June 3, 1965, British Prime Minister Harold Wilson sent the following cable to President Johnson, gently but firmly taking issue with U.S. policy in Vietnam. What did Wilson find most objectionable?

I was most grateful to you for asking Bob McNamara [secretary of defense] to arrange the very full briefing about the two oil targets near Hanoi and Haiphong that Col. Rogers gave me yesterday. . . .

I know you will not feel that I am either unsympathetic or uncomprehending of the dilemma that this problem presents for you. In particular, I wholly understand the deep concern you must feel at the need to do anything possible to reduce the

---

[3]*Pentagon Papers,* New York Times edition (1971), pp. 448–449.

losses of young Americans in and over Vietnam; and Col. Rogers made it clear to us what care has been taken to plan this operation so as to keep civilian casualties to the minimum.

However, . . . I am bound to say that, as seen from here, the possible military benefits that may result from this bombing do not appear to outweigh the political disadvantages that would seem the inevitable consequence. If you and the South Vietnamese Government were conducting a declared war on the conventional pattern . . . this operation would clearly be necessary and right. But since you have made it abundantly clear—and you know how much we have welcomed and supported this—that your purpose is to achieve a negotiated settlement, and that you are not striving for total military victory in the field, I remain convinced that the bombing of these targets, without producing decisive military advantage, may only increase the difficulty of reaching an eventual settlement. . . .

The last thing I wish is to add to your difficulties, but, as I warned you in my previous message, if this action is taken we shall have to dissociate ourselves from it, and in doing so I should have to say that you had given me advance warning and that I had made my position clear to you. . . .

Nevertheless I want to repeat . . . that our reservations about this operation will not affect our continuing support for your policy over Vietnam, as you and your people have made it clear from your Baltimore speech onwards. But, while this will remain the Government's position, I know that the effect on public opinion in this country—and I believe throughout Western Europe—is likely to be such as to reinforce the existing disquiet and criticism that we have to deal with.

4. Defense Secretary Robert McNamara Foresees a Stalemate (1965)

Despite intense air attacks on North Vietnam and swelling contingents of U.S. troops, the United States and its South Vietnamese allies made little headway in Vietnam. At home, conservative critics demanded that the military be given a free hand to deliver a knockout blow to the communist forces. The government's policy, however, was to increase its application of force only in carefully measured increments. In an assessment of the war effort in December 1965, Secretary of Defense Robert S. McNamara suggested one reason for this policy of cautious escalation. What did he see as the greatest restraint on U.S. ability to raise the stakes in Vietnam?

. . . We believe that, whether or not major new diplomatic initiatives are made, the U.S. must send a substantial number of additional forces to VN [Vietnam] if we are to avoid being defeated there. (30 Nov program; concurred in by JCS [Joint Chiefs of Staff])

IV. Prognosis assuming the recommended deployments

Deployments of the kind we have recommended will not guarantee success. Our intelligence estimate is that the present Communist policy is to continue to prosecute the war vigorously in the South. They continue to believe that the war will be a long one, that time is their ally, and that their own staying power is supe-

---

[4]*Pentagon Papers,* New York Times edition (1971), pp. 489–490.

rior to ours. They recognize that the U.S. reinforcements of 1965 signify a determination to avoid defeat, and that more U.S. troops can be expected. Even though the Communists will continue to suffer heavily from GVN [government of Vietnam] and U.S. ground and air action, we expect them, upon learning of any U.S. intentions to augment its forces, to boost their own commitment and to test U.S. capabilities and will to persevere at higher level of conflict and casualties (U.S. KIA [killed in action] with the recommended deployments can be expected to reach 1000 a month).

If the U.S. were willing to commit enough forces—perhaps 600,000 men or more—we could ultimately prevent the DRV/VC [Democratic Republic of Vietnam/Viet Cong] from sustaining the conflict at a significant level. When this point was reached, however, the question of Chinese intervention would become critical. (We are generally agreed that the Chinese Communists will intervene with combat forces to prevent destruction of the Communist regime in the DRV. It is less clear whether they would intervene to prevent a DRV/VC defeat in the South.) The intelligence estimate is that the chances are a little better than even that, at this stage, Hanoi and Peiping would choose to reduce the effort in the South and try to salvage their resources for another day; but there is an almost equal chance that they would enlarge the war and bring in large numbers of Chinese forces (they have made certain preparations which could point in this direction).

It follows, therefore, that the odds are about even that, even with the recommended deployments, we will be faced in early 1967 with a military standoff at a much higher level, with pacification still stalled, and with any prospect of military success marred by the chances of an active Chinese intervention. . . .

5. Secretary McNamara Opposes Further Escalation (1966)

By the end of 1966 Vietnam was beginning to look like a bottomless pit into which the United States was dumping precious money and more precious men. Secretary of Defense McNamara, one of the original architects of U.S. involvement, was among the first high-level officials to grow disenchanted with the course of the war. In his report to the president, given here, he records his increasingly pessimistic assessment of U.S. prospects in Southeast Asia. Such views did not endear him to President Johnson, who clung to the hope that the United States could salvage some kind of victory from the Vietnam quagmire, and McNamara soon resigned. But when military men in the spring of 1968 requested an additional 200,000 troops for Vietnam, Johnson at last drew the line. He put a ceiling on U.S. troop commitments and withdrew from the 1968 presidential race so as to pursue peace more effectively. For Johnson, it was too little, too late. There was no peace in 1968 (the war dragged on five more years), and his party lost the White House in that year to the Republican candidate, Richard M. Nixon. Nixon soon announced a policy of "Vietnamization"—increasing the role of the Vietnamese in their own war, while simultaneously decreasing the U.S. role. In what ways does McNamara's 1966 report foreshadow Nixon's approach? Why was McNamara pessimistic? What was his view of the bombing operation over North Vietnam?

[5]*Pentagon Papers,* New York Times edition (1971), pp. 542–551.

1. Evaluation of the situation. In the report of my last trip to Vietnam almost a year ago, I stated that the odds were about even that, even with the then-recommended deployments, we would be faced in early 1967 with a military stand-off at a much higher level of conflict and with "pacification" still stalled. I am a little less pessimistic now in one respect. We have done somewhat better militarily than I anticipated. We have by and large blunted the communist military initiative—and military victory in South Vietnam the Viet Cong may have had in mind 18 months ago has been thwarted by our emergency deployments and actions. And our program of bombing the North has exacted a price.

My concern continues, however, in other respects. This is because I see no reasonable way to bring the war to an end soon. Enemy morale has not broken—he apparently has adjusted to our stopping his drive for military victory and has adopted a strategy of keeping us busy and waiting us out (a strategy of attriting our national will). He knows that we have not been, and he believes we probably will not be, able to translate our military successes into the "end products"—broken enemy morale and political achievements by the GVN [government of Vietnam]. . . .

Pacification is a bad disappointment. We have good grounds to be pleased by the recent elections, by [President] Ky's 16 months in power, and by the faint signs of development of national political institutions and of a legitimate civil government. But none of this has translated itself into political achievements at Province level or below. Pacification has if anything gone backward. As compared with two, or four, years ago, enemy full-time regional forces and part-time guerrilla forces are larger; attacks, terrorism and sabotage have increased in scope and intensity; more railroads are closed and highways cut; the rice crop expected to come to market is smaller; we control little, if any, more of the population; the VC [Viet Cong] political infrastructure thrives in most of the country, continuing to give the enemy his enormous intelligence advantage; full security exists nowhere (not even behind the U.S. Marines' lines and in Saigon); in the countryside, the enemy almost completely controls the night.

Nor has the Rolling Thunder program of bombing the North either significantly affected infiltration or cracked the morale of Hanoi. There is agreement in the intelligence community on these facts. . . .

In essence, we find ourselves—from the point of view of the important war (for the complicity of the people)—no better, and if anything, worse off. This important war must be fought and won by the Vietnamese themselves. We have known this from the beginning. But the discouraging truth is that, as was the case in 1961 and 1963 and 1965, we have not found the formula, the catalyst, for training and inspiring them into effective action.

2. Recommended actions. In such an unpromising state of affairs, what should we do? We must continue to press the enemy militarily; we must make demonstrable progress in pacification; at the same time, we must add a new ingredient forced on us by the facts. Specifically, we must improve our position by getting ourselves into a military posture that we credibly would maintain indefinitely—a posture that makes trying to "wait us out" less attractive. I recommend a five-pronged course of action to achieve those ends.

a. Stabilize U.S. force-levels in Vietnam. It is my judgment that, barring a dramatic change in the war, we should limit the increase in U.S. forces in SVN [South

Vietnam] in 1967 to 70,000 men and we should level off at the total of 470,000 which such an increase would provide. . . .*

b. Install a barrier. A portion of the 470,000 troops—perhaps 10,000 to 20,000—should be devoted to the construction and maintenance of an infiltration barrier. Such a barrier would lie near the 17th parallel—would run from the sea, across the neck of South Vietnam (choking off the new infiltration routes through the DMZ [demilitarized zone] and across the trails in Laos. This interdiction system (at an approximate cost of $1 billion) would comprise to the east a ground barrier of fences, wire, sensors, artillery, aircraft and mobile troops; and to the west—mainly in Laos—an interdiction zone covered by air-laid mines and bombing attacks pinpointed by air-laid acoustic sensors. . . .

c. Stabilize the Rolling Thunder program against the North. Attack sorties in North Vietnam have risen from about 4,000 per month at the end of last year to 6,000 per month in the first quarter of this year and 12,000 per month at present. Most of our 50 percent increase of deployed attack-capable aircraft has been absorbed in the attacks on North Vietnam. In North Vietnam, almost 84,000 attack sorties have been flown (about 25 percent against fixed targets), 45 percent during the past seven months. . . . I recommend, as a minimum, against increasing the level of bombing of North Vietnam and against increasing the intensity of operations by changing the areas or kinds of targets struck.

Under these conditions, the bombing program would continue the pressure and would remain available as a bargaining counter to get talks started (or to trade off in talks). But, as in the case of a stabilized level of U.S. ground forces, the stabilization of Rolling Thunder would remove the prospect of ever escalating bombing as a factor complicating our political posture and distracting from the main job of pacification in South Vietnam.

At the proper time, as discussed . . . below, I believe we should consider terminating bombing in all of North Vietnam, or at least in the Northeast zones, for an indefinite period in connection with covert moves toward peace.

d. Pursue a vigorous pacification program. . . .

3. The prognosis. The prognosis is bad that the war can be brought to a satisfactory conclusion within the next two years. The large-unit operations probably will not do it; negotiations probably will not do it. *While we should continue to pursue both of these routes in trying for a solution in the short run, we should recognize that success from them is a mere possibility, not a probability.* [Emphasis in original.]

The solution lies in girding, openly, for a longer war and in taking actions immediately which will in 12 to 18 months give clear evidence that the continuing costs and risks to the American people are acceptably limited, that the formula for success has been found, and that the end of the war is merely a matter of time. All of my recommendations will contribute to this strategy, but the one most difficult to implement is perhaps the most important one—enlivening the pacification program. The odds are less than even for this task, if only because we have failed consistently since 1961 to make a dent in the problem. But, because the 1967 trend of pacification will,

---

*Admiral Sharp has recommended a 12/31/67 strength of 570,000. However, I believe both he and General Westmoreland recognize that the danger of inflation will probably force an end 1967 deployment limit of about 470,000. [Footnote in the original.]

I believe, be the main talisman of ultimate U.S. success or failure in Vietnam, extraordinary imagination and effort should go into changing the stripes of that problem. . . .

6. The Soldiers' War (1966)

Hundreds of thousands of young Americans served in Vietnam; more than fifty thousand lost their lives there during the decade-long conflict (it was the United States' longest war). Much of the fighting was not conventional warfare, with front lines and well-identified foes facing one another. Instead, the Americans faced guerrilla adversaries and their civilian supporters, who were indistinguishable from the "friendly" South Vietnamese. In the absence of a defined front, there was no "rear," and U.S. troops often felt themselves to be adrift in a hostile sea of treacherous enemies. Brutality was inevitable in this kind of environment. Two wartime letters from U.S. servicemen follow. What opinion did the writers have of the war? of their own role in it? of antiwar protesters at home?

Dear Mom, . . .

Yesterday I witnessed something that would make any American realize why we are in this war. At least it did me. I was on daylight patrol. We were on a hill overlooking a bridge that was out of our sector. I saw a platoon of Vietcong stopping traffic from going over the bridge. They were beating women and children over the head with rifles, clubs, and fists. They even shot one woman and her child. They were taking rice, coconuts, fish, and other assorted foods from these people. The ones that didn't give they either beat cr shot. I think you know what I tried to do. I wanted to go down and kill all of those slant-eyed bastards. I started to and it took two men to stop me. Those slobs have to be stopped, even if it takes every last believer in a democracy and a free way of life to do it. I know after seeing their brave tactics I'm going to try my best. So please don't knock [President] Johnson's policy in Vietnam. There is a good reason for it. I'm not too sure what it is myself, but I'm beginning to realize, especially after yesterday. . . .

Love,
Bill

How are the people taking to the war in Portland? I've read too much . . . about the way some of those cowardly students are acting on campuses. They sure don't show me much as far as being American citizens. They have the idea that they are our future leaders. Well, I won't follow nobody if he isn't going to help fight for my freedom.

A few weeks ago, I had the chance to talk with some Marines who had come to Okinawa for four (lousy) days of leave. They were more than happy because they had been fighting for six months with no let-up. We sat in a restaurant all the time, and I wish I could have taped it on my recorder. What they had to say would have had an impact on the people back home. One showed me where he had been shot. I asked if it hurt, and he didn't feel it. Not until after he got the ———— that shot him. He was more angry than hurt. They told me of some of their patrols and how they would be talking to a buddy one minute and watch him die in the next. Or wake up

---

[6]Glenn Munson, ed., *Letters from Viet Nam* (New York: Parallax Publishing Co., 1966), pp. 104, 118.

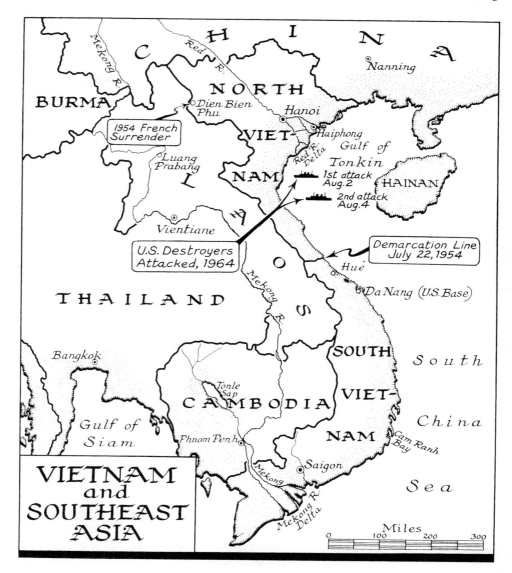

VIETNAM and SOUTHEAST ASIA

in the morning and see a friend hung from a tree by hooks in his armpits with parts of his body cut and shoved into his mouth. From what they said, the Vietcong aren't the only ruthless ones. We have to be, too. *Have* to. You'd be surprised to know that a guy you went to school with is right now shooting a nine-year-old girl and her mother. He did it because if they got the chance they would kill him. Or throwing a Vietcong out of a helicopter because he wouldn't talk.

One guy (who had broke down and cried) said that his one desire is to get enough leave to go home and kick three of those demonstrators in a well-suited place and bring him back. I tell you, it's horrible to read a paper and see our own people aren't backing you up.

7. The Dilemma of Vietnam (1966)

By 1966, many Americans were agonizing about their country's involvement in Southeast Asia, and a bitter argument over the Vietnam War was intensifying. In the following image, from the Chicago Sun-Times, *renowned cartoonist Bill Mauldin ridiculed both the pro-war and antiwar factions. Was his criticism fair? What is the cartoonist's own view of the war? What policy choices other than escalation and withdrawal were there?*

The Strategists

---

[7] Bill Mauldin © *The Chicago Sun-Times,* 1966.

E. The Politics of Protest in the 1960s

1. Students for a Democratic Society Issues a Manifesto (1962)

The civil rights struggle and the continuing Cold War inspired many young people who came of age in the 1960s to take a radically critical look at U.S. society—even before the worsening Vietnam imbroglio made radical disenchantment almost fashionable among the young. One of the earliest and most thoughtful expressions of this incipient youthful radicalism was the Port Huron Statement, drafted by Tom Hayden and adopted by the fledgling Students for a Democratic Society (SDS), then in a relatively moderate phase of development, at its national convention at Port Huron, Michigan, in 1962. This statement later proved enormously influential in shaping the political views of many young activists. What aspects of the U.S. situation does it find most deplorable? How truly "radical" are the sentiments it expresses?

We are people of this generation, bred in at least modest comfort, housed now in universities, looking uncomfortably to the world we inherit.

When we were kids the United States was the wealthiest and strongest country in the world; the only one with the atom bomb, the least scarred by modern war, an initiator of the United Nations that we thought would distribute Western influence throughout the world. Freedom and equality for each individual government of, by, and for the people—these American values we found good, principles by which we could live as men. Many of us began maturing in complacency.

As we grew, however, our comfort was penetrated by events too troubling to dismiss. First, the permeating and victimizing fact of human degradation, symbolized by the Southern struggle against racial bigotry, compelled most of us from silence to activism. Second, the enclosing fact of the Cold War, symbolized by the presence of the Bomb, brought awareness that we ourselves, and our friends, and millions of abstract "others" we knew more directly because of our common peril, might die at any time. We might deliberately ignore, or avoid, or fail to feel all other humor problems, but not these two, for these were too immediate and crushing in their impact, too challenging in the demand that we as individuals take the responsibility for encounter and resolution.

While these and other problems either directly oppressed us or rankled our consciences and became our own subjective concern, we began to see complicated and disturbing paradoxes in our surrounding America. The declaration "all men are created equal . . ." rang hollow before the facts of Negro life in the South and the big cities of the North. The proclaimed peaceful intentions of the United States contradicted its economic and military investments in the Cold War status quo.

We witnessed, and continue to witness, other paradoxes. With nuclear energy whole cities can easily be powered, yet the dominant nation-states seem more likely

---

[1]From the Port Huron Statement. Reprinted by permission of Tom Hayden, a founding member of Students for a Democratic Society and principal author of the Port Huron Statement. He was elected to the California legislature in 1982.

to unleash destruction greater than that incurred in all wars of human history. Although our own technology is destroying old and creating new forms of social organization, men still tolerate meaningless work and idleness. While two-thirds of mankind suffers undernourishment, our own upper classes revel amidst superfluous abundance. Although world population is expected to double in forty years, the nations still tolerate anarchy as a major principle of international conduct and uncontrolled exploitation governs the sapping of the earth's physical resources. Although mankind desperately needs revolutionary leadership, America rests in national stalemate, its goals ambiguous and tradition-bound instead of informed and clear, its democratic system apathetic and manipulated rather than "of, by, and for the people."

Not only did tarnish appear on our image of American virtue, not only did disillusion occur when the hypocrisy of American ideals was discovered, but we began to sense that what we had originally seen as the American Golden Age was actually the decline of an era. The worldwide outbreak of revolution against colonialism and imperialism, the entrenchment of totalitarian states, the menace of war, overpopulation, international disorder, supertechnology—these trends were testing the tenacity of our own commitment to democracy and freedom and our abilities to visualize their application to a world in upheaval.

Our work is guided by the sense that we may be the last generation in the experiment with living. But we are a minority—the vast majority of our people regard the temporary equilibriums of our society and world as eternally functional parts. In this is perhaps the outstanding paradox: we ourselves are imbued with urgency, yet the message of our society is that there is no viable alternative to the present. Beneath the reassuring tones of the politicians, beneath the common opinion that America will "muddle through," beneath the stagnation of those who have closed their minds to the future, is the pervading feeling that there simply are no alternatives, that our times have witnessed the exhaustion not only of Utopias, but of any new departures as well. Feeling the press of complexity upon the emptiness of life, people are fearful of the thought that at any moment things might be thrust out of control. They fear change itself, since change might smash whatever invisible framework seems to hold back chaos for them now. For most Americans, all crusades are suspect, threatening. The fact that each individual sees apathy in his fellows perpetuates the common reluctance to organize for change. The dominant institutions are complex enough to blunt the minds of their potential critics, and entrenched enough to swiftly dissipate or entirely repeal the energies of protest and reform, thus limiting human expectancies. Then, too, we are a materially improved society, and by our own improvements we seem to have weakened the case for further change.

Some would have us believe that Americans feel contentment amidst prosperity—but might it not better be called a glaze above deeply felt anxieties about their role in the new world? And if these anxieties produce a developed indifference to human affairs, do they not as well produce a yearning to believe there *is* an alternative to the present, not something *can* be done to change circumstances in the school, the workplaces, the bureaucracies, the government? It is to this latter yearning, at once the spark and engine of change, that we direct our present appeal. The search for truly democratic alternatives to the present, and a commitment to social experimentation with them, is a worthy and fulfilling human enterprise, one which moves us and, we hope, others today. On such a basis do we offer this document of our convictions and analysis: as an effort in understanding and changing the conditions of humanity in the late twentieth century, an effort rooted in the ancient, still unfulfilled conception of man attaining determining influence over his circumstances of life.

2. The Young Americans for Freedom Make a Statement (1960)

Meeting at the Sharon, Connecticut, home of conservative activist and National Review *publisher William F. Buckley, Jr., in September 1960, a group of college students drafted the following statement of principles as the founding charter of Young Americans for Freedom. YAF became a rallying point for young conservatives through the tumultuous 1960s and provided organizational support for the eventual conservative Republican resurgence that culminated in the election of Ronald Reagan in 1980. In what ways do the ideas in the following "Sharon Statement" resemble those in the Manifesto of Students for a Democratic Society (the previous document)? In what ways do they differ? How might one account for the subsequent political fates of the two ideologies and the two groups?*

The Sharon Statement

Adopted by the Young Americans for Freedom in conference at Sharon, Conn., September 9-11, 1960

In this time of moral and political crisis, it is the responsibility of the youth of America to affirm certain eternal truths.

We, as young conservatives, believe:

That foremost among the transcendent values is the individual's use of his God-given free will, whence derives his right to be free from the restrictions of arbitrary force;

That liberty is indivisible, and that political freedom cannot long exist without economic freedom;

That the purposes of government are to protect these freedoms through the preservation of internal order, the provision of national defense, and the administration of justice;

That when government ventures beyond these rightful functions, it accumulates power which tends to diminish order and liberty;

That the Constitution of the United States is the best arrangement yet devised for empowering government to fulfill its proper role, while restraining it from the concentration and abuse of power;

That the genius of the Constitution—the division of powers—is summed up in the clause which reserves primacy to the several states, or to the people, in those spheres not specifically delegated to the Federal Government;

That the market economy, allocating resources by the free play of supply and demand, is the single economic system compatible with the requirements of personal freedom and constitutional government, and that it is at the same time the most productive supplier of human needs;

---

[2]Reprinted from *National Review,* September 24, 1960, p. 173 by permission of the publisher.

That when government interferes with the work of the market economy, it tends to reduce the moral and physical strength of the nation; that when it takes from one man to bestow on another, it diminishes the incentive of the first, the integrity of the second, and the moral autonomy of both;

That we will be free only so long as the national sovereignty of the United States is secure; that history shows periods of freedom are rare, and can exist only when free citizens concertedly defend their rights against all enemies;

That the forces of international Communism are, at present, the greatest single threat to these liberties;

That the United States should stress victory over, rather than coexistence with, this menace; and

That American foreign policy must be judged by this criterion: does it serve the just interests of the United States?

3. A War Protester Decides to Resist the Draft (1966)

No other issue did more to breed disenchantment among young people in the 1960s than the Vietnam War. As revelations spread about the deepening U.S. involvement there, and as the government in Washington proved increasingly unable to justify the conflict to the American public, countless people, especially college youths, expressed their disaffection. For many young men of draft age, their relationship with the Selective Service System became both a political and a moral issue. One young man who decided to resist the draft was David Harris, a former Boy-of-the-Year from Fresno, California, and, in 1966, president of the student body at Stanford University. With his friend Dennis Sweeney—who a decade and a half later would be convicted of murdering former Congressman Allard K. Lowenstein, another antiwar activist—Harris helped to organize a draft resistance movement among college students. In the following passage, Harris describes his own decision to become a draft resister. (He would later spend nearly two years in a federal penitentiary as a consequence.) What were his motives? Was he justified in reaching his decision?

The more we learned about the war, the worse it seemed. Late in July, Cooley Street attended a lecture by a Canadian journalist who had just returned from North Vietnam. Dennis and the Channing Street group were at the lecture as well.*

With what amounted to only a fledgling air defense system, explained the journalist, North Vietnam had no hope of turning the American Force back. Theoretically, strategic air power destroys the enemy's industrial, logistic, and transportation systems, but North Vietnam possessed little centralized industry and only a rudimentary transportation system. Consequently, the target increasingly became the population itself. The American strategy's starting point was a calculation by Defense Department planners that it took only two Vietnamese to deal with one of their dead countrymen, but one wounded required five. Mass woundings, it was as-

---

[3]*Dreams Die Hard: Three Men's Journey Through the Sixties* by David Harris, pp. 146–148. Copyright © 1982 by David Harris. Reprinted by permission of St. Martin's/Marek, New York.

*Cooley and Channing are two streets in the Palo Alto, California, area where Harris and other antiwar activists lived in the 1960s.

sumed, would tie the enemy's hands, and the American arsenal had developed wounding devices in great variety.

The CBU 46 was a small explosive package stuffed with hundreds of one-inch steel darts, each shaped with fins, designed to "peel off" the outer flesh, make "enlarged wounds," and "shred body organs" before "lodging in the blood vessels." They were dropped a thousand at a time from 30,000 feet. The BLU 52 was 270 pounds of "riot control" chemical that induced vomiting, nausea, and muscle spasms, occasionally fatal to old people and children. The M-36 was an 800-pound casing containing 182 separate "incendiary bomblets," the most horrendous of which were manufactured from phosphorus, commonly lodging in the flesh and continuing to burn for as long as fifteen days, causing its victims' wounds to glow with an eerie green light.

The two antipersonnel weapons then in most common use were versions of the BLU 24/26. The "pineapple bomb" was the earliest model. A yellow cylinder, it contained 250 steel ball-bearing pellets packed around an explosive charge. On impact, its pellets fired out horizontally. A batch of a thousand pineapples would cover an area the size of four football fields, leaving anything above ground level a casualty. The "guava bomb" was the pineapple's successor. Gray and round, it doubled the number of pellets and had a fuse that let it either explode at a set altitude or on impact. Since it fired its pellets diagonally instead of on the horizontal, the Guava also fired into the holes where people might be hiding.

After the program was over, we all decided to proceed to a place we called End of the World Beach. It was the edge of a causeway supporting the eastern approach to the Dumbarton Bridge, where beer bottles, old tires, two-by-fours, tennis shoes, condoms, dead fish, and seaweed were strung out for half a mile. It captured the devastation still haunting everyone's thinking. At one point, Dennis and I stood next to each other, staring across the refuse at the blinking lights of civilization on the other side of the bay.

Without looking at Dennis, I spoke up.

"You know," I said, "those bastards have got to be stopped."

When I turned to Sweeney, he was nodding his head like he knew exactly what I meant.

Three weeks later I sat at my typewriter and wrote local Draft Board 71 in Fresno, California, a letter "To whom it may concern." I enclosed a Selective Service classification card indicating that the bearer, David Victor Harris, possessed a student deferment. The letter informed my draft board that I could no longer in good conscience carry the enclosed document or accept the deferment it signified. It was a privilege I found unwarranted for any student. It also signified tacit assent on my part for both the task the Selective Service System was performing and the power it had assumed over my life. Being even implicitly a party to the destruction of Indochina was not part of my plans. If they ordered me for induction, I warned them, I would refuse to comply.

I feel as though I have explained that act of defiance a million times in the intervening years without ever quite capturing it. The repetition eventually burdened my explanation with a shell of distance and matter-of-factness that distorts what I did. It was an act of wonderment and impulse, taken in the calmest and most practical frame of mind. I was prepared to abandon what seemed a promising future and pit myself against the war one on one, believing I would redeem my country and realize myself in the process. It seemed that to do anything else would have dishonored both. There was nothing matter-of-fact or distant about it that August. I took my life in my hands and it was the bravest I have ever been. It was also, I think, the most right. That I have never doubted. Times change and I am no longer the same person, but my past and I are still directly related.

I remember mailing that letter at the mailbox next to the neighborhood store, scuffing along in the dust at the road edge, wearing Levis, moccasins, and a brown khaki work shirt. My moustache had become a full beard and my hair covered the top of my ears. I was both frightened and exhilarated. The last barrier was down. Henceforth, I was my own soldier advancing in my own kind of war.

My adrenaline didn't diminish until long after midnight. Lying in my bed, I pictured the penitentiary as a very cold and lonely place that I planned to endure for the sake of us all.

4. Stewart Alsop Senses the End of an Era (1970)

Stewart Alsop (1914–1974), along with his brother Joseph, was among the most famous and influential American journalists of his day. A veteran of World War II and a staunch cold warrior, he was a member of the generation that had survived the Great Depression, defeated the Nazis and the Japanese, ridden the fabulous wave of postwar prosperity, and held the Soviets at bay in the post–World War II years. His was also a generation that was deeply disillusioned by the protests over the Vietnam War and the emergence of the counterculture in the 1960s. His brother Joseph used a remark of Stewart's as the title of his autobiography, I've Seen the Best of It *(1992), a phrase that captured the two journalists' sense that the country had taken a turn for the worse in the 1960s. In Stewart Alsop's editorial that follows, what does he see as the principal ill afflicting American society in the 1960s? Were WASPS (an acronym for White Anglo-Saxon Protestants) the only elite threatened by the cultural and political upheavals of the decade? Did the 1960s really witness a fundamental shift in American values?*

In a recent *Harper's*, Peter Schrag had an interesting piece—"The Decline of the Wasp." He made the point that the era has ended when this country was dominated intellectually and politically by a small minority of people with Anglo-Saxon names. The point is valid, and important, politically and in other ways.

The Nixon Administration is a Waspish administration, but it is Rotarian-Waspish. The Eastern Ivy League Wasps, whose special preserve was the making of foreign policy, have almost wholly faded from the Washington scene. The old Wasp elite, in fact, is dying and it may be dead.

The Wasp elite was never the only American elite, of course. The United States used to be managed by a kind of network of elites. But the other elites seem to be dying too. The church-centered, Irish-dominated Catholic elite is moribund—the au-

---

[4]Stewart Alsop, "The Disintegration of the Elite," from *Newsweek*, June 8, 1970. Copyright 1970 by Stewart Alsop. Reprinted by permission of the Stewart J. D. Alsop Trust.

thority of the church, which used to hold politicians and movie magnates in thrall, is fading, as even the priests defy their bishops.

The authority of "Our Crowd," the Zionist-oriented Jewish elite, is also much reduced—a symbol of its weakening is the anti-Zionism of many young Jewish radicals. The Negro elite, which once acted as a racial bridge, is enfeebled too—its three pillars, the church, the NAACP, and the Urban League, are dismissed by young blacks as havens for Uncle Toms.

Yet the decline of the Wasp elite is the most important development politically, for it is the central elite. Like Charles II, it has been an unconscionable time a-dying. The decline began in the Depression, when a midget sat in J. P. Morgan's lap, and when, in the pictures of Richard Whitney entering the paddy wagon on his way to Sing Sing, the Porcellian Club emblem was clearly visible on the properly buttoned waistcoat.*

Still, even in that era, foreign policy was safely in the hands of a couple of undoubted elitists—Franklin Roosevelt and Sumner Welles. Under that distinctly non-Ivy League Wasp, Harry Truman, the Wasp elite enjoyed a kind of Indian summer. Foreign policy was made in those days by such elitists as Dean Acheson (Yale), Averell Harriman (Yale), James Forrestal (Princeton), Robert Lovett (Yale), Charles Bohlen (Harvard), George Kennan (Princeton), and Paul Nitze (Harvard).[†]

McCarthyism was basically an assault on the Wasp elite—it was no accident that Senator McCarthy chose Dean Acheson, whose mustache provided the perfect symbol of Eastern elitism, as his principal target. The assault was beaten back, but the Wasp elite never fully recovered its old dominance of foreign policy.[‡]

With a few exceptions (the Dulles brothers, Christian Herter, Thomas Gates) the Eisenhower regime was dominated by the Rotarian-Wasps, not the Eastern elitists. President Kennedy always gave the Wasp elite a hearing—McGeorge Bundy was its principal voice—but those really close to the throne, aside from the clan, were Kennedy's fellow Catholics of the Irish Mafia. In the Johnson and Nixon eras the decline of the Wasp elite has been rapid and is now almost total.[§]

There may be a factor in the decline which has been overlooked. This is the collapse of Great Britain as a world power. The collapse occurred suddenly and completely immediately after the Suez disaster in 1956, when Harold Macmillan sent

---

*In a notorious publicity stunt in the 1930s, a photographer contrived to have a midget sit in banker J. P. Morgan's lap and then quickly snapped a photograph of Morgan's astonished reaction. The episode typified the ridicule and contempt showered upon the former "titans of industry" in the midst of the economic catastrophe of the Great Depression. Richard Whitney was the former president of the New York Stock Exchange, a respected Wall Street banker, and a pillar of the northeastern elite establishment until he was convicted in 1938 of grand larceny charges for fraudulent stock dealings. He had belonged to the exclusive Porcellian Club as a Harvard undergraduate.

[†]Sumner Welles was undersecretary of state in the Franklin Roosevelt administration. Dean Acheson served as Harry Truman's secretary of state. Averell Harriman was for a time ambassador to the Soviet Union. James Forrestal served as secretary of the navy and then as the first secretary of defense. Robert Lovett, Charles Bohlen, George Kennan, and Paul Nitze were all prominent government officials in the early Cold War era.

[‡]Joseph McCarthy was the senator from Wisconsin who accused numerous government officials of having pro-communist sympathies (see p. 441).

[§]Allen Dulles was the long-time director of the CIA. His brother John Foster Dulles served as Dwight Eisenhower's secretary of state, as, briefly, did Christian Herter. Thomas Gates was secretary of defense in the Eisenhower administration. McGeorge Bundy, a former Harvard dean, was John F. Kennedy's national security adviser.

a cable to his old friend President Eisenhower: OVER TO YOU. The meaning was clear: Britain was opting out as a world power.*

The collapse of Britain as a world power had a curious effect on the Wasp elite in this country. In its period of foreign-policy dominance, the Wasp elite was molded in about a dozen preparatory schools and three universities. Education in these institutions was patterned on the British model, and it was permeated by Anglophilia.

The archetypical forcing ground for the Wasp elite in its heyday was Groton School, which produced such elitists as Franklin Roosevelt and Sumner Welles, those non-biodegradable elder statesmen Acheson and Harriman, and whole slews of Bundys, Morgans, Whitneys, Dillons, lesser Roosevelts, and so on. Education at Groton was an indoctrination in British culture and British attitudes—a boy was stuffed to the gills with English history and literature while American history and literature were passed over as though they scarcely existed.

The result of this kind of education was a sort of love-hate complex. Franklin Roosevelt, very typically, combined a rather naive anti-colonialism with a profound and instinctive Anglophilia. The basic assumption of the Wasp elite was that Britain, while arrogant and capable of burning down the White House, was (a) a great world power, and (b) a power on which the United States could rely in time of trouble. These were the basic assumptions of American foreign policy, from the Federal period right through to 1956. Suez knocked them into a cocked hat.

It was as though an irritating but powerful parent had turned quite suddenly into a lean and slippered pantaloon. Britannia, instead of ruling the seas, produced the Beatles and Carnaby Street. The British collapse contributed in a subtle and unmeasurable but real way to the erosion of self-confidence of the Wasp elite. It wrecked their whole system of thinking about the world, and even about themselves.

This erosion of confidence has had something, and perhaps quite a lot, to do with the erosion of authority which is the most pervasive and significant phenomenon in American life today. Pat Moynihan was remarkably foresighted when he warned President Nixon before he took office that "all the major domestic problems facing you derive from the erosion of the authority of the institutions of American society."[†]

The *Wall Street Journal,* in a brilliant editorial, maintained that "the source of the pathology is in the elite," which has failed in its duty "to supply the bonds that hold together diverse and potentially competing factions." But perhaps the trouble is not that the elite has failed, but that it has ceased to exist. Because the Wasp elite, in a predominantly Wasp country, was the keystone of the arch, the other elites have collapsed with it.

The Wasp elite was quite often arrogant and quite often wrong, and the lesser elites—the Catholic elite especially—could be parochial and even reactionary. But our present situation suggests that it may be better to have an arrogant or reactionary elite than no elite at all. For a society without a self-respecting and respect-

---

*Britain, France, and Israel invaded Egypt in 1956 in a controversy over the control of the Suez Canal. They expected American support, but President Eisenhower did not give it to them.

[†]Daniel Patrick Moynihan, later a Democratic senator from New York state, was a domestic policy adviser to Richard Nixon.

commanding elite is a society without authority, and a society without authority is one short step away from becoming an authoritarian society.

Thought Provokers

---

1. Was the Cuban missile crisis a turning point in the Cold War? Who actually "won" the confrontation over the missiles? Was President Kennedy's diplomacy in the crisis courageous or foolhardy?

2. In what ways was Lyndon Johnson an innovative political leader? What did the Great Society program owe to the New Deal? Can the United States afford the kinds of programs that Johnson dreamed of?

3. Was Martin Luther King, Jr., a "radical"? Would there have been a civil rights movement in the 1950s and 1960s without him? What motivated the sit-ins and freedom rides? What did they accomplish? King took part of his inspiration from the nonviolent tactics of Mohandas Gandhi's campaign for independence in India. What conditions are necessary for nonviolence to succeed as a political technique? Who deserves more credit for the civil rights advances of the 1960s, Martin Luther King or Lyndon Baines Johnson?

4. Why did the United States become involved in Vietnam? Why did it fight the war in the gradually escalating way that it did? Why did the war last so long? In what ways did the Vietnam imbroglio alter the U.S. role in the world?

5. Why did a radical movement well up in the 1960s? How truly radical was it? What legacy have the 1960s movements left behind? Are the issues on which they focused dead?

40

The Stalemated Seventies, 1968–1980

> I pledge to you the new leadership will end the war
> and win the peace in the Pacific.
>
> *Presidential Candidate Richard Nixon, 1968*

Prologue: Richard Nixon, elected by a minority of voters in the bitterly contested election of 1968, gave his highest priority to foreign affairs, especially to ending the war in Vietnam. He sought "peace with honor"—a combination that took him nearly five years to achieve. When Nixon sent U.S. troops into Cambodia in the spring of 1970, the nation's already seething college campuses erupted. Nixon weathered the subsequent storm of unpopularity and finally succeeded in extricating the United States from Vietnam. In the process he established diplomatic contact with the People's Republic of China and initiated a period of détente, or relaxed relations, with the Soviet Union. Nixon also had the opportunity to appoint several Supreme Court justices. He expected them to share his conservative judicial philosophy, which emphasized "law and order" and frowned on the kind of judicial activism on behalf of minorities that had characterized the Court in the 1950s and 1960s under Chief Justice Earl Warren. Nixon handily won reelection in 1972 but was soon ensnared in a controversy concerning his role in a break-in at the Democratic party offices in Washington's Watergate apartment complex. Threatened with formal impeachment and trial, Nixon resigned the presidency in August 1974. Gerald Ford, who had been apppointed vice president after Nixon's original running mate, Spiro Agnew, had resigned amid scandalous accusations, became the first person ever elevated to the presidency solely by act of Congress. He speedily lost the public's confidence when he extended an unconditional pardon to the fallen Nixon. Little-known Jimmy Carter of Georgia, promising that he "would never lie," capitalized on public disgust with Nixon and Ford to win the presidency in 1976.

A. Richard Nixon's Cambodian Coup

1. The President Defends His Incursion (1970)

Nixon's scheme for ending the Vietnam War and winning the peace came to be known as Vietnamization. Pursuant to his "Guam Doctrine" or "Nixon Doctrine" of turning over Asia's wars to Asians, he announced on November 3, 1969, that he

---

[1] *Weekly Compilation of Presidential Documents* 6 (1970): 597ff.

would gradually withdraw U.S. troops from Vietnam in the expectation that an ever-stronger South Vietnam would take up the slack and hold its own. On April 30, 1970, Nixon dramatically appeared on nationwide television. Pointing out that areas along the border of supposedly neutral Cambodia were being used as hideouts from which enemy troops had long been attacking U.S. and South Vietnamese forces, Nixon announced that he was taking steps to wipe out these sanctuaries. Which of the reasons that he gives for doing so seem the most valid and which the least valid? How could an extension of the fighting save American lives?

Cambodia . . . has sent out a call to the United States, to a number of other nations, for assistance. Because if this enemy effort succeeds, Cambodia would become a vast enemy staging area and a springboard for attacks on South Vietnam along 600 miles of frontier—a refuge where enemy troops could return from combat without fear of retaliation.

North Vietnamese men and supplies could then be poured into that country, jeopardizing not only the lives of our own men but the people of South Vietnam as well.

Now confronted with this situation, we have three options.

First, we can do nothing. Well, the ultimate result of that course of action is clear. Unless we indulge in wishful thinking, the lives of Americans remaining in Vietnam after our next withdrawal of 10,000 would be gravely threatened. . . .

Our second choice is to provide massive military assistance to Cambodia itself. Now unfortunately, while we deeply sympathize with the plight of 7 million Cambodians whose country is being invaded, massive amounts of military assistance could not be rapidly and effectively utilized by the small Cambodian Army against the immediate threat. . . .

Our third choice is to go to the heart of the trouble. That means cleaning out major North Vietnamese and Vietcong occupied territories, these sanctuaries which serve as bases for attacks on both Cambodia and American and South Vietnamese forces in South Vietnam. Some of these, incidentally, are as close to Saigon as Baltimore is to Washington. . . .

In cooperation with the armed forces of South Vietnam, attacks are being launched this week to clean out major enemy sanctuaries on the Cambodian-Vietnam border. . . .

This is not an invasion of Cambodia. The areas in which these attacks will be launched are completely occupied and controlled by North Vietnamese forces. Our purpose is not to occupy the areas. Once enemy forces are driven out of these sanctuaries and once their military supplies are destroyed, we will withdraw. . . .

Now let me give you the reasons for my decision.

A majority of the American people, a majority of you listening to me, are for the withdrawal of our forces from Vietnam. The action I have taken tonight is indispensable for the continuing success of that withdrawal program.

A majority of the American people want to end this war rather than to have it drag on interminably. The action I have taken tonight will serve that purpose.

A majority of the American people want to keep the casualties of our brave men in Vietnam at an absolute minimum. The action I take tonight is essential if we are to accomplish that goal.

We take this action not for the purpose of expanding the war into Cambodia but for the purpose of ending the war in Vietnam and winning the just peace we all desire. We have made and we will continue to make every possible effort to end this war through negotiation at the conference table rather than through more fighting on the battlefield. . . .

Tonight, I again warn the North Vietnamese that if they continue to escalate the fighting when the United States is withdrawing its forces, I shall meet my responsibility as Commander in Chief of our Armed Forces to take the action I consider necessary to defend the security of our American men.

The action that I have announced tonight puts the leaders of North Vietnam on notice that we will be patient in working for peace, we will be conciliatory at the conference table, but we will not be humiliated. We will not be defeated. We will not allow American men by the thousands to be killed by an enemy from privileged sanctuaries. . . .

If, when the chips are down, the world's most powerful nation, the United States of America, acts like a pitiful, helpless giant, the forces of totalitarianism and anarchy will threaten free nations and free institutions throughout the world.

It is not our power but our will and character that is being tested tonight. The question all Americans must ask and answer tonight is this: Does the richest and strongest nation in the history of the world have the character to meet a direct challenge by a group which rejects every effort to win a just peace, ignores our warning, tramples on solemn agreements, violates the neutrality of an unarmed people, and uses our prisoners as hostages?

If we fail to meet this challenge, all other nations will be on notice that despite its overwhelming power the United States, when a real crisis comes, will be found wanting.

During my campaign for the Presidency, I pledged to bring Americans home from Vietnam. They are coming home.

I promised to end this war. I shall keep that promise.

I promised to win a just peace. I shall keep that promise.

We shall avoid a wider war. But we are also determined to put an end to this war.

2. *The* St. Louis Post-Dispatch *Dissents (1970)*

The sudden invasion of "neutral" Cambodia by U.S. troops, at a time when Nixon was supposedly winding down the war rather than widening it, provoked an angry uproar in the United States. No doubt taken aback by the furor, Nixon gave assurances that U.S. forces would withdraw within two months (as they did) and penetrate no farther than about twenty miles (which they did). Some stores of rice, arms, and trucks were captured. The assumption was that the enemy forces would return, as they did, when the Americans left. Nixon was widely upbraided for having turned the Vietnam War into an Indochina war (which to a degree it already was), and this

---

[2]*St. Louis Post-Dispatch*, May 3, 1970. By permission of the publisher.

charge was redoubled when, in February 1971, a U.S.-supported South Vietnamese force invaded Laos and was quickly driven back. The St. Louis Post-Dispatch, *a prominent Democratic newspaper, found the Cambodian incursion illogical and deceptive. Which of its various criticisms seems most trenchant in the light of subsequent events?*

President Nixon now has his own Indochina war and his own credibility gap. Neither one is inherited any longer. In asking the American people to support the expansion of the Vietnam war to Cambodia, as he has already expanded it to Laos, he asks them to believe the same false promises which have repeatedly betrayed them against their will into ever deeper involvement on the mainland of Asia.

They are asked to seek peace by making war; to seek withdrawal of our troops by enlarging the arena of combat; to diminish American casualties by sending more young men to their death; to save the lives of 450,000 American troops by one more round of escalation. And all this Mr. Nixon asks in the name of preserving the credibility of America as a great power!

Such an exercise in double-think and double-talk would be unbelievable if the whole nation had not seen an uneasy President floundering in illogic and misrepresentation before its very eyes. It is still hard to understand how a President who saw his predecessor destroyed by manipulating the people into an unwanted war would now attempt to manipulate them into enlarging the war he promised to end.

When all of Mr. Nixon's patchwork rationalizations are stripped away, it is quite clear what has happened. His policy of Vietnamization is a failure. It always was a fatuous assumption that as American troops withdrew the South Vietnamese would become stronger and Hanoi would be intimidated into accepting defeat. Now that the assumption has been exposed as false—now that the Communists refuse to give up fighting on Mr. Nixon's command—the Pentagon has sold him the bill of goods that escalation will rescue a bankrupt policy.

It is the same bill of goods, slightly worn, that the generals sold Lyndon Johnson. First they promised that a merciless air war would bring Hanoi to its knees; and it didn't. Then, 500,000 ground troops would cow the Viet Cong; and they didn't. Now, "cleaning out" the bases on the Cambodian border, which our forces have lived with for five years, will suddenly win the war—and who can believe, honestly, that it will?

Nor can rational men honestly believe that sending American troops into Cambodia is necessary to save the lives of our garrison in Vietnam. The 450,000 men there, equipped and armed to the hilt, are perfectly able to protect themselves and Mr. Nixon knows it. So he fuzzes up the argument by saying that the object is to protect the lives of those Americans who will be left in Vietnam after mid-1971, when the current withdrawal schedule has been fulfilled.

This adds up to an interesting confession that Mr. Nixon intends to leave some 300,000 troops in Vietnam after his third year in office, but it is no more persuasive than the other. The plain truth is that Vietnamization has failed, the withdrawal schedule is threatened, Mr. Nixon because of his marriage to the Thieu-Ky regime [in South Vietnam] refuses to negotiate a compromise political settlement, and so he buys the old, battered nostrum of escalation. . . .

It is no wonder that moderate and thoughtful men like Republican Senator Mark Hatfield of Oregon are coming to the conclusion that the only way left to carry out the public will is to exercise the constitutional powers of Congress in a way that guarantees an end to the war. . . . Senator Hatfield is proposing that Congress stipulate a cut-off date after which no more funds will be appropriated for military operations in Indochina.

We favor such a measure. The cut-off date could be set far enough ahead to avoid any perils of precipitate withdrawal. It would not interfere with, but would reinforce, an orderly and secure disengagement. It would do no more than to write into law what Mr. Nixon claims to be his policy of ending the war. Its most immediate effect, we imagine, would be to compel Mr. Nixon to negotiate a reasonable political settlement based on a coalition government, to be followed by elections in which the Vietnamese people determine their own future. And what is wrong with that?

3. Henry Kissinger Dissects the Dissenters

Henry Kissinger, a brilliant, German-born former Harvard professor, was serving in 1970 as President Nixon's national security assistant—a powerful position from which he exerted great influence on foreign policy. (He would later exercise still more power as secretary of state in both the second Nixon administration and the short-lived Ford administration.) In the following passage from his memoirs, he offers his view of the antiwar protesters who convulsed the country in the wake of the Cambodian incursion. How does he judge the behavior of the Nixon administration toward the protesters? What is his assessment of their motives? of their effect on policy? What did the crisis do to his relations with his one-time academic colleagues?

. . . I had entered government with the hope that I could help heal the schisms in my adopted country by working to end the war. I sympathized with the anguish of the students eager to live the American dream of a world where ideas prevailed by their purity without the ambiguities of recourse to power. The war in Vietnam was the first conflict shown on television and reported by a largely hostile press. The squalor and suffering and confusion inseparable from any war became part of the living experience of Americans; too many ascribed its agony to the defects of their own leaders.

Repellent as I found the self-righteousness and brutality of some protesters, I had a special feeling for the students. They had been brought up by skeptics, relativists, and psychiatrists; now they were rudderless in a world from which they demanded certainty without sacrifice. My generation had failed them by encouraging self-indulgence and neglecting to provide roots. I spent a disproportionate amount of time in the next months with student groups—ten in May alone. I met with protesters at private homes. I listened, explained, argued. But my sympathy for their an-

---

[3]From Henry Kissinger, *White House Years,* pp. 510–517. Copyright © 1979. Reprinted by permission of Kissinger Associates.

guish could not obscure my obligation to my country as I saw it. They were, in my view, as wrong as they were passionate. Their pressures delayed the end of the war, not accelerated it; their simplifications did not bring closer the peace, of the yearning for which they had no monopoly. Emotion was not a policy. We had to end the war, but in conditions that did not undermine America's power to help build the new international order upon which the future of even the most enraged depended. . . .

. . . The President's statements, oscillating between the maudlin and the strident, did not help in a volatile situation where everything was capable of misinterpretation. His May 1 off-the-cuff reference to "bums . . . blowing up campuses," a gibe overheard by reporters during a visit to the Pentagon, was a needless challenge, although it was intended to refer only to a tiny group of students who had fire-bombed a building and burned the life's research of a Stanford professor. When on May 4, four students at Kent State University were killed by rifle fire from National Guardsmen dispatched by Ohio Governor James Rhodes to keep order during several days of violence, there was a shock wave that brought the nation and its leadership close to psychological exhaustion.

The Administration responded with a statement of extraordinary insensitivity. [Press secretary] Ron Ziegler was told to say that the killings "should remind us all once again that when dissent turns to violence it invites tragedy."

The momentum of student strikes and protests accelerated immediately. Campus unrest and violence overtook the Cambodian operation itself as the major issue before the public. Washington took on the character of a besieged city. A pinnacle of mass public protest was reached by May 9 when a crowd estimated at between 75,000 and 100,000 demonstrated on a hot Saturday afternoon on the Ellipse, the park to the south of the White House. Police surrounded the White House; a ring of sixty buses was used to shield the grounds of the President's home. . . .

All this accelerated the processes of disenchantment. Conservatives were demoralized by a war that had turned into a retreat and liberals were paralyzed by what they themselves had wrought—for they could not completely repress the knowledge that it was a liberal Administration that had sent half a million Americans to Indochina. They were equally reluctant to face the implications of their past actions or to exert any serious effort to maintain calm. There was a headlong retreat from responsibility. Extraordinarily enough, all groups, dissenters and others, passed the buck to the Presidency. It was a great joke for undergraduates when one senior professor proclaimed "the way to get out of Vietnam is by ship." The practical consequence was that in the absence of any serious alternative the government was left with only its own policy or capitulation.

The very fabric of government was falling apart. The Executive Branch was shell-shocked. After all, their children and their friends' children took part in the demonstrations. Some two hundred and fifty State Department employees, including fifty Foreign Service Officers, signed a statement objecting to Administration policy. The ill-concealed disagreement of Cabinet members showed that the Executive Branch was nearly as divided as the country. Interior Secretary Walter Hickel protested in public. The *New York Times* on May 9 reported that the Secretary of State had prohibited any speculation on his own attitude—hardly a ringing endorsement of the President. A group of employees seized the Peace Corps building and flew a Viet Cong flag from it. Robert Finch, Secretary of Health, Education, and Welfare, refused to disagree publicly with his President and old friend—as indeed he did privately—and a large number of his officials occupied the department's auditorium in protest. The President saw himself as the firm rock in this rushing stream, but the turmoil had its effect on him as well. Pretending indifference, he was deeply wounded by the hatred of the protesters. He would have given a great deal to gain a measure of the affection in which the students held the envied and admired Kennedys. In his ambivalence Nixon reached a point of exhaustion that caused his advisers deep concern. His awkward visit to the Lincoln Memorial to meet students at 5:00 A.M. on May 9 was only the tip of the psychological iceberg.

Exhaustion was the hallmark of us all. I had to move from my apartment ringed by protesters into the basement of the White House to get some sleep. Despite the need to coordinate the management of the crisis, much of my own time was spent with unhappy, nearly panicky, colleagues; even more with student and colleague demonstrators. I talked at some length to Brian McDonnell and Thomas Mahoney, two young pacifists who announced they would fast in Lafayette Park until all American troops had been withdrawn. I talked in the Situation Room with groups of students from various colleges and graduate schools about the root causes, as I saw them, of their despair, which I thought deeper than anxiety about the war.

I found these discussions with students rather more rewarding than those with their protesting teachers. When I had lunch in the Situation Room with a group of Harvard professors, most of whom had held high governmental posts, at their request, I offered to engage in a candid discussion of the reasoning behind the decision, but on an off-the-record basis. Most had been my close colleagues and friends. They would not accept this offer. They were there not as eminent academicians but as political figures representing a constituency at home, a campus inflamed by the Kent State tragedy as much as by the war. They had proclaimed to the newspapers beforehand—but not to me—that they were there to confront me; they announced that they would henceforth refuse any research or advisory relationship with the government.

Their objections to the Cambodian decision illustrated that hyperbole was not confined to the Administration. One distinguished professor gave it as his considered analysis that "somebody had forgotten to tell the President that Cambodia was a country; he acted as if he didn't know this. Had we undertaken a large commitment to Cambodia? If we had, this was rotten foreign policy. If we hadn't, this was rotten foreign policy." He was convinced that this action "clearly jeopardized American withdrawals"—though in fact it did the opposite. This professor was prepared to believe, on the basis of no evidence whatsoever, that Secretary of Defense Laird had been unaware of the military operations before the President announced them. He held the amazing view that "it was a gamble that shouldn't have been taken even if it succeeds on its own terms." Others said the decision was "incomprehensible," "more horrible than anything done by LBJ," "dreadful." One professor advanced the extraordinary hypothesis that an operation lasting eight weeks to a distance of twenty-one miles might lead our military commanders to believe that the use of nuclear weapons was now conceivable. Another declared that we had provoked all the actions of the other side.

The meeting completed my transition from the academic world to the world of affairs. These were the leaders of their fields; men who had been my friends, academicians whose lifetime of study should have encouraged a sense of perspective. That they disagreed with our decision was understandable; I had myself gone through a long process of hesitation before I became convinced that there was no alternative. But the lack of compassion, the overweening righteousness, the refusal to offer an alternative, reinforced two convictions: that for the internal peace of our country the war had to be ended, but also that in doing so on terms compatible with any international responsibility we would get no help from those with whom I had spent my professional life. The wounds would have to be healed after the war was over; in the event, these were not.

Cambodia was *not* a moral issue; neither Nixon nor his opponents should ever have presented it in those terms. What we faced was an essentially tactical choice: whether the use of American troops to neutralize the sanctuaries for a period of eight weeks was the best way to maintain the established pace and security of our exit from Vietnam and prevent Hanoi from overrunning Indochina. Reasonable men might differ; instead, rational discussion ended. The President's presentation that elevated his decision to the same level of crisis as some of the crucial choices of World War II was countered by the critics with the image of an out-of-control President acting totally irrationally, who had provoked the enemy and whose actions were immoral even if they *succeeded*.

But it was not the incursion into Cambodia that was the real subject of debate. It was the same issue that had torn the country during the Moratorium the previous year: whether there were any terms that the United States should insist on for its honor, its world position, and the sacrifices already made, or whether it should collapse its effort immediately and unconditionally. A political settlement as urged by Senator Fulbright—other than the quick imposition of a Communist government in Saigon—was precisely what Hanoi had always rejected, as Le Duc Tho had confirmed to me in the most unqualified terms not three weeks earlier. What none of the moderate critics was willing to admit was that if we followed their recommendations of refusing aid to Cambodia, we would soon have no choice but to accept Hanoi's terms, which none of them supported. Our opponents kept proclaiming an assumption for which there did not exist the slightest evidence—that there was some unspecified political alternative, some magic formula of neutrality, which was being willfully spurned. The panicky decision to set a June 30 deadline for the removal of our forces from Cambodia was one concrete result of public pressures. . . .

Unfortunately, the arguments for a withdrawal deadline had not improved with age. Either the deadline was compatible with Vietnamization, in which case it coincided with our own policy but would deprive us of negotiating leverage. Or it was arbitrary, in which case it was euphemism for a collapse; and it would have been nearly impossible to justify risking lives in the interval before the deadline expired. So we ended the Cambodia operation still on the long route out of Vietnam, confronting an implacable enemy and an equally implacable domestic opposition.

B. Winding Down the Vietnam War

I. Nixon's Grand Plan in Foreign Policy (1968–1969)

Richard Nixon built his prepresidential career on a strong reputation as a hawkish cold warrior—and thus, ironically, he was in a particularly favorable position to bring some thaw to the chilly Cold War. As a certified conservative, he had a freedom of maneuver that would not have been available to a liberal Democrat, who would have been vulnerable to criticism from the very right wing that Nixon could easily control. Nixon shrewdly saw the implications of the split between China and the Soviet Union that had developed in the 1960s, and he was determined to turn that split to U.S. advantage. In the following passage from his memoirs, Nixon describes his thinking about global affairs as he embarked upon his presidency. What does he mean when he says that "the key to a Vietnam settlement lay in Moscow and Peking rather than in Hanoi"?

In the late 1940s and during the 1950s I had seen communism spread to China and other parts of Asia, and to Africa and South America, under the camouflage of parties of socialist revolution, or under the guise of wars of national liberation. And, finally, during the 1960s I had watched as Peking and Moscow became rivals for the role of leadership in the Communist world.

Never once in my career have I doubted that the Communists mean it when they say that their goal is to bring the world under Communist control. Nor have I ever forgotten Whittaker Chambers's chilling comment that when he left communism, he had the feeling he was leaving the winning side. But unlike some anticommunists who think we should refuse to recognize or deal with the Communists lest in doing so we imply or extend an ideological respectability to their philosophy and their system, I have always believed that we can and must communicate and, when possible, negotiate with Communist nations. They are too powerful to ignore. We must always remember that they will never act out of altruism, but only out of self-interest. Once this is understood, it is more sensible—and also safer—to communicate with the Communists than it is to live in icy cold-war isolation or confrontation. In fact, in January 1969 I felt the relationship between the United States and the Soviet Union would probably be the single most important factor in determining whether the world would live at peace during and after my administration.

I felt that we had allowed ourselves to get in a disadvantageous position vis-à-vis the Soviets. They had a major presence in the Arab states of the Middle East, while we had none; they had Castro in Cuba; since the mid-1960s they had supplanted the Chinese as the principal military suppliers of North Vietnam; and except for Tito's Yugoslavia they still totally controlled Eastern Europe and threatened the stability and security of Western Europe.

There were, however, a few things in our favor. The most important and interesting was the Soviet split with China. There was also some evidence of growing,

---

[1]Reprinted by permission of Warner Books, Inc., New York, New York, U.S.A. From *RN: The Memoirs of Richard Nixon* by Richard Nixon. Copyright © 1978 by Richard Nixon. All rights reserved.

albeit limited, independence in some of the satellite nations. There were indications that the Soviet leaders were becoming interested in reaching an agreement on strategic arms limitation. They also appeared to be ready to hold serious talks on the anomalous situation in Berlin, which, almost a quarter century after the war had ended, was still a divided city and a constant source of tension, not just between the Soviets and the United States, but also between the Soviets and Western Europe. We sensed that they were looking for a face-saving formula that would lessen the risk of confrontation in the Mideast. And we had some solid evidence that they were anxious for an expansion of trade.

It was often said that the key to a Vietnam settlement lay in Moscow and Peking rather than in Hanoi. Without continuous and massive aid from either or both of the Communist giants, the leaders of North Vietnam would not have been able to carry on the war for more than a few months. Thanks to the Sino-Soviet split, however, the North Vietnamese had been extremely successful in playing off the Soviets and the Chinese against each other by turning support for their war effort into a touchstone of Communist orthodoxy and a requisite for keeping North Vietnam from settling into the opposing camp in the struggle for domination within the Communist world. This situation became a strain, particularly for the Soviets. Aside from wanting to keep Hanoi from going over to Peking, Moscow had little stake in the outcome of the North Vietnamese cause, especially as it increasingly worked against Moscow's own major interests vis-à-vis the United States. While I understood that the Soviets were not entirely free agents where their support for North Vietnam was concerned, I nonetheless planned to bring maximum pressure to bear on them in this area.

I was sure that [Soviet leaders] Brezhnev and Kosygin had been no more anxious for me to win in 1968 than Khrushchev had been in 1960. The prospect of having to deal with a Republican administration—and a Nixon administration at that—undoubtedly caused anxiety in Moscow. In fact, I suspected that the Soviets might have counseled the North Vietnamese to offer to begin the Paris talks in the hope that the bombing halt would tip the balance to [Hubert] Humphrey in the election—and if that was their strategy, it had almost worked.

After the election Johnson proposed that as President and President-elect he and I attend a summit meeting with the Soviets in the period before my inauguration. I understood his desire to make one last dramatic demonstration of his dedication to peace, but I saw no solid basis for concluding that the Soviet leaders were prepared to negotiate seriously on any critical issue. Nor did I want to be boxed in by any decisions that were made before I took office.

The most that might come from such a last-minute summit would be a "spirit," like the "Spirit of Glassboro" that followed Johnson's meeting with Kosygin in New Jersey in 1967 or the "Spirit of Camp David" that followed Eisenhower's meeting with Khrushchev in 1959. It was my feeling that such "spirits" were almost entirely spurious and that they actually worked heavily to the Soviets' advantage. Since public opinion played no role whatever in the Communist system, such summit "spirit" was a one-way street in their direction, because the optimistic attitudes that characterized American public opinion after a summit made it harder for us to assume a tough line in our postsummit dealings with the Soviets.

During the transition period Kissinger and I developed a new policy for dealing with the Soviets. Since U.S.-Soviet interests as the world's two competing nuclear superpowers were so widespread and overlapping, it was unrealistic to separate or compartmentalize areas of concern. Therefore we decided to link progress in such areas of Soviet concern as strategic arms limitation and increased trade with progress in areas that were important to us—Vietnam, the Mideast, and Berlin. This concept became known as linkage.

Lest there be any doubt of my seriousness in pursuing this policy, I purposely announced it at my first press conference when asked a question about starting SALT [Strategic Arms Limitation Talks] talks. I said, "What I want to do is to see to it that we have strategic arms talks in a way and at a time that will promote, if possible, progress on outstanding political problems at the same time—for example, on the problem of the Mideast and on other outstanding problems in which the United States and the Soviet Union acting together can serve the cause of peace."

Linkage was something uncomfortably new and different for the Soviets, and I was not surprised when they bridled at the restraints it imposed on our relationship. It would take almost two years of patient and hard-nosed determination on our part before they would accept that linkage with what we wanted from them was the price they would have to pay for getting any of the things they wanted from us.

We made our first contacts with the Soviets during the transition period. In mid-December Kissinger met with a Soviet UN diplomat who was, as we knew, actually an intelligence officer. I wanted it made clear that I was not taken in by any of the optimistic rhetoric that had characterized so much of recent Soviet-American relations. Kissinger therefore stated that while the tendency during the last few years had been to emphasize how much our two nations supposedly had in common, the Nixon administration felt that there were real and substantial differences between us and that an effort to lessen the tension created by these differences should be the central focus of our relationship. Kissinger also said that I did not want a pre-inauguration summit meeting and that if they held one with Johnson I would have to state publicly that I would not be bound by it. Nothing was heard about this summit project.

We received a prompt reply from Moscow. Our UN contact reported that the Soviet leadership was "not pessimistic" because of the election of a Republican President. He said that the Soviet leadership had expressed an interest in knowing if I desired to "open channels of communication.' It was with this in mind that I said in my inaugural address, "After a period of confrontation, we are entering an era of negotiation. Let all nations know that during this administration our lines of communication will be open."

2. Nixon's Address to the Nation (1973)

President Nixon had inherited the unwanted Vietnam War, but he kept the bloodshed going for more than four years—longer than the United States' participation in

---

[2]*Weekly Compilation of Presidential Documents* 9 (1973): 43–44.

either World War I or World War II. When the North Vietnamese balked at the peace table in Paris in 1972, Nixon launched his awesome "Christmas blitz" against the North Vietnamese capital, thus prompting the so-called cease-fire that Nixon hailed as "peace with honor." By its terms, the United States retrieved some 560 prisoners of war and withdrew its remaining 27,000 troops. The South Vietnamese government of dictatorial President Thieu was permitted to receive replacements of weapons from the United States, as well as other kinds of nontroop support. Yet the North Vietnamese forces still occupied about 30 percent of South Vietnam, and they were allowed to retain there about 145,000 troops that were in a position to renew hostilities. Such was the "honorable" peace that North Vietnam immediately flouted and that vanished in about two years. To what extent does Nixon gloss over the truth in this section of his televised report to the nation on January 23, 1973?

Good evening. I have asked for this radio and television time tonight for the purpose of announcing that we today have concluded an agreement to end the war and bring peace with honor in Vietnam and in Southeast Asia. . . .

We must recognize that ending the war is only the first step toward building the peace. All parties must now see to it that this is a peace that lasts, and also a peace that heals, and a peace that not only ends the war in Southeast Asia, but contributes to the prospects of peace in the whole world.

This will mean that the terms of the agreement must be scrupulously adhered to. We shall do everything the agreement requires of us and we shall expect the other parties to do everything it requires of them. We shall also expect other interested nations to help insure that the agreement is carried out and peace is maintained.

As this long and very difficult war ends, I would like to address a few special words to each of those who have been parties in the conflict.

First, to the people and Government of South Vietnam: By your courage, by your sacrifice, you have won the precious right to determine your own future and you have developed the strength to defend that right. We look forward to working with you in the future, friends in peace as we have been allies in war.

To the leaders of North Vietnam: As we have ended the war through negotiations, let us now build a peace of reconciliation. For our part, we are prepared to make a major effort to help achieve that goal. But just as reciprocity was needed to end the war, so, too, will it be needed to build and strengthen the peace.

To the other major powers [China, the Soviet Union] that have been involved even indirectly: Now is the time for mutual restraint so that the peace we have achieved can last.

And finally, to all of you who are listening, the American people: Your steadfastness in supporting our insistence on peace with honor has made peace with honor possible. I know that you would not have wanted that peace jeopardized. With our secret negotiations at the sensitive stage they were in during this recent period, for me to have discussed publicly our efforts to secure peace would not only have violated our understanding with North Vietnam, it would have seriously harmed and possibly destroyed the chances for peace. Therefore, I know that you now can understand why, during these past several weeks, I have not made any public statements about those efforts.

The important thing was not to talk about peace, but to get peace and to get the right kind of peace. This we have done.

Now that we have achieved an honorable agreement, let us be proud that America did not settle for a peace that would have betrayed our allies, that would have abandoned our prisoners of war, or that would have ended the war for us but would have continued the war for the 50 million people of Indochina. Let us be proud of the 2½ million young Americans who served in Vietnam, who served with honor and distinction in one of the most selfless enterprises in the history of nations. And let us be proud of those who sacrificed, who gave their lives so that the people of South Vietnam might live in freedom and so that the world might live in peace.

3. Canadians See Neither Peace nor Honor (1973)

Much of the free world, in addition to the communist countries, had deplored the U.S. intervention in Vietnam. Canada, to which many draft dodgers had fled, was conspicuous among the critics. The "peace with honor" that Nixon announced was actually violated in a wholesale fashion by both sides from the day of signing in January 1973 until the disgraceful rout in April 1975. During the first year of "peace" alone, an estimated fifty thousand Vietnamese were killed. To what extent does the following editorial from the Toronto Star *seem justified in the light of the facts?*

It's evidently impossible for a president of the United States to come clean about Viet Nam; there is too much shame and failure in the American record there to be even hinted at. Thus President Nixon kept proclaiming the achievement of "peace with honor" last night, when all he can really promise is that the Americans are going to pull out of that wretched war in fairly good order, with their prisoners returned, instead of fleeing in abject humiliation.

"Exit with face saved" would have been a more accurate phrase than peace with honor; for, whatever the terms of the Paris agreement may say, it's obvious that there is no guarantee of peace between North and South Viet Nam. Hanoi maintains its goal of unifying all Viet Nam under Communist rule, while the government of South Viet Nam and a considerable number of its people mean to resist that dubious blessing.

The president felt obliged to insist that the principal war aim of the United States had been achieved; he told the South Vietnamese that their right to determine their own future has been won. That's uncertain, to put it mildly, since they have so far been incapable of defeating the Communists with the full participation of the United States on their side.

It would have been enough good news for Nixon to say what he can say credibly, that the United States is getting out. Not that the basic purpose of the American intervention—to keep South Viet Nam from being taken over by the Communists—

---

[3]The *Toronto Star,* January 24, 1973. Reprinted with permission of the *Toronto Star.*

was dishonorable. But the way the Americans fought the war has been calamitous for both Viet Nam and the United States.

The United States waged war with incredible stupidity and callousness. Counting social as well as material and human destruction, it probably harmed its ally South Viet Nam more than its enemy North Viet Nam. The land was transformed from one of hamlets and villages to one of shantytown cities living off the American war machine. Bombing and clearance orders—in South Viet Nam—created millions of refugees and caused hundreds of thousands of civilian casualties. In terms of military efficiency, the profligate American operation was comparable to shooting mosquitoes with a machine-gun. The Viet Cong and the North Vietnamese troops were equally callous, but couldn't match the American power to destroy and disrupt.

Let us hope that peace is indeed near for the tortured people of Viet Nam. But the prospects are highly doubtful, and depend heavily on the willingness of the Soviet Union and China on one side, and the United States on the other, to restrain their respective allies. For now, it is sufficient to know that the most blunderingly destructive element of all—the American presence—is to be removed.

4. The Expulsion from Vietnam (1975)

Early in 1975 the North Vietnamese launched a furious assault, and the South Vietnamese defenses crumpled like cardboard. As Saigon was caving in, helicopters airlifted out U.S. personnel and also rescued an estimated 140,000 Vietnamese who were supposedly marked for extermination by the victors. The escape from Vietnam was a defeat not so much for the United States as it was for the U.S. policy of supporting communist-threatened regimes in distant parts of the globe. The U.S. forces had fought the enemy to a standstill and had withdrawn "with honor" after fighting to at least a stalemate in 1973. The South Vietnamese, with continued U.S. military supplies, lost the war, and the United States consequently lost face. In the light of these circumstances, was the Des Moines Register *unduly critical in its assessment?*

The war in Vietnam, like the war in Cambodia, has ended with a victory for the Communist-led revolutionary forces and a defeat for the upholders of the old ruling classes. That includes the United States, which for 25 years—since the first aid to France in support of that country's effort to maintain its Indochina colony—has been upholding the old regimes.

The incredible thing, still, is the stubborn failure of United States leaders to see what was going on, to see the hopelessness of their cause and to get out. A quarter of a century!

The American public and press must share the blame for this disaster of American foreign policy. With rare and honorable exceptions, Americans went along, bemused by the concept of American leadership of a "free world" struggle against Communism.

---

[4]*Des Moines Register,* April 30, 1975. Reprinted with permission of the *Des Moines Register.*

A succession of American presidents, secretaries of state, defense secretaries and generals told the people over and over that America was winning. They distorted the evidence; they told outright lies. The facts were that the side America was supporting was losing.

Each American president since Eisenhower has had the opportunity to move toward a political compromise in Vietnam. Each one lacked the courage to take a step which he feared might look like an American "defeat" or, as President Ford and Secretary Kissinger have been putting it, like a failure to make good on a commitment.

In the end, this policy led to a much worse defeat and a much worse discrediting of America's international behavior than early withdrawal would have meant.

The fear of Communist takeovers, of a phony "domino" theory of collapsing "democracies," has been dominant in U.S. policy—even after the moves toward détente with the big communist countries.

The misguided quarter century is now behind America, as President Ford said recently, although not in those words. Instead of losing face or encouraging Communism or losing confidence of the rest of the world, the United States probably will gain in these respects from finally ending its military role in Asia.

The nation would have gained respect sooner if the government had acted on its own—10, 15 or more years ago. Instead, action to end the Indochina connection came only after the arousal of public opinion which drove one president out of public life, and led to the near-impeachment of another on charges of abuse of constitutional power. Even the ending was a foot-dragging business with Ford, Kissinger and Ambassador Graham Martin holding the line in Saigon.

But public opinion finally did prevail; the machinery of democracy did work, though slowly. The country will be stronger, wiser and more effective in world affairs, we believe, as a result of ending this misadventure. The illusions of imperialism, of world leadership in terms of military power, of executive primacy in foreign affairs—those illusions, we hope and believe, are vanishing.

C. The Supreme Court "Coddles" Criminals

1. The Outlawing of Third-Degree Confessions (1966)

In the 1960s and even earlier, the Supreme Court was a target for abuse by conservative groups. The more vocal extremists raised the insulting cry "Impeach Earl Warren" against the liberal chief justice. Conservatives were first outraged by a series of rulings that extended constitutional guarantees to communists and that ordered desegregation in the schools. Then, in 1962 and 1963, came two decisions banning the recitation of prayers in the public schools. Such a practice was declared to be in violation of the First Amendment, which required a separation of church and state.*

---

[1]*Official Reports of the Supreme Court,* vol. 384 U.S. pt. 3 (Preliminary Print), pp. 444–481, passim.

*The Court also decreed reapportionment in the state legislatures (1962) and in the congressional districts (1964) on the basis of "one man, one vote" rather than on the lopsided basis that often gave agricultural areas greater voting power than more populous urban areas.

In 1963 an epochal decision held that accused criminals must be provided with lawyers in noncapital offenses. In 1964 and 1966 other decisions decreed that confessions obtained by the police in private (and hence under suspicion of physical force) could not be used to convict. The Fifth Amendment had long barred self-incrimination. Finally, on June 13, 1966, the Supreme Court, in a five-to-four decision, reversed the conviction of a confessed kidnapper-rapist, Ernesto Miranda, together with three men accused of other felonies. Chief Justice Warren, speaking for the majority, ruled in part as follows. In view of the fact that the crime rate was rising alarmingly and that this decision would make convictions harder to obtain, was the Court to be commended for emphasizing the rights of the individual at the expense of social order?

Prior to any questioning, the person must be warned that he has a right to remain silent, that any statement he does make may be used as evidence against him, and that he has a right to the presence of an attorney, either retained or appointed.

The defendant may waive effectuation of these rights, provided the waiver is made voluntarily, knowingly and intelligently.

If, however, he indicates in any manner and at any stage of the process that he wishes to consult with an attorney before speaking, there can be no questioning.

Likewise, if the individual is alone and indicates in any manner that he does not wish to be interrogated, the police may not question him. The mere fact that he may have answered some questions or volunteered some statements on his own does not deprive him of the right to refrain from answering any further inquiries until he has consulted with an attorney and thereafter consents to be questioned.

The constitutional issue we decide in each of these [four] cases is the admissibility of statements obtained from a defendant questioned while in custody and deprived of his freedom of option. In each, the defendant was questioned by police officers, detectives, or a prosecuting attorney in a room in which he was cut off from the outside world. In none of these cases was the defendant given a full and effective warning of his rights at the outset of the interrogation process. In all the cases, the questioning elicited oral admissions, and in three of them, signed statements as well which were admitted at their trials.

They all thus share salient features—incommunicado* interrogation of individuals in a police-dominated atmosphere, resulting in self-incriminating statements without full warnings of constitutional rights. . . .

From extensive factual studies undertaken in the early [19]30s . . . it is clear that police violence and the "third degree" flourished at that time. In a series of cases decided by this Court long after these studies, the police resorted to physical brutality—beatings, hanging, whipping—and to sustained and protracted questioning incommunicado in order to extort confessions. The 1961 Commission on Civil Rights found much evidence to indicate that "some policemen still resort to physical force to obtain confessions."

The use of physical brutality and violence is not, unfortunately, relegated to the past or to any part of the country. Only recently in Kings County, N.Y., the police brutally beat, kicked and placed lighted cigarette butts on the back of a potential

---

*That is, without outside communication.

witness under interrogation for the purpose of securing a statement incriminating a third party. . . .

The examples given above are undoubtedly the exception now, but they are sufficiently widespread to be the object of concern. . . .

Even without employing brutality, the "third degree" or the specific stratagems described above, the very fact of custodial interrogation exacts a heavy toll on individual liberty and trades on the weakness of individuals. . . .

If an individual indicates that he wishes the assistance of counsel before any interrogation occurs, the authorities cannot rationally ignore or deny his request on the basis that the individual does not have or cannot afford a retained attorney.

The financial ability of the individual has no relationship to the scope of the rights involved here. The privilege against self-incrimination secured by the Constitution applies to all individuals. The need for counsel in order to protect the privilege exists for the indigent as well as the affluent. . . .

This does not mean, as some have suggested, that each police station must have a "station-house lawyer" present at all times to advise prisoners. It does mean, however, that if police propose to interrogate a person they must make known to him that he is entitled to a lawyer and that, if he cannot afford one, a lawyer will be provided for him prior to any interrogation. . . .

Our decision is not intended to hamper the traditional function of police officers in investigating crime. . . . When an individual is in custody on probable cause, the police may, of course, seek out evidence in the field to be used at trial against him. Such investigation may include inquiry of persons not under restraint.

General on-the-scene questioning as to facts surrounding a crime or other general questioning of citizens in the fact-finding process is not affected by our holding. It is an act of responsible citizenship for individuals to give whatever information they may have to aid in law enforcement. In such situations the compelling atmosphere inherent in the process of in-custody interrogation is not necessarily present.

In dealing with statements obtained through interrogation, we do not purport to find all confessions inadmissible. Confessions remain a proper element in law enforcement. Any statement given freely and voluntarily without any compelling influence is, of course, admissible in evidence. . . .

In announcing these principles, we are not unmindful of the burdens which law-enforcement officials must bear, often under trying circumstances. We also fully recognize the obligation of all citizens to aid in enforcing the criminal laws.

2. The Minority Supports the Police (1966)

An angered, fist-pounding Mr. Justice John Harlan, speaking for three of the four dissenters, put his finger on some of the weaknesses of the majority opinion. In these excerpts from his dissent, is he more realistic than the majority in his approach to the problem, and if so, in what respects?

---

[2]*Official Reports of the Supreme Court,* vol. 384 U.S. pt. 3 (Preliminary Print), pp. 504–517, passim.

I believe the decision of the Court represents poor constitutional law and entails harmful consequences for the country at large. How serious these consequences may prove to be only time can tell. But the basic flaws in the Court's justification seem to me readily apparent, now once all sides of the problem are considered. . . .

The new rules are not designed to guard against police brutality or other unmistakably banned forms of coercion. Those who use "third degree" tactics and deny them in court are equally able and destined to lie as skillfully about warnings and waivers.

Rather, the thrust of the new rules is to negate all pressures, to reinforce the nervous or ignorant suspect, and ultimately to discourage any confession at all. The aim, in short, is toward "voluntariness" in a utopian sense, or, to view it from a different angle, voluntariness with a vengeance.

To incorporate this notion into the Constitution requires a strained reading of history and precedent and a disregard of the very pragmatic concerns that alone may on occasion justify such strains. . . .

What the Court largely ignores is that its rules impair, if they will not eventually serve wholly to frustrate, an instrument of law enforcement that has long and quite reasonably been thought worth the price paid for it.

There can be little doubt that the Court's new code would markedly decrease the number of confessions. To warn the suspect that he may remain silent and remind him that his confession may be used in court are minor obstructions. To require also an express waiver by the suspect and an end to questioning whenever he demurs must heavily handicap questioning. And to suggest or provide counsel for the suspect simply invites the end of the interrogation.

How much harm this decision will inflict on law enforcement cannot fairly be predicted with accuracy. Evidence on the role of confessions is notoriously incomplete. . . .

We do know that some crimes cannot be solved without confessions, that ample expert testimony attests to their importance in crime control, and that the court is taking a real risk with society's welfare in imposing its new regime on the country. The social costs of crime are too great to call the new rules anything but a hazardous experimentation.

3. A Green Light for Criminals (1966)

The increase of crimes of violence in the large cities had become frightening, particularly stabbings, "muggings" (assaults to commit robbery), rapes, and murders. In Washington, D.C., where citizens were frequently attacked within sight of the Capitol dome, one newspaper responded to the Miranda *decision under the heading "Green Light for Criminals." In what additional respects does this commentary strengthen the view of the Court's minority as to the visionary character of the majority decision?*

---

[3]© **1966, The Washington Post. Reprinted with permission.**

The Supreme Court's 5 to 4 ruling on police questioning of criminal suspects will be received with rejoicing by every thug in the land. For without a doubt it is a ruling which will grievously handicap the police and make it much easier for a criminal to beat the rap.

The murky torrent of words embodied in Chief Justice Warren's opinion tends to obscure some aspects of the ruling. But the salient points come through clearly enough.

Henceforth, once the police have taken a suspect into custody, they cannot lawfully ask him any questions unless four warnings have been given. (1) The suspect must be plainly advised that he need not make any statement. (2) He must be informed that anything he says may be used against him in a trial. (3) He must be told that he has a right to have an attorney *present* throughout the questioning. (4) If the suspect is an indigent, he must be assured that he will be furnished a lawyer free of charge. Unless all of these conditions are met no confession or other evidence obtained during an interrogation can be used against the suspect.

The Chief Justice makes the remarkable observation that "our decision is not intended to hamper the traditional function of police officers in investigating crime." Intent aside, he must know that this is in fact a decision which will not only hamper but will largely destroy the traditional police function, at least as far as interrogation is concerned.

Why? Because any lawyer called in to sit beside a guilty prisoner is going to tell him to say nothing to the police. He would be derelict in his duty were he to do otherwise. In the face of this, the Chief Justice blandly suggests that there is nothing in the decision which requires "that police stop a person who enters a police station and states that he wishes to confess to a crime." How true! And how often in the proverbial blue moon will this happen?

The deplorable fact is that this ruling, as far as the public is concerned, will most directly affect the vicious types of crime—the murders, the yokings,* the robberies and the rapes where it often is impossible to assemble enough evidence, without a confession, to obtain convictions. All the criminal need do is to demand a lawyer—and then the police, under the practical effect of this decision, will be unable to ask him question No. 1. What was it the President said about ridding our cities of crime so law-abiding citizens will be safe in their homes, on the streets and in their places of business?

The dissents by Justices Harlan, Clark, Stewart and White were sharply-worded. It is necessary to read them to understand the frailty of the grounds upon which the majority rests this unprecedented ruling.

[An extreme case of the application of the Miranda *ruling came in February 1967. In Brooklyn a factory worker had confessed to stabbing to death his common-law wife and her five children. But he had not been advised of his "right to silence," and, in the absence of concrete evidence, he was turned loose. The presiding judge remarked, "Even an animal such as this one . . . must be protected with all legal safeguards. It is repulsive to let a thing like this out on the streets." (*Time, *March 3, 1967, p. 49.)]*

---

*Beating or humiliating another person into submission.

4. President Nixon Outlines His Judicial Philosophy (1971)

Before his election, Nixon made clear his determination to change the complexion of the liberal Warren Court. He clearly wished to reverse some recent landmark decisions. Two of his early appointees, Justices Warren Burger and Harry Blackmun, were distinguished conservatives. Two other nominees, both rejected by the Senate, were of a similar stripe, though conspicuously less able and obviously chosen to discharge a political debt to the South. The next nominees were Lewis F. Powell, Jr., and William H. Rehnquist, both rock-ribbed conservative lawyers with noteworthy intellectual qualifications. In presenting these two nominees, the president set forth at length his judicial philosophy. How did it differ from the values that animated the Warren Court?

These are the criteria I believe should be applied in naming people to the Supreme Court.

First, the Supreme Court is the highest judicial body in this country. Its members, therefore, should, above all, be among the very best lawyers in the Nation. Putting it another way: In the legal profession, the Supreme Court is the fastest track in the Nation, and it is essential that the Justices on that Court be able to keep up with the very able lawyers who will appear before that Court arguing cases. The two individuals I am nominating to the Court meet that standard of excellence to an exceptional degree.

The second consideration is the judicial philosophy of those who are to serve on the Court. Now, I emphasize the word "judicial" because whether an individual is a Democrat or a Republican cannot and should not be a decisive factor in determining whether he should be on the Court.

By "judicial philosophy" I do not mean agreeing with the President on every issue. It would be a total repudiation of our constitutional system if judges on the Supreme Court, or any other Federal court, for that matter, were like puppets on a string pulled by the President who appointed them.

When I appointed Chief Justice Burger, I told him that from the day he was confirmed by the Senate, he could expect that I would never talk to him about a case that was before the Court.

In the case of both Chief Justice Burger and Mr. Justice Blackmun and in the case of the two nominees that I shall be sending to the Senate tomorrow, their sole obligation is to the Constitution and to the American people and not to the President who appointed them to their positions.

As far as judicial philosophy is concerned, it is my belief that it is the duty of a judge to interpret the Constitution and not to place himself above the Constitution or outside the Constitution.

He should not twist or bend the Constitution in order to perpetuate his personal political and social views.

Now, this does not mean that judges who adhere to this philosophy that I have just described will find that they always agree on their interpretation of the Constitution. You seldom find two lawyers who will agree on any close question.

---

[4] *Weekly Compilation of Presidential Documents* 7 (1971): 1431–1432.

We have an excellent example of this in the record of the two judges whose vacancies I now have the duty to fill, Mr. Justice Black, Mr. Justice Harlan. When they retired from the Court a month ago, most observers labeled Mr. Justice Black as a liberal and Mr. Justice Harlan as a conservative. There was a measure of truth in this, but I would say that both were constitutionalists.

It is true, they disagreed sharply in many cases, but as I learned, not only from reading their opinions over the years, but from appearing twice before them and arguing a case before the Supreme Court, both were great judges with the brilliant ability to ask questions that went to the heart of a matter and then to make a decision based on their honest interpretation of the Constitution.

In the debate over the confirmation of the two individuals I have selected, I would imagine that it may be charged that they are conservatives. This is true, but only in a judicial, not in a political sense.

You will recall, I am sure, that during my campaign for the Presidency, I pledged to nominate to the Supreme Court individuals who shared my judicial philosophy, which is basically a conservative philosophy.

Now, let me give you an example of what that philosophy means.

Twenty-one months ago, Mr. Walter Lippmann wrote, ". . . the balance of power within our society has turned dangerously against the peace forces—against governors and mayors and legislatures, against the police and the courts." I share this view.

Over the past few years, many cases have come before the court involving that delicate balance between the rights of society and the rights of defendants accused of crimes against society. And honest and dedicated constitutional lawyers have disagreed as to where and how to maintain that balance.

As a judical conservative, I believe some court decisions have gone too far in the past in weakening the peace forces as against the criminal forces in our society. In maintaining, as it must be maintained, the delicate balance between the rights of society and defendants accused of crimes, I believe the peace forces must not be denied the legal tools they need to protect the innocent from criminal elements. And I believe we can strengthen the hand of the peace forces without compromising our precious principle that the rights of individuals accused of crimes must always be protected.

It is with these criteria in mind that I have selected the two men whose names I will send to the Senate tomorrow.

D. The Move to Impeach Nixon

1. The First Article of Impeachment (1974)

During the Nixon-McGovern campaign of 1972, a bungled burglary had occurred in the Democratic Watergate headquarters in Washington, D.C. After Nixon's reelection, evidence turned up that the culprits, with close White House connections, had been working for the Republican Committee for the Reelection of the President (which came to be known as CREEP). A Senate investigating committee uncovered

---

[1]*House of Representatives Report No. 93–1305* (House Calendar No. 426), 93d Cong., 2d sess., pp. 1–2.

proof that the president had secretly recorded relevant White House conversations on tape. After much foot-dragging and legal obstruction by Nixon, enough of the damning tapes were surrendered to prove beyond doubt that he had known of the attempted cover-up from an early date and had actively participated in it. After extensive hearings, the House Judiciary Committee voted three articles of impeachment, of which the following, relating to the crime of obstructing justice, was the first. This article was approved on July 27, 1974, by a committee vote of twenty-seven to eleven, with all the Democrats being joined by six Republicans. Assuming that these charges were true, did they add up to "high crimes and misdemeanors" as specified by the Constitution?

Article I

In his conduct of the office of President of the United States, Richard M. Nixon, in violation of his constitutional oath faithfully to execute the office of President of the United States and, to the best of his ability, preserve, protect, and defend the Constitution of the United States, and in violation of his constitutional duty to take care that the laws be faithfully executed, has prevented, obstructed, and impeded the administration of justice, in that:

On June 17, 1972, and prior thereto, agents of the Committee for the Re-election of the President committed unlawful entry of the headquarters of the Democratic National Committee in Washington, District of Columbia, for the purpose of securing political intelligence. Subsequent thereto, Richard M. Nixon, using the powers of his high office, engaged personally and through his subordinates and agents, in a course of conduct or plan designed to delay, impede, and obstruct the investigation of such unlawful entry; to cover up, conceal and protect those responsible; and to conceal the existence and scope of other unlawful covert activities.

The means used to implement this course of conduct or plan included one or more of the following:

1. making or causing to be made false or misleading statements to lawfully authorized investigative officers and employees of the United States;

2. withholding relevant and material evidence or information from lawfully authorized investigative officers and employees of the United States;

3. approving, condoning, acquiescing in, and counseling witnesses with respect to the giving of false or misleading statements to lawfully authorized investigative officers and employees of the United States and false or misleading testimony in duly instituted judicial and congressional proceedings;

4. interfering or endeavoring to interfere with the conduct of investigations by the Department of Justice of the United States, the Federal Bureau of Investigation, the Office of Watergate Special Prosecution Force, and Congressional Committees;

5. approving, condoning, and acquiescing in, the surreptitious payment of substantial sums of money for the purpose of obtaining the silence or influencing the testimony of witnesses, potential witnesses or individuals who participated in such unlawful entry and other illegal activities;

6. endeavoring to misuse the Central Intelligence Agency, an agency of the United States;

7. disseminating information received from officers of the Department of Justice of the United States to subjects of investigations conducted by lawfully authorized investigative

officers and employees of the United States, for the purpose of aiding and assisting such subjects in their attempts to avoid criminal liability;

8. making false or misleading public statements for the purpose of deceiving the people of the United States into believing that a thorough and complete investigation had been conducted with respect to allegations of misconduct on the part of personnel of the executive branch of the United States and personnel of the Committee for the Re-election of the President, and that there was no involvement of such personnel in such misconduct; or

9. endeavoring to cause prospective defendants, and individuals duly tried and convicted, to expect favored treatment and consideration in return for their silence or false testimony, or rewarding individuals for their silence or false testimony.

In all of this, Richard M. Nixon has acted in a manner contrary to his trust as President and subversive of constitutional government, to the great prejudice of the cause of law and justice and to the manifest injury of the people of the United States.

Wherefore Richard M. Nixon, by such conduct, warrants impeachment and trial, and removal from office.

2. Impeachment as a Partisan Issue (1974)

The second and third articles of impeachment approved by the House Judiciary Committee related to repeated abuses of presidential power and to prolonged contempt of Congress. The second article passed the committee by a tally of 28 to 10; all the Democrats, as well as 7 Republicans, voted yea. The third article charged Nixon with contempt of Congress for refusing to comply with eight subpoenas for the White House tapes. It was regarded as the least damaging of the three, for it failed to gain broad partisan backing when it squeezed through by a narrow vote of 21 to 17. Even after his complete disgrace, Nixon had millions of supporters who believed that his removal was unjustified. The following is a part of the minority report of the House Committee, signed by 10 of its 17 Republican members, and dated August 20, 1974, eleven days after Nixon's formal resignation. What light does it throw on the alleged partisanship of the impeachment move?

Richard Nixon served his country in elective office for the better part of three decades and, in the main, he served it well. Each of the undersigned voted for him, worked for and with him in election campaigns, and supported the major portion of his legislative program during his tenure as President. Even at the risk of seeming paradoxical, since we were prepared to vote for his impeachment on proposed Article I had he not resigned his office, we hope that in the fullness of time it is his accomplishments—and they were many and significant—rather than the conduct to which this Report is addressed for which Richard Nixon is primarily remembered in history.

---

[2]*House of Representatives Report No. 93–1305* (House Calendar No. 426), 93d Congress, 2d sess., p. 361.

We know that it has been said, and perhaps some will continue to say, that Richard Nixon was "hounded from office" by his political opponents and media critics. We feel constrained to point out, however, that it was Richard Nixon who impeded the FBI's investigation of the Watergate affair by wrongfully attempting to implicate the Central Intelligence Agency; it was Richard Nixon, who created and preserved the evidence of that transgression and who, *knowing that it had been subpoenaed by this Committee and the Special Prosecutor,* concealed its terrible import, even from his own counsel, until he could do so no longer. And it was a unanimous Supreme Court of the United States which, in an opinion authored by the Chief Justice whom he appointed, ordered Richard Nixon to surrender that evidence to the Special Prosecutor, to further the ends of justice. [Emphasis in original.]

The tragedy that finally engulfed Richard Nixon had many facets. One was the very self-inflicted nature of the harm. It is striking that such an able, experienced and perceptive man, whose ability to grasp the global implications of events little noticed by others may well have been unsurpassed by any of his predecessors, should fail to comprehend the damage that accrued daily to himself, his Administration, and to the Nation, as day after day, month after month, he imprisoned the truth about his role in the Watergate cover-up so long and so tightly within the solitude of his Oval Office that it could not be unleashed without destroying his Presidency.

3. Nixon Incriminates Himself (1972)

By August 5, 1974, much evidence of presidential misconduct and wrongdoing had been uncovered, but where was the high crime? Where was the "smoking pistol"? It finally surfaced on that day, when Nixon, forced by a unanimous decision of the Supreme Court to yield crucial tape recordings, revealed a White House conversation of June 23, 1972. In it the president was heard instructing his chief aide, H. R. Haldeman, to use the Central Intelligence Agency to quash an investigation by the Federal Bureau of Investigation. Obstruction of justice of this type was a clear-cut crime. Support for Nixon in Congress collapsed, and he was faced with the dilemma of resigning or being thrown out of office without retirement benefits amounting to more than $150,000 a year. He wisely chose to announce his resignation on August 8. How damning is the evidence in the following transcript of the conversation of June 23, 1972?

Transcript of a Recording of a Meeting Between the President and H. R. Haldeman, the Oval Office, June 23, 1972, from 10:04 to 11:39 A.M.

Haldeman. Okay—that's fine. Now, on the investigation, you know, the Democratic break-in thing, we're back to the—in the, the problem area because the FBI is not under control, because [acting director of the FBI, Patrick] Gray doesn't exactly know how to control them, and they have, their investigation is now leading into some productive areas, because they've been able to trace the money,

---

[3]*Statement of Information,* Appendix 3, *Hearings before the Committee on the Judiciary,* House of Representatives, 93d Cong., 2d sess., pursuant to H.R. 803, p. 39.

not through the money itself, but through the bank, you know, sources—the banker himself. And, and it goes in some directions we don't want it to go. Ah, also there have been some things, like an informant came in off the street to the FBI in Miami, who was a photographer or has a friend who is a photographer who developed some films through this guy, Barker, and the films had pictures of Democratic National Committee letter head documents and things. So I guess, so it's things like that are gonna, that are filtering in. [U.S. Attorney General, John] Mitchell came up with yesterday, and [presidential counselor] John Dean analyzed very carefully last night and concludes, concurs now with Mitchell's recommendation that the only way to solve this, and we're set up beautifully to do it, ah, in that and that . . . the only network that paid any attention to it last night was NBC . . . they did a massive story on the Cuban . . .

President. That's right.

Haldeman. . . . thing.

President. Right.

Haldeman. That the way to handle this is for us to have [deputy director of the CIA, Vernon] Walters call Pat Gray and just say, "Stay the hell out of this . . . this is ah, business here we don't want you to go any further on it." That's not an unusual development, . . .

President. Um huh.

Haldeman. . . . and, uh, that would take care of it.

President. What about Pat Gray, ah, you mean he doesn't want to?

Haldeman. Pat does want to. He doesn't know how to, and he doesn't have, he doesn't have any basis for doing it. Given this, he will then have the basis. He'll call [assistant director of the FBI] Mark Felt in, and the two of them . . . and Mark Felt wants to cooperate because . . .

President. Yeah.

Haldeman. . . . he's ambitious . . .

President. Yeah.

Haldeman. Ah, he'll call him in and say, "We've got the signal from across the river to, to put the hold on this." And that will fit rather well because the FBI agents who are working the case, at this point, feel that's what it is. This is CIA.

President. But they've traced the money to 'em.

Haldeman. Well they have, they've traced to a name, but they haven't gotten to the guy yet.

President. Would it be somebody here?

Haldeman. [GOP fundraiser] Ken Dahlberg.

President. Who the hell is Ken Dahlberg?

Haldeman. He's ah, he gave $25,000 in Minnesota and ah, the check went directly in to this, to this guy [Watergate burglar, Bernard L.] Barker.

President. Maybe he's a . . . bum. . . . He didn't get this from the committee though, from [finance chairman for the Committee for the Re-election of the President, Maurice] Stans.

Haldeman. Yeah. It is. It's directly traceable and there's some more through some Texas people in—that went to the Mexican bank which they can also trace to the Mexican bank . . . they'll get their names today. And [*pause*].

President. Well, I mean, ah, there's no way . . . I'm just thinking if they don't cooperate, what do they say? They they, they were approached by the Cubans. That's what Dahlberg has to say, the Texans too. Is that the idea?

Haldeman. Well, if they will. But then we're relying on more and more people all the time. That's the problem. And ah, they'll stop if we could, if we take this other step.

President. All right. Fine.

Haldeman. And, and they seem to feel the thing to do is get them to stop?

President. Right, fine.

Haldeman. They say the only way to do that is from White House instructions. And it's got to be to [CIA director, Richard] Helms and, ah, what's his name . . . ? Walters.

President. Walters.

Haldeman. And the proposal would be that Ehrlichman [*coughs*] and I call them in . . .

President. All right, fine.

Haldeman. . . . and say, ah . . .

President. How do you call him in, I mean you just, well, we protected Helms from one hell of a lot of things.

Haldeman. That's what Ehrlichman says.

President. Of course, this is a, this is a [Watergate burglar and former CIA employee, E. Howard] Hunt, you will—that will uncover a lot of things. You open that scab there's a hell of a lot of things and that we just feel that it would be very detrimental to have this thing go any further. This involves these Cubans, Hunt, and a lot of hanky-panky that we have nothing to do with ourselves. Well what the hell, did [U.S. Attorney General John] Mitchell know about this thing to any much of a degree?

Haldeman. I think so. I don't think he knew the details, but I think he knew.

President. He didn't know how it was going to be handled though, with Dahlberg and the Texans and so forth? Well who was the asshole that did? [*unintelligible*] Is it [legal counsel for the Committee for the Re-election of the President, G. Gordon] Liddy? Is that the fellow? He must be a little nuts.

Haldeman. He is.

President. I mean he just isn't well screwed on is he? Isn't that the problem?

Haldeman. No, but he was under pressure, apparently, to get more information, and as he got more pressure, he pushed the people harder to move harder on . . .

President. Pressure from Mitchell?

Haldeman. Apparently.

President. Oh, Mitchell, Mitchell was at the point that you made on this, that exactly what I need from you is on the—

Haldeman. Gemstone, yeah.

President. All right, fine, I understand it all. We won't second-guess Mitchell and the rest. Thank God it wasn't [presidential aide, Charles] Colson.

Haldeman. The FBI interviewed Colson yesterday. They determined that would be a good thing to do.

President. Um hum.

Haldeman. Ah, to have him take a . . .

President. Uh hum.

Haldeman. An interrogation, which he did, and that, the FBI guys working the case had concluded that there were one or two possibilities, one, that this was a White House, they don't think that there is anything at the Election Committee, they think it was either a White House operation and they had some obscure reasons for it, nonpolitical. . . .

President. Uh huh.

Haldeman. . . . or it was a . . .

President. Cuban thing—

Haldeman. Cubans and the CIA. And after their interrogation of, of . . .

President. . . . Colson.

Haldeman. Colson, yesterday, they concluded it was not the White House, but are now convinced it is a CIA thing, so the CIA turnoff would . . .

President. Well, not sure of their analysis, I'm not going to get that involved. I'm [*unintelligible*].

Haldeman. No, sir. We don't want you to.

President. You call them in. . . . Good. Good deal. Play it tough. That's the way they play it and that's the way we are going to play it.

Haldeman. O.K. We'll do it.

President. Yeah, when I saw that news summary item, I of course knew it was a bunch of crap, but I thought, ah, well it's good to have them off on this wild hair thing because when they start bugging us, which they have, we'll know our little boys will not know how to handle it. I hope they will though. You never know. Maybe, you think about it. Good! . . . When you get in these people . . . when you get these people in, say: "Look, the problem is that this will open the whole, the whole Bay of Pigs thing, and the President just feels that" ah, without going into the details . . . don't, don't lie to them to the extent to say there is no involvement, but just say this is sort of a comedy of errors, bizarre, without getting into it, "the President believes that it is going to open the whole Bay of Pigs thing up again. And, ah because these people are plugging for, for keeps and that they should call the FBI in and say that we wish for the country, don't go any further into this case," period!

Haldeman. O.K.

President. That's the way to put it, do it straight [*unintelligible*].

Haldeman. Get more done for our cause by the opposition than by us at this point.

President. You think so?

Haldeman. I think so, yeah.

Transcript of a Recording of a Meeting Between the President and H. R. Haldeman, the Oval Office, June 23, 1972, from 1:04 to 1:13 P.M.

[*Background noise, sound of writing and some unintelligible conversation*]

Haldeman. [*On the phone*] [*Unintelligible*] Where are they? Okay. I'll be up in just a minute.

[*40-second pause, with sounds of writing*]

Haldeman. I see a time way back [*unintelligible*] might find out about that report before we do anything.

President. [Unintelligible]

[*35-second pause*]

President. Okay [*unintelligible*] and, ah, just, just postpone the [*unintelligible, with noises*] hearings [*15-second unintelligible, with noises*] and all that garbage. Just say that I have to take a look at the primaries [*unintelligible*] recover [*unintelligible*] I just don't [*unintelligible*] very bad, to have this fellow Hunt, ah, you know, ah, it's, he, he knows too damn much and he was involved, we happen to know that. And that it gets out that the whole, this is all involved in the Cuban thing, that it's a fiasco, and it's going to make the FB, ah CIA look bad, it's going to make Hunt look bad, and it's likely to blow the whole, uh, Bay of Pigs thing which we think would be very unfortunate for CIA and for the country at this time, and for American foreign policy, and he just better tough it and lay it on them. Isn't that what you . . .

Haldeman. Yeah, that's, that's the basis we'll do it on and just leave it at that.

President. I don't want them to get any ideas we're doing it because our concern is political.

Haldeman. Right.

President. And at the same time, I wouldn't tell them it is not political . . .

Haldeman. Right.

President. I would just say "Look, it's because of the Hunt involvement," just say [*unintelligible, with noise*] sort of thing, the whole cover is, uh, basically this [*unintelligible*].

Haldeman. [*Unintelligible*] Well they've got some pretty good ideas on this need thing.

President. George Shultz did a good paper on that, I read it . . .

[*Unintelligible voices heard leaving the room*]

4. A Critical Canadian Viewpoint (1974)

From the objective vantage point of Canada, the Toronto Star *newspaper pronounced this judgment on Nixon's resignation. It is unduly harsh?*

Richard Nixon leaves the presidency the way he operated it—dishonestly.

The man who approved the Watergate cover-up six days after the break-in continued to hide his guilt right to the end. In his resignation speech last night, there was no admission of wrong-doing, no acceptance of personal responsibility for the scandal that ripped apart U.S. society, paralyzed its government and, for a time, threatened to destroy public confidence in the democratic system.

It is happily true that ultimately the process that forced Nixon from office was a triumph of the system he tried to subvert. A free press in its role as watchdog uncovered the scandal and an independent judiciary affirmed the principle that under the rule of law, no men are above the law. The checks and balances needed to make democracy work came through when it counted.

All this is the positive side of Watergate, and its significance is great. An open

---

[4]The *Toronto Star,* August 9, 1974. Reprinted with permission of the *Toronto Star.*

society has openly met its problems and emerged healthier and stronger. The American system has shown that it could meet stern tests. The confidence of ordinary people in the institutions that govern them has been restored, and they can make a fresh start with a fresh president. The western world, which depends on U.S. leadership, is grateful.

But it wasn't the rule of law and his own personal culpability that Nixon cited as his reason for leaving office. No one would know from his speech last night that he had done anything wrong. Oh, some errors in judgment, sure. But nothing serious. The reason he gave for leaving rested on the narrow base that he had lost the political support in Congress that he needed both to stay in office and to fight the attempts to oust him.

If 20 or so senators hadn't changed their minds, he'd still be in there fighting.

That in effect is what he was saying.

This manner of leaving does not satisfy the rule of law, for if it is true that no man is above the law, it must also be true that all men are equal before it.

So what is Richard Nixon's punishment for breaking the law? The $60,000 pension that he gets because he resigned and which he would have lost if he had been ousted by impeachment? Where is the equality in a jail sentence for John Dean, the former presidential counsel whose Watergate testimony first accused Nixon, while the man who gave him his orders goes free? Where is equality in proceeding with cover-up charges against former presidential chief-of-staff H. R. Haldeman with the prime evidence a tape on which Nixon is approving the cover-up?

If Nixon had openly admitted his guilt and responsibility, then it would at least be clear that his resignation was his punishment. This was the formula followed by Spiro Agnew when he resigned as vice-president. He pleaded guilty but avoided jail. One might then argue whether the punishment fitted the crime, but at least the record would be clear about guilt.

At present there is no such clear-cut record. Nixon is out, but he has admitted nothing. Congress, by halting the impeachment process, has not declared its judgment of his actions.

This judgment may yet come. Leon Jaworski, the special Watergate prosecutor, has made it clear he is prevented by no agreement or understanding from bringing charges against Nixon. State courts or even private citizens could bring suits against him. More taped conversations are to be made public and some of the material may have an impact on the public's judgment about whether a former president should be pursued like a common criminal.

But don't count on it. The Americans have been sweating through Watergate for a long time and many are tired of it. There is a strong feeling that a man shouldn't be kicked when he is down. Many undoubtedly will argue that every effort should go towards a fresh start rather than try further to cleanse the past.

If this is the course then America will be whole again, but the stain will remain. Nixon's manipulations will have succeeded. The phony transcripts. The lies. The obstruction. They did not save his office but they saved him from the law.

He left politics as he arrived. Tricky Dick.

[Despite the three long categories of accusations voted by the House Judiciary Committee, Nixon was not impeached by the full House, tried by the Senate, or even

convicted in the courts of any crime. The closest he came to conviction was his un-contested disbarment as a lawyer by the appellate division of the state supreme court of New York. The decision (July 8, 1976), by a four-to-one vote, was the most severe punishment that this body could impose. As for obstruction of justice, the court found Nixon guilty on five specifications, including improper interference with an FBI investigation of the Watergate break-in; improper authorization of bribes to si-lence conspirators; and improper encouragement of others to commit perjury by concealing evidence of wrongdoing.]

5. Nixon Accepts a Presidential Pardon (1974)

To complicate the Watergate uproar, Vice-President Agnew, facing unrelated crimi-nal charges, had avoided jail by resigning in August 1973. Nixon, pursuant to the Twenty-fifth Amendment to the Constitution, had chosen as his successor Gerald R. Ford, the House minority leader. For about a month the nonelected president en-joyed a "honeymoon," which he abruptly ended by granting Nixon "a full, free, and absolute pardon" for "all offenses against the United States which he, Richard Nixon, has committed or may have committed or taken part in" during his presidency. Nixon promptly accepted the pardon but was careful not to confess that he had com-mitted any crimes. Mistakes, indecision, poor judgment, yes—but crimes, no. Yet, as President Ford agreed, testifying before a House Judiciary Committee, acceptance of the pardon is "tantamount to an admission of guilt." Moreover, many of Nixon's ad-mirers felt that he had humbled himself enough by admitting remorse for acts he had committed in the line of duty for what he regarded to be the good of the country. Is Nixon's self-justification convincing?

I have been informed that President Ford has granted me a full and absolute pardon for any charges which might be brought against me for actions taken during the time I was President of the United States.

In accepting this pardon, I hope that his compassionate act will contribute to lifting the burden of Watergate from our country.

Here in California, my perspective on Watergate is quite different than it was while I was embattled in the midst of the controversy, and while I was still subject to the unrelenting daily demands of the presidency itself.

Looking back on what is still in my mind a complex and confusing maze of events, decisions, pressures and personalities, one thing I can see clearly now is that I was wrong in not acting more decisively and more forthrightly in dealing with Wa-tergate, particularly when it reached the stage of judicial proceedings and grew from a political scandal into a national tragedy.

No words can describe the depths of my regret and pain at the anguish my mis-takes over Watergate have caused the nation and the presidency—a nation I so deeply love and an institution I so greatly respect.

I know many fair-minded people believe that my motivations and action in the Watergate affair were intentionally self-serving and illegal. I now understand how

---

[5]*San Francisco Chronicle*, September 9, 1974.

my own mistakes and misjudgments have contributed to that belief and seemed to support it. This burden is the heaviest one of all to bear.

That the way I tried to deal with Watergate was the wrong way is a burden I shall bear for every day of the life that is left to me.

E. The Revitalization of the Feminist Movement

1. The National Organization for Women Proclaims the Rebirth of Feminism (1966)

The publication of Betty Friedan's The Feminine Mystique *in 1963 sparked a new "second-wave" feminist revival, the first concerted effort to advance women's standing in American society since the Nineteenth Amendment had crowned the women's suffrage campaign with success in 1920. One of the main vehicles of the new feminist movement was the National Organization for Women, founded in 1966. What are the guiding assumptions of its original statement of purpose? What tactics and strategies does it advocate?*

We, men and women who hereby constitute ourselves as the National Organization for Women [NOW], believe that the time has come for a new movement toward true equality for all women in America, and toward a fully equal partnership of the sexes, as part of the world-wide revolution of human rights now taking place within and beyond our national borders.

The purpose of NOW is to take action to bring women into full participation in the mainstream of American society now, exercising all the privileges and responsibilities thereof in truly equal partnership with men.

We believe the time has come to move beyond the abstract argument, discussion and symposia over the status and special nature of women which has raged in America in recent years; the time has come to confront, with concrete action, the conditions that now prevent women from enjoying the equality of opportunity and freedom of choice which is their right as individual Americans, and as human beings.

NOW is dedicated to the proposition that women first and foremost are human beings, who, like all other people in our society, must have the chance to develop their fullest human potential. We believe that women can achieve such equality only by accepting to the full the challenges and responsibilities they share with all other people in our society, as part of the decision-making mainstream of American political, economic and social life.

We organize to initiate or support action, nationally or in any part of this nation, by individuals or organizations, to break through the silken curtain of prejudice and discrimination against women in government, industry, the professions, the churches, the political parties, the judiciary, the labor unions, in education, science, medicine, law, religion and every other field of importance in American society. . . .

There is no civil rights movement to speak for women, as there has been for

[1]Reprinted by permission of The National Organization for Women. This is a historical document, and it does not reflect the current language or priorities of the organization.

Negroes and other victims of discrimination. The National Organization for Women must therefore begin to speak.

WE BELIEVE that the power of American law, and the protection guaranteed by the U.S. Constitution to the civil rights of all individuals, must be effectively applied and enforced to isolate and remove patterns of sex discrimination, to ensure equality of opportunity in employment and education, and equality of civil and political rights and responsibilities on behalf of women, as well as for Negroes and other deprived groups.

We realize that women's problems are linked to many broader questions of social justice; their solution will require concerted action by many groups. Therefore, convinced that human rights for all are indivisible, we expect to give active support to the common cause of equal rights for all those who suffer discrimination and deprivation, and we call upon other organizations committed to such goals to support our efforts toward equality for women.

WE DO NOT ACCEPT the token appointment of a few women to high-level positions in government and industry as a substitute for a serious continuing effort to recruit and advance women according to their individual abilities. To this end, we urge American government and industry to mobilize the same resources of ingenuity and command with which they have solved problems of far greater difficulty than those now impeding the progress of women.

WE BELIEVE that this nation has a capacity at least as great as other nations, to innovate new social institutions which will enable women to enjoy true equality of opportunity and responsibility in society, without conflict with their responsibilities as mothers and homemakers. In such innovations, America does not lead the Western world, but lags by decades behind many European countries. We do not accept the traditional assumption that a woman has to choose between marriage and motherhood, on the one hand, and serious participation in industry or the professions on the other. We question the present expectation that all normal women will retire from job or profession for ten or fifteen years, to devote their full time to raising children, only to reenter the job market at a relatively minor level. This in itself is a deterrent to the aspirations of women, to their acceptance into management or professional training courses, and to the very possibility of equality of opportunity or real choice, for all but a few women. Above all, we reject the assumption that these problems are the unique responsibility of each individual woman, rather than a basic social dilemma which society must solve. True equality of opportunity and freedom of choice for women requires such practical and possible innovations as a nationwide network of child-care centers, which will make it unnecessary for women to retire completely from society until their children are grown, and national programs to provide retraining for women who have chosen to care for their own children full time.

WE BELIEVE that it is as essential for every girl to be educated to her full potential of human ability as it is for every boy—with the knowledge that such education is the key to effective participation in today's economy and that, for a girl as for a boy, education can only be serious where there is expectation that it will be used in society. We believe that American educators are capable of devising means of imparting such expectations to girl students. Moreover, we consider the decline in the proportion of women receiving higher and professional education to be evidence of discrimination. This discrimination may take the form of quotas against the admission of women to colleges and professional schools; lack of encouragement by parents, counselors and educators; denial of loans or fellowships; or the traditional or arbitrary procedures in graduate and professional training geared in terms of men, which inadvertently discriminate against women. We believe that the same serious attention must be given to high school dropouts who are girls as to boys.

WE REJECT the current assumptions that a man must carry the sole burden of supporting himself, his wife, and family, and that a woman is automatically entitled to lifelong support by a man upon her marriage, or that marriage, home and family are primarily woman's world and responsibility—hers, to dominate, his to support. We believe that a true partnership between the sexes demands a different concept of marriage, an equitable sharing of the responsibilities of home and children and of the economic burdens of their support. We believe that proper recognition should be given to the economic and social value of homemaking and child care. To these ends, we will seek to open a reexamination of laws and mores governing marriage and divorce, for we believe that the current state of "half-equality" between the sexes discriminates against both men and women, and is the cause of much unnecessary hostility between the sexes.

WE BELIEVE that women must now exercise their political rights and responsibilities as American citizens. They must refuse to be segregated on the basis of sex into separate-and-not-equal ladies' auxiliaries in the political parties, and they must demand representation according to their numbers in the regularly constituted party committees—at local, state, and national levels—and in the informal power structure, participating fully in the selection of candidates and political decision-making, and running for office themselves.

IN THE INTERESTS OF THE HUMAN DIGNITY OF WOMEN, we will protest and endeavor to change the false image of women now prevalent in the mass media, and in the texts, ceremonies, laws, and practices of our major social institutions. Such images perpetuate contempt for women by society and by women for themselves. We are similarly opposed to all policies and practices—in church, state, college, factory, or office—which, in the guise of protectiveness, not only deny opportunities but also foster in women self-denigration, dependence, and evasion of responsibility, undermine their confidence in their own abilities and foster contempt for women.

NOW WILL HOLD ITSELF INDEPENDENT OF ANY POLITICAL PARTY in order to mobilize the political power of all women and men intent on our goals. We will strive to ensure that no party, candidate, President, senator, governor, congressman, or any public official who betrays or ignores the principle of full equality between the sexes is elected or appointed to office. If it is necessary to mobilize the votes of men and women who believe in our cause, in order to win for women the final right to be fully free and equal human beings, we so commit ourselves.

WE BELIEVE THAT women will do most to create a new image of women by *acting* now, and by speaking out in behalf of their own equality, freedom, and human dignity—not in pleas for special privilege, nor in enmity toward men, who are also victims of the current half-equality between the sexes—but in an active, self-respecting partnership with men. By so doing, women will develop confidence in their own ability to determine actively, in partnership with men, the conditions of their life, their choices, their future and their society.

2. The Case for the Equal Rights Amendment (1970)

The Equal Rights Amendment, or ERA, declared simply, "Equality of Rights under the law shall not be denied or abridged by the United States or by any State on account of sex." First put forth in the 1920s, the proposed ERA was ratified by a two-thirds vote of the House of Representatives in 1970 and by the same majority of the Senate in 1972. But the ERA eventually fell short of ratification by the requisite three-fourths of all the states, and it quietly disappeared from consideration in the 1980s. For a time, the ERA, along with abortion rights, was a defining issue for many feminists. In the pro-ERA statement to Congress reprinted here, what arguments are brought to bear in favor of ERA? How persuasive are they?

The proposed equal rights amendment to the U.S. Constitution would provide that "Equality of rights under the law shall not be denied or abridged by the United States or by any State on account of sex," and would authorize the Congress and the States to enforce the amendment by appropriate legislation. . . .

The purpose of the proposed amendment would be to provide constitutional protection against laws and official practices that treat men and women differently. At the present time, the extent to which women may invoke the protection of the Constitution against laws which discriminate on the basis of sex is unclear. The equal rights amendment would insure equal rights under the law and official practices without differentiation based on sex. . . .

Since the proposed equal rights amendment has failed to pass Congress for the past forty-seven years, it may appear to be a loser, although admittedly it took women more than fifty years to secure the adoption of the 19th amendment. However, a revival of the feminist movement has occurred during the past four years and it is greatly increasing in momentum, especially among younger women. Thus the demand for equal rights and support for the amendment is becoming more widespread, with a corresponding increase in likelihood of early adoption of the amendment. . . .

Numerous distinctions based on sex still exist in the law. For example:

1. State laws placing special restrictions on women with respect to hours of work and weightlifting on the job;

2. State laws prohibiting women from working in certain occupations;

3. Laws and practices operating to exclude women from State colleges and universities (including higher standards required for women applicants to institutions of higher learning and in the administration of scholarship programs);

4. Discrimination in employment by State and local governments;

5. Dual pay schedules for men and women public school teachers;

6. State laws providing for alimony to be awarded, under certain circumstances, to ex-wives but not to ex-husbands;

7. State laws placing special restrictions on the legal capacity of married women or on their right to establish a legal domicile;

8. State laws that require married women but not married men to go through a formal procedure and obtain court approval before they may engage in an independent business;

---

[2]Citizen's Advisory Council on the Status of Women, "Memorandum on the Proposed Equal Rights Amendment, March 26, 1970," *Congressional Record,* 91st Cong., 2d sess., pp. 9684–9688.

9. Social Security and other social benefits legislation which give greater benefits to one sex than to the other;

10. Discriminatory preferences, based on sex, in child custody cases;

11. State laws providing that the father is the natural guardian of the minor children;

12. Different ages for males and females in (a) child labor laws, (b) age for marriage, (c) cutoff of the right to parental support, and (d) juvenile court jurisdiction;

13. Exclusion of women from the requirements of the Military Selective Service Act of 1967;

14. Special sex-based exemptions for women in selection of State juries;

15. Heavier criminal penalties for female offenders than for male offenders committing the same crime.

Although it is possible that these and other discriminations might eventually be corrected by legislation, legislative remedies are *not* adequate substitutes for fundamental constitutional protection against discrimination. Any class of persons (i.e., women) which cannot successfully invoke the protection of the Constitution against discriminatory treatment is by definition comprised of "second class citizens" and is inferior in the eyes of law. . . .

Following is a five-point analysis of the impact the equal rights amendment will have on the various types of Federal and State laws which distinguish on the basis of sex:

1. *Strike the Words of Sex Identification and Apply the Law to Both Sexes.* Where the law confers a benefit, privilege or obligation of citizenship, such would be extended to the other sex, i.e., the effect of the amendment would be to strike the words of sex identification. Thus, such laws would not be rendered unconstitutional but would be extended to apply to both sexes by operation of the amendment, in the same way that laws pertaining to voting were extended to Negroes and women under the 15th and 19th amendments. . . .

Any expression of preference in the law for the mother in child custody cases would be extended to both parents (as against claims of third parties). Children are entitled to support from *both* parents under the existing laws of most States. . . .

2. *Laws Rendered Unconstitutional by the Amendment.* Where a law restricts or denies opportunities of women or men, as the case may be, the effect of the equal rights amendment would be to render such laws unconstitutional.

Examples are: the exclusion of women from State universities or other public schools; State laws placing special restrictions on the hours of work for women or the weights women may lift on the job; laws prohibiting women from working in certain occupations, such as bartenders; laws placing special restrictions on the legal capacity of married women, such as making contracts or establishing a legal domicile.

3. *Removal of Age Distinctions Based on Sex.* Some laws which apply to both sexes make an age distinction by sex and thereby discriminate as to persons between the ages specified for males and females. Under the foregoing analysis, the ages specified in such laws would be equalized by the amendment by extending the benefits, privileges or opportunities under the law to both sexes. This would mean that as to some such laws, the *lower* age would apply to both sexes. . . .

4. *Laws Which Could Not Possibly Apply to Both Sexes Because of the Difference in Reproductive Capacity.* Laws which, as a practical matter, can apply to only one

sex no matter how they are phrased, such as laws providing maternity benefits and laws prohibiting rape, would not be affected by the amendment. The extension of these laws to both sexes would be purely academic since such laws would not apply differently if they were phrased in terms of both sexes. In these situations, the terminology of sex identification is of no consequence.

5. *Separation of the Sexes.* Separation of the sexes by law would be forbidden under the amendment except in situations where the separation is shown to be necessary because of an overriding and compelling public interest and does not deny individual rights and liberties.

For example, in our present culture the recognition of the right to privacy would justify separate restroom facilities in public buildings.

As shown above, the amendment would not change the substance of existing laws, except that those which restrict and deny opportunities to women would be rendered unconstitutional under the standard of point two of the analysis. In all other cases, the laws presently on the books would simply be equalized, and this includes the entire body of family law. . . .

3. Phyllis Schlafly Upholds Traditional Gender Roles (1977)

The feminist upsurge of the 1970s provoked a backlash, and not all of it from men. Phyllis Schlafly, a prominent conservative, emerged as one of the most critical opponents of the new feminists' agenda, especially the ERA. In the selection that follows, what are Schlafly's principal objections to the feminist position? How does she conceive of the "Positive Woman"? What differences does she see between men and women?

The first requirement for the acquisition of power by the Positive Woman is to understand the differences between men and women. Your outlook on life, your faith, your behavior, your potential for fulfillment, all are determined by the parameters of your original premise. The Positive Woman starts with the assumption that the world is her oyster. She rejoices in the creative capability within her body and the power potential of her mind and spirit. She understands that men and women are different, and that those very differences provide the key to her success as a person and fulfillment as a woman.

The women's liberationist, on the other hand, is imprisoned by her own negative view of herself and of her place in the world around her. This view of women was most succinctly expressed in an advertisement designed by the principal women's liberationist organization, the National Organization for Women (NOW), and run in many magazines and newspapers and as spot announcements on many television stations. The advertisement showed a darling curlyheaded girl with the caption: "This healthy, normal baby has a handicap. She was born female."

This is the self-articulated dog-in-the-manger, chip-on-the-shoulder, fundamental dogma of the women's liberation movement. Someone—it is not clear who,

---

[3]From *The Power of the Positive Woman* by Phyllis Schlafly. Used by permission of Arlington House, a division of Random House, Inc.

perhaps God, perhaps the "Establishment," perhaps a conspiracy of male chauvinist pigs—dealt women a foul blow by making them female. It becomes necessary, therefore, for women to agitate and demonstrate and hurl demands on society in order to wrest from an oppressive male-dominated social structure the status that has been wrongfully denied to women through the centuries.

By its very nature, therefore, the women's liberation movement precipitates a series of conflict situations—in the legislatures, in the courts, in the schools, in industry—with man targeted as the enemy. Confrontation replaces cooperation as the watchword of all relationships. Women and men become adversaries instead of partners.

The second dogma of the women's liberationists is that, of all the injustices perpetuated upon women through the centuries, the most oppressive is the cruel fact that women have babies and men do not. Within the confines of the women's liberationist ideology, therefore, the abolition of this overriding inequality of women becomes the primary goal. This goal must be achieved at any and all costs—to the woman herself, to the baby, to the family, and to society. Women must be made equal to men in their ability *not* to become pregnant and *not* to be expected to care for babies they may bring into the world.

This is why women's liberationists are compulsively involved in the drive to make abortion and child-care centers for all women, regardless of religion or income, both socially acceptable and government-financed. Former Congresswoman Bella Abzug has defined the goal: "to enforce the constitutional right of females to terminate pregnancies that they do not wish to continue."

If man is targeted as the enemy, and the ultimate goal of women's liberation is independence from men and the avoidance of pregnancy and its consequences, then lesbianism is logically the highest form in the ritual of women's liberation. Many, such as [feminist author] Kate Millett, come to this conclusion, although many others do not.

The Positive Woman will never travel that dead-end road. It is self-evident to the Positive Woman that the female body with its baby-producing organs was not designed by a conspiracy of men but by the Divine Architect of the human race. Those who think it is unfair that women have babies, whereas men cannot, will have to take up their complaint with God because no other power is capable of changing that fundamental fact. . . .

The third basic dogma of the women's liberation movement is that there is no difference between male and female except the sex organs, and that all those physical, cognitive, and emotional differences you *think* are there, are merely the result of centuries of restraints imposed by a male-dominated society and sex-stereotyped schooling. The role imposed on women is, by definition, inferior, according to the women's liberationists.

The Positive Woman knows that, while there are some physical competitions in which women are better (and can command more money) than men, including those that put a premium on grace and beauty, such as figure skating, the superior physical strength of males over females in competitions of strength, speed, and short-term endurance is beyond rational dispute. . . .

Does the physical advantage of men doom women to a life of servility and subservience? The Positive Woman knows that she has a complementary advantage which is at least as great—and, in the hands of a skillful woman, far greater. The Divine Architect who gave men a superior strength to lift weights also gave women a different kind of superior strength.

The women's liberationists and their dupes who try to tell each other that the sexual drive of men and women is really the same, and that it is only societal restraints that inhibit women from an equal desire, and equal enjoyment, and an equal freedom from the consequences, are doomed to frustration forever. It just isn't so, and pretending cannot make it so. The differences are not a woman's weakness but her strength. . . .

The new generation can brag all it wants about the new liberation of the new morality, but it is still the woman who is hurt the most. The new morality isn't just a "fad"—it is a cheat and a thief. It robs the woman of her virtue, her youth, her beauty, and her love—for nothing, just nothing. It has produced a generation of young women searching for their identity, bored with sexual freedom, and despondent from the loneliness of living a life without commitment. They have abandoned the old commandments, but they can't find any new rules that work.

The Positive Woman recognizes the fact that, when it comes to sex, women are simply not the equal of men. The sexual drive of men is much stronger than that of women. That is how the human race was designed in order that it might perpetuate itself. The other side of the coin is that it is easier for women to control their sexual appetites. A Positive Woman cannot defeat a man in a wrestling or boxing match, but she can motivate him, inspire him, encourage him, teach him, restrain him, reward him, and have power over him that he can never achieve over her with all his muscle. How or whether a Positive Woman uses her power is determined solely by the way she alone defines her goals and develops her skills.

The differences between men and women are also emotional and psychological. Without woman's innate maternal instinct, the human race would have died out centuries ago. There is nothing so helpless in all earthly life as the newborn infant. It will die within hours if not cared for. Even in the most primitive, uneducated societies, women have always cared for their newborn babies. They didn't need any schooling to teach them how. They didn't need any welfare workers to tell them it is their social obligation. Even in societies to whom such concepts as "ought," "social responsibility," and "compassion for the helpless" were unknown, mothers cared for their new babies.

Why? Because caring for a baby serves the natural maternal need of a woman. Although not nearly so total as the baby's need, the woman's need is nonetheless real.

The overriding psychological need of a woman is to love something alive. A baby fulfills this need in the lives of most women. If a baby is not available to fill that need, women search for a baby-substitute. This is the reason why women have traditionally gone into teaching and nursing careers. They are doing what comes naturally to the female psyche. The schoolchild or the patient of any age provides an outlet for a woman to express her natural maternal need. . . .

Finally, women are different from men in dealing with the fundamentals of life itself. Men are philosophers, women are practical, and 'twas ever thus. Men may philosophize about how life began and where we are heading; women are concerned about feeding the kids today. No woman would ever, as Karl Marx did, spend years reading political philosophy in the British Museum while her child starved to death. Women don't take naturally to a search for the intangible and the abstract. The Positive Woman knows who she is and where she is going, and she will reach her goal because the longest journey starts with a very practical first step.

4. Betty Friedan Has Second Thoughts (1981)

Widely recognized as the founding mother of second-wave feminism, Betty Friedan assumed near-iconic status in the women's movement of the 1960s and 1970s. But in later years, she distanced herself somewhat from the very movement she had helped to launch. In this selection, what are her principal criticisms of the ongoing feminist movement? Is she consistent with her own early beliefs?

Around 1969, when that anti-man, anti-family, bra-burning image of "women's lib" was built up in *Newsweek* and *Time* cover stories exaggerating the antics of the most extremist voices in the movement, I remember the helpless feeling shared by the founding Mothers of NOW: "But that's not what we meant, not at all." For us, with our roots in the middle American mainstream and our own fifties' families, equality and the personhood of women never meant destruction of the family, repudiation of marriage and motherhood, or implacable sexual war against men. That "bra-burning" note shocked and outraged us, and we knew it was wrong—personally and politically—though we never said so, then, as loudly as we should have. We were intimidated by the conformities of the women's movement and the reality of "sisterhood is powerful," as we never would have been by "the enemy."

But in the late sixties and the seventies, young radical women, scarred early by the feminine mystique, and without firm roots in family or career, gave vent to their rage in a rhetoric of sexual politics based on a serious ideological mistake. And they, and later daughters who based personal and political strategies on their distortion, locked themselves and the movement into a reaction that perpetuates, in reverse, the very half-life they were reacting against.

Consider, for instance, the personal reality of some of those valiant women who produced fantasies of mounting Amazonian armies against men, wrote SCUM manifestos (Society for Cutting Up Men), or would shock and titillate suburban matrons at meetings of the League of Women Voters and the National Conference of Christians and Jews by proclaiming, "All married women are prostitutes," and "Only honest prostitutes are heroines." Consider the ones who said women would never be free unless the family was abolished and women forswore motherhood and sexual intercourse with men. "Let babies be bred in test tubes!" they cried. Or they created elaborate rationales reducing every relation of man to woman, and the military and economic depredations of the nation, to rape. The rhetoric ranged from the ridiculous (the members of the consciousness-raising group deciding that if they go home and sleep with their husbands, from now on they must be "on top"; the belief that masturbation or sex with a woman was superior to any "submission" to man's

---

penis) to the sublime (the high preaching of the new feminist theologians against every manifestation of "God, the father," or Mary Daly's image of man as vampire who feeds "on the bodies and minds of women . . . like Dracula, the he-male has lived on woman's blood"). "The personal is political" was the motto: not shaving your legs or underarms, refusing to go to the beauty parlor or wear makeup, not letting him pay the restaurant bill or hold the door open, not making his breakfast or dinner, or washing his socks. . . .

The rhetoric of sexual politics resonated and dignified the mundane, daily buried rage of countless "happy" suburban housewives and sweetly efficient secretaries, nurses and stewardesses. But its origin was the extreme reaction of the "chicks" and "earth mothers" of the radical student movement of the sixties against their own situation in the so-called revolutionary counterculture where, in fact, the feminine mystique reached its apogee.

The position of women in that hippie counterculture was, as a young radical black male leader preached succinctly, "prone." Tom Hayden and others might like to forget it now, but those early male leaders of the radical student movement and counterculture of the sixties, white and black, were more blatantly male chauvinist pigs than their conservative fathers. From the communes of Haight-Ashbury and Big Sur and Vermont to the seized and trashed academic fortresses of Harvard and Columbia, women were supposed to wash the pots and pans and cook the spaghetti and be good girls at the mimeograph machine—the "woman trip"—while the men made the revolutionary decisions, smoking their pot around the commune fire and taunting "the pigs" under the television lights.

And when these radical "chicks" were finally infected by our first feminist stirrings, and saw through the feminine mystique in the radical movement itself, and introduced their resolutions for "women's liberation" at Berkeley or Cornell, the radical young men just laughed. So the women walked out of the larger radical "movement" and formed their separate "women's lib" groups—like black separatism, right? No men allowed; man was the *enemy*.

Their personal truth as women in the counterculture or radical student movement of the sixties was doubly humiliating when viewed through the lens of revolutionary equality: the ideology of class warfare they had learned to apply to oppressed races and masses, black, brown and pink.

They made a simple, though serious, ideological error when they applied the same political rhetoric to their own situation as women versus men: too literal an analogy with class warfare, racial oppression. It was heady, and made headlines, to vent the venom earlier directed against "whitey" or "boss finks" against *men*—your own man and the whole damn sex—and use all that sophisticated Marxist jargon to make a new revolutionary case for destruction of "the patriarchal nuclear family" and the "tyranny" of sexual biology as the source of all oppression. The media seized on the rhetoric. A "revolutionary in every bedroom" was both sexier and less threatening to vested economic and political interests (it was not political at all, merely personal) than the mainstream actions of the women's movement: breaking through sex discrimination in employment, professions, education, the church; gaining women some measure of the economic independence and self-respect they so desperately needed, control over their own bodies and reproductive process and simple, nonhumiliating police protection against rape. . . .

The women's movement has for some years been the scapegoat for the rage of threatened, insecure housewives who can no longer count on husbands for lifelong support. Recently I've been hearing younger women, and even older feminists, blame the women's movement for the supposed increase of male impotence, the inadequacy or unavailability of men for the "new women." Some even suggest that the recent explosion of rape, "battered wives," "battered children" and violence in the family is a reaction to, or byproduct of, feminism.

The women's movement is being blamed, above all, for the destruction of the family. Churchmen and sociologists proclaim that the American family, as it has always been defined, is becoming an "endangered species," with the rising divorce rate and the enormous increase in single-parent families and people—especially women—living alone. Women's abdication of their age-old responsibility for the family is also being blamed for the apathy and moral delinquency of the "me generation."

Can we keep on shrugging all this off as enemy propaganda—"their problem, not ours"? I think we must at least admit and begin openly to discuss feminist denial of the importance of family, of women's own needs to give and get love and nurture, tender loving care.

What worries me today is the agonizing conflicts young and not-so-young women are facing—or denying—as they come up against the biological clock, at thirty-five, thirty-six, thirty-nine, forty, and cannot "choose" to have a child. I fought for the right to choose, and will continue to defend that right, against reactionary forces who have already taken it away for poor women now denied Medicaid for abortion, and would take it away for all women with a constitutional amendment. But I think we must begin to discuss, in new terms, the choice to *have* children.

What worries me today is "choices" women have supposedly won, which are not real. How can a woman freely "choose" to have a child when her paycheck is needed for the rent or mortgage, when her job isn't geared to taking care of a child, when there is no national policy for parental leave, and no assurance that her job will be waiting for her if she takes off to have a child? . . .

This uneasy sense of battles won, only to be fought over again, of battles that should have been won, according to all the rules, and yet are not, of battles that suddenly one does not really want to win, and the weariness of battle altogether—how many women feel it? What does it mean? This nervousness in the women's movement, this sense of enemies and dangers omnipresent, unseen, of shadowboxing enemies who aren't there—are they paranoid phantoms, and if so, why do these enemies always win? This unarticulated malaise now within the women's movement—is something wonderful dulling, dwindling, tarnishing from going on too long, or coming to an end too soon, before it is really finished?

Though the women's movement has changed all our lives and surpassed our dreams in its magnitude, and our daughters take their own personhood and equality for granted, they—and we—are finding that it's not so easy to *live,* with or without men and children, solely on the basis of that first feminist agenda. I think, in fact, that the women's movement has come just about as far as it can in terms of women alone. The very choices, options, aspirations, opportunities that we have won for women—no matter how far from real equality—and the small degree of new power women now enjoy, or hunger for, openly, honestly, as never before, are converging on and into new economic and emotional urgencies. Battles lost or won are being fought in terms that are somehow inadequate, irrelevant to this new personal, and political, reality. I believe it's over, that first stage: the women's movement. And yet the larger revolution, evolution, liberation that the women's movement set off, has barely begun. How do we move on? What are the terms of the second stage?

In the first stage, our aim was full participation, power and voice in the mainstream, inside the party, the political process, the professions, the business world. Do women change, inevitably discard the radiant, enviable, idealized feminist dream, once they get inside and begin to share that power, and do they then operate on the same terms as men? Can women, will women even try to, change the terms?

What are the limits of the true potential of women's power? I believe that the women's movement, in the political sense, is both less and more powerful than we realize. I believe that the personal is both more and less political than our own rhetoric ever implied. I believe that we have to break through our own *feminist* mystique now to come to terms with the new reality of our personal and political experience, and to move into the second stage.

All this past year, with some reluctance and dread, and a strange, compelling relief, I've been asking new questions and listening with a new urgency to other women again, wondering if anyone else reads these signs as beginning-of-the-end, end-of-the-beginning. When I start to talk about them, it makes some women, feminists and antifeminists, uncomfortable, even angry.

There is a disconcerted silence, an uneasy murmuring, when I begin to voice my hunches out loud:

The second stage cannot be seen in terms of women alone, our separate personhood or equality with men.

The second stage involves coming to new terms with the family—new terms with love and with work.

The second stage may not even be a women's movement. Men may be at the cutting edge of the second stage.

The second stage has to transcend the battle for equal power in institutions. The second stage will restructure institutions and transform the nature of power itself.

The second stage may even now be evolving, out of or even aside from what we have thought of as our battle.

I've experienced before the strange mix of shock and relief these hunches arouse. It happened twenty years ago when I began to question the feminine mystique. It happened before when I put into words uncomfortable realities women had been avoiding because they meant we'd have to change. Even the makers of change, self-proclaimed revolutionaries, women no less than men, resist change of the change that has become their security, their power.

If we put these symptoms I have hinted at to the test of full consciousness . . . facing clearly, openly, publicly what they mean, will we find that the women's movement is, in fact, harboring some incurable cancer, dooming it to imminent death? Inconceivable—never has the women's movement, and the movement of women in the largest sense, seemed stronger, more endurable, irreversible. Three generations of women, millions upon millions, in this and other lands, are living, moving, changing, frantically grasping a new life, or trying to hold on to life, in terms of feminism.

I and other feminists dread to admit or discuss out loud these troubling symptoms because the women's movement has, in fact, been the source and focus of so much of our own energy and strength and security, its root and support, for so many years. We cannot conceive that it will not go on forever the same way it has for nearly twenty years now. But we can't go on denying these puzzling symptoms of distress. If they mean something is seriously wrong, we had better find out and change direction yet again—as much as we ourselves resist such change now—before it is too late.

"How can you talk about the second stage when we haven't even won the first yet?" a woman asks me at a Catholic college weekend for housewives going back to work. "The men still have the power. We haven't gotten enough for ourselves yet. We have to fight now just to stay where we are, not to be pushed back."

But that's the point. Maybe we have to begin talking about the second stage to keep from getting locked into obsolete power games and irrelevant sexual battles that never can be won, or that we will lose by winning. Maybe only by moving into the second stage, and asking the new questions—political and personal—confronting women and men trying to live the equality we fought for, can we transcend the polarization that threatens even the gains already won, and prevent the ERA from being lost and the right to abortion and the laws against sex discrimination reversed. . . .

Thought Provokers

1. Was Nixon's Cambodian incursion courageous or foolhardy? Did it shorten or lengthen the war? What effect did the public outcry against the incursion have on the administration's conduct of foreign policy?

2. What was the connection between détente and the end of the Vietnam War? Did Nixon's policies toward the Soviet Union and China mark a fundamental reorientation in U.S. foreign policy, or were they simply a convenient maneuver to extricate the United States from the Indochina war?

3. What is the role of the Supreme Court in the American governmental system? Is its independence compromised because the president has the exclusive power to nominate justices? Would some other system—for example, national election of justices—be better? What, precisely, were the differences between the Warren Court of the 1950s and 1960s and the Burger Court of the 1970s and 1980s?

4. Why was the resolution to impeach President Nixon passed? What exactly did it name as the grounds for impeachment? Nixon later said that he gave his enemies a sword and they cut him down with it. Is that an accurate description of what happened? Should a president be forgiven for lying to the public under some circumstances?

5. How did "second-wave" feminism compare with the Feminist movements of the nineteenth and early twentieth centuries? It has been argued that women are the social group most disrupted by the demands of modernity. Comment.

41

The Resurgence of Conservatism, 1980–2000

While [communists] preach the supremacy of the state, declare its omnipotence over individual man, and predict its eventual domination of all peoples on the Earth, they are the focus of evil in the modern world.

President Ronald Reagan, March 8, 1983

Prologue: Ronald Reagan, the most conservative president in half a century, emerged victorious in the election of 1980. He set out immediately to implement a virtual revolution in U.S. politics. He attacked head-on the big-government legacy of the New Deal and the Great Society. He slashed the federal budget for social programs and induced Congress to pass a sweeping tax cut. He simultaneously called for massive increases in defense spending, and federal budget deficits soared to nearly $200 billion a year in the mid-1980s. But "Reaganomics" did slay the ogre of inflation that had stalked the economy for more than a decade. Reagan took a hard line with the Soviet Union and announced a major shift in U.S. strategic doctrine in 1983, when he called for the construction of a space-based defense system against intercontinental ballistic missiles. Jolted, the Soviets made the abandonment of this so-called Star Wars scheme the precondition for any further discussion of arms control. Reagan meanwhile flexed his military muscle in the Caribbean by dispatching U.S. troops to invade the tiny island of Grenada in 1983. Central America posed more frustrating problems, as Reagan struggled against congressional opposition to send aid to rebels seeking to overthrow the leftist government in Nicaragua. The Reagan administration's frustrations over congressional opposition to its Central American policies led to the scandalous Iran-contra affair. Meanwhile, new Soviet leader Mikhail Gorbachev undertook some dramatic initiatives that seemed to spell an end to the Cold War—or at least a truce. Triumphantly reelected in 1984, Reagan embraced some emotional social issues such as prayer in the schools and the anti-abortion crusade. He found support among many fundamentalist religious groups, as well as among a group of intellectuals known as neoconservatives.

A. The Reagan "Revolution" in Economic Policy

1. The Supply-Side Gospel (1984)

Since New Deal days, Keynesian economic theory had dominated federal policy. Named for the brilliant British economist John Maynard Keynes, who had developed his ideas most conspicuously in The General Theory of Employment, Interest and Money *in 1936, Keynesian theory emphasized the role of government spending, including deficit financing, in stimulating the economy. Now, so-called supply-side economists argued that continual reliance on government spending sapped money and initiative from the private sector, ballooned deficits, and contained an inherently inflationary bias. The supply-siders came into their own with Ronald Reagan's election in 1980. Here one of them explains the basics of their approach. What is innovative about it? In the light of the unprecedented deficits chalked up in the Reagan years, can supply-side theory be said to have worked?*

Ronald Reagan campaigned for the presidency on a supply-side platform. It gave him an employment policy that did not rely on inflation and government programs. It gave him an anti-inflation policy that did not rely on the pain and suffering of rising unemployment. And it gave him a budget policy that eliminated the deficit through economic growth instead of balancing the budget on the backs of taxpayers. Reagan was a different kind of candidate because he emphasized the capabilities of the people and the American economy. He campaigned on a message of hope that sparked a rebirth of confidence in the people. Reagan's optimism was so unfamiliar to the Republican establishment that its candidate, George Bush, called it "voodoo economics."

The political themes of failures and limits, themes that had created and reinforced insecurities in the people leading them to accept more government programs and controls over their lives, were not a part of Reagan's message. He spoke the language of an American renaissance. His message invigorated the hopes of people whose lives, pocketbooks, and prospects were cramped by a politics that closed all frontiers except those serviced by the federal budget. Here was a man breaking all of the ingrained political rules, and he was winning. . . .

The President-elect wanted to get on with his business of using incentives to rebuild the U.S. economy. He ruled out both wage and price controls and the continuation of demand management—the economic cycle of fighting inflation with unemployment and unemployment with inflation. In place of a stop-go monetary policy ranging from too tight to too loose, there would be steady, moderate, and predictable growth in the money supply. And instead of pumping up demand to stimulate the economy, reliance would be placed on improving incentives on the supply side.

This is the policy package that became known as Reaganomics. Its controversial feature is its belief that the economy can enjoy a rise in real gross national product

---

[1]Reprinted by permission of the publisher from *The Supply-Side Revolution: An Insider's Account of Policymaking in Washington* by Paul C. Roberts, Cambridge, Mass.: Harvard University Press. Copyright © 1984 by the President and Fellows of Harvard College.

while inflation declines. Monetary policy would first stabilize and then gradually reduce inflation, while tax cuts would provide liquidity as well as incentives and prevent the slower money growth from causing a recession. By creating the wrong
incentives and damaging the cash flow of individuals and businesses, the tax system
had produced a nation of debt junkies. With the economy strung out on credit, it
had to be carefully rehabilitated so as not to produce a liquidity crisis.

A decade of taxflation (inflation and rising marginal tax rates) had taken most
of the gains in individual incomes, leaving people no recourse but to turn to debt
to finance their gains in consumption. Since the interest on debt is tax-deductible,
being in debt was the only way for people to get some of their income back from
the government and experience a rise in living standards. Businesses were equally
encouraged by the tax system to go into debt. The only way out of this dilemma
is to improve production incentives and the cash flow of individuals and businesses, while gradually reducing the rate of money growth. The tax cuts had two
purposes. One was to lower tax rates and improve incentives. The other was to prevent a reduction in money growth from causing liquidity problems in the private
sector. With incentives restructured, money growth would be used to finance the
growth of real goods and services rather than to bid up the prices of houses and
commodities. . . .

Keynesian theory explained the economy's performance in terms of the level of
total spending. A budget deficit adds to total spending and helps keep employment
high and the economy running at full capacity. Cutting the deficit, as the Republicans wanted to do, would reduce spending and throw people out of work, thereby
lowering national income and raising the unemployment rate. The lower income
would produce less tax revenue, and the higher unemployment would require
larger budget expenditures for unemployment compensation, food stamps, and
other support programs. The budget deficit would thus reappear from a shrunken
tax base and higher income-support payments. Patient (and impatient) Democrats,
economists, columnists, and editorial writers had explained many times to the ob-
durate Republicans that cutting the deficit would simply reduce spending on goods
and services, drive the economy down, and raise the unemployment rate. Keyne-
sians argued that the way to balance the budget was to run a deficit. Deficit spending would lift the economy, and the government's tax revenues would rise, bringing
the budget into balance. Since cutting the deficit was believed to be the surest way
to throw people out of work, there were not many Republican economists. When
Democrat Alice Rivlin was asked why there were no Republican economists on her
"nonpartisan" Congressional Budget Committee staff, she was probably telling the
truth when she said she could not find any.

The focus on the deficit had left the Republicans without a competitive political
program. They were perceived by the recipients of government benefits as the party
always threatening to cut back on government programs such as social security,
while the taxpaying part of the electorate saw Republicans as the party that was always threatening to raise taxes in order to pay for the benefits that others were receiving. The party that takes away with both hands competes badly with the party
that gives away with both hands, and that simple fact explained the decline of the
Republican Party, which had come to be known as the tax collector for Democratic
spending programs.

Supply-side economics brought a new perspective to fiscal policy. Instead of stressing the effects on spending, supply-siders showed that tax rates directly affect the supply of goods and services. Lower tax rates mean better incentives to work, to save, to take risks, and to invest. As people respond to the higher after-tax rewards, or greater profitability, incomes rise and the tax base grows, thus feeding back some of the lost revenues to the Treasury. The saving rate also grows, providing more financing for government and private borrowing. Since Keynesian analysis left out such effects, once supply-side economics appeared on the scene the Democrats could no longer claim that government spending stimulated the economy more effectively than tax cuts.

2. President Reagan Asks for a Tax Cut (1981)

Ronald Reagan scored a stunning electoral victory over Jimmy Carter in 1980, and after his inauguration he set out energetically to cut the federal budget and reduce federal taxes. A former actor and television personality, Reagan used the electronic media with more effectiveness than almost any other modern president—earning for himself the title of Great Communicator. In his nationally televised address of July 27, 1981, reproduced here, Reagan called on Congress to grant a three-year, 25 percent personal income tax cut across the board to all U.S. taxpayers. Why did he feel that such a cut was necessary?

It's been nearly 6 months since I first reported to you on the state of the Nation's economy. I'm afraid my message that night was grim and disturbing. I remember telling you we were in the worst economic mess since the Great Depression. Prices were continuing to spiral upward, unemployment was reaching intolerable levels, and all because government was too big and spent too much of our money.

We're still not out of the woods, but we've made a start. And we've certainly surprised those longtime and somewhat cynical observers of the Washington scene, who looked, listened, and said, "It can never be done; Washington will never change its spending habits." Well, something very exciting has been happening here in Washington, and you're responsible.

Your voices have been heard—millions of you, Democrats, Republicans, and independents, from every profession, trade and line of work, and from every part of this land. You sent a message that you wanted a new beginning. You wanted to change one little, two little word—two letter word, I should say. It doesn't sound like much, but it sure can make a difference changing "by government," "control *by* government" to "control *of* government."

In that earlier broadcast, you'll recall I proposed a program to drastically cut back government spending in the 1982 budget, which begins October 1st, and to continue cutting in the '83 and '84 budgets. Along with this I suggested an across-the-board tax cut, spread over those same 3 years, and the elimination of unnecessary regulations which were adding billions to the cost of things we buy.

---

[2]*Weekly Compilation of Presidential Documents* 17, no. 31 (August 3, 1981): 814–820.

All the lobbying, the organized demonstrations, and the cries of protest by those whose way of life depends on maintaining government's wasteful ways were no match for your voices, which were heard loud and clear in these marble halls of government. And you made history with your telegrams, your letters, your phone calls and, yes, personal visits to talk to your elected Representatives. You reaffirmed the mandate you delivered in the election last November—a mandate that called for an end to government policies that sent prices and mortgage rates skyrocketing while millions of Americans went jobless.

Because of what you did, Republicans and Democrats in the Congress came together and passed the most sweeping cutbacks in the history of the Federal budget. Right now, Members of the House and Senate are meeting in a conference committee to reconcile the differences between the two budget cutting bills passed by the House and Senate. When they finish, all Americans will benefit from savings of approximately $140 billion in reduced government costs over just the next 3 years. And that doesn't include the additional savings from the hundreds of burdensome regulations already cancelled or facing cancellation.

For 19 out of the last 20 years, the Federal Government has spent more than it took in. There will be another large deficit in this present year which ends September 30th, but with our program in place, it won't be quite as big as it might have been. And starting next year, the deficits will get smaller until in just a few years the budget can be balanced. And we hope we can begin whittling at that almost $1 trillion debt that hangs over the future of our children.

Now, so far, I've been talking about only one part of our program for economic recovery—the budget cutting part. I don't minimize its importance. Just the fact that Democrats and Republicans could work together as they have, proving the strength of our system, has created an optimism in our land. The rate of inflation is no longer in double-digit figures. The dollar has regained strength in the international money markets, and businessmen and investors are making decisions with regard to industrial development, modernization and expansion—all of this based on anticipation of our program being adopted and put into operation.

A recent poll shows that where a year and a half ago only 24 percent of our people believed things would get better, today 46 percent believe they will. To justify their faith, we must deliver the other part of our program. Our economic package is a closely knit, carefully constructed plan to restore America's economic strength and put our Nation back on the road to prosperity.

Each part of this package is vital. It cannot be considered piecemeal. It was proposed as a package, and it has been supported as such by the American people. Only if the Congress passes all of its major components does it have any real chance of success. This is absolutely essential if we are to provide incentives and make capital available for the increased productivity required to provide real, permanent jobs for our people.

And let us not forget that the rest of the world is watching America carefully to see how we'll act at this critical moment.

I have recently returned from a summit meeting with world leaders in Ottawa, Canada, and the message I heard from them was quite clear. Our allies depend on a strong and economically sound America. And they're watching events in this country, particularly those surrounding our program for economic recovery, with close attention and great hopes. In short, the best way to have a strong foreign policy abroad is to have a strong economy at home.

The day after tomorrow, Wednesday, the House of Representatives will begin debate on two tax bills. And once again, they need to hear from you. I know that doesn't give you much time, but a great deal is at stake. A few days ago I was visited here in the office by a Democratic Congressman from one of our Southern States. He'd been back in his district. And one day one of his constituents asked him where he stood on our economic recovery program—I outlined that program in an earlier broadcast—particularly the tax cut. Well, the Congressman, who happens to be a strong leader in support of our program, replied at some length with a discussion of the technical points involved, but he also mentioned a few reservations he had on certain points. The constituent, a farmer, listened politely until he'd finished, and then he said, "Don't give me an essay. What I want to know is are you for 'im or agin 'im?"

Well, I appreciate the gentleman's support and suggest his question is a message your own Representatives should hear. Let me add, those Representatives honestly and sincerely want to know your feelings. They get plenty of input from the special interest groups. They'd like to hear from their home folks.

Now, let me explain what the situation is and what's at issue. With our budget cuts, we've presented a complete program of reduction in tax rates. Again, our purpose was to provide incentive for the individual, incentives for business to encourage production and hiring of the unemployed, and to free up money for investment. Our bill calls for a 5-percent reduction in the income tax rates by October 1st, a 10-percent reduction beginning July 1st, 1982, and another 10-percent cut a year later, a 25-percent total reduction over 3 years.

But then to ensure the tax cut is permanent, we call for indexing the tax rates in 1985, which means adjusting them for inflation. As it is now, if you get a cost-of-living raise that's intended to keep you even with inflation, you find that the increase in the number of dollars you get may very likely move you into a higher tax bracket, and you wind up poorer than you would. This is called bracket creep.

Bracket creep is an insidious tax. Let me give an example. If you earned $10,000 a year in 1972, by 1980 you had to earn $19,700 just to stay even with inflation. But that's before taxes. Come April 15th, you'll find your tax rates have increased 30 percent. Now, if you've been wondering why you don't seem as well-off as you were a few years back, it's because government makes a profit on inflation. It gets an automatic tax increase without having to vote on it. We intended to stop that.

Time won't allow me to explain every detail. But our bill includes just about everything to help the economy. We reduce the marriage penalty, that unfair tax that has a working husband and wife pay more tax than if they were single. We increase the exemption on the inheritance or estate tax to $600,000, so that farmers and family-owned businesses don't have to sell the farm or store in the event of death just to pay the taxes. Most important, we wipe out the tax entirely for a surviving spouse. No longer, for example, will a widow have to sell the family source of income to pay a tax on her husband's death.

There are deductions to encourage investment and savings. Business gets realistic depreciation on equipment and machinery. And there are tax breaks for small and independent businesses which create 80 percent of all our new jobs.

This bill also provides major credits to the research and development industry. These credits will help spark the high technology breakthroughs that are so critical to America's economic leadership in the world. There are also added incentives for small businesses, including a provision that will lift much of the burden of costly paperwork that government has imposed on small business.

In addition, there's short-term but substantial assistance for the hard pressed thrift industry, as well as reductions in oil taxes that will benefit new or independent oil producers and move our Nation a step closer to energy self-sufficiency. Our bill is, in short, the first real tax cut for everyone in almost 20 years. . . .

If I could paraphrase a well-known statement by Will Rogers that he had never met a man he didn't like, I'm afraid we have some people around here who never met a tax they didn't hike. . . .

In a few days the Congress will stand at the fork of two roads. One road is all too familiar to us. It leads ultimately to higher taxes. It merely brings us full circle back to the source of our economic problems, where the government decides that it knows better than you what should be done with your earnings and, in fact, how you should conduct your life. The other road promises to renew the American spirit. It's a road of hope and opportunity. It places the direction of your life back in your hands where it belongs.

I've not taken your time this evening merely to ask you to trust me. Instead, I ask you to trust yourselves. That's what America is all about. Our struggle for nationhood, our unrelenting fight for freedom, our very existence—these have all rested on the assurance that you must be free to shape your life as you are best able to, that no one can stop you from reaching higher or take from you the creativity that has made America the envy of mankind.

One road is timid and fearful; the other bold and hopeful.

In these 6 months, we've done so much and have come so far. It's been the power of millions of people like you who have determined that we will make America great again. You have made the difference up to now. You will make the difference again. Let us not stop now.

Thank you. God bless you, and good night.

3. The New York Times *Attacks Reagan's Policies (1981)*

Critics of President Reagan's budget-slashing and tax-cutting policies fumed furiously but ineffectively during Reagan's first year in office. The new president appeared to be a masterful politician whose will was impossible to thwart. Some observers, however, worried about the real purposes behind Reagan's deft display of presidential leadership. In the following editorial from the New York Times, *what are alleged to be Reagan's true intentions? What does the editorial mean when it states that Reagan "gathers power for the purpose of denigrating its value in shaping America"? Is this assessment fair?*

---

[3]Editorial, "The Reagan Paradox," August 2, 1981. Copyright © 1981 by The New York Times Co. Reprinted by permission.

One thing is surely settled: the Presidency is no feeble office. Let a shrewd President single-mindedly pursue a policy broadly grounded in his election mandate, and he can put it across.

It does not follow that Mr. Reagan's economic program is therefore wise or efficient, or that a different program, without tax cuts, could have fared so well. But conservatives did not invent the technique of buying votes with Federal monies; democracy tilts toward gratifying private wants. It is plainly untrue, however, as many have complained, that the democracy of Congress is bound to frustrate the democratic will that elects Presidents.

Nor is it true that Presidential power requires a telegenic face. Rest in peace, Lyndon Johnson. Power lies in circumstance and in the skill with which it is exploited. The Democrats who opposed Mr. Reagan's budget and tax bills played weak hands, but they played them badly. By turning for help to special-interest lobbies, they only challenged the President to outbid them. By forcing a showdown when they lacked decisive strength, they only magnified the drama of his victory.

But is this President's paradoxical triumph also the nation's? He gathers power for the purpose of denigrating its value in shaping America. He does not say the nation is overextended financially. He does not say guns are momentarily more important than butter. He does not rerank the nation's needs or argue against assorted remedies. He denounces all Federal government as oppressive, as the cause of economic distress and a threat to liberty.

So Mr. Reagan has arranged to shrink annual Federal spending by 1984 by about $150 billion and cut taxes to let individuals and businesses spend that sum instead. Economically, that is mostly a transfer of purchasing power which cannot much reduce inflation or unemployment, the Federal deficit or debt. On the contrary, a big increase in military spending will enlarge the deficit unless the President finds further huge savings in civilian programs. And the pressure to find them— wherever—is what he values most about his accomplishment.

But why does the President boast that he has thus improved economic prospects? Because he holds, as a matter of faith, that a dollar spent privately creates more wealth than a dollar spent by Government.

That is surely sometimes true: a Government-run railroad that is politically beholden to its unions will tolerate more waste than a private bus company. But it surely also is sometimes untrue: a Government investment in a student or road or depressed community can stimulate more productive activity than the same sum spent by private citizens on diamonds or cameras. Government may be incompetent to achieve some of its social goals. But uncoordinated private spending is notoriously inefficient in meeting large public needs.

Take the obvious, urgent need to cool inflation. Mr. Reagan's answer is a tortuous chain of incentives: cut a family's taxes by $500 and the money goes to banks and merchants who invest in more businesses and machines which will be more efficient and hold down prices. Also: reduce a citizen's tax on the *next* earned dollar from 29 to 25 cents and he'll work harder longer and thus reduce costs.

But if it were primarily interested in economic results, Government has surer ways to achieve those results—as even Mr. Reagan's plan recognizes. For it aims large tax reductions directly at businesses that buy cost-reducing machines or job-producing plants. A still more efficient plan would have aimed more precisely at the most wanted machines and at workers who hold down wages or communities that reduce sales taxes.

The unavoidable conclusion is that Mr. Reagan wants to use his power primarily to diminish Government—even where that dilutes economic recovery and prevents efficient allocation of resources.

That the President's plan will revive the economy remains to be proved. What is no longer in doubt is that his economic remedies mask an assault on the very idea that free people can solve their collective problems through representative Government. One day soon Americans will rediscover that their general welfare depends on national as well as parochial actions. And then they will want not just a powerful President but one who cherishes the power of Government to act for the common good.

B. Reagan's Foreign Policies

1. Reagan Sees Red in Nicaragua (1986)

Central America was shaken by political turmoil in the Reagan years. El Salvador, thrown into chaos by a coup in 1979, was finally stabilized only with the help of U.S. military "advisers." In the same year, a revolution in Nicaragua against the dictator Somoza brought to power a leftist government (the Sandinistas) that President Reagan regarded as a festering thorn in his flesh. He tried repeatedly to win congressional approval for sending military aid to the Nicaraguan "contras," or antigovernment rebels. But American memories of the bloody disaster of Vietnam were still vivid, and Congress balked at giving the president the authority he wanted. On March 16, 1986, President Reagan made the following case for his policy in an emotional television address. What are his strongest and weakest arguments? How convincing are his historical analogies?

My fellow Americans, I must speak to you tonight about a mounting danger in Central America that threatens the security of the United States. This danger will not go away; it will grow worse, much worse, if we fail to take action now.

I am speaking of Nicaragua, a Soviet ally on the American mainland only two hours' flying time from our own borders. With over a billion dollars in Soviet-bloc-aid, the Communist Government of Nicaragua has launched a campaign to subvert and topple its democratic neighbors.

Using Nicaragua as a base, the Soviets and Cubans can become the dominant power in the crucial corridor between North and South America. Established there they will be in a position to threaten the Panama Canal, interdict our vital Caribbean sea lanes and, ultimately, move against Mexico. Should that happen, desperate Latin

---

[1]*New York Times,* March 17, 1986, p. 8.

peoples by the millions would begin fleeing north into the cities of the southern United States, or to wherever some hope of freedom remained.

The United States Congress has before it a proposal to help stop this threat. The legislation is an aid package of $100 million for the more than 20,000 freedom fighters struggling to bring democracy to their country and eliminate this Communist menace at its source. But this $100 million is not an additional $100 million. We are not asking for a single dime in new money. We are asking only to be permitted to switch a small part of our present defense budget—to the defense of our own southern frontier.

Gathered in Nicaragua already are thousands of Cuban military advisers, contingents of Soviet and East Germans and all the elements of international terror—from the P.L.O. [Palestine Liberation Organization] to Italy's Red Brigades. Why are they there? Because, as Colonel Qaddafi has publicly exalted: "Nicaragua means a great thing, it means fighting America near its borders. Fighting America at its doorstep."

For our own security the United States must deny the Soviet Union a beachhead in North America. But let me make one thing plain, I am not talking about American troops. They are not needed; they have not been requested. The democratic resistance fighting in Nicaragua is only asking America for the supplies and support to save their own country from Communism.

The question the Congress of the United States will now answer is a simple one: Will we give the Nicaraguans' democratic resistance the means to recapture their betrayed revolution, or will we turn our backs and ignore the malignancy in Managua until it spreads and becomes a mortal threat to the entire New World?

Will we permit the Soviet Union to put a second Cuba, a second Libya, right on the doorsteps of the United States?

How can such a small country pose such a great threat? It is not Nicaragua alone that threatens us, but those using Nicaragua as a privileged sanctuary for their struggle against the United States.

Their first target is Nicaragua's neighbors. With an army and militia of 120,000 men, backed by more than 3,000 Cuban military advisers, Nicaragua's armed forces are the largest Central America has ever seen. The Nicaraguan military machine is more powerful than all its neighbors combined. . . .

If maps, statistics and facts aren't persuasive enough, we have the words of the Sandinistas and Soviets themselves. One of the highest-level Sandinista leaders was asked by an American magazine whether their Communist revolution will—and I quote—"be exported to El Salvador, then Guatemala, then Honduras, then Mexico?" He responded, "That is one historical prophecy of Ronald Reagan's that is absolutely true."

The Soviets have been no less candid. A few years ago, then Soviet Foreign Minister Gromyko noted that Central America was "boiling like a cauldron" and ripe for revolution. In a Moscow meeting in 1983, Soviet Chief of Staff, Marshal Ogarkov, declared: "Over two decades ago there was only Cuba in Latin America. Today there are Nicaragua, Grenada and a serious battle is going on in El Salvador."

But we don't need their quotes; the American forces who liberated Grenada captured thousands of documents that demonstrated Soviet intent to bring Communist revolution home to the Western Hemisphere.

So, we are clear on the intentions of the Sandinistas and those who back them. Let us be equally clear about the nature of their regime. To begin with, the Sandinistas have revoked the civil liberties of the Nicaraguan people, depriving them of any legal right to speak, to publish, to assemble or to worship freely. Independent newspapers have been shut down. There is no longer any independent labor movement in Nicaragua nor any right to strike. . . .

Like Communist governments everywhere, the Sandinistas have launched assaults against ethnic and religious groups. The capital's only synagogue was desecrated and firebombed—the entire Jewish community forced to flee Nicaragua. Protestant Bible meetings have been broken up by raids, by mob violence, by machine guns. The Catholic Church has been singled out—priests have been expelled from the country. Catholics beaten in the streets after attending mass. The Catholic Primate of Nicaragua, Cardinal Obando y Bravo, has put the matter forthrightly: "We want to state clearly that this Government is totalitarian. We are dealing with an enemy of the church."

Evangelical pastor Prudencio Baltodano found out he was on his Sandinista hit list, when an army patrol asked his name: "You don't know what we do to the evangelical pastors. We don't believe in God," they told him. Pastor Baltodano was tied to a tree, struck in the forehead with a rifle butt, stabbed in the neck with a bayonet—finally his ears were cut off, and he was left for dead. "See if your God will save you," they mocked. Well, God did have other plans for Pastor Baltodano. He lived to tell the world his story—to tell it, among other places, right here in the White House.

I could go on about this nightmare—the blacklist, the secret prisons, the Sandinista-directed mob violence. But, as if all this brutality at home were not enough, the Sandinistas are transforming their nation into a safe house, a command post for the international terror.

The Sandinistas not only sponsor terror in El Salvador, Costa Rica, Guatemala and Honduras—terror that led last summer to the murder of four U.S. marines in a cafe in Salvador—they provide a sanctuary for terror. Italy has charged Nicaragua with harboring their worst terrorists, the Red Brigades.

The Sandinistas have been involved themselves in the international drug trade. I know every American parent concerned about the drug problem will be outraged to learn that top Nicaraguan Government officials are deeply involved in drug trafficking. This picture, secretly taken at a military airfield outside Managua, shows Federico Vaughn, a top aide to one of the nine commandantes who rule Nicaragua, loading an aircraft with illegal narcotics, bound for the United States.

No there seems to be no crime to which the Sandinistas will not stoop—this is an outlaw regime. . . .

Through this crucial part of the Western Hemisphere passes almost half our foreign trade, more than half our imports of crude oil and a significant portion of the military supplies we would have to send to the NATO [North Atlantic Treaty Organization] alliance in the event of a crisis. These are the choke points where the sea lanes could be closed.

Central America is strategic to our Western alliance, a fact always understood by foreign enemies. In World War II, only a few German U-boats, operating from bases 4,000 miles away in Germany and occupied Europe, inflicted crippling losses on U.S. shipping right off our southern coast.

Today, Warsaw Pact engineers are building a deep-water port on Nicaragua's Caribbean coast, similar to the naval base in Cuba for Soviet-built submarines. They are also constructing, outside Managua, the largest military airfield in Central America—similar to those in Cuba, from which Russian Bear bombers patrol the U.S. East Coast from Maine to Florida.

How did this menace to the peace and security of our Latin neighbors—and ultimately ourselves—suddenly emerge? Let me give you a brief history.

In 1979, the people of Nicaragua rose up and overthrew a corrupt dictatorship. At first the revolutionary leaders promised free elections and respect for human rights. But among them was an organization called the Sandinistas. Theirs was a Communist organization, and their support of the revolutionary goals was sheer deceit. Quickly and ruthlessly, they took complete control.

Two months after the revolution, the Sandinista leadership met in secret, and, in what came to be known as the "72-hour document," described themselves as the "vanguard" of a revolution that would sweep Central America, Latin America and finally the world. Their true enemy, they declared: the United States.

Rather than make this document public, they followed the advice of Fidel Castro, who told them to put on a facade of democracy. While Castro viewed the democratic elements in Nicaragua with contempt, he urged his Nicaraguan friends to keep some of them in their coalition—in minor posts—as window dressing to deceive the West. That way, Castro said, you can have your revolution, and the Americans will pay for it.

And we did pay for it. More aid flowed to Nicaragua from the United States in the first 18 months under the Sandinistas than from any other country. Only when the mask fell, and the face of the totalitarianism became visible to the world, did the aid stop.

Confronted with this emerging threat, early in our Administration I went to Congress and, with bipartisan support, managed to get help for the nations surrounding Nicaragua. Some of you may remember the inspiring scene when the people of El Salvador braved the threats and gunfire of Communist guerrillas—guerrillas directed and supplied from Nicaragua—and went to the polls to vote decisively for democracy. For the Communists in El Salvador it was a humiliating defeat.

But there was another factor the Communists never counted on, a factor that now promises to give freedom a second chance—the freedom fighters of Nicaragua.

You see, when the Sandinistas betrayed the revolution, many who had fought the old Somoza dictatorship literally took to the hills, and like the French Resistance that fought the Nazis, began fighting the Soviet bloc Communists and the Nicaraguan collaborators. These few have now been joined by thousands.

With their blood and courage, the freedom fighters of Nicaragua have pinned down the Sandinista Army and bought the people of Central America precious time. We Americans owe them a debt of gratitude. In helping to thwart the Sandinistas and their Soviet mentors, the resistance has contributed directly to the security of the United States.

Since its inception in 1982, the democratic resistance has grown dramatically in strength. Today it numbers more than 20,000 volunteers and more come every day. But now the freedom fighters' supplies are running short, and they are virtually defenseless against the helicopter gunships Moscow has sent to Managua.

Now comes the crucial test for the Congress of the United States. Will they provide the assistance the freedom fighters need to deal with Russian tanks and gunships—or will they abandon the democratic resistance to its Communist enemy?

In answering this question, I hope Congress will reflect deeply upon what it is the resistance is fighting against in Nicaragua:

Ask yourselves, what in the world are Soviets, East Germans, Bulgarians, North Koreans, Cubans and terrorists from the P.L.O. [Palestine Liberation Organization] and the Red Brigades doing in our hemisphere, camped on our own doorstep? Is that for peace?

Why have the Soviets invested $600 million to build Nicaragua into an armed force almost the size of Mexico's, a country 15 times as large, and 25 times as populous? Is that for peace?

Why did Nicaragua's dictator, Daniel Ortega, go [to] the Communist Party Congress in Havana and endorse Castro's cause for the worldwide triumph of Communism? Was that for peace?

Some members of Congress asked me, Why not negotiate? Good question—let me answer it directly. We have sought—and still seek—a negotiated peace and a democratic future in a free Nicaragua. Ten times we have met and tried to reason with the Sandinistas. Ten times we were rebuffed. Last year, we endorsed church-mediated negotiations between the regime and the resistance. The Soviets and the Sandinistas responded with a rapid arms buildup of mortars, tanks, artillery and helicopter gunships.

Clearly, the Soviet Union and the Warsaw Pact have grasped the great stakes involved, the strategic importance of Nicaragua. The Soviets have made their decision—to support the Communists. Fidel Castro has made his decision—to support the Communists. Arafat, Qaddafi, and the Ayatollah have made their decision—to support the Communists. Now, we must make our decision. With Congress' help, we can prevent an outcome deeply injurious to the national security of the United States.

If we fail, there will be no evading responsibility, history will hold us accountable.

This is not some narrow partisan issue; it is a national security issue, an issue on which we must act not as Republicans, not as Democrats, but as Americans.

Forty years ago, Republicans and Democrats joined together behind the Truman Doctrine [see p. 412]. It must be our policy, Harry Truman declared, to support peoples struggling to preserve their freedom. Under that doctrine, Congress sent aid to Greece just in time to save that country from the closing grip of a Communist tyranny. We saved freedom in Greece then—and with that same bipartisan spirit we can save freedom in Nicaragua today.

Over the coming days, I will continue the dialogue with members of Congress, talking to them, listening to them, hearing out their concerns. Senator Scoop Jackson, who led the fight on Capitol Hill for an awareness of danger in Central America, said it best: On matters of national security, the best politics is no politics.

You know, recently one of our most distinguished Americans, [former Congresswoman and Ambassador] Clare Booth Luce, had this to say about the coming vote.

"In considering this crisis," Mrs. Luce said, "My mind goes back to a similar moment in our history—back to the first years after Cuba had fallen to Fidel. One day during those years, I had lunch at the White House with a man I had known since he was a boy—John F. Kennedy. 'Mr. President,' I said, 'no matter how exalted or great a man may be, history will have time to give him no more than one sentence. George Washington—he founded our country. Abraham Lincoln—he freed the slaves and preserved the union. Winston Churchill—he saved Europe.'"

"'And what, Clare,' John Kennedy said, 'do you believe my sentence will be?'"

"'Mr. President,' she answered, 'your sentence will be that you stopped the Communists—or that you did not.'"

Tragically, John Kennedy never had the chance to decide which that would be. Now, leaders of our own time must do so. My fellow Americans, you know where I stand. The Soviets and the Sandinistas must not be permitted to crush freedom in Central America and threaten our own security on our own doorstep.

Now the Congress must decide where it stands. Mrs. Luce ended by saying: "Only this is certain. Through all time to come, this, the 99th Congress of the United States, will be remembered as that body of men and women that either stopped the Communists before it was too late—or did not."

So tonight I ask you to do what you have done so often in the past. Get in touch with your representatives and senators and urge them to vote yes; tell them to help the freedom fighters—help us prevent a Communist takeover of Central America.

I have only three years left to serve my country, three years to carry out the responsibilities you have entrusted to me, three years to work for peace. Could there be any greater tragedy than for us to sit back and permit this cancer to spread, leaving my successor to face far more agonizing decisions in the years ahead? The freedom fighters seek a political solution. They are willing to lay down their arms and negotiate to restore the original goals of the revolution. A democracy in which the people of Nicaragua choose their own government, that is our goal also, but it can only come if the democratic resistance is able to bring pressure to bear on those who have seized power.

We still have time to do what must be done so history will say of us, We had the vision, the courage and good sense to come together and act—Republicans and Democrats—when the price was not high and the risks were not great. We left America safe, we left America secure, we left America free, still a beacon of hope to mankind, still a light [u]nto the nations.

Thank you and God bless you.

2. A Journalist Urges Caution in Nicaragua (1986)

Tad Szulc, an experienced reporter on Caribbean affairs, saw some disturbing parallels between Reagan's proposed steps in Central America and the failed Bay of Pigs invasion during John F. Kennedy's presidency. How convincing is he? What similarities in the two situations are most disturbing?

---

[2]"Nicaragua, an Echo of the Bay of Pigs" by Tad Szulc, *New York Times,* March 16, 1986. Copyright © 1986 by The New York Times Co. Reprinted by permission.

April 17 marks the nearly forgotten 25th anniversary of the invasion of the Bay of Pigs in Cuba—organized, financed and directed by the United States. That sorry enterprise provides an uncannily real analogy with President Reagan's latest efforts to arm the Nicaraguan contras in order finally to oust the Sandinistas. Congress may do well to ponder this analogy as it prepares to vote on President Reagan's request for $100 million in new aid to the rebels.

There is, to begin with, an eerie similarity in the assumptions underlying United States involvement in Cuba 25 years ago and in Nicaragua today. There are also parallels in the sequence of policy making decisions that gradually linked United States geopolitical objectives, first with Cuba, now with Nicaragua.

In the case of Nicaragua, the White House began by asserting that the Sandinistas were threatening to spread the virus of Communism throughout Central America. A secret decision was made, apparently in the early days of the Reagan Administration, in the National Security Council to uproot Managua's Marxist-Leninist leadership. This was followed by the self-serving declaration that most Nicaraguans were determined to be rid of the Sandinistas and that all it would take to help them accomplish this would be clever paramilitary support provided by the Central Intelligence Agency.

In the case of Cuba, the National Security Council met on March 10, 1959, to discuss, in secret, ways to "bring another Government to power." This was barely two months after Fidel Castro swept into power with overwhelming national support for his social revolution.

On March 17, 1960, President Dwight D. Eisenhower approved "A Program of Covert Action Against the Castro Regime" because Fidel Castro was moving toward Communism and a stronger relationship with the Soviet Union. Meanwhile, his Administration had begun to develop a paramilitary force outside of Cuba for "future guerrilla action."

On Feb. 3, 1961, the Joint Chiefs of Staff approved a "Military Evaluation of the C.I.A. Paramilitary Plan—Cuba," but with the warning that "it is obvious that ultimate success will depend upon political factors, i.e., a sizable popular uprising or substantial follow-on forces."

However, the C.I.A. misled President John F. Kennedy about the likelihood of an uprising after the landing of the Cuban exiles' brigade. Secretary of State Dean Rusk later told a Presidential board of inquiry "that the uprising was utterly essential to success."

No major uprising occurred in Cuba along with the landing, and not only because Mr. Castro had had the foresight to round up thousands of potential opponents. Even those who had become increasingly disenchanted with Mr. Castro refused to welcome what they suspected to be a United States-engineered return to the status quo of the Fulgencio Batista dictatorship—indeed, the invading forces included several Batista officers.

Let us now turn to the Nicaraguan rerun of the Bay of Pigs operations.

Obviously, the conditions are not identical. The Sandinista commandantes have been in power for nearly seven years, and, notwithstanding their generally appalling leadership they have managed to consolidate their police and political hold on the population. Bad as life is in Nicaragua, and repressive as the Government's internal policies may be, the masses have not rushed to join or support the contras after nearly four years of C.I.A. entreaties.

In other repressive societies, the people have risen against well-armed dictatorships—as in Poland with Solidarity, and in the Philippines—without C.I.A. manipulations. They have had convincing reasons to rebel, and they have done so with clean hands. Clearly, this point entirely escapes President Reagan when he compares the contras with the Filipinos or *real* freedom fighters elsewhere in the world.

Despite its failures, the Nicaraguan revolution of 1979 has brought considerable social justice and care to Nicaragua's impoverished people. The United States cannot ignore this fact any more than it can ignore the strong nationalistic sentiments of the Nicaraguan people arising, in part, from earlier armed interventions by United States Marines.

Nor can it ignore the fact that the leadership of the contras is probably as repugnant to ordinary Nicaraguans as the leadership of the Bay of Pigs force was to the ordinary Cuban 25 years ago. That the contras are led by key officers of the old Somoza dictatorship's National Guard, the main oppressors of the population in the old days, is either sheer C.I.A. folly or a confession that no better leaders could be produced.

The Administration confronts this argument by pointing out that respected democrats from the first Sandinista regime, including Arturo Cruz and Alfonso Robelo, are members of the umbrella political organization attached to the contras, and that this in turn suggests the existence of widespread support inside Nicaragua for the anti-Sandinista effort.

Here again the Cuban experience is instructive. The C.I.A.-backed Democratic Revolution Front was headed by José Miró Cardona, the first Prime Minister after the Cuban revolution, and included Manuel Ray, who had been Mr. Castro's liberal-minded public works minister. But despite their individual popularity, and the fact that they had been dismissed by an increasingly radical Fidel Castro, they did not have significant backing inside Cuba, and when the invasion came, the C.I.A.-controlled Democratic Revolutionary Front turned out to be totally useless.

Just as the C.I.A. misled the Kennedy Administration about the internal support for the exiles' invasion, the Reagan Administration—equally misleadingly—applies self-fulfilling prophecies to the Nicaraguan dispute. The President says he is willing to forget the contras if Managua agrees to negotiate, but what he evidently means by negotiation is either a Sandinista capitulation or power-sharing with the contra-backed opposition outside the country.

Since, as President Reagan must realize, this is an unacceptable proposition to any government, he will be able to proclaim that, having turned down his peace-making ultimatum, Nicaragua is now fair game for the use of force. And at that juncture he will have trapped himself.

Recent history shows that the United States can impose its will in Latin America only by applying or threatening the use of its armed forces. The leftist regime in Guatemala was thrown out in 1954 by a ragtag guerrilla army directed by United States officers, ushering in a corrupt rightist dictatorship. In 1965, it took two United States combat divisions to make the civil war in the Dominican Republic come out our way. In 1983, tiny Grenada was simply knocked out by American forces.

What happens, therefore, in Nicaragua if the contras, even with a fresh $100 million, fail to win their war? Will President Reagan, in desperation, order the use of American troops there? This is the one thing that John F. Kennedy chose not to do at the Bay of Pigs.

3. An Editor Analyzes the Iran-Contra Affair (1987)

In November 1986 the American people were shocked to learn that representatives of the Reagan administration had secretly entered into negotiations to sell armaments to the government of Iran—a government that Ronald Reagan himself had called "Murder Incorporated." The public was further stunned by subsequent revelations that profits from the Iranian arms sales were funneled to the "contra" rebels in Nicaragua, in blatant defiance of a congressional ban on military aid to the contras. Later congressional hearings and inquiries—especially the report of the Tower Commission—and court trials hinted at a shadowy network of secret government operations, involving National Security Adviser John Poindexter and his aide, Marine Colonel Oliver North. President Reagan maintained that he knew nothing of all these covert operations, but questions about his role stubbornly refused to go away. In the following selection, Harper's Magazine *editor Lewis H. Lapham speculates on the meaning of the Iran-contra affair for the American governmental system. What picture of Ronald Reagan as president emerges? How valid is Lapham's concept of "two governments"? Can a president be held fairly accountable for all the actions of his subordinates? To what does Lapham attribute the political recklessness that led to Iran-contra?*

As expected, the Tower Commission's report depicted the President of the United States as a matinee idol held captive by his retinue of zealous, vain, and remarkably inept subalterns. Although muffled in the language of bureaucratic euphemism, the text makes it plain enough that President Reagan knew as much about the Iranian arms deals as he knows about the dark side of the moon. The National Security Council did as it pleased—trading weapons for hostages, ignoring whatever laws it didn't care to understand, furnishing the President with the lies that he obligingly and uncomprehendingly read into the television cameras.

If with regard to the habitual somnambulism of the Reagan Administration the report confirmed what had been obvious for some years, it raised further and more difficult questions about the paranoid mechanics of any American presidency. Why is it that so many seemingly enlightened politicians (a.k.a. "the leaders of the free world") insist on making mockeries of their own dearest beliefs? How does it happen that they repeatedly entangle themselves in the coils of scandal and the nets of crime? How does it come to pass that President Kennedy approves the doomed invasion at the Bay of Pigs and sets in motion the idiot *Realpolitik* of the Vietnam War, or that President Johnson sponsors the escalation of that war with the contrived incident in the Tonkin Gulf, or that President Nixon orders the secret bombing of

---

Cambodia and entrusts his reputation to the incompetent thugs sent to rifle a desk at the Watergate?

At least some of the answers follow from two sets of fantastic expectations assigned to the office of the presidency.

1. *The two governments.* In response to the popular but utterly implausible belief that it can provide all things to all people, the American political system allows for the parallel sovereignty of both a permanent and a provisional government. The permanent government—the Congress, the civil and military services, the media, the legion of Washington lawyers and expensive lobbyists—occupies the anonymous hierarchies that remain safely in place no matter what the political truths voted in and out of the White House on the trend of a season. It is this government—sly and patient and slow—that writes the briefing papers and the laws, presides over the administrative routine, remembers who bribed whom in the election of 1968, and why President Carter thought it prudent to talk privately to God about the B-1 bomber.

Except in the rare moments of jointly opportune interest, the permanent government wages a ceaseless war of bureaucratic attrition against the provisional government that once every four or eight years accompanies a newly elected president to Washington. The amateur government consists of the cadre of ideologues, cronies, plutocrats, and academic theorists miraculously transformed into Cabinet officials and White House privy counselors. Endowed with the virtues of freebooting adventurers, the *parvenu* statesmen can be compared with reasonable accuracy either to a troupe of actors or to a swarm of thieves. They possess the talents and energies necessary to the winning of elections. Although admirable, these are not the talents and energies useful to the conduct of international diplomacy.

An American presidential campaign resembles a forced march through enemy country, and the president's companions-in-arms—whether Robert Kennedy, John Mitchell, Hamilton Jordan, or William Casey—inevitably prove to be the sort of people who know how to set up advance publicity in a shopping mall, how to counterfeit a political image or bully a congressman, how to buy a vote or rig a stock price. They seldom know anything of history, of languages, of literature, of political economy, and they lack the imaginative intelligence that might allow them to understand any system of value that can't be learned in a football stadium or a used-car lot.

The president and his confederates inherit a suite of empty rooms. The media like to pretend that the White House is an august and stately institution, the point at which all the lines of power converge, the still center of the still American universe. The people who occupy the place discover that the White House bears a more credible resemblance to a bare stage or an abandoned cruise ship. The previous tenants have removed everything of value—the files, the correspondence, the telephone numbers, the memorabilia on the walls. The new repertory company begins at the beginning, setting up its own props and lights, arranging its own systems of communications and theory of command, hoping to sustain, at least long enough for everybody to profit from the effect, the illusion of coherent power.

All other American institutions of any consequence (the Chase Manhattan Bank, say, or the Pentagon) rely on the presence of senior officials who remember what happened twenty years ago when somebody else—equally ambitious, equally new—proposed something equally foolish. But the White House is barren of institutional memory. Maybe an old butler remembers that President Eisenhower liked sugar in his tea, but nobody remembers the travel arrangements for the last American expedition to Iran.

Because everybody in the White House arrives at the same time (all of them contemporaries in their newfound authority), nobody, not even Nancy Reagan, can invent the pomp and majesty of a traditional protocol. The ancient Romans at least had the wit to provide their triumphant generals with a word of doubt. The general was allowed to ride through the streets of the capital at the head of a procession of captured slaves, but the Senate assigned a magistrate to stand behind him in the chariot, holding the wreath over his head and muttering into his ear the constant reminder that he was mortal. But who in the White House can teach the lessons of humility?

Within a week of its arrival in Washington, the provisional government learns that the world is a far more dangerous place than anybody had thought possible as recently as two months ago, when the candidate was reciting the familiar claptrap about the Russians to an airport crowd somewhere south of Atlanta. Alarmed by the introductory briefings at the Defense Department, the amateur statesmen feel impelled to take bold stands, to make good on their campaign promises, to act.

Being as impatient as they are vain, they know they have only a short period of time in which to set up their profitable passage back into the private sector (i.e., to make their deals with a book publisher, a consulting business, or a brokerage firm), and so they're in a hurry to make their fortunes and their names. Almost immediately they find themselves checked by the inertia of the permanent government, by the congressional committees, by the maze of prior agreements, by the bureaucrats who bring up the niggling reasons why a thing can't be done.

Sooner or later, usually sooner, the sense of frustration incites the president's men to "take it inside" or "move it across the street," and so they make of the National Security Council or the White House basement the seat of "a loyal government" blessed with the will to dare and do. The decision inevitably entails the subversion of the law and excites the passion for secrecy. The technological possibilities presented by the available back channels, map overlays, and surveillance techniques tempt the would-be Metternichs to succumb to the dreams of omnipotence. Pretty soon they start speaking in code, and before long American infantrymen begin to turn up dead in the jungles of Vietnam or the streets of Beirut.

2. *The will to innocence.* Every administration has no choice but to confront the world's violence and disorder, but the doctrines of American grace oblige it to do so under the banners of righteousness and in the name of one or another of the fanciful pretexts ("democracy," "civilization," "humanity," "the people," etc.) that preserve the conscience of the American television audience. The electorate expects its presidential candidates to feign the clean-limbed idealism of college sophomores, to present themselves as honest and good-natured fellows who know nothing of murder, ambition, lust, selfishness, cowardice, or greed. The pose of innocence is as mandatory as the ability to eat banquet food. Nobody can afford to say, with Talleyrand, that he's in it for the money, or, with Montaigne, that a statesman must deny himself, at least during business hours, the luxuries of conscience and sentiment.

After having been in office no more than a few months, the provisional government no longer knows when it's telling the truth. The need to preserve the illusion of innocence gets confused with the dream of power, and the resident fantasts come to believe their own invented reality—the one they made out of smoke and colored lights when they first arrived in Washington.

During the early years of the Reagan Administration, the President's advisers were wise enough to remember that they had been hired to work on a theatrical production. They staged military pageants in the Caribbean, the eastern Mediterranean, and New York harbor, sustained the illusion of economic prosperity with money borrowed from the Japanese, dressed up the chicanery of their politics in the sentiment of Broadway musicals. They were as lucky as they were clever, and for a surprisingly long time their enemies in the permanent government stood willing to judge the show a success.

The media's applause prompted the President and his companions to mistake the world behind the footlights for the world outside the theater. Flattered by a claque of increasingly belligerent and literal-minded ideologues (among them Vice Admiral John Poindexter, Lieutenant Colonel Oliver North, and Patrick Buchanan) and encouraged by the pretensions of his wife, Reagan came to imagine himself a real, not a make-believe, president. He took to wearing his costume in the street, delivering his lines to passing strangers (among them Mikhail Gorbachev and the Ayatollah Khomeini) with the fond expectation that they would respond with dialogue appropriate to the scene. The most recent reports from Washington suggest that he apparently believed he was leading a Republican renaissance in America, that he had gathered around him not a gang of petty charlatans but a host of selfless idealists, and that in exchange for a Bible and a key-shaped cake, the Iranian despotism would abide by the rules of decorum in effect at the Los Angeles Country Club.

Despite having been repeatedly warned of his possible assassination that last weekend in November 1963, President Kennedy went to Dallas in the firm belief that he couldn't be killed. President Reagan invited the Tower Commission to examine his nonexistent foreign policy and his sentimental variations on the theme of America the Beautiful in the belief that his enemies would accept his ignorance as proof of his virtue.

4. Four Views on the End of the Cold War (1994)

At an extraordinary gathering in the summer of 1994, four of the major figures who played roles in ending the four-and-one-half-decade-long Cold War met in Colorado to assess the process by which the Cold War at last reached its finale. Margaret Thatcher was prime minister of Britain for the entire decade of the 1980s; François Mitterrand was president of France; George Bush served as Ronald Reagan's vice president and was elected president himself in 1988; and Mikhail Gorbachev was the principal architect of the enormous changes that swept through the Soviet Union in the 1980s. How do they agree, and how do they differ, in their appraisals of what happened and why in that momentous decade? Which explanation is most credible?

[4]From M. Gorbachev, M. Thatcher, G. Bush, F. Mitterrand, and B. Mulroney, "What Did We End the Cold War For?," *New Perspectives Quarterly*, 13:1, Winter 1996, pp. 18–28. Copyright © 1996. Reprinted by permission of Blackwell Publishers, U. K.

Who should get the lion's share of the credit for ending the Cold War? Which of these leaders is most prophetic about the future?

Margaret Thatcher. There was one vital factor in the ending of the Cold War: Ronald Reagan's decision to go ahead with the Strategic Defense Initiative (SDI).

The point of SDI was to stop nuclear weapons from reaching their objective. The first nation that got it would have a tremendous advantage because the whole military balance would change. So, it was of supreme importance.

This was a completely different level of defense. It required enormous computer capability, which he knew at the time the Soviet Union could not match. And that was the end of the arms race as we had been pursuing it. I told Mr. Gorbachev when he first visited me that I was all for President Reagan going ahead with SDI and that some of our scientists would help if needed.

From that particular moment, everything was not so easy in my relationship with Mr. Gorbachev. At the same time it was clear that (with Gorbachev) we could negotiate in a different way with a different kind of person who was beginning to allow people in the Soviet Union to have freedom of worship and freedom of speech.

So the end of the Cold War had a great deal to do with Ronald Reagan and a great deal to do with Mr. Gorbachev.

Mikhail Gorbachev. I cannot agree that the SDI initiative had this much importance. SDI-type research was also done in our country. We knew that in the defense sector we could find a response. So, SDI was not decisive in our movement toward a new relationship with the West. If you accept that reforms in the Soviet Union started under the pressure from the West, particularly as a result of the implementation of SDI, that would distort the real picture and offer the wrong lesson for the future.

Of decisive importance were the changes within the Soviet Union. They necessarily preceded any change in our external relations.

We had to go a long way from a critical reassessment of the Communist model that was forcibly imposed on our country and that was sustained by repressive measures. With technological progress and the improvement of the educational and cultural level, the old system began to be rejected by people who saw that their initiative was suppressed, who saw they were not able to realize their potential.

Therefore, the first impulses for reform were in the Soviet Union itself, in our society which could no longer tolerate the lack of freedom, where no one could speak out or choose their own party or select their own creed. In the eyes of the people, especially the educated, the totalitarian system had run its course morally and politically. People were waiting for reform. Russia was pregnant.

So, the moment was mature to give possibility to the people. And we could only do it from above because initiative from below would have meant an explosion of discontent. This was the decisive factor, not SDI.

François Mitterrand. From the first moment Ronald Reagan mentioned SDI to me I made known my firm opposition. I believed this was an excessive project, and it has since been abandoned. . . .

In the Soviet Union, the need for change went back long before Gorbachev arrived on the scene. Nikita Khrushchev and even Leonid Brezhnev were sufficiently intelligent to transform trends into habits. They made reforms; but the purpose of reform was to guarantee their power. For this reason, Soviet public opinion never trusted or believed in reform. That changed with Mr. Gorbachev. Under him reforms were carried out for the sake of reforms. That is the difference.

George Bush. I supported SDI, but you have got to remember that Ronald Reagan was very idealistic on nuclear weapons. Ronald Reagan felt SDI was a way to reduce nuclear terror. As you remember, he offered to share the technology with all countries.

At Reykjavik, he and Mikhail almost hammered out a deal to get rid of nuclear weapons altogether. And Margaret had a fit about it, as did a lot of people in the United States. I suspect François wasn't too pleased either because of the French deterrent.

I disagree with Margaret, though, about the degree to which it forced reform or accelerated change inside the Soviet Union. We had huge defense budgets at that time and they continued on through my administration. SDI was part of that, but it was nothing compared to the overall deployment of nukes all around the world. . . .

Gorbachev. During the Chernenko* funeral, when I spoke with George Bush (then Vice President) and Margaret Thatcher, I was also talking with the leaders of the Eastern European countries. I said to all of them: "I want to assure you that the principles that used to just be proclaimed—equality of states and non-interference in internal affairs—will now be our real policy. Therefore you bear responsibility for affairs in your own country. We need *perestroika* [restructuring] and will do it in our own country. You make your own decision." I said this was the end of the Brezhnev Doctrine.†

I must say they all took a rather skeptical attitude. They thought, "Well, Gorbachev said something about troop reductions at the UN. He is talking about reform at home. He must be in bad shape. He will improve things a little, and then the Soviet Union will go back to its old ways. This is playing the game that is usual with Soviet leaders."

During my years in power we stuck to the policy I announced. We never interfered, not militarily and not even politically. When Gustav Husak from Czechoslovakia and others came to us, we told them we would help them to the extent possible, but "your country is your responsibility."

Bush. We were skeptical (about Gorbachev's proclamations on non-interference). We were cautious. We were prudent. We didn't want to provoke something inside these Eastern European countries that would compel the Soviet leadership to take action. . . .

---

*Konstantin Chernenko was the head of the Soviet Union from February 1984 until his death in March 1985.
†On the occasion of the Soviet invasion of Czechoslovakia in 1968, Soviet leader Leonid Brezhnev announced the "Brezhnev Doctrine," asserting the right of the Soviet Union to intervene militarily in any Eastern European country where Communist rule was threatened.

Mitterrand. What brought everything down was the inability to control the fantastic migration out of East Germany into Hungary and Czechoslovakia, and later to West Germany. That was the end for the Soviet empire.

If Gorbachev had chosen to use force in those countries under Soviet sway, none could have resisted. But he made it known that he considered that option an historical blunder. The very moment that Gorbachev said to the president of the GDR (East Germany) that he did not intend to use force to solve the crisis, that this was a new day and a new deal, that was the end. This was when the big shift occurred. The fault line was not in Warsaw or Prague. It was in East Berlin.

So, the Communist leaders in Germany continued to be Communist leaders, but they no longer led anything. This was a truly popular, peaceful revolution against which they could do nothing. After that, it all broke down, leading to the transformation of Europe and to German unity.

Bush. When the Berlin Wall came down, we didn't know whether there were elements inside the Soviet Union that would say "enough is enough, we are not going to lose this crown jewel, and we already have troops stationed there."

In an interview at the time in the Oval Office, I was asked why I didn't share the emotion of the American people over the fall of the Berlin Wall. Leaders of the opposition in Congress were saying that I ought to go and get up on top of the Berlin Wall with all those students to show the world how we Americans felt.

I felt very emotional, but it was my view that this was not the time to stick our fingers in the eyes of Mikhail Gorbachev or the Soviet military. We were in favor of German unity early on and felt events were moving properly.

So, we didn't want to do something stupid, showing our emotion in a way that would compel elements in the Soviet Union to rise up against Gorbachev.

Gorbachev. We were not naive about what might happen. We understood that what was underway was a process of change in the civilization. We knew that when we pursued the principle of freedom of choice and non-interference in Eastern Europe that we also deprived the West from interfering, from injecting themselves into the processes taking place there.

As for what was happening within the Soviet leadership at the time, I wouldn't have been able to launch the far-reaching process of reforms alone. There was a group of reformers around me in the very first months of being in office and we set out to change personnel, including in the Politburo and in the provinces, and replace them with fresh forces. It was also at this time—in 1986 and 1987—when I thought that we should expand the democratic process. If we didn't involve the citizens the bureaucrats would eventually suppress all reforms. Without these changes I would have met the fate of Khrushchev. Of course, it was not a smooth process.

Thatcher. Unlike George Bush, I was opposed to German unification from early on for the obvious reasons. To unify Germany would make her the dominant nation in the European community. They are powerful and they are efficient. It would become a German Europe.

But unification was accomplished, really, very much without consulting the rest of Europe. We were always amazed that it happened. My generation, of course, remembers that we had two world wars against Germany, and that it was a very racist society in the second. Those things that took place in Germany could never happen in Britain.

I also thought it wrong that East Germany, whom, after all, we fought against, should be the first to come into the European Community, while Poland and Czechoslovakia, whom we went to war for, had to wait. They should have been free in 1945 but were kept under the Communist yoke until the collapse of the Soviet Union and, even now, are not sufficiently integrated into Europe and suffer from protectionism.

Bush. To be very frank, we had our differences with Lady Thatcher and François Mitterrand. Perhaps it was because I didn't share their concerns based on the histories of the two world wars. Maybe it is because America is removed and separated.

But I felt that German unification would be in the fundamental interest of the West. I felt the time had come to trust the Germans more, given what they had done since the end of World War II.

I was convinced, also, that Helmut Kohl would not take a united Germany out of NATO [the North Atlantic Treaty Organization]. I was convinced he would opt for the West and not neutrality between NATO and the Warsaw Pact as Mr. Gorbachev wanted. The whole process moved faster than any of us thought, including Chancellor Kohl. . . .

Gorbachev. The German question was the nerve center of our European policy. You will recall that the Soviet position after World War II was that Germany should be united—but as a democratic, neutral and demilitarized country. But that did not happen.

When West German President Richard von Weiszacker came to see me when I had first become general secretary and asked about my views on Germany, I told him that as result of the war and the system created after the war, two Germanys were an historic reality. History had passed its judgment. Perhaps Germany would reunify in five or ten—or a hundred—years. That was my position then.

At the same time, the Helsinki Process,* begun in 1975, was underway. That consolidated the postwar realities, among them of a divided Germany, and made it possible for us to normalize relations with Europe. We then became engaged in widespread cooperation with West Germany. Together, East and West Germany were our biggest economic and trade partners. The Federal Republic, to my mind, had also settled all those frontier issues President Mitterrand raised by signing treaties with Poland and Czechoslovakia. All this created the groundwork for the movement to a new situation.

Of decisive importance, though, was the launching of perestroika in the Soviet Union. It affected public opinion in all the central and eastern European countries, but especially in East Germany.

When I went to the GDR to participate in the 40th anniversary celebrations

---

*Representatives of thirty-four nations met in Helsinki, Finland in July 1975 and officially ended World War II. The agreements signed at Helsinki recognized the Soviet-dictated boundaries of divided Germany, Poland, and other East European countries. In return, the Soviets agreed to liberalization of educational and other exchanges between East and West. The Helsinki accords also stimulated dissident movements throughout Eastern Europe to organize and assert claims for political and human rights.

in October 1989 there was a torchlight parade organized by the leaders. The marchers were carefully selected from 28 districts around the GDR. They were people who were supposed to be "reliable." But they began to shout slogans demanding democracy and perestroika for the GDR.

The Polish premier came to me and said: "This is the end." This had become the reality. And politicians have to accept realities.

For us the German reunification issue was the most difficult one. For President Bush and the US Administration the key issue was the future of NATO. And, today, as we see how NATO is being pushed forward instead of a European process of building common institutions, we understand why it was their concern. That is a problem.

The president of France was concerned about borders and territory. Mrs. Thatcher had geopolitical concerns about who would dominate Europe. Everyone had questions.

But I can tell you those questions cannot even be compared with the problems the Soviet leadership was facing given our enormous sacrifices during the war. So, for us, taking the decision on German unification was not easy. We had to go a very long way. We thought the process would take a long time and would be coordinated with the building of new European institutions under the umbrella not of the Americans, but of a European process.

Like Chancellor Kohl, we thought that initially there would be some kind of association of German states, a confederation perhaps.

Then history began to speak when the masses created a new reality more rapidly than any of us were prepared for. Suddenly all these questions were put in a new frame.

We had ended the Cold War and said, as George Bush and I did in Malta, that we would no longer regard each other as enemies. We had come a long way in opening freedom in our country. We dismantled the totalitarian system, launched perestroika in the Soviet Union and reforms in Eastern Europe. The entire world had moved into a new stage of development.

Was all this to be sacrificed by trying to stop what the Germans themselves wanted by moving in troops? No. Only the political process was available to us. And the political process is constrained by the realities of what the people want. We had to recognize the free expression of the Germans.

President Bush was right about Germany. The Germans had accepted democratic values. They had behaved responsibly. They had recognized their guilt. They had apologized for that past, and that was very important.

So, as difficult as it was, it was inevitable that the Soviet leadership took decisions consistent with this reality. . . .

Mitterrand. We too wanted to avoid the military test in the Baltics because this would jeopardize the position of Mikhail Gorbachev. At the same time, for him to accept the unconditional independence of revolting nations was to accept dislocation of the whole. . . .

I believe that in the next century a new synthesis must be found between the two requirements stressed by President Gorbachev—the need for integration as well as the need to affirm individual personality, sovereignty and rights in different areas. And this is by no means a done deal.

The separation of the Czechs and Slovaks is a good example, but there will be other less harmonious separations in Europe. And let us hope it is not contagious and spreads to the American continent.

The aspiration for national identity is clearly understandable after what Mrs. Thatcher called the fallen empires—certainly the main feature of the 20th century. The end of empire releases ethnic and tribal groups. Each goes it alone, wanting to enjoy all the trappings of sovereignty. But that is not possible. It clashes with the other basic trend of globalization.

So, a synthesis is necessary. Though Lady Thatcher does not agree, that is what we are doing within the European community. Shall we succeed in effecting a synthesis between this need for great aggregates and this incipient need of each small community to affirm itself as such?

Absurd, would it not be, to encourage each splinter of a truth to lead an independent international life? And yet, it is injustice to prevent anyone from doing so.

So, in the next century the world must create the rule of law that protects minorities, enabling them to live freely with most of the attributes that makes it possible to meet their national aspirations. At the same time national organizations must be created so that each country can maintain its cohesiveness.

If we do not do this, we shall see a tremendous scattering and breaking away. No one will be immune. The need for decentralization in the US or Canada will prevail over a federal state. And it will be the same in Brazil, in Spain, in Belgium. There would be no end, no way out.

Will we have political leaders capable of conceiving the organization of this huge world with a few major coordination centers obeying international laws set by the international community, and at the same time making minority rules that enable each to live according to his or her yearning?

Enough said. A new generation is rising. They will have to answer this question.

C. Social Issues Enter Politics

1. Newt Gingrich and Lowell Weicker Debate School Prayer (1984)

Two Supreme Court decisions in the early 1960s effectively prohibited the recitation of prayers in public schools: Engel v. Vitale *(370 U.S. 421 [1962]) and* Abington School District v. Schempp *(374 U.S. 203 [1963]). The ban has rankled many churchgoing Americans ever since. They found their champion in Ronald Reagan, who called for a constitutional amendment to permit prayer in the schools, and also*

---

[1]From Pro and Con—"Permit Prayers by Students in Public Schools?," *U.S. News & World Report,* 1984. Copyright 1984 U.S. News & World Report, L.P. Reprinted with permission.

appealed to conservatives with his denunciation of abortion. Some critics spotted an inconsistency in Reagan's opposition to abortion and his support for school prayer. As the New Republic *put it in 1984: "The man who has made a career out of talking about getting government off the backs of the people starts his campaign by pledging to expand government authority over the private lives of women and the spiritual lives of children." In the following exchange, Congressman Newt Gingrich of Georgia and Senator Lowell Weicker of Connecticut, both of them Republicans, debate the school-prayer issue. Who has the more convincing arguments? What constitutional principles are at stake in the school-prayer controversy?*

Interview with Representative Newt Gingrich, Republican of Georgia

Q. Representative Gingrich, why do you favor a constitutional amendment to permit organized recitation of prayers by students in public schools?

A. Because the schools occupy our children's lives for 12 years, and a nation that prohibits recognizing God for 12 years is, in fact, actively against religion and not neutral about religion.

Q. The Supreme Court ruled in 1962 that government-sponsored school prayer violates the First Amendment's prohibition against any law "respecting the establishment of religion." Wouldn't restoring such prayers breach the traditional separation of church and state?

A. No. That's basic misreading of American history. For most of our history, there were prayers in school. The Founding Fathers clearly believed that there was a relationship between a Supreme Being and the survival of the United States.

    Our money bears the inscription "In God We Trust," and Thomas Jefferson said that our inalienable rights come from our Creator. The prohibition in the Constitution was meant to apply to a state religion, not to religion itself.

Q. Some critics say that the push for organized prayers in schools is motivated by a desire to associate religious practice with good citizenship in children's minds—

A. George Washington said that without religion it's impossible to preserve freedom, and this is probably true. Traditional values are the framework within which a free society flourishes, and a purely secular, radical-lifestyle society is, I think, unlikely to sustain freedom.

Q. How would you accommodate nonbelievers or those who don't want to say the prayer used in the school?

A. I'm not sure that we would have a particular prayer. In fact, the President's proposed amendment would prohibit any specific state-written prayer.

Q. Who would decide the content of the prayer?

A. It would be decided differently in different areas, but I would hope ultimately we would just let one of the children volunteer to lead the prayer each day.

Q. Wouldn't students become the butt of ridicule from their schoolmates if they did not participate in the prayers?

A. In an age when we have peer pressure to use drugs and alcohol and to engage in sex at 15, it's not all that bad to have some peer pressure to pray. We are in greater danger of becoming a pornographic-viewing, drug-addicted culture than of becoming an abstinence-dominated theocracy.

Q. Why hasn't Congress voted for a prayer amendment?

A. Because our liberal national elite doesn't believe in religion. In the House, the liberal-Democratic power structure for 20 years has smothered school prayer and not allowed it to be brought to a vote. It'll require real pressure from the public to force a vote on the issue.

Interview with Senator Lowell Weicker, Republican of Connecticut

Q. Senator Weicker, why do you oppose organized recitation of prayer in public schools?

A. No part of our Constitution is more important or unique to the United States than the First Amendment, which clearly sets out the separation of government and religion. This nation was founded by people fleeing from religious persecution, and we must continue to make sure that all faiths—today's and tomorrow's—can be practiced in this country.

The essence of the debate over school prayer is whether religion is going to remain a personal rather than an official act in the United States.

Q. Advocates of prayer in schools say that prayers were permitted until 22 years ago because it was recognized that the Founding Fathers had intended to prohibit the establishment of a state religion—not to bar all public expressions of religion.

A. James Madison, the author of the First Amendment, said: "We are teaching the great truth that governments do better without kings and nobles than with them. The merit will be doubled by the other lesson that religion flourishes in greater purity without than with the aid of government."

As for school prayer being permitted for many years, habit and tradition are no substitute for the Constitution. For example, we had discrimination toward the handicapped and rampant racism in this country as habits and traditions until the Constitution was enforced.

When the Supreme Court announced its decision to ban school prayer, President Kennedy said there was an easy remedy: Families should pray more often at home and attend church more faithfully.

Q. In view of the polls showing widespread public support for prayer in public schools, why shouldn't Congress pass an amendment to the Constitution permitting school prayer, and then leave it up to the states to ratify or defeat it?

A. I'm not so sure that, if you offered the Bill of Rights of the Constitution as a referendum to the voters today, they'd pass it. So I look upon the debate on school prayer in the Senate as a historic opportunity to remind people that the origins of our greatness as a nation are in the Constitution and not the ephemeral morality of the New Right.

Q. Will the Senate pass a school-prayer amendment?

A. In an election year, there is a pretty good chance. It is very easy to demagogue the school-prayer issue. No one running for office wants to be accused of being against the Bible.

But my purpose is to re-educate the American people on our Constitution. I won't filibuster, but it will take a full debate to rouse a constituency for religious freedom and against state prayer.

It should be remembered that most religious spokesmen support the position I am espousing. So I would hope all faiths would stand up and speak forcefully from the pulpits of this country on what is their freedom.

2. The Agonizing Debate over Abortion (1984)

The Supreme Court's 1973 decision upholding a woman's right to an abortion during the early months of pregnancy (Roe v. Wade, 410 U.S. 113) *set off a bitter battle between pro-abortion ("pro-choice") and antiabortion ("pro-life") groups. Feminists were conspicuous in the pro-choice camp, and Roman Catholics and members of other religious denominations in the pro-life camp. President Reagan strongly aligned himself with the latter forces and made his opposition to abortion a prominent theme in his 1984 election campaign. "Unless and until it came to be proven that the unborn child is not a living entity," he told the National Association of Evan-*

gelicals in 1983, "then its right to life, liberty, and the pursuit of happiness must be protected." The president's public stand stirred an already boiling pot of moral, constitutional, and political questions. Democrats, many of them Roman Catholics such as New York State Governor Mario Cuomo and 1984 vice-presidential candidate Geraldine Ferraro, felt compelled to express their own personal opposition to abortion but stopped short of joining the president's crusade for antiabortion legislation. How do the following commentaries evaluate their position? Which commentator has the sounder arguments? What is the proper relation of personal morality and public policy in a democracy?

a. A Pro-Life Spokesman Equates Private and Public Morality*

The debate over the appropriate role of religion in politics is befogged by a crucial misunderstanding about the nature of abortion, which is in essence a matter of public and not merely private morality.

Governor Mario Cuomo, Representative Geraldine A. Ferraro and Senator Edward M. Kennedy maintain that they personally oppose most abortions but that they do not want to impose their morality by law. They believe abortion should be legal and that abortions for the poor should be publicly funded, and they criticize the Roman Catholic bishops' view that it is "not logically tenable" to separate "personal morality and public policy."

Yet the proper dichotomy is not, as some contend, between law and morality: most laws are grounded in moral concepts. Instead, it is between moral principles that relate to the individual conduct of one's own life, with which the law should not deal, and moral principles that relate to actions that may cause harm to others, with which the law must deal.

Senator Kennedy came close to articulating this point last week. "Issues like nuclear arms," he said, "are inherently public in nature; we must decide them together as a nation; and here, religion and religious values must appeal to our common conscience—and to the decision of Government itself. . . . But this cannot mean that every moral command should be written into law—that Catholics should seek to make birth control illegal; that Orthodox Jews should seek to ban business on the Sabbath."

So far, Senator Kennedy is correct. But there is a problem in applying this principle to abortion. If the fetus is not yet a human person, abortion, like contraception, does not affect others, and religious and other moral leaders should not ask the law to interfere. However, if the fetus is a human person, then an abortion causes harm to someone other than the mother, and abortion is a matter of public morality—one about which laws may properly be advocated by religious leaders.

Since the status of the fetus is the very matter most in dispute, it begs the question to rule religious leaders out of the debate on the ground they are illicitly advocating

---

[2a]"Abortion: A General Concern" by Burke J. Balch, *New York Times,* September 20, 1984. Copyright ©1984 by The New York Times Co. Reprinted by permission.

*The author of this selection, Burke J. Balch, was the staff counsel for the Americans United for Life Legal Defense Fund.

private morality in the public sphere. In their view, they are not asking the state to impose private morality but to protect the rights of others.

Senator Kennedy, Governor Cuomo and others seem to anticipate this point, but they also make a larger claim: that when we are deeply divided about whether an issue is one of public or private morality, the state should not intervene.

But the notion that division of opinion should end rather than foster debate is an unfortunate one. For decades, we were deeply divided about whether race prejudice was a private matter, and for years the argument against civil rights laws was that Government can't legislate morality. In reply, Dr. Martin Luther King Jr. used to point out that the law cannot make one love one's neighbors, but it can—and should—keep one from lynching them. He did not hesitate to invoke the Bible in support of his position.

As Dr. King well knew, the mere existence of disagreement cannot justify politicians, religious leaders or anyone else in tolerating injustice—still less in assisting it. What would one think of a politician who was "personally opposed" to rape but objected to imposing that morality on rapists who believe that "women want it"? What if the same politician worked to provide tax funds to buy weapons for rapists unable to afford their own? Would we denounce a religious leader who cried "inconsistency"?

Mr. Cuomo, Mrs. Ferraro and Mr. Kennedy may have unusual grounds to oppose abortion, unrelated to the rights of the fetus. But if their reasoning is the same as that given by their church (as well as by other denominations and by agnostics like myself), they must believe that the fetus is a human person whom abortion unjustly destroys. There is an untenable inconsistency between that conviction and a public policy permitting and funding abortion. Religious leaders who put this out do not breach the separation of church and state. They act in the best tradition of public debate in a justice-seeking republic.

b. A Catholic Urges Restraint*

In early August, Bishop James M. Malone, president of the United States Catholic Conference of Bishops, stated that it is "not logically tenable" for political candidates to draw a dichotomy between their personal morality and public policy. Archbishop John J. O'Connor of New York more recently made the same point. In doing so, they expressed a common belief about the moral integrity required of the politician: we don't like hypocrites or those who think that private belief and behavior are irrelevant to public office.

Yet that view overlooks a no less important demand upon the politician in a pluralistic society: that he or she understand the importance of self-restraint in moving from morality to legislation. For the sake of our collective freedom, we need politicians who know how and when to curb personal convictions. Since that capacity is a less dramatic civic virtue, it is all too easy to overlook. But it has been publicly invoked by Representative Geraldine A. Ferraro and Governor Mario Cuomo to explain their political stands on abortion.

[2b]"Restraint Serves Pluralism" by Daniel Callahan, *New York Times,* September 20, 1984. Copyright ©1984 by The New York Times Co. Reprinted by permission.

*The author of this selection, Daniel Callahan, was the director of the Institute for Social Ethics and the Life Sciences at the Hastings Center in New York.

Politicians are asked why they are reluctant to work legislatively against abortion when on other issues such as hunger and child abuse their personal positions regularly produce proposals for action. While I can't answer for Mrs. Ferraro and Mr. Cuomo, I can suggest reasons why on some issues a politician would hesitate to translate personal belief into public policy. The hesitation can occur at two points: in considering the certainty of the moral judgment and then moving from that judgment to a policy conclusion.

Most of us can think of standards we have set for ourselves that we would not demand of others, especially by law, or hold moral beliefs for reasons we find personally compelling but need not be persuasive to others. I decided late in my teens that hunting for sport is morally damaging, but I am not certain that my own feeling of repugnance can be strongly enough justified to turn it into a universal ethical prescription.

One of the more damaging demands we make of politicians is that they have a bushel basket of moral certainties on any and all subjects. Ambivalence is not readily allowed. Just about everyone agrees that abortion is a difficult moral issue. Why should we expect politicians any more than others to have such high moral certitude on the matter that they will know exactly what kind of public policy would be best? I am not saying that moral certainty is insupportable on any subject. I only argue that on some issues our personal convictions will not seem to us sufficiently well grounded to insist that others accept them, yet we can and will find them sufficiently strong to impose upon ourselves.

What if we are certain about our moral beliefs and conclude that they seem to require some action on our part? Does that immediately entail their being embodied in public policy? Not necessarily. We might well conclude (as many politicians do in the case of abortion) that effective and fair laws could not readily be devised, that too few others share one's personal convictions (however sensible) or that some moral issues should be left within the realm of personal choice, even if there are some moral costs in a policy of that kind.

There must be a dichotomy on many (though by no means all) issues between what is correct for private behavior and what is rightly to be demanded of public behavior. That is a necessary assumption of a pluralistic society, dedicated as it is to the toleration of diversity and the sparing use of government power in the moral sphere. It must take special care in making the move from morality to law. In most circumstances, it should be exceedingly reluctant to do so.

The great hazard of the self-restraint that pluralism requires is that it will be confused with moral indifference or vacuity. A solution to that is more public discussion of the private moral life. Politicians should tell us more about how they think through moral issues, not that we might condemn them or insist they turn their convictions into law, but because they may have something to say of importance to the rest of us. To say that a moral issue or decision ought to remain private should be the beginning and not the end of moral discourse.

D. A Philosophy for Neoconservatism

1. Editor Irving Kristol Defines Neoconservatism (1983)

Liberalism was the dominant political religion for most American intellectuals for at least a generation after the New Deal and World War II. Liberals pursued a vision of a just, equitable society, and they looked to government as the means to achieve that vision. In the 1960s, however, a reaction set in, as some intellectuals—many of them refugees from liberalism—began to express growing doubts about egalitarian "excesses" and governmental inefficiencies, as well as about the "softness" of liberal foreign policy toward the Soviet Union. One of the leading thinkers in this conservative renaissance was Irving Kristol, editor of the Public Interest, *which became a prominent journal for the expression of neoconservative ideas. Kristol here defines the essence of the neoconservative outlook. What are its leading features? How does it compare to and contrast with the liberal outlook?*

It should be clear by now that I do think there really is such a thing as neoconservatism—but it is most misleading to think of it as any kind of "movement." It holds no meetings, has no organizational form, has no specific programmatic goals, and when two neoconservatives meet they are more likely to argue with one another than to confer or conspire. But it is there, nevertheless—an impulse that ripples through the intellectual world; a "persuasion," to use a nice old-fashioned term; a mode of thought (but not quite a school of thought).

What are its distinctive features? I shall list them as I see them—but to say that this listing is unofficial would be the understatement of the decade.

1. Neoconservatism is a current of thought emerging out of the academic-intellectual world and provoked by disillusionment with contemporary liberalism. Its relation to the business community—the traditional source of American conservatism—is loose and uneasy, though not necessarily unfriendly.

2. Unlike previous such currents of thought—for example, the Southern Agrarians or the Transcendentalists of the nineteenth century—neoconservatism is antiromantic in substance and temperament. Indeed, it regards political romanticism—and its twin, political utopianism—of any kind as one of the plagues of our age. This is but another way of saying it is a philosophical-political impulse rather than a literary-political impulse. Or, to put it still another way: Its approach to the world is more "rabbinic" than "prophetic."

3. The philosophical roots of neoconservatism are to be found mainly in classical—that is, premodern, preideological—political philosophy. Here the teaching and writing of the late [University of Chicago philosopher] Leo Strauss . . . are of importance, though many neoconservatives find him somewhat too wary of modernity. Neoconservatives are admiring of Aristotle, respectful of Locke, distrustful of Rousseau.

4. The attitude of neoconservatives to bourgeois society and the bourgeois ethos is one of detached attachment. In the spirit of Tocqueville, neoconservatives do not think that

---

[1]From *Reflections of a Neoconservative: Looking Back, Looking Ahead* by Irving Kristol, pp. 75–77, 263–264. Copyright © 1983 by Basic Books, Inc. Reprinted by permission.

liberal-democratic capitalism is the best of all imaginable worlds—only the best, under the circumstances, of all possible worlds. This *modest* enthusiasm distinguishes neoconservatism from the Old Right and the New Right—both of which are exceedingly suspicious of it.

5. Neoconservatism is inclined to the belief that a predominantly market economy—just how "predominant" is a matter for some disagreement—is a necessary if not sufficient precondition for a liberal society. (Daniel Bell, as the theoretician for what may be called our "social-democratic wing," would presumably take issue with this judgment.) It also sees a market economy as favorable to economic growth.

6. Neoconservatives believe in the importance of economic growth, not out of any enthusiasm for the material goods of this world, but because they see economic growth as indispensable for social and political stability. It is the prospect of economic growth that has made it possible to think—against the grain of premodern political thought—of democracy as a viable and enduring sociopolitical system.

7. Neoconservatives, though respecting the market as an economic mechanism, are not libertarian in the sense, say, that [conservative economists] Milton Friedman and Friedrich A. von Hayek are. A conservative welfare state—what once was called a "social insurance" state—is perfectly consistent with the neoconservative perspective. So is a state that takes a degree of responsibility for helping to shape the preferences that the people exercise in a free market—to "elevate" them, if you will. Neoconservatives, moreover, believe that it is natural for people to want their preferences to be elevated. The current version of liberalism, which prescribes massive government intervention in the marketplace but an absolute laissez-faire attitude toward manners and morals, strikes neoconservatives as representing a bizarre inversion of priorities.

8. Neoconservatives look upon family and religion as indispensable pillars of a decent society. Indeed, they have a special fondness for all of those intermediate institutions of a liberal society which reconcile the need for community with the desire for liberty.

Karl Marx once wrote that the human race would eventually face the choice between socialism and barbarism. Well, we have seen enough of socialism in our time to realize that, in actuality as distinct from ideality, it can offer neither stability nor justice, and that in many of its versions it seems perfectly compatible with barbarism. So most neoconservatives believe that the last, best hope of humanity at this time is an intellectually and morally reinvigorated liberal capitalism. . . .

It is the fundamental fallacy of American foreign policy to believe, in face of the evidence, that all peoples, everywhere, are immediately "entitled" to a liberal constitutional government—and a thoroughly democratic one at that. It is because of this assumption that our discussions of foreign policy, along with our policy itself, are constantly being tormented by moral dilemmas, as we find ourselves allied to nonliberal and nondemocratic regimes. These dilemmas are guilt-inducing mechanisms which cripple policy—an attitude that no nation can sustain for long—or else we take flight into sweeping crusades for "human rights," which quickly brings us up short before intractable realities.

Now, there is nothing inevitable about this state of affairs. As a matter of fact, it is only since World War I—a war fought under the Wilsonian slogans of "self-determination for all nations" and "make the world safe for democracy"—that American foreign policy began to disregard the obvious for the sake of the quixotic pursuit of impossible ideals. Before World War I, intelligent men took it for granted that not all peoples, everywhere, at all times, could be expected to replicate a Western constitutional democracy. This was a point of view, incidentally, shared more or less equally by conservatives, liberals, and socialists.

It was only with World War I and its aftermath that thinking about foreign policy lost its moorings in the real world and became utterly ideologized. . . .

For Americans, the transition occurred via the utopian enthusiasm of Woodrow Wilson, preaching "self-determination," "human rights," "one man, one vote," "a world without war" as if these were in fact unproblematic possibilities. The consequence has been a foreign policy that is intellectually disarmed before all those cases where a government is neither totalitarian nor democratic, but authoritarian in one way or another, to one degree or another. We could, if we were sensible, calmly accept this basic reality of world politics, while using our influence to edge unenlightened despotisms toward more enlightened behavior, or enlightened despotisms toward more liberal and humane behavior. Instead, we end up in either an unstable, guilt-ridden and seemingly "immoral" alliance with them or displaying a haughty censoriousness that helps "destabilize" them.

2. Journalist Peter Steinfels Criticizes the Neoconservatives (1979)

One of the first commentators to identify neoconservatism as a distinct body of thought was Peter Steinfels, editor of the Catholic periodical Commonweal. *In his book of 1979 about the neoconservative movement, he is sharply critical of many of its doctrines. What does he find most objectionable in neoconservative thought? What does he find most valuable?*

The great virtue of neoconservatism is the serious attention it pays to the moral culture that is a fundament of our political and economic life. There is barely a serious school of liberal or even Marxist thought that holds humans to be economically determined and values, culture, and beliefs the mere reflection of socioeconomic forces. And yet in practice liberals, radicals, and socialists concentrate on questions of economic deprivation or physical pain rather than of meaning or moral capacity. They do not deny the importance of culture and values; but when they would act upon them, they almost inevitably propose to enter the chain of causes at the point of providing material support or physical well-being. Otherwise, the Left, broadly speaking, has been primarily concerned with culture by way of removing constraints—commercial pressures, government censorship, insufficient funding, traditional taboos, established conventions. The New Left did criticize liberalism in the sixties for its rendering of politics as procedure and its presentation of social science as value-free. Irving Kristol and the New Left were thus agreed on the necessity of "republican virtue" (though the New Left, unlike Kristol, would not rally to the "bourgeois ethic"). But the New Left's concern dissolved into assorted dogmatisms on the one hand, and into the cultural *laissez-faire* of "do your own thing" on the

---

other. It was left to neoconservatism, sworn enemy of the New Left, to be the serious force reminding us that the capacity of self-government and self-direction is not a given which simply emerges once restraints are removed. It is an active power that must be fostered, nourished, and sustained; that requires supporting communities, disciplined thinking and speech, self-restraint, and accepted conventions. In a number of ways neoconservatism is not itself faithful to this insight, even contradicts it; but it has put the moral culture of society on the public agenda and no doubt will keep it there.

The second virtue of neoconservatism is its rejection of sentimentality. By sentimentality I mean the immediate emotional response that renders a reality all of a piece and "obvious." When sentimentality governs our responses to the world's ills, it clings to the visible or physical evils at hand and tends to ignore the less apparent, more diffuse, and distant dangers. It leaps to solutions and short-circuits reflection. Neoconservatism has countered this sentimentality by forcing back the discussion of many political issues to first principles and by its delight in exposing unintended consequences of well-meant measures. There is a good bit of sentimentality in neoconservatism; there is even a sentimentality of anti-sentimentality— a reflexive granting of credibility to whatever, through irony, paradox, or complexity, appears to resist the pull of sympathy, and an equally automatic suspicion of whatever appears untutored or unguarded in its registration of experience. And there is also the tendency toward that hard-headed constriction of feeling that Dickens, in *Hard Times,* fixed in the very name as well as character of Gradgrind. Nonetheless, the neoconservative presence in public controversy has certainly reduced the likelihood that the "obvious" will escape questioning. Is money what the poor need? Or better schools the solution to illiteracy? Does poverty breed crime? Should more people vote? Or campaign spending be limited? Is equality desirable? To some people, the very posing of such questions is an annoyance and a diversion. To those, however, who believe that the unexamined proposal is not worth pursuing, the neoconservative attitude appears salutary.

The third virtue of neoconservatism is related to the second: the thoroughgoing criticisms that it has made of liberal or radical programs and premises. This is less an attitude, like its anti-sentimentality, than a self-assigned agenda. Neoconservatism has taken pride in frontally challenging the excesses of the New Left and the counterculture; more important—because those excesses were probably self-liquidating and already on the wane when neoconservatism set to work—have been the detailed and often technically superior critiques of mainstream liberal notions. Despite the polemical overkill that too frequently mars such critiques, they provide a much more factually informed and sophisticated debating partner for liberal or left-wing thought than has traditional American conservatism, in any of its rugged individualist, agrarian aristocrat, or super-nationalist manifestations.

To every virtue a vice. The outstanding weaknesses of neoconservatism have already been amply suggested: its formulation of an outlook largely in negative terms; its lack of internal criticism; its unwillingness to direct attention to socioeconomic structures and to the existing economic powers; its exaggeration of the adversarial forces in society; its lack of serious respect for its adversaries. If neoconservatism is to construct a convincing defense of an outlook emphasizing a stoic rationality, public restraint, and the maintenance of an ethic of achievement and excellence, it will have to confront the extent to which such an ideal challenges contemporary capitalism. If it is to defend freedom in a bureaucratic age, it will have to understand freedom in a richer sense than anti-Communism and a derived anti-statism. If it is to defend high culture and intellectual rigor, it will need to celebrate the enlarging and life-giving force of superior work and not merely issue self-satisfying strictures on the inferior or fashionable.

Neoconservatism began as an antibody on the left. Many of its leading figures originally conceived of it that way and perhaps still do: it was a reaction to what they considered the destabilizing and excessive developments of the sixties, and when these had been quelled, it would once again be indistinguishable from main-stream liberalism. Its own excesses, or at least its somewhat narrow focus of atten-tion on one set of adversaries, would be balanced by the native strengths of the liberalism of which it was part. That, of course, has not turned out to be the case. Neoconservatism is now an independent force. To return to the biological analogy, antibodies which overreact can destroy the organism. The great danger posed by and to neoconservatism is that it will become nothing more than the legitimating and lubricating ideology of an oligarchic America where essential decisions are made by corporate elites, where great inequalities are rationalized by straitened cir-cumstances and a system of meritocratic hierarchy, and where democracy becomes an occasional, ritualistic gesture. Whether neoconservatism will end by playing this sinister and unhappy role, or whether it will end as a permanent, creative, and con-structive element in American politics, is only partially in the hands of neocon-servatives themselves. It will also be determined by the vigor, intelligence, and dedication of their critics and opponents.

E. Assessing the Reagan Presidency

1. Author Frances FitzGerald Laments the Reagan Legacy (1988)

Ronald Reagan was only the second president since World War II to serve two full consecutive terms. (The other was Dwight D. Eisenhower.) Indeed, he was only the fourth president since Ulysses S. Grant to serve consecutively in office for eight or more years. Thus, his longevity alone seemed bound to make him a consequential— and controversial—president. Even before he left office, the debate about his histori-cal place had begun. In the selection below, Frances FitzGerald, a Pulitzer Prize–winning author, finds much to criticize in the Reagan record. What are her principal objections?

Along the way, somewhere along the road between Denver and Dubuque, when the music was the brightest, the clowns the most droll, when the spangled girls on the dappled horses seemed to walk on air, the tightrope artist missed a step

---

[1]"Death of a Salesman: How Reagan Failed," by Frances FitzGerald, from *Rolling Stone,* February 25, 1988. Copyright by Straight Arrow Publishers, Inc. 1988. All Rights Reserved. Reprinted by Permission.

and almost fell. He recovered—it was a matter of a moment—but there was an intake of breath, an instant of doubt, before the crowd applauded. In the end they cheered as loudly as crowds had been cheering the same performance for years, but looking back, looking back, that seemed to be the moment when the luck of the troupe changed. In the next town the lion tamer was cuffed by the youngest and sleekest of his beasts. He snapped the cub back into place, but blood was drawn, and the mothers in the audience covered their children's faces with their hands.

After that the show went on as usual for a while; the stands were packed, the balloon sellers made good money, and the spangled girls smiled. But then all at once the fat lady took sick, the horses unseated their bareback riders, the elephant's breath turned sour, and the children laughed at the mess he left behind him. Such things, of course, had happened before—this was show business—but this time word of their troubles seemed to ride ahead of them from town to town. Fewer people came; the applause diminished; the hotel rooms were smaller and dingier. The troupe members encouraged one another, practicing new acts, new flourishes, but they could not seem to regain the magic they once had. Even the spangles and the sequins seemed to tarnish. They blamed the lights, they blamed their agents, and finally they blamed one another. The ringmaster alternately stormed about and told stories of the old days of glory. All of them knew something was wrong, but none of them knew what it was.

. . . Now the Reagan administration is on its way out, just like the Carter, the Nixon and the Johnson administrations before it. Everyone knows the names of the stops along the way: Libya disinformation, Daniloff, Reykjavik, Iran-*contra,* Bork, Ginsburg, the crash on Wall Street. Where once each slip, each failure, was seen as an isolated event and quickly forgotten, now audiences are remembering the old ones and adding the new ones to a sequence, like beads to a string. Even clear successes—such as the Gorbachev visit to Washington—do not stop this addition. White House officials, of course, keep denying that such a sequence exists: yes, mistakes were made, but they are now behind us, and the show goes on as before. But they find persuasion hard, for pundits have fashioned the sequence into a narrative of decline and fall: the administration, once so powerful, can no longer cope; the president, once so compelling, is old and distracted; the magic has faded; there is no one there anymore.

But is this narrative the right one? A simple story can never be wholly accurate, and this one has some obvious flaws. The president is still high in the polls, his administration is virtually a new one with respect to foreign policy, and he may yet surprise us by concluding an unprecedented strategic-arms-reduction treaty with the Soviet Union. Then, too, the incidents strung together in sequence could tell a completely different story: not one of decline but one of consistency within the administration for six or seven years. Certainly not one of these incidents is wholly out of line with the past and what we already know about the administration's "management style" and its core philosophy.

The nomination of Judge Robert Bork to the Supreme Court was, after all, merely the latest in a long line of attempts by Attorney General Edwin Meese and the Justice Department to reverse thirty years of Supreme Court jurisprudence. The nomination of Douglas Ginsburg was yet another example of the bullying carelessness Meese is well known for. The White House disinformation campaign in the summer of 1986 to persuade the press that the United States was about to attack Libya for a second time followed upon numerous other attempts by the National Security Council (NSC) staff to mislead the press. The president's sudden embrace of total nuclear disarmament at Reykjavik surprised many, but it was wholly consistent with his vision of Star Wars as an invulnerable defensive shield. As for the budget deficits that Wall Street analysts began to complain about after Black Monday [October 19, 1987, when stocks on the New York Stock Exchange lost nearly 23 percent of their value in a single day], they had mounted steadily for five years. Lack of economic leadership from Washington was a principle with the president: those who now complain about it had applauded a thousand Reagan speeches on the unique wisdom of the market.

In a sense the Iran-*contra* affair was the only true surprise. Who, after all, would have imagined that Ronald Reagan would be selling arms to a government he called "Murder Incorporated"? The secret *contra* resupply operation was easier to understand, given the president's deep and longstanding commitment to reversing the revolution in Nicaragua. But few would have credited Reagan with the duplicity required for it. The amount of sheer incompetence displayed in both operations was out of the ordinary for the administration—as was the extent of the willingness to break the law.

But extraordinary as the Iran-*contra* affair was, it, too, fit certain patterns within the administration. As Larry Speakes, Reagan's press secretary for six years, said recently, "The Reagan administration is more of a crusade or a revolution, as we liked to call it in the first years." From the beginning it had an ideological radicalism unique among Republican administrations of the twentieth century and a habit of bending laws and regulations to realize its vision of the greater good. At the same time it had an unserious, even farcical quality to it that distinguished it sharply from the Nixon administration. Nixon invaded Cambodia—Reagan, Grenada.

The Reagan administration was also astonishingly corrupt. Before the Iran-*contra* affair came to light, almost 100 senior administration officials had been indicted or charged with serious violations of the government code of ethics. Only after the affair did the press begin to add the scandals up. Radicalism, buffoonery, corruption—this is not all the administration is or was. But just as particular crimes express the nature of the society that commits them—just as Watergate expressed the ever-present strain of paranoia within the Nixon administration—so the Iran-*contra* affair, with all of its paradoxes, pointed to certain distinctive characteristics of the Reagan administration. . . .

Much of this was not entirely surprising. Ronald Reagan, after all, had never been known for having a detailed grasp of the issues. According to David Stockman, his first director of the Office of Management and Budget (OMB), he "seemed as far above the detail work of supply side as a ceremonial monarch is above politics." The presidential mind—to use [former White House chief of staff] Donald Regan's phrase—was not cluttered with facts. And as White House staffers told Leslie Gelb of *The New York Times* in 1985, it was not at all analytical. It contained a number of precepts, each one backed up by a quotient of anecdotes and personal reminiscences—some of which had a basis in fact. A few months ago the Speaker of the House, Jim Wright, was quoted as saying that Reagan was "a person with whom you can't seriously discuss serious issues. . . . The minute the subject gets on to anything of substance, he clams up and wants to recite the shibboleths that form his ideological matrix." Not the most eloquent way to put it perhaps, but at the time Wright was fighting with Reagan over the Central American peace plan, and he had just run into Reagan's legendary stubbornness.

Reagan, as Gelb demonstrated, took his precepts and maxims extremely seriously and would return to them over and over again as the basis for action. His famous "management style" was to trust his advisers to figure out a means to reach his goals—while he sold these goals to the public. Just as a salesman is not helped by harboring doubts about the quality of his product, so Reagan, as Garry Wills has pointed out in *Innocents at Home,* was unfailingly optimistic.

This was Reagan's great strength. But it was also the cause of some detachment from reality; Reagan had great difficulty assimilating bad news. Thus while the budget deficits rose into the hundreds of billions, Reagan remained steadfastly against a tax increase and refused to do what was politically necessary to cut the budget—that is, to reduce military as well as social spending. Apparently he believed that the economy would grow to absorb the debt or that the Democrats would have to give up and cut all social programs. . . .

For some months this summer and fall, it looked very much as if the president would go down for good, his popularity sinking under the Iran-*contra* affair and the added burden of Bork and Ginsburg that Meese had put upon him. But then with the visit of Gorbachev to Washington, he bobbed right back up again in the polls. As his staff members told Leslie Gelb, people always underestimate Reagan, and that is his strength. But in this instance the president outdid himself. Not only did he sign an arms-control treaty and allow Gorbachev the opportunity to take the spotlight and outshine him, but also he gave up the role he had been playing for twenty-five years and took on another one. In interviews, Reagan said that the Soviet Union under Gorbachev did not seek world domination, that Gorbachev was not responsible for Afghanistan and that many opponents of the treaty on the American right believe nuclear war to be inevitable. He said all this with his usual sweet sincerity. With the same sincerity, he then told an interviewer that he had never sold arms to Iran in exchange for hostages.

Before next January, Reagan may actually succeed in concluding a treaty with the Soviet Union reducing strategic nuclear weapons by fifty percent. If he succeeds, it will be thanks in part to the exposure of the Iran-*contra* affair, which forced upon him a White House and NSC staff actually capable of managing a summit. It will also be thanks to the huge budget deficits that are removing the greatest obstacle in a Soviet agreement by drawing down funds of his cherished Star Wars program. Most probably it will also be thanks to Nancy Reagan, who, as long ago as Reykjavik, told friends that her husband needed an arms-control treaty to assure his place in history.

Since the Washington summit, "movement conservatives" have been quite vociferously impolite, calling the president stupid, frivolous and lightweight. In fact, they have been calling him the same names under their breath for some time. Over the past seven years, Reagan has failed them on many counts. He has never worked hard to push their social agenda—for example, on school prayer and abortion—through Congress. And he has never advanced their foreign policies—e.g., victory for the *contras*—at the expense of civil unrest in the United States. As for abolishing the New Deal state, he has given up on that. Over the years the administration has managed to pinch a few pennies from the domestic budget—cutting programs for the poor by twenty percent and reducing funds for health, education, transportation, and the protection of the environment. But it has not touched popular entitlement programs—such as social security and Medicare.

Reagan's deep commitment to his own popularity has, in other words, saved the nation from the Reagan revolution. It has, however, cost the country a good deal. The price tag might be said to be $2 trillion, since that is the amount the national debt has risen as a result of huge—and hugely popular—tax cuts and large annual increases in military spending. But the cost is actually a good deal more than that. For one thing, Pentagon planners used their wealth to buy the first installments on a vast array of new weapons systems—with the balance yet to be paid for. For another, the administration has simply put off expenditures in the civilian sector, such as the repair of roads and bridges, that cannot be put off forever. Most important, however, Reagan's muddled economic policies—or what might be described as supply-side Keynesian monetarism—have failed to increase productivity as anticipated. In spite of business tax cuts and record-high farm subsidies, American industry and agriculture have lost their competitive edge in the global economy. Six years of growing trade deficits and capital borrowing have turned the United States from the largest creditor into the largest debtor nation in the world.

Finally it must be said that certain Americans have paid a great deal more than others. Through its tax and monetary policies, the administration has redistributed the wealth of the country from the young to the old and from the poor to the rich. Twenty percent of all American children are now estimated to live below the poverty line, and the income disparity between poor and rich is the widest it has been since World War II. But now even the rich are worried, for, as it turns out, the prosperity of the Reagan years has been a sleight of hand—a shell game of borrowing from the future.

In the not-so-distant future, American opinion may turn on the Reagan presidency, charging it with corruption and heartless frivolity and blaming it for every woe. This, then, may be the only moment for nostalgia— the last time to give the man his due. Ronald Reagan, after all, has done a very good job, not just of playing president but of representing the country to itself. Standards of probity and fiscal responsibility were, after all, not much higher on Wall Street or in state and municipal governments than they were in Washington during the Reagan years. And Reagan was the perfect spokesman for those millions of Americans who espouse traditional family values but do not practice them. He has worn the robes of the imperial presidency in an age of military impotence. His rhetorical flourishes and symbolic victories fill patriotic bosoms with a pride unmitigated by the consequences of a real and bloody war fought by American troops. Until recently, at least, his optimism—his almost superhuman cheerfulness—has permitted most Americans to keep their minds off such unpleasant subjects as the budget and trade deficits. Transcending the corruption around him, he has personified American innocence in a wicked world. Though a man in his seventies, he has given us faith in a land of eternal youth. This was not easy, because as all performers know, the world of illusion is a delicate thing. So let us applaud the acrobats and the spangled girls going round and round, for when the music stops, we will be left to put on our galoshes and feel our way out into the dark.

2. Columnist Robert Samuelson Praises the Reagan Record (1989)

Columnist Robert Samuelson conspicuously disagrees with FitzGerald about the Reagan presidency. How can two observers come to such different conclusions? Which of them is more persuasive? Why?

A huge puzzle hangs over Ronald Reagan's presidency. By conventional measures, it's been enormously successful. Double-digit inflation is gone. The economy is in its second-longest expansion since World War II. Reagan championed the most sweeping tax reform in decades. He proposed—and Congress enacted—a program of catastrophic health insurance for the elderly and a major overhaul of welfare. Abroad, he signed the first arms control agreement (the INF [intermediate nuclear forces] treaty) that actually reduces nuclear stockpiles. All these achievements enjoy widespread bipartisan approval. If anyone else (say, Jimmy Carter) had compiled this record, he'd be leaving to loud cheers. Reagan's reputation, however, is more complex.

Everyone concedes his popularity and accomplishments. But he's also treated with casual contempt, as if his success were a fluke. James Reston of *The New York Times* recently ridiculed "Reagan's easy optimism, his amiable incompetence, his tolerance of dubs and sleaze, his cronyism, his preoccupation with stars, his indifference to facts and convenient forgetfulness." This captures the conventional wisdom. Reagan's seen as a public relations president, often ignorant of policy. The picture is more than journalistic invention. The memoirs of White House aides (David Stockman, Donald Regan) show a man aloof from everyday government. So there's the puzzle: How did someone who worked so little at being president do so well at it? The answer is that you don't have to work hard to be a good president.

It's no accident that Reagan is the first two-term president since Eisenhower. Nor is it a coincidence that, despite high personal popularity, both these presidents have been held in low esteem by the journalistic and political elites who dominate presidential commentary. There's an unspoken idea of what a successful president should be like, and neither Eisenhower nor Reagan has conformed. This ideal president should be a forceful leader and activist. He should have a clear national vision and the political savvy to get Congress and the public to follow him. Eisenhower never fit this mold, and Reagan seemed to only at first—when the "Reagan revolution" was a popular political and media myth. Both men reacted to events. Each seemed disengaged. Ike played golf. Ron chopped wood.

The trouble with the idealized president is that it has little to do with the real world. Presidents do not succeed based on how well they advance a personal agenda. These agendas were usually overwhelmed by outside events. Truman is best remembered for the Marshall Plan: a program he didn't design for a problem that barely existed when he replaced Roosevelt. Presidents succeed or fail by how well they make sound judgments on a few issues—where presidential decisions count—that vitally affect the nation's future. Everyday management of government (including most congressional actions) doesn't matter much. Reagan bungled

---

[2]Robert J. Samuelson, "The Enigma," January 16, 1989, pp. 21–23. Reprinted by permission of *The New Republic,* © 1989, The New Republic, Inc.

important matters, most obviously the budget deficits. But these lapses were outweighed by his good judgment on inflation, dealing with the Soviets, and tax reform. By contrast, most other recent presidents have failed the good judgment test.

If Presidents Ford and Kennedy aren't counted—because each served only briefly—Reagan is the first president since Eisenhower not to leave the country in a state of acute crisis. For Lyndon Johnson, the crisis was Vietnam. For Nixon, it was Watergate. For Carter, it was mainly spiraling inflation. These presidents had accomplishments: the enactment of Medicare and Medicaid for Johnson; the opening of China for Nixon; the Israeli-Egyptian peace treaty for Carter. But their achievements were overshadowed. The contrast with Reagan and Eisenhower simply confirms that the president's main job is custodial: it is to deal with the central national problems that occur on his watch, whether the problems are inherited or emerge along the way.

Reagan has been given little credit for having done well at this basic task. His glitzy lifestyle, relaxed work habits, and sugary rhetoric all suggested a man who excelled at performing ceremonial functions but disdained doing the actual job of governing. This vindicated the widely held view that Reagan was a mere actor who didn't deserve to be president. The imagery is false. His last feature movie opened in 1957. For a quarter century he's been involved in politics. For 16 of those years he's held two of the nation's highest elective offices. If he's not a professional politician, who is?

To explain Reagan's success, his critics are full of theories. One is "luck." Reagan had little to do with his administration's achievements and everything to do with its failures. Thus: Paul Volcker (former chairman of the Federal Reserve Board and a 1979 appointee of Carter) defeated double-digit inflation; Treasury Secretary James A. Baker III engineered tax reform; Secretary of State George Shultz (and the rise of Mikhail Gorbachev) made arms control possible; other subordinates handled catastrophic health insurance and welfare reform. But Reagan's incompetence led to the fiascos, from budget deficits to Iran-*contra*. Yet how did such a dopey president (tolerant of "cronyism" and "sleaze") manage to have so many competent subordinates? And if the president was merely manipulated by his subordinates, how was it that he repeatedly ignored their advice in many areas—the budget deficits being the best example?

The good-luck theory clearly fails to explain Reagan's greatest accomplishment and the pillar of his popularity: the reduction of double-digit inflation. The idea that Volcker ought to receive all the credit, and Reagan none, is preposterous. It's true that Volcker led the attack. But though nominally "independent" of the White House, the Federal Reserve cannot long oppose presidential wishes without facing intense political pressures that no agency of technocrats can easily withstand. William Greider's *Secrets of the Temple*—a chronicle of Volcker's time at the Fed— shows that his politics had Reagan's encouragement and backing. After one 1981 session between the two men, David Stockman concluded: "Volcker couldn't have come out of that meeting thinking anything but that the White House wanted tightening."

The ensuing 1981–82 recession was more severe than anyone anticipated. Unemployment reached a peak of 10.8 percent in late 1982. But Volcker did not relax the tough, high interest rate policies until inflation was clearly broken—and Reagan didn't force his hand by blasting the Fed in public. That's the important point. It's easy to forget now how much economists agonized in the late 1970s over the difficulty of controlling inflation. Reagan and Volcker showed that government could govern. With nerve and patience, someone could take the unpopular decisions that had huge long-term benefits. Would Carter have done the same? The answer surely is no.

Carter had trouble sticking with any anti-inflation policy. He tinkered with price and credit controls. As unemployment passed nine percent, he probably would have panicked and forced Volcker to relent. The risk would have been continued stagflation. With inflation at six to eight percent (down from 1979's 13.3 percent), fear of going back into double digits would have inhibited the recovery. Carter partisans say he's unfairly maligned. They blame his inflation on oil prices and credit him for naming Volcker. The first argument is wrong. By 1978—before the second oil shock—inflation had reached nine percent, up from 4.8 percent in 1976, and was rising. As for Volcker, he was an afterthought. Carter was firing Treasury Secretary W. Michael Blumenthal and replacing him with Fed Chairman G. William Miller. Someone had to run the Fed, and Volcker wasn't even the first choice.

Another anti-Reagan theory is that his success is a mirage. The press was hypnotized by his charm or manipulated by media advisers. This theory is also crazy. First, the press dwelled on Reagan's failures, bad habits, and embarrassments, from the disastrous Lebanon policy to his press conference errors to Nancy's astrologer. Second, the theory makes his popularity a media contrivance separate from public approval of his performance. Opinion polls contradict that. In his first two years Reagan's average approval ratings were below those of every president—except Ford—since Truman, as sociologists Michael Shudson and Elliot King of the University of California, San Diego, have pointed out. In his second year, for instance, Reagan's approval rating averaged 43 percent compared with Carter's 46 percent, Nixon's 56 percent, Johnson's 67 percent, Kennedy's 72 percent, and Eisenhower's 65 percent. The ratings rose after people found the Reagan presidency more to their liking: that is, after inflation dropped and the 1981–82 recession ended.

Where Reagan's critics hit pay dirt are the budget deficits. There were times (especially after his landslide 1984 re-election) when more energetic leadership might have broken the deadlock. The president held back. Either he wouldn't risk unpopular actions or believed that the deficits would restrain government spending. So the deficits persist. But his failure needs to be kept in perspective. The apocalyptic language often used to describe it has a political purpose: to portray the deficits as such a catastrophe—such an awesome act of irresponsibility—that they cancel any Reagan achievements. This view misrepresents both the politics and economics of deficits.

By 1980 Americans simply wanted more government than they were willing to pay for. They thought taxes were too high and defense spending too low. They opposed cuts in government services, especially entitlements such as Social Security or Medicare. No one wanted budget deficits. These preferences couldn't all be met simultaneously. Reagan emphasized lower taxes and higher defense spending. Congress resisted cuts in domestic spending. Deficits emerged because they're the least painful political alternative. For all of Reagan's stubbornness on taxes, he didn't cut them so much as stabilize them. In the past three years [1986–1989] they've averaged 18.9 percent of gross national product, compared with 18.8 percent in the Carter years and 20.1 percent in 1981. Congress has halted the defense buildup. The deficits endure because they reflect genuine conflicts in popular demands.

It's true, as charged, that the United States has lived beyond its means. Part of Reagan's prosperity was borrowed from the future. Our excess spending was covered by imports. Now that the trade deficit is dropping, choices can't be postponed indefinitely. There are two ways to restrain our excess national spending: we can do so explicitly by reducing the budget deficits; or we can let the market do the job through higher interest rates, exchange rate changes, more inflation, or some other mechanism that will restrain private spending. The danger of leaving the job to the market is that the ultimate social costs may be higher. For example, higher interest rates could depress private investment, which might harm future productivity growth and living standards.

These economic consequences are serious, but not calamitous. The economy's main problem is actually the poor growth of productivity—the ability to raise our national wealth. This is the basic cause of the budget deficits. When productivity rose rapidly in the 1950s and '60s, people felt they could afford more government and more private spending. Now the conflict is acute. Economists don't fully understand the productivity slowdown. Nor can government easily cure it. But the Reagan years coincided with an improvement. Since 1979 business productivity has grown 1.4 percent annually. That's twice the 0.6 percent rate between 1973 and 1979, but below the 1947–73 average of three percent. Despite budget deficits and other problems—stubborn poverty and the savings and loan crisis, to mention two—the economy is far healthier today than a decade ago.

A president can't do everything. The presidency is, as political scientist Richard Neustadt has argued, a weak institution. Other centers of power abound, as do opportunities for political failure. The president cannot determine every piece of legislation, which, regardless of his personal views, will be largely shaped by bureaucrats, interest groups, and congressional committees. Foreign relations with most countries have their own drift. A president who tries to do too much risks seeing his reputation sink under the weight of all the visible (and inevitable) setbacks. He must pick and choose what he considers important. Unlike Johnson, Nixon, and Carter, Reagan preserved the authority of his office.

In this, he also resembles Eisenhower. When historians rummaged through Eisenhower's presidency, they discovered that the general was far more crafty and calculated than contemporaries had thought. Perhaps historians will decide the same of Reagan. But perhaps not: the inside of the White House is far more visible today—with tidal waves of media leaks and every janitor writing a memoir—than in Eisenhower's era. Maybe Reagan acted, or didn't, mostly on instinct. But whatever the case, Eisenhower and Reagan shared a common characteristic disparaged by their critics: an ability to stay above events.

Eisenhower was criticized for being too "non-political." Reagan was more ideological and partisan, but his partisanship was often only cosmetic and rhetorical. His social agenda (anti-abortion, school prayer), which antagonized majorities of Americans, was pursued halfheartedly. Where Reagan strayed too far from the mainstream, he was frustrated by Congress, interest groups, or public opinion. But he accepted these restraints. There was no fanatical fight to keep James Watt in the Cabinet. Like Eisenhower, Reagan sensed that a president cannot succeed unless he is a unifying figure. And he cannot be that if he becomes too deeply embroiled in too many political firefights.

The truth is that the Reagan presidency falls firmly in the centrist tradition of U.S. politics. A liberal could as easily boast of his major accomplishments: inflation's decline, tax reform, the arms control treaty, welfare reform. Reagan gets blamed for many things that would have happened even if he hadn't become president. Government social spending would have been squeezed anyway, simply because there was less money to pay for old and new programs. Granting this, Reagan's changes to government were modest. He didn't demolish the welfare state or end demands for more government services. Indeed, his success in lowering inflation "had the unintended consequence of ending the revolt against government," as analyst William Schneider has noted.

By the same token, Reagan didn't transform the political landscape. The Great Communicator didn't create a conservative majority. In 1987 only 20 percent of college freshmen considered themselves "conservative," while 25 percent labeled themselves "liberal" and 56 percent "middle of the road." The figures have hardly changed since 1980, when conservatives were 18 percent; liberals, 22 percent; and middle-of-the-roaders, 60 percent. The conservatives are disappointed that Reagan didn't do more. But they misunderstand what happened. "We underestimated the stamina of liberalism," Edwin J. Feulner, Jr., head of the Heritage Foundation, recently complained. No, they misjudged Reagan. His presidency has been more cautious than conservative. In the end, it's been a triumph of competence, not ideology.

3. The Reagan Revolution in Historical Context (1982)

As a young man in the 1930s, Ronald Reagan voted for Franklin Roosevelt. When he was elected president in 1980, however, Reagan proclaimed that the real loser in the election of that year was not his opponent, Jimmy Carter, but the liberal tradition associated with the Square Deal of Theodore Roosevelt, the New Deal of Franklin Roosevelt, and the Fair Deal of Harry Truman, as illustrated in the cartoon that follows. Did Reagan actually overthrow the liberal reform tradition? In what ways did Reagan's presidency resemble the others represented here? In what ways did it differ from them?

---

[3]Copyright John Trever, *The Albuquerque Journal.*

Thought Provokers

1. Did Reagan's electoral victory in 1980 ring the death knell for the philosophy of the New Deal and the Great Society? Did the Reagan administration constitute a true revolution in U.S. politics?
2. Did Reagan's massive military buildup make the world a safer place? Did the prospect of a Star Wars defense stabilize or destabilize the international scene? To what degree was U.S. foreign policy responsible for the changes in Russia and Eastern Europe in the late 1980s and early 1990s? Were there any positive features of the Cold War?
3. Why were social issues like school prayer and abortion forced onto the political agenda in the 1980s? Do they belong in the formal political arena? Once there, can they ever be removed?
4. What developments gave rise to the neoconservative philosophy? What has been the impact of neoconservatism? Are ideas important in politics?
5. How will the future judge Ronald Reagan, the man, as *president?* How will it judge his *presidency?*

42

The American People
Face a New Century

As our case is new, so we must think anew and act
anew. We must disenthrall ourselves, and then we
shall save our country.

Abraham Lincoln, 1862

Prologue: Americans were still an affluent people as the twentieth century
neared its sunset, yet they worried if prosperity would be as secure, and as widely
shared, as it had been in the fabulously productive post–World War II years. Powerful economic forces and dizzying technological changes seemed to be dividing
American society into those who had very much and those who had relatively little,
an alarming prospect for the stability of a democratic society. Women, who were
among the principal beneficiaries of the explosive boom of the postwar era, continued to debate the implications of their changing economic and social roles. Social
issues affecting women, particularly abortion rights, moved to the forefront of the
nation's political agenda and contributed to a widening political "gender gap" between men and women. A no less ominous gap appeared to be opening between
the generations, as the society grew progressively older, and more and more retirees
depended on fewer and fewer active workers to keep the Social Security system sol-
vent. One major source of new workers was immigration, but immigration too generated its own problems, particularly in California, home to some 40 percent of the
nation's immigrants by the 1990s. Meanwhile Americans debated, as they had for
more than two centuries, how best to make their experiment in multicultural
democracy serve the needs of all citizens.

A. An Unequal Society?

I. Lester Thurow Decries Growing Inequality (1995)

*Evidence mounted in the 1990s that the American economy had undergone a fun-
damental shift in the 1970s. By about 1973, the long post–World War II wave of
increasing productivity and mounting prosperity apparently crested, and was followed by decades of slow economic growth and stagnant real incomes. Although*

economists and historians remained puzzled over the precise causes of this change, its consequences were increasingly apparent and troublesome. The economist Lester Thurow here describes the basic contours of the transformation and points especially to its impact on income distribution. What does he see as the most disturbing implication of the new economic order? What remedies does he envision?

The year 1968 was among the worst years this century for the United States—assassinations, riots, campus uprisings and the infamous Democratic National Convention in Chicago. But an event that attracted little or no attention at the time may ultimately prove to have the most lasting and destabilizing effects of all. Suddenly that year, like a surge in a long immobile glacier, economic inequality started to rise.

Among men working full time—the group most sharply affected—inequalities in earnings between the top 20 percent of wage earners and the bottom 20 percent doubled in the next two and a half decades. By 1973, the median wage for all men working full time began to fall.

Over the next 20 years, men's earnings fell 11 percent, from $34,048 to $30,407, even though the earnings of the top 20 percent grew steadily and the real, per-capita gross domestic product (G.D.P.) rose 29 percent.

Within the family, American women came to the rescue of American men. Mostly by working many more hours per year, women kept median household incomes slowly rising until 1989. In 1989, however, median real wages for women working full time year-round also began to fall. Preliminary data for 1994 and early 1995 indicate that these wage declines are accelerating. As a result, since 1989 median household incomes have fallen more than 7 percent after correcting for inflation and family size, to $31,241 in 1993, from $33,585. Already working full time, women had no more extra hours of work effort to contribute to the family's income.

The same sharp rise in inequality has occurred in the distribution of wealth. The share of total net worth of the top one-half of 1 percent of the population rose from 26 to 31 percent in just six years, between 1983 and 1989. By the early 1990's the share of wealth (more than 40 percent) held by the top 1 percent of the population was essentially double what it had been in the mid-1970's and back to where it was in the late 1920's, before the introduction of progressive taxation.

These are uncharted waters for American democracy. Since accurate data have been kept, beginning in 1929, America has never experienced falling real wages for a majority of its work force while its per-capita G.D.P. was rising. In effect, we are conducting an enormous social and political experiment—something like putting a pressure cooker on the stove over a full flame and waiting to see how long it takes to explode.

Behind these changes lie technological shifts that demand a more skilled work force, competition from lower-paid but well-educated workers in the rest of the world and two decades of Federal Reserve Board policies of creating unemployment to fight inflation. There also has been a big shift in the implicit contract between owners and workers.

After World War II, white-collar workers and managers came to expect lifetime employment with rising wages, assuming their firms remained profitable. Blue-collar workers, who also expected and received real annual-wage increases, did face the prospect of occasional layoffs. But these were restricted mostly to younger workers, who could expect to be recalled in the next boom. This implicit contract has been smashed by companies with high and rising profits that are nevertheless reducing wages, eliminating fringe benefits and permanently laying off hundreds of thousands of workers from what had been society's best jobs.

The middle class is scared, and it should be. The supports for its economic security are being kicked out from under it. The remedy must include a huge program of re-educating and retraining the bottom 60 percent of the work force, investments in research and high-tech infrastructure and a willingness to run the economy with tight labor markets so that labor shortages push wages upward. But it takes organization to do that, and it's not clear that America has the will to get organized to solve its problems.

Historically, some very successful societies have existed for millennia with enormous inequalities of wealth and income—ancient Egypt, imperial Rome, classical China, the Incas, the Aztecs. But all these societies had political and social ideologies that fit this economic reality. None believed in equality in any sense—not theoretically, not politically, not socially, not economically. Democracies have a problem with rising economic inequality precisely because they believe in political equality—"one person, one vote."

One solution to this divergent distribution of power is to drive out the economically weak. A 19th-century economist, Herbert Spencer, introduced the idea of "survival of the fittest" capitalism, a phrase that Charles Darwin appropriated to explain evolution. Spencer believed that it was the duty of the economically strong to drive the economically weak into extinction; that drive was in fact the secret of capitalism's strength.

Until recently, Spencer's suggested solution was roundly rejected, and democratic governments systematically worked to reduce earnings and wealth inequalities. A state-financed safety net protected the weak (the old, the sick, the unemployed, the poor) from economic extinction. Social investments in education, infrastructure and research and development helped raise the earning power of the middle class. The capitalist's power to exploit his work force was legally limited, and a combination of social and legal pressures insured that rising output was shared with the work force.

The Republicans' balanced-budget plan essentially offers a return to Spencer's survival-of-the-fittest capitalism. It raises taxes on working Americans and lowers them for the wealthy. It shreds the safety net, apparently on the theory that individuals facing starvation will knuckle down and work. Fear will make them hold on so tightly to the economic trapeze that they won't fall off.

No one has ever tried survival-of-the-fittest capitalism for any extended period in a modern democracy, so we don't know how far rising inequality and falling real wages can go before something snaps. Social systems can certainly snap; the recent implosion of the Soviet Union is a good example. But to snap, there must be some alternative banner under which the population can quickly regroup. In the case of Communism, that alternative banner was capitalism. But if capitalism does not produce acceptable results, there simply isn't any alternative system under which the people can quickly regroup. As a result, a sudden social collapse is highly unlikely.

What is more likely is a vicious cycle of individual disaffection, social disorganization, falling incomes and a slow downward spiral, something like the long slide from the peak of the Roman Empire to the bottom of the Middle Ages. There were those in the Middle Ages, for example, who knew everything the Romans knew about fertilizing crops. What later Europeans lost was the ability to get organized to fertilize. Without fertilization, crop yields fell so far that the best land yielded only three pieces of grain for each one that was planted. Put aside one seed to plant next year, subtract seeds eaten or spoiled by vermin and there is very little left to sustain life through the winter. There simply were not enough calories available to sustain vigorous activity, and the quality of life inevitably declined.

Today we are refusing to make the investments in the modern equivalents of fertilization—education, infrastructure, research and development. Public spending on infrastructure, as a percentage of G.D.P., has been cut in half in the last two decades and is scheduled to be reduced even further by Washington's budget cutters.

Rome's downward spiral did not begin with an external defeat. It began with a period of uncertainty and disorientation. Further military expansion no longer made sense, since Rome was at its natural geographic limits and facing empty deserts, steppes and forests. Our equivalent is the disorientation that came at the end of the cold war. The enemy was gone, yet defense budgets had to be maintained.

Rome was faced with huge numbers of immigrants who wanted to attain the higher standard of living they saw before them, But Rome had lost the ability to make them into Romans. Perhaps Proposition 187 in California means that America has also lost that ability.

Literacy, widespread in the Roman Empire, was restricted to a few cloistered monks in the depths of the Middle Ages. Today functional illiteracy is on the rise even amid a sharp escalation in the educational requirements for productive workers.

During the medieval era, banditry became widespread and was widely accepted (remember Robin Hood) as a populist revenge upon the defenders of the political and social order. Unwalled cities and free citizens were replaced by walled manor houses and serfs. Walled and gated communities are once again on the rise. Twenty-eight million Americans live in such communities, if one counts privately guarded apartment houses, and the number is expected to double in the next decade.

No one can know what will happen if inequality continues to rise and a large majority of our families experience falling real incomes. But if capitalism does not deliver rising real wages in a period when the total economic pie is expanding, its hold on the political allegiance of the population will be threatened. Similarly, if the democratic political process cannot reverse the trend to inequality, democracy will eventually be discredited. What we do know is that a large group of hostile voters who draw no benefits from the economic system and don't think the government cares is not a particularly promising recipe for economic or political success.

2. Michael Walzer Sees Dangers for Democracy (1996)

The philosopher Michael Walzer sees not only an economic change in the years after the early 1970s, but a momentous political shift as well, in which the liberal, activist-

---

[2]Michael Walzer, "Gulf Crisis," *The New Republic,* August 5, 1996, p. 25. Reprinted by permission of *The New Republic.* Copyright © 1996, The New Republic, Inc.

government programs of the New Deal and post–World War II years gave way to the conservative, small-government policies of the 1980s and 1990s. What is the relationship between these economic and political developments in American society in the past quarter century? What does Walzer mean by "countervailing power"? Is it likely to be an effective answer for the problems he identifies?

For much of the last decade, academic and public debate has focused intensely on whether multiculturalism—sometimes interpreted as healthy pluralism, sometimes as frightening division—is leading, in [historian] Arthur Schlesinger's words, to the "The Disuniting of America." But lost in the arguments over race, gender and immigration is the threat to American culture posed by a different division: the one between rich and poor. A recent U.S. Census Bureau report reveals that in 1994, the last year for which complete data are available, the richest 20 percent of Americans earned close to 50 percent of the country's total income while the poorest 20 percent earned only a little more than 5 percent.

Though we've come to treat such news as inevitable, it isn't. The free movement of capital, labor and commodities obviously makes for inequality, but not necessarily for the gulf we now see in the U.S. While inequality has been increasing for the past twenty-five years, before that it declined for several decades. The reasons for both the recent increase and the previous decline are more political than economic.

The modestly increasing egalitarianism of American society in the 1940s and '50s depended on what John Kenneth Galbraith called "countervailing power." A key example was the power of the labor movement to counter corporate America's search for profits. The development of this balance, [John Kenneth] Galbraith wrote forty-four years ago in *American Capitalism,* is a "normal economic process." But Galbraith recognized that, to succeed, countervailing power requires the intervention of the state. Workers organize naturally to strengthen their market position, but they will just as naturally be repressed by owners and managers unless they receive political protection.

Today's income inequality stems from a dramatic loss of such protection. Despite a recent spate of good publicity stemming from the AFL-CIO's effective attacks on Republican congressional candidates, labor's influence remains in deep decline. Ronald Reagan's 1981 replacement of striking air traffic controllers crippled the effectiveness of strikes, and their frequency has diminished substantially in recent years. Bill Clinton's unfulfilled 1992 campaign promise to outlaw the hiring of replacement workers notwithstanding, the federal government remains indifferent to labor's plight. And labor's weakness has made possible a series of aggressive campaigns—first by the Reagan administration, and now by the Gingrich Congress—on behalf of greater inequality. These campaigns—which combine a celebration of the free market with attacks on government regulation, federal welfare entitlements and the progressive income tax—combine theory and practice in ways that would have made the old left envious.

Business's need to remain globally competitive is part of the reason for these campaigns, but, more importantly, it is the rationale. No doubt, the new global economy poses a hard question: How much room to maneuver do national governments have in regulating their economies and providing welfare services? The example of our European and Asian competitors, who face the same pressures to cut public spending, suggests there is, given the political will, at least room enough to avoid the kinds of inequality now developing in the U.S. Third World standards (sweat shops, unenforced safety rules, intensified discipline on the shop floor, loss of health insurance, lower wages, and so on) are not being imposed on American workers to "save" their jobs. The imposition has at least something to do with the prospect of Third World fortunes for American owners and managers.

Galbraith describes countervailing power as a feature of American capitalism. It is better described, it seems to me, as a feature of liberal democracy, a political order that systematically limits the use of power. The limits work in the market only if they work in state and society as well. They depend upon civil responsibility and popular liveliness as much as upon entrepreneurial invention.

The kind of inequality toward which we are drifting will make it harder to sustain this responsible and lively public. With rare exceptions, men and women do not enter the political arena on their own. They come in parties and movements, organized for a purpose, defending their interests and ideals. We still have groups like that: feminists, environmentalists, Christian rightists, and so on. But the news media's homogenization of American life, and the resulting erosion of distinctive working-class cultures, means that material interests and egalitarian ideals are difficult to defend today, difficult even to represent coherently. Hence the general decrease in political participation, especially at lower educational and income levels.

What follows from this decline is uncertain. One possibility is populism of a kind that has long been absent from American life: a frightened, angry and disorganized mass periodically mobilized by demagogues, cult figures and tinhorn charismatics. This kind of populism, perhaps foreshadowed by Pat Buchanan, Ross Perot and Louis Farrakhan, is the product of a certain sort of inequality: where the differences are radical, where they are not mediated by strong middling groups, where the "lower orders" are without their own institutions or habits of collective action.

So inequality is dangerous for liberal democracy. And the dangers are self-perpetuating: disparities of wealth make it difficult to organize countervailing powers, and the absence of countervailing powers makes for increasingly radical disparities. The long-term effect of this process, the characteristic product of radical inequality, is tyranny in everyday life: the arrogance of the wealthy, the humbling of the poor. We are not there yet, but the demonizing of "welfare mothers," the challenge to universal entitlements such as Medicare and Social Security, the drift toward means-tested, stigmatized welfare programs like AFDC [Aid to Families with Dependent Children] and Medicaid—these are early examples of social tyranny. That there is so little resistance to these trends suggests we are already feeling the cumulative impact of inequality.

Democracy is at risk when the fellowship of citizens resonates so weakly, when we are so unready to come to each other's aid. Yet we still have a fairly strong economy, a multitude of voluntary associations and social movements, large numbers of politically competent men and women, a basically liberal state with constitutional protections for dissent and protest. We still have a fundamentally decent politics. What the Census Bureau report means is that all this is at risk. And our political system is paralyzed when it comes to addressing it. I am not sure about specific policies, but we might well begin by reviving the theory and practice of countervailing power.

B. American Women: New Roles, New Problems

1. Nannerl Keohane Analyzes the "Glass Ceiling" (1991)

Spurred by a militant feminist movement, women marched by the millions into the workforce and into all kinds of previously all-male strongholds in the 1970s, 1980s, and 1990s. But they rarely marched at the head of the column; rather, leadership positions remained a virtual male monopoly, and a "pink-collar ghetto" of predominantly female occupational categories emerged. Nannerl Keohane, then president of Wellesley College, an all-women's institution, here describes the particular problems women face in the modern era. What does she see as the principal obstacles to women's further advancement in the workplace? How likely are those obstacles to be overcome in the future?

My topic is leadership—a sorely needed skill in our country and our world these days; and particularly women leaders—an even scarcer phenomenon; and how we might prepare more women to be leaders in the future.

Thinking about women in leadership can lead to very different conclusions depending on where you look, and how you look at it. It's like the old joke about the optimist—who thinks this is the best of all possible worlds—and the pessimist—who agrees with her.

First, the optimist's perspective:

More and more women are holding leadership positions around the world these days. There are women generals and women judges, women neurosurgeons and opera conductors and newspaper editors and even, occasionally, a woman CEO.

Such new leaders join the legions of strong women who have traditionally been leaders in more familiar fields: in early childhood education, on the boards of symphonies and art museums, in the soup kitchens and in the peace movement, in all kinds of non-profit organizations that so enrich our lives.

There are more women in politics, as well, more women governors, mayors, even presidential and vice-presidential candidates these days. If someone had said ten years ago that the mayors of several of America's largest cities in 1990 would be women, or that one-half the cabinet, one-half the legislature, and the prime minister of Norway would be female, they would have been laughed out of court.

The clearest indicator that women have made our mark in positions of leadership in our society may be that we have begun to engage in some traditional male behavior surrounding leadership. I read not too long ago about a typical political "roasting session," with one unusual feature: all the participants were well-known women political figures. Some of the feminist old guard—Bella Abzug, Gloria Steinem and so forth—were roasting Geraldine Ferraro.* One of the questions went

---

[1]"Educating Women for Leadership" by Nannerl O. Keohane, delivered to the City Club of Cleveland, April 26, 1991. Reprinted by permission of Nannerl O. Keohane, President of Duke University.

*Bella Abzug was a U.S. Representative from New York in the 1970s; Gloria Steinem, a prominent feminist, founded *MS* magazine; Geraldine Ferraro was a U.S. Representative from New York and as Walter Mondale's running mate on the Democratic ticket in 1980, she became the first woman nominated for vice president by a major political party.

as follows: "What can we learn about women in politics from Geraldine Ferraro's vice-presidential candidacy?" The answer: "Don't get married."

Still, the pessimist insists, the examples I've cited of women at the top can hardly be taken to be typical of us all. Many things still stand in the way of women ambitious for leadership in politics, in corporate life, in colleges and universities. It is true that women are gaining *entry* to many fields in increasing numbers; but there are still very few women at the top, however visible and successful those few may be. The problem lies not in getting your Ph.D. or your MBA—but in moving from the troops to the top jobs, through the shoals of middle management, where most women seem to founder. What happens between the bottom and the top?

A first cut at an explanation holds that it's simply a matter of time. The women who are coming in today will be the leaders of tomorrow, in a kind of "trickle-up" phenomenon. Thus, all we have to do is wait for them to make their progress up the ladder in numbers commensurate to the MDs and MBAs, and then the problem will be solved. But this is surely too sanguine; for there is a specific problem area five or ten years after young women are hired and begin their professional development, when it's time to get the big promotion, become a partner, run for office, or get tenure. At this point, many women get sidetracked, lower their ambitions, downplay their careers.

A great deal has been written about this: images have been used—especially the "glass ceiling." Using a metaphor from one of my favorite sports—running—I like to call this problem "the Wall." It's like hitting a wall when you're running smoothly. All of a sudden you run out of steam, bumping into an obstacle that seems almost physical, blocking your path. What causes this depressingly familiar phenomenon in our careers? And how can women break through "the wall," or the "glass ceiling" to become leaders in corporate, political and professional careers?

According to one explanation, the problem lies with men: men control the gateways to success, and they are reluctant to let women in. Men fear successful women, are uncomfortable with women leaders, resist threats to male bonding and changes in the familiar scenery. So when it comes time for the big promotion, they look for reasons to promote a man instead.

We cannot discount male chauvinism; it still accounts for a significant part of the obstacles that women face. But there are many confident CEOs and political leaders who really want women to succeed—either because they have become sensitive to women's talents and needs (perhaps because of an ambitious and eager daughter), or because they can do the cold arithmetic about the changing work force or the demographics of the women's vote.

Other kinds of explanations for the glass ceiling attribute the problem to something that is wrong with women—perhaps we lack ambition; perhaps women do not really want other women to succeed. These explanations may have worked in the past, when ambitions were systematically suppressed and even ridiculed; when the rare woman who made it to the top had fought so hard that she could not bring herself to accept the fact that young women coming up behind her might make it more easily, with her help. But today, young women fresh out of business school or law school seem just as ambitious as their brothers, and they show no fear of the successes that come to them at the start of their careers. And many successful women nowadays do indeed want other women to succeed, and go out of their way to help them do so.

One more suspicion may be lurking about an explanation for the glass ceiling. Maybe women most of all want to have babies, and when the biological clock begins ticking in our thirties, our bodies realize this and no matter how ambitious or energetic we had been about our jobs, we go back to nature. Of course, men want to have families as well, and they may also succumb to the lure of hearth and home at about that same age. But the *consequences* of heeding the biological clock are very different for women and for men.

Traditionally, at least, when the young bachelor marries, he acquires a loving helpmate who prepares his meals and raises his children and gives smashing dinner parties to advance his career; all of which, if he marries wisely, wins the approval of his superiors and his peers, and gives him new advantages in the competition for professional success, smoothing his way to the top. But the young woman who marries is expected to take on a second job, as busy as the first, and become a successful homemaker and mother at the same time as she struggles for professional recognition.

We are all aware of the difficulties of combining career and family; even with the cooperative and supportive partner, the demands are enormous. And women still take responsibility for almost all the housework and a large proportion of childcare. As we also know, statistics show that a large and growing majority of women of child-bearing age are employed outside the home. Yet jobs are still constructed with the expectation that there will be one partner in the home, and the other in the workforce, even though only a small percentage of Americans actually live that way these days.

High-powered jobs, leadership jobs, mean you have to be available many nights and weekends. Such jobs make no allowance for the fact that Johnny might get sick or Mary have the starring role in the school play. Our society has woefully inadequate support systems for young children and working parents, and these facts bear most heavily on mothers. In such a setting, it is hardly surprising that few women manage to sustain their ambitions long enough to make it to the top. For significant change to occur in the pattern of women in leadership, there will need to be more flexibility in our expectations for how one performs in high-powered jobs at different stages in one's life, and also changes in the support systems for working parents. . . .

2. Women Assault The Citadel (1995)

In 1995, after lengthy legal proceedings to clear the way, Shannon Faulkner became the first woman to enroll at The Military College of South Carolina (known as The Citadel), a historically all-male military college in Charleston, South Carolina. Within days, she withdrew, prompting a nationwide debate on the suitability of

---

2"A Lesson from the Citadel in Double Standards," *San Francisco Chronicle,* August 25, 1995. Cynthia Tucker's column is reprinted courtesy Chronicle Features, San Francisco, California. All rights reserved.

women in certain institutions and occupations and on the traditional definitions of gender roles. The following editorial places Faulkner's experience in the context of other "firsts." To what extent did her fate at The Citadel mirror larger issues of managing social change and breaking established stereotypes? Are all social roles infinitely malleable? Are there any limits of nature or custom that need to be acknowledged when thinking about gender roles?

During the week that Shannon Faulkner departed The Citadel, at least 34 other "knobs" quit—burned out, exhausted, fed up, depressed or had suddenly come to their senses. You heard very little about them. They were all men.

Faulkner was not allowed to go quietly, as they were. Colleagues in the corps of cadets did not cheer the departures of those young men, as they so childishly cheered Faulkner's.

There are lessons in Faulkner's departure from The Citadel, but not the ones offered by her ready defenders or detractors. Her experience says next to nothing about whether women can stand up to the rigors of The Citadel.

Instead, the controversy surrounding her departure merely bears out an old truth: Women and people of color are judged by a double standard. Our failures are magnified.

Nowhere is that more true than for those who take up the daunting challenge of being "firsts"—kicking open doors, knocking down walls, breaking through glass ceilings. Theirs is not a task for mere mortals.

Read the memoirs of any "first black" or "first woman" who broke through a significant barrier. The challenge they chose to accept required mental toughness, strength of character, an endurance hard to imagine.

Before she entered the corps at The Citadel, Faulkner might have benefited from reading the story of Benjamin O. Davis Jr., who was graduated from the U.S. Military Academy at West Point in 1936, the first black man in the 20th century to achieve that distinction. Throughout his career at West Point, he endured searing isolation.

Of course, it is no accident that so many of those "firsts"—especially in the civil rights movement—did so well. Many were chosen by strategists who wanted them to succeed and were acutely aware of the burdens that trailblazers would bear. Fair or not, every black person would be judged by the actions of those "firsts."

"MacNeil/Lehrer NewsHour" correspondent Charlayne Hunter-Gault, the first black woman to attend the University of Georgia, recounts the search for black students able to withstand both intense scrutiny and harsh circumstances: "They would have to find two squeaky-clean students who couldn't be challenged on moral, intellectual or educational grounds . . . ," she writes in her memoirs, *In My Place.*

In his prize-winning book, *Bearing the Cross,* historian David Garrow recounts a similar search for the right person to challenge the system of segregated buses in Montgomery, Ala.

Before Rosa Parks stood up to white authorities, Claudette Colvin, a 15-year-old high school student, refused to surrender her seat to a white rider. Colvin had courage, but lacked the rest of the necessary credentials: She was pregnant out of wedlock. While pregnant black girls deserved to be able to sit at the front of the bus, black activists were not about to allow her to be their standard-bearer. Her frailties were too obvious.

Jackie Robinson, the first black man to play major league baseball, was chosen as much for his temperament as his athletic talents. He was expected to quietly and gracefully endure the indignities, the taunts, the constant abuse without so much as a sullen look. He had to be better than most of us.

Shannon Faulkner's sin was that she turned out to be less than superhuman. The 34 young men who dropped out of The Citadel in their first week paid no great penalty for that. Faulkner did. So did the cause she championed.

3. The "Gender Gap" in Politics (1996)

Political analysts in the 1980s and 1990s detected remarkable correlations between voters' political views and their gender. Increasingly, men and women seemed to be politically divided along lines of gender difference. In the following discussion of the "gender gap," what issues seem to be most potent in creating that gap? How have the political parties contributed to creating it? How have they responded to it? Are women likely to sustain a distinctive voting bloc over the long term? Why—or why not?

The gap is suddenly hot, very hot. It has already been around for nearly a generation, a 5 to 9 percentage point difference between the sexes in the candidates they support for President and a smaller gap in Congressional races. Early in the Clinton-Dole campaign, however, the gap turned epic—20 percent or more in some surveys. . . .

A century ago, suffrage leaders predicted that when women got the right to vote, they'd vote as a bloc for clean government, peace, temperance and progressive programs to protect children and families from the worst ravages of the Industrial Revolution. "That was the hope and expectation," says Lynn Sherr, a biographer of Susan B. Anthony and an ABC correspondent. Anthony told an interviewer in 1871 that when enfranchised, women "propose to do away with vice and immorality, to prevent the social evil"—prostitution—"by giving women remunerative employment, to forbid the sale of spiritous liquors and tobacco, and to teach men a higher and nobler life than the one they now follow."

Politicians, fearing for their lives as suffrage approached, passed a slew of laws on consumer protection, child labor and prenatal care in the early 1920's. But then nothing much happened. Women seemed to vote the same way men did, except in fewer numbers. Interest in women as a voting class vanished, and the prenatal-care program ran out of money.

When I was studying at the University of Massachusetts in 1969, women's political behavior took up a grand total of two paragraphs in our American politics textbook. The author, John H. Fenton, believed that women tended to cluster to the far left and far right, because they had little experience with the real world. "If a man

---

[3]Excerpted from "Wooing the Women," *The New York Times Magazine,* July 28, 1996. Copyright © 1996 by The New York Times Co. Reprinted by permission.

becomes interested in extreme politics, his views are likely to be challenged by both his associates at work and his neighborhood friends," the book said. "Typically, women have a less variegated history of friendship and associations, and when they acquire extreme political views they are less likely to have them challenged by their friends or their experience." Fenton died recently, and I never had a chance to find out how he explained the Michigan Militia.

Studying women's voting behavior was difficult back then. Most researchers were poring over election data, trying to figure out where the Hungarians and Germans and WASP's [white Anglo-Saxon Protestants] and Jews lived and to chart the ebbs and flows of their precincts. Women had no special neighborhoods. They were all mixed in with men, difficult to quantify. It was easiest to assume that women voted the same way their husbands did.

Gallup polls did show differences between the sexes in voting in the post–World War II years, but they did not reveal a major difference in the way men and women regarded the political world. Women liked Ike better than male voters, and contrary to all the legends about John Kennedy's sexual charisma, they split, 51–49, for Nixon in 1960, while men voted for Kennedy, 52–48. Women were slightly more favorable to Hubert Humphrey than men in 1968 only because more men voted for the third-party candidate, George Wallace. Four years later, in Nixon's landslide over George McGovern, there was virtually no sex difference in the vote. But if only women had been voting in 1976, Jimmy Carter would have never beaten Gerald Ford.

Flash forward to 1979. The Republican pollster Richard B. Wirthlin, working on the Reagan campaign, peered into a stew of data and discerned an amazing new element floating just beneath the surface: women were pulling away from Ronald Reagan and toward the Democrats, while men were being drawn deeper into the orbit of the Republican Party. "It was one of those things that once you see it, you can't take your eyes off it," says Wirthlin reverently, in the tones of a scientist who has just discovered a new variation of the Ebola virus.

The gender gap had arrived. It was not exactly the mass movement the suffragists promised, but in the hypersensitive world of modern politics, a gap is almost as good as a bloc. Women were going off on their own, requiring special treatment. By 1984, Reagan was running ads on daytime television trying to convince housewives that he had really done something about inflation.

The cause of the gap seems to be remarkably basic. Both Republican and Democratic pollsters agree that women, as a group, believe in an activist government— particularly the social safety net—more than men do. . . .

A fascinating thing about the gender gap is the number of theories it has spawned about who is gapping and why. Among the more interesting:

Women Didn't Go Anywhere—It's the Men Who Took a Hike

If women are voting for candidates who will protect Medicare, Social Security, aid to education and a safety net for the poor, they're only behaving as both sexes did before the Reagan revolution. Barbara Ehrenreich, the essayist, argued in *Newsweek* that because of late marriage, single motherhood and the invention of 24-hour sports channels, "men are living in a state of radical disconnection from the women-and-children part of the human race," which still has to worry about caring for elderly parents and finding affordable day care and decent schools.

This theory is popular with people who resent the idea that men should always be regarded as the norm. Nancy Cott, a professor of American Studies at Yale University, complains that when newly enfranchised women started voting like their husbands, no one considered the possibility that "the husbands were voting the way their wives wanted all along."

Gender Pride

Women may have deserted the Republican Party, this theory goes, because it does not seem hospitable to women. "American women need to see other faces of the party to show that there's more diversity," says [polling expert Linda] DiVall. This theory is popular among Republicans (particularly the women), partly because the cure is so simple: nominate more Republican women for races they can win and appoint more Republican women to high-profile government positions.

The G.O.P. has actually made strides on this front, and Dole's team of top advisers certainly contains more women than Clinton's. But the Republicans have to erase a lot of old memories. Who can forget the golden moment in the 1992 Presidential debate when President Bush, trying to prove that he had plenty of key female advisers, pointed to Rose Zamaria, an aide assigned to duties like handing out Presidential souvenirs, and praised her as "about as tough as a boot."

It's Abortion, Stupid

Abortion-rights advocates frequently take credit for the gender gap, but a look at the polls shows that men and women do not really differ on abortion. Men, in fact, turn out to be more supportive of abortion rights in some polls. But abortion, like gun control, is an intensity-of-preference issue: the power resides with the minority of voters who will change candidates over that single question.

Since 1989, when the Supreme Court shifted to a more restrictive stance on abortion, the swing voters have been pro-choice. A study by Debra L. Dodson of the Center for the American Woman and Politics found that among people who voted for George Bush in 1988 but not in 1992, the greatest drop-off came among pro-choice women.

The Loudness Factor

Women are so turned off by any hint of aggression, says [Democratic pollster] Celinda Lake, that they even reject propositions about curing the trade imbalance that lean too hard on the idea of competition, or "beating" the other countries. In other words, women will not vote for men who yell. Loud-candidate rejection would explain the relative shortage of women at Pat Buchanan rallies, the gender gap in the George Wallace campaigns and the fact that women who'd voted for Republican candidates in 1994 started deserting the new Congress as soon as Newt Gingrich began appearing on the evening news. It does not account for women's relative lack of enthusiasm for Reagan and Bush. But it may have been at least partly to blame for Ted Kennedy's gap problem during the Democratic primaries in 1980. One of his former campaign workers says: "He'd go out and scream on the podium, and I'd think, imagine you're a retired woman, having your dinner in front of the TV in your nice quiet house, and you see this out-of-control, red-faced guy yelling. Maybe the gap had as much to do with that as Chappaquiddick."

Does Character Count?

Conventional wisdom has always held that female voters are particularly concerned about the Inner Candidate—a politician's personality and character. How then to explain their enormous preference for Clinton, a man subject to investigations into his personal finances and political ethics, and dogged by questions about his own past sexual behavior? The answer may be that women are not all that obsessed with character issues, at least when they're choosing a President. Lake has asked voters whether they would rather support a candidate they agree with on the issues but who had character flaws or a candidate with a good character but with whom they disagree. Both sexes chose the candidate they agreed with on the issues, by a wide margin. . . .

Little of this gnawing over the gender gap, you will notice, has had much impact on actual government policy. By virtually every account, the most important single factor splitting women from men in the voting booth is women's greater confidence in government's ability to help people and their concern about the reduction in services for the young, old and needy. And ever since the gap first cropped up, the country has been moving away from activist government and the social safety net.

"Ouch," says Ann Lewis of the Clinton re-election campaign, when I suggest that the political response to the gender gap has been mainly cosmetic. "I know women have made a difference. Give me a second to think about this. I'm clutched over in pain." DiVall, meanwhile, says that Dole's campaign can appeal to women by doing "more personalizing." This means talking about his war injuries. Both parties still seem to regard the gap as a marketing problem that can be addressed by buying more advertising time on the Lifetime channel.

The gender gap era is just another stage in the evolution of the female voter that began with the struggle for suffrage. For generations after, politicians believed that to get women's votes, they had only to win over their husbands. Far more humiliating was when powerful campaign strategists thought what female voters wanted was a really cute guy. (Remember Dan Quayle?) Then there were all those campaigns in which Washington was obsessed with the angry white male. Now, women voters have reached a new plateau: They've arrived at the pander zone.

C. The Continuing Debate on Abortion _____

1. The Furor over "Partial-Birth Abortions" (1996)

In 1996, Congress passed a bill outlawing a medical procedure called "partial-birth abortion" (described in the selection that follows). President Clinton vetoed the bill,

_____
[1]Jonathon Alter, "When Facts Get Aborted," from *Newsweek,* October 7, 1966. Copyright © 1996, Newsweek, Inc. All rights reserved. Reprinted by permission.

initiating yet another round in the apparently endless debate between "pro-choice" abortion advocates and "pro-life" abortion opponents. Partial-birth abortions raised especially troubling moral and political questions because they could be performed on well-developed fetuses relatively late in pregnancy. What does the author of this selection identify as the most difficult moral issues posed by partial-birth abortions? What does he see as the political implications of this debate? What does he advise the pro-choice movement to do about partial-birth abortions? Is the abortion issue politically resolvable?

When Bill Clinton and the Democrats were down, abortion was about the only issue working for them. Now they are up, and abortion—partial-birth abortion, to be precise—may be just about the only issue working against them. Not this year, perhaps, but the pro-choice forces are in danger of turning themselves into extremists on this one. While anti-abortion activists failed last week to override Clinton's veto of a ban on the partial-birth procedure, they succeeded in opening a promising new front in their struggle. Their arguments even managed to rouse the consciences of basically pro-choice types like me, who are beginning to doubt the National Rifle Association–style zealotry of the home team. But it turns out the pro-lifers are playing loose with the details, too. Give me flip-flopping mushy compromise any time. When politics meets moral conviction, the truth usually gets aborted.

Especially if nobody knows the facts. About the only thing all sides can agree on is that "partial-birth abortion," the term coined by anti-abortion activists for a medical procedure known officially as "intact dilation and evacuation," is horrific. Doctors bring the fetus down into the birth canal, then crush the skull so that the head can be pulled out of the uterus. Sen. Daniel Patrick Moynihan, a Catholic Democrat who generally votes pro-choice, says it is "as close to infanticide as anything I've come upon." How many such procedures are performed each year? Here's where it gets complicated. Pro-lifers rightly complain that statistics on abortion are gathered mostly by abortion-rights activists, not by the government or some independent authority. And although both sides agree that there are about 1.5 million abortions performed a year, the type and timing of the practice is in dispute. When the partial-birth-abortion debate took shape last year, pro-choice groups insisted the procedure was extremely rare. The number 500 to 600 was tossed around, with the president and others explaining that it was reserved for heart-wrenching cases involving women whose tests show severely deformed fetuses or whose health was at risk. Not so. When deemed medically appropriate, it is used much more commonly—perhaps several thousand times a year (although a New Jersey clinic denies widespread reports that it performed 1,500 a year). The *Washington Post* surveyed physicians and found that most of those patients receiving partial-birth abortions were young, poor, single women without health problems. They simply wanted abortions, and in the second trimester it is sometimes the recommended procedure, though pro-life former surgeon general C. Everett Koop says this type of abortion is never truly medically necessary. If progressives listen raptly to Koop on tobacco, they at least owe him a hearing on obstetrics.

Even so, the pro-life camp has been equally misleading in suggesting that "late-term" abortions are common. They are not. Supporters of the ban made it seem as if a healthy woman could find herself not fitting into her prom dress, walk into an abortion clinic 40 weeks pregnant and get an abortion. This is against the law in 41 states, and Vicki Saporta of the National Abortion Federation insists this "simply does not happen in the United States; the doctors won't perform them." Maybe so, but Gary Bauer of the Family Research Council points out that courts have expanded *Roe* v. *Wade* to allow "the health of the mother" to include psychological health, a standard so broad as to render it meaningless and allow late-term abortion on demand. Yet neither he nor other anti-abortion activists have produced any examples of women who aborted normal fetuses in the third trimester. Indeed, the total number of abortions performed after 24 weeks is tiny. Only two clinics in the country even perform third-trimester abortions.

This year's ban may have been too sweeping, but pro-choice forces are too uncompromising. They see any regulation as a slippery slope to the bad old days of illegal abortions—just as the NRA sees banning assault weapons as the first step to the confiscation of all guns. In both cases lobbies with a reasonable claim on the mainstream risk marginalizing themselves by overreacting to the slightest move from the other side. This is what happens when politics is ruled by rigid principles. Compromise becomes tantamount to selling out bedrock belief, and each camp's position hardens.

The partial-abortion clash will resonate, but how? "I get irritated when I hear our supporters say, 'This is a good strategy to pick up Senate seats' or 'It will help Dole close a 20-point gap'," says Gary Bauer. But hey, we're less than a trimester away from the election. In the short run, partial-birth abortion will now help Dole with swing-vote Catholics and evangelicals (many of whom have been, amazingly enough, leaning toward Clinton). In the medium run, it all but wrecks the national political aspirations of New Jersey Gov. Christine Todd Whitman. A pro-choice Republican has a slight enough chance for his or her party's nomination in 2000; a pro-partial-birth-abortion Republican like Whitman has virtually no chance. In the long run, the debate should help us recognize the mistake we made leaving abortion to the courts, where judges have spent years trying to plant principle in the soggy soil of emotion. This has rendered the post-*Roe* wrangling fiercer than it needed to be. Other Western countries have experienced less rancor by debating abortion legislatively, then regulating it. Ultimately, that's the best way to answer the really tough questions in a democracy—by compromising, with the common sense that Americans have long and reliably applied to their own lives.

2. A Christian Conservative Urges Moderation (1996)

Abortion was the main issue that galvanized Christian conservatives in the era after the pro–abortion rights Roe v. Wade *decision of 1973. Ralph Reed, a leader of the religious right and chairman of the Christian Coalition, offered the following thoughts on the politics of abortion during the 1996 presidential campaign. How does he envision the reconciliation of faith and tolerance that he suggests? Is his proposed rec-*

onciliation realistic? Would overturning the Roe *decision settle the abortion debate? Where are the grounds for compromise on abortion?*

The most dangerous thing that could happen to the pro-family movement would be to gain political power without first learning how to turn the levers of government slowly, deliberately, and cautiously. No lobbying or arm-twisting can take the place of a change in public attitudes through moral persuasion. If religious conservatives are wise, they will resist the temptation to replace the social engineering of the left with the social engineering of the right by forcing compliance with the moral principles that motivate us so deeply.

As a community of faith, we stand at a crossroads. Down one path lies the fate of many other great religiously-inspired political movements of the past: irrelevance and obscurity. It is a path defined by its spiritual arrogance and by its faulty assumption that the most efficacious way to change hearts is through the coercive power of the state. This is the path taken by the prohibitionists, the Social Gospel advocates, the New Dealers, and the architects of the Great Society. It is not the right path for our movement. Fortunately, there is another way to go, and at the end of it lies not simply wider influence and greater political impact, but a changed society and a thoroughly Judeo-Christian culture. To get there, religious conservatives must shun harsh language on critical issues—chiefly abortion, Clinton-bashing, and homosexuality—and learn to speak of our opponents with charity.

Currently there is a fractious and, I believe, healthy debate within the pro-life community about whether to pursue cultural remedies and persuasion that will lead to fewer abortions, or whether to seek a legal ban on abortion. Even Americans describing themselves as "pro-choice" would not deny that 1.6 million abortions a year is a national tragedy.

Some, like [former Secretary of Education] Bill Bennett and scholar Marvin Olasky, argue that adoption and abstinence offer the greatest hope of reducing the number of abortions. The problem with this "moral suasion" argument is that it is a little like arguing in 1963 that a Civil Rights Act would be unnecessary because people could read *To Kill a Mockingbird.* Do we need moral arguments and changes in public opinion before we end the tragedy of abortion? Of course we do. But the law is also an effective teacher—it is part of a cultural solution, not a substitute for it.

True, we have already made enormous progress. Pro-life political action has undeniably helped stigmatize abortion. What else would provoke President Clinton to promise to make abortion "rare," or abortion-rights lobbyist Kate Michelman to admit that it was "a bad thing"?

Yet, undeniably, the votes cannot currently be found in Congress for the ultimate goal of the pro-life movement, a constitutional amendment to ban abortion. This presents a political dilemma. Until public opinion shifts on a political solution to abortion, outlawing all abortions by constitutional fiat would create the same dilemma for pro-lifers that the prohibitionist movement faced. What is the answer? The right to life is inalienable, and this is a matter of principle for us upon which we cannot compromise. But as a purely tactical matter, it is true that amending the Constitution may be the most remote weapon at our disposal at this time. Still, we must never retreat from our ultimate goal of protecting the sanctity of life in our laws and in the Constitution.

In the short term, though, the most effective strategy for us is to seek to overturn *Roe* through the appointment of pro-life judges, to pass pro-life laws in every state possible, to eliminate tax subsidies for abortion and the organizations that perform them, and to reduce the incidence of abortion through cultural and moral suasion. To change public attitudes, we must also repudiate the demonization of women who are pregnant out of wedlock, condemn violence at abortion clinics in unequivocal terms, and pour out greatest efforts into education, persuasion, and prayer—not politics alone.

The Republican Party's pro-life position is a winning one that has given the party landslides in three of the past four presidential elections. It has served the party well and should not be retreated from, not only as a moral principle, but as a purely political matter because standing down would cost the party the support of millions of pro-family citizens. The pro-life community's hopes, however, do not hinge on the existing wording of the GOP platform, but on the principle behind it. I have supported the existing plank since 1980, and I will do so again. The current platform calls for a Human Life Amendment that would ban abortion. To some in the pro-life community, any change in the wording is anathema, but pro-lifers could draft language that would be as morally compelling. Here is my effort at a pro-life plank:

> We are a party that respects the sanctity of innocent human life as the basis of all civil rights. We will seek by all legal and constitutional means to protect the right to life for the elderly, the infirm, the unborn, and the disabled. We oppose physician-assisted suicide, euthanasia, and the rationing of health care because they threaten the lives of the elderly. We deplore abortion on demand as a grave evil and a national tragedy. We oppose the taxpayer subsidies for abortion and those organizations that promote and perform them, a practice that millions of our citizens believe is the taking of an innocent human life. We agree with Mother Teresa's statement: "Abortion is the greatest destroyer of peace in the world today." We seek compassionate and humane alternatives to abortion, such as adoption services, and favor reforms of our foster-care and adoption system, such as greater facilitation of transracial adoptions, to provide loving homes for children who need them. We urge all Americans to work together to create what Pope John Paul II has called a "culture of life."

Let me be clear: these words are my own. They do not reflect the policy of the Christian Coalition.

Beyond abortion, an important principle in a theology of political activism is grace and humility. There are two contradictory qualities that faith should bring to politics. The first is an uncompromising sense of right and wrong. The second is mercy. Our political witness should reflect not only God's judgment but also His forgiveness. For He loves everyone—including our political foes.

Every word we say should reflect God's grace. This is easy when dealing with allies, but the Bible tells us to love our enemies. Nowhere is this principle more important than in our opposition to Bill Clinton. Some of the opposition has been deeply personal, attacking his character rather than his policies, and in so doing it risks permanent damage to the office he occupies. I oppose President Clinton's policies, but I do not despise him. If Bill Clinton is a sinner, he is no worse than you or me.

We will be judged by history and by our God not according to the political victories we achieve, but by whether our words and our deeds reflect His love. When one of the nation's leading evangelical preachers suggests that the president may be a murderer, when a pro-life leader says that to vote for Clinton is to sin against God, and when conservative talk-show hosts lampoon the sexual behavior of the leader of the free world, their speech reflects poorly on the gospel and on our faith.

True Christianity loves the sinner, but hates the sin. But how we criticize is important, as are our motives. Do we chasten in love, seeking repentance and reconciliation? Or do we seek the political destruction of our foes? The answer to that question makes all the difference.

This is especially important in our approach to the issue of homosexuality. Calling gays "perverts" or announcing that AIDS is "God's judgment" on the gay community is not consistent with our Christian call to mercy. A Liberty Alliance fund-raising letter in 1995 claimed that "the radical homosexual onslaught of America is raging!" The evidence? Al and Tipper Gore had opened the vice-presidential residence to a "horde of homosexual leaders." The letter went on to assert that "if we do not act now, homosexuals will 'own' America." We have all been guilty of excessive hyperbole in fund-raising letters (the harangues against conservative Christians by groups on the left are notorious), but I would hope both sides will resist attacking individuals and stick to policy differences. We must never retreat from our principled defense of the traditional, marriage-based family as the foundation of our society. We oppose the granting of minority status based on one's sexual preference. But we must always speak and move in love, seeking redemption rather than condemnation.

Especially in this election year, we should resist the temptation to identify our religious convictions with the platform of a party of the platitudes of favored politicians. At heart, what America needs is not political revolution but spiritual renewal.

D. Social Security and the Looming War Between the Generations _____

1. Mortimer B. Zuckerman Foresees a Catastrophe (1996)

As the average age of Americans rose steadily in the last years of the twentieth century, anxiety intensified about the financial integrity and even the long-term solvency of the Social Security system, enacted during the New Deal in the 1930s as a means to alleviate poverty among the elderly. The huge size of the "baby boom" demographic cohort, born in the post–World War II decade and destined to begin passing into retirement in about 2012, posed especially difficult problems for the Social Security system. The following selection, by U.S. News and World Report *publisher Mortimer B. Zuckerman, outlines the fiscal dimensions of the approaching crisis in Social Security financing. How convincing is the "dismal arithmetic" he presents? Why is Social Security such a difficult issue for politicians to deal with?*

---

[1]From "Recognizing the Shades of Gray," *U.S. News & World Report,* May 13, 1996, p. 96. Copyright 1996 U.S. News & World Report, L.P. Reprinted with permission.

Social Security is on the verge of being neither social nor secure.

It will not be secure because irresponsible politicians have promised to pay more in benefits over the coming decades than Social Security will collect in revenues. Proof: Social Security will begin running a cash deficit by the year 2013, when the first wave of the baby boom generation will have reached 65 and begun the largest ever migration into retirement. By the year 2030, with the last of that generation past 65, Social Security will be running a staggering annual cash deficit estimated at $766 billion. This is asking for trouble—not just accountancy trouble but trouble between people. If the benefit level is maintained, financially strapped workers will resent the unavoidable doubling or tripling of the payroll tax. Expect the biggest tax revolt in our history. On the other hand, if the benefit level is slashed, millions of the poorer senior citizens will be in jeopardy.

The background of the coming crisis reminds me of the man who jumped off the roof of a 60-story building and shouted as he passed the 30th floor: "Don't worry, nothing's happened yet!" This despite the fact that the Social Security system's trustees have been warning for years that demographic trends were undermining the system's integrity. Consider: The ratio of workers, who support the system with their payroll taxes, to retirees has gone from 16 in 1 in 1950 to under 4 to 1 today; it is anticipated to decline to 2 to 1 by the year 2030 and to slip below that by the time today's newborns reach the peak of their earning years. At that point each married couple will, in effect, be supporting the Social Security cost of some anonymous retired household in addition to whatever they can do for their parents.

Compounding the difficulty is an increasingly inequitable distribution. A majority of today's beneficiaries are getting back far more than they ever paid in FICA contributions, while 25-year-olds today can expect to get back less than half of what they have paid.

The other piece of dismal arithmetic lies in the demographics of aging. We will become a nation of Floridas in the early part of the next century. One in 5 of us will be over the age of 65 by 2030. By that same year, as many as 48 million of us will be over 70—twice as many as today. The cumulative result is that we will have more people in the wagon for a longer period of time and fewer people pulling it. As Pete Peterson points out in a stunning article in the current *Atlantic Monthly*, it is tantamount to robbing Peter Jr., as well as Peter, to pay Paul. The politicians' purpose, of course, is to ensure the voting support of Paul.

The sum of it all is that the burden on future generations threatens the very existence of Social Security, an excellent idea now put in jeopardy by cowardly politicians. Both Democrats and Republicans, fearing the voting power of the elderly, play off seniors' concerns rather than confront the changes needed. Their chief lobbying group, the American Association of Retired Persons (AARP), worries that any change, even at the margins, will sooner or later lead to slashing government checks to the elderly. Any legislator who does not swear to protect the existing system risks defeat. But such a guardianship of today's benefits is inconsistent with the fact that action, not inertia, is the only way to protect Social Security.

The changes to save the Social Security system and its sibling, Medicare, can be relatively small if they are made sooner rather than later. The longer change is delayed the greater will be the magnitude of change needed. It is better to restructure the scheme now and not in the last two minutes of the game, when the immense claims of the retiring baby boomers will have sent the system into shock—and stalemate. A huge block of pensioners fiercely invested in the status quo will confront a younger generation that won't want to pay, and politicians will run ever faster from the scene of the disaster.

In 1983, a bipartisan commission headed by current Federal Reserve Chairman Alan Greenspan unveiled a plan that provided political cover for both parties and saved the system temporarily. It is time to call on Greenspan again. The gears must be shifted now so that we do not roar recklessly downhill but gain control of our speed. As Pete Peterson writes, "The real question is will America grow up before it grows old?"

2. *The* National Review *Urges Privatization of Social Security (1996)*

The National Review, *an influential conservative magazine, acknowledges the reality of the crisis that the previous selection described, and urges a specific solution: privatizing the Social Security system, at least partly. Liberal critics of this proposal charge that privatization would lead to unacceptably wide differences in income among the elderly and would even break the "social contract" in which all Americans have participated since New Deal days, thereby eroding the very fabric of shared citizenship. How persuasive is the privatization solution?*

Social security is going broke. Maybe. There's a growing awareness that insolvency, currently projected for 2029, can be postponed, perhaps indefinitely, if surplus funds are invested wisely. Over the next twenty years Social Security revenues will exceed benefit payments by a whopping $2 trillion. These surpluses are "lent" to the government. (Although Washington spends the cash, the gimmick helps to keep the deficit below $200 billion today, and to balance it by 2002.) Meanwhile, the retirement fund earns just 2.3 per cent per annum, after inflation, on the money. Had the funds been invested in common stocks—in effect privatizing part of the system—the return would have been close to 7 per cent.

Had an average-income worker born in 1970 been allowed to invest his Social Security taxes in stocks, he would receive nearly six times the retirement benefits obtainable under Social Security—as much as $11,729 per month. Even a low-wage earner would triple the return on Social Security.

But no matter how shrewdly you invest them, the surpluses are too small and short-lived to postpone insolvency by more than a year or two. At their peak, in 2010, a rebate of $880 per worker would be possible. Starting in 2012, as baby boomers retire, benefit payments exceed payroll-tax collections. Over the long haul Social Security faces a $12-trillion gap between future benefits and revenues.

---

[2]Reprinted from *National Review,* August 12, 1996, p. 23, by permission of the publisher.

A realistic privatization plan must address this enormous unfunded liability. Congressman Nick Smith's Social Security Solvency Act does just that. He envisions a two-tier benefit system. Tier one provides a basic retirement benefit financed by payroll taxes. The second tier's size will depend on money invested privately. Mr. Smith's bill would permit workers to divert 2.3 per cent of their income—subtracting this from the current 12.4 per cent payroll tax (employee and employer combined)—into privately held savings accounts. Over time the permissible amount rises to 10 per cent.

Mr. Smith does not provide a free lunch, however. To pay for private accounts he shrinks the size of the government component. Retirees making more than $50,000 a year would—once they have recovered everything they and their employers paid into Social Security, plus interest—receive smaller Social Security benefits. The age at which workers can get reduced benefits, currently 62, would gradually rise to 65, while the normal retirement age, currently slated to rise to 67, would be pushed up to 69.

Mr. Smith would also rejigger the formula used to compute basic benefits so as to reduce the share of an upper-income salary replaced by Social Security. And workers who put money into private accounts will, upon retirement, have their Social Security (tier one) benefits reduced by the amount accumulated in their private account.

Computer models suggest that with modest wage growth and a 4.3 per cent real rate of return, the private accounts will eventually provide benefits larger than those available from the government program. At that point, some time late in the next century, payroll taxes will no longer be needed to finance retirement benefits. Social Security will be completely privatized.

Purists invariably point to Chile. In 1981 that nation privatized its retirement system almost overnight. But Chile faces no baby-boom retirement bulge. Investment capital is scarce. This enabled private retirement funds to generate returns averaging 14 per cent per year—roughly twice our stock-market growth rate. Last, but not least, are the large budget surpluses Chile ran to help pay off pensioners in the old state-run system. That might be difficult to emulate in a country not run by a junta.

3. A Younger Generation Looks to the Future (1996)

When Social Security began in the 1930s, a huge army of workers paid for the support of a tiny cohort of retirees. But early in the next century, every two workers will, in effect, be supporting one retiree through the Social Security system. Many younger Americans, like Heather Lamm, a lobbyist for Social Security reform, whose remarks follow, find that prospect indefensible. What most upsets her? How justified are her concerns? How viable is her proposed solution?

---

[3]Heather Lamm, "Retirement in the 21st Century," delivered to 1996 Mutual Funds and Investment Management Conference, March 26, 1996. Reprinted by permission of Heather Lamm.

I come before you as a member of a group of people born after 1960 who are concerned about the future of America. Third Millennium's mission is to redirect our country's attention from the next election cycle to the next generational cycle and, in the process, inspire our generation to action. The issue before us today is not about what size piece of the American entitlement pie one generation gets compared to the next. It is not about generational warfare. The issue before us is about looking toward the future and realizing the severity of the problems awaiting us. It is about dealing with those facts and those problems now, before they deal with us. Mark Weinberger has outlined the fiscal realities confronting this nation on its current course: unsustainable entitlement programs, a skyrocketing national debt, the potential for unbearable tax rates. Would you invest in a company that had the balance sheet of this country?

It is my opinion that this nation can no longer afford to question whether or not Social Security is in trouble. The facts speak for themselves. From Alan Greenspan to the Public Trustees of Social Security to Mark Weinberger and Carolyn Weaver, the experts agree that Social Security is on a collision course with bankruptcy. By 2030, the program will run out of money. But by 2013, the date we really should focus on, the trust fund is projected to begin running deficits. This crisis is not a result of "trust fund looting," or of waste, fraud and abuse in the system. The trust fund will begin to run deficits as a result of the forces of demographics and simple arithmetic. America is experiencing a demographic shift that will double the number of Americans over age 70 from 24 million today to 48 million in 2030.

Thus the question before us is when and how we act to change the course of Social Security. While Social Security's collapse may seem very distant to some, to my generation it is a reality that is literally right around the corner. Last year Third Millennium commissioned a national survey that found that nearly twice as many young adults believe in the existence of UFOs as believe Social Security will exist by the time they retire. The crisis of confidence in federal retirement programs among young people is astounding; our lack of faith in this system has broadened into a cynicism about government in general that will not be healthy in the long run.

Imagine for a moment that we are in the year 2013. For years Congress and the President have been ensnared by special interests and partisan bickering, and as a result have denied the need for Social Security reform. Social Security is now running a deficit, and every year plunges the United States further into debt. The nation is faced with a horrendous decision. We must raise payroll taxes on young workers by 25 percent immediately to balance the program, or we must slash all benefit checks dramatically, leaving many needy seniors unprepared and without vital benefits. The nation is of course outraged. Why must a country as great and wealthy as America have to choose between burdening its workers with unbearable tax rates, and denying poor senior citizens adequate benefits?

We will not have to make that drastic decision if we act soon. We can ensure that Social Security continues to provide benefits to those who need them and we can maintain reasonable tax rates if we have the courage to face the situation today rather than tomorrow. But if we wait, the issue of "age" in the 21st century could become as divisive as gender and race were in this century.

Let's set some priorities immediately. Our government has a responsibility to oversee a national retirement plan, but our government also has the responsibility to strengthen the economy for future generations and provide them with reasonable retirement expectations. Let's acknowledge the moral imperative of supporting poor seniors to keep them out of poverty. But let's also come to the table and discuss real reforms which will ensure that retirement security will always be there for those who need it in today's generation of senior citizens, and tomorrow's.

Now is a good time to recall the admonition of the 1937–38 Advisory Council on Social Security: "The protection of the aged must not be at the expense of adequate protection of dependent children, the sick, the disabled, or the unemployed; or at the cost of lowering the standard of living of the working population."

In the words of Lawrence Kotlikoff of Boston University: "For over four decades, government at the federal, state, and local levels has been shifting fiscal burdens from current to future generations. This process of 'pass the generational buck' has left today's young and middle-aged Americans paying such a high fraction of their labor earnings in net taxes that many have little wherewithal from which to save for their old age."

Imagine your paycheck. Imagine that you work for wages at $10/hour. You have worked 100 hours and expect $1000. Yet you receive $666 substantially less. You know that your money is being taken out for taxes, and you know that a large percentage goes to Social Security. But you are happy to be getting paid, and the government will take what it has to. Now imagine that $600 of that same $1000 is taken by the government, leaving you with $400 of your hard earned money. This is my generation's future under current trends. Now imagine trying to pay your living expenses, pay back loans, support your children, cover home and car payments, and save for your own retirement. This is virtually impossible.

Let us acknowledge that Social Security, when enacted, provided a crucial boost to the economy, but that if left unreformed, it will soon become a tremendous drain on our economy and on young workers.

Third Millennium's national survey last year found that 82 percent of young Americans want to be given the freedom to invest part of their Social Security payments in private retirement accounts that they would own, control and even pass along to their children or grandchildren. Allowing workers to contribute part of their payroll taxes to individual retirement accounts would lead to a tremendous boost in savings and capital formation. It would keep interest rates low and provide billions of dollars to the economy which could be used for new plants and equipment, research and development and worthwhile investment projects.

Private pensions would not only encourage households to plan for their own future, they would also greatly reduce the cost burden of the public portions of our retirement system over the long term. I believe, however, that a personal investment plan option would only really work if it is mandatory—otherwise, too many individuals might opt out and end up as a part of the public burden.

A mandatory pension plan is not a miracle cure for the problems that plague Social Security. Other structural reforms must accompany any personal investment plan in order to ensure that Social Security will be able to fulfill its promises to those currently in retirement or close to retirement.

Additionally, young workers are going to have to accept the fact that we must save more for our own retirement, as well as bear a share of our parents' Social Security benefits. For individual pensions to accumulate and provide an adequate retirement income, they will have to be based on substantial contributions. This means that workers will have to continue to pay a portion of Social Security, contribute the rest to a personal, mandatory account, and contribute additional savings to their personal account. But it is my belief that young workers will accept this burden if they are given the opportunity and the incentive to save more money themselves, watch their money grow and know that the money will be there for them when they retire.

A recent Third Millennium study found that 62% of young people would be more likely to support a presidential candidate who advocated a personal investment plan. That figure compares with only 6% of young people who said they would be less likely to vote for such a candidate. This issue will grow in importance and urgency as young people continue to realize where their FICA taxes go under the current system, and where that money could go under a different system.

I believe our nation's ultimate challenge is farsightedness. Would a private business, knowing that financial disaster is pending, wait until tomorrow to deal with the situation? Would an individual family, realizing it is running into financial troubles, wait until tomorrow to change course? Why, then, should the Federal government be held to any lower standard?

Every generation of Americans has its own assets and liabilities, and I truly don't believe that most people in my generation are whining about the future we are inheriting. But we can no longer sit idly by as politicians compromise our economic future and, more importantly, the future of our children, to pacify powerful special interest groups. Young people have an obligation, both as citizens and as the parents of the next generation, to offer solutions, to have a voice and to demand action. We are willing to sacrifice because we know the consequences to our generation and to future generations if we do not. We are willing to accept reduced benefits and an increased retirement age. But we are not willing to accept inaction on the part of today's leaders. And I do not think my generation will accept increased payroll taxes for programs that the experts all tell us will be bankrupt by the time we retire.

It is crucial for all Americans that we begin to confront Social Security today. To avoid action now is a moral and economic assault on future generations. If we seize the opportunity, however, I believe we can embark on a course that will boost national savings, invest in the future and secure our ailing retirement system.

E. Can the United States Still Afford to Be a Nation of Immigrants? _____

1. The Puzzling Economics of Immigration (1996)

America has long been an immigrant nation, and most Americans are proud of their heritage. But as immigration rose to unprecedented levels in the 1970s,

---

[1]From Susan Dentzer, "Adding and Subtracting," *U.S. News & World Report,* April 29, 1996, p. 37. Copyright 1996 U.S. News & World Report, L.P. Reprinted with permission

1980s, and 1990s, debate intensified about the desirability of keeping the immigration doors open. Among the most contentious aspects of the controversy was the question of whether immigration imposed economic costs or conferred economic benefits on American society. The following selection attempts to sort out the economic dimension of immigration—a surprisingly complex and challenging task. What are the principal questions that must be answered before this issue might be settled? Should immigration policy be based on economic considerations alone? Why, or why not?

> *Give me your tired, your poor,*
> *Your huddled masses yearning to breathe free—*
> *And I will perform a cost-benefit analysis*
> *To determine if immigrants are a good deal for America.*

Fortunately, Emma Lazarus was a poet, not a policy wonk, and thus never wrote those lines. But given the tenor of the current immigration debate, it's easy to imagine such sentiments being carved today beneath the Statue of Liberty. Consider the economic and pseudo-economic arguments for and against immigration. On one hand, somewhat inconsistently, immigrants are said to run up the tab for programs such as welfare and to steal jobs from the native born. On the other, immigrants are extolled as ethnic Horatio Alger characters who work hard, study hard, launch new businesses and add, like Albert Einstein, to the nation's store of human resources.

The reality is that even though research in the field has flowered in recent years, we still know little that is definitive about immigration's economic consequences. Economists bitterly debate the range of topics—for example, whether or not immigrants pay more in taxes than they soak up in benefits like welfare or Medicaid. Still worse, from the standpoint of fairness, we seem to know far more about the probable costs of immigration than we know about its often unmeasurable benefits, like the value of a diverse workplace in an era of global markets. But this doesn't mean the anti-immigration arguments carry the day. What it does mean is that it's futile to try to determine whether immigration is a net economic plus or minus—and about as useful as evaluating motherhood, patriotism or other tried-and-true American values on the basis of costs and benefits.

Hard questions. It's tough to answer the big economic questions about immigration—for example, what impact the inflow of foreigners has had on overall U.S. economic growth. One key reason is that it is hard to figure out which came first, the immigrants or the growth: While immigration may have spurred America's growth, foreigners have been attracted here because the economy was growing. Probably the best we can safely say is that the arrival of tens of millions of foreigners has not had a significant adverse effect on the economy. Consider employment: More legal immigrants flooded into the United States during the 1980s than during any other decade since the peak flows of 1900–1910. Even so, overall job growth boomed during the '80s, and by 1989 the unemployment rate had fallen to a low 5.3 percent.

Immigration's most discernible effects have probably been on wages. When new immigrants arrive, their primary effect is to drive down the wages of immigrants who came earlier, since a bigger pool of similarly situated people is now competing for similar jobs. That's a long-standing phenomenon that can be traced back at least to the 19th century, when New York's immigrant garment workers lost ground when the next wave showed up, says Harvard economic historian Claudia Goldin. But today, immigration may also have noticeable effects on the wages of low-skilled, native-born workers.

Consider today's immigrants, roughly four fifths of whom are from Asia and Latin America, and who on average have had fewer years of schooling than native-born Americans. Harvard economists George Borjas, Richard Freeman and Lawrence Katz argue that this influx of less-educated people helps explain as much as one third of the widening pay gap between low-skilled and highly educated U.S. workers during the 1980s. Other economists dispute that—and at any rate, Borjas and his colleagues agree that immigration probably has played no larger role in America's widening wage gap than the decline of labor unions and the growth of trade. Moreover, immigration almost certainly played a smaller part in the growing gap than the biggest contributor yet identified: rapidly changing technology that dried up opportunities for America's low-skilled workers.

If immigration has some role in pushing down the wages of low-skilled Americans, it may also be pushing them around, period. From 1990 to 1995, notes University of Michigan demographer William Frey, 2 out of 3 immigrants newly arrived in the United States ended up in just 10 metropolitan areas, including New York, Los Angeles, Chicago and Houston. At the same time, tens of thousands of low-skilled Americans seemed to be leaving many of those areas—for example, departing California, which suffered a recession during much of that period, for new homes in Nevada or the Pacific Northwest. What role immigrants played in decisions to move isn't clear, Frey says. "But it would be nice if we could distribute immigrants around the country somewhat more evenly," he adds, to blunt the effect on native-born people in already heavily populated areas.

What other effects might the influx of low-skilled immigrants have on the broader economy? It sounds callous, but for many Americans, the results may not be all bad. If immigrants drive down wages for restaurant workers or lower the price of dry cleaning, that means cheaper meals and cleaning bills for better-off people, says Yale economist Jennifer Hunt, currently a national scholar at Stanford's Hoover Institution. This dynamic underscores a potentially important economic aspect of immigration: It effectively transfers wealth from native workers to those who use the services of immigrants.

Perhaps the most contentious question is whether immigrants "pay their own way"—that is, whether they pay enough in taxes to offset the costs they impose on society. Depending on what you count, it is possible to answer yes or no. For example, Urban Institute researcher Jeffrey Passel calculates that in 1992, the taxes paid by immigrants who arrived in 1970 or later outstripped their costs for welfare and other social services by $27 billion. But economist Borjas says that reckoning neglects immigrants' heavy use of schools and other public services. In fact, he contends, immigrants didn't pay their way that year, to the tune of about $16 billion.

Uneven burdens. Now consider what happens when you add immigrants'

Social Security and Medicare taxes—benefits that working-age immigrants won't collect for years. Under the calculus, immigrants more than pay their way, contends Stephen Moore, an economist at the Cato Institute in Washington. Perhaps all we can say with confidence is that immigrants may be "overpaying" their way at the federal level and "underpaying" at the state and local level, which funds the lion's share of services like schools and roads. That could argue for federal "impact aid" to areas with the biggest immigrant populations.

Even if immigrants impose some higher costs on society, it could be that it is worth making that investment in order to capture other benefits from immigration. Unfortunately, we know almost nothing about those benefits, since few economists have evaluated them. An exception is George Borjas, himself a Cuban immigrant, who tried to come up with what he calls a "back of the envelope" estimate of how much immigration increases the national income each year. His conclusion: somewhere between $7 billion and $25 billion—a pittance in a $7 trillion economy.

In the absence of more work in this vein, all we really have are disjointed anecdotes about immigration's benefits. For example, a new report published by the UCLA Asian American Studies Center and the Leadership Education for Asian Pacifics, a nonprofit group, calculates that businesses owned by Asian-Pacific Americans had sales of more than $33 billion by the late 1980s and employed more than 350,000 workers. Then there's Social Security: The fact that immigrants have higher birth rates than the native population means the system is somewhat healthier than it otherwise would be, since more younger workers—the offspring of immigrants—are helping foot the bill for oldsters' pensions. In fact, the Cato Institute estimates that cutting legal immigration by almost half, as some lawmakers have proposed, would require raising taxes or cutting Social Security benefits by $5.6 billion a year to avoid worsening the system's long-run insolvency.

Given how little we know about the economics of immigration, how, if at all, should we amend our immigration policies? If the objective of immigration is solely to increase the nation's wealth—and that's a big "if"—we might do two things. We'd enforce our immigration laws better to stem the flow of largely unskilled illegal workers—and we'd shift to a system of legal immigration that admitted people primarily based on their level of skills, rather than on their family ties, as the current system does. The infusion of better-educated people would take less of a toll on low-skilled workers' wages and expand the nation's stock of human capital. Yet while this might make economic sense, as a society, we seem in conflict: We're troubled that highly skilled workers might also see their wages fall—or lose their jobs—when foreign-born professionals showed up, willing to work for lower pay. "The U.S. has this 'terrible' problem," says Yale economist (and Australian native) Hunt. "The smartest people in the world want to come here"—and we can't get over it.

On the other hand, lest we fret too much about the low-skilled immigrants arriving on our shores, it is useful to remember that Americans don't have a good track record in predicting how immigrants will fare. It's also an apparent obligation of U.S. citizenship to complain that the next boatload to arrive won't be as great as your own boatload was. Benjamin Franklin once carped that German immigrants to

America would never master the English language or assimilate into American society. Two centuries later, this writer, descended from a 19th-century immigrant from Bavaria, would have to disagree.

2. Immigration and Poverty (1996)

Columnist Robert Samuelson argues in the selection below that the issues of widening income inequality and immigration are related. How sound is his analysis? What does he think of proposals to deny immigrants access to public services, such as education? What are likely to be the long-term contributions—or costs—of the massive immigrant wave of the past three decades?

As a nation, we are importing poverty. That is the clearest consequence of the surge of immigration that began in the early 1970s. I do not say this to be alarmist or to advocate any type of immigration legislation. I say it merely to highlight an important truth that's usually overlooked in our political discussions of other social issues, ranging from poverty to the lack of health insurance. We deceive ourselves by discussing these matters as if immigration has had little effect on them.

The silent assumption is that the population is static. If poverty hasn't declined, then something must be making it harder for people to escape poverty. If more people lack health insurance, then insurance must be much less available. If income inequality has risen, then something must be widening the gap between the "haves" and "have-nots." But the population isn't static. Many people at the bottom are immigrants, and because they arrive poor, they instantly aggravate all these problems. They take lousy jobs with low wages and no insurance.

In any one year, new immigrants (about 800,000 of them legal and perhaps 300,000 illegal) don't much alter social conditions. But the cumulative impact is significant. Between 1970 and 1994, immigrants rose from 4.8 percent to 8.7 percent of the population. Counting their American-born children amplifies the effect. And the new immigrants come from different countries than the old. In the 1950s, two-thirds of a much smaller number came from Europe and Canada. By the 1980s, nearly half came from Mexico, other parts of Latin America and the Caribbean; almost 40 percent came from Asia.

It is not simply that many new immigrants are desperately poor and don't speak English. That's often been true. More important, many don't achieve the rapid income gains of some earlier immigrants. Wages of many European immigrants approached (or even exceeded) the levels of native-born Americans after 10 or 15 years. A new study by the Rand Corp., a research organization, shows that this is still true for Europeans and also applies to many Asian immigrants. In 1990 wages for European immigrants who arrived in the late 1970s were 10 percent above those of American-born workers; for Asians who arrived in the late 1970s, wages were 15 percent higher in 1990.

---

[2]Robert Samuelson, "Importing Poverty," © **1996,** *Newsweek.* **Reprinted with permission.**

But the picture for Mexican and many other Hispanic immigrants is much different, reports Rand. Mexicans arriving in the late 1970s received wages half the level of natives; by 1990 their wages were still about half. Simply as a matter of arithmetic, all these poor workers worsen our poverty indicators. Unfortunately, gauging the effect is hard, because the subject hasn't been rigorously studied. Immigrants are examined in isolation: How fast do they assimilate? Do economic benefits outweigh costs?

By contrast, I have tried—from various government reports—to estimate the broader impacts. To do so, I used the classification "Hispanic" as a substitute for "immigrants," because most reports don't identify immigrants separately. Admittedly, this is crude. All Hispanics aren't immigrants, and all immigrants aren't Hispanic. Still, immigration has propelled the rise of the Hispanic population, and so the connection—though loose—is real. Here's what the reports imply:

Poverty: Perhaps a quarter to a half of the increase in poverty since the early 1970s reflects immigration. Between 1973 and 1994, the number of people with incomes below the government's official poverty line rose by 15 million. Of those, 6 million were Hispanic.

No health insurance: The impact is similar. Between 1987 and 1994, the number of Americans without health insurance rose by 8.7 million; of these, 3.3 million (38 percent) were Hispanic. (The Census Bureau has data before 1987 but says that it isn't exactly comparable with later figures.)

Economic inequality: Immigration has aggravated it, though by how much is hard to say. In 1994 nearly one in eight households among the poorest fifth of Americans was Hispanic. In 1974 the Hispanic share was only one in 20. And as the Rand study shows, average wages for immigrants have fallen compared with those of natives.

Don't misunderstand me. Immigration didn't cause these problems. It simply made them worse—as it has crime and student test scores. Nor am I saying that the ill effects can easily be erased by legislation. Many poor immigrants arrive illegally. If we could halt that, we would already have done so. Indeed, some anti-immigration measures could backfire. For example, one proposal now before Congress would allow states to deny schooling to children of illegal immigrants. That's unwise. Thousands of children could be ejected. And because many might stay in the United States, they could ultimately end up poorer.

Finally, I'm not predicting a new permanent underclass. Though that's a possibility, it's only one of many. Just because people arrive poor does not mean their families stay poor forever. Later generations of Mexican-Americans do better than immigrants, reports a study by economist Stephen Trejo of the University of California, Santa Barbara. Among men, average wages for second- and third-generation Mexican-Americans rise to about 80 percent of those of whites. That's the good news; the bad news is that the gap hasn't yet vanished altogether.

America's powerful tides of assimilation may work as they have in the past—or they may not. No one can say, because the surge in immigrants is too recent to permit sweeping conclusions. Absorbing them is clearly one of the great challenges we now face. My aim here is more modest. It is not to predict the outcome of this struggle but to contest the convention of viewing immigration separately from many other social problems. My message is less about immigrants than about how we judge our condition.

It's unreasonable to think that so many poor newcomers could be assimilated instantly or effortlessly. Immigration inevitably depresses our indicators of national well-being. If we ignore that, we'll wrongly conclude that we're doing worse than we are.

3. Clamping Down on Immigrants in California (1994)

California received far more immigrants—many of whom entered the country illegally—than any other state in the closing decades of the twentieth century. Hardly surprisingly, immigration emerged as a major political issue in California, especially in the wake of a sharp statewide recession in the early 1990s. As part of his reelection campaign in 1994, California governor Pete Wilson supported a measure, known as Proposition 187, that sought to deny public services to illegal immigrants. The measure passed by a wide margin, and Wilson was handily reelected. Yet doubts persisted about the wisdom of Proposition 187, and the courts blocked implementation of many of its provisions. What does this Los Angeles Times *editorial identify as the most troublesome implications of Proposition 187? Should there be any restrictions at all on immigration to the United States?*

In the passions that swirl around this election's [1994] now most controversial decision—Proposition 187—voters who still haven't made up their minds should understand that in their hands lie one of the most significant matters they will ever confront in a polling booth.

Many Californians—including Gov. Pete Wilson, who is fighting for reelection—are embracing this deeply flawed measure in part out of pent-up frustration with the federal government's failure to enforce basic border control and its refusal to provide the money to help impacted border states cope with increased immigration.

Even if California defines illegal immigration as nothing but a problem—thereby ignoring the powerful economic benefits that derive from this valuable labor pool—there is no wisdom in lashing out in precipitous action that the state would come to regret.

Indeed, almost everything about Proposition 187 is wrong. It is wrong morally, because it would cast an indiscriminate shadow on people whose only real sin is to try to escape grinding poverty and make something of themselves. It is wrong politically, because the proposition's very presence on the ballot is dividing the state into two emotionally polarized camps at the very time all Californians should be working together. Nothing is ever accomplished when the people are divided, as they

[3]From *Los Angeles Times,* November 4, 1994. Copyright © 1995, Los Angeles Times. Reprinted by permission.

certainly are now over this ill-named "Save Our State" initiative—which surely would prove to be a "Tear Our State Apart" consensus-wrecker.

Perhaps the most telling argument against Proposition 187 is in a document called "Summary of Legislative Analyst's Estimate of Net State and Local Government Fiscal Impact," which appears in the California General Election Pamphlet, given to every registered voter.

The state legislative analyst's office is nonpartisan; Republican and Democratic legislators alike avail themselves of its penetrating and time-proven analyses to help determine the likely impact of legislation. The professionals who work in the agency are highly regarded: When they have done their work on a pending bill and then speak out, legislators generally listen.

So listen to what these experts say about Proposition 187:

Their analysis raises the specter of unintended consequences. Rather than save money, 187 might deprive the state of money: The ballot measure, they conclude, "places at risk billions of dollars annually in federal funding for state and local education, health and welfare programs due to conflicts between the measure's provisions and federal requirements."

They worry about considerable administrative disarray: "This measure does not set out any specific requirements as to how verification of citizenship or legal presence in the United States would be done."

They suggest that any savings from denying services to immigrants might be offset by the administrative costs of verification: "Ongoing annual costs could be in the tens of millions of dollars, with the first-year costs considerably higher (potentially in excess of $100 million)."

They say that 187 might save money at first, but not in the long run: "Denying some medical services to illegal immigrants could result in future increased state and local health costs. For example, eliminating prenatal services to illegal immigrant women could result in higher Medi-Cal* costs for their infants, who would be citizens. In addition, failure to treat and control serious contagious diseases, such as tuberculosis, among illegal immigrants could increase future costs to treat the disease in the general population."

Faced with such a finding from the legislative analyst concerning some ordinary bill, as opposed to this monumental ballot measure, most state lawmakers would back away, return the bill to committee, do some more homework and work up a better measure. That's exactly what California should do with Proposition 187: Hold off and do something more intelligent. For if this initiative passes on Nov. 8, that would be much harder to do. Yes, the courts might invalidate one portion or another, but the counterproductive statement will have been made. In the end, maybe the only people who will truly benefit will be the lawyers on either side collecting fees for litigating this whole misconceived thing.

---

*Medi-Cal is the state of California's publicly financed health care system for indigent Californians.

Yes, let's get control of U.S. borders, but let's not lose sight of our principles or abandon all reason. Vote "no" on Proposition 187.

4. Immigrants and the Law (1995)

Well before Californians passed Proposition 187, Texas had tried to close the public schools to the children of illegal immigrants, but it was prevented from doing so by the U.S. Supreme Court in the case of Plyler v. Doe (1982). *The selection below analyzes that decision and its applicability to California. What was the essence of the Court's reasoning in the* Plyler *case? Would denying illegal immigrants (or their children) access to schools save taxpayers' money in the long run? Would it be wise social policy?*

The latest earthquake out in California is political, not seismic. The reverberations of Proposition 187, the anti–illegal immigrant initiative on the state's November 1994 ballot, have already registered high on the Richter scales in state capitals and Washington, where politicians see that Pete Wilson's firm identification with Proposition 187 was largely responsible for his sweeping re-election victory. The law's aftershocks are even unsettling Europe, where leaders in almost every country face their own immigration crises, desperately seek solutions, and often look to U.S. experience for guidance.

Is Proposition 187 a firebell in the night (as was said of the Dred Scott decision), warning of imminent civil conflict? Or is it instead just a flash in the pan, one more California exotic that flourishes in that state's unique climate but fails to take firm root elsewhere? Proposition 187, I believe, lies somewhere in between. It is less a spasm of nativist hatred than an expression of public frustration with a government and civil society that seem out of touch and out of control, and with external convulsions that our borders can no longer contain. Although the alarms that motivated Proposition 187 are exaggerated and widely misunderstood, the law is nevertheless a warning—a primal scream, as one political commentator called it—to all of us who are friends of immigration and have slumbered in the wistful hope that illegal residents and the political problems that they create would, quite literally, go away.

Proposition 187 is a melange of different policies that seeks to stem the flow of illegal aliens into California, encourage the state's roughly 1.4 million residents to go home, and expel the rest. The most controversial provisions would bar anyone who is not a citizen, legal permanent resident (green card holder), or legal temporary visitor from receiving public social services, health care, and education. The provisions differ slightly for each service, but they generally impose three duties on all service providers: to verify the immigration status of all who seek services, to promptly notify state officials and the INS [Immigration and Naturalization Service] about whoever is "determined or reasonably suspected to be" violating the immigration laws, and to notify the alien (or in the case of children, their parent or guardian) of their

---

[4]Peter H. Schuck, "The Meaning of 187: Facing Up to Illegal Immigration." Reprinted with permission from *The American Prospect* #21, Spring 1995. Copyright © 1995 The American Prospect, P.O. Box 383080, Cambridge, MA 02138.

apparently illegal status. Proposition 187 is no ordinary law; it provides that the legislature cannot amend it "except to further its purposes" and then only by a recorded supermajority vote in each house of the legislature or by another voter initiative.

As a practical matter, the parts of Proposition 187 that would deny public services may never be implemented. Immediately after voters approved it, immigrant advocate groups and some local officials filed a blizzard of legal challenges to the constitutionality of the heart of the measure's service denial and reporting provisions. (Since Proposition 187 provides that its sections are severable, some might survive even if others were struck down.) A federal judge immediately enjoined it pending trial, and most commentators believe that the courts will ultimately strike down some if not most of the measure.

But the legal challenge against Proposition 187 is not nearly as solid as many say. Indeed, a closer look at the relevant constitutional precedents suggests that the courts could uphold the law if they have a mind to do so.

The courts have long prohibited the states from discriminating against legal immigrants, largely on the grounds that the state's authority in this area is subordinate to the federal government's. But until recently, the courts had never addressed *illegal* immigration. It simply had not been a major issue.

That started changing about 30 years ago. INS arrests—a very crude, unsatisfactory indicator of illegal entries—swelled from 1.6 million during the 1960s to 8.3 million in the 1970s, and then continued to rise in the early 1980s. When states and localities sought to protect their education and health care budgets by imposing restrictions on the newcomers' access to benefits, the courts could no longer duck the issue. In 1982, the Supreme Court decided *Plyler* v. *Doe,* a class-action suit brought on behalf of undocumented Mexican children living in Texas. Upholding the ruling of a lower court, a five-to-four majority struck down a statute that withheld from local school districts any state funds for the education of any child who was not legally admitted into the United States.

The constitutional challenge to 187 rests mainly on this precedent. Writing for the *Plyler* majority, Justice William Brennan had argued that the Texas law would inevitably harm children. These children would eventually obtain legal status in this country, yet would be "permanently locked into the lowest socioeconomic class." Brennan acknowledged that the state had some leeway in such matters: Under equal-protection principles, illegal alien status is not a "suspect class" like race or religion, and education is not a "fundamental right." Hence, it did not require heightened judicial scrutiny. Nevertheless, Brennan said, a law that denied children "the ability to live within the structure of our civic institutions . . . can hardly be considered rational unless it furthers some substantial goal of the State."

Brennan conceded that keeping illegal aliens out of the state might be a legitimate state goal. But the trial court had found that the Texas law had neither the purpose nor the effect of doing that, and Brennan agreed. The Texas law might save some money, according to Brennan, but Texas failed to establish that illegal aliens imposed a significant fiscal burden on state coffers or that their exclusion would improve the quality of education. Besides, Brennan said, federal immigration policy was not concerned with conserving state educational resources, much less with denying an education "to a child enjoying an inchoate federal permission to remain." (This referred to the possibility that an illegal alien might obtain discretionary relief from deportation.) All the Texas law would serve to do, Brennan said, was promote "the creation and perpetuation of a subclass of illiterates," who would be socially dysfunctional and a burden to society. That, he said, clearly was not something the states were allowed to do.

The parallels to Proposition 187 are obvious. Both would in effect bar undocumented children from the public schools; if anything, California's new ban on enrolling such children is even more categorical and rigid than the Texas statute invalidated in *Plyer,* which simply denied state funding for those who were enrolled. Any court that accepted Brennan's premises in *Plyler* would have a hard time sustaining Proposition 187.

F. The Dilemmas of Difference in a Democratic Society

1. The Controversy over Bilingual Education (1995)

The millions of immigrants flooding into America in the last part of the twentieth century posed thorny dilemmas for many institutions, especially schools. Should non–English speaking students be immediately placed in English-only classes, or should they be gradually introduced to English while keeping up to speed in other subjects through instruction in their native tongue? Could schools afford to offer classes in several different languages? Might transitional bilingual instruction become long-term maintenance of foreign tongues, and thereby retard the process of assimilation?

Javier Sanchez speaks English like the proud American he is. Born in Brooklyn, N.Y., the wiry 12-year-old speaks English at home, and he speaks it on the playground. He spoke it in the classroom, too—until one day in the third grade, when he was abruptly moved to a program that taught him in Spanish all but 45 minutes a day. "It was a disaster," says his Puerto Rican–born mother, Dominga Sanchez. "He didn't understand Spanish." Sanchez begged the teacher to return her son to his regular class. Her request was met with amazement. "Why?" the teacher asked. "Don't you feel proud to be Hispanic?"

Along with crumbling classrooms and violence in the hallways, bilingual education has emerged as one of the dark spots on the grim tableau of American public education. Started 27 years ago to help impoverished Mexican-Americans, the program was born of good intentions, but today it has mushroomed into a $10 billion-a-year bureaucracy that not only cannot promise that students will learn English but may actually do some children more harm than good. Just as troubling, while children like Javier are placed in programs they don't want and may not need, thousands more children are foundering because they get no help with English at all.

Bilingual education was intended to give new immigrants a leg up. During earlier waves of immigration, children who entered American schools without speaking

[1]From Susan Haeddan, "Tongue Tied in the Schools," *U.S. News & World Report,* September 25, 1995, p. 44. Copyright 1995 U.S. News & World Report, L.P. Reprinted with permission.

English were left to fend for themselves. Many thrived, but others, feeling lost and confused, did not. Their failures led to Title VII of the Elementary and Secondary Education Act, which ensured supplementary services for all non-English-speaking newcomers to America.

Significantly, the law did not prescribe a method for delivering those services. But today, of the funds used to help children learn English, 75 percent of federal money—and the bulk of state and local money—goes toward classes taught in students' native tongues; only 25 percent supports programs rooted in English. That makes bilingual education the de facto law of the land.

Historically, Hispanics have been the largest beneficiaries of bilingual education. Today, however, they compete for funding with new immigrant groups whose urge to assimilate, some educators say, may be stronger. Further, not many school districts can offer classes in such languages as Armenian and Urdu. So for practical reasons, too, children of other nationalities are placed in English-based classes more often than children of Hispanics. The problem, as many see it, is that students are staying in native-language programs far too long. In a typical complaint, the mother of one New York ninth grader says her daughter has been in "transitional" bilingual education for nine years. "We support bilingual education," says Ray Domanico of the New York Public Education Association. "But it is becoming an institutionalized ghetto."

In theory, bilingual education is hard to fault. Students learn math, science and other "content" subjects in their native tongues, and they take special English classes for a small part of the day. When they are ready, ideally within three or four years, they switch to classes taught exclusively in English. The crucial advantage is that students don't fall behind in their other lessons while gaining competence in English. Further, supporters claim, bilingual education produces students fluent in two languages.

That would be great, if it were true. Too often it is not. What is sometimes mistaken for dual-language instruction is actually native-language instruction, in which students hear English for as little as 30 minutes a day. "Art, physical education and music are supposed to be taught in English," says Lucy Fortney, a third-grade teacher from Sun Valley, Calif. "But that is absolutely not happening at all."

Assignments to bilingual programs are increasingly a source of complaint. Many students, parents say, are placed in bilingual classes not because they can't understand English but because they don't read well. They need remedial, not bilingual, help. Others wind up in bilingual programs simply because there is no room in regular classes. Luz Pena says her third-grade son, born in America, spoke excellent English until he was moved to a bilingual track. Determined to avoid such problems with her daughter, she registered her for English kindergarten—only to be told the sole vacancies were in the Spanish class.

In some cases, the placements seem to defy common sense. In San Francisco, because of a desegregation order, some English-speaking African-Americans end up in classes taught partly in Chinese. Chinese-speakers, meanwhile, have been placed in classes taught partly in Spanish. Presented with evidence that blacks in bilingual programs scored well below other blacks on basic skills tests, school officials recently announced an end to the practice.

Whether a child is placed in a bilingual program can turn on criteria as arbitrary as whether his name is Miller or Martinez. In Utah, federal records show that the same test scores that identified some students as "limited English proficient" (LEP) were used to identify others as learning disabled. The distinction depended on the student's ethnic group: Hispanics were designated LEP, while Native Americans who spoke Navajo or Ute were labeled learning disabled. In New York City, where public schools teach children in 10 different languages, enrollment in bilingual education has jumped by half since 1989, when officials raised the cut-off on a reading test. Critics say that 40 percent of all children are likely to fail the test—whether they speak English or not.

Misplacement, however, is only part of the problem. At least 25 percent of LEP students, according to the U.S. Department of Education, get no special help at all. Other children are victims of a haphazard approach. In Medford, Ore., LEP students received English training anywhere from three hours a day, five days a week to 30 minutes a day, three days a week. The results? Of 12 former LEP students reviewed by education department officials, seven had two or more F's and achievement scores below the 20th percentile. Four more had D's and test scores below the 30th percentile. In Twin Falls, Idaho, three high-school teachers had no idea that their students needed any help with English, despite their obvious LEP background and consistently failing grades.

Poorly trained teachers further complicate the picture. Nationwide, the shortage of teachers trained for bilingual-education programs is estimated at 170,000. The paucity of qualified candidates has forced desperate superintendents to waive some credentialing requirements and recruit instructors from abroad. The result is teachers who themselves struggle with English. "You can hardly understand them," said San Francisco teacher Gwen Carmen. In Duchesne, Utah, two teachers' aides admitted to education department inspectors that they had no college credits, no instructional materials and no idea what was expected of them.

What all these problems add up to is impossible to say precisely, but one statistic is hard to ignore. The high-school dropout rate for Hispanic students is nearly 30 percent. It remains by far the highest of any ethnic group—four times that of whites, three times that of blacks—and it has not budged since bilingual education began.

Although poverty and other problems contribute to the disappointing numbers, studies suggest that confining Hispanic students to Spanish-only classrooms also may be a significant factor. A New York study, published earlier this year, determined that 80 percent of LEP students who enrolled in English-immersion classes graduated to mainstream English within three years, while only half the students in bilingual classes tested out that quickly. A similar study released last fall by the state of California concluded that students stayed in native-language instruction far too long. It followed an independent investigation in 1993 that called native-language instruction "divisive, wasteful and unproductive."

Not everyone agrees. More than half of American voters, according to a new *U.S. News* poll, approve of bilingual education. Jim Lyons, executive director of the Bilingual Education Association, says the recent studies are flawed because they fail to measure mastery of academic content: "They don't even pretend to address the issue of the full education," he says. Learning English takes time, insists Eugene Garcia of the education department. "And it's well worth the wait."

The alternative to native-language instruction is to teach children exclusively in

English, pulling them out of class periodically for lessons in English as a second language. Lucy Fortney taught exclusively white American-born children when she started her career 30 years ago; now her classroom is almost entirely Vietnamese, Cambodian and Armenian. "I can't translate one single word for them," she says, "but they learn English."

Today, bilingual education is creeping beyond impoverished urban neighborhoods to rural and suburban communities likely to expose its failings to harsher light. Until now, no constituency has been vested or powerful enough to force the kind of reforms that may yet come with civil-rights lawsuits. "Everybody's appalled when they find out about the problems," says Linda Chavez, onetime director of the Commission on Civil Rights and a dogged opponent of bilingual education, "but the fact is, it doesn't affect their kids." That may have been true in the past. But as a rainbow-hued contingent of schoolchildren starts filling up the desks in mostly white suburbia, it is not likely to be the case for long.

2. Affirmative Action on the Rocks (1996)

Affirmative-action programs unquestionably did much to accelerate the social and economic advancement of women, African-Americans, and other minorities in the late twentieth-century United States. But after three decades of "preferential treatment" of historically underprivileged groups, many Americans seemed to be losing patience with affirmative action. Minority set-aside programs and special college admissions procedures for targeted minorities came increasingly under fire, beginning with the Supreme Court's Bakke *decision in 1978. By the 1900s, the Court seemed bent on circumscribing affirmative-action measures ever more narrowly. As discussed in the selection below, in* Adarand v. Pena *(1995) the Court ruled against the practice, in place for more than two decades, of earmarking some federal contracts for minority bidders. In* Hopwood v. Texas *(1996), the Court curtailed a preferential admissions program for minority applicants at the University of Texas Law School. Did these decisions spell the end of an era? On what grounds—constitutional, moral, or political—might affirmative action be defended?*

Affirmative action is in crisis, and proponents find themselves fighting a rearguard action for its survival. The Supreme Court in *Adarand* v. *Pena* (1995) made it clear that the use of racial preferences to remediate past wrongs will be subject to strict scrutiny and will have to be justified in painstaking detail. What may remain as the last constitutional justification for racial preferences is the diversity rationale. Its roots can be traced to Supreme Court Justice Lewis Powell's opinion in *Regents of the University of California* v. *Bakke* (1978), wherein he opined that race could be taken into account for achieving diversity within a student body.

The diversity rationale soon was adopted by most universities and many companies and became a powerful tool for affirmative action. Since it required no proof of historic discrimination, the diversity rationale had fewer legal hurdles to over-

---

[2]Robert Bresler, "Affirmative Action on the Rocks," from *USA Today Magazine,* July 1996. Reprinted by permission of USA Today Magazine.

come. On its face, the concept of diversity in the university or in the workplace engendered little opposition. The problems were to come in its implementation and with the inevitable issue of racial proportionalism. Who could define diversity so as to satisfy all claimants? If the diversity rationale were to address the problems of the underrepresentation of certain minorities, the issue of overrepresentation of other minorities would not lurk far behind.

In California, a state teeming with racial and ethnic diversity, the issue already has risen with ugly overtones, pitting one minority group against another. Asian students at the University of California's Berkeley campus were felt to be overrepresented due to their outstanding academic performance and actually were placed at a disadvantage under certain affirmative action programs. In Los Angeles County, affirmative action goals were raised for Hispanics, who, as a result of immigration, have become almost 40% of the county, and lowered for blacks, who represent 12% of the population and have 30% of the county jobs. Unsurprisingly, new tensions have developed between blacks and Hispanic leaders over this question.

In the spring of 1996, a Federal court dealt what may be a fatal blow to the constitutional standing of the diversity rationale. In *Hopwood* v. *Texas,* a three-judge panel of the U.S. Court of Appeals for the Fifth Circuit struck down an affirmative action program adopted by the University of Texas Law School that set lower minimum standards for Law School Admission Tests (LSATs) and grade point averages for blacks and Mexican-American applicants than for other groups. The Appellate Court ordered university officials, under pain of punitive damages, to adopt a color-blind admissions process immediately. Judge Jerry Smith, speaking for the Fifth Circuit, stated that "the use of race to achieve a diverse student body cannot be a state interest compelling enough to meet the steep standard of strict scrutiny. Within the general principles of the Fourteenth Amendment, the use of race in admission for diversity in higher education contradicts, rather than furthers, the aims of equal protection. Diversity fosters, rather than minimizes, the use of race. It treats minorities as a group, but, just as likely, may promote improper racial stereotypes, thus fueling racial hostility." Smith argued that a university could consider "a host of factors—some of which may have some correlation with race—in making admissions decisions . . . diversity can take many forms. To foster such diversity, state universities and law schools and other governmental entities must scrutinize applicants individually, rather than resorting to the dangerous proxy of race."

Hopwood is being appealed to the Supreme Court, which may hear the case next term. Given the Court's increasingly skeptical attitude toward racial preferences, it well may uphold Judge Smith's opinion.

In California, a new civil rights initiative would amend its constitution with this language: "The State shall not discriminate against, or grant preferential treatment to, any individual or group on the basis of race, sex, color, ethnicity, or national origin in the operation of public employment, public education, or public contracting." Its sponsors have collected the necessary 700,000 signatures to place the measure on the November ballot, and polls consistently have showed it to have overwhelming support.

In a presidential swing state, Ohio Gov. George Voinovich, mentioned as a possible running mate for [presidential candidate Robert] Dole, asked the General Assembly to change set-aside programs so that they benefit "socially and economically disadvantaged" people instead of those in racial-minority groups. An Ohio poll, taken in March, showed nearly 80% of white voters opposed to racial preference in hiring and promotion. No matter how the Supreme Court decides or what law and initiatives are passed, it is unlikely that the days of all-white schools and white male domination of the elite professions and jobs ever will return. Social norms and personal values have changed markedly since the time of segregation. In higher education, there are numerous devices available to admissions committees to create a diverse class—economic disadvantage, geographic dispersal, and special skills are a few that come to mind. Nor will corporations, eager to reach people of color here and abroad, want to show just a white face to their customers.

The fact that most Americans oppose affirmative action programs is not evidence of growing racism. The concept that rights are rooted in each individual, not in any group, is fundamental to the American creed. The civil rights movement in its one-time commitment to "color-blindness" drew strongly on that creed, and consequently inspired a nation. It is time to return to that tradition without fear.

3. Californians Trash Affirmative Action (1996)

Just as Californians had led the reaction against immigration in 1994, so did they lead the charge against affirmative action in 1996. California voters overwhelmingly approved ballot Proposition 209, known as the California Civil Rights Initiative, which prohibited all discrimination—positive or negative in intent—on the basis of race or gender. In the editorial below, the San Francisco Chronicle *sharply condemned the ballot measure. What are its strongest arguments? Its weakest? Has affirmative action outlived its usefulness? What information would be necessary to answer that question?*

Make no mistake. Proposition 209 is about abolishing affirmative action, even though the initiative makes no mention at all of the 30-year civil rights program that has made significant progress in opening long-closed doors for blacks, other minorities and women.

The initiative would prohibit the state from "discriminating against or giving preferential treatment to any individual or group in public employment, public education, or public contracting on the basis of race, sex, color, ethnicity or national origin."

The upshot of that seemingly benign language would be to prevent public agencies from maintaining affirmative-action practices designed to change their ethnic and gender makeup to better reflect the diversity of the community and state.

Those practices have made a big difference in the lives of women and minorities. They have helped lead to a growing black middle class; they have helped close the wage gap between men and women. But the job clearly is not done.

Look around. In most workplaces, diversity is not even close to a reality in the upper echelons. According to the U.S. Bureau of Labor Statistics, white men held 88.8 percent of managerial positions in 1994.

---

[3]"Keep Affirmative Action: Vote 'No' on Prop. 209," from *San Francisco Chronicle,* October 6, 1996. © San Francisco Chronicle. Reprinted by permission.

Discrimination comes in many forms, many of which are not necessarily rooted in sexism or racism. Still, the biases against women and minorities are very real.

If affirmative action were eliminated, there is reason to worry that managers would revert to the days when jobs were handed out based on word-of-mouth references and when no one questioned the general tendency to hire in one's own image.

While meaning no ill, those in positions of authority could also decide that the risk of workplace friction was not worth hiring people of different backgrounds and cultures and outlooks. Since white males still control most hiring decisions, it takes a special effort to change the ethnic and gender face of an office or construction site or college.

Affirmative action is not quotas; it is not hiring an unqualified woman or minority over a qualified white male; and it is not a permanent solution. It is a bridge to a society of more equal opportunity for women and minorities.

Unfortunately, we are not there yet. As General Colin Powell said in opposing Proposition 209: "There are those who rail against affirmative-action preferences, while living lives of preference, who do not understand that the progress achieved over the past generation must be continued if we wish to bless future generations."

An end to affirmative action now will restore obstacles that have made it so difficult for historically disenfranchised groups to enter the economic mainstream and realize the American Dream.

Thought Provokers

1. What were the major strengths and weaknesses of the American economy as the twentieth century approached its end? Which of the following factors most affected American economic performance: foreign competition, the demography of the workforce, government policies, including taxation and education, or technological change?
2. What forces have most dramatically influenced the changing status of women in American society in the past three decades? What political issues are peculiarly in women's province? What changes has the women's movement made in men's lives?
3. What are the major points at issue in the abortion debate? What similarities are there between the debate over abortion in the late twentieth century and the debate over slavery in the mid-nineteenth century?
4. Is there a possibility of a future intergenerational war? Is demography always destiny?
5. How does the latest wave of immigrants differ, if at all, from waves in the nineteenth and early twentieth centuries? What causes anti-immigrant sentiment? Is it stronger or weaker now than one hundred years ago?
6. Is America as a society more committed to equality or to opportunity? Has affirmative action imposed penalties on those who are not its beneficiaries? If so, are such penalties justifiable for the health of the larger society?

Constitution of the United States of America

[Boldface headings and bracketed explanatory matter have been inserted for the reader's convenience. Passages that are no longer operative are printed in italic type.]

Preamble

We the people of the United States, in order to form a more perfect union, establish justice, insure domestic tranquillity, provide for the common defense, promote the general welfare, and secure the blessings of liberty to ourselves and our posterity, do ordain and establish this CONSTITUTION for the United States of America.

Article I. Legislative Department

Section I. Congress

Legislative power vested in a two-house Congress. All legislative powers herein granted shall be vested in a Congress of the United States, which shall consist of a Senate and a House of Representatives.

Section II. House of Representatives

1. The people to elect representatives biennially. The House of Representatives shall be composed of members chosen every second year by the people of the several States, and the electors [voters] in each State shall have the qualifications requisite for electors of the most numerous branch of the State Legislature.

2. Who may be representatives. No person shall be a Representative who shall not have attained to the age of twenty-five years, and been seven years a citizen of the United States, and who shall not, when elected, be an inhabitant of that State in which he shall be chosen.

3. Representation in the House based on population; census. Representatives and direct taxes[1] shall be apportioned among the several States which may be included within this Union, according to their respective numbers, *which shall be determined by adding to the whole number of free persons, including those bound to service for a term of years* [apprentices and indentured servants], *and excluding*

---

[1]Modified in 1913 by the Sixteenth Amendment authorizing income taxes.

Indians not taxed, three-fifths of all other persons [slaves].[1] The actual enumeration [census] shall be made within three years after the first meeting of the Congress of the United States, and within every subsequent term of ten years, in such manner as they shall by law direct. The number of Representatives shall not exceed one for every thirty thousand, but each State shall have at least one Representative; *and until such enumeration shall be made, the State of New Hampshire shall be entitled to choose three, Massachusetts eight, Rhode Island and Providence Plantations one, Connecticut five, New York six, New Jersey four, Pennsylvania eight, Delaware one, Maryland six, Virginia ten, North Carolina five, South Carolina five, and Georgia three.*

4. Vacancies in the House to be filled by election. When vacancies happen in the representation from any State, the Executive authority [governor] thereof shall issue writs of election [call a special election] to fill such vacancies.

5. The House to select its officers; to vote impeachment charges (i.e., indictments). The House of Representatives shall choose their Speaker and other officers; and shall have the sole power of impeachment.

Section III. Senate

1. Senators to represent the states. The Senate of the United States shall be composed of two Senators from each State, *chosen by the legislature thereof,*[2] for six years; and each Senator shall have one vote.

2. One-third of Senators to be chosen every two years; vacancies. *Immediately after they shall be assembled in consequence of the first election, they shall be divided as equally as may be into three classes. The seats of the Senators of the first class shall be vacated at the expiration of the second year, of the second class at the expiration of the fourth year, and of the third class at the expiration of the sixth year,* so that one-third may be chosen every second year; *and if vacancies happen by resignation or otherwise, during the recess of the legislature of any State, the Executive* [governor] *thereof may make temporary appointments until the next meeting of the legislature, which shall then fill such vacancies.*[3]

3. Who may be Senators. No person shall be a Senator who shall not have attained to the age of thirty years, and been nine years a citizen of the United States, and who shall not, when elected, be an inhabitant of that State for which he shall be chosen.

4. The Vice-President to preside over the Senate. The Vice-President of the United States shall be President of the Senate, but shall have no vote, unless they be equally divided [tied].

5. The Senate to choose its other officers. The Senate shall choose their other officers, and also a President pro tempore, in the absence of the Vice-President, or when he shall exercise the office of President of the United States.

6. The Senate to try impeachments. The Senate shall have the sole power

---

[1] The word *slave* appears nowhere in the Constitution; *slavery* appears in the Thirteenth Amendment. The three-fifths rule ceased to be in force when the Thirteenth Amendment was adopted in 1865.

[2] Repealed in favor of popular election in 1913 by the Seventeenth Amendment.

[3] Changed in 1913 by the Seventeenth Amendment.

to try all impeachments. When sitting for that purpose, they shall be on oath or affirmation. When the President of the United States is tried, the Chief Justice shall preside:[1] and no person shall be convicted without the concurrence of two-thirds of the members present.

7. Penalties for impeachment conviction. Judgment in cases of impeachment shall not extend further than to removal from office, and disqualification to hold and enjoy any office of honor, trust or profit under the United States: but the party convicted shall nevertheless be liable and subject to indictment, trial, judgment and punishment, according to law.

Section IV. Election and Meetings of Congress

1. Regulation of elections. The times, places and manner of holding elections for Senators and Representatives shall be prescribed in each State by the legislature thereof; but the Congress may at any time by law make or alter such regulations, except as to the places of choosing Senators.

2. Congress to meet once a year. The Congress shall assemble at least once in every year, and such meeting *shall be on the first Monday in December, unless they shall by law appoint a different day.*[2]

Section V. Organization and Rules of the Houses

1. Each House may reject members; quorums. Each house shall be the judge of the elections, returns and qualifications of its own members, and a majority of each shall constitute a quorum to do business; but a smaller number may adjourn from day to day, and may be authorized to compel the attendance of absent members, in such manner, and under such penalties, as each house may provide.

2. Each House to make its own rules. Each house may determine the rules of its proceedings, punish its members for disorderly behavior, and with the concurrence of two-thirds, expel a member.

3. Each House to publish a record of its proceedings. Each house shall keep a journal of its proceedings, and from time to time publish the same, excepting such parts as may in their judgment require secrecy; and the yeas and nays of the members of either house on any question shall, at the desire of one-fifth of those present, be entered on the journal.

4. Both Houses required to agree on adjournment. Neither house, during the session of Congress, shall, without the consent of the other, adjourn for more than three days, nor to any other place than that in which the two houses shall be sitting.

Section VI. Privileges of and Prohibitions upon Congressmen

1. Congressional salaries; immunities. The Senators and Representatives shall receive a compensation for their services, to be ascertained by law and paid out of the treasury of the United States. They shall in all cases except treason, felony and breach of the peace, be privileged from arrest during their attendance at the

---

[1]The vice-president, as next in line, would be an interested party.
[2]Changed in 1933 to January 3 by the Twentieth Amendment.

session of their respective houses, and in going to and returning from the same; and for any speech or debate in either house, they shall not be questioned in any other place [i.e., they shall be immune from libel suits].[1]

2. Congressmen not to hold incompatible federal civil offices. No Senator or Representative shall, during the time for which he was elected, be appointed to any civil office under the authority of the United States, which shall have been created, or the emoluments whereof shall have been increased, during such time; and no person holding any office under the United States shall be a member of either house during his continuance in office.

Section VII. Method of Making Laws

1. Money bills to originate in the House. All bills for raising revenue shall originate in the House of Representatives; but the Senate may propose or concur with amendments as on other bills.

2. The President's veto power; Congress may override. Every bill which shall have passed the House of Representatives and the Senate, shall, before it become a law, be presented to the President of the United States; if he approve he shall sign it, but if not he shall return it with his objections to that house in which it shall have originated, who shall enter the objections at large on their journal, and proceed to reconsider it. If after such reconsideration two-thirds of that house shall agree to pass the bill, it shall be sent, together with the objections, to the other house, by which it shall likewise be reconsidered, and, if approved by two-thirds of that house, it shall become a law. But in all such cases the votes of both houses shall be determined by yeas and nays, and the names of the persons voting for and against the bill shall be entered on the journal of each house respectively. If any bill shall not be returned by the President within ten days (Sundays excepted) after it shall have been presented to him, the same shall be a law, in like manner as if he had signed it, unless the Congress by their adjournment prevent its return, in which case it shall not be a law [this is the so-called pocket veto].

3. All measures requiring the agreement of both Houses to go to the President for approval. Every order, resolution, or vote to which the concurrence of the Senate and House of Representatives may be necessary (except on a question of adjournment) shall be presented to the President of the United States; and before the same shall take effect, shall be approved by him, or being disapproved by him, shall be repassed by two-thirds of the Senate and House of Representatives, according to the rules and limitations prescribed in the case of a bill.

Section VIII. Powers Granted to Congress

Congress possesses certain enumerated powers:

1. Congress may lay and collect taxes. The Congress shall have power to lay and collect taxes, duties, imposts, and excises, to pay the debts and provide for the common defense and general welfare of the United States; but all duties, imposts and excises shall be uniform throughout the United States;

---

[1]In the 1950s, Senator Joseph R. McCarthy was accused of abusing this privilege.

2. Congress may borrow money. To borrow money on the credit of the United States;

3. Congress may regulate foreign and interstate trade. To regulate commerce with foreign nations, and among the several States, and with the Indian tribes;

4. Congress may pass naturalization and bankruptcy laws. To establish an uniform rule of naturalization, and uniform laws on the subject of bankruptcies throughout the United States;

5. Congress may coin money and regulate weights and measures. To coin money, regulate the value thereof, and of foreign coin, and fix the standard of weights and measures;

6. Congress may punish counterfeiters. To provide for the punishment of counterfeiting the securities and current coin of the United States;

7. Congress may establish a postal service. To establish post offices and post roads;

8. Congress may issue patents and copyrights. To promote the progress of science and useful arts by securing for limited times to authors and inventors the exclusive right to their respective writings and discoveries;

9. Congress may establish inferior courts. To constitute tribunals inferior to the Supreme Court;

10. Congress may punish crimes committed on the high seas. To define and punish piracies and felonies committed on the high seas [i.e., outside the three-mile limit] and offenses against the law of nations [international law];

11. Congress may declare war, may authorize privateering. To declare war,[1] grant letters of marque and reprisal,[2] and make rules concerning captures on land and water;

12. Congress may maintain an army. To raise and support armies, but no appropriation of money to that use shall be for a longer term than two years;[3]

13. Congress may maintain a navy. To provide and maintain a navy;

14. Congress may regulate the army and navy. To make rules for the government and regulation of the land and naval forces;

15. Congress may call out the state militia. To provide for calling forth the militia to execute the laws of the Union, suppress insurrections, and repel invasions;

16. Congress shares with the states control of militia. To provide for organizing, arming, and disciplining the militia, and for governing such part of them as may be employed in the service of the United States, reserving to the States respectively the appointment of the officers, and the authority of training the militia according to the discipline prescribed by Congress;

17. Congress makes laws for the District of Columbia and other federal areas. To exercise exclusive legislation in all cases whatsoever, over such district (not exceeding ten miles square) as may, be cession of particular States, and the acceptance of Congress, become the seat of government of the United States,[4] and to

---

[1]Note that the president, although he can provoke war or wage it after it is declared, cannot declare it.

[2]Papers issued to private citizens in time of war authorizing them to capture enemy ships.

[3]A reflection of fear of standing armies earlier expressed in the Declaration of Independence.

[4]District of Columbia, ten miles square, was established in 1791.

exercise like authority over all places purchased by the consent of the legislature of the State, in which the same shall be, for the erection of forts, magazines, arsenals, dock-yards, and other needful buildings;—and

Congress has certain implied powers:

18. **Congress may enact laws necessary to enforce the Constitution.** To make all laws which shall be necessary and proper for carrying into execution the foregoing powers, and all other powers vested by this Constitution in the government of the United States, or in any department or officer thereof.

Section IX. Powers Denied to the Federal Government

1. **Congressional control of slave trade postponed until 1808.** *The migration or importation of such persons as any of the States now existing shall think proper to admit shall not be prohibited by the Congress prior to the year 1808; but a tax or duty may be imposed on such importation, not exceeding $10 for each person.*

2. **The writ of habeas corpus[1] not to be suspended; exception.** The privilege of the writ of habeas corpus shall not be suspended, unless when in cases of rebellion or invasion the public safety may require it.

3. **Attainders[2] and ex post facto laws[3] forbidden.** No bill of attainder or ex post facto law shall be passed.

4. **Direct taxes to be apportioned according to population.** No capitation [head or poll tax], or other direct, tax shall be laid, unless in proportion to the census or enumeration herein before directed to be taken.[4]

5. **Export taxes forbidden.** No tax or duty shall be laid on articles exported from any State.

6. **Congress not to discriminate among states in regulating commerce; interstate shipping.** No preference shall be given by any regulation of commerce or revenue to the ports of one State over those of another; nor shall vessels bound to, or from, one State, be obliged to enter, clear, or pay duties in another.

7. **Public money not to be spent without Congressional appropriation; accounting.** No money shall be drawn from the treasury, but in consequence of appropriations made by law; and a regular statement and account of the receipts and expenditures of all public money shall be published from time to time.

8. **Titles of nobility prohibited; foreign gifts.** No title of nobility shall be granted by the United States: and no person holding any office of profit or trust under them, shall, without the consent of the Congress, accept of any present, emolument, office, or title, of any kind whatever, from any king, prince, or foreign state.

---

[1]A writ of habeas corpus is a document that enables a person under arrest to obtain an immediate examination in court to ascertain whether he is being legally held.

[2]A bill of attainder is a special legislative act condemning and punishing an individual without a judicial trial.

[3]An ex post facto law is one that fixes punishment for acts committed before the law was passed.

[4]Modified in 1913 by the Sixteenth Amendment.

Section X. Powers Denied to the States

Absolute prohibitions on the states:

1. **The states forbidden certain powers.** No State shall enter into any treaty, alliance, or confederation; grant letters of marque and reprisal [i.e., authorize privateers], coin money; emit bills of credit [issue paper money]; make anything but gold and silver coin a [legal] tender in payment of debts; pass any bill of attainder, ex post facto law,[1] or law impairing the obligation of contracts, or grant any title of nobility.

Conditional prohibitions on the states:

2. **The states not to levy duties without the consent of Congress.** No State shall, without the consent of the Congress, lay any imposts or duties on imports or exports, except what may be absolutely necessary for executing its inspection laws: and the net produce of all duties and imposts, laid by any State on imports or exports, shall be for the use of the treasury of the United States; and all such laws shall be subject to the revision and control of the Congress.

3. **Other federal powers forbidden the states.** No State shall, without the consent of Congress, lay any duty of tonnage [i.e., duty on ship tonnage], keep [non-militia] troops or ships of war in time of peace, enter into any agreement or compact with another State, or with a foreign power, or engage in war, unless actually invaded, or in such imminent danger as will not admit of delay.

Article II. Executive Department

Section I. President and Vice-President

1. **The President the chief executive; his term.** The executive power shall be vested in a President of the United States of America. He shall hold his office during the term of four years,[2] and, together with the Vice-President, chosen for the same term, be elected as follows:

2. **The President to be chosen by state electors.** Each State shall appoint, in such manner as the legislature thereof may direct, a number of electors, equal to the whole number of Senators and Representatives to which the State may be entitled in the Congress; but no Senator or Representative, or person holding an office of trust or profit under the United States, shall be appointed an elector.

A majority of the electoral votes needed to elect a President. *The electors shall meet in their respective States, and vote by ballot for two persons, of whom one at least shall not be an inhabitant of the same State with themselves. And they shall make a list of all the persons voted for, and of the number of votes for each; which list they shall sign and certify, and transmit sealed to the seat of government of the United States, directed to the President of the Senate. The President of the Senate shall, in the presence of the Senate and House of Representatives, open all the certifi-*

---

[1]For definitions see footnotes 2 and 3 on preceding page.

[2]No reference to reelection; clarified by the anti–third term Twenty-second Amendment.

cates, and the votes shall then be counted. *The person having the greatest number of votes shall be the President, if such number be a majority of the whole number of electors appointed; and if there be more than one who have such majority, and have an equal number of votes, then the House of Representatives shall immediately choose by ballot one of them for President; and if no person have a majority, then from the five highest on the list the said house shall in like manner choose the President. But in choosing the President the votes shall be taken by States, the representation from each State having one vote; a quorum for this purpose shall consist of a member or members from two-thirds of the States, and a majority of all the States shall be necessary to a choice. In every case, after the choice of the President, the person having the greatest number of votes of the electors shall be the Vice-President. But if there should remain two or more who have equal votes, the Senate shall choose from them by ballot the Vice-President.*[1]

3. Congress to decide time of meeting of Electoral College. The Congress may determine the time of choosing the electors and the day on which they shall give their votes; which day shall be the same throughout the United States.

4. Who may be President. No person except a natural-born citizen, *or a citizen of the United States at the time of the adoption of this Constitution,* shall be eligible to the office of President; neither shall any person be eligible to that office who shall not have attained to the age of thirty-five years, and been fourteen years a resident within the United States [i.e., a legal resident].

5. Replacements for President. In case of the removal of the President from office or of his death, resignation, or inability to discharge the powers and duties of the said office, the same shall devolve on the Vice-President, and the Congress may by law provide for the case of removal, death, resignation, or inability, both of the President and Vice-President, declaring what officer shall then act as President, and such officer shall act accordingly, until the disability be removed, or a President shall be elected.

6. The President's salary. The President shall, at stated times, receive for his services a compensation, which shall neither be increased nor diminished during the period for which he shall have been elected, and he shall not receive within that period any other emolument from the United States, or any of them.

7. The President's oath of office. Before he enter on the execution of his office, he shall take the following oath or affirmation:—"I do solemnly swear (or affirm) that I will faithfully execute the office of President of the United States, and will to the best of my ability preserve, protect and defend the Constitution of the United States."

Section II. Powers of the President

1. The President has important military and civil powers. The President shall be commander in chief of the army and navy of the United States, and of the militia of the several States, when called into the actual service of the United States; he may require the opinion, in writing, of the principal officer in each of the executive departments, upon any subject relating to the duties of their respective offices,

---

[1]Repealed in 1804 by the Twelfth Amendment.

and he shall have power to grant reprieves and pardons for offenses against the United States, except in cases of impeachment.[1]

2. The President may negotiate treaties and nominate federal officials. He shall have power, by and with the advice and consent of the Senate, to make treaties, provided two-thirds of the Senators present concur; and he shall nominate, and by and with the advice and consent of the Senate, shall appoint ambassadors, other public ministers and consuls, judges of the Supreme Court, and all other officers of the United States, whose appointments are not herein otherwise provided for, and which shall be established by law: but the Congress may by law vest the appointment of such inferior officers, as they think proper, in the President alone, in the courts of law, or in the heads of departments.

3. The President may fill vacancies during Senate recess. The President shall have power to fill up all vacancies that may happen during the recess of the Senate, by granting commissions which shall expire at the end of their next session.

Section III. Other Powers and Duties of the President

Submitting messages; calling extra sessions; receiving ambassadors; executing the laws; commissioning officers. He shall from time to time give to the Congress information of the state of the Union, and recommend to their consideration such measures as he shall judge necessary and expedient; he may, on extraordinary occasions, convene both houses, or either of them, and in case of disagreement between them, with respect to the time of adjournment, he may adjourn them to such time as he shall think proper; he shall receive ambassadors and other public ministers; he shall take care that the laws be faithfully executed, and shall commission all the officers of the United States.

Section IV. Impeachment

Civil officers may be removed by impeachment. The President, Vice-President, and all civil officers[2] of the United States shall be removed from office on impeachment for, and on conviction of, treason, bribery, or other high crimes and misdemeanors.

Article III. Judicial Department

Section I. The Federal Courts

The judicial power lodged in the federal courts. The judicial power of the United States shall be vested in one Supreme Court, and in such inferior courts as the Congress may from time to time ordain and establish. The judges, both of the Supreme and inferior courts, shall hold their offices during good behavior, and shall, at stated times, receive for their services a compensation which shall not be diminished during their continuance in office.

---

[1]To prevent the president's pardoning himself or his close associates.

[2]That is, all federal executive and judicial officers, but not members of Congress or military personnel.

Section II. Jurisdiction of Federal Courts

1. **Kinds of cases that may be heard.** The judicial power shall extend to all cases, in law and equity, arising under this Constitution, the laws of the United States, and treaties made, or which shall be made, under their authority;—to all cases affecting ambassadors, other public ministers and consuls;—to all cases of admiralty and maritime jurisdiction;—to controversies to which the United States shall be a party;—to controversies between two or more States;—*between a State and citizens of another State;*[1]—between citizens of different States;—between citizens of the same State claiming lands under grants of different States, and between a State, or the citizens thereof, and foreign states, citizens or subjects.

2. **Jurisdiction of the Supreme Court.** In all cases affecting ambassadors, other public ministers and consuls, and those in which a State shall be party, the Supreme Court shall have original jurisdiction.[2] In all the other cases before mentioned, the Supreme Court shall have appellate jurisdiction,[3] both as to law and fact, with such exceptions, and under such regulations, as the Congress shall make.

3. **Trial for federal crime to be by jury.** The trial of all crimes, except in cases of impeachment, shall be by jury; and such trial shall be held in the State where the said crimes shall have been committed; but when not committed within any State, the trial shall be at such place or places as the Congress may by law have directed.

Section III. Treason

1. **Treason defined; necessary evidence.** Treason against the United States shall consist only in levying war against them, or in adhering to their enemies, giving them aid and comfort. No person shall be convicted of treason unless on the testimony of two witnesses to the same overt act, or on confession in open court.

2. **Congress to fix punishment for treason.** The Congress shall have power to declare the punishment of treason, but no attainder of treason shall work corruption of blood, or forfeiture except during the life of the person attained.[4]

Article IV. Relations of the States to One Another

Section I. Credit to Acts, Records, and Court Proceedings

Each state to respect the public acts of the others. Full faith and credit shall be given in each State to the public acts, records, and judicial proceedings of every other State.[5] And the Congress may by general laws prescribe the manner in which such acts, records, and proceedings shall be proved [attested], and the effect thereof.

---

[1]The Eleventh Amendment restricts this to suits by a state against citizens of another state.

[2]That is, such cases must originate in the Supreme Court.

[3]That is, it hears other cases only when they are appealed to it from a lower federal court or a state court.

[4]That is, punishment only for the offender; none for his heirs.

[5]For example, a marriage valid in one is valid in all.

Section II. Duties of States to States

1. Citizenship in one state valid in all. The citizens of each State shall be entitled to all privileges and immunities of citizens in the several States.

2. Fugitives from justice to be surrendered by the states. A person charged in any State with treason, felony, or other crime, who shall flee from justice, and be found in another State, shall on demand of the executive authority [governor] of the state from which he fled, be delivered up, to be removed to the State having jurisdiction of the crime.

3. Slaves and apprentices to be returned. *No person held to service or labor in one State, under the laws thereof, escaping into another, shall, in consequence of any law or regulation therein, be discharged from such service or labor, but shall be delivered up on claim of the party to whom such service or labor may be due.*[1]

Section III. New States and Territories

1. Congress to admit new states. New States may be admitted by the Congress into this Union; but no new State shall be formed or erected within the jurisdiction of any other State; nor any State be formed by the junction of two or more States, or parts of States, without the consent of the legislatures of the States concerned as well as of the Congress.

2. Congress to regulate federal territory and property. The Congress shall have power to dispose of and make all needful rules and regulations respecting the territory or other property belonging to the United States; and nothing in this Constitution shall be so construed as to prejudice any claims of the United States, or of any particular State.

Section IV. Protection to the States

Republican form of government guaranteed; also protection against invasion and rebellion. The United States shall guarantee to every State in this Union a republican form of government, and shall protect each of them against invasion; and on application of the legislature, or of the executive [governor] (when the legislature cannot be convened), against domestic violence.

Article V. The Process of Amendment

The Constitution may be amended in one of four ways. The Congress, whenever two-thirds of both houses shall deem it necessary, shall propose amendments to this Constitution, or, on the application of the legislatures of two-thirds of the several States, shall call a convention for proposing amendments, which, in either case, shall be valid to all intents and purposes, as part of this Constitution, when ratified by the legislatures of three-fourths of the several States, or by conventions in three-fourths thereof, as the one or the other mode of ratification may be proposed by the Con-

---

[1]Invalidated in 1865 by the Thirteenth Amendment.

gress; provided *that no amendments which may be made prior to the year one thousand eight hundred and eight shall in any manner affect the first and fourth clauses in the ninth section of the first article,*[1] *and* that no State, without its consent, shall be deprived of its equal suffrage in the Senate.

Article VI. General Provisions

1. **The debts of the Confederation secured.** All debts contracted and engagements entered into, before the adoption of this Constitution, shall be as valid against the United States under this Constitution, as under the Confederation.

2. **The Constitution, federal laws, and treaties the supreme law of the land.** This Constitution, and the laws of the United States which shall be made in pursuance thereof; and all treaties made, or which shall be made, under the authority of the United States, shall be the supreme law of the land; and the judges in every State shall be bound thereby, anything in the Constitution or laws of any State to the contrary notwithstanding.

3. **Federal and state officers bound by oath to support the Constitution; religious tests forbidden.** The Senators and Representatives before mentioned, and the members of the several State legislatures, and all executive and judicial officers, both of the United States and of the several States, shall be bound by oath or affirmation to support this Constitution; but no religious test shall ever be required as a qualification to any office or public trust under the United States.

Article VII. Ratification of the Constitution

The Constitution to become effective when ratified by nine states. The ratification of the conventions of nine States shall be sufficient for the establishment of this Constitution between the States so ratifying the same.

Done in Convention by the unanimous consent of the States present, the seventeenth day of September in the year of our Lord one thousand seven hundred and eighty-seven and of the Independence of the United States of America the twelfth. In witness whereof we have hereunto subscribed our names.

[Signed by]

G° Washington
Presidt and Deputy from Virginia
[and thirty-eight others]

---

[1]This clause, relating to slave trade and direct taxes, became inoperative in 1808.

AMENDMENTS TO THE CONSTITUTION

Article I. Religious and Political Freedom (1791)

Congress not to interfere with freedom of religion, speech or press, assembly, and petition. Congress shall make no law respecting an establishment of religion, or prohibiting the free exercise thereof; or abridging the freedom of speech, or of the press; or the right of the people peaceably to assemble, and to petition the government for a redress of grievances.

Article II. Right to Bear Arms (1791)

The people secured in their right to bear arms. A well-regulated militia being necessary to the security of a free State, the right of the people to keep and bear arms [i.e., for military purposes] shall not be infringed.

Article III. Quartering of Troops (1791)

Quartering of soldiers on the people restricted. No soldier shall, in time of peace, be quartered in any house without the consent of the owner, nor in time of war, but in a manner to be prescribed by law.

Article IV. Searches and Seizures (1791)

Unreasonable searches forbidden. The right of the people to be secure in their persons, houses, papers, and effects, against unreasonable searches and seizures, shall not be violated, and no [search] warrants shall issue but upon probable cause, supported by oath or affirmation, and particularly describing the place to be searched, and the persons or things to be seized.

Article V. Right to Life, Liberty, and Property (1791)

Individuals guaranteed certain rights when on trial and the right to life, liberty, and property. No person shall be held to answer for a capital, or otherwise infamous, crime, unless on a presentment [formal charge] or indictment of a grand jury, except in cases arising in the land or naval forces, or in the militia, when in actual service in time of war or public danger; nor shall any person be subject for the same offense to be twice put in jeopardy of life or limb; nor shall be compelled in any criminal case to be a witness against himself, nor be deprived of life, liberty, or property, without due process of law; nor shall private property be taken for public use [i.e., by eminent domain] without just compensation.

Article VI. Protection in Criminal Trials (1791)

Accused persons assured of important rights. In all criminal prosecutions, the accused shall enjoy the right to a speedy and public trial, by an impartial jury of the State and district wherein the crime shall have been committed, which district shall have been previously ascertained by law, and to be informed of the nature and cause of the accusation; to be confronted with the witnesses against him; to have compulsory process [subpoena] for obtaining witnesses in his favor, and to have the assistance of counsel for his defense.

Article VII. Suits at Common Law (1791)

The rules of common law recognized. In suits at common law, where the value in controversy shall exceed twenty dollars, the right of trial by jury shall be preserved, and no fact tried by a jury shall be otherwise re-examined in any court of the United States, than according to the rules of the common law.

Article VIII. Bail and Punishments (1791)

Excessive bail, fines, and punishments forbidden. Excessive bail shall not be required, nor excessive fines imposed, nor cruel and unusual punishments inflicted.

Article IX. Concerning Rights Not Enumerated (1791)

The people to retain rights not here enumerated. The enumeration in the Constitution, of certain rights, shall not be construed to deny or disparage others retained by the people.

Article X. Powers Reserved to the States and to the People (1791)

Powers not delegated to the federal government reserved to the states and the people. The powers not delegated to the United States by the Constitution, nor prohibited by it to the States, are reserved to the States respectively, or to the people.

Article XI. Suits Against a State (1798)

The federal courts denied authority in suits by citizens against a state. The judicial power of the United States shall not be construed to extend to any suit in law or equity, commenced or prosecuted against one of the United States by citizens of another State, or by citizens or subjects of any foreign state.

Article XII. Election of President and Vice-President (1804)

1. Changes in manner of electing President and Vice-President; procedure when no presidential candidate receives electoral majority. The electors shall meet in their respective States, and vote by ballot for President and Vice-President, one of whom, at least, shall not be an inhabitant of the same State with themselves; they shall name in their ballots the person voted for as President, and in distinct ballots the person voted for as Vice-President, and they shall make distinct lists of all persons voted for as President, and of all persons voted for as Vice-President, and of the number of votes for each, which lists they shall sign and certify, and transmit sealed to the seat of government of the United States, directed to the President of the Senate;—the President of the Senate shall, in the presence of the Senate and House of Representatives, open all the certificates and the votes shall then be counted;—the person having the greatest number of votes for President shall be the President, if such number be a majority of the whole number of electors appointed; and if no person have such majority, then from the persons having the highest numbers not exceeding three on the list of those voted for as President, the House of Representatives shall choose immediately, by ballot, the President. But in choosing the President, the votes shall be taken by States, the representation from each State having one vote; a quorum for this purpose shall consist of a member or members from two-thirds of the States, and a majority of all the States shall be necessary to a choice. And if the House of Representatives shall not choose a President whenever the right of choice shall devolve upon them, before *the fourth day of March*[1] next following, then the Vice-President shall act as President, as in the case of the death or other constitutional disability of the President.

2. Procedure when no vice-presidential candidate receives electoral majority. The person having the greatest number of votes as Vice-President shall be the Vice-President, if such number be a majority of the whole number of electors appointed; and if no person have a majority, then from the two highest numbers on the list the Senate shall choose the Vice-President; a quorum for the purpose shall consist of two-thirds of the whole number of Senators, and a majority of the whole number shall be necessary to a choice. But no person constitutionally ineligible to the office of President shall be eligible to that of Vice-President of the United States.

Article XIII. Slavery Prohibited (1865)

1. Slavery forbidden. Neither slavery[2] nor involuntary servitude, except as a punishment for crime whereof the party shall have been duly convicted, shall exist within the United States, or any place subject to their jurisdiction.

2. Congress shall have power to enforce this article by appropriate legislation.

---

[1] Changed to January 20 by the Twentieth Amendment.

[2] The only explicit mention of slavery in the Constitution.

Article XIV. Civil Rights for Blacks, etc. (1868)

1. **Citizenship defined; rights of citizens.** All persons born or naturalized in the United States, and subject to the jurisdiction thereof, are citizens of the United States and of the State wherein they reside. No State shall make or enforce any law which shall abridge the privileges or immunities of citizens of the United States; nor shall any State deprive any person of life, liberty, or property, without due process of law; nor deny to any person within its jurisdiction the equal protection of the laws.

2. **When a state denies [blacks] the vote, its representation shall be reduced.** Representatives shall be apportioned among the several States according to their respective numbers, counting the whole number of persons in each State, excluding Indians not taxed. But when the right to vote at any election for the choice of Electors for President and Vice-President of the United States, Representatives in Congress, the executive and judicial officers of a State, or the members of the legislature thereof, is denied to any of the male inhabitants of such State, being twenty-one years of age and citizens of the United States, or in any way abridged, except for participation in rebellion, or other crime, the basis of representation therein shall be reduced in the proportion which the number of such male citizens shall bear to the whole number of male citizens twenty-one years of age in such State.

3. **Certain ex-Confederates ineligible for federal and state office; removal of disability.** No person shall be a Senator or Representative in Congress, or Elector of President and Vice-President, or hold any office, civil or military, under the United States, or under any State, who, having previously taken an oath, as a member of Congress, or as an officer of the United States, or as a member of any State legislature, or as an executive or judicial officer of any State, to support the Constitution of the United States, shall have engaged in insurrection or rebellion against the same, or given aid or comfort to the enemies thereof. But Congress may, by a vote of two-thirds of each house, remove such disability.

4. **Public debt valid; debt of rebels void.** The validity of the public debt of the United States, authorized by law, including debts incurred for payment of pensions and bounties for services in suppressing insurrection or rebellion, shall not be questioned. But neither the United States nor any State shall assume or pay any debt or obligation incurred in aid of insurrection or rebellion against the United States or any claim for the loss or emancipation of any slave; but all such debts, obligations, and claims shall be held illegal and void.

5. **Enforcement.** The Congress shall have power to enforce, by appropriate legislation, the provisions of this article.

Article XV. Black Suffrage (1870)

Restrictions on denial of vote. *1.* The right of citizens of the United States to vote shall not be denied or abridged by the United States or by any State on account of race, color, or previous condition of servitude.

2. The Congress shall have power to enforce this article by appropriate legislation.

Article XVI. Income Taxes (1913)

Congress empowered to lay and collect income taxes. The Congress shall have power to lay and collect taxes on incomes, from whatever source derived, without apportionment among the several States, and without regard to any census or enumeration.

Article XVII. Direct Election of Senators (1913)

Senators to be elected by popular vote. *1.* The Senate of the United States shall be composed of two Senators from each State, elected by the people thereof, for six years; and each Senator shall have one vote. The electors in each State shall have the qualifications requisite for electors of [voters for] the most numerous branch of the State legislatures.

2. When vacancies happen in the representation of any State in the Senate, the executive authority of such State shall issue writs of election to fill such vacancies: Provided, that the Legislature of any State may empower the executive thereof to make temporary appointments until the people fill the vacancies by election as the Legislature may direct.

3. This amendment shall not be so construed as to affect the election or term of any Senator chosen before it becomes valid as part of the Constitution.

Article XVIII. National Prohibition (1919)

The manufacture, sale, or transportation of intoxicating liquors forbidden. *1. After one year from the ratification of this article the manufacture, sale, or transportation of intoxicating liquors within, the importation thereof into, or the exportation thereof from the United States and all territory subject to the jurisdiction thereof, for beverage purposes, is hereby prohibited.*

2. The Congress and the several States shall have concurrent power to enforce this article by appropriate legislation.

3. This article shall be inoperative unless it shall have been ratified as an amendment to the Constitution by the legislatures of the several States, as provided by the Constitution, within seven years from the date of the submission thereof to the states by the Congress.[1]

Article XIX. Woman Suffrage (1920)

Women permitted to vote. *1.* The right of citizens of the United States to vote shall not be denied or abridged by the United States or by any State on account of sex.

2. Congress shall have power to enforce this article by appropriate legislation.

---

[1]Repealed in 1933 by the Twenty-first Amendment.

Article XX. Presidential and Congressional Terms (1933)

1. **Presidential, vice-presidential, and Congressional terms of office to begin in January.** The terms of the President and Vice-President shall end at noon on the 20th day of January, and the terms of Senators and Representatives at noon on the 3rd day of January, of the years in which such terms would have ended if this article had not been ratified; and the terms of their successors shall then begin.

2. **New meeting date for Congress.** The Congress shall assemble at least once in every year, and such meeting shall begin at noon on the 3rd day of January, unless they shall by law appoint a different day.

3. **Emergency presidential and vice-presidential succession.** If, at the time fixed for the beginning of the term of the President, the President-elect shall have died, the Vice-President-elect shall become President. If a President shall not have been chosen before the time fixed for the beginning of his term, or if the President-elect shall have failed to qualify, then the Vice-President-elect shall act as President until a President shall have qualified; and the Congress may by law provide for the case wherein neither a President-elect nor a Vice-President-elect shall have qualified, declaring who shall then act as President, or the manner in which one who is to act shall be selected, and such persons shall act accordingly until a President or Vice-President shall have qualified.

4. The Congress may by law provide for the case of the death of any of the persons from whom the House of Representatives may choose a President whenever the right of choice shall have devolved upon them, and for the case of the death of any of the persons from whom the Senate may choose a Vice-President whenever the right of choice shall have devolved upon them.

5. Sections 1 and 2 shall take effect on the 15th day of October following the ratification of this article.

6. This article shall be inoperative unless it shall have been ratified as an amendment to the Constitution by the legislatures of three-fourths of the several States within seven years from the date of its submission.

Article XXI. Prohibition Repealed (1933)

1. **Eighteenth Amendment repealed.** The eighteenth article of amendment to the Constitution of the United States is hereby repealed.

2. **Local laws honored.** The transportation or importation into any State, Territory, or Possession of the United States for delivery or use therein of intoxicating liquors, in violation of the laws thereof, is hereby prohibited.

3. This article shall be inoperative unless it shall have been ratified as an amendment to the Constitution by conventions in the several States, as provided in the Constitution, within seven years from the date of the submission thereof to the States by the Congress.

Article XXII. Anti–Third Term Amendment (1951)

The President limited to two terms. *1.* No person shall be elected to the office of President more than twice, and no person who has held the office of President, or acted as President, for more than two years of a term to which some other person was elected President shall be elected to the office of President more than once. But this article shall not apply to any person holding the office of President when this article was proposed by the Congress [i.e., Truman], and shall not prevent any person who may be holding the office of President, or acting as President, during the term within which this article becomes operative [i.e., Truman] from holding the office of President or acting as President during the remainder of such term.

2. This article shall be inoperative unless it shall have been ratified as an amendment to the Constitution by the legislatures of three-fourths of the several States within seven years from the date of its submission to the States by the Congress.

Article XXIII. District of Columbia Vote (1961)

1. **Presidential Electors for the District of Columbia.** The District constituting the seat of Government of the United States shall appoint in such manner as the Congress may direct:

A number of electors of President and Vice-President equal to the whole number of Senators and Representatives in Congress to which the District would be entitled if it were a State, but in no event more than the least populous State; they shall be in addition to those appointed by the States, but they shall be considered for the purposes of the election of President and Vice-President, to be electors appointed by a State; and they shall meet in the District and perform such duties as provided by the twelfth article of amendment.

2. **Enforcement.** The Congress shall have the power to enforce this article by appropriate legislation. [Adopted 1961].

Article XXIV. Poll Tax (1964)

1. **Payment of poll tax or other taxes not to be prerequisite for voting in federal elections.** The right of citizens of the United States to vote in any primary or other election for President or Vice-President, for electors for President or Vice-President, or for Senator or Representative in Congress, shall not be denied or abridged by the United States or any State by reason of failure to pay any poll tax or other tax.

2. **Enforcement.** The Congress shall have the power to enforce this article by appropriate legislation. [Adopted 1964].

Article XXV. Presidential Succession and Disability[1] (1967)

1. **Vice-President to become President.** In case of the removal of the President from office or of his death or resignation, the Vice-President shall become President.[2]

---

[1]Passed by a two-thirds vote of both houses of Congress in July 1965; ratified by the requisite three-fourths of the state legislatures, February 1967, or well within the seven-year limit.

[2]The original Constitution (Art. II, sec. I, para. 5) was vague on this point, stipulating that "the powers and duties" of the president, but not necessarily the title, should "devolve" on the vice-president. President Tyler, the first "accidental president," assumed not only the power and duties but the title as well.

2. Successor to Vice-President provided. Whenever there is a vacancy in the office of the Vice-President, the President shall nominate a Vice-President who shall take office upon confirmation by a majority vote of both Houses of Congress.

3. Vice-President to serve for disabled President. Whenever the President transmits to the President pro tempore of the Senate and the Speaker of the House of Representatives his written declaration that he is unable to discharge the powers and duties of his office, and until he transmits to them a written declaration to the contrary, such powers and duties shall be discharged by the Vice-President as Acting President.

4. Procedure for disqualifying or requalifying President. Whenever the Vice-President and a majority of either the principal officers of the executive departments or of such other body as Congress may by law provide, transmit to the President pro tempore of the Senate and the Speaker of the House of Representatives their written declaration that the President is unable to discharge the powers and duties of his office, the Vice-President shall immediately assume the powers and duties of the office as Acting President.

Thereafter, when the President transmits to the President pro tempore of the Senate and the Speaker of the House of Representatives his written declaration that no inability exists, he shall resume the powers and duties of his office unless the Vice-President and a majority of either the principal officers of the executive department[s] or of such other body as Congress may by law provide, transmit within four days to the President pro tempore of the Senate and the Speaker of the House of Representatives their written declaration that the President is unable to discharge the powers and duties of his office. Thereupon Congress shall decide the issue, assembling within forty-eight hours for that purpose if not in session. If the Congress, within twenty-one days after receipt of the latter written declaration, or, if Congress is not in session, within twenty-one days after Congress is required to assemble, determines by two-thirds vote of both Houses that the President is unable to discharge the powers and duties of his office, the Vice-President shall continue to discharge the same as Acting President; otherwise, the President shall resume the powers and duties of his office.

Article XXVI. Lowering Voting Age (1971)

1. Ballot for eighteen-year-olds. The right of citizens of the United States, who are eighteen years of age or older, to vote shall not be denied or abridged by the United States or by any State on account of age.

2. Enforcement. The Congress shall have power to enforce this article by appropriate legislation.

Article XXVII. Restricting Congressional Pay Raises (1992)

Congress not allowed to increase its current pay. No law varying the compensation for the services of the Senators and Representatives shall take effect, until an election of Representatives shall have intervened.

Index